1953-
In pursuit of the
natural sign

In Pursuit
of the Natural Sign

In Pursuit
of the Natural Sign

Azorín and the Poetics of Ekphrasis

Gayana Jurkevich

Lewisburg
Bucknell University Press
London: Associated University Presses

Associated University Presses
440 Forsgate Drive
Cranbury, NJ 08512

Associated University Presses
16 Barter Street
London WC1A 2AH, England

Associated University Presses
P.O. Box 338, Port Credit
Mississauga, Ontario
Canada L5G 4L8

The paper used in this publication meets the requirements of the American National Standard for Permanence of Paper for Printed Library Materials Z39.48-1984.

Library of Congress Cataloging-in-Publication Data

Jurkevich, Gayana, 1953–
    In pursuit of the natural sign : Azorín and the poetics of
Ekphrasis / Gayana Jurkevich.
        p.   cm.
    Includes bibliographical references and index.
    ISBN 0-8387-5413-9
    1. Azorín, 1873–1967—Knowledge—Art.   2. Landscape painting,
Spanish.   3. Landscape painting—19th century—Spain.   4. Ekphrasis.
I. Title.
PQ6623.A816Z64   1999
868'.6209—dc21   99-13041
                                                                                      CIP

PRINTED IN THE UNITED STATES OF AMERICA

For Marshall J. Schneider, a true friend in deed.

Y también a Pepe y a Madín, y la Casa-Museo Azorín, mil gracias.

Contents

List of Illustrations

Black and White Figures

9

Color Plates

Plates 1 to 16 appear after page 64.

Acknowledgments

I would like to express my thanks to all those who helped see *In Pursuit of the Natural Sign* come to fruition: to Professor E. Inman Fox for putting the idea for this project into my head many years ago over glasses of *pacharán* one sultry afternoon at the Residencia de Estudiantes in Madrid; to Professor Roberta L. Johnson who very generously provided me with diskettes of her then unpublished catalogue of Azorín's personal and family libraries at Monóvar, and to both Professors Fox and Johnson for their willingness to act as sounding-boards throughout the book's long gestational process.

Thanks also to the PSC/CUNY Research Foundation for three generous grants awarded over the summers of 1993, 1994, and 1995 that allowed me to work at the Biblioteca Nacional in Madrid and the Casa-Museo Azorín in Monóvar. My gratitude to the "Program for Cultural Cooperation between Spain's Ministry of Culture and United States' Universities" for a sabbatical grant awarded in 1995–1996 that gave me the time to complete a first draft of this book. A second, generous grant awarded in 1998 by the "Program for Cultural Cooperation," as well as financial support from Baruch College and its Department of Modern Languages and Comparative Literature, helped offset the exorbitant costs of publishing a book with plenty of color illustrations.

My gratitude to the Caja de Ahorros del Mediterráneo (CAM), holders of the copyright to Azorín's *Obras Completas*, for allowing me to quote from the *Complete Works* at length. I could never have done without the cooperation and hospitality of Don José Payá Bernabé, and especially Magdalena Rigual Bonastre, directors of the Casa-Museo Azorín, who always made my stays in Alicante so productive and whose willingness to return long-distance telephone calls and faxes, engage in research on my behalf, tireless efforts to ferret out transparencies and art catalogues from all over the Spanish Peninsula, not to mention the rich conversation over many fabulously long lunches in and around Monóvar, I will never forget.

I would like to express my appreciation to Drs. Marcus Burke, Priscilla Muller, and Patrick Lenaghan of the Hispanic Society of America in New York who very generously shared their art-historical expertise with me when I needed guidance in a field whose protocols were not at all familiar when I first dared to cross its threshold. Professor Angel Alcalá of Brooklyn College provided valuable guidance on the history of the Catholic Church in Spain, the lives and careers of various popes and saints, as well as the telephone number of his son-in-law, Dr. Miguel Falomir, conservator at the Prado Museum. Professor Lane Kauffmann of Rice University rescued me from a twelfth-hour crisis by unearthing in his university library the dimensions of a painting that had eluded me for quite some time. My colleague at Baruch College, the inveterate Francophile, Professor Scott Bryson, did much to improve my translations from French into English; Professor Joan Ramon Resina of Cornell University did the same for my inchoate efforts to render Catalán into English: my gratitude to both of them. Since there are so few translations of Azorín into Engish, I must assume full credit for the dubious results.

Many thanks to the editors and publishers of *Revista Hispánica Moderna*, *MLN*, and the *Bulletin of Hispanic Studies* (Glasgow) for permission to incorporate into my book portions of articles I had published previously in their journals. Special mention should go to the Fundación Cultural MAPFRE Vida and Rosario López at the Banco Central-Hispano, both in Madrid, and to Ariadna Blanc of the Museu Nacional d'Art de Catalunya in Barcelona for their generosity and unbelievable speed in responding to my requests for transparencies. I am very much in debt to Don Juan Sunyé, Cónsul para Asuntos Culturales, and Don Federico Palomera, Cónsul General Adjunto of the Spanish Consulate in New York City for their assistance in prodding several recalcitrant provincial museums in Spain to respond to requests for transparencies. Many thanks also to Don Javier Goliszewski, Cultural Attaché at the Consulate General of Argentina in New York City, and his assistant Ms. Verónica Mijelshon, for their help in obtaining transparencies from the Museo Nacional de Bellas Artes in Buenos Aires. Special recognition goes to that Museum, as well as the Museo de Arte Contemporáneo of Toledo, the Museo Municipal de San Telmo of San Sebastián, Don José María Yudego Marín, Encargado General of the Museo Municipal de Marceliano Santa María at Burgos, and Anna Llanes i Tuset, Conservadora de Museos at the Patrimoni de Sitges, for waiving reproduction rights or transparency rental fees of paintings belonging to the collections of their museums. My gratitude also to several anonymous *bedeles* at Madrid's Biblioteca Nacional, without whose surreptitious and unsanctioned photocopying my research there would have been much more labor-intensive and time-consuming.

A heartfelt thanks to Thomas Mermall for managing to find the time and the energy to help me through many an Azorinian snafu while in the throes of completing his critical edition of *La rebelión de las masas*. And finally, to my father, Igor Jurkevich (1928–1996), for whose doctorate in astrophysics I finally discovered some use while grappling with the content of my last chapter. I would have liked him to be able to see the finished product.

List of Abbreviations

AE	*Amada España*
BILE	*Boletín de la Institución Libre de Enseñanza*
CM	*El cine y el momento*
EC	*El efímero cine*
EdC	*Ejercicios de castellano*
EL	*En Lontananza*
EP	*Españoles en París*
LM	*Los médicos*
PCQ	*Pintar como querer*
PQ	*Pasos quedos*
VH	*Varios hombres y alguna mujer*
VL	*Los valores literarios*

Introduction
Through a Painter's Eyes

On 15 January 1996 the Peruvian Nobel laureate, Mario Vargas Llosa, commemorated his highly unusual election to the Real Academia Española with an investiture speech titled "Las discretas ficciones de Azorín."[1] Declaring that he never traveled without taking along a book by Azorín, Vargas Llosa proposed that Azorín was a precursor of the *nouveau roman*, he spoke of Azorín's influence on his own writing, and he dedicated a portion of his talk to Azorín's importance as a literary "archaeologist" who resurrected the forgotten classics of Spanish literature in critical essays, frequently recasting their themes and protagonists in modern dress. The idea is not a new one. In "Lectura y literatura (en torno a la inspiración libresca de Azorín)," first published in 1967, E. Inman Fox documented what has by now become indisputable fact among students of Azorín's modus operandi as a writer. And the facts are these: everything that Azorín wrote was occasioned and informed by some kind of printed material, and because he scrupulously acknowledged sources, Azorín ensured that comparing his texts against their provenance would be as relatively manageable and productive an enterprise as it was fascinating.[2]

The truth of the matter, however, is that throughout his life Azorín also maintained an ongoing dialogue with the world of art, yet while his "inspiración libresca" entered the scholarly vernacular as a kind of axiom, systematic inquiry into the extent to which the visual arts constitute the "other" text that informs and contextualizes Azorín's thematics, style, and the structure of individual works, is still to appear. This book is a long overdue testimonial to the significance of the visual arts in Azorín's writing. Over the years some critics have noted in passing the importance of painting to Azorín. In 1949 Manuel Granell observed that critics had all but ignored the influence of art in Azorín's work, remarking that he could not identify any generation of writers, and no single author within a generation, more concerned with color and painterly techniques. Although Granell deemed the subject worthy of study, and his own book was suggestively titled *Estética de Azorín*, he declared that he had no time to explore the topic at length (93–94). In *Panorama de la literatura española*, which has gone through several editions since its initial appearance in 1956, Torrente Ballester noted that Azorín had the soul of an intellectual but the eyes of a painter (240); Antonio Risco also reflected on the influence of visual art on all aspects of Azorín's writing (1980, 240), while Antonio Espí Valdés wrote in 1976 that the more one reads Azorín, the more convinced one could become that had Azorín not chosen to be a writer, he might have turned to painting instead (71). Luis Granjel briefly discusses the plastic nature and pictorial values evident throughout Azorín's writing in his *Retrato de Azorín* (167), but unfortunately, the promising title of Manuel Ferrand's 1974 study, "Azorín y la pintura," dispenses half-truths and errors to the effect that, more than having an interest in painting, Azorín demonstrated greater concern with painters (76); that he rarely spoke of contemporary art or artists, and even less about the aesthetic revolution that occurred in the visual arts during the first decades of the twentieth century (77–78); that Azorín's interest in painting did not go beyond Courbet and the realists, and that he remained indifferent to Impressionism (180).

Of all the Generation of 1898 writers it is Azorín who is best remembered for his appreciation of the visual arts, his friendships with contemporary painters, his respectable knowledge of European landscape history, his familiarity with the collections of the French and Spanish national museums, his essays on classical and contemporary art, and the painterly nature of his prose. Torrente's observation that Azorín saw through a painter's eyes is confirmed time and again by Azorín himself. Ghostwriting the biography of his thinly disguised alter ego, "X," Azorín recalled that he was drawn to the visual arts from childhood and that while an adolescent boarding student with the Piarist fathers in Yecla, he took lessons in drawing, consuming "many little tubes of paint daubing" his favorite subject: ships on the high seas. Perhaps because he recognized painting and writing as sign systems within which vision was an essential component, in *Memorias Inmemoriales* Azorín wrote that as an adult he was attracted by painters and that when he sat down at his typewriter, he imagined himself not as a writer, but as a painter with palette and brush in hand.[3]

Since his memory was eidetic and the plastic arts were such an integral part of his sensibility, Azorín indicated that the visual element ineluctably made itself felt in everything that he wrote: "The main point is, I believe, that since his memory [that of X] was visual, as his books attest, painting fueled that instinct of his" (8:441).[4] The anonymous poet who speaks in the first person in the evocatively titled "Poeta sin nombre (Autobiografía)," reveals that he always keeps on his worktable a reproduction of a famous painting because "painting has always been a stimulant for me." In the past, the place of honor had been occupied by Mantegna's *Parnaso*, Ribera's *Santa María Egipciaca*, and Rembrandt's *Filósofo ante el libro abierto*, while the current painting of choice was Turner's *The Evening Star*.[5] As we shall see in the chapters that follow, the paintings mentioned by this "anonymous" poet also happen to be Azorín's personal favorites.

Azorín considered much of what he thought and wrote about in terms of the visual arts. He was obsessed (the word choice is his) with identifying in daily life people who resembled well-known iconographic images, once finding Tintoretto's Susana and Correggio's Antiope on the streets of Paris and Madrid. He described the patrons of the Pombo café made famous by Gómez de la Serna's *tertulia*, as physical types he'd never seen anywhere before except in the paintings of social satirists like Goya, Ortego, and Alenza (*EL* 169). Azorín's descriptions of place are often couched in terms of analogies to old prints and photographs: wanting to portray the archetypal milieu of Avila, he relied on an old print depicting a spacious plaza with a lone gentleman in a top hat and a lady carrying a parasol, dressed in a voluminous crinoline skirt, to do it for him (4:505); when he needed to describe attics converted into convalescent centers for wounded French soldiers during his tour as a World War I newspaper correspondent, Azorín could not refrain from comparing "these French attics—so different from ours—" to ones he had seen in elegant, rococo "prints from the eighteenth century" (3:909). He even expressed the evolution of language from the Renaissance style of Ronsard to the innovations of Verlaine by identifying analogous transformations of sensibility in landscapes painted by Claude Lorrain in the seventeenth century and those executed in the nineteenth by Claude Monet (2:795). As a distinguished predecessor of Vargas Llosas's at the Real Academia, Azorín was eligible to participate in the Academy's periodic revision of the Spanish language, an exercise that consisted in the admission of new lexical expressions to the official *Dictionary of the Spanish Language*. Ramón Gómez de la Serna reported that one of the two or three words Azorín sponsored was the noun *gavilar*, derived from *gavilla* (a sheaf of grain), to mean a "heap of sheaves." Yet even in this case, Azorín's Academy-sanctioned neologism was inspired by Goya's painting of summer's bounty, titled *Verano* (181).

The minutely detailed descriptions for which Azorín is especially known are decidedly visual since, as Roland Barthes put it, "every literary description is a *view*" (Berg 1992, 149). In some cases Azorín's descriptions stress color, or they might suggest, or outrightly name, a specific painting, artist, artistic movement, or even imitate a painter's style—this is particularly true in the case of Azorín's reliance on impressionist techniques for landscape description. In other instances, he provides unmistakable indications that a scene is intended to have pictorial qualities, such as a painted vista from *El oasis de los clásicos*: "Beside us rises not a fragrant cedar, but an elegant poplar. The poplar is the tree of Castile. Due to the effect of perspective, we perceive the poplar as being taller than the tower of the cathedral" (9:959). Azorín's creativity was stimulated by his continual incursions into the art world, facilitated either through the literature of painting in the form of the many books on art, museum guides, artist biographies, and picture postcards of master paintings he collected, or to the countless visits he made to the Louvre and Prado Museums where he was able to see firsthand many of Europe's greatest paintings.[6] When he defended appending *Los clásicos futuros* to his 1945 *Los clásicos redivivos*, Azorín chose to do so with a visual arts analogy. Observing that the Prado Museum would do well to follow the Louvre's example and include the work of modern masters in its collections so that the museum visitor would have a complete picture of the history of art, Azorín pleaded his own case: "And why can't I, in these ruminations, consider the ancients alongside the moderns?," in the same way that deep in the heart of the Louvre, in a gallery hung with classical art, "the magnificent portrait of Whistler's mother, painted by the artist, is displayed on an easel" (8:89).

Azorín's contacts with the artistic community, his sensitivity to visual stimuli and use of painterly techniques complement both his critical essays on painting as well as his works of fiction. The paintings and painters, whether fictional or historically real, that play important roles in his creative work become exegetical tools which illuminate the importance of interart relations within individual texts and constitute, as well, invaluable metaliterary

statements providing insights into Azorín's stylistics. Allusions to art and to the art world make their presence felt throughout Azorín's writing in all literary genres: his novels and stories are replete with references to the visual arts and characters who are painters, art collectors or gallery owners; his language is rich in plastic metaphor; the essays on art and museums, in many cases first written for the periodical press, were frequently accompanied by photographic reproductions of the paintings under discussion. Azorín's favorite trope was the simile, a figure of speech more innately visual than any other since its copulae, based on "like" or "as if" structures, invite visual activity on a reader's part. Azorín, however, often makes his similes doubly visual by having a painting stand in for one of the elements in his terms of comparison, as occurs in a telegraphic juxtaposition of Eastern opulence in the film *The Thief of Baghdad* to the lush, Renaissance canvases of Paolo Veronese: "Producer: Alexander Korda, infatuated with the Orient, lavish in the first scenes of *The Thief of Baghdad*, just like a huge canvas by Veronese" (*CM* 35).

Azorín was equally partial to the ekphrastic topos—the verbal description of art objects—which bears an uncanny resemblance to the visual arts simile: both trope and topos, meaning to be "like" a point of reference in the world of art, utilize verbal means of representation to invoke objects first presented visually. A few words on the nature of literary ekphrasis are pertinent since the term will be used frequently throughout the chapters that follow. In *De Gloria Atheniensium*, Plutarch attributed to Simonides of Ceos (c.556–467 B.C.) the saying that "painting is mute poetry and poetry a speaking picture." The notion was restated by Horace in his famous adage "ut pictura poesis"—a poem is like a painting. The close relationship between the sister arts remained relatively intact until the eighteenth century when Gotthold Ephraim Lessing (1729–1781) inveighed against interart intrusions and determined to divorce poetry from painting in the *Laocoön* by insisting that poetry, with its time-bound nature, had no business attempting to incorporate the spatiality of visual art into its midst. The term *ekphrasis* derives from the Greek *ekphrassein* which suggests speaking out or expressing (G. Scott 301), and was originally used to refer to the rhetorical stratagem of giving voice to mute objects in order to achieve *enargeia*, or the creation of vivid pictorial images before the mind's eye of an audience. Ekphrasis gradually evolved to mean literary embellishment, a self-contained piece that described a visual art object, regardless of whether it had voice or not; whether it was fictional or real, but having no specific function other than one of aesthetic finality (Barthes 143). In its broadest meaning, ekphrasis can refer to any kind of "word painting" that emulates the visual and spatial properties of the arts in words (Krieger 1992, 9); in modern usage, it often takes the form of an intertextual reference that provides metacommentary on the text within which it is inscribed.[7] The inherent paradox of the ekphrastic moment is two-fold: first, the art object it manifests verbally is made present in a reader's imagination only through an awareness of its physical absence; second, as the successive temporality of the verbal art form is temporarily arrested in order to accommodate the spatial and atemporal qualities of the linguistically created visual image, the resulting bi-generic confrontation provokes what James Heffernan calls a "paragonal struggle for power between word and image" (1993, 93). Implicit in any use of ekphrasis is the writer's ambition to have words outlast their visual arts subject, displacing visual with verbal representation; the unstable natural signs of painting with the arbitrary, but more permanent signs of writing. Foucault, while admitting that the relation of painting to writing is infinite, points to the otiose nature of this type of enterprise since neither painting nor writing can be reduced to the other's terms. "It is in vain," he observes, "that we say what we see; what we see never resides in what we say."[8]

Ekphrastic interpolation tends to "spatialize" literature in much the same way that Joseph Frank, in his groundbreaking essay "Spatial Form in Modern Literature" (1945), and subsequently Gérard Genette, using a more sophisticated taxonomy, argued that interfering with the time flow of literary sequentiality through mise-en-abyme, analepsis, prolepsis, or parataxis, interrupted the linearity of textual discourse, thereby spatializing its form. Because it attempts to imitate the spatial simultaneity of a work of art within the temporal unfolding of narrative, the ekphrastic passage temporarily suspends narrative continuity and stills the "turning world" of literature as it bends discursive linearity into the shape of a circular mimesis germane to plastic art forms (Krieger 1992, 265–66). W. J. T. Mitchell proposed three types of spatial representation in literature: shaped, or iconic, poetry; ekphrasis; and fictional description (1989, 95). Azorín utilizes two of these three forms with great frequency, and it might be worth our while to speculate why the ekphrastic topos so engaged his imagination. Murray Krieger holds that as a time-bound art form, ekphrasis bestows on literature the unique capability to arrest its own movement by producing the illusion of simultaneity and stasis within a normally temporal dynamics; as such, literature's progressive evolution is always accompanied by the "archetypal principle of repetition, of eternal return" (1967, 125). In his most recent work, Krieger refers to the self-reflexive, circular movement and shape suggested by the literary ekphrasis as an "ouroboros" which, in Modern literature, converts chronological time into the mythic time of the eternal return (1992, 226–27). All this has obvious implications in terms of Azorín's preference for description and the ekphrastic topos, as well as his favorite thematic hobby-horses, the personal burden of time and the repetition of "history" that he reformulated into his own version of Nietzsche's eternal recurrence. Aside from his partiality to ekphrasis, we know that Azorín had always been concerned with the transposition of diachronic sequentiality into the synchrony of simultaneous coexistence, melding—as Inman Fox observed—"the present and the past with the intention of undoing the destructive force of linear time and of creating a new reality determined by shared rhythms and sensibilities (1988, 154).

In addition to his preference for the "still movement" of ekphrasis, Azorín was also partial to converting the linearity of time into circular patterns through the use of present perfect verb tenses. José Ortega y Gasset noted that when Azorín wrote "he estado" [I have been] rather than "estuve" [I was], or "he llamado" [I have called] instead of "llamé" [I called], he was not being capricious or precious. Rather, the present perfect tense enabled Azorín to freeze the subject in a state that Ortega dubbed "virtual stillness," a temporality of pure presentness which had somehow not yet slipped into an irretrievable past.[9] Azorín himself explained his predilection for the present perfect in the 1938 "El pretérito perfecto." Assuming the identity of his favorite verb tense ("Soy el Pretérito Perfecto"), he wrote that the past was his territory and, as an expert on the subject, he could say that there was a remote past as well as an imminent past which expresses a time that has not yet come to a definitive end, "and from which vestiges appear to trickle down to us" (5:995). The static nature of the present perfect captures the fleeting moment in a timeless, "forever now" zone, and is a way of defying the absolute "pastness" of the preterit with its implications of chronology; of physical activity completed; of life marching onward inexorably toward death.[10] Azorín perhaps best expressed his thoughts on time in a decidedly visual image that juxtaposed the eternal symbolism of the cypress against the fugacious nature of the rose: "The cypress . . . is always the same, and from its pointed top it can look down, among the rose bushes, at the continuous renewal of the roses . . . how they flower in the spring and how they disappear in autumn. This . . . was like an image of life, of changeless eternity, always the same, and of beautiful, transient things that disappear with time" (2:632).

William Carlos Williams, a poet whose sensitivity to the visual arts and involvement with the art world in New York City are well-known, wrote that Modernism often fused poetry and painting, and that it was a period of time, unlike the one that preceded it, when words went beyond themselves to express tactile qualities to become closely allied with painting (Steiner 1982, 72). More recently, Murray Krieger distinguished Modernism from the post-Modern period when he noted that the preference for ekphrasis which appears to characterize Modern literature, expresses the writers' "lingering semiotic desire for the natural sign, and leads them to resort to verbal analogies to painting in a struggle to create emblems out of words" (1992, 22, 233). Azorín not only created visual emblems out of words in his own work, but he was intrigued by the ekphrastic topos in the work of other writers. In his copy of J.-K. Huysmans's *A Rebours*, the most heavily annotated passage is the one in which des Esseintes acquires two paintings, one of them Gustave Moreau's *Salomé*, before which he dreams the nights away. What caught Azorín's attention is a lengthy ekphrasis of the painting by Huysmans in which color-coded words and concepts emphasize the painting's visual sensuality.[11] In my study of the impact the visual arts had upon Azorín's creative writing, as well as on his es-

says and literary criticism, I have included a chapter on his positive response to intercrarts parallels in the work of other authors; there are also chapters on the ckphrastic imperative in the novel *Doña Inés*, the short story "La casa cerrada," and another on the influence Cézanne and the cinema may have had on *Salvadora de Olbena*. Still other chapters of the book examine Azorín's construction of the visual art or portrait simile, its importance to his stylistics, and its role in the novel *Don Juan* and the play *Comedia del arte*. I also study Azorín's affinities with Spanish and French painters who were his contemporaries, his vast knowledge of the Prado and Louvre museums, and the role played by paintings in his writing.

No discussion of Azorín's interest in, and deep involvement with, the visual arts, however, would be complete without addressing the significance literary and plastic landscape had on his work. To understand that significance, we must first understand what the landscape—in particular the classical landscape of Castile—meant not only to Azorín, but to all the writers and painters who comprise the so-called Generation of 1898 in Spain. It is with this pivotal moment in Spanish cultural history that the first part of my book begins. Contrary to what is popularly believed, it was the previous generation of intellectuals, painters, and art historians associated with the Institución Libre de Enseñanza and the liberal "Revolution of 1868" that deposed the monarchy of Queen Isabel II, who first semantisized a rebuilding of Spain in terms of landscape art and literature.

As it did elsewhere in Europe, the second half of the nineteenth century in Spain coincided with the emergence of landscape painting as an academically sanctioned genre, and from this point it was only a short step for the educational reformer, Francisco Giner de los Ríos (1839–1915), to supplement the teaching of geology and geography at the Institución Libre de Enseñanza with the participation of visual artists in celebrating the Spanish national terrain in paint. Manuel Bartolomé Cossío (1857–1935), a colleague of Giner's at the Institución Libre, and one of Spain's first internationally renowned modern art historians, directed his scholarly attention to the study of El Greco and Velázquez, discovering that both painters frequently employed not only Castilian landscape scenery in their paintings, but that they also resorted to Impressionist painting techniques hundreds of years before these were "reinvented" by French painters in the last third of the nineteenth century. There are uncanny coincidences that I explore in Chapter 1, between the nation-building role ascribed to landscape painting and writing by the Generations of 1868 and 1898 in Spain, both of them galvanized by the political events of the short-lived revolution of 1868, in the one case, and by Spain's ignominious defeat in the Spanish-American War in the other, and the nationalistic subtext of French landscape Impressionism that coalesced as a movement shortly after the disastrous Franco-Prussian War of 1870–1871.

Growing demand for work by El Greco on the European art market, coupled with Édouard Manet's interest in and intertextal use of work by Velázquez, proved of liminal importance to developments in Spain. While the rekindling of international interest in the great Spanish masters enabled the intellectuals of the Institución Libre to situate both painters in the mainstream of contemporary European art as formidable precursors, it also allowed the younger group of Spanish writers and painters, those eventually baptized as the "gente nueva" of Spanish Modernism (to which the men of 1898 also belonged), to incorporate commentary on El Greco and Velázquez into their essays and fiction, and to utilize impressionist techniques in their writing as a way of challenging the su-

perannuated aesthetics of a complacent Spanish bourgeoisie. As the iconoclastic anarchist he liked to play, at least in the first years of his career, Azorín inevitably became one of the first "new writers" to popularize El Greco and Velázquez in fiction and newspaper articles. However, as I point out in Chapter 3, while he first turned to these two painters as representatives of new and unconventional aesthetics, with time Azorín transformed the classics of Spanish literature and art into the keystones of a conservative political agenda.

Landscape painting, nevertheless, and in particular the Impressionist movement, maintained its position of privilege throughout Azorín's long life and literary career (1873–1967). As I show in Chapter 4, Azorín's knowledge of European landscape art history was quite remarkable, and his favorite artists, whose paintings inform many essays on landscape, are those from whom art historians trace the evolution of Impressionist painting. Given his personal preferences, it is not surprising that Azorín continued to employ literary techniques and themes drawn from the Impressionist movement well into the 1940s. The fifth, and last chapter of Part One, addresses the significance of landscape to Azorín's aesthetics and explores the salient role played by Impressionist art and artists in his essays, short stories, and the novels *La Voluntad* and *María Fontán*.

In Pursuit
of the Natural Sign

Part I
Narrating the Nation: The Castilian Landscape in Spanish Literature and Art, 1868–1898

1
Defining Castile: *Institucionismo*, the Generation of '98, and the Origins of Modern Spanish Landscape

ON CONSIDERING THE LEGACY OF THE SO-called Generation of 1898, what frequently comes to mind is the attention its writers paid to the Spanish landscape, particularly that of Castile. José Martínez Ruiz (Azorín), the self-appointed theorist of the Generation, gave this group credit for legitimizing landscape as a literary genre: "Landscape attracted us . . . landscape for the sake of landscape as the only protagonist of a novel, story or poem . . . was a real innovation" (6:215). A natural development of the Generation's literary interest in landscape was the writers' interest in landscape painting which Azorín saw as part of the triad informing the aesthetic orientation of his day: "la escuela del 98, el wagnerismo y los paisajis-tas" (6:292). He attributed a heuristic function to landscape genre, suggesting that it was non-existent in the eyes of the general public until interpreted by a painter or a writer: "Yes; from the moment a writer or painter describes the landscape, the landscape exists. The artist has created the landscape; from that moment on, everyone will be able to see what nobody had seen before" (9:759). Azorín argued that it was not explorers who discovered and familiarized the world with new lands, but painters and writers. Africa, he maintained, was "created"

for the majority of Frenchmen and incorporated to the French national consciousness through the paintings of Delacroix as well as the painting and travel diaries of Eugène Fromentin (9:758–60).[1] In his view it was also the travel-ogues of French writers like Dumas, Achard, and especially Gautier's *Voyage en Espagne* that revealed the Spanish landscape, in particular the magnificent Guadarrama mountain range, to the young men of '98 who were just beginning "to love the old Castilian towns" (2:911) and "to observe, to feel, to describe the Castilian landscape" (2:891). The Guadarrama mountains, which appear so often in paintings by Velázquez and Goya, played a significant role in the ideological programs of both the Generations of 1868 and 1898, intellectuals, writers, and artists who saw their mission as that of reviving a Castilianophile consciousness in the minds of Spaniards.

Less well-known is that perhaps no other group of writers and intellectuals had such strong ideological and aesthetic affinities with the painters of their time as did those working in finisecular Spain, and that the painters associated with the Generation of 1898 were just as vital in endorsing and promulgating the ideological cast given to the notion of the Spanish landscape as were their literary counterparts.[2] According to testimony, again offered by Azorín, the group of '98 authors "was very fond of art. Painting influenced the writers of the group a great deal"; "those writers lived in a painterly ambience" (6:218, 239). Indeed, the writers of '98 were avid visitors to museums, some were amateur painters themselves, and nearly all counted among their friends contemporary painters on whose work, as well as matters artistic and literary, they often contributed newspaper and magazine articles. The same men of letters frequently were inspired by contemporary and classical works of art, often incorporating into their poems, novels, and essays modern (chiefly impressionistic), painterly techniques.[3]

Although Azorín gave the Generation of 1898 artists and writers credit for putting landscape on the Spanish cultural map—"The group of writers so talked about here, has incorporated landscape to literature in a systematic way" (6:216)—a closer examination of nineteenth-century Spanish cultural history calls for a revision of Azorín's claim, which to this day is accepted by many historians and critics of literature. The legitimization of landscape as a literary and artistic genre was the principal endeavor of a group of intellectuals who came to national prominence at the time of "La Gloriosa" (1868); namely, the second-generation Krausists with Francisco Giner de los Ríos at their helm. This select coterie of university professors was also affiliated with the beginnings of religious modernism in Spain, subscribing to a rational Christianity unencumbered by the accouterments of dogma and revealed mysteries. An attempt was made in December 1864 to squelch modern, neo-Catholicism in Europe by Pius IX in his encyclical *Quanta cura*, the decree *Syllabus errorum*, and finally, in 1870, with the pronouncement of the Pope's infallibility (Jiménez García 173). In Spain the Marqués de Orovio, Minister of Public Works and the Economy, reinforced the Vatican's position with his own 1866 circular admonishing the increasingly vocal Krausist and liberal, neo-Catholic professorate to respect the teaching of Catholic beliefs in their university classrooms. Orovio's second decree of 1875 provoked organized protest by faculty against his demand that only an approved curriculum be taught and that it not contradict Catholic dogma, attack the monarchy, or lead students astray to moral or social "error." This infringement of academic freedoms and personal religious belief, and the attendant outcry on the part of liberal faculty, led to the dismissal of Giner de los Ríos and other liberal university professors from their positions. The time these men spent in exile, or detained in the provinces, was passed in an intense epistolary exchange devoted to the planning of an educational establishment free of religious and academic ties to the State, whose aim it would be to regenerate Spain through a reform of national education.[4] The *Institución Libre de Enseñanza* (hereafter *ILE*) was founded in 1876, and once classes began, its faculty set about putting into practice their declared mission of rediscovering Spain's long-lost *señas de identidad*.

Deeply influenced by positivistic determinism, especially Taine's notion of *race, moment et milieu*, and by the concomitant emergence of geology and geography as discrete scientific disciplines from the general rubric of "natural history," the founders of the *ILE* were among the first to study the Spanish terrain. Familiarity with and appreciation of the national landscape were considered indispensable, since the prevailing belief held that a nation's physical environment (*medio ambiente*) shaped the indigenous population and its history, and might account for the current deplorable state of the Spanish nation. At the *ILE* scientific exploration of the national terrain was considered a patriotic enterprise that could lead the Spanish people not only to self-recognition through an understanding of their environment, but also to an awareness of the backward state of their country which it was so crucial to restore and regenerate. Similarly, geology and geography as a patriotic undertaking formed a significant part of '98 ideology. Unamuno warned that only by submerging themselves in the landscape could Spaniards recover faith in a promising national future (1:432), while in *Un pueblecito. Ríofrío de Avila* (1916), Azorín wrote that knowledge of geography was the foundation of patriotism. Echoing a pronouncement Unamuno had made in *En torno al casticismo* (1895), he argued, "We will not love our country, we will not love it well, if we are not familiar with it. Let us feel our landscape; let the landscape imbue our spirit" (3:561).[5]

Because Giner believed, as did most educated men of his day, that there was a correlation between "the geological composition, the relief of the land, the climate, the environment . . . and man, a relationship that imprints itself on the constitution of the body . . . from where it extends to our tastes, habits and arts" (1865, 43), he placed a great deal of emphasis on the study of geology and geography at the *ILE* as primary sources that would help revive the slumbering national collective consciousness and lead to the recovery of Spain's autocthonous artistic, historic, political, and racial identity.[6] Giner's advocacy of hands-on field experience prior to class lectures and laboratory practice in all areas of instruction (10:80), led to the Institute's famous pedagogy of "excursionism." The impact this methodology had on students is attested by Leopoldo Palacios, one of Giner's disciples:

> Y la cátedra no terminaba en la Universidad . . . continuaba a la salida, en la calle . . . y seguía los domingos en el campo, o en la Sierra, o en los pueblos aldeanos . . . o en los museos y las viejas ciudades castizas, reviviendo el Arte y la Historia, y donde él [Giner] nos descubría realmente a España, a la pasada y a la por venir—¡la eterna!—, ¡despertándonos en la verdadera adoración hacia ella! (Giner 1933b, 12:10)

> [And the classroom did not end at the University . . . it continued afterwards, in the street . . . and during Sunday excursions to the countryside, or to the mountains, or to rural villages . . . or to the museums and the typical old Spanish cities, reviving Art and History, and where he [Giner] revealed an authentic Spain to us, the Spain of the past and the Spain of the future—the eternal one— awakening in us a genuine adoration for her!]

As geography, geology, and topography became solidly established academic pursuits, its pioneers turned to field excursions to compile data, collect samples, and sketch the terrain to be studied and mapped. This confluence of new methodologies sparked interest in the aesthetic aspects of the landscape; the development of landscape painting followed soon afterward.

Of all the subfields of geology, the most popular appears to have been orography. Nearly every issue of the *Boletín de la Institución Libre de Enseñanza* (hereafter *BILE*) is replete with news items on conferences, excursions, and book reviews dealing with mountain geology. One of the groups most active at the *ILE* in the practice of excursionism was the faculty of geology which in 1886, under the leadership of José Macpherson, founded the "Sociedad para el estudio del Guadarrama." Scientific study of the Guadarrama coincided with an appreciation of its aesthetic possibilities: the founding protocols of the newly constituted Society were also signed by the painter Aureliano de Beruete and the art historian Manuel Bartolomé Cossío.[7] Excursionism was also important to the writers of '98, most of whom demonstrated great interest in travel and the reading and writing of travel literature, rich in the visual evocation of place. Azorín's partiality to geographical dictionaries and tracts on topography is well-documented by the large number of books on the subject in his Monóvar library, and he reminisced about having traveled "throughout Spain" with Pío Baroja at a time when the study of landscape and landscape writing was an "unusual thing in literature" (8:144). Baroja himself reported in "Nuestra Generación" on the Generation's desire to become familiar with the land where they lived, to travel, to know the countryside, to make excursions to the provincial cities (7:660). His reportage in "A las orillas del Duero" of a trip he took with his brother Ricardo through Old Castile—Soria, Covaleda, Numancia, the Laguna Negra, and el Urbión— immediately recalls Machado's epic poem "La tierra de Alvargonzález" (8:803–12). Ricardo's own memoir of a trip he and Pío made in the company of Paul Schmitz through the Guadarrama, El Paular, Avila, El Escorial, and Toledo (1952, 125), was fictionalized by Pío in *Camino de perfección*, a novel Azorín called one of the first "collections of landscapes" produced by the Generation of 1898 (2:891).

Giner's attention was drawn to the Guadarrama mountains when, as part of his program of reviving an authentic Spanish legacy, he turned to the study of classical literature and art, and discovered that the Guadarrama appeared repeatedly in the backgrounds of paintings by Velázquez and Goya. Soon the painters and art historians associated with the *ILE* were undertaking excursions of their own, either to paint in the mountains or to museums to study the largely forgotten works of the Spanish masters. Although the *Institución Libre* undoubtedly was responsible for giving landscape painting the impetus it needed to become a genre recognized and accepted by the Academy, plein-air painting was not entirely the product of revolutionary attitudes promoted at the Institute. Landscape painting in Europe was a phenomenon of the nineteenth century. In

France the Prix de Rome for landscape was established in 1817; in Barcelona's Escola de Nobles Artes landscape painting was introduced as a subject of study in 1824, while in Madrid it was not until 1844 that the Academy of Fine Arts (San Fernando) approved a professorship of landscape painting, whose first occupant was Jenaro Pérez Villaamil (1807–1854) (Pl. 1).[8] Painting directly from nature, however, was not taught in Madrid until 1857 when Carlos de Haes (1826–1898), a painter of Belgian descent who studied abroad and maintained close contact with artistic movements in Europe, took possession of the Landscape Chair at the Academy. Years after the fact, Aureliano de Beruete—a student of Haes's—recalled that during the competitive examinations for the Chair of Landscape Painting, the technique and color Haes employed were so unusual that his work caused a furor among his rivals, leading the jury to demand an examination of Haes's paint box to uncover possible irregularities. What they found there, Beruete wryly observed, was nothing but "the fruit of wise teaching, based on the study of nature," radically different from the mannered conventionalisms prevalent in Spanish landscape painting at the time (1898, 379).

The novelty of Haes's approach was his view of nature as a protagonist worthy of painting for its beauty alone. Azorín recalled that when first elected to the Academy of Fine Arts in 1860, Haes presented an entirely fresh approach to landscape painting by insisting in his inaugural address that an artist's responsibility was to record on canvas a scene exactly as it was observed by the painter's eye (6:293). Preferring to work from natural models, he urged a move away from slavish imitation of formulaic landscape "recipes" sanctioned by the Academy: "In landscape exactitude of reproduction is worth more than an impossible ideal. Nature does not easily tolerate the work of the imagination. . . . Her countless accidents and combinations leave little for us to invent" (293). In his lecture Haes also championed the depiction of rock formations, plants, and trees as they appeared in nature, and not as the painter would like them, or needed them, to appear ideally in his work. Haes's mature paintings include mountainscapes, a reflection of the growing popularity of orography and mountaineering that took place toward the latter part of his career. He also paid special attention to the mineralogical composition and physical geography of the rock formations that he painted; the titles given these canvases demonstrate the painter's knowledge of a specialized technical vocabulary: *Paisaje del Guadarrama con pico en granito; Desfiladero de la Hermida en calizas, Peñas de Alsasúa, Paisaje de Montaña* (Pl. 2).

Haes was especially known for his treatment of trees, insisting they were the true protagonists of landscape, each having its own "language," physiognomy, and preferred soil and climate in which to take root. "The artist who might wish to paint them," he wrote, "must be familiar with their expression and, as it were, with their habits and preferences . . ." (294). Carmen Pena noted that Haes initiated the marked interest trees would acquire as a motif in the essays and creative work of the Generation of 1898 (1982, 102). Azorín knew and quoted from Haes's "Discurso de Recepción," especially the painter's comments on the individuality of trees in the landscape (6:294). Similar to the artist's plea for appreciating the regional idiosyncracies of landscape, Azorín recognized that a fundamental distinction had to be made between a generic and indeterminate landscape and "a concrete landscape, relative to a specific geography" (2:801). In "Los árboles y el agua," Azorín condemned the lack of respect for trees and water in Castile, tracing the "traditional antipathy for trees" as far back in Spanish history as the *Relaciones topográficas* compiled during the reign of Felipe II (4:58). He took special interest in the deforestation of Castile: bibliophile that he was, Azorín's personal library contains an annotated copy of Guillermo Bowles's *Introducción a la historia natural y a la geografía física de España* (1789), in which he marked passages where Bowles observed that Castile's isolated elm and walnut trees indicated the presence of subterranean water reserves and was a clear sign that successful reforestation could be undertaken. However, Bowles observed, the task would not be an easy one since the Spanish people had an aversion to trees and claimed they only encouraged the presence of nesting birds that damaged the grape and wheat harvests (265–66).[9]

In his speech at the Academy of Fine Arts, Haes took the opportunity to address the Government, pleading that in its "paternal solicitude" the State not skimp on its support of landscape painting and approve the reforms necessary to modernize and perfect its teaching

(296). While the pedagogical methods he used were met with disapproval, and were even considered "seditious" by the old guard, subsequent generations of painters and art historians recognized Haes as having introduced "a novel and rational and progressive manner of interpreting Nature" (Beruete y Moret 111–12). Recognizing landscape as indicative of a nation's specific geographical character, and establishing it as a legitimate genre was viewed by critics from Giner to Azorín and Ortega as the arrival of a thoroughly "modern" element on the Spanish cultural scene. The Generation of 1898 was especially fond of emphasizing that the ancients had used landscape sketchily, as a decorative element only, and often quoted Sainte Beuve's argument that modern landscape writing was initiated by Jean Jacques Rousseau.[10] Observing that the taste for nature in literature was a thoroughly modern phenomenon, among the many pronouncements Azorín made on aesthetics in his 1902 novel *La Voluntad*, was the opinion that "a writer will be that much more an artist the better he is able to interpret the emotion of the landscape. . . . It is a thoroughly, almost thoroughly, modern emotion" (Fox 1968, 130). José Ortega y Gasset, Spain's quintessential modernist, advanced similar thoughts on the matter, writing that the discovery of Nature "as a contemplative delight is a feat of the Modern Age"; "the invention of a plastically beautiful landscape was reserved for our time" (2:604, 605).

Haes established for himself a reputation not only as the first painter to bring progressive (i.e., modern) approaches to his choice of technique and subject matter, but through his many excursions to paint and sketch in the countryside, as the first contemporary Spanish artist able to capture something of a particularly Spanish "essence" in his work. Older than Giner de los Ríos, and never formally associated with the *Institución Libre*, Haes's *excursionismo*, often in the company of students whom he treated as equals, anticipated the spirit of the ILE and brought him attention as a precursor to Giner (exhib. cat. *Darío de Regoyos* 66). Aureliano de Beruete fondly recalled the excursions on which Haes took his classes on spring mornings to the Pardo, teaching his students to work out of doors, and of having had the privilege to accompany Haes on an extensive painting campaign in the Picos de Europa during the summer holidays in 1874 (1898, 379). In the closing remarks of his 1860 speech at the Academy of San Fernando, Haes stated that he would consider himself lucky should he, in his capacity as Professor of Landscape Painting, be able to contribute to the development of the discipline. Indeed, it was from his studio that the painters most closely associated with the *ILE*, and later with the Generation of 1898, emerged: Aureliano de Beruete, Agustín Lhardy, Casimiro Sainz, and Juan Espina (Pantorba 47).

Azorín's personal "maestro de estética" was Aureliano de Beruete (1845–1912), a transitional figure between Carlos de Haes and the post-Impressionism of younger painters like Darío de Regoyos. Born into a wealthy family of distinguished political figures, Beruete never seriously pursued a career in law for which he had trained, nor a career in the national political arena where some of his family members were active. Instead he became an internationally acclaimed art historian, and he painted: mostly Castilian landscapes that became visual and ideological emblems for the Castilianophile intellectuals of the Generations of 1868 and 1898. Because he frequently exhibited abroad and served on juries of international exhibitions, foreign art critics commented on Beruete's exceptional knowledge of Spain based on his extensive travel and observation. In a 1907 issue of *L'Art et les Artistes*, William Ritter noted that "M. de Beruete has travelled extensively in the course of his painting campaigns: he knows his Spain, and everything related to Spain, better than anyone." Referring to Beruete as the Spanish landscapist par excellence, the painter of Toledo, and the artist who best depicted the bare, gray earth, arid rocks, and snowy mountain peaks of Castile, Ritter praised the artist for meeting the challenge of painting landscapes from which the customary motifs of vegetation and "anything that makes for a smiling landscape" were entirely absent (198). Since he painted for pleasure, Beruete did not feel the need to make a name for himself by exhibiting at the biannual National Art Expositions, so he was not well-known outside artistic and literary circles in Madrid. Azorín observed the paradox in a 1913 essay, remarking that he admired "Beruete like no one else. Until now, he's been a painter known only to a very small public: critics, art connoisseurs and men of letters" (7:241). It was only during a retrospective of the painter's work organized by Joaquín Sorolla several months after Beruete's death on 5

January 1912 that the public at large became aware of his cultural significance.[11]

Closely allied from his student days to the Colegio Internacional and to Nicolás Salmerón whose approach to pedagogical reform anticipated that of the *Institución Libre de Enseñanza*, Beruete formed a lasting friendship with Giner and was among the first *accionistas* to support the *ILE*. For a time he taught at the Institute and he educated his son, Aureliano de Beruete y Moret, who was to become a notable art historian and director of the Prado Museum, at the Institute.[12] Having spent his formative years in the studios of Carlos de Haes, it is not at all surprising that Beruete's familiarity with the excursionist methodology and his painter's eye trained to appreciate the Spanish terrain, would be welcome not only at the *ILE*, but also among the founding members of the "Sociedad para el estudio del Guadarrama." Beruete's parallel interests in geology and art perhaps furnish the clearest evidence that the consecration of landscape painting and the aesthetics of *paisajismo* which characterize the last third of the nineteenth century in Spain, were encouraged by the Institute's "excursionismo en su doble versión geográfica y artística" (exhib. cat. *A. de Beruete* 14, 35). As a result of the *ILE*-sponsored excursionism, Giner turned his attention to the aesthetic aspects of the terrain, developing what he called an "aesthetics of geology." As was the case of titles Haes gave to his mountainscapes, Giner's landscape descriptions include similar technical vocabulary: "The earth, the solid crust of the planet, as an element of the landscape . . . in and of itself offers enough data to create what could be termed an 'aesthetics of geology.' The first of these is the character of the materials that make it up. There are, for example, granitic, basaltic, alluvial landscapes, etc." (1965, 40). The other factor in this equation for Giner was the purely aesthetic aspect of geology. A significant portion of his pedagogical philosophy thus revolved first, around the study of nature, and second, around landscape painting as highly effective visual stimuli which he thought could lead students to a recovery and definition of the Spanish nation and its character.

Giner himself was a passionate lover of nature; Azorín included him, along with Nietzsche and Fray Luis de Granada, as three writers whose understanding of Nature was paradigmatic in that they considered landscape to be more than an insignificant background accessory to painting (4:147). Despite the sometimes considerable geographical, linguistic, historical, and cultural differences among the provinces of the Spanish Kingdom, Giner and his colleagues defined the nation in terms of Castile, the "mother lode" of Spain from which the modern Spanish State was to emerge: its spiritual core, center of past imperial glories, and cultural home of renowned classical poets, painters, and statesmen. The view that "Spanishness" was determined and circumscribed by the historically dominant Kingdom of Castile was not in itself a novel idea: in *A Handbook for Travellers in Spain*, Richard Ford noted that "The Castilian . . . claims to be synonymous with the Spaniard . . . and gives his name to the Kingdom, nation, and language."[13] The *institucionistas* resurrected this notion in the last half of the nineteenth century and made it an integral plank of their regenerationist platform. The concept was developed and given scholarly endorsement by the revisionist historiography that emerged with the new generation of intellectuals associated with the *ILE*: the research and publications of historians and sociologists such as Rafael Altamira and Joaquín Costa, the philologist Ramón Menéndez Pidal, and the art historian Manuel B. Cossío all revolved around a Castilian-centered frame of reference. To understand and value Castile, to restore her to former greatness through the careful, broad education of a new cadre of intellectual leaders, would regenerate the entire nation. This premise was embraced by the Generation of 1898. Like it or not, according to Azorín, Castile, which had set the tone for national development and had defined the national character in early modern history, was currently, of all the Spanish provinces, the most in need of stimulus and intervention: her cities were deserted and on the verge of collapse; her lands lay uncultivated and sterile. Azorín called on his readers, men of the twentieth century, to restore life to Castile, "that most glorious part of Spain to which we owe our soul."[14]

Accuracy in representing the Castilian landscape was of utmost importance to Giner. Artists like Beruete, who preferred the soft light and verdant gray-green landscape of the north early in his career, turned his gaze, under Giner's influence, to the arid landscape of Castile and to its historically significant cities and their environs: Toledo, Avila, Segovia, and the suburbs of Madrid. Baroja recalled Ramón y Cajal's observation that only the eyes of a caterpillar could remain insensitive to the poetry of the gray, yellow, brown and blue colors in the Madrid landscape, and he pointed out that when speaking of the chromaticity of the Madrid suburbs, Ramón y Cajal "was repeating the axiom of the day, very much in line with the Institución Libre de Enseñanza" (7:927). The change of physical venue in Beruete's painting called for a corresponding change of palette that highlighted color tones often found in Giner's geological observations or Azorín's landscape writing. The art historian Francisco Calvo Serraller noted that Beruete's "poetic sublimation of the Castilian desert" brought about the painter's "new chromatic scale, based on sienna, brown and mauve, and revealed the value of restrained, spare, glaringly linear structures, like a reflection of mountain geography" (77). The change did not go unnoticed by the writers of '98 and was most likely instrumental in producing the ideological and aesthetic rapprochement that developed between them and the older painter. Although Baroja observed the artist's change of palette—"Beruete, a landscapist from Haes's school, who had used a palette of dark green and gray, eventually became very Sorollesque, and painted using a lot of red and yellow" (7:887)—Azorín noted that "Little by little the master began to focus his love on the Castilian terrain" (7:242) (Pls. 3 and 4).[15]

In 1912 Azorín dedicated *Castilla* to this "marvelous painter of Castile" whose ideological concept of the landscape had obvious appeal to the writers and intellectuals of 1868 and 1898, and their task of revaluating and restoring Castile to her lost primacy of historical and cultural importance. Beruete's sober, dusty, ruined Castilian plains and villages closely approximated those described by the Generation's writers, and his Madrid landscapes often featured the Guadarrama mountains, reminding his contemporaries of paintings by Goya and Velázquez in which the same mountain range frequently appeared. Azorín commented on the painter's singular ability to portray the diaphanous atmosphere characteristic of the Madrid sky: "The clarity of the sky around Madrid, the diaphanous nature of those horizons above the high Manchegan tableland: no one has interpreted them on canvas, after Velázquez and Goya, like Aureliano de Beruete" (7:244).

The association Giner made between landscape—as material for both geological study and as an example of the environment that had forged the Spanish national character, and landscape as the subject of aesthetic praxis—led him to what can be described best as the elaboration of a "landscape pedagogy": an attempt to (re)create the country (*país*) through the plastic (re)presentation of the countryside (*paisaje*). According to W. J. T. Mitchell, the most ambitious of literatures—and, I would add, of visual arts—are "nation-making" texts (1994a, 321). Contemporary theorists acknowledge landscape as an ideological construct of signifiers through which a specific group of persons chooses to define themselves and through which they communicate to their peers the social relation they imagine themselves as having with nature.[16] Thus landscape painting is not necessarily an innocuous genre meant for tranquil contemplation; rather, it is a suggestive form of metaphor which may encode historical, political, cultural, or aesthetic values often allied with nationalistic ideals (Mitchell 1994b, 14, 29–30). The avenues of inquiry opened up in the nineteenth century by the new disciplines of ethnography, linguistics, social psychology and folklore further contributed to establishing unique national identities and boundaries between peoples, witnessing the birth of the idea of national states, a development that also embraced the visual arts as a reflection of the sociopolitical milieu.

In his much quoted and often reproduced 1885 essay "Paisaje," Giner stated that the most integral and encompassing of all artistic genres was landscape painting since it was charged with ethical and ideological connotations and was therefore capable of uplifting the moral condition of the society that produced and consumed it.[17] He clearly intuited that the production of cultural forms involved a transaction between image-makers and image-receivers, that landscape was a represented as well as a presented space which, through the aesthetics of reception, provided a venue whereby the revised image of Castile produced at the *ILE* could be promoted and communicated effectively to a large receptor-public whose historical consciousness he intended to rouse.[18] Giner felt that classical art, and landscape painting in particular, was a crucible that distilled pure (*castizo*) Spanish history and tradition from the baggage of corruption they had acquired over a period of many centuries. Calvo Serraller pointed out that the critical nationalism which issued forth from the *ILE* inspired not only the best landscape painting and the most important writing on art history produced in contemporary Spain, but that it was also responsible for linking Spain to European modernity (1985, 76). In the process of reinventing Spain as Castile, Giner and his colleagues elaborated a scientific-artistic discourse adopted by their disciples and associates who, in turn, were to form a most influential sector within the next generation of Spanish intellectual leadership; a significant portion of this discourse found its way into the thinking of the Generation of 1898.

In his essay "Sobre la educación artística de nuestro pueblo," Giner called for Spain to follow educational trends in Europe by instituting courses in the fine arts as early as the primary grades (12:57). Art appreciation, as he observed in "Espíritu y naturaleza," is a "'preparation for nature,' in the broad sense of the term; an education that teaches us to see it and feel it" (1899, 167). In the same essay Giner argued for a "pedagogical mission" of aesthetics, suggesting that appreciation of landscape painting was crucial not so much to developing a student's knowledge of technique, line, and color but, more importantly, "it has no other function than to make us notice the beauty of the countryside, to understand it, to take pleasure in it . . ." (1965, 167). Giner's fine arts landscape pedagogy found a niche in the early reformist ideology of the Generation of 1898. For Azorín, solving the "Spanish problem" was not so much a question of "hydrologic or agricultural politics" (4:60–61), but one of reorganizing the educational system in order to nurture "generations familiar with the Spanish terrain and its history, its art . . . the beauty of its landscapes and cities" (*PCQ* 56). In *La Voluntad* he outlined a pedagogical mission for art closely approximating Giner's affirmation that art for art's sake alone had little educational value: "Art must *serve* a humanitarian purpose, it must be *useful* . . . that is to say, it is a *means*, not an *end* . . . and let's consider how a new criticism might begin to push works of pure art out of the way . . ." (Fox 1968, 176–77). Landscape pedagogy also had a place in the thought of Ortega who was partial to "this pursuit of landscapes that constitutes excursionism" (2:419), and in "La pedagogía del paisaje," he argued that landscape is a better teacher than the most gifted of pedagogues (1:54). As did Giner,

Ortega believed that landscapes "teach us morals and history, two exalted disciplines of which Spaniards have not a little need" (1:56). Referring to the "paisaje-maestro" of the Guadarrama, he observed that the mountain range communicated to him "a lesson in 'Celt-Iberianism,' and it has clarified for me those ethnic secrets that the men painted by El Greco attempt to reveal to us in brightly lit museums with a slight tremor of their pointed beards" (1:56).[19]

Special attention was paid at the *ILE* to the work of El Greco, Velázquez and Goya not only because the landscape backgrounds of their paintings were inspired by the Castilian *paisaje*, but also because the artists' spirit carried the imprint of the Castilian environment which enabled them to convey something of the Spanish *genio nacional* in their work, thus providing the viewer a sense of historic and artistic continuity with the past (Giner 3:325; 12:82). Cossío, author of the first modern biography and *catalogue raisonné* on El Greco, suggested that although the painter could never fully dissociate himself from his native Cretan environment, he became so imbued with his adopted, Castilian *medio ambiente* that he immortalized in his art the innermost Spanish soul: "the sky, the landscape, the race and the legends of Castile" (1908, 1:199, 509).[20] This opinion entered unchanged into the '98 canon. Commenting on the El Greco collection at the Prado, Baroja observed: "I don't think there exists anything to explain better the work of a painter than the land in which he lives . . ." (8:829). Azorín elaborated similar views in *La Voluntad* where he noted that the Castilian psyche, as its landscape, is "clear, rigid, uniform . . . to see the austere and harsh panorama of the *cigarrales* around Toledo, is to see and understand the contorted and anguished physical types painted by El Greco" (Fox 1968, 211). Despite the claim Baroja had made in the inimitable fashion so characteristic of his old age that Giner and Cossío thought "an exhibit of earthenware or porcelain was much more worthy of attention than a work by Nietzsche or Dostoyevsky. To meditate on paintings by El Greco more important than understanding Kant or Einstein" (7:887), in "De la raza" Azorín argued that painters and writers were best qualified to represent racial (read: national) archetypes (9:1385). As Azorín observed in his "Discurso de Aranjuez," landscape appreciation was linked to an appreciation of Spanish history, the legacy of its classics, and the racial constitution of the Spanish people (9:1183).

When allying themselves with contemporary landscape painters, the writers of '98 preferred artists who shared their desire to portray an authentic vision of Spain. For both painters and writers this vision converged around the patriotic impulse of capturing on canvas or in print the spirit of the Spanish "race." Aureliano de Beruete, Joaquim Mir, Darío de Regoyos, Agustín Lhardy, Juan Espina, Santiago Rusiñol, Ignacio Zuloaga, and Joaquín Sorolla were just as involved in the creation and propagation of a Castilian (in most cases) and, more generally, a Spanish national paradigm in their art as were their literary contemporaries—the essayists, poets, and novelists of 1898. Azorín observed that Lhardy, together with Beruete and Espina, created a "cosa muy española" (6:264), while Ramiro de Maeztu singled out Zuloaga, Regoyos, Iturrino, and Guiard—Spanish painters (in addition to Rusiñol), with strongest ties to and multiple exhibitions in Paris—as revealing to the Parisian public "los caracteres tradicionales de la raza" (1903, 14). When asked why he did not paint the landscape of his native Basque country, Zuloaga responded that as an artist he was fascinated by contrasts, the more abrupt the better, and only Castile offered him those contrasts: "That's why I love Castile so much, that's why Castile has given me the fullness of her blinding light and shadows . . . the only definitive landscapes that my palette has preserved" (Lafuente Ferrari 1948a, 439). In the suggestively titled "La labor patriótica de Zuloaga," Unamuno identified in Zuloaga's work a plastic equivalent of *intrahistoria*, a concept he developed in the essays of *En torno al casticismo*: "In his paintings, replete with men beyond the pale of time and history, Zuloaga has given us a mirror of the nation's soul" (7:768).[21] He preferred Zuloaga to other painters because the Basque artist was a genuine "exemplar of our race, he has earned glory and has bestowed it upon his caste and his native land, resurrecting the ancient and pure Spanish painting, Castilian painting" (7:729). The "ancient painting" Unamuno saw as surviving and finding new life in the work of Zuloaga was the heritage of Velázquez who, together with El Greco and Goya, was restored to national consciousness by the *ILE* as a painter representative of the Castilian spirit. For Ortega, Zuloaga's work also synthe-

sized classical traditions epitomized by the painting of El Greco, Velázquez, and Goya (1:537). In 1910 he suggested that a synoptic exhibition of the Basque painter's work could provide the public pedagogic instruction since Zuloaga's painting was so forceful it would lead viewers to an examination of national consciousness. This legacy, according to Ortega, was "the greatest, most glorious thing a Spanish artist can do for the future of his race: to put it into contact with itself . . . until completely awakening its sensibility" (1:140). Azorín interviewed Zuloaga in 1917 and, like Unamuno, he wrote that rather than painting the historical and architectonic monuments of Spain, Zuloaga preferred to paint, as did the writers of his generation, the ordinariness of forgotten Castilian villages whose unexceptional, centuries-old ambience and unremarkable inhabitants formed the marrow of Castilian history. He observed that Zuloaga understood Castile so well because the "pueblo popular vasco" of the twentieth century incarnated the "pueblo castellano" of the sixteenth and seventeenth centuries (Pl. 5).[22]

By all accounts, however, the Generation of 1898 considered Darío de Regoyos (1857–1913) to be "their painter" (Azorín 6:295). In a posthumous homage offered by Catalonia to Regoyos, who spent the last years of his life in Barcelona, the critic J. Torres-García remembered the artist as "el único pintor de raza, auténticamente 'castellano'," and the essence of his work as a genuine portrayal of the Spanish landscape, while Calvo Serraller saw Regoyos as incorporating in his painting not only an ideological interpretation of the landscape, but also as including innuendos of patriotic regeneration characteristic of the moral and psychological crisis lived by the writers and painters of finisecular Spain (exhib. cat. *D. de Regoyos* 44, 14). Regoyos first came to the Generation's attention via the illustrations he provided for *La España negra*, a collection of poems by the Belgian writer Émile Verhaeren and etchings by Regoyos commemorating a trip the two had made through Spain in 1888. While their collaborative efforts were published immediately in the Brussels periodical *L'Art Moderne*, they were serialized for the first time in Spain only ten years later in the Barcelona review *Luz*; publication in book form followed in 1899. Regoyos's pessimistic vision of Spain as an ignorant, silent, sinister, and crudely provincial

country fit remarkably well with the early ideological and aesthetic position adopted by the
writers of 1898. According to Ramiro de Maeztu
La España negra caught the Generation's attention in the crucial year of the "Disaster," wield-
ing a great deal of influence on the menacing
and truculent aspects of Azorín's *La Voluntad*
and Baroja's *Camino de perfección* (D. de Regoyos 56).[23] Regoyos spent many years studying, painting, and actively participating in the
Bohemian life of the arts communities in Brussels and Paris. Unlike Zuloaga, who made his
home permanently in the French capital, Regoyos returned to Spain at the end of the century and became as vociferous a critic of the
aesthetic and intellectual vulgarity and mediocrity rampant in Spanish artistic circles as were
his friends Unamuno, Baroja, and Azorín; he
was frequently a signatory to collective writer-
painter manifestoes that appeared in the press.
And it has been all but forgotten that while Ortega possessed (as did so many writers of the
Generation of 1898), a reproduction of El Greco's *El caballero de la mano al pecho*, he also
owned a landscape by Regoyos: it was this picture of a train on the international bridge at
Bidasoa that inspired his seminal essay "Meditación del Marco" (2:308).

While still publishing as José Martínez Ruiz,
in the first issue of *Alma Española*, the future
"Azorín" exhorted his correligionaries to eschew art for art's sake and instead to employ
literature and art to create "una patria nueva."
If one loves Spain, writes Martínez Ruiz, if the
artist is moved by his country's historical sites,
has studied the national traditions, and is permeated by the spirit of the *pueblo*, the artist
must not fail, for the sake of Spain, to respond
to her call in all artistic endeavors (1904, 5). Curiously enough, most of the second-generation
participants in this nation-building project
were not Castilian natives: Unamuno, the Baroja and Maeztu brothers, as well as Zuloaga
were Basque; Azorín was born in the Levant;
Regoyos in Asturias; Sorolla, Mir, and Rusiñol
were Catalonian; Valle-Inclán was from Galicia; and the Machado brothers hailed from Andalusia. Yet each of them lived and defined the
Castilian consciousness and the Castilian landscape with a fervor and passion that were quite
remarkable. The group's ties to the land and its
description were just as evident in the visual
arts as they were in the creative work of its
writers. All were united in the quest for na-

tional identity and perceived themselves as participating in the construction of a modern,
national State. Landscape description, noted
Azorín, was the order of the day, the goal being
to force Spaniards to learn to "see" an authentic
image of their country and to generate in the
public conscience a pride in its land: one has
only to recall Unamuno's *Andanzas y visiones
españolas* or the painstakingly detailed Basque
landscapes of *Paz en la guerra*; Baroja's travel-
ogue of Castile, the Guadarrama, and the Levant in *Camino de perfección*; Azorín's
impressionistic landscapes in *La Voluntad*; the
mystical, medieval Galicia evoked by Valle-Inclán in *Sonata de otoño* or *Romance de lobos*
and *Divinas palabras*; and Machado's *Campos
de Castilla*.

Azorín understood the alliance of artists and
writers in his generation as having the same
mission: first, to focus attention on the contradiction between the false political rhetoric and
aesthetic values of "official" Spain and the dis-
mal reality of the nation; and second, to replace
that rhetoric with the *castizo* values of an authentic but forgotten Castile (Rozas 188). This
commonality of purpose that characterized the
Generation of 1898 landscape painters and
writers produced a confluence of friendships,
mutual exchange, and influence, as well as an
intertextuality wholly absent in the work of the
preceding generation. Azorín recognized that
the history of contemporary aesthetics could no
longer be written without accounting for the influence painting had upon literature and that of
literature upon art, and he considered the
craftsmanship involved in painting and writing
to be completely analogous (*PCQ* 96, 202), observing that creative persons working in the
same country, during the same historical moment, were apt to be influenced by the same
"mysterious emanations" (6:295).

Azorín's sensitivity to literature and art led
him to note that the manner in which the
painter-writer José Gutiérrez Solana (1886–
1945) described the various Spanish cities and
the social commentary he made in his books
replicated the plastic representation of the
same places and customs depicted in his painting (9:1357). Fernández Almagro confirmed
Azorín's observations: "Everything in Solana is
one and the same. His writing explains his
painting completely, and these two aspects of
his personality are both in consonance with the
sharp edge of his ideas about Spanish reality,

learned at the altar of Goya, the promotor, among other things, of 'Black Spain'" (1948, 192). Although Ramón Gómez de la Serna drew comparisons between Solana's painting and Valle-Inclán's *esperpento*, he concluded that it was pointless to search for influences in Solana's work: it was unique since the motivation behind it was solely that of racial continuity (1944, 44, 12). Solana's grim, expressionistic vision of Spain and the life of the underprivileged also has close affinities to Zuloaga's "temas de la España negra," the work of both painters traceable to the early graphic themes and style of Darío de Regoyos, as well as to the critical spirit of '98 (Barrio-Garay 55). In a 1917 essay, "Darío de Regoyos," a highly critical appraisal of the ideological orientation the Generation's writers had championed in their youth, José María Salaverría excoriated them, as well as Regoyos, for their negative vision of Spain and, in the painter's case, for returning to Spain laden with the baggage of Belgian and French "impressionistic modernity." Worse than falling into the "revolutionary tendencies" of Monet, Manet, and Pissarro, Regoyos was guilty of providing the graphics for *La España negra*, "that idiotic book by the poet Verhaeren." Salaverría suggested that Regoyos's vision was exacerbated by the intellectual climate in Spain which at the time was passing through the "zona triste del 98." It was this odious ambience that had shaped both Regoyos and Zuloaga; but in Salavería's view, whereas Zuloaga continued to stoke the "perverse" vision of Spain held by foreigners, Regoyos came to his senses and quickly abandoned his "wretched" thematics.[24]

Although Baroja did not care for either Zuloaga or Solana, and he categorically refuted any comparison between his work and theirs (7:886, 908), Fernández Almagro wrote that it was not difficult to identify similarities between the landscapes, domestic interiors, scenes, and physical types in *Camino de perfección* or *La Voluntad* and the "local color" that typified Zuloaga's most characteristic paintings. Baroja observed that if analogies were to be made between writers and painters, perhaps the greatest resemblance was between Zuloaga and Azorín, although he conceded Azorín's protagonists were more serene and in harmony with their environment than Zuloaga's "violently contorted" figures who appear to be at odds with the ambience in which they are portrayed

(7:892–93). Baroja himself felt special affection for Darío de Regoyos. Concurring with Azorín's assessment that "From Regoyos to Baroja, from one landscape to the other, from the plastic to the literary, there is but one step" (6:216), Baroja indicated that "one would have to put me in the same pigeonhole as Regoyos; he wanted to express, as did I, so many things with a faulty technique" (7:891–92) (Pl. 6).[25] In *Camino de perfección*, his own version of travels through "black Spain," Baroja referred to Regoyos, along with Zuloaga and Rusiñol, as vanguard painters whose work was reviled by the bourgeois art establishment; Ricardo Baroja supported fiction with fact when he recalled his submission to one National Art Exhibition as being hung in the "Sala del Crimen," alongside paintings by Regoyos and the young Pablo Picasso (40). The painter Daniel Vázquez Díaz also told the anecdote of how his two entries for the 1905 National Exhibition were hung in the infamous "Sala del Crimen" together with canvases by Solana, who introduced him to Regoyos, all three painters consoling each other on their unhappy fate (51). Nevertheless, Pío Baroja speculated correctly that with time Regoyos, a friend and traveling companion, might be considered the most original of all Spanish landscape painters.

Although Azorín wrote that the Generation of 1898 identified with Darío de Regoyos because he shared "our color and our precision," its members also recognized Carlos de Haes as their "brother" because he demonstrated the same "perseverance and enthusiasm that we had." Azorín recalled being a frequent visitor to the Carlos de Haes gallery at the Museum of Modern Art and wrote that he learned to create verbal landscape during his meditations on Haes's paintings: "There I meditated on the plastic landscape, and I gathered strength to persevere—to persevere and to polish—my landscape descriptions" (6:216). Of all the Generation's painters, however, it is with Beruete and his ramshackle country inns, painted almost as if they were natural outcroppings of the terrain, his dusty landscapes, and the special attention he paid to cloud formations in his paintings of the Castilian *meseta*, that Azorín's literary landscapes are most often compared (exhib. cat. *A. de Beruete* 20, 100; Faraldo 31). Marín Valdés attributed the affinity between artist and writer to Azorín's visual sensibility, noting that "there are passages in Azorín that evoke landscapes by Beruete, in the same way that some landscapes by Beruete seem to be the equivalent of Azorín's prose (1993, 100). Beruete, along with Ricardo Baroja and Solana, was also inspired by the outskirts of Madrid and its lower-class neighborhoods. Ricardo Baroja, especially, is remembered for his interest in the low-life of Madrid, his engravings of ragpickers, the illustrations he provided for his brother's early novels, and for the graphics he contributed to a sociological tract on delinquency and prostitution, *La mala vida en Madrid* (Moral 23, 61).[26]

Ancillary to the rise of geology and geography, and the stimulus these sciences provided to the development of orography, mountaineering, and the painting and literary description of mountain ranges, was a growing enthusiasm for botany, horti- and floriculture. As was to be expected, the *ILE* provided its students with laboratories, instruction, and excursions to study the flora of Castile and was instrumental in reviving and expanding Madrid's Botanical Gardens. In literature, the abandoned symbolist gardens of Antonio Machado, Valle-Inclán, and Juan Ramón Jiménez have visual counterparts in the musty gardenscapes, often illuminated by a melancholy, autumnal sun, of the painter, poet, and playwright Santiago Rusiñol (1861–1931), whose work Azorín admired and defended in several essays (9:1185–86; *PCQ* 118). Other than Solana, of the entire '98 group, it was Rusiñol who straddled most successfully both painting and writing, becoming well-known as a lyrical and visual literary stylist whose art reflected in both tone and content that of his writing. Despite the appearance of a cultivated decadence that may have had a superficial association with the non-ideological attitude characteristic of "pure" art, Rusiñol's painting appealed to his contemporaries. His moribund gardens, literary and painterly, made elegiac and plastic reference to the inexorable decrepitude of a nation once great and splendid, capable of constructing magnificent, aristocratic parks that now mirrored the general decay of "black Spain" and its myopic people. Pompeyo Gener described these gardens as emblematic of "a nation that was great, but today is in the most profound decay. These gardens symbolize the end of a race . . . they even lead us to gentle pity for the nearly defunct civilizations that possess gardens such as these" (Martínez Sierra 20–21).

Martínez Sierra, editor of *Jardines de España* (1914), a collection of Rusiñol's paintings accompanied by verse and prose contributions from numerous members of the *gente nueva*, observed that Rusiñol drew inspiration from the tragic contradiction between Spain's former imperial greatness and her present lifelessness. The painter's flora and vegetation are dead or decaying; architectural details crumble; statues are worn away; the cypresses characteristic of the Castilian landscape are worm-eaten; fallen leaves and stagnant water fill the marble fountains (Pl. 7). It was obviously the sense of time standing still and the wistful melancholy of Rusiñol's work that appealed to Azorín's sensibilities. His own contribution to the volume, "Jardín junto a la vía," is clearly an attempt to re-create verbally Rusiñol's painterly style: "Santiago Rusiñol has painted the gardens of Spain . . . its cypresses, and at the foot of the cypresses, thick rose bushes, from which the withered petals fall silently; the old gardens of dilapidated Castilian mansions, abandoned gardens, in whose depths stands a palace with broken windows and locked doors . . ." (9:1185).[27] The only sign of life is the railroad that passes outside the garden gates but where the train undoubtedly never stops. Obviously Azorín found in Rusiñol's oxymoron of time-bound train and a palace garden that time had somehow forgotten, an iconographic analogue of his personal interest in time and eternity which he often metaphorized by juxtaposing trains or railroad tracks against symbols of the changeless, usually drawn from images of classical (e.g., sixteenth or seventeenth century) Spain. The train of "Jardín junto a la vía," associated with the historical world of "toil, sadness, desire, bitterness," penetrates the ahistorical milieu of palace garden where "all is silence, peace and death." Only the strident blast of the locomotive's whistle bridges the gap between time and space, momentarily conflating the two disparate worlds (9:1186).[28]

Perhaps it was also Azorín, the most "painterly" of the Generation's authors, who paid greatest homage to the collaborative ideological and aesthetic enterprise pursued by the painters and writers of his youth. As he waited out the Spanish Civil War in Paris, Azorín wrote his nostalgic *Sintiendo a España*. Significantly, he chose as his alter ego a painter, Gaspar Salgado; even more significantly, Salgado is a landscape painter who one day recollects his youth and training in Spain, thereby allowing Azorín to indulge in commemorating his favorite artists:

Doy preferencia al paisaje. He pintado todos los paisajes de España. Y tengo el culto de los paisajistas españoles. A Casimiro Sainz . . . que andaba errante por los montes de Santander, le debo mucho. Y al patriarca don Carlos Haes. Y a Joaquín Mir, poseo de la pintura, y a Darío de Regoyos, que ha pintado paisajes maravillosos en su elementalidad. No debo olvidar a don Aureliano de Beruete y al elegante bodegonero de la carrera de San Jerónimo, Agustín Lhardy. (6:704–5)

[I have a predilection for landscape. I've painted all the landscapes of Spain. And I worship the Spanish landscapists. To Casimiro Sainz . . . who wandered about the mountains of Santander, I owe a great deal. And to the patriarch Carlos Haes. And to Joaquín Mir, the control of paint, and to Darío de Regoyos, who painted landscapes, magnificent in their simplicity. I must not forget don Aureliano de Beruete, and the elegant restaurateur from San Jerónimo Street, Agustín Lhardy].

On Saturdays Gaspar Salgado gathers his canvases and takes them to the Durand-Ruel gallery in the hope of eking out a meager sustenance in Paris (6:703–4). In the pages which follow, it will become apparent that Azorín's choice of Durand-Ruel, a historically extant gallery specializing in Impressionist painting, was far from arbitrary.

While the Generation of 1898 admitted its debt to Giner and the *Institución Libre*—"How else, but thanks to the *Institución*, could this group of young writers and artists have taken heart?," wrote Azorín—this is not to say that he and his generational colleagues always had amicable relations with their elders. One of the ways in which the younger group attempted to distinguish itself from nineteenth-century, bourgeois society was to cast their generation as the Adamic initiators of a fresh beginning for Spanish history and culture. The new era, according to Azorín, was dateable to the liminal year 1898 and the infamous military defeat of the colonial "Disaster" that unleashed the pessimism and psychological crisis lived by the nation at century's end. He saw the *gente nueva* as rising from the ashes of this debacle to reconstruct Spain and direct it away from the ruinous political path down which the country had been led by its misguided and inept leadership (*PCQ* 39). According to Azorín's retrospective mus-

ings, the resurrection of Spain began when young people turned away from contemplating the national navel toward Europe in order to compare their country against "lo extranjero"; that is, to the social structure of other European nations to and, above all, to foreign culture, especially to Dickens, Ibsen, Dostoyevsky, Flaubert; the philosophers Nietzsche and Bergson—in short, all that was considered new, subversive, or anarchic.[29] What they thought they saw in this comparison provoked a cataclysmic reaction governed by the three "Rs": rupture, rebellion, and reaction to what the *gente nueva* perceived as the exhausted and putrified formulas of late nineteenth-century Spain. Speaking in 1921 at a retrospective exhibition of work by Regoyos, Ramiro de Maeztu reminded his audience that while the ideals and aesthetics espoused by the *gente nueva* remained in force, those of the old guard had long been eclipsed:

. . . porque nada serviría que los hombres del 98, los "modernistas," como se nos llamaba entonces, desperdiciaríamos esta ocasión solemne de mostrar que los valores que nosotros afirmábamos están vivos y en pie, cuando los más de los que combatíamos, sepulto o insepultos, muertos están y putrefactos.
(exhib. cat. *D. de Regoyos* 53)

[. . . because the men of '98, the "modernists" as we were then called, would accomplish nothing if we wasted this solemn occasion without showing that the values we espoused back then are still alive and well, while the greater part of those we fought against, entombed or not, are dead and putrefied].

Among other forms of European culture, the *gente nueva* viewed literary and painterly Impressionism as anarchic, anti-bourgeois, and a thoroughly modern form of artistic expression. In a 1909 article published in *La Lectura*, Adrián de Loyarte referred to Darío de Regoyos as belonging to the "modernist camp"; that is, as a member of "the French impressionist, modernist school, however you want to call it." Loyarte went on to explain Impressionism as an art movement that broke all ties with traditional painting, holding its rules, formulas, and academic technicalities in contempt (156). When writing on the influence of Impressionism outside France, Camille Mauclair, art critic of the *Mercure de France*, noted a consonance between Zuloaga and Manet. He pointed out that Sorolla was nourished by Impressionism, and he singled out Darío de Regoyos as the Spanish painter who practiced pointillist technique with greatest assiduity (210). Of all the Spanish landscapists linked to the Generation of 1898, Regoyos developed strong ties to the artistic vanguard in France: he exhibited regularly in Paris; his work was favorably reviewed by the *Mercure de France, L'Art Moderne*, and *La Jeune Belgique*; he organized an exhibition of Spanish Basque art in 1902 at the Silberberg Gallery in Paris; he maintained friendships and correspondence with Georges Seurat and Paul Signac even after his return to Spain; and he remained in close contact with the Parisian art world. Although his work was not enthusiastically received in Spain, Durand-Ruel, the Parisian art dealer famous for supporting the Impressionists in their difficult first days, began to represent Regoyos and offer his work for sale at his gallery as early as 1897.[30]

While in France by century's end, the Impressionist vision had become a mimetic convention naturalized by tradition, in finisecular Spain where any form of innovation in the visual arts was labeled "modernist" and regarded with suspicion, Impressionism was still a hotly debated topic (Pena 1982, 89). Battle lines were drawn between the "moderns"—the disaffected *gente nueva* who supported anything new and revolutionary in European art—and the "ancients" who regarded Impressionism as a subversive foreign import. The conflict came to a head in 1901 when the *gente nueva* were galvanized by the address of a member-elect to the Academy of Fine Arts who, according to Azorín, "adopted an aggressive stance with regard to Impressionism in painting" (9:130). In response to the attack, the magazine *Juventud* printed a spirited, intelligent editorial by Darío de Regoyos, outlining the true precepts of Impressionist art.[31] The editorial states that Impressionism needed to be brought to the attention of the general public since neither the work of foreign or Spanish Impressionist painters had yet been shown at the official, National Art Exhibitions in Madrid, thus keeping the public in complete ignorance of new directions in which Manet, Cézanne, Renoir, Monet, Pissarro, Guillaumin, and Sisley had taken contemporary art.[32] In practical terms, the situation is best illustrated in the evolution of the personal views and technique used by Aureliano de Beruete. Although he spent some part of every year traveling abroad, mostly in France and Germany,

and he was thoroughly familiar with Impressionist painting, Beruete was slow to adopt its technical innovations. In a 1901 essay on Joaquín Sorolla, he observed that although the younger painter employed an abbreviated brushstroke and protagonized light in his painting, he had avoided falling into the "exaggerations of the so-called impressionists."[33] Nevertheless, by 1903, Beruete himself had begun to employ a brighter color palette as well as a looser brushstroke that imparted a much less smooth facture to his mature canvases. Fully developed impressionist technique appears in his work by 1905–1906 and it is these mature paintings that constitute the artist's most critically acclaimed work, earning him the sobriquet "father of Spanish Impressionism" (Rodríguez Alcalde 101, 112). By 1908, four years before he died, Beruete published a highly favorable essay on his friend and fellow artist Martín Rico (1833–1908), the first modern Spanish, proto-Impressionist who left Spain in 1862 to study and paint in France and Italy.[34]

Spanish Impressionist painters had the full support of their literary colleagues. In a retrospective assessment of Zola's novel *L'Oeuvre*, whose painter-protagonist allegedly was modeled on Cézanne, Azorín observed that both painting and writing involve analogous struggle: neither artist is ever assured that his work will be understood, nor that he will be able to give cogent expression to that which he most desires to communicate (*PCQ* 201–2). In his memoir of life in the Bohemian circles of Madrid, Ricardo Baroja wrote that although fluid in configuration, the fraternity of "moderns" who gathered in the cafés for the customary *tertulia*, included as many painters as it did writers: Ruiz Picasso, Meifrén, Mir, the Zubiaurre brothers, Regoyos, Rusiñol, Zuloaga, the caricaturist Sancha and the sculptors Macho and Mani (the latter fictionalized by Pío Baroja in *Mala hierba*); the Spanish writers Martínez Ruiz, Valle-Inclán, the Machado and Baroja brothers, Corpus Barga, Silverio Lanza, and the Spanish-Americans Rubén Darío, Amado Nervo, and Santos Chocano (50). In *Memorias Inmemoriales*, Azorín's alter ego "X" states that he was always an advocate of "the moderns" in painting, as well as in literature, and that he would prefer to have in his study a landscape by Renoir who emblematized an entire era: "Preference for that Impressionist was by then a symptom. On expressing a predilection for this modern, one automatically rejected the ancients" (8:352). Pío Baroja, too, said that of all the "French moderns" he was especially fond of Degas, and among the landscapists, Sisley and Van Gogh (7:718); should he have been in a position to purchase original masterworks, Baroja wrote that in addition to landscapes by Watteau, Lorrain, and Breughel, he would like to own "paintings by the modern Impressionists" (7:884).

Impressionism in Spanish art concided with the incorporation of its techniques into literature. One does not often think of Unamuno as an impressionist, yet he was familiar with the Impressionists' discovery that objects constantly change color, depending on how they are affected by light and atmosphere, and he was aware of their claim that nuances of color stand out with greater clarity in the more subtle atmospheres of northern climates or hours of the day when the sun did not strike with greatest intensity (7:739). His 1899 article, "Puesta de sol (recuerdo del 16 de diciembre de 1897)," is worth citing at length because it reveals an impressionist style in the early Unamuno unfamiliar to most readers. Describing the efflorescence of a winter sky at sunset, Unamuno, as all good Impressionists, seems intent on capturing the transitory nature of time and its corresponding effect on color, atmosphere, and light:

> . . . de un remolino de áurea nube, irradiaban, cual inmensos pétalos, otras nubes esplendorosas. Fingía una de ellas inmenso dorso de mitológica bestia, lanuda piel de vellones de abrasado oro. . . . Corríanse otras por el cielo de un lado a otro vistiéndose de abrasado rosa, algunas con tornasoladas tintas de profundo violeta en el cuerpo y en los contornos de ascua de oro. (615)[35]

> [. . . from a swirl of golden cloud, other magnificent clouds radiated, like gigantic petals. One of them resembled the huge back of a mythological beast, its wooly fur made of golden fleece. . . . Still other clouds, decked out in burnished rose, some with iridescent hues of deep violet in the body, and flecks of gold at the edges, scurried from one end of the sky to the other].

Unamuno infuses his description with additional references to color—"un verdoso mar celeste"; "nubecillas cenicientas"; "arrebolado esplendor" [a greenish celestial sea, ashy cloudlets, reddish splendor]—and he arranges his noun-adjective combinations in choppy phrases separated by commas, reminiscent of the comma-like, truncated brushstroke of the Impressionist painter. If the analogy were not obvious enough, Unamuno, who himself sketched and painted, exclaims:

> ¡Si pudiese pintarla para siempre y no verter aquí el rastrojo que de aquellos feraces momentos ha quedado en la tumba de mi memoria! . . . Era todo aquello cual escultórica idealización de nuestra pobre tierra; estatuas de sierras y de campos inundados, en incendio de colores vivificantes. Frente a las superficies meramente visuales para nosotros de aquellas esculturas, la áspera tierra se empequeñecía a punto de perder su grosera realidad tangible." (616)

> [If only I could immortalize it in paint forever and not pour out here the stubble of those lush moments ingrained in the pit of my memory!. . . . All of it was like a sculptural idealization of our poor earth; statues of mountain ranges and flooded fields blazing with life-giving colors. For us, faced with the mere visual, surface areas of those sculptures, the rugged earth became so small as to lose its coarse, tangible reality].

He concludes by transforming the fiery turbulence of clouds and atmosphere into a lyrical evocation of the spectacle of Genesis and the emergence of the universe from pre-telluric clouds and gases.

There are remarkable analogies of historical circumstance motivating aesthetic development that account for the affinity the Generation of 1898 felt for the Impressionist movement in literature and art which go beyond their early politics of *europeización* and need to portray themselves as modern and iconoclastic. In France the national identity crisis and subsequent need to define the nation as "French" that followed on the heels of the country's defeat in the Franco-Prussian War (19 July 1870–29 January 1871), resembles the situation in Spain both after the failure of "La Gloriosa" in 1868 and following the imperial collapse of 1898. The French Impressionists are thus positioned exactly between the two Spanish generations with which we are concerned: chronologically perhaps closer to 1868 (in age and as a school), but more influential in the ideology and aesthetics of the Generation of 1898. In the aftermath of the French Revolution and the subsequent turmoil engendered by a succession of reactionary governments, in the first half of the nineteenth century French prestige and power were involuntarily ceded to an in-

creasingly industrialized and capitalist England, Germany, and America. The appeals
made in Spain for national unity in 1898 by the
intellectuals in their sociological, economic
and literary pamphlets, monographs, and public
statements were the same in spirit and intent
as those published in France after the invasion
of Paris and the loss of Alsace-Lorraine to the
Germans.[36] It was in this atmosphere of national uncertainty and loss of direction that
French landscape painting developed, first with
the Barbizon School of the mid-1840s through
the 1860s, followed by the more daring vision
of the younger painters who would eventually
coalesce as the Impressionist movement of the
1870s to the 1890s. Similar to the failed revolution of 1868 and the subsequent restoration of
the monarchy in Spain, the Franco-Prussian
War was followed by the radical and short-lived
Commune (March-May 1871), brutally put
down by government troops. As in the case of
Spain's defeat by an upstart United States in
1898, France was forced to sign a treaty with
Germany, a much smaller nation that the
French had always considered "inconsequential." Reading assessments made by French historians of culture, we need only change the
word "France" to "Spain" for relevant passages
of French historiography to sound as if they had
been written about Spain: "How the nation
dealt with this bitter defeat and internal tragedy
is critical to understanding France in the late
nineteenth century. For the Third Republic
continually defined itself . . . in relation to these
disasters and their enduring legacies" (Tucker
1990, 7–8). Contemporaries often referred to
the Franco-Prussian War as the "year of disaster," while French literary historians saw the
pessimism and feeling of national decadence in
the literary generation that came to maturity
after the War as having originated in the "tragic
experiences of the national defeat" which had
shattered, as they also did in Spain, the illusion
of national complacency and international political and cultural superiority. Those who criticized the failure of French foreign policy often
compared France to Spain and Italy, "Latin"
countries that had endured foreign policy set-
backs throughout the nineteenth century
(Swart 123–39). As would occur in Spain, the
sense of decay and decadence that permeated
the work of French artists and writers inspired
works of significant and lasting artistic value.

Although antedating the revisionist historiography of the Spanish *Institución Libre de Enseñanza*, one of the nationalist projects that
emerged from the confusion of postrevolution-
ary France was a similar revaluation of French
history. Led by Jules Michelet (1798–1874),
nineteenth-century French historians no longer
saw history as the chronicling of royal dynas-
ties, armies, treaties, and great men of state, but
as the history of ordinary French people and the
landscape of France, as a "vast national theatre
for the actions of her people" (Brettell 1984, 33–
34). These historians, like those who emerged
from the *ILE* in Madrid, intended to reconnect
France with her most authentic past while side-
stepping the break in continuity represented by
the nation's more recent historical and political
reversals of fortune. Essentially reactionary at
its foundations in France, as it was also in
Spain, this new historiography provided the
same kind of catalyst in France, leading to a
similar study of local monuments, archives,
and museums; the same excursionism and publication of travel guides and literature illustrated with views of architecturally or
historically important French sites considered
emblematic of the nation's former grandeur.

Coincidental with the crisis in national self-
confidence and the desire to recover and reinvigorate a lost, national identity, was the emergence of Impressionist painting whose favorite
subjects most often derived from the French
landscape. As did the Spanish landscape painters, the Impressionists, although they depicted
some of their country's historical monuments
and urban leisure activities, preferred the landscape of the Ile de France—the territory in
which Paris, the nation's capital from the beginning of France's existence as a country—was
located. For the French, the Ile de France was
France itself, and it possessed the same historical significance as did Castile for the Generations of 1868 and 1898 in Spain. Because the
Impressionist vision has become so widely accepted as a "natural" way of seeing, the role
played by Impressionist painters in the nationalist project of recovering the French national
consciousness has frequently been overlooked,
as has also the fact that the painters in question
lived and worked in a climate saturated with
ideological diversity and pleas for national
unity within which landscape painting was
linked by many intellectuals, including Ernest
Renan, to the "national soul" (Brettell 1984,
27–28). Art critic Camille Mauclair described

the ideological motivation of these painters with words that recall those the Generation of 1898 might have used to speak of Beruete, Regoyos or Zuloaga: "Ils ont été les decouvreurs fervents du terroir national, et notamment de l'Ile de France. . . . Ils ont aimé la terre française avec sincerité et fraîcheur. Ce sont vraiment nos peintres. . . . Ils ont été émus par la campagne . . ."[37] [162; They were enthusiastic discoverers of the national landscape, especially the Ile de France. . . . They loved the French land with sincerity and spontaneity. They're truly our painters. . . . They were moved by the countryide . . .]. Like their Spanish counterparts, the Impressionists were considered by Mauclair as having injected new life into an art that had been reified by stagnant canonical views of what constituted acceptable forms of beauty.

National pessimism and lack of self-confidence in France continued with varying degrees of intensity for more than two decades after the Franco-Prussian War. Monet's renewed interest in the 1890s in agricultural scenes from the French countryside was ancillary to renewed French recognition that the nation no longer held a position of leadership in the Western world (Tucker 1990, 73). Impressionist art thus once again participated in a nationalist project of redirecting French energies to focus on what was thought to be substantial and ineradicable about the nation: its wealth of natural resources and the beauty of its landscape (112). As was true in the case of Spanish intellectuals and artists at the turn of the century, the Impressionists and their supporters saw themselves as utterly "modern." T. J. Clark suggests that the increasing lack of importance, even the absence of the human figure in Impressionist painting, was perhaps due to the absence of "heroism" in modern life (15), while Robert Herbert refers to the Impressionists as the "first generation of modernists" to concern themselves almost exclusively with contemporary life (1988, xv). Spanish contemporaries of the Impressionist movement also ascribed the change of direction in French painting to the advent of a new and modern era. Martín Rico dated the change to 1865 "when the first symptoms of this modernist fever began to appear" (109); Aureliano de Beruete y Moret, recognizing the heterogeneous nature of the Impressionist group, wrote that for lack of a better label, these painters should be considered exponents of "Modernism" (135).

Fernando Araujo, writing in *La España Moderna* in 1909, stated that the Impressionist program was simply an expression of the artists' desire to paint "contemporary life" (174). As did Giner in 1895, Camille Mauclair wrote that the "réalistes-impressionistes" concerned themselves with daily habits and expressions characteristic of the late nineteenth century: "scenes of dance-halls . . . streets, the countryside, factories, contemporary interiors" (38–39). Aside from being differentiated from their predecessors as the painters of "modern life," the Impressionists' novelty lies in their artistic response to the new rhythms and directions taken by that life: much of their theoretical apparatus was based on advances made in the field of optics; their loose, abbreviated brushstroke mirrored the fragmentation, increased momentum, and spontaneity of daily life; the random effects of light and atmosphere on objects with which they were concerned instigated a new way of perceiving space, time, and the material world (Sypher 171).

The Impressionists' objective distance from their subject matter in which the "author's presence was hidden from the viewer" (Herbert 1988, 304), and their insistence, for the first time in the history of art, on the viewer's participation in reconstituting paint on canvas into a composite whole, clearly anticipated the aesthetic orientation of "high Modernism" with its preference for "readerly" rather than "writerly" texts. The fragmentation of vision in painting and of language in literature, which have by now become Modern "clichés," is what particularly angered (or intrigued) the public about this new way of painting. While Camille Lemonnier, in his review of the Universal Exposition of 1878, criticized the Impresssionists for "specializing" in making fragments of observation and thus lacking a "sense of the picture," by 1882 Georg Brandes responded more positively to pictures that left out details and reproduced "reality" as if viewed from a distance. Rather than presenting objects as a whole, the Impressionist reproduces mood and motif "declaring a painting 'finished' as soon as this aim apparently has been accomplished, regardless of how incomplete it may seem according to ordinary conceptions . . ."[38] Modern life incurred directly upon and affected the Impressionist sensibility in ways other than through the incipient cultural crisis associated with the beginnings of Modern aesthetics. The Impressionists' vision of the wide Parisian boulevards, well-groomed parks, and leisure activities newly available in and around the city, are considered by art historians to be the direct result of Baron Haussmann's modernization of Paris. "Haussmannization," as it was cynically termed, ostensibly meant to clean up the crowded, ancient quarters of Paris by widening the streets, razing old buildings, reconfiguring neighborhoods, and ushering in a healthier atmosphere of light and air (while simultaneously discouraging the building of barricades and the formation of seditious revolutionary cells to which the old quarters had lent themselves in the past). The architectural and social changes engendered by the fashionably redesigned open spaces of Paris—the boulevards, hippodromes, department stores, imposing railway stations, and middle-class access to leisure activities—could not have but affected contemporary painters (Herbert 1988, 28).[39]

Similar to the great diversity among the members of the Spanish *gente nueva*, too diverse according to some literary historians to constitute a true "generation," the Impressionist painters, although born approximately within the same decade, came from heterogeneous social backgrounds, subscribed to different conceptions of and tendencies in art, but like the Generation of 1898, they shared the same politico-ideological experiences and were united by their opposition to the officially sanctioned salons. The group that met at the Café Guerbois, very much like the Madrid *tertulia* of modern artists and writers described by Ricardo Baroja, was so vastly individual in the ways they sought to distinguish themselves from the traditional art world, that at first they were dubbed "le groupe des Batignolles" and not a "school" of painters defined by a specificity of subject matter, lifestyle, or artistic education (Rewald 205). Although it was Pío Baroja who first protested Azorín's designation of the *gente nueva* as a "generation" precisely because of its excessively diverse composition, ironically it was Azorín who noted that at the inception of the Impressionist movement all the painters were grouped indiscriminately together; only with the passage of time were the nuances between painters such as Monet and Manet or Manet and Degas, understood (*PCQ* 117).[40]

Camille Mauclair noted that the Impressionist movement in art evolved from the same revolution in aesthetics as did the naturalist novel

of Flaubert, Zola, and the brothers Goncourt (165), all contemporaries of the Impressionist painters. Similar to the cooperation between the painters and writers of the Spanish Generation of 1898, the French naturalist writers perceived the early ideological orientation of the Impressionists as complementary to their own. In seeking to establish intellectual and aesthetic affinities between themselves and their painter-colleagues, literary naturalists found commonality of purpose in their shared reaction to the dominance of an impotent yet still prevalent Romanticism in art and literature, and their mutual interest in describing a "natural" vision of modern French life without the constraints of convention. In establishing this affinity the naturalists also found a convenient way to prove that their literature was in no way incompatible with beauty and delicacy of psychological expression. Without specifying what they were, Mauclair pointed out that Manet's "modernist ideas" were quickly seized by naturalist writers and adapted to their commentary on and descriptions of the daily lives and habits of their protagonists (165).

Aside from his early choice of Romantic and idealized Spanish subject matter, it was indeed Manet who first committed himself to painting modern themes, identifying as suitable topics for "serious" art, material drawn from popular illustrated French news and periodical magazines (Hanson 133). As did Spanish writers like Baroja, the "marginals" Manet portrayed in early paintings such as *The Ragpicker* (1869) or *The Old Musician* (1862) were admired by fellow artists and writers (Herbert 1988, 63). As was true in the case of the *gente nueva*, French naturalist literature and the new movement in art quickly became synonymous with "Modernism." In France the connection was made by none other than Zola in a remark closely resembling in word choice and turns of phrase those that could just as easily have been made by finisecular art critics, writers, or painters in Spain: "It's that naturalism, impressionism, modernity, however you want to call it, dominates today in the official Salons" (Berg 1992, 34).[41] To speak of the naturalists Zola, Flaubert, and the Goncourt brothers, according to Mauclair, was to speak of the Impressionist painters since they were all motivated by the same ideas and the same choice of subject matter. However erroneous the notion proved to be in the final analysis, parallels were drawn between the work of painters such as Degas and Manet and the naturalist writers' concern with avoiding false idealism in their portrayal of modern psychological truths (Mauclair 38, 165). Conversely, the Impressionist protagonization of light and color and the ocular-centrism of their techniques had a noticeable effect on naturalist literature. Notwithstanding their eventual parting of the ways, the partnership between the more established French writers and the somewhat younger Impressionist painters resembled the heterogeneous, yet, for the most part, mutually supportive group that coalesced in Spain at the turn of the century. Baudelaire, Edmond and Jules de Goncourt, Zola, Mallarmé, and Flaubert were all involved to one degree or another in the public support of new art, the writing of art reviews, prefaces to exhibition catalogues, artist biographies, the collecting of art work, forging personal friendships, and, in some cases, protagonizing vanguard painters in their fiction.

In their role as anti-establishment artists, literary naturalists and Impressionist painters rallied together around Wagner's provocative challenge to bourgeois taste in music. In addition to the novelty of the music itself, the German composer's epic sense of landscape and his resolve to integrate all the arts into productions of gargantuan proportions, often with nationalistic intent, was a hotly debated issue in France in the 1860s that appealed to the Impressionist painters (Rewald 116). Frédéric Bazille, a member of the Batignolles group, was a passionate admirer of Wagner's, as were Baudelaire and the painter Henri Fantin-Latour, another Batignolles member. Bazille and Renoir attended the opera together where Bazille was often instrumental in organizing pro-Wagnerian claques; Cézanne contemplated painting an *Ouverture du Tannhäuser*, while in 1864 Fantin completed a canvas he called *Tannhäuser: Venusberg* (Rewald 116; Fried 213). Renoir visited Wagner in Palermo in 1882 where he painted the composer's portrait; the symbolist writer Édouard Dujardin (1861–1949) recalled that in creating his 1888 novel *Les Lauriers sont coupés*, he was motivated by the "foolish ambition of transposing into literature Wagnerian devices" which he understood to be the expression of mental life via musical motives realized through an indefinite succession of impressionistic thoughts, feelings, and sensations, expressed by short sentences in a succession

without logical order (Mukarovsky 101–2). Although Dujardin's experiment is said to have influenced what we know today as James Joyce's "stream of consciousness," Dujardin's own description of his artistic intent reflects not only the influence of Wagner, but that of Impressionist painting as well.

The same debate took place in Spain, although it began several decades later: *Tannhäuser* was first performed in Madrid in 1890; *Die Meistersinger* in 1894; *Siegfried* in 1901; by 1905, among true connoisseurs in Spain, there was no longer a rift between *wagnerianos* and *antiwagnerianos*, and by 1909 the "Ring" trilogy, first performed at Bayreuth in 1876, was also staged in Madrid (Alfaro López 240–41). The introduction of Wagner to Madrid and the acceptance of his music by the *gente nueva* had as much to do with the exaltation of the landscape in Wagnerian aesthetics as it did with the connection between the German composer's glorification of the hero and the superman, also extolled by Nietzsche, a philosopher much admired by the Spanish moderns.[42] In his memoirs Pío Baroja recalled the finisecular vogue for Wagner in Madrid (7:916), while Azorín remembered pianists in Madrid cafés regaling patrons with endless arrangements from *Tannhäuser* and *Lohengrin* (6:35). As was usually the case, aesthetic innovations from abroad entered Spain through Barcelona. In his article "Wagnerismo" (*ABC*, 5 April 1952), Azorín recalled that a book on Wagner had been published in the Catalonian capital in 1878 by Marsillach. In the same essay he also wrote that the first Spanish novel to have been influenced by Wagnerian aesthetics was Blasco Ibáñez's *Entre naranjos* (1900), which Azorín called a "fervent exaltation of Wagner—and his disciple Hans Kaller . . . set in the splendid orange groves of Alcira." In his personal copy of Félix Borrell's 1912 monograph *El Wagnerismo en Madrid*, Azorín annotated passages relevant to the years in which there were performances of Wagner operas in Madrid, the audience reaction, newspaper reviews, which producers were supporters or detractors of the German composer, etc. At the end of his life Azorín recognized the fundamental contradiction between the Dionysian Wagner and his own preference for classical (i.e., Apollonian) restraint (*PQ* 50). Yet, try as he might, Azorín concluded that "neither could I resist Wagner's music which, for me, has been and continues to be, an intoxicating potion."[43] Baroja chose to dissociate himself completely at the end of his life from any youthful enthusiasm for Wagner, stating that his music always seemed "like reinforced concrete or papier maché"; however, he did make an interesting remark that he found the English landscapists Constable and Turner appealing, and that Turner's extraordinary imagination was somewhat "Wagnerian" in nature (7:916, 772). As was to be expected, among Spanish painters, it was Aureliano de Beruete and Darío de Regoyos who most appreciated Wagner, perhaps because their ties to Europe were the strongest. In *La España negra*, Regoyos wrote that he and Émile Verhaeren once had occasion to contemplate a sunset and the return of fishing boats to port from the Castillo de la Mota. The description is an interesting melange of verbal impressionism married to Wagnerian simile:

> . . . mirando hacia Francia eran las velas de diferentes blancos, según la distancia y dispuestas en escala como notas de música: las lejanas de un blanco sucio y fundidas con el gran azul; las más cercanas, de blancura planchada, como inmensos cisnes de Lohengrin, pero dominadas por otro blanco aún más potente, el de las olas rompiéndose abajo en las rocas y espumando entre el verde vidrioso del agua su complementario de nieve rosa.[44]

> [. . . looking toward France, the sails appeared to be of different white hues depending on the distance and arranged to scale, like musical notes: those furthest away were of a dirty white and merged with the great blue expanse; the closest ones, a flat white, like gigantic swans from *Lohengrin*, were overpowered by another, even more intense white: that of the waves crashing below on the rocks and foaming between the vitreous green of the water and its complementary of snowy rose].

It was Beruete who proved to be, yet again, one of the most liberal-minded men in Spanish intellectual and artistic circles when he became one of Wagner's most ardent supporters. Intrigued by the critical importance of landscape to Wagner's totalizing vision of the musical work, Beruete attended the Bayreuth festival on a regular basis and even executed a series of paintings at the site.[45]

In addition to having its origins in the raising of national consciousness in various countries during periods of critical need for historical self-recognition, landscape painting in modern history often developed alongside environmental despoliation (Bazarov 6). Beginning with the late eighteenth century, and certainly by the early nineteenth, landscape painting in England, France, and eventually Spain, was stimulated by modern urbanization. In England landscape painting developed in the late eighteenth century, and while it portrayed scenes of archetypal rural serenity, the genre's evolution coincided with a moment when the face of the countryside was being reconfigured by enclosure, industrial expansion, and urban development (Bermingham 1, 9, 15). In France the same process began a generation later, roughly corresponding in the visual arts to the birth of the Barbizon School. To escape the urban sprawl and overcrowding of Paris, landscape painters began to visit Fontainebleau Forest in the mid-1820s (Adams 8). Significantly the same group became the first environmental activists in France: Théodore Rousseau was involved in a campaign to prevent the deforestation of Fontainebleau; Daubigny, the painter of rivers and riverbank scenes, decried the diversion of water for industrial power and the incipient pollution of the waterways; the rapid expansion of railways encroached upon the countryside, making it more accessible to human and industrial invasion. For the Barbizon painters, depicting the peasant way of life in the rural and asperous forest scenes of Fontainebleau and its environs was a way of preserving the countryside and its inhabitants when these had largely been replaced by the urban laborer (Herbert 1962, 46, 65). The forest itself was no longer as unspoiled or removed from the industrial and demographic crises of Paris as the paintings of Barbizon artists would lead us to believe (Adams 8, 166). As they did for Carlos de Haes in Spain, trees and their portrayal directly from nature became symbolic of permanent and enduring solidity. For Théodore Rousseau trees were emblematic of the immutable element in history: "If only I could speak their language," he wrote, "I would be using the tongue of all ages." In similar fashion Jean-François Millet, who settled in the Forest in 1849, observed in a letter that humans no longer understood what "those fellows" (the trees) said to each other because man and nature no longer spoke the same language (Herbert 1962, 14, 42, 65).

In Spain, although it was established much later, the Escola d'Olot, frequently called the

"Barbizon of Spain," was established in the province of Gerona. Generationally comparable to Giner de los Ríos and the *institucionistas* of Madrid, a group of painters organized by Joaquim Vayreda (1843–1894) retreated in 1874 from an increasingly urban Barcelona to the village of Olot. Since Vayreda had studied the painters of Barbizon in Paris, whose plein air technique and color palette he brought back to Spain with him, it was natural for the Escola d'Olot to be compared to the Barbizon School (Pl. 8 and 9).[46] Parallel to the rehabilitation and revival of Castile taking place within the *institucionista* circles of the Spanish capital, the painters of Olot took an active interest in the rural landscape and the ways of life of this agricultural community, heavily dependent for its livelihood on the cultivation of beans. Comparable to the situation at Fontainebleau, at the time the Escola d'Olot was founded, the rural agriculture that had sustained this community for countless generations was threatened with extinction by advancing Catalonian modernization. The painters of Olot, like many of their counterparts among the Madrid landscapists, were also poets and playwrights, and they hoped to use both media to focus public attention on the life and traditions of the Olot region to promote interest in preserving and regenerating the community whose extensive, picturesque vistas of bean fields became as emblematic as the gnarled, ancient oaks of Fontainebleau were for the painters of Barbizon. Memorializing the landscape of Olot in literature and art thus had "a clear nation-building implication, since it meant deepening the knowledge of their own land whose history the anxious residents were beginning to recover . . .", an ideological program similar to the one generated in Madrid, and one that the Vayreda brothers, Joaquim and Marià, together with their colleague Josep Berga i Boix, hoped would occasion the "moral regeneration of the land" (exhib. cat. *L'Escola d'Olot* 20, 42).

Similar to the ideological project designed to revitalize interest in Castile launched by Giner and the *Institución Libre*, eternalizing the Olot landscape and transmitting its visual image to an oblivious receptor-public informed the ideology operating at the Escola d'Olot. Unlike the situation in Castile, however, the invention and exportation of Olot was largely a myth comparable to the attempted preservation of Fontainebleau, and for the same reasons. In both instances attention was focused on the landscape as a repository of symbolic and changeless values when great changes, indeed, were taking place at all levels of French and Catalonian life. In an attempt to counteract this eradication, the artists of Olot represented the region as an idyllic and idealized enclave about to be lost to indiscriminate urbanization when, in reality, their proposal was no longer viable. To a great extent the same type of casuistry motivated the French Impressionists who frequently poeticized their views of the environs around Paris when these areas had already been invaded by industrial development. At the time they began to protagonize the Impressionist canvas, the Ile de France and its idyllic villages—Asnières, Marly, Argentcuil, Bougival—frequently give no indication that the sites had suffered industrial encroachment and despoliation (Herbert 1988, 202). This illusory portrayal of the countryside perhaps reflects the ambiguous position the Impressionists occupied within the social restructuring of modernized France. The industrialized society that had emerged in the mid-1850s witnessed unprecedented growth in the numbers and economic power of the small bourgeoisie to which, with few exceptions, the Impressionist painters also belonged. This social group, however, remained "classless" in the sense that while they took care to distinguish themselves from the proletariat, they were also rebuffed by the *grande bourgeoisie* to which they aspired as social members and as "partners" in the business of seeking desirable clients and marketing their work. Thus the "documentary" nature of the Impressionist landscape often consciously eschews portraying the results of its invasion by industrial forms of employment as well as by leisure activities associated with the lower classes.[47] Ironically, the new character and tenor of society, and the changes it effected in the landscape, were the products of the very same modernity with which the painters identified and saw themselves as representing. A similar ambiguity obtains in the Spanish Generation of 1898. The crisis of *petit bourgeois* consciousness which the *gente nueva* lived and emblematized was instigated by a self-image in conflict with existing social realities. Perhaps Pío Baroja summed it up best in "Nuestra Generación" where he observed that "Rebuffed in nearly all sectors of public and practical life, the young people in liberal professions, in a great majority of cases, tended to take refuge in private life and in literature" (7:659). The solution to the crisis of social and class consciousness among the French Impressionists and the Spanish *gente nueva* eventually came to rest upon literary and artistic evasion and a compendium of ideals largely sustained by an inauthentic existential status.[48]

T. J. Clark argues that the paradox of Modern art is both its link to the emerging *couches sociales* and the construction of suburbs and leisure activities made available by "new," modern lifestyles, while at the same time it is characterized by a desire for distance from the *petite bourgeoisie* that sustained the very same modernity which so fascinated the Impressionist painters and with which they, too, in their opposition to traditional art forms, identified (202, 235). In considering the legion of paintings executed at Gennevillier, Asnières, or Argenteuil, for example, one would never imagine that the Seine at Asnières and the land surrounding the town were poisoned by a giant "collector sewer" that dumped waste from Paris into the river and then carried the sewage downstream to Argenteuil, causing local complaints of poisoned soil and malodorous crops.[49] A parallel situation existed between an increasingly urbanized Madrid and the painters who memorialized the city's suburban wastelands and lower-class neighborhoods near the Manzanares River. The modernization of the city through projects like the building of the Gran Vía left many of the lower classes homeless, forcing a sizeable number of people into makeshift housing on the outskirts of town where they literally had to engage in urban, guerilla warfare in order to stay alive. Pío Baroja aptly titled an early trilogy *La lucha por la vida* (*The Struggle for Life*): three sociological novels that document incursions and forays into the city by the socially and economically disenfranchised and their failed attempts to carve out a legitimate place for themselves in society. Aside from the laundresses of the Manzanares River, the wastelands of suburban Madrid were the territory of ragpickers who engaged in the ancillary business of the commercial raising of chickens and hogs fed on edible scrap culled from the collection of urban garbage. The consumption of these animals sold for food, or eaten by the *traperos* themselves, was under constant attack as a source of public health hazards and epidemics. As in the case of foul-smell-

ing produce raised on the banks of the Seine, the meat of the hogs and eggs of the chickens raised on Madrid garbage not only smelled badly but, as an analysis of meat from one Madrid slaughterhouse showed, it was infected by trichinosis spread to the hogs by the rats with whom they shared the trash heaps (Moral 61–62).

Interpreting these suburbs in paint differed widely in the work of Aureliano de Beruete, on the one hand, and Ricardo Baroja and José Gutiérrez Solana on the other. Although Spanish art historians agree that Beruete was the "painter of Madrid and its suburban landscape," and they claim that his lyrical views of the *arrabales* were not artificially "beautified," the discrepancy between Beruete's vision and that of the other two painters is striking.[50] Beruete's suburbs, "in which Solana and Baroja documented so much ugliness," are harmonious and pleasant, replete with radiant chromatic effects, not because of any idealized vision on the artist's part, but due to "the light's own reality . . . that imparts harmony and translucency to those impoverished scenes" (Rodríguez Alcalde 107). As the Impressionists tended to do, Beruete eliminated anecdote and narrative from his work which may account for, as it also did among the French painters, his visual detour around the more crude sociological implications that could be found in the suburban landscape, thereby avoiding slippage into the kind of naturalism that characterized the work of his brother Ricardo and that of Gutiérrez Solana (Pl. 10). Unlike the realist-naturalist painters, the impressionist Beruete, as Bazille had remarked of his French colleagues, was more interested in the handling of subject, than in the subject itself.[51] Contrary to the persistent and by now clichéd parallels art historians establish between Beruete's paintings and the early novels of Pío Baroja that chronicle life among Madrid's underclass, it is much more suitable to compare Beruete's "sad poetry of dusty and ruined Castile" to Azorín's verbal landscapes of the *meseta*.[52] Pío Baroja's *aledaños madrileños* are more analogous to the painting and writing of José Gutiérrez Solana, or the etchings and lithographs of his brother Ricardo who provided the graphics for Pío's trilogy *La lucha por la vida*. Although the elder Baroja also painted landscapes, with the possible exception of Solana, his artistic vision had a greater sociological orientation than did that of other painters associated with the Generation of 1898. The life of Madrid's underworld fascinated the artist whose reputation was made on his depiction of prostitutes, gypsies, beggars, ragpickers, and the habitués of seedy taverns. It was Ricardo Baroja who received the commission to provide illustrations for *La mala vida en Madrid, estudio psico-sociológico con dibujos y fotografías del natural* (1901), authored by two *institucionistas*, P. C. Bernaldo de Quirós and J. M. Llanas Aguilaniedo. Baroja's sketches include low-life taverns, scenes of beggars, pimps and prostitutes, in perfect consonance not only with those described by the authors of the monograph, but also with those fictionalized by Pío in his famous trilogy or the short stories of *Vidas Sombrías* (1900).

José Gutiérrez Solana (1886–1945), though somewhat younger than most of the artists associated with the Generation of '98, was influenced by the early work of Darío de Regoyos (e.g., *La España negra*), as well as the fiction and art work of Pío and Ricardo Baroja. His *Chulos y Chulas* series, which dates from 1906, and his first book *Madrid, escenas y costumbres* (completed in 1909; published in 1913), show an unmistakable visual and textual debt to the Baroja brothers (Barrio-Garay 48). Solana's *Los Caídos* series (1915) was also inspired by literature, borrowing its title from a section of *La mala vida en Madrid* that distinguished people who had somehow lost a former, legitimate standing in society from those who had been recruited willingly into questionable lifestyles. By collating paintings and photographs in his *catalogue raisonné* and biography of Solana, Barrio-Garay demonstrated that the men and women portrayed in canvases Solana titled *Delinquent Prostitute, Homosexual Transvestite,* and *Drunkard Prostitute* were all inspired by photographs reproduced in the text of *La mala vida en Madrid* (69–71) (Fig. 1).

In the same way that the Impressionist landscape was circumscribed by events in French political history, Claude Monet began to turn his attention to trains in the landscape, railway bridges, and train stations as subjects for study, an interest fueled perhaps by a postwar need to rebuild the nation's infrastructure after the Franco-Prussian War (Herbert 1988, 220).[53] By the time the Impressionists coalesced as a new movement in art, train travel was no longer as daunting an enterprise as it had been in the 1840s. Rather, the laying of roads and rail lines

had become, as Flaubert remarked, emblematic of modern resourcefulness: in cutting through nature, society, and geography, all three were opened up to communication and human control (Graña 40). Railway lines made the landscape accessible to painters and tourists alike, and they made possible the development of commuter exurbs and the expansion of industrial sites to the countryside. Trains, train travel, and their impact on Nature became part of the "discourse of industrial society" and were associated with that other Modern phenomenon, the concept of Time (Ermarth 43–44). The Impressionists thus lived a transitional moment in history during which landscape painting evolved from a genre that invited tranquil aesthetic contemplation to one that was compelled by the unfolding of history to participate in the adventure of modern industrialization. While travel by carriage had allowed both the sensorial perception of familiar, animal power as well as a leisurely, ocular appreciation of variations in the landscape traversed, train travel broke the sense of human contact with the landscape at the same time that it shattered the traditional understanding of time-space affiliations. For writers and painters who lived during the era of great railway expansion, trains often embodied the transitory, fleeting nature of time. It was not surprising, then, that the Impressionist painter, whose greatest aesthetic concern was to portray the effects of time's passage on color, light, and objects, should have been fascinated by this intrusion of modern life into the countryside (Schivelbusch 25).[54] The first train landscape Monet painted was the 1870 *Train in the Countryside*, followed by *The Train* (1872) and *The Railroad Bridge, Argenteuil* (1873), where the painter appears not so much interested in trains crossing the bridge as he is in the bridge itself as a feat of modern engineering (Herbert 1988, 219–20). More familiar and evocative, however, are the twelve paintings which comprise Monet's 1877 *Gare Saint-Lazare* suite. As Robert Herbert argues, a painting that depicts a locomotive in a trainshed, rather than suggesting the train's power and speed, communicates the obverse feeling of timelessness: puffs of steam emanating from the undercarriage of the locomotive hide the engine's wheels, diminishing for the viewer any implication of potential motion; instead, the visual interest of the painting centers on the atmosphere of light, steam, and smoke that

Fig. 1 José Gutiérrez Solana, *Los Caídos*, 1915. Oil on canvas, 208 × 170.5 cm. Colección del Museo Nacional de Bellas Artes. Buenos Aires, Argentina.

envelop the train (1988, 20, 28).[55] The Pont de l'Europe, a street bridge completed in 1868 that spanned the tracks at Saint Lazare, was painted by Manet (*Le Chemin de fer* 1873) and Monet (*Le Pont de l'Europe* 1877), while Gustave Caillebotte memorialized both train station and bridge in several paintings, the most famous of which is the eponymous canvas of 1876, so accurate in its reproduction of the bridge's architectural details and engineering that it seems almost photographic. While living in England during the Franco-Prussian War, Pissarro painted trains in London's Penge and Lordship Lane stations, and Zola protagonized the railway in his novel *La Bête humaine* (1889).

After a sluggish start, hampered by political infighting and budgetary snafus, the second half of the nineteenth century in Spain witnessed unprecedented growth in railway communication. By 1895 Spain had approximately 13,000 kilometers of extant railway; by 1901 nearly 12,000 additional kilometers of track had been put down (Litvak 1991, 16). As was to be expected, the construction projects impacted upon aesthetics: the photographer J. Laurent documented the building of railroads, bridges and tunnels both as works-in-progress and as finished products; Aureliano de Beruete wrote a play, *Entre rocas*, set in the context of blasting a railroad through the mountains; Darío de Regoyos painted trains in both urban and rural settings; Azorín had a life-long passion for trains. In *Madrid, guía sentimental*, he wrote that "never in our life have we stopped being affected by the magic of railroads, trains, locomotives, and train stations" (3:1292). Although trains and train travel figure widely in all of Azorín's work, the first two essays of *Castilla*—"Los ferrocarriles" and "El primer ferrocarril castellano"—are the best known.[56] Azorín's interest in trains dates back to the 1903 novel *Antonio Azorín* which includes a particularly vivid description of a train departure during evening hours, focusing on the fluidity of shifting, colorful light effects that results in an overtly impressionistic verbal "painting":

El tren parte. Cruzan los verdes y rojos faros . . . una muchedumbre de lucecillas imperceptibles brilla, parpadea, desaparece, surge de nuevo, torna a ocultarse . . . sobre la gran ciudad, aparece—emanación de los focos eléctricos—como una tenue, difuminada claridad de aurora. En el coche,

la mortecina luz de la lamparilla cae sobre los cuadros, rojos, azules, negros, de una manta, resbala sobre la uniformidad parda de la pañosa castellana, se desliza, medrosa, entre las largas y argentadas hebras de la barba del anciano. (Fox 1970, 176–77)

[The train departs. Red and green headlights intersect . . . a crowd of imperceptible, small lights shines, twinkles, disappears, twinkles again, vanishes . . . above the big city—emanating from the electric lights—appears a tenuous, diffuse clarity similar to the glimmer of dawn. In the train car, the dying light of a lantern falls on the red, blue, black squares of a shawl, slides down the smooth brown of a typical Castilian cape, and slithers, fearful, among the long, silvery threads of an old man's beard].

Like all those who sensed that modernity ushered in radical changes in ideas, aesthetics, and lifestyles, Azorín responded to the apparent increase in the speed of life around him.[57] The train not only symbolized modern life, but its ability to compress time and space via speed made it a perfect allegory of his well-known, idiosyncratic concerns with those same issues. One of Azorín's favorite analogies was the frequent juxtaposition of a train and the paradigmatic *caserón vetusto* (dilapidated mansion), the jarring contrast between them providing a perfect emblem of modernity versus eternity. The pattern perhaps begins with "Una lucecita roja" (*Castilla*), in which the regular passage of a train during evening hours abolishes the need for clocks: time, instead, is measured by the little red light of the caboose. Part of the "historical" world of schedules and routines, the train is as invariable in its mechanical regularity and as impervious as the clock to the "intra-history" of those who may perceive the little red light from widely divergent frames of reference, contextualizing it within the perspective of individual tragedies or celebrations. By the 1944 "Un tren que pasa," however, the train—although still allegorizing the invasion of the eternal Castilian village by diachronic, modern time—elicited a negative response from Azorín. Having escaped to the country from the bustle of Madrid, the narrator of this short story feels that a weight has been lifted from his shoulders. His reverie is quickly interrupted by a train which, we are told, passes by daily at the same time. It jolts the narrator into recognizing the inexorable nature of time and its circumscription of modern life: "Why now, suddenly, when

I thought myself to be in a new modality of my being, my psyche, this distant plume of smoke, this smoke that has disappeared so quickly, imbues my spirit with emotion and has left me quivering silently and almost anxiously?" As the narrator and his companion abandon the site, they turn back for one last glimpse of the Castilian plain and its city, "the unruffled city, the dead city, with its silence, with its immutability, with its stillness of centuries, centuries, and centuries" (7:388). The only indication that this rural "city" may actually exist in the twentieth century is the railroad track and train that pass through it on the way to somewhere else.[58]

As Elizabeth Ermarth points out in her study of crisis in the representation of time in the modern and postmodern periods, analogies between time and trains; clock-time and locomotion appeared in the literature and iconography of train travel from its inception (43–45). The train "accelerated" time, effecting substantial changes in how things were perceived through the windows of rapidly moving train cars. Azorín acknowledged the role of trains in similar fashion. He recognized, first, that landscape appreciation and its protagonism in literature might have been promoted by its greater accessibility to increasing numbers of people through train travel; he also appreciated the fact that the train had significantly altered the perception of landscape since it could no longer be contemplated at the same leisurely pace that coach travel had permitted.[59] Antonio Risco observed that while travel in Azorín's early work is usually accomplished in carts or coaches, thus allowing for detailed landscape "painting," in his mature work travel tends to involve fast-moving trains or automobiles which produce verbal landscape descriptions that dissolve into cinematographic flashes or imaginary, surreal dreamscapes (1985, 346).

Rusiñol, and especially Regoyos—like the Impressionists Monet, Guillaumin, and Pissarro—painted the effects of encroaching industry on the landscape. Many of Regoyos's paintings of the Basque countryside include allusions, and sometimes direct references, to the effect industry was having on the Basque cities and towns where many of Spain's most industrialized rivers and ports were located. As did some Impressionists, Regoyos painted landscapes such as *Altos Hornos de Bilbao* (1908), in which a spectacular sunset dominates the painting, but whose distant background might

also include smoke rising from factory chimneys (Pl. 11 and 12), or a beachscape whose middle-ground shows oxen and cranes unloading cargo from a lone ship (*El arco iris* 1900). Regoyos also painted trains. The exhibition catalogue of a retrospective of his work (Madrid, November 1986–January 1987) contains eight urban or rural landscapes, the earliest dated 1883, which directly protagonize trains. As they did for Azorín, trains for Regoyos had an inherent association with clock time, as indicated in his painting *El tren de las 16 horas* (1900), and perhaps there is more than a coincidence of title between Azorín's "El tren que pasa" (1944) and Regoyos's *Pancorbo. El tren que pasa* (1901). In this picture the train, like Azorín's, passes forward through the canvas in the viewer's direction. A mountain village forms the background which the train will quickly leave behind, while two indistinct human figures in the middle-ground, similar to those of Azorín's story, face the train and wave it on its way out of their bucolic surroundings. In Regoyos's iconology trains became emblematic of changes wrought in the traditional understanding of time-space relationships; he was struck by the incongruity of trains passing through seemingly eternal Castilian villages untouched by historical time. Paintings such as *Viernes Santo en Castilla* (Pl. 13) juxtapose a great, arching railway overpass with a looming black engine rushing headlong in one direction, while underneath the pass, moving slowly on an opposite course, is a group of figures shrouded in black, filing off to, or perhaps home from, the observance of Good Friday services. In *El túnel de Pancorbo* (1902), on a high trestle above the road, a freight train is about to enter a tunnel while down below, moving in the opposite direction, is a horse-drawn covered wagon. The painting draws together in one canvas the many changes train travel implied: the train as synonymous with modern life; the loss of sensorially perceived animal power; the disappearance of leisurely contemplation of the landscape that accompanied the advent of much more rapid forms of mechanical transport; the tunnel as a suspension in the relationship between the human eye and the landscape. Some critics called Regoyos's train canvases "thesis paintings": in a rather petulant article written in 1917, José María Salaverría commented that when Regoyos returned to Spain from many years abroad, he brought back with him a "tendentious aesthetic," producing "thesis paintings. . . . I remember one small canvas that showed . . . a procession of monks along a road, and above them, on a bridge, a smoking train traveling at full speed, topics that excited a lot of people back then" (n.p.).

The eye, its ability to perceive space, and human perception as affected by the modern phenomena of train travel and advances made in optical science, all precipitated significant changes in the way human beings saw their world. Writers and painters in Spain and France immediately recognized the implications these changes had for aesthetics and tried to find ways of incorporating them to their work. As William Berg indicates in his study of vision and the visual in Zola, theories of "pure visuality" abounded in all forms of late nineteenth-century intellectual life, from science to art criticism, to painting and literature (1992, 60). In his studies on Velázquez, José Ortega y Gasset, the most prominent chronicler and quantifier of Spanish Modernism, reformulated Kant's *Critique of Pure Reason* to propose that Veláz-quez had reduced painting to something like an impressionistic "critique of pure retinality" (8:477). The notion that Velázquez and El Greco were Impressionists before the fact had already surfaced at the *Institución Libre de Enseñanza* in the revisionist art histories of Manuel B. Cossío and Aureliano de Beruete. In their mission to reestablish a sense of continuity between a past spiritual and cultural life that promised more fruitful lessons for the present than those offered by the ignominy and chaos of recent Spanish history, Cossío and Beruete, with a little help from Manet's interest in Velázquez, cast both El Greco and Velázquez as aesthetic innovators who had used impressionist techniques centuries before the "new" art form reared its head in France. In doing so they found a way to contextualize Spanish art within the European mainstream, and thus to promote national pride in and awareness of the great classical painters. Azorín's transformation of this program into a fully realized political and aesthetic ideology, and his inclusion of work by El Greco and Velázquez in his essays and fiction, are the topics of the following two chapters.

2

El Greco and Velázquez: Two Spanish Proto-Impressionists

El Greco

Francisco Giner de los Ríos argued that a nation's originality was determined by, among other factors, the continuity of a national tradition within each moment of a people's history (3:171). An important component of Giner's pedagogical mission to restore the diminished national self-esteem of his country was to focus public attention on the positive aspects of the Spanish past. José Luis Bernal argues that because Spain lacked an uninterrupted tradition of scientific, musical, or philosophical achievement, the nineteenth-century quest for a national heritage that could be restored to a pride of place in the nation's conscience fell on the literature and art of Spain's dazzling Golden Age (1990, 70). Rafael Altamira, a disciple of Giner's who was to become one of the most important "new" historians associated with the *Institución Libre,* recalled that art history field trips led either by Giner or Cossío were fundamental in guiding students to a more profound understanding of Spanish "History" (Gómez Molleda 107).

The project of revalorizing and restoring Spanish classical art was essentially the work of Giner, Manuel B. Cossío, and Aureliano de Beruete who focused their attention on the painters El Greco, Velázquez, and Goya. Because their work embodied the severe grandeur, nobility, and inner strength of the landscape and people of Castile, El Greco and Velázquez were thought best qualified to represent the character and poetics of Castile to which Giner referred as the "backbone of Spain" (1915, 365). With the exception of Jacinto Octavio Picón's book on Velázquez (1899), the work of all three painters had largely been consigned to oblivion in Spain. Azorín indicated that even Jovellanos, one of the most enlightened minds of the eighteenth century, considered Mengs superior to Goya, and wrote in 1790 (at the time Goya was forty-four years old and already an established artist), that Mengs was the most important painter in Spain (4:331). As for El Greco, Azorín observed that his work was not particularly well-known during the painter's own lifetime, and even the "enlightened" eighteenth century laughed at his paintings. He cited the case of Francisco Gregorio de Salas who, in his *Nuevas poesías serias y jocosas,* attempted a satirical ekphrastic re-creation of the typical nobleman in El Greco's iconography:

> Este original del *Greco*
> acartonado y enjuto,
> fue de color de escorbuto,

carilargo y anquiseco;
habló grave, tosió hueco,
y fue un grandísimo maza . . . (7:726)

[This odd character of El Greco's
withered and skinny,
was sallow of complexion,
long in the face and lean;
solemn of speech, hollow of cough,
and he was a terrific bore . . .]

In another piece on El Greco, Azorín reviewed the thesis put forth by a Dr. Beritens who argued that, had El Greco access to modern ophthalmology and eye wear to correct his impaired vision, he never would have portrayed reality in the anomalous fashion that he did. Azorín concluded his observations with the tongue-in-cheek query as to what effect corrective eyewear might have had on Degas, Sisley, Pissarro, and Monet who also were accused of "visual extravagance" (PCQ 76–77).

Daniel Vázquez Díaz (1882–1969), a post-Impressionist painter who lived in Paris during the first decades of the new century, recalled that in his childhood (the 1890s), El Greco was the "laughingstock of visitors to the Prado" (Benito 289), while in his definitive study of Velázquez, published in 1898, Aureliano de Beruete observed that El Greco had only recently come to attention outside of Spain (1906, 45). It was due to the consistent educative and public relations campaigns undertaken by Giner, Cossío, and Beruete that El Greco, Velázquez, and Goya slowly found a place in the minds of Spaniards. As was to be expected, the gente nueva responded immediately to these painters who, as Azorín observed, represented "authentic Spanish tradition" (9:1142). Among the less liberal-minded, however, the triumvirate of classical painters was at the center of heated polemical discussion.

Manuel B. Cossío, Giner's closest collaborator and resident art historian at the ILE, almost single-handedly restored El Greco to the visual arts canon in Spain. In the preface to his book on the painter, Cossío stated that his personal interest in El Greco had been stimulated by, then coalesced over the years, through preparations he made to teach the life and work of the master at the ILE, and by repeated visits he undertook with generations of students to the Prado Museum and Toledo. Finally, Cossío observed that he felt the need to synthesize his many years of meditation on El Greco and to

publish the fruit of his research in book form in order to contribute further to the painter's "rehabilitation" (1:x–xi).[1] José Giner Pantoja, a student at the Institución Libre in the early 1900s, left valuable observations on the methodology used by Giner and Cossío: prior to embarking on field excursions to Toledo, Giner prepared students by illustrating his talks with J. Laurent's photographs of the historical sites through which Cossío would later guide them. Giner Pantoja also had the good fortune to still be enrolled at the ILE when Cossío's book was published, and he recalled that, during one excursion to Toledo, students had the privilege of hearing Cossío read his chapter on El Entierro del Conde de Orgaz while the group was actually seated before the painting in the church of Santo Tomé (55).

Spanish classical art may not have been especially valued in Spain, nor, for that matter, were El Greco, Velázquez, and Goya household names in Europe, but there was an increasing demand for their work on the international art market which unmindful and frequently insolvent Spanish officials were only too willing to supply. Although in his series of articles on the Generation of 1898, Azorín claimed the conservancy of national art treasures to be the provenance of the gente nueva, it was Giner and Cossío who first stirred public outcry against the careless squandering abroad of the patrimonio nacional. Giner deplored the lack of government control and conservation of art, and he condemned the clergy for outright theft of art and artifacts from their own churches for the purpose of selling whatever they could to antiquarians (20:279–81). In his book on El Greco, Cossío related the arrival in Toledo of an unfamiliar automobile whose equally unidentified occupants removed two Greco canvases from the Chapel of San José during a summer siesta and later, under the cover of night, absconded with the paintings (1:704–5). A significant number of paintings by El Greco are actually copies made to replace originals that had been sold or otherwise removed: such was the case with the Asunción in the Church of Santo Domingo in Toledo where an inferior duplicate by José Aparicio replaced the original, sold in 1830 by Don Sebastián de Borbón, a member of the royal family. The original painting resurfaced in 1904 at the Durand-Ruel gallery in Paris (1:33). Cossío also gave an account of inept and tasteless restorations, and the harrowing story of a nearly concluded sale by the government in 1902 of the *Entierro del Conde de Orgaz* to a foreign dealer (1:312). He argued that rather than pilfer a heritage that in no way could be considered the personal property of the government, nobility, or clergy, these same officials should be held responsible for cataloguing and controlling the nation's art treasures; for conserving and displaying them at the sites they were meant to occupy by their creators. But, in order to preserve the national artistic heritage, Cossío pointed out that the nation had to be deserving of it, and to become deserving of their patrimony, the public first had to evince an interest in the art itself, and then bring pressure to bear on the government to comply with its responsibilities to the people: "It's not enough to complain. Agitating and channeling public opinion, not only with words, but with deeds, promoting wherever possible local societies and missions for the protection of art, influencing the government . . . is the duty of anyone who is seriously distressed by such shameful neglect" (1:312 n. 1).

Although Cossío's two-volume study of El Greco was published in 1908, articles on the painter began to appear in the last two decades of the previous century. Giner first mentioned Velázquez and El Greco in his 1885 essay "El Paisaje"; in 1894 Martín Rico published a piece on the painter in *El Liberal*, followed three years later by Cossío's detailed commentary on the painter in his guide to Toledo, published in 1897 in the *BILE* (*PCQ* 80). Cossío's interpretation of El Greco was essentially a determinist one; this position would also be the view adopted by the Generation of 1898: although he was born in Crete and studied painting in Italy, because the immigrant El Greco adapted so easily to the Castilian environment and empathized with its ambience so profoundly, he was able to portray the Castilian landscape and the psyche of its people with utmost realism (1:198–99). Azorín, perhaps the '98 writer who adhered to determinist notions with most consistency for an appreciable number of years, wrote that to absorb visually the interminable plains and bald hillocks of Castile was to understand the inspiration behind her literature and art (Fox 1968, 211). The untamed savagery of the countryside, its indomitable harshness, wrote Azorín in *La ruta de Don Quijote*, invariably leads one to understand how this land produced the reclusive, "hallucinated, fantastic

souls" of Castilian warriors, mystics, and conquistadores (Ramsden 42–43).

In Cossío's opinion Toledo, El Greco's adoptive city, was of paramount importance in circumscribing the evolution of his idiosyncratic style. For the *institucionistas* Toledo represented a composite of "all that the genuine Spanish land and civilization have been": the landscape around the city was a synthesis of the most salient features of the "high Castilian tableland"; any comprehension of the national racial type memorialized in the iconography of the sixteenth and seventeenth centuries was, therefore, dependent upon an appreciation of Toledo and the models El Greco used for his figure paintings (Cossío 1897, 4–5). Of all paintings by El Greco, *El Entierro del Conde de Orgaz* was, in Cossío's view, "one of the most truthful pages in the history of Spain," preserving in one canvas everything that represented the body and soul of Castile during the last years of the reign of Felipe II (1:236) (Pl. 14). So authentic was the documentary realism of this painting that Cossío argued the entire past of the Spanish people could be reconstructed on the basis of its example, as well as those gleaned from the *romancero* and the drama and novel of the Golden Age (1:238). El Greco's "realism" consisted in a felicitous merging of the physical and moral ambience of Castilian society with the artist's signature "nervous accent and cool color tones" that Cossío thought especially apt to portray El Greco's models and the landscape in which they lived (1:225). El Greco's figure paintings are not imaginary, idealized physical types, but reflect the commingling of pessimism and melancholy with the violence, anxiety, pomposity, and impulsiveness characteristic of the people and spiritual climate in Castile during the late sixteenth and early seventeenth centuries (1:241). The sallow, lean, angular physical type, whose deep-set eyes sometimes reflected melancholy and at others, the burning light of fanatical passion, became a human objective correlative of the arid, gray and ochre Castilian plain through which, in the environs of Toledo, the Tajo River had cut one of the deepest and most spectacular gorges in Spain. The saffron-colored city, rising dramatically on a high outcrop of land above the meandering river at the bottom of its ravine, contrasted violently with the *cigarrales* on the outskirts below where the vegetation and orchards were plentifully supplied with water from the Tajo. These dissonant visual contrasts echoed the conflictive dichotomies of the Castilian mentality, and represented a vivid incarnation of the lack of parity between external form and internal content that defined the national *élan vital* during El Greco's lifetime (Cossío 1908, 1:110, 279).

While most of El Greco's painter contemporaries preferred an Italiante palette of warm, xanthic colors, Cossío suggested that on his arrival in Toledo, El Greco systematically began to use a cyanic color scheme in which a cool blue, violet, and silver palette "traduce fielmente, con perfecto sabor realista, el tono de la raza y de la tierra castellana" (1:512).[2] Although Cossío rightfully deserves credit for rescuing El Greco from the oblivion into which he had fallen by undertaking the first modern research to reconstruct the painter's life, analyze his work, authenticate and catalogue the paintings, Cossío himself recognized that popularizing El Greco to a larger, nonspecialized public was the work of "the young Spanish writers, the most recent generation of 'intellectuals'" (1:530). The notion that El Greco, Velázquez, and Goya represented the authentic, *castizo* spirit of Spain was embraced wholeheartedly by the *gente nueva* who continued the labor of salvaging whatever they thought positive and exemplary from the detritus of Spain's former greatness. The turn of the century proved auspicious for the task at hand, witnessing a flurry of commemorative activities and scholarly publications: 1899 coincided with the tercentenary of Velázquez's birth, preceded the year before by the publication in France of Aureliano de Beruete's study and *catalogue raisonné* of the painter's work; a special exhibition of paintings by Velázquez was organized at the Prado Museum; in 1900 there was a sizeable Goya retrospective; in 1902 a commemorative exhibition of paintings by El Greco was held in conjunction with the many festivities that marked the coming of age of Alfonso XIII; and, finally, in 1908 Cossío published his long-awaited, monumental study of the painter.

Although Azorín sometimes attributed primacy of recognizing El Greco's importance to the artists and writers of Barcelona, more often than not, he credited the Castilianophile Generation of 1898 with putting El Greco at the center of their cultural activities.[3] However, it was, indeed, the group of Catalonian *modernistas*, organized by Santiago Rusiñol, who were

the first to elevate El Greco to the stature of a cult figure. Rusiñol had purchased some land and a dilapidated house in Sitges, outside Barcelona, where he planned to house his growing collection of art, including significant holdings of antique Spanish wrought iron, hence the name "Cau Ferrat" given to the property. Although Rusiñol did not take up official residence there for quite some time, whenever he happened to come through Barcelona, Cau Ferrat became a hotbed of artistic activity. The most Bohemian of players in the pipeline between Paris and Barcelona, Rusiñol was active in bringing European culture to Spain: a champion of Ibsen, Nietzsche, and Maeterlinck, he also encouraged young musicians, the composition of new music, and was among the first to recognize the importance of El Greco. It was in Sitges, in 1900, that Rusiñol organized, as Cossío put it, "a group of Catalonian writers and artists educated in Montmartre . . . those who most live the universal life in Spain," to erect a statue in El Greco's honor. Zuloaga donated two paintings attributed to El Greco that were featured in a procession commemorating the event, and later deposited at Rusiñol's ever-expanding "museum" at Cau Ferrat where they still hang today (1907, 378).

Not to be outdone, Madrid's *gente nueva* also did their part to fan the flames of El Greco's growing popularity. In 1900 they dedicated the only number of *Mercurio*, one of their many short-lived "little magazines," to the painter, and they began to feature Toledo and paintings by El Greco in their creative writing and contributions to the periodic press. In an article anticipating the tercentenary commemoration of El Greco's death (April 1614), Azorín noted that by 1900 another group—"of Castilian writers"—had also proclaimed their devotion and enthusiasm for El Greco (2:842–43). Ignoring his own role in the endeavor, he wrote that the admiration for El Greco generated in Catalonia was headed in Madrid by Pío and Ricardo Baroja who spread the "fervent admiration for El Greco among the Spanish youth," and he called especially significant in this context Pío Baroja's 1902 novel, *Camino de perfección* (2:847). A large part of the book is set in Toledo, traditionally considered the spiritual capital of Spain, and its structure appears to follow that of a mystical journey leading to purification and perfection. The novel also features important paintings by El Greco cast in meaningful, supportive roles, as are the various churches and chapels in which these paintings are housed.

Cossío supported Azorín's claim (*PCQ* 234) that El Greco was "resurrected" by writers, observing that it was the "young intellectuals" who kept the painter in the public eye, who were inspired by his work, who visited and wrote about the places where El Greco lived and painted, who recognized his cultural importance, and who devoted themselves to the pedagogical task of carving out a niche for El Greco in the public consciousness (1:530). In his essay "Los cuadros del Greco" (1900), Baroja wrote that he visited Illescas and Toledo to see for himself the places where El Greco executed his most famous paintings and to contemplate the same landscape El Greco would have contemplated (8:829). The association between the new-found enthusiasm for El Greco and the significance of the Castilian landscape and Castilian towns was also made by Azorín, who indicated that the rediscovery of El Greco was ineluctably tied to the recent popularity of "old Spanish cities, especially Toledo. From there originates the concern in art—poetry, novel, painting—with the Castilian landscape and its ancient cities" (2:847).[4]

It would be useful to consider why Giner and Cossío would have chosen El Greco, Velázquez, and, secondarily, Goya, over other Spanish painters on whom to focus their efforts of redeeming long-neglected, national cultural traditions. As Carmen Pena put it so aptly, these "recently nationalized" painters represented for the *institucionistas* and the *gente nueva* a realist temperament that adumbrated by many centuries contemporary European art (1993, 45). In a retrospective essay Cossío suggested that both Goya and El Greco, because they responded to the ferment, exploits, and uneasiness of their respective historical moments, most closely approximated the spiritual climate that, from the mid-nineteenth century on, had been called "modernismo" (1931, 273). In his view, El Greco was not fully understood or appreciated "until our time" because no other period in Spanish history demonstrated such close affinities as those between contemporary art and the vision of Domenico Theotocópuli (1:535).

In the Introduction to his book, Cossío noted that only the moderns in their anti-academic posture and rejection of "good taste" in art were able to complete the rehabilitation of El Greco initiated by the French Romantics, finally rescuing him from the oblivion or, at best, the lack of regard, to which he had been consigned (1:vii).[5] The homologies Cossío identified between El Greco's style and the Modern sensibility were based on his view that the same ideology, the same profound spiritual desolation and pessimism that informed contemporary art—Maeterlinck's *L'Intruse*, Ibsen's *Ghosts*, Whistler's portrait of Carlyle, Renoir's landscapes, and Rusiñol's abandoned gardens—was the same "funereal sadness" that imbued El Greco's paintings.[6] He postulated that the current of unease and potential for social and political destabilization flowing just beneath the surface of an outwardly undisturbed nation and its people, as implied in the painting of El Greco, was echoed by the sense of mutability, loss of faith in the "real," and established society that characterized modern times, thereby explaining contemporary empathy with the Toledan painter (1:536). Cossío further argued that, given contemporary disturbances in the social and cultural milieu, the moderns could not help but find El Greco's broken lines, explosive brushstrokes, preference for color over line, his "singlemindedness, anxiety, and violent color," suggestive of their own anxieties, the social instability of their own environment, and their rebellion against obdurate classicism. Because the new movement in contemporary aesthetics felt itself untrammeled by convention, the moderns could freely applaud "any aberration, any monstrosity" as long as the work of art was infused with, or able to provoke an impression of, life. For the first time El Greco—who had been censured for so long as "outlandish," "scandalous," even insane—was not only understood, but eulogized and admired all the more for his idiosyncracies (1:537). He was thus both classical and modern; a painter whose aesthetic vision was so far ahead of its time that it could be appreciated only hundreds of years after his death by the kindred sensibilities of the late nineteenth- and early twentieth-century Moderns.

Cossío, as well as critics of art, culture, and literature who followed him—among them Azorín—drew further parallels between contemporary and classical aesthetics when they proposed Góngora and Gracián as literary moderns whose "subtle, writhing, disjointed" conceptist style, bursting with energy and motility, they interpreted as verbal and spiritual analogues to El Greco's visual discourse (1:535). In Cossío's view, El Greco's paintings demanded the same kind of intellectual acuity as did the poetry of his friend Góngora; it possessed the same kind of subtlety and produced similar complications and distortions of style, securing for both painter and poet roles as prototypes of Modern aesthetics in their respective media (1907, 379).[7] In his guide to Toledo, Cossío was the first to suggest that El Greco be considered the only Spanish antecedent to explain the roots and genesis of Velázquez's art. In subsequent publications he stated overtly that, while it was true Velázquez had gained public acceptance and renown before El Greco, El Greco's influence on the younger painter was decisive and his ensuing popularity was assured by the kinship between them (1:xii, 533). The Generation of 1898 accepted Cossío's judgment, and the opinion Pío Baroja expressed regarding Velázquez as the "logical development of certain pictorial features of El Greco," generally reflected that of the *vox populi*. He also made the intriguing observation that in the composition of El Greco's *El Entierro del Conde de Orgaz* (Pl. 14) lay the seeds of Velázquez's *La rendición de Breda* (8:833).

Cossío further promoted El Greco by arguing that for the "ultra-modernistas," the painter was not only Velázquez's "great precursor," but he also maintained that modernists even considered El Greco to be the superior of the two artists. The reason for this preference on the part of the "super-modernists," Cossío explained, was that in the last phase of his artistic evolution, Theotocópuli discovered the technique of juxtaposing complementary primary colors, and he understood as well that light was modified by the reflections given off by adjacent color tones. He staunchly defended El Greco as the precursor of Impressionism against those who accorded primacy of place to Velázquez (1:528–29), observing that it was logical to consider El Greco the "father of Impressionism," a fact anyone could verify by visiting the sizeable collection of Impressionist art the painter Caillebot [sic] had recently bequeathed to the Musée de Luxembourg (1:xii). According to Cossío, the Impressionists discovered in El Greco a "consecrated" painter to whose work they might allude in order to bolster and gain support for their own (1897, 7). This view was defended decades later by Bermúdez-Cañete who observed that appreciation of El Greco and Impressionist painting—as well as the study of parallels between literature, art, and music—were all common features of Modernism (1:163). A similar notion was advanced by the art historian Enrique Lafuente Ferrari in his book on Zuloaga where he argued that El Greco had always utilized impressionist technique, being especially taken by the sense of motion an unblended brushstroke could produce and that, like the Impressionists, El Greco was a "destructor de la forma" who shared, with Velázquez and Goya, a sensitivity to the challenges presented a painter by the variability of color and light (1950, 121).

In a 1903 essay on Góngora, Navarro Ledesma referred to El Greco and Góngora as great innovators and immortal Modernists, writing that both painter and poet were "twin souls," one of them urged on by a superhuman desire to find new colors, unexpected nuances, and unusual tonalities of the palette; the other by a need to discover untested lexical expression, unspoiled verbal constructions, and chaste idiom (477–78). Azorín, in "El momento y la sensación" (6:285–89), undoubtedly meant to evoke affinities between El Greco and impressionist technique, took the parallels Cossío had established between Góngora and El Greco further into the realm of Modernity by outrightly declaring Góngora to be an Impressionist. He pointed out that while most painters and writers found "antecedents and consequences" indispensable to mimesis, the great innovation of Góngora and El Greco, like that of the Impressionists, was to suggest a more natural vision by, paradoxically, eliminating from reality some of its "realism" so that no excess might obscure the quintessence of the work. Just as Góngora communicated volumes of concepts and conceits through a mere "isolated sensation," so El Greco consciously touched and retouched his canvases in order to leave his colors "distinct and disjointed," relying on the same disjunction in paint as did Góngora on paper to freeze and make tangible the transient, phenomenological moment (6:286).[8]

Temporality, the mutability of light and color, the unblended brushstroke and juxtaposition of complementary primary colors, formed the backbone of impressionist technique, the most extraordinary revolution in aesthetics since the discovery of linear perspective during the Renaissance. In this scheme of things, Spain was thus not a cultural backwater of Europe, but rather the birthplace of writers and painters whose modernity was only now being rediscovered and appreciated. In his essay on Góngora in *Los dos Luises*, Azorín noted that "above all, Góngora gives the impression of modernity; of all the classics, he is the most modern" (4:194). Góngora not only influenced modern poetry and prose, observed Azorín in *Leyendo a los clásicos*, but his reach also extended to the visual arts. Writing two years before the poets of Spain's Generation of 1927 organized their commemorative activities around Góngora's tercentenary, Azorín suggested that the Golden Age poet deserved "a tribute, not merely locally, but nationally, to the man who influenced modern art so thoroughly and intensely" (7:720).[9] He maintained that innovative writers, by virtue of the verbal medium's greater accessibility to the public, had a much easier time in disseminating their work than did painters, citing the example of Góngora who was already considered a "classic" shortly after his death, while it took El Greco centuries to achieve the same status (1908b, 10). Although so much time had elapsed between El Greco's death and his belated recognition, his ambitious handling of the challenges light and color always presented to painters, his prescient awareness of the effect complementary colors have when placed in close proximity to one another, adumbrate the same challenges to which the Impressionist painters responded. While Camille Mauclair insisted that Claude Monet discovered "the division of tonalities through dabs of juxtaposed color, reconstituting at a distance in the eye of the viewer the true color of the objects represented" (16), in his 1909 article on Impressionism, Fernando Araujo argued that, although the juxtaposition of complementary primary colors was traditionally attributed to Monet via Turner, this was not a new discovery but a technique known to "all colorists and is classic in all painters' studios" (175–76).

In his tireless promotion of El Greco as a precursor of Impressionism, Cossío maintained that the painter's chief interest was the "problem of color," and that he was not aware of any painter prior to El Greco who "so resolutely and consciously sought to show the influence of one tone on its surroundings" (1:350).[10] The impressionist El Greco was also the one adopted and popularized by the Generation of 1898. In a speech he made inaugurating a retrospective exhibition of work by Darío de Regoyos, Ra-

miro de Maeztu observed that Tintoretto and El Greco both anticipated Chevreul's "discovery" of heightening chromatic effects by juxtaposing gradations of the same hue that, when viewed at a distance, are perceived by the human eye as an unbroken, blended sweep of color. Maeztu then traced this technique to the Impressionist painters via Constable, Delacroix, and the Barbizon School.[11] In an early article on El Greco, Baroja noted that the "gentle, filtered light that entered through the green and yellow stained glass windows," its delicately shaded chiaroscuro dappling a group of worshippers he contemplated in a church at Illescas, re-created the subtle gradations of pigment and multicolored shadows of an Impressionist painting, leading him to speculate that El Greco's daily visual contact with such phenomena might explain the evolution of a proto-impressionist technique in his work (8:829). Unamuno's El Greco, like Azorín's, was much more a "realist" than that prescribed by conventional standards. El Greco aimed to eternalize the fugitive moment, made possible only by awarding an "impression" the full value that it merits. Unamuno compared El Greco's paintings to snapshots "taken instantaneously with the blinding light of a lightning flash . . . like those imprinted on magnesium, but snapshots of art and color." In Unamuno's opinion El Greco was "the first apostle of naturalistic Impressionism"—a naturalist because his art communicates to the spectator "an impression of nature" rather than a reality accessed through familiar and clichéd prescriptions for realism (7:756).

The final apotheosis of El Greco as an Impressionist consisted in making direct connections between his work and that of specific Impressionist painters. Cossío was adamant in his insistence that the cool, monochromatic backgrounds of El Greco's canvases, his unusual contrasts of light and dark pigment amid spots of exuberantly heightened color, passed first through Goya and later found their way into paintings by Whistler and Manet (1:228). He went on to say that not only was Manet influenced by El Greco's portraiture, but that even neo-Impressionism with its disdain for form, its tendency to communicate the isolated sensation, its eagerness to simplify and eliminate the superfluous, its "displays of impropriety," could trace its etiology to El Greco (1907, 379–80). Ortega y Gasset more accurately recognized in Manet the influence of Velázquez, but agreed with the German art historian Julius Meier-Graefe that "Cézanne serves as an introduction to El Greco" (1:98). Indeed, contemporary historians of Cubism and Cubo-Futurism frequently note Delaunay's identification of El Greco, Turner, and Constable as painters whose interest in light and color anticipated the Impressionists' response to the same issues (Golding 184).

Spanish vanguard artists with ties to the French art world were only too happy to encourage the Impressionists to visit their country and to act as personal tour guides through the Velázquez, El Greco, and Goya collections at the Prado Museum, the Escorial, and the churches of Toledo. Darío de Regoyos traveled through Spain in the company of painters Toulouse-Lautrec, Constantin Meunier, Theo von Rysselberghe, and in 1888 with the Belgian poet Émile Verhaeren (Rodríguez Alcalde 176); in 1904 Aureliano de Beruete entertained Claude Monet in Madrid and wrote of him, "he's a young old man, strong as an oak, somewhat like Martín Rico . . . he walked away amazed by Greco, Velázquez, above all by Goya. The rest didn't impress him at all" (Marín Valdés 89). Azorín noted that Marceliano Santa María hosted Rodin on his visit to Spain in 1905 (8:450), for which Zuloaga, a good friend of the sculptor's, organized a banquet on 9 June and a visit to the bullfights on 12 June.[12] Maurice Barrès, friend to both painters and writers of '98, first visited Toledo in 1902 in the company of Aureliano de Beruete, and eventually published a book, *Greco, ou le secret de Tolède*, in which he remarked that the Castilian plains, "their low, unchangeable slopes, their land noble like Zurbarán, striking like El Greco, their fertile plains rich like Velázquez, also contain the colors of our Manet" (64 n. 4). In his necrology of Zuloaga, Azorín noted that the idea of "Spain" was perhaps best embodied in modern aesthetics by the Cid of Leconte de Lisle, Baudelaire's Don Juan, and Manet's *Le Torero mort* (1946a). Manet visited Spain for about ten days in late August and early September of 1865. There seems to have been no record made of his visit by Spaniards, although it is known that Manet lodged in the newly built, luxurious Grand Hôtel de Paris at the Puerta del Sol, and that he visited Burgos, Valladolid, Toledo, and spent a full week in Madrid where he made numerous visits to the Prado, being especially impressed with Velázquez whom he called "the painter of painters" in letters written to friends after his return to France on 13 September (Wilson-Bareau 16–17). Robert Herbert points out that there is a "heavy 'Spanish' touch" in Manet's early work reminiscent of techniques used by Velázquez and other Spanish painters of the seventeenth century (1988, 63). What Manet could have absorbed in so short a visit to Spain is moot since, as a young man, he might have visited the extensive Galerie Espagnole at the Louvre, a collection of more than 500 Spanish paintings either looted earlier in the century by Napoleon or bought subsequently by Louis-Philippe (the gallery was dismantled, together with the July Monarchy, in 1848). In the early years of his career, Manet also had access to the popular Spanish dance troupes that visited Paris on a regular basis, and whose performers would occasionally pose for him. Although he might have aimed for Velázquez's subdued color palette and objective realism, Manet's "Spanish" canvases are infused with a Romantic flavor absent from the work of the seventeenth-century Spanish masters. Nevertheless, it was the association of an impressionist Velázquez as Manet's precursor, first advanced by Aureliano de Beruete and later championed by the *gente nueva*, that once again meant to position Spanish aesthetics on the cutting edge of European art at a moment when Spain was most prostrate and isolated from the mainstream, and national morale was at its nadir. The rehabilitation of El Greco and Velázquez not only redeemed these painters from languishing in undeserved oblivion but, as we shall see, also contributed to a revalidation of the Spanish cultural present.

Velázquez

Cossío wrote that the phenomenon of Velázquez could not have materialized in Spanish art without the precedent of El Greco; that El Greco was Velázquez's only master; Velázquez El Greco's only disciple (1:514–15, 518). He supported his contention by referring to the opinion of the "highest authority" that he knew on matters concerning Velázquez: that of his colleague at the *ILE*, Aureliano de Beruete. In his seminal book on the Spanish master, Beruete, "despite all his circumlocutions," wrote Cossío, "has come to confirm my opinion on this point" (1907, 373). Although Cossío recognized El Greco was Castilian by adoption only, he argued that because the painter expressed in his canvases the character of the Castilian landscape and that of the Castilian race "with perfect realist flavor," he was able to exercise such profound influence on Velázquez, the greatest of all Spanish painters (1907, 346). Because El Greco and Velázquez were both interested in the topical rather than the ideal, and because both responded to the problems color and light presented to painters, together they paved the way for modern art (1907, 377). To support his argument, Cossío cited Richard Muther, professor of art history at the University of Breslau, who stated categorically that the most topical and noteworthy difficulty all modern painters sought to resolve was the representation of objects not as they were defined by line and form, but as they appeared in their individual atmospheres of light and air; a problem according to Muther, that no painter other than Velázquez had previously addressed.[13] Cossío concluded that Velázquez was the indisputable "influjo capital" modern art had been fortunate enough to inherit from classical painting, and that both contemporary Realism and Impressionism benefited from valuable instruction subsumed in examples provided by the paintings of the great artist (1:527).

In 1898 Aureliano de Beruete published in French—in a limited, luxury edition—what Gaspar Gómez de la Serna called "the first Spanish work of note on Velázquez" (40).[14] Although the German art critic Karl Justi published an important book on Velázquez in 1889, and Jacinto Octavio Picón's monograph followed one year after Beruete's much more scholarly study, Beruete's contribution was the first exhaustive, modern scholarship on Velázquez, as well as the first effort to produce a *catalogue raisonné* of authenticated paintings. Because he was independently wealthy, Beruete could travel extensively in England, France, and Germany to examine paintings attributed to Velázquez housed in public and private collections to which he gained access due to his international stature as a painter and art historian. None other than Cossío admired Beruete as "the most practical and intelligent Spanish critic of our time" (1:508). William Ritter, writing for the French journal *L'Art et les Artistes* in 1907, spoke of Beruete not only as "the Spanish landscapist par excellence," but also as the Spanish critic who best knew Velázquez (197). Ritter observed that in many of his own paint-

ings, Beruete featured the same Guadarrama mountains that Velázquez often painted in the backgrounds of his royal portraits (198). In a suggestive, deterministic assessment of the two painters, Ritter considered the possible reasons that might explain why Beruete would have employed a color palette dominated by pearl gray, rose gray, green and brown grays, to achieve the same "refined, dissonant harmonies" as did Velázquez centuries before. The most obvious explanation was the inevitable influence Velázquez would have exerted on the painting of his biographer who spent years steeped in the master's style and technique. Ritter, however, also mused that Beruete might have chosen his palette even without the "intervention" of Velázquez, basing his conclusions on the observation that the same gray-based color scheme dominated in the apparel crafted by Spanish tailors and seamstresses that was worn by the subjects of Velázquez's portraits. The Spanish taste for gray was, therefore, conditioned by "the very same elements within which this taste was formed" (199).[15] In an uncanny anticipation of Orteguian *sinfronismo*, Ritter concluded that there was no better explanation for Beruete's affinity with Velázquez than the mysterious lines of communication that linked material objects to human beings and history to a race of people, bridging the gaps between "the most remote subjects, the most contradictory epochs, and the most disparate among men" (199).

Although Beruete rarely submitted his work to the biannual National Art Exhibitions held in Madrid, and he was awarded medals and prizes even less frequently by the "official" art establishment, he enjoyed considerable reputation as an art historian and was asked by the Spanish government to organize and inaugurate a Velázquez gallery at the Prado Museum for the tercentenary celebrations of the painter's birth. The celebrations coincided with a revival of public interest in Velázquez that had germinated within artistic and intellectual communities at an earlier date. Martín Rico, who left Spain in 1862 to study with Charles Daubigny, a painter later acknowledged as the father of French Impressionism, was astounded to find how similar Daubigny's palette was to that used by Velázquez. In the last decades of the century knowledgeable Spaniards were aware of, and only too eager to exploit, the alleged influence Velázquez had on Manet, and even post-

Impressionists like the Catalonian painter Joaquim Mir acknowledged that "el meu mestre és i ha estat sempre Velázquez" (Plá 693). Until recently the art historian Carmen Pena argued that Velázquez actually impeded the development of Impressionism in Spain at the turn of the century because Spanish painters were too much under the sway of "Velazquean luminism" to be able to accept and assimilate fully the "technical excesses" of the French. Pena's contention makes no sense given the fact that the very same painters and art historians who rehabilitated Velázquez at century's end were the same painters and art historians who were adamant in their belief that Impressionism could not be explained without a Velazquean antecedent.[16] In her most recent publications Pena concedes that in the last years of his career Beruete was able to achieve a happy synthesis of Spanish tradition and French modernity, observing that "such a combination was made possible by the identification in certain Spanish painting, the foundations of a certain modernity, first by the foreign romantics, then by the Impressionists who, like Manet, gleaned from Velázquez's visual text lessons for the future" (1993, 86).[17]

As did Cossío with El Greco, Beruete went out of his way to present Velázquez as a Modern before the fact. He often shored up his positions by referring to similar ones expressed in the publications of "authoritative" figures from abroad, citing the words of Paul Lefort who wrote that "modern art will certainly find in Velázquez . . . the means of expression which are best suited to its aspirations. Velázquez is . . . the initiator of modern art . . . so much in advance of his day that he seems rather to belong to ours." Beruete also quoted the same passage from Richard Muther's *Geschichte der Malerei* that Cossío would use some years later to support his conviction that Velázquez influenced a significant number of modern artists and that the problem of representing objects in their individual atmospheres of light and air "is a new problem in the history of art, the work of Velázquez alone excepted" (1906, 140, 143–44).

Although José Ortega y Gasset first published his hermeneutic study of Velázquez's painterly vocation in 1943, the Spanish philosopher began to write about Velázquez as early as 1906.[18] In an article on the German art critic Julius Meier-Graefe, among the first art historians to publish serious critical work on Impressionism, Ortega, like most Spaniards of his day, took the opportunity to mention Manet's debt to Velázquez, quoting Meier-Graefe's observation that "Manet . . . shows contemporary men that which is eternal in Velázquez" (1:98). In "Del realismo en pintura" (1912), Ortega, like Cossío and Beruete, noted that Velázquez had to wait for English and French painters in the second half of the nineteenth century to place his work at the apex of modern art and to "instruct" Spaniards how to view his work properly (1:566).[19] Similar to the observation T. J. Clark made regarding the absence of heroism in the Modern age, and thus its absence from modern art, Ortega proposed that Velázquez was "our painter" because he prepared the way for "our era bereft of gods" in which a spade is called a spade and, referring to Velázquez's *Los borrachos*, circumlocutory dithyrambs to Dionysius were replaced by unselfconscious commentary on alcoholism (2:58). In Velázquez's hands, Bacchus became a nonexistent mystification, the Bacchanalia was replaced by booze, and gods were supplanted by *ganapanes* [hustlers] (2:57). To account for some of the claims made regarding Manet's debt to Velázquez, one has only to recall the French painter's *Olympia* (1863) or *Le Déjeuner sur l'herbe* (1863), paintings inspired by classical nudes that the artist summarily chose to transmogrify, wrenching them from their customary mythological settings of scallop shells, forest glades, and putti-filled entourages, and transplanting them to the contemporary, intranscendental world of middle-class picnickers and prostitution, leading scandalized contemporaries to proclaim Manet a "realist." In commentary similar to Ortega's on Velázquez, Robert Herbert, referring to Manet's paintings, writes that the artist "makes fun of tradition by clothing mythological figures in contemporary costume," thereby demythifying the historical and mythological subject matter considered de rigueur for serious art in his day (1988, 61–62).

In his reading of Velázquez, Ortega saw in the painter's courageous preference for the trivial and the quotidian a highly subversive rejection of the idealized and the sublime that were expected to protagonize officially patronized art (2:57).[20] The penchant contemporary artists had for portraying ordinary people and objects— what Ortega would immortalize in his famous oxymoron as the exquisite vulgarity of the commonplace—was anticipated by Velázquez's nominalism in the seventeenth century. But, warned Ortega, to call Velázquez a "realist" was to say nothing at all about his art (8:475). Had depicting "las cosas, las *res* o las naturas de las cosas" been all that mattered to Velázquez, his painting would be indistinguishable from Flemish genre pieces or the Italian Quattrocento (1:566). Ortega saw Velázquez's originality and modernity emblematized by the manner in which he chose to depict and particularize the material world. Flying in the face of accepted European artistic convention in which realism was determined by the senses of sight and touch, Velázquez paradoxically achieved the pinnacle of realistic illusion by eliminating from his work the representation of volumetric solidity and suggestions of the tactile. Contrary to the practice of his contemporaries, the Spanish master portrayed reality by selecting just enough of its elements to produce a visual illusion: "No one has copied from reality," wrote Ortega, "fewer of its components." Velázquez, therefore, was not a realist at all, but an "unrealist" (8:477). Azorín, like Ortega, interpreted Velázquez's art as having wrested organic materiality from the idealized shackles where it had been imprisoned by tradition and restoring to his subjects their individual ordinariness. Yet, writes Azorín, Velázquez never pretends to surpass phenomenological perception as did the "otra pintura modernísima" (perhaps an allusion to Cubism), that narrowed artistic vision to the infinite combinations made possible by abstract linearity. Even in such cases, the abstract painter could never surpass Nature since pure linearity, in the form of crystallography, also had a place in the natural realm (*PCQ* 235–36).[21]

Ortega's novel interpretation of Velázquez, however, was anticipated by Aureliano de Beruete who noticed that the Spanish master made a practice of doing away with useless details, conserving only "the purely essential for the realisation of the work" (1906, 142–43). Azorín was also partial to the elimination of useless detail. He recalled that as a young, inexperienced writer he filled countless notebooks with annotations of landscape or human physical types for possible later use in his work. With maturity, however, one realizes that it is better to suggest through innuendo rather than to spell everything out for the reader. A firm believer in the adage *maximus in minimus*, for Azorín supreme artistic achievement lay in dis-

carding the profuse, the useless, and the ornamental (9:1195). In his essay "La eliminación," an unusual articulation of what would become one of the most important tenets in the Modern canon, Azorín championed what Roland Barthes was to call the "readerly" text: "La eliminación nos enseña a saltar intrépidamente, sin la preocupación de la incoherencia, de un matiz a otro matiz. Los intersticios que otros rellenan, con fatiga del lector, quedan suprimidos. Elipsis, sí: pero elipsis, principalmente, no gramatical, sino psicológica" [6:32; Elimination shows us how to jump fearlessly, without worrying about incoherence, from one nuance to another. The gaps that others fill, to the reader's weariness, are eliminated. Ellipsis, yes; although mainly not grammatical, but psychological]. In his 1907 essay "Sobre la pintura," Azorín pointed out that Velázquez was also an advocate of eliminating the unnecessary, a thoroughly modern approach that signaled the definitive end of realism (*PCQ* 27).

José Antonio Maravall, like Azorín and Ortega before him, saw Velázquez's great innovation as having renounced the absurd pretense of duplicating reality on canvas (1987, 45). His formidable accomplishment—like that of Rembrandt—resided in the elimination of detail. But, while reality in the painting of Rembrandt is effaced because chiaroscuro overwhelms the represented space, Velázquez is more audacious because he effaces details that are fully illuminated, patently exposing their sketchiness to the spectator's gaze. Velazquean mimesis, accomplished with a minimum of detail, relies more on suggestion than on replication, a manner of painting that provoked accusations of a "lack of finish" to his work and anticipated identical criticism directed at the Impressionists by a public accustomed to the smooth, blended facture characteristic of academic painting (Maravall 1987, 56). Maravall concluded that everything about Velazquez's methodology anticipated Impressionism and that Impressionism would not have evolved as it did without the example of Velázquez through whom the French painters "discovered" their revolutionary techniques (85).

The Impressionists, indeed, undertook a reconsideration of human perception similar to that of Velázquez. As historians of the Impressionist movement remind us, one of its principal innovations was to expand our understanding of what the term "realism" commonly em-

Pl. 1   Jenaro Pérez Villaamil, *Los Picos de Europa en la Serranía de Covadonga*, 1847. Oil on canvas, 98 × 129 cm. Colección del Patrimonio Nacional, Palacio de la Moncloa, Madrid.

Pl. 2   Carlos de Haes, *Picos de Europa*, 1876. Oil on canvas, 168 × 123 cm. Casón del Buen Retiro, Museo del Prado, Madrid.

Pl. 3   Aureliano de Beruete y Moret, *Orillas del Avia*, 1883. Oil on canvas, 76 × 46 cm. Museo del Prado, Madrid.

Pl. 4   Aureliano de Beruete, *Paisaije de Toledo entre cigarrales*, 1910. Oil on canvas, 67 × 100 cm. Museo de Arte Contemporáneo, Toledo.

Pl. 5   Ignacio Zuloaga, *Torerillos en Turégano*, 1912–15. Oil on canvas, 248 × 300 cm. Museo Municipal de San Telmo, San Sebastián, Spain.

Pl. 6   Darío de Regoyos, *Aurresku con lluvia en Mondragón*, 1905. Oil on wood panel, 34 × 46 cm. Museo de Bellas Artes de Bilbao. © Archivo fotográfico del Museo de Bellas Artes de Bilbao, Spain.

Pl. 7   Santiago Rusiñol, *Jardí d'Aranjuez*, 1911. Oil on canvas, 79.5 × 97 cm. Museu Nacional d'Art de Catalunya, Barcelona. © MNAC (Calaveras / Mérida / Sagristà).

Pl. 8   Jean-Baptiste Camille Corot, *Forest of Fontainebleau*, c.1846. Oil on canvas, 90.2 × 128.8 cm. (35¹/₂ × 50³/₄ in.). Gift of Mrs. Samuel Dennis Warren. Courtesy, Museum of Fine Arts, Boston.

Pl. 9   Joaquim Vayreda, *L'Estiu*, 1877. Oil on canvas, 128 × 263 cm. Museu Nacional d'Art de Catalunya, Barcelona. © MNAC (Calaveras / Mérida / Sagristà).

Pl. 10   Aureliano de Beruete, *Las Afueras de Madrid (Barrio de Bellas Vistas)*, 1906. Oil on canvas, 57 × 81 cm. Casón del Buen Retiro, Museo del Prado, Madrid.

Pl. 11   Darío de Regoyos, *Altos hornos de Bilbao*, 1908. Oil on canvas, 26.5 × 35 cm. Colección Central Hispano, Madrid. Photograph by Gonzalo de la Serna.

Pl. 12   Armand Guillaumin, *Soleil couchant à Ivry*, c.1869–71. Oil on canvas, 65 × 81 cm. Musée d'Orsay, Paris. Giraudon / Art Resource, New York.

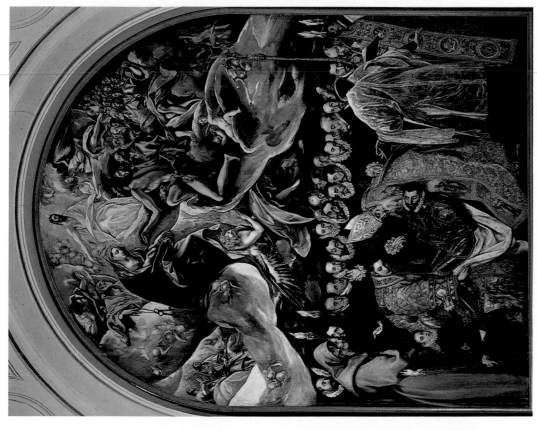

Pl. 14   Dominico Theotocopuli (El Greco), *Entierro del Conde de Orgaz*, c.1586. Oil on canvas, 4.80 × 3.60 m. Church of Santo Tomé, Toledo, Spain. Giraudon / Art Resource, New York.

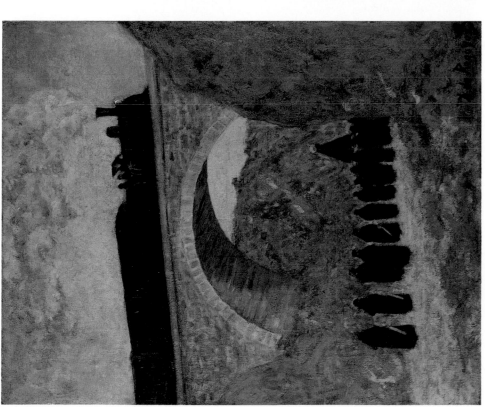

Pl. 13   Darío de Regoyos, *Viernes Santo en Castilla*, 1904. Oil on canvas, 81 × 65 cm. Museo de Bellas Artes de Bilbao. © Archivo fotográfico del Museo de Bellas Artes de Bilbao, Spain.

Pl. 15   Diego Rodríguez de Silva y Velázquez, *Vista del jardín de la 'Villa Medici,' de Roma*, 1630. Oil on canvas, 44 × 38 cm. Museo del Prado, Madrid.

Pl. 16   Diego Rodríguez de Silva y Velázquez, *Vista del jardín de la 'Villa Medici,' de Roma*, 1630. Oil on canvas, 48 × 42 cm. Museo del Prado, Madrid.

braced. For the Impressionist painter the term went beyond an objective portrayal of natural phenomena, and extended to how those phenomena were processed by the human eye (Torgovnick 16). Their subjective, phenomenological manner of perception, determined by values of light and the fluid instability of matter, could not be further removed from that of realist painters whose vision, as Ortega pointed out, was circumscribed by volume and the material corporeality of objects (1:567).[22] This "nueva manera de ver las cosas" in the work of Velázquez was not considered "normal" until the Impressionists, after a long and arduous battle, succeeded in conquering a public unprepared to "see" beyond the rigid standards set for "realism" by the academies. Modern aesthetics are also eminently time-bound. Enrique Lafuente Ferrari related Velázquez's concern with the passing moment to the general way in which the seventeenth century confronted the issue of time. In Velázquez's day, time had acquired a "historial" dimension measurable by clocks, leading as well to the realization that the tangible world perceived by the human eye was vulnerable to its passage. From this new contextualization of time and the ephemeral nature of the material world derives the sense of objective, unsentimental melancholy just beneath the surface of Velázquez's paintings. Although his canvases usually portray some specific instance of the present moment frozen in time and enveloped by its own luminous aura, they also allude to the irrepeatability of the historical present and the impermanent nature of physical bodies whose superficial presence is perpetuated only by dint of conscious selections made by the subjective vision of a painter (Lafuente 1970, 230–31). While El Greco, Rubens, Poussin, and the Carracci brothers all painted objects in motion, Velázquez's *Los borrachos* portrays the moment a latter-day Bacchus places a crown of grape leaves on the head of a common drunkard; *Las Lanzas*, the moment in which a vanquished general turns over the keys of his city to a victorious army; and *Las Meninas*, a specific scene that occurred in the painter's palace studio (Ortega 8:486).

It was the time-bound quality of Velázquez's thematics, as well as his method of execution, that invited still further comparison between the Spanish master and Impressionist painters. As Unamuno had remarked of El Greco's "pin-

tura de istantáneas [sic]," Aureliano de Beruete suggested that Velázquez painted *Las Meninas* and *Las Hilanderas* "after the manner of an instantaneous photograph" (1906, 113).[23] Velázquez's phenomenological approach to artistic praxis, his internalization of objects at the moment they appeared before his eyes, imbued his painting with the illusion of having momentarily detained the fluid temporality of life and required the same economy of representation practiced by the Impressionists as they grappled with the problematic issue of how to represent the transient nature of human perception on canvas. In the introduction to his study on Velázquez, Beruete cites Bonnat's description of the painter's modus operandi that bears a striking resemblance to techniques used by Impressionist painters: ". . . he painted in everything at the first touch. The shadows . . . are merely rubbed in, and only the high lights [sic] are thickly painted; and the whole, with its fine gradations of tone, is so broadly and rapidly executed, and is so precise in colour . . . so exact in its values, and so true in drawing, that the illusion [of reality] is complete, and the resulting work a marvel" (1906, xxi).[24]

Velázquez's aesthetic sensitivity toward time, its fleeting nature, and his seizing of the moment in paint appealed to Azorín who shared the same interests and felt special empathy for the artist. The most important stylistic qualities he advocated in "La eliminación" approximate Velázquez's (and Impressionism's) repudiation of the belabored procedures of academic realism: "Fluidity and speed: those are two essential conditions of style, above those prescribed in the classrooms and the academies: purity and exactness" (6:32). Antonio Risco noted that Azorín's "battle against the clock," and the more general absorption of Modern life with the issue of time, produced a rapidity of execution in literature and painting that introduced into Modern discourse its characteristic fragmentariness and sketchy qualities. He concluded that Azorín's style, as could be said of Modern aesthetics generally, was presentative rather than representative, and succeeded in impeding the flow of movement by freezing it photographically, arresting the elusive sensation, fixing the instantaneous impression through rapid annotation, the sketch, or allusive suggestion, thereby avoiding the ponderous agglomeration of fact and detail in order to reproduce an illusion of the "real" (1980, 212, 118).

Like the Impressionists—and to a great extent the Barbizon painters—Velázquez shied away from a conventionally generic treatment of landscape. The backgrounds of his portraits were inspired by landscape views in and around Madrid: the grounds of the royal palace, panoramas of the Escorial, and the evergreen oaks of the Pardo thrown into relief by the reddish-gray soil in which they grew (Beruete 1906, 54). Beruete argued that it was precisely because Velázquez looked to the direct study of nature for inspiration that late nineteenth-century painters and art historians considered him the "greatest of innovators" (113). In his article "Las montañas" (1909), Azorín reviewed a *Guía alpina del Guadarrama* published by the *institucionista* Bernaldo de Quirós, but he could not refrain from mentioning Velázquez's love for the Guadarrama to which he referred as "one of the most beautiful, noble, austere, magnificent mountain ranges of our country" (1909a, 13). The Velazquean landscape was the same landscape recuperated by the *Institución Libre*, protagonized in the art of Beruete, as well as the literary landscapes of Azorín, Baroja, Machado, and Unamuno. Considered paradigmatic of the Castilian spirit, Velázquez's landscapes compelled in turn-of-the-century regenerationalist art critics and writers a melancholy contemplation of the decaying empire and society traditionally associated with the Spanish Baroque (Pena 1982, 67). Azorín wrote that Velázquez's only pure landscapes, two small paintings executed on the grounds of the Villa Medici in Rome, were not expressions of landscape per se, but depicted a spiritual "melancolía, idealidad," evoked by the ambience of the house and bare wall portrayed in the paintings (2:959–60). Executed during Velázquez's second trip to Italy (1649–51), it was the technique he used in the Villa Medici landscapes (Pl. 15 and 16) that produced additional comparisons to Impressionist painting, evident in the vibrating shimmer of midday sun in one picture and the more composed shadow atmosphere of late afternoon light in the other. Light is the only protagonist in these two paintings, both of which anticipate the importance light would acquire in Velázquez's last major works, *Las Meninas* (1656) and *Las Hilanderas* (1657).[25]

For Azorín the two greatest painters of light and air were Rembrandt and Velázquez (1906b, 80–81). Ortega agreed that the most significant development in the history of art occurred during the relatively short period of time that had elapsed between Caravaggio (1569–1609) and Velázquez (1599–1660), and it entailed the passage of art from tenebrism to the "land of luminosity" (8:851). As far as Ortega was concerned, Velázquez was the first painter to protagonize light, the "substance with which God created the world" (8:628). Referring to the Villa Medici paintings, Gaya Nuño observed that conceiving landscape for no purpose other than to explore in paint its visual modification engendered by changes in light and atmosphere, attested to the lack of parity between the historical moment in which Velázquez was fated to live and paint, and his highly unorthodox technique, one that Susan Brown considered anticipatory of Constable, Corot, Théodore Rousseau, and the French Impressionists.[26] Aureliano de Beruete was partial to Velázquez's *San Antonio abad y San Pablo ermitaño*, a painting in which the diaphanous, nearly watercolor technique that allows canvas to show through the paint in some instances, anticipated by two centuries "what is known as the impressionist school" (1906, 122–23). In his review of Aman-Jean's book on Velázquez, Azorín focused on the French painter-critic's opinion that the landscape background of *St. Anthony and St. Paul* made Velázquez "one of the greatest of great landscape painters." What better accolade could be given a painter, queried Azorín, than to say that he has allowed himself to be affected by Nature to such an extent (7:240)? Aman-Jean also pointed out that of all the Moderns, Corot was the first to disabuse his fellow painters of the notion that shadow had to be painted black, but that Corot himself had learned the technique from Velázquez. In the French critic's opinion, all Modern painters descended from Velázquez and Corot, who together re-educated the human eye to a new manner of seeing and feeling nature through "impressions" (140). The American art critic Christian Brinton, a contemporary of Aman-Jean's, remarked that from Velázquez on, all Spanish painters "have been a race of pictorial impressionists" to whom Manet and the rest of the Moderns were obliged to turn as they searched for ways "with which to combat the false classicism and flamboyant rhetoric of the mid-century in France" (*Eight Essays* 1:437). Camille Mauclair saw the influence of Velázquez and Goya in the work of Manet (49), as did Aureliano de Beruete y Moret who noted that in his early realist phase Manet was especially indebted to Goya and Velázquez (133). The French painter Jean-François Rafaëlli also argued that Manet was long under the tutelage of Frans Hals, Velázquez, and Goya before finding his way to the plein air luminism practiced by the Impressionists, his somewhat younger contemporaries (147).[27]

The mirror Manet placed at the back of *A Bar at the Folies-Bergère* (1881–82), extending the picture space beyond its compositional frame, and the mirrors Degas painted in some of his dance studio canvases, function in much the same way as does the mirror Velázquez placed at the back of *Las Meninas*. The Goncourts report Degas as acknowledging Velazquean influence in his work, especially in his painting *The Rehearsal* (1874) where translucent tones and unmodeled edges permit the melding of form with atmosphere so dear to Impressionist goals, and recalling, for Degas, Velázquez's "tender softness" (Herbert 1988, 121). Ortega made a similar observation when he noted that by eliminating the linear boundaries of formal modeling, Velázquez allowed objects to flow into and out of each other's "pores." He pointed out that in *Las Meninas* it is impossible to distinguish where a hand begins and where it ends; the *menina* who offers a ewer of water to the Infanta is as elusive as shadow, and should we try to grasp her, a mere "impression" is all that would remain in our hands (1:567). T. J. Clark mentions that leaving "markers" in their paintings of where the illusion of reality almost dissipates, as practiced by some seventeenth-century painters, "only served to make the likeness, where it was achieved, the more compelling" because the technique conferred an appearance of salvaging the image from slipping into formless chaos at just the appropriate moment. In Clark's view, Manet and his colleagues looked back for instruction of this kind especially to Velázquez and Fans Hals, but what intrigued them most was the visibly tangible inconsistency inherent in this practice rather than the fact that it somehow preserved the image from permanent eradication (10).

The Spanish have always taken pride and, to some extent, consolation in the "empréstitos españoles" taken by Manet and the Impressionists from El Greco, Velázquez, and Goya (Gaya Nuño 4). Ortega wrote that the "Velázquez de Manet, el Velázquez impresionista" was not the same Velázquez observed by Felipe IV through his myopic eyes (1:566–67). A contemporary of Ortega's, Bernardino de Pantorba, went even further in his exaggerated claim that impressionist style undeniably originated with Velázquez and that Manet, no matter how admirable a painter, culled impressionist technique directly from "our sublime Velázquez and Goya" (23–24). Cristina Arteaga proposed a direct line of evolution from El Greco to Velázquez and from Velázquez to Goya, maintaining that the work of this "great triumvirate" reached its pinnacle in that of Zuloaga. She accounted for this coincidence by arguing that Zuloaga was not an indiscriminate copyist, but rather that his painting reflected the predominance of heritage and race over the diversity of genius (145). The art critic Juan de la Encina observed in 1917 that when Zuloaga first came to public attention in Paris, French art critics always mentioned his name in tandem with Velázquez who was very much in fashion at the time because Manet had educated the French to appreciate Velázquez's sensibility. "From then on," he concluded, "painters who best represent the sensibility of the last half of the nineteenth century studied him with real passion."[28]

Turn-of-the-century revalidation of El Greco, Velázquez, and Goya in Spain was therefore not simply a matter of erudite specialists resurrecting forgotten painters for their own academic pursuits, but represented, instead, one way that contemporary Spaniards could make some sense of their history by having their seemingly barren present reconfigured within an uninterrupted historical continuum connecting the past and present, and attesting to the ineradicability of Spanish cultural heritage as well as its impact on modern European aesthetics.

3

Azorín's Classics: El Greco and Velázquez in Essays and Fiction

JOEL WEINSHEIMER PROPOSES THAT "THE PAST conceived as continuous and indivisible from the present" is analogous to a classic that is traditionary, enduring, and universal. When time is thought of as "elastic" and uninterrupted, the classic can be linked to succeeding generations; passed on through institutions of cultural conservation, it imparts a sense of spatial community as well as temporal continuity between generations and historico-cultural time periods. Yet, according to Weinsheimer, in order to partake of the "eternal return," every genuine classic must also be a "neo-classic"; that is, it must have the ability to survive and endure, and to speak to myriad generations of cultural consumers. The true classic is deathless and, because it is eternal, it is an emblem of the uninterrupted continuity of time. Quoting T. S. Eliot's *On Poetry and Poets*, Weinsheimer notes Eliot's "organic" approach to the continuity of tradition which postulates a classic is produced only when the language and literature of a civilization reach a peak of maturity, a "ripeness" prepared for by the work of preceding generations. A mature literature, in Eliot's view, must be supported by the armature of continuity within each culture's individual history.[1]

A cultural classic insinuates certain ideologi-
cal connotations because it serves as a "locus of unity" within the diversity of a national history; a kind of magnet that organizes and unifies history around itself, the classic is a symbol of national continuity. Both form and content, it is passed from one generation to the next, actively participating in establishing tradition and a "community mind" among those who inherit it, while disenfranchising those who do not (Weinsheimer 139). Because the classic embodies that which a community tacitly agrees to share as intelligble and apparent without any need for explanation, it also bestows a sense of coherence on the body politic that chooses to recognize its validity as such. This notion of cultural continuity and national coherence across time is an ideologically conservative one, and it speaks very much to the position Azorín adopted in his cultural politics.[2] This approach to history was further reinforced by the determinist philosophy—also inherently a conservative one—to which both the Generations of 1868 and 1898 subscribed. The cultural archaeology upon which Giner and his disciples embarked derived from the notion that if human beings are conditioned by race, environment, and historical circumstance, then it would follow that cultural heritage circum-

scribes the development of a people. Restoring and revalidating the classics was thus not only a way of demonstrating the continuity of culture across the centuries, and of promoting a sense of national cohesion, but also a venue by which to comprehend, evaluate, and explain the present national circumstance. Because he viewed the course of Spanish political history as having been rendered discontinuous by developments inconsistent with the nation's historically determined potential, Azorín resolved to restore lost national unity by reconnecting the gaps, as it were, via a proposed composite view of Spain's literary and artistic history as continuous and cogent, a process José Antonio Maravall likened to Velázquez's "broken, separate daubs" that, when viewed at a distance, seemed to blend together to give the impression of unity in diversity (1968, 54). Thus in 1905 Azorín argued that the masterpieces of Spanish art in the Prado Museum should be accorded profound, almost religious veneration, because they embodied and transmitted to present generations the "soul of Spain" (7:484).

Although the political enemies of Giner and the *institucionistas* perceived them as revolutionaries, the group's ideological evolution proved to be grounded in the notion of constancy and stability in tradition. It should not be at all surprising that, as he transformed the *ILE*'s enterprise of cultural revaluation into a politically conservative position aligned with Juan de la Cierva and the conservative party, Azorín should have invoked the Krausists and Giner de los Ríos (Maravall 1968, 76). As Inman Fox points out, even while Azorín was most active in conservative party ranks, he never stopped speaking well of the Krausists whom he perceived as correligionaries because they, too, mediated the corrupt and frivolous Spanish milieu through the predication of a harmonious, emotionally disengaged and unaggressive rationalism (1988, 119). As did many of his generational companions, Azorín abandoned the radical stance of his early years when he became convinced that much-desired governmental reforms could be implemented only by the forcefully stated and well-organized program of de la Cierva and the conservative party.[3]

Weinsheimer noted that the revolutionary process invariably entails ousting the immediate past, represented by the "father," while conserving the "grandfather's" more authoritative legacy. Accordingly, in such cases where one classic replaces another, even the most radical of transformations ultimately preserves the continuity of tradition in the midst of revolution (142). It was this type of reasoning that enabled Azorín to proclaim himself a progressive during the same period of time when he was shifting his political allegiance to the conservative party. In *Un Discurso de La Cierva*, he claimed the preservation of historic patrimony to be an enterprise initiated by the Generation of 1898. Rather than demolish old churches, Azorín urged the dismantling of a mentality that could bring itself to raze a historical building fallen into disrepair: "Don't knock the old church down! Let it stand! Demolish, by all means, whatever is necessary so that the ancient structure can be preserved for all time. To conserve is to renew" (3:136). Azorín declared that although it was possible to label the Generation of 1898 "conservative" because as a group its members were interested in conserving national cultural traditions and historical monuments, they were actually partisans of progressive ideas. "To conserve is to renew," he insisted; "It is not a paradox to say that the Generation of 1898—and especially some of its members—has accomplished a deeply conservative and patriotic task" (3:136). In a classic example of paronomasia, Azorín breached the implied contradiction in terms by assigning a new meaning to the verb *conservar* that metamorphosed it from its commonplace acceptance in the realm of politics, where it carries a mildly pejorative connotation, and relocating it within the unfamiliar reference frame of aesthetics. Here the verb assumes a novel, completely antonymic significance associated with liberal progressivism, change, and renewal, whereby *conservar* (to conserve) is shifted to mean *recuperar-revalorar* (to recuperate; to reappraise), and finally, to mean *renovar* (to renew or to revise).

In the suggestively titled "La continuidad nacional" (1910), Azorín deployed the argument that true progress is based on national continuity rather than the misguided notion of abrupt and absurd rupture, and that continuity is achieved by creating a consciousness among Spaniards of "who we are." This national consciousness is determined principally by religion—a clear reference to the long-extant Catholic tradition of Spain—as well as by artists and writers. It is the Spanish classics (Velázquez, Cervantes, El Greco, Garcilaso, Santa

Teresa, Goya) that Azorín considers the "real promoters and driving forces of progress, and not the 'moderns,' 'the progressives,' and the 'Europeans'" (*PCQ* 42–43).[4] In a 1907 essay, "Sobre pintura," he observed that the same reconsideration of the classics that was taking place in the literary world was also occurring in the Spanish art-historical canon. The current generation of painters abandoned their predecessors' taste for a "theatrical, flashy, *internationalist* painting," in favor of a more intimate, "Spanish" kind of art. Azorín observed that while the Museum of Modern Art was filled with paintings based on scenes from Spanish life and national history, there was nothing at all Spanish about these canvases, since they did not allude to anything of a particularly Spanish essence. The artists associated with the *gente nueva*, however, chose to study Velázquez and El Greco, observing the classical painters' methods, tendencies, and style. This produced two important results according to Azorín: "one of them the establishing of a true concept of classicism; the other, the discarding of the last vestiges of the 'realist' aesthetic that predominated in art during the preceding period," which he considered unresponsive to autochthonous Spanish needs, and exponential of exactly the kind of historical and cultural discontinuities against which he took such a profound ideological stand (*PCQ* 24–25).

Because Azorín viewed the classics as intrahistoric repositories of Spanish tradition and the Spanish soul, he spent the second decade of the twentieth century dusting off the literary classics which he hoped would reorient the future direction of Spain toward order, continuity, and coherence while also providing him with a justification and explanation of the conservative political agenda he had begun to advocate so enthusiastically (Fox 1988, 98–99).[5] Thus, in his preface to *Lecturas españolas* (1912), Azorín restated his favorite theme which he admitted linked all the essays of the collection: "Coherence rests on a curiosity about what it is that constitutes the Spanish environment—landscapes, literature, art, people, cities, interiors —and in a preoccupation with a future of wellbeing and justice for Spain" (2:531). The same operation continues in *Clásicos y Modernos* (1913) which Azorín considered a sequel to *Lecturas españolas*, inspired by the same "national problem," or the desire to identify the Spanish spirit in the classics which, leaving

aside any archaic lessons they might impart, he felt must be reviewed and reconsidered in a new, modern light (2:737). Azorín's view of the Generation's collective enterprise of rehabilitating the classics finds resonance and support in Ricardo Baroja's recollections of the same period. The elder Baroja observed that while it was more common for young artists and writers to be concerned with contemporary developments in their field, the Generation of 1898 aimed to reestablish connections with the past, preferring Velázquez to Pradilla; El Greco to Muñoz Degrain; Lope to Echegaray; Berruguete to Querol. He also noted the inherent paradox in the name *modernistas* that was derisively applied to the Generation by its more old-fashioned contemporaries, when a more appropriate term might have been *arcaístas* or *futuristas*: either one would do since Baroja and his peers wanted to "accomplish something . . . very difficult: to be ahead of our time, or to retreat to the past" (49).

In an uncanny anticipation of Borges's Pierre Menard, and consonant with Unamuno's provocative assertions that literature is largely circumscribed by the contributions and recontextualizations brought to it by individual readers or reinterpreters of text, in his "Nuevo Prefacio" to the second edition of *Lecturas españolas*, Azorín proposed that the classics were not written by their alleged authors, but rather by their readers: "Cervantes hasn't written the *Quijote*, nor Garcilaso the *Églogas*, nor Quevedo *Los sueños*. The *Quijote*, the *Églogas*, the *Sueños*, have been written by the different men who, over time, have seen their own sensibility reflected in those works. The more a literary classic lends itself to change, the more vital it is" (2:534). According to this definition of the literary classic, any work that resisted change was lifeless and not worthy of revival. Literary works that continued to speak to succeeding generations, however, were classics because in them was preserved the marrow of *intrahistoria*, palpitating with life and capable of striking a responsive chord in contemporary sensibilities (2:535). Therefore, the Generation of 1898 consulted the great masters of the cultural past in order to learn the proper technical elements with which to elaborate new aesthetics more compatible with a genuine Spanish circumstance (*PCQ* 128).

Dating from the same year as his *La deshumanización del arte* (1925), Ortega's essay "El arte en presente y en pretérito," presents a theory of what constitutes a "classic" that resembles those put forth by Azorín. Taking his cue from the visual arts, Ortega writes that interest in schools of art from the past is always, and paradoxically, maintained by the most contemporary of painters. Because new styles are actually the end products of their past, new art revalidates and imbues the old with life, as in the case of Manet's rediscovery of Velázquez. Whereas all works of art are capable of giving enjoyment to one degree or another, not all paintings can be confused with, or substitute for, the true aesthetic experience. When it becomes a lifeless, archaeological relic, a painting loses its aesthetic effectiveness, an artistic legacy that Ortega concludes "is not art, but was art" (3:422). Azorín's notion of what constituted a "classic" appears to anticipate elements from the two paradigms established by Ortega and Weinsheimer. Similar to the "traditional" classic Weinsheimer suggested endures in a past "conceived as continuous and indivisible from the present" (149), Azorín postulated the validity of a classic's survival within the present historical circumstance because he considered time as a synchronous entity in which the past, present, and future were indivisible. Yet his assertion that in order to endure and maintain relevance, a classic must also renew itself perpetually, corresponds to Weinsheimer's "deciduous" classic whose chameleon-like qualities permit self-renewal and adaptation to the "different times and cultures in which it returns" (149–50). Therefore Azorín also defined a "classical" author as one who reflects modern sensibilities. He explained the paradox thus: "a classical author won't amount to anything; that is to say, he will not be a classic if he doesn't reflect our sensibility." In his view a literary classic is irrelevant unless it constantly evolves in accordance with the changes and transformations incurred within succeeding generations of readers. For Azorín a classic somewhat resembled a literary version of Nietzsche's eternal recurrence, existing in a constant state of formation, rebirth, and self-renewal (2:534).

Azorín's personal aesthetic and political agenda of "continuity and coherence," based on the revalidation of classical Spanish literature, and of rendering it accessible to a broad reading public, was fabulously successful. Also rooted in this literary archaeology was his interest in reviving the subtleties and infinite variations of popular phraseology subsumed in classical texts which he considered a philological treasure trove fallen into oblivion and disuse. As did Unamuno, Azorín suggested that the expressive, plastic language of the classics remained extant in popular parlance. Because the rich and varied character of this idiom had disappeared from the usage of city folk, he recommended mining the philological wealth available in forgotten literary texts as a way to revitalize the language, particularly in the case of politicians and public figures who might rely on popular turns of phrase and lexicon to appeal to the imagination of their audiences (2:423). In his own work Azorín practiced what he preached, making it a point to challenge readers through the liberal use of unfamiliar words and unusual forms of linguistic expression.[6] Although he generously attributed to Unamuno (PCQ 247) the "love for the classics" and exhumation of modismos submerged in popular turns of phrase, it is Azorín who was almost single-handedly responsible for this monumental project. The enormity and significance of this enterprise did not go unnoticed by his contemporaries. Pío Baroja recalled that at the time Azorín took up the mission of restoring lost fluency to the Spanish lexicon, no one else followed his example. In Baroja's opinion there were only two modern writers whose perseverance and struggle with the language was worth mentioning: Azorín and Ortega y Gasset (8:939). Ortega himself recognized the importance of this contribution: when Azorín failed to win election to the Royal Academy of the Language in 1913, Ortega protested, commenting in a letter to Roberto Castrovido, editor of the newspaper ABC, not only on the cultural value of Azorín's efforts but, more importantly, that Azorín had provided a bridge between modern sensibilities and the spirit of the Spanish classics: ". . . it's an undeniable, indisputable fact that Azorín is the Spanish writer who today promotes with greatest efficacy, among the gente joven, the reading of castizo literature. He's discovered the breach through which a modern sensibility can penetrate the space of our old classics" (1:263).[7]

As the new awareness of things archetypally Castilian took hold among the gente nueva, cultural classics and the historically significant cities and landscape of Castile began to enjoy tremendous popularity as locales in which to set literary or pictorial action. In their early fiction Azorín and Pío Baroja, more than the others, turned their attention to the painting of El Greco and the city of Toledo which they visited individually on several occasions. One visit, however, was made together in December 1900, and the shared experiences there were powerful enough to be re-created fictionally by Azorín in *Diario de un enfermo* (1901) and *La Voluntad* (1902), and by Baroja in *Camino de perfección* (1902), three novels in which the city of Toledo and paintings by El Greco not only circumscribe theme, action, and setting, but character development as well.

El Greco: *Diario de un enfermo*

Azorín had an abiding, lifelong interest in the visual arts and he constantly referred to the visual nature of his memory (Campos 163). His work in all literary genres is distinguished by painterly qualities and a pronounced emphasis on the visual. While a visual image is not a text, because the visual and verbal realms have always been considered as sharing a special kinship, authors who choose to allow the plastic arts to inform their writing must, of necessity, wield a visual language which, unlike pure verbal discourse, is characterized by its own semiotic system sensitive to the inherent opposition between the verbal and the visual, the temporal and the spatial, the arbitrary and the natural sign. If, for the moment, we narrow our consideration to prose fiction only, there are two ways in which visual representation can be narrated: either through allusion, whereby a work of art is invoked by the author with decorative, ideological or hermeneutic purposes in mind, or through ekphrasis, involving a verbal imitation of the plastic arts. Although Azorín slightly favored allusive and theoretical reference to the relations between the verbal and visual arts, on many occasions he would strive for plastic equivalence in words. Very often he alluded to works of art, the style of a specific painter, or a school of painting as a means of lending polysemic richness to verbal metaphor that otherwise would remain abstract, by relying on visual art analogies from the concrete, referential world. He frequently used works of art or artistic images for thematic projection, to further character development, or to contextualize a character's evolving consciousness and approach to life through his or her response to the visual arts.

In "Lectura y literatura (En torno a la inspiración libresca de Azorín)," Inman Fox points out that as diverse as it was, much of Azorín's writing is informed by the textual discourse of others gleaned from a wide-ranging and avid history of reading that spanned the centuries and literary genres (1988, 121). While, in the same article, Fox limits his commentary on Azorín's visual art sources to a footnote (125), it is important to bear in mind that unlike the literary sources that provided Azorín with subject matter for his writing, and factual material for his arguments, the plastic arts not only inspired him, but also stimulated his well-developed pictorial sensibilities and conscious intent to evoke the painterly while transposing it to the verbal medium. In the case of *Diario de un enfermo* (1901), Azorín engages both literary and visual sources of inspiration. Although Manuel B. Cossío's book on El Greco was published after Azorín's novel, Cossío's groundbreaking articles on the painter, dating from the turn of the century, were much discussed in intellectual circles and provide the intertext for Azorín's descriptions of Toledo and specific paintings by El Greco.[8] Paintings are also used hermeneutically in the novel to establish a homologous relationship between the tortured spirituality commonly attributed by art historians—Cossío among them—to El Greco's figure paintings and the neurasthenic anguish of Azorín's protagonist.

In *Memorias Inmemoriales*, "X" announces that in his youth he had been "one of the first promoters of the cult for El Greco." With time, as "X" developed a preference for the direct and the straightforward, he says that Rembrandt displaced El Greco in his personal pantheon and that he now considered the Dutch artist to be "the intellectual painter par excellence" (8:352).[9] Azorín wrote that Góngora's sonnet on El Greco's tomb became a symbolic banner for the 1898 writers (*PCQ* 243), and in *La Voluntad*—as he did elsewhere in his writing—Azorín gave Pío Baroja, fictionalized as the character Olaiz, credit for inspiring among the young, Castile-based intellectuals, a love for the Cretan painter (Fox 1968, 234). According to Azorín, the writers of '98 looked to El Greco for stylistic lessons they could incorporate into their own literary revisionism (Campos 32). What they found most attractive was the painter's mysterious, exalted idealism, which they transposed to their writing as the pursuit of the infinite and the inscrutable, two concepts expressed by the shibboleth of the moment: "Eternidad" (6:220).

Indeed, because of their active role in promoting El Greco and Toledo, both painter and city became synonymous with the Generation of 1898. In summarizing the contents of a 1914 issue of the journal *Contemporary Review*, Madrid's *La Lectura* excerpted sections relevant to El Greco in which it was stated that the painter is essentially an artist for the twentieth century because his work, judged to be so individual and original, could not but encourage people to take refuge from the rampant materialism of the day in the pure intellectuality and mysticism of El Greco's paintings. The review also noted El Greco's influence on contemporary Spanish literature, especially the work of Azorín, Baroja, and Valle-Inclán.[10] The most advanced Spanish painters of the early twentieth century—Beruete, Rusiñol, and Zuloaga—also expressed interest in El Greco. Beruete owned two paintings, including an alleged self-portrait by El Greco; Zuloaga was also an early collector, having purchased two canvases, *San Pedro arrepentido* and *La Magdalena*, that he later donated to Rusiñol's museum at Cau Ferrat (Lafuente Ferrari 1950, 38–39). El Greco's self-portrait, like that of the anonymous *caballero* featured in the painting popularly known as the *Caballero de la mano al pecho*, became emblematic of the Generation's interest in the painter: reproductions of the portrait graced many a writer's or fictional protagonist's studio (Fig. 2). The eponymous hero of *Antonio Azorín* (1903) has a photograph of El Greco's self-portrait above his desk. Not quite a complete literary ekphrasis, the description is one of Azorín's first verbal imitations of a work of plastic art: "Destacan en la negrura la mancha blanca de la calva y los trazos de la blanda gorguera; sus mejillas están secas, arrugadas, y sus ojos, puestos en anchos y redondos cajos, miran con melancolía a quien frente por frente a él va empujando palabras en las cuartillas" [1:1011; The white patch of his pate and the folds of the soft ruff stand out against the blackness; his cheeks are withered, wrinkled, and his eyes, set in wide, round sockets, peer with melancholy at the writer seated facing him, pushing words around on sheets of paper].

In *Las confesiones de un pequeño filósofo*, a hybrid of fiction and intellectual autobiography published in 1904, Azorín describes a portrait of his great-grandfather for which Pío Baroja—"the great admirer of El Greco"—had taken a special liking. The invocation of El Greco is not fortuitous, for what follows is a verbal evocation of the portrait that bears striking analogies to El Greco's painted noblemen:

> . . . mi bisabuelo es un viejecito con la cara afeitada . . . sus ojos son pequeños, a medio abrir, como si mirara algo lejano y brillante. . . . El traje es negro; lleva también una capa negra . . . y por entre sus pliegues, a la altura del pecho, aparece la mano amarilla y huesosa . . . medio extendida, como señalando . . . cuatro o seis infolios que se destacan a la derecha . . . (2:70–71)

> [. . . my great grandfather is a clean-shaven, little old man . . . his eyes are small, half-open, as if he were looking at something bright in the distance. . . . His suit is black; he's also wearing a black cloak . . . and through its folds, at chest height, appears his yellow and bony hand . . . half outstretched, as if pointing . . . to four or six folios that stand out at the right].

Due to his own interests in the literature of the sixteenth and seventeenth centuries, Azorín had many occasions on which to re-create the archetypal Castilian gentleman for whom he always chose a visual referent from the El Greco repertoire. The *caballero* of "Lo fatal" (*Castilla*) ends his days in Toledo, where it is rumored "Domenico Theotocópuli, llamado *el Greco*," painted his portrait. The narrator of the story affirms the popular attribution by detailing some aspects of the painting that reflect the unmistakable traits of El Greco's style: "worthy of the master are the sharp, elongated face; a sparse beard plays against the clean ruff; high on the forehead some ashy wisps of hair. His eyes are sunken, deep set, and in them there is—as in someone who sees death approaching—a glow of eternity" (Fox 1991, 171). In his edition of *Castilla* Inman Fox argues that "the El Greco painting which inspires Azorín here is undoubtedly *El caballero de la mano al pecho*" (171 n. 18). The anonymous gentleman depicted in that portrait, however, is a relatively young man with full moustache and beard, certainly not the sparse beard and sunken eyes of the man near death Azorín describes in "Lo fatal." The portrait invoked may very well be El Greco's "self-portrait," which Azorín obviously knew, having referred to it in *Las confesiones*

Fig. 2   Dominico Theotocopuli (El Greco), *El caballero de la mano al pecho*, 1577. Oil on canvas, 81 × 86 cm. Museo del Prado, Madrid.

de un pequeño filósofo; alternately, it could be a composite of the self-portrait and the *Caballero de la mano al pecho* in which case Azorín's verbal "painting" would be a notional (i.e., fictional) ekphrasis "after the manner of" El Greco.[11]

Azorín attributed the genesis of *Diario de un enfermo* to the general enthusiasm for El Greco and Toledo shared by members of the Generation of 1898, and specifically to a trip he made to Toledo in 1900 in the company of his friend and fellow writer, Pío Baroja (Campos 31–32). During that visit, the two friends witnessed a protracted scene at dusk of a man attempting to deliver a child's coffin to a residence whose correct address he appeared not to have been given by the mortuary. The resulting black comedy of errors, including the man's peregrination through the darkening streets of Toledo with the persistently slipping and increasingly burdensome coffin on his shoulder, his equivocal conversations bordering on the grotesque with sundry residents who attempt to identify the house where a child may have died, made such an impression that both writers fictionalized the episode in their first novels.[12] In *Camino de perfección*, Baroja narrated a second adventure involving Toledo and El Greco that assumed legendary proportions as it passed into the mythological lore of '98. Ignacio Zuloaga was studying in Paris at the end of the nineteenth century where he shared a makeshift ménage with the struggling Catalonian painters Ramón Casas, Santiago Rusiñol, and Miquel Utrillo. If we are to believe Rusiñol's account of the story, as Zuloaga waded through Impressionism, Modernism, and Symbolism in search of his own identity as a painter, one day he was struck by the "lightning bolt" of El Greco and the old Spanish masters through whose work he finally was able to find a direction for his own (Lafuente 1950, 97). Zuloaga's passion for El Greco was a common denominator he shared with the Generation of 1898, and so ardent a defender of El Greco's genius did he become that his coterie of painter friends in Paris rebaptized Zuloaga "le Greco" (Lafuente 1950, 38–39). A robust man, bursting with an indomitable energy that he conserved into old age, Zuloaga decided that he had to visit Toledo in order to see El Greco originals *in situ*. Taking the first train out of Paris, without so much as a stop in Madrid to recoup, he arrived in Toledo at night and impetuously decided he wanted to

see the *Entierro del Conde de Orgaz* without further delay. After much coaxing, persuading, and finally bribing the night watchman, Zuloaga managed to view the painting by torchlight (Lafuente 1950, 31). In *Camino de perfección*, a postprandial discussion of El Greco among the protagonists leads to a recounting of Zuloaga's exploit: "Afterwards they mentioned El Greco. Someone said that two Impressionist painters, one from Catalonia, the other a Basque, had gone to see *El entierro del Conde de Orgaz* at night, by the light of candles" (117).[13] This motivates the group to duplicate the experience in order to see for themselves what effect candlelight would have on El Greco's masterpiece. This second episode is based on a nocturnal visit to the church of Santo Tomé in which Baroja himself participated, along with Julio Burell, a respected journalist, future government minister, and mentor to the writers of '98, who was then governor of Toledo.[14]

Because the public generally associated the *gente nueva* with El Greco, and because the group, by antonomasia, was linked with the new, the modern, and just as frequently, the decadent, El Greco, too, was popularly thought to be a "decadent" painter. Cossío himself, although without any pejorative connotation, contributed to this widespread assumption: how could the contemporary schools of painting that consistently strive for the intellectual, the subtle, the twisted, the fragmentary, and the inventive, Cossío observed, not but identify El Greco as a model when he was the first to fragment line and drawing in order to infuse his art with energy and movement. "In this respect he has to be a model," wrote Cossío, "for all kinds of symbolists and decadents, for intimists, for painters of high-strung elegance" (1907, 379). El Greco's style as frenzied, anxiety-ridden, and contorted became a universally accepted view. Azorín reported that Zuloaga considered Velázquez too "perfect" and controlled for his taste, preferring the spiritual anxieties (*"inquietudes"*) El Greco's painting stirred in the most recondite eddies of his soul (*VH* 255). Ortega referred to El Greco as "the frenetic Greek from Toledo" (2:307), while more recently Jiménez Placer commented that El Greco was a milestone in the history of art because he was the first painter to abandon an idealized interpretation of reality by filtering its image through the intimacy of his own emotions before transposing it to canvas via his singularly expressionistic manner (602).[15]

It is the expressionist, neurotic, mannered El Greco who sets the tone in Azorín's *Diario de un enfermo*. The novel comes to its reader second hand through José Martínez Ruiz, who edits a journal chronicling the nameless protagonist's intense, albeit brief, pursuit, courtship, and marriage to a young woman who dies of consumption. It is the progress of the bride's illness and the inevitability of her death that strike at the depths of the protagonist's soul, inducing external behavioral symptoms of feverish agitation and paroxysms of despair that alternate with bouts of spiritualized melancholia. The novel's dedication—"A la memoria de Domenico Theotocopuli"—presumably was made by the journal's "author," who apparently drew parallels between his own neurotic emotional state and the spirit emanating from the environment of Toledo, as well as El Greco's figure paintings. Of equal significance is a suggestive note to the reader appended by the editor regarding his "friend's" literary style: "the prose vibrates, sings, moans beneath his pen; infatuated with the classics, he borrowed from them vigor in style and sobriety in painting" (1:691). The dedication of the book to El Greco "by the author" supports Martínez Ruiz's claim that the Generation of 1898 took the painter as a model for their early writing. However, whether the *dedicace* originates with the author of the *Diario* or its editor is somewhat ambiguous, and the editor further confuses distinctions between reality and fiction by acknowledging the incongruity of his editorship since his friend and author of the memoir is a sensitive, aggrieved artist, whereas the editor's own style (it seems that he, too, is a writer), has been called impassive and cold by the distinguished (and historically real) literary critic, González Serrano (1:691).[16]

The journal entries of *Diario de un enfermo* record the protagonist's chance meeting in the street of a young woman clothed in black whose bloodless skin and feverish eyes immediately connote disease, yet with whom the protagonist is taken to the point of obsession. The spiritual anxiety and frustrated longing generated in him by the mysterious young lady leads the protagonist to imagine they had known each other, even shared a life together, in some previous form of existence (1:697). His fascination with the woman enervates the protagonist,

affecting his psychological state as well as his ability to write; he literally becomes ill as a result: "I am devoured by fever. Yesterday I was writing all afternoon, all night, rapidly, frenetically" in a failed effort to somehow find external expression for "the vision of a landscape (e.g., the inner landscape of the soul), that I want to make visible and plastic" (1:700–701). In his exalted emotional condition, the author cannot sleep, his face is flushed, his head pounds, his body trembles. When determining who the young woman is or where she lives proves elusive, the protagonist flees Madrid to Toledo in an attempt to find consolation in the city's spiritually heightened atmosphere. The change of location is not fortuitous since the landscape setting and artistic milieu of Toledo provide a perfect expressionistic backdrop for the protagonist's nearly hysterical emotional state. Laureano Bonet indicates that Toledo already had been utilized as an objective correlative of this type by Castelar, Bécquer, and Galdós (1987, 146); Maurice Barrès likewise observed in *Du sang, de la volupté et de la mort* (1894) that, rather than being a mere city, Toledo was a place significant to the soul. Hermetic, inflexible, "in that harsh, burning terrain, Toledo looms out like an image of exaltation stranded in the desert, a cry in the wilderness" (28).[17]

Authorial invocation of a work of art, a painter's personal style, or the style of a specific school of painting, can be one of the most efficient ways in which to establish tangible, because visual, analogues for the emotional condition, whether conscious or unconscious, of a fictional character. Azorín himself wrote that he liked to speculate on the extent to which painting was able to influence writing. What he especially admired in painters, and what he surmised exercised the greatest influence on him, was the psychology operative in aesthetic creation: why an artist would choose certain colors over others, why he would arrange them in the ways that he did; how he might imagine the perfect composition in a reverie before his canvas (6:352). The psychological process involved in aesthetic, especially visual creation, fascinated Azorín who thought he shared with painters "that eagerness to express a specific moment, a specific affliction, a psychological state" (*PCQ* 174). Thus, in *Diario de un enfermo*, the impact of El Greco is not so much through allusion to specific paintings, but in the evocation of the painter's style to inform the protagonist's psychic and emotional states of mind.[18]

Undoubtedly Azorín was inspired by the El Greco rehabilitated and "re-created" by Manuel B. Cossío. The art historian observed that Spanish painting generally is as melancholy as the character of its people (1:242). Nowhere was this more evident than in the archetypal environment of Toledo to which El Greco responded immediately upon his arrival to the Imperial City. Cossío maintained that in order to understand the painter, one had to travel to Spain, and in order to appreciate El Greco in all his glory, one had to journey to the "inharmonious Castilian city where his spirit was made flesh" (1:vii–viii). For Cossío, Toledo personified both in form and content the ambience of Castile. In the days of El Greco the city was, and still continued to be in the late nineteenth and early twentieth centuries, the most complete and characteristic example of the genuine civilization and landscape of Castile; the most evocative summation of what constituted the national history of Spain (1:109). According to Cossío, Toledo found in El Greco a painter capable not only of holding his own among the artistic treasures accumulated there prior to his arrival, but also one who could interpret its character, identify with its history, and internalize its spiritual temperament in order to express in his painting the cool tones of its local color and the enervated pessimism of its spiritual and social climate (1:112).[19] Because his psyche absorbed both the spirit and the landscape of his adopted environment, El Greco was able to reproduce the physiological characteristics of the Castilian with great historical accuracy. In Cossío's view, one of the first elements El Greco changed about his technique in response to his new surroundings was his color palette, abandoning the warm tones of the Venetian School for the cool, blue-violet hues of his most characteristic work (1:511–12).

The significance of El Greco's specifically Toledan color palette was not lost on Azorín who incorporated the language of Cossío's color values to his own descriptions in *Diario de un enfermo*. Meditating on the effect El Greco's paintings had on him, the protagonist of *Diario* notes that "Este divino *Greco* me hace llorar de admiración y de angustia. Sus personajes alargados, retorcidos, violentos . . . en negruzcos tintes, azulados violentos, violentos rojos, palideces cárdenas, dan la sensación angustiosa de la vida febril, tumultuosa, atormentada, trágica" [1:720–21; This divine Greco makes me weep with admiration and anguish. His elongated, contorted, violent figures . . . in blackish, violent blues, violent reds, livid pallor, give the anguished sensation of feverish, tumultuous, tormented, tragic life]. Like Azorín and Cossío, Maurice Barrès also was struck by the "sweeping, monochromatic movements of that purplish, ochre land" (65), two colors that dominate not only El Greco's Toledan landscapes, but also those Aureliano de Beruete utilized in his paintings of the Toledan countryside. These are the same hues Azorín reproduced whenever he needed to re-create the same landscape. Some of his descriptions, such as the following from *Los pueblos*, even invoke El Greco's name directly: ". . . on the other bank of the deep Tajo River, unfolds the austere, sober, intense, dark blue, muted ochre, murky green panorama—El Greco's colors—, of the extensive orchard gardens" (203). The landscape description of Toledo in *Diario de un enfermo* is similar in tone, reminiscent of the many pictures Beruete painted of the Toledan *cigarrales*: "Squares of green tilled land, extensive tracts of blackish fallow earth, promenades of leafless elms stretch into the distance of the ravine. And further away, abandoned, almost barren, the earth takes on gray, light green, dirty green, bluish, reddish, black tones" (1:717).

The Toledan environment that circumscribed both El Greco as a human being and his style as a painter was one of brusque geographical and visual contrasts which, according to Cossío, produced a frenetic, nervous race of people. In his opinion, El Greco's characteristically violent intensity of expression and movement were suggested by the equally violent contrasts of the Castilian *meseta*; the harsh light of the sky on the cold, monotonous ashgray of the earth was reflected in the "hardness and angularity of body and spirit of an exaggeratedly nervous, excitable race . . . and the general tendency to affectation and mannered complication in Castilian literature and art" (1:206). The men who appeared in El Greco's portraits were Castilians shaped by this harsh environment: "lean, angular, withered and hard of body and spirit, like the arid plains and granitic mountains where they live" (1:241). A journal entry the protagonist of *Diario de un enfermo* makes after viewing El Greco's por-

trait of Cardinal Juan de Tavera (Pl. 17), reproduces the flavor of El Greco's style as "seen" in
Cossío's descriptions of El Greco's portraiture,
and includes the constantly reiterated adjectives *violento, retorcido,* and *tortuoso:*

> ¡Qué retrato el del cardenal Tavera! Irradia luz
> sombría su cara larga, angulosa, huesuda, tintada
> de gris, hundidos los ojos, secas las mejillas,
> rígida, autoritaria, fanática. El brazo extendido, la
> fina mano . . . viven y se mueven. . . . Todas las
> manos del *Greco* son violentas, puestas en extra-
> ordinarias actitudes de retorcimientos, cris-
> paduras, súplicas, éxtasis. Todas sus caras son
> largas, cenceñas, amojamadas, pizarrosas, cárde-
> nas. (1:721)

> [What a portrait, the one of Cardinal Tavera! His
> long, angular, bony, grayish face radiates shadowy
> light; the eyes, sunken; cheeks, withered, rigid,
> authoritarian, fanatic. The arm extended, the fine
> hand . . . all live and move. . . . All of El Greco's
> hands are violent, placed in extraordinarily
> twisted, contorted, supplicant, ecstatic positions.
> All his faces are long, lean, emaciated, slate-col-
> ored, livid.]

The sense of motility, spiritual transport, in-
flexibility of character, and physiological distortion Azorín brings to his verbal description
are all trademarks of El Greco as filtered
through Cossío's analyses of the painter's work.

As Aureliano de Beruete observed, El Greco's
religious paintings, rather than depicting
human beings, portray "spectres of exaggerated
proportions and livid faces," whose peculiar
brand of mysticism still manages to exude the
sublime (1906, 45–46). Rather than calming the
shattered nerves of *Diario's* protagonist, the
ambience of Toledo, pregnant with El Greco's
anguished and frenetic expressionism, only ex-
acerbates his neurasthenic emotional state. The
contemplation of a "Dolorosa" by El Greco during early morning Mass at Santo Domingo el
Antiguo does not bring solace but additional de-
spondency stimulated by the "contorted, enervated, gray, black, sinister characters" that
jump out at the protagonist from the gilt retable
above the altar (1:715).

The protagonist sees in the large, anguished
eyes of El Greco's self-portrait an artist who, in
his ceaseless pursuit of the "essential" and the
"spiritual," much like himself, nearly became
mad:

> Exasperado, febril, loco, lucha ante el lienzo,
> pinta, repinta, borra, vuelve a pintar; se cansa; se
> fatiga, se extenúa, hasta que la visión exacta
> queda limpia, fija, inalterable, en "crueles bo-
> rrones," en tormentoso dibujo que expresa el
> dolor, la fe ardiente . . . la audacia, la fuerza avasa-
> lladora de un pueblo de aventureros locos y locos
> místicos (1:721)

> [Exasperated, feverish, mad, he struggles before
> the canvas, paints, retouches, rubs out, paints
> again; he tires; he becomes fatigued and weak,
> until the image is left exact, clear, permanent, un-
> alterable, the "harsh smudges," the tormented
> modeling express the pain, the ardent faith . . . the
> audacity, the overpowering strength of a nation of
> adventurers gone mad and mad mystics.]

The expression "crueles borrones" (harsh
smudges) placed in quotation marks by Martínez Ruiz is an example of the specialized language he borrowed from the realm of art
criticism, in this instance, courtesy of Salvador
Viniegra, associate director of the Prado Museum. In his essay "El momento y la sensación," Azorín refers to the preface Viniegra
wrote to accompany the 1902 exhibition catalogue of a retrospective of work by El Greco. As
quoted by Azorín, Viniegra cited an observation
made by Velázquez's father-in-law, Francisco
Pacheco, regarding El Greco's working methods: "Retocaba muchas veces sus cuadros para
dejar los colores *distintos* y *desunidos* y daba
aquellos crueles borrones para afectar valentía"
[6:286; He retouched his canvases many times
in order to leave the colors *distinct* and *unblended* and he produced those harsh smudges
in order to affect boldness].[20] The fictional author of the journal entries made in *Diario de un
enfermo* experiences similar frustration in his
pursuit of the most exact form of verbal expression. His passion does not allow him rest or
sleep; the difficulty of the exercise leaves him
excited and agitated; he thinks he may be deliri-
ous and implicitly compares his working methods to that of an artist through terminology
borrowed from engraving and sculpture:
". . . the pen runs vertiginously, vibrates, skips,
crosses out nervously, reworks the phrase,
struggles, fights obstinately and fiercely . . .
until the sentence emerges radiant and limpid;
leaving the suggestive emotion as if engraved or
sculpted (1:700).[21]

Azorín continued to subscribe to a determinist view of the Castilian personality as shaped
by its harsh environment well beyond the publication of *Diario de un enfermo.*[22] Assessments

similar to those made in *Diario* of the Castilian as mad, tortured or hallucinatory occur as early as the 1897 collection of short stories *Bohemia* in which Azorín remarks that the gloomy landscape of La Mancha calls to mind the frenetic excesses of the Spanish mystics, the ascetics of the Middle Ages, or the mob of illuminati wandering over the plain in pursuit of some phantasmagoric ideal the contemporary painter and sculptor Mariano Benlliure (1862–1947) had portrayed in one of his paintings (1:322). In *La ruta de Don Quijote* (1905), a collection of impressions Azorín recorded while retracing, either on foot or by train and horse-drawn cart, the trajectory of Don Quijote's wanderings around Castile, he reports that after trekking about for many hours one day, he felt himself overwhelmed by the interminable, changeless plain, the infinite expanse of the horizon, and began to understand how only this inaccessible land could have produced the misguided, frenetic knight-errant who, like Castilians past and present, yearned for something spiritually ineffable, anxiously pursuing his chimera over the endless Castilian plains (31). In this monotonous and monochromatic environment the human mind lies dormant, having succumbed to the uneventful passage of time, as monotonous in its infinity as the endless vistas of the landscape. Nevertheless, this pervasive lethargy could be shattered by short-lived outbursts of energy in response to extraordinary or fantastic events that tend to stimulate the Castilian into momentarily intense reaction: the appearance of a visionary knight or enervated mystic is enough to provoke slumbering imaginations that "until then were in repose, but now thrill madly and hurl themselves at dreams. . . . Isn't this the insane, irrational, and impetuous fantasy that suddenly shatters inertia in order to fall unproductively into apathy all over again?" (Ramsden 1966, 68).[23]

While Azorín continued to subscribe to deterministic interpretations of humankind and human society for many more years than did his generational companions, after the publication of *Diario de un enfermo* his novelistic interest in El Greco seems to have waned considerably. Although he continued to write essays on the painter, never ceasing to acknowledge El Greco's importance in the art-historical canon, his interest shifted to Velázquez with whom he maintained a constant dialogue throughout his writing, and who proved to be an important source of thematic inspiration, painterly metaphor, and structural paradigm during the remainder of Azorín's very long literary career.

Velázquez: The Essays

According to Gaspar Gómez de la Serna, mention of Velázquez is practically absent from the literature of the Generation of 1898. He attributed this lack of interest to a spiritual rift between the "aesthetes" of the Generation who identified more easily with the refined, elegant distortions of El Greco than with the human realism of Velázquez (42–43). Velázquez's name is likewise absent from Antonio Risco's list of Azorín's favorite painters (1980, 240). The truth of the matter, however, is quite different from what Gómez de la Serna and others would have us believe.[24] Although it is indisputable that Baroja and Azorín were instrumental in the rehabilitation of El Greco, what Azorín did for Velázquez and the significance of the painter to his work remains almost unexplored.

As we know, the year 1899 coincided with the tercentenary of Velázquez's birth, commemorated in Spain by the organization of a "Velázquez Gallery" at the Prado Museum under the direction of Aureliano de Beruete, and the publication in France the year before of Beruete's *catalogue raisonné* of the master's work. Azorín held Beruete in high regard, and in 1912 he dedicated *Castilla*, his seminal book of essays, to this "pintor maravilloso de Castilla." Perhaps because of his friendship with Beruete, Azorín took an early and profound interest in Velázquez. He was familiar with contemporary bibliography on the painter, including Beruete's impeccable contribution to Velázquez scholarship, as well as the studies of the French painter-art critics Edmond Aman-Jean and Jean François Rafaëlli. That Azorín kept up with current Velázquez bibliography, at least during the first decade and a half of the twentieth century, is evident in essays such as "El arte nacional" (1904) where he discusses a previously unknown painting by Velázquez that he saw reproduced in *La Ilustración Española* "that does not appear in the books that have been written about the master, nor has it been popularized through photographs" (4:49–50). Azorín also wrote two review essays of Aman-Jean's *Velázquez* (Paris, 1913): "Cuestiones de actualidad: Velázquez" and "El Museo y Velázquez."[25]

Azorín was drawn to Aman-Jean's book for the same reasons he found the book published by Beruete attractive: art history when written by painters who understand the problems of artistic practice yield aspects of the plastic arts with which laypersons are not ordinarily conversant (PCQ 101). He noted that Aman-Jean's interpretation of Velázquez was based on the deterministic notions of Taine and Barrès who put great emphasis on the influencing factor of the milieu within which a painter's artistic vocation evolved (7:237). Azorín pointed out that Aman-Jean refers to Barrès's study of El Greco as a model by which to examine the roots of any artist's formation, and he reports that much more than Taine's focus on the physical aspects of milieu, Aman-Jean places greater importance on Barrès's notion of the "accidentes espirituales" crucial to an artist's development (PCQ 104). Due to his own determinist leanings, Azorín concluded that the book's greatest interest was in the connections Aman-Jean made between the Castilian landscape and Velázquez's technique and aesthetics (PCQ 110). Similar to Cossío's attribution of the dominant cianic tones in El Greco's palette to the Toledan landscape, Aman-Jean observes that while it is customary to think of Spain as a land of vibrant, bright color, nothing could be further from the truth. More than any other Mediterranean country, the intensity of the sun in Spain washes out color, leaving the impression of monochromatic tones of black, white, and gray. Thus, in Aman-Jean's opinion, Velázquez can never be considered a great colorist comparable to Rembrandt, Delacroix, or Watteau (7:238–39).[26] Azorín himself intuited much the same phenomenon when he observed that while it was common to think of Valencia as a land of "painters betrothed to light," and of Joaquín Sorolla as a great colorist, the truth of the matter was that the sun's intensity dissolves all color into a symphony of grays, and in Valencia especially, the dominant color is white (6:108).[27] Though not a voluptuary as was Titian, Aman-Jean wrote that Velázquez was a colorist whose sober yet resonant palette ranged the spectrum from "a beautiful red to all the varied hues of purple . . . to the pinks which he knows how to pair with a black that, quietly, allows them to sing gently" (123–24). Drawing conclusions similar to those Cossío made re-

garding El Greco's limited, but extremely realistic use of pigment, Aman-Jean argued that Velázquez proved one could paint effectively without the use of heightened color, and that his "exquisite refinement of gray tones," which became the trademark of Velázquez's style, reappeared in modern painting to emerge as one of the bases of contemporary art (127–28).

Aman-Jean devoted a great deal of space in his book to detailed, verbal ekphrases of some of Velázquez's most important paintings. Especially suggestive are those of the female members of the royal household whose overly large mouchoirs (handkerchiefs) seem to have had great appeal for Aman-Jean. His ekphrasis of a portrait in which Queen Mariana wears an enormous silver-gray dress includes the description of "a large handkerchief that slithers down along her enormous dress"; the whiteness of handkerchief made even more salient by the rich purple-red of the curtain against which the Queen is posed (81). He throws a portrait of the Infanta Margarita into visual relief by comparing the child's tiny body, engulfed by the exaggerated proportions of the sleeves and skirt of her dress, to that of a tiny butterfly with enormous wings. The princess's slender arms are forced to the side of her body by the voluminous quantity of fabric that envelops her; in one hand she holds "un mouchoir, l'autre est chargée d'une rose" (90–91). Given Azorín's penchant for seeking inspiration, often in the most insignificant details of texts created by others—whether visual or verbal—Aman-Jean's emphasis on the mouchoir is particularly suggestive since, whenever Azorín wanted to evoke the atmosphere of courtly life in Golden Age Spain, he often called upon the Spanish infantas "Con sus guardainfantes y sus pañuelos de batista en la mano, como en los retratos de Velázquez" [With their voluminous farthingales and fine linen handkerchiefs in their hands, like those of Velázquez's portraits] to do it for him.[28]

In everything Azorín read about Velázquez, what interested him most was the color controversy raging among art critics and historians. This debate extended well into the twentieth century and is still evident in the writing of Ortega y Gasset. That Azorín was intrigued by the issue of whether Velázquez was a great colorist is not surprising, since he had a well-developed painter's eye, and the evocation of color in his own work was of great importance to him.

There is a well-annotated copy of A. M. Perrot's *Manuel du coloriste* (1834) in Azorín's personal library; he likewise knew and wrote about the importance of using expensive, chemically stable pigment in order to ensure the longevity of a painting; and he frequently observed that for writers and painters, good color technique was an extremely treacherous ocean to negotiate well: should either painter or writer not have the proper navigational skills, shipwreck would surely follow.[29] In the essay "El color" (*Madrid*), a memoir of Bohemian life in the Spanish capital at the turn of the century, Azorín recalled that the young writers' ambition to render the exact impression of things in their work led them to emphasize color which they considered the most expressive external characteristic any object could possess (6:239). In "El momento y la sensación" Azorín discussed finisecular aesthetics that he thought particularly emphasized "feeling for the sake of feeling" (evident in his own *Diario de un enfermo*), and the use of color for color's sake, citing Antonio Machado's "las ascuas de un crepúsculo morado . . ." as exemplary of this movement in early twentieth-century Spanish literature (6:287).

Color also forms the basis of Azorín's discussion of Rafaëlli's commentary on Velázquez. He reports that while this painter-turned-art-historian maintains it is impossible to describe Velázquez's use of line or his manner of composition, the Spanish master was unquestionably the most extraordinary of colorists (*PCQ* 113).[30] As Ortega would point out decades later in his metaphor regarding the fluidity of line in Velázquez's work that permitted adjacent objects to flow into and out of each other's "pores," Rafaëlli observed that Velázquez's color tones "flow one into the other without ever revealing how or where, as they do in mother-of-pearl," each painting being a harmonious assembly of pearl gray, black, rose, and ivory hues (116). Rafaëlli considered Velázquez an even greater colorist than Rubens, but he admitted that some would find the categorical nature of his statement controversial given that "in the Spanish master, there is not one tone that isn't a luminous gray": white is never pure white and the deepest black is never wholly black. The secret to the success of Velázquez's gray-based palette is that the rainbow of delicate grays he prefers is suffused with light, reflections, and a true depth of atmosphere. A genuine colorist, concludes Rafaëlli, is not the painter who throws vivid pigment onto his canvas, but one who can "see" and make distinctions among the infinite gray hues available to him, utilizing them to greatest effect in his painting (39).

The controversy over whether Velázquez was a colorist or not had begun in the previous century. Azorín's own views on the matter were influenced by, among others, those the painter, novelist, and art historian Eugène Fromentin (1820–1876) expressed in *Les Maîtres d'autrefois* (1876), a seminal monograph on Dutch and Flemish painters which Azorín knew and occasionally quoted (*PCQ* 24). Fromentin's scholarship has withstood the test of time: the art historian Meyer Schapiro considered it unique in the art-historical canon because the book is a "critical study of painting by an accomplished artist who is also a first-rate writer" (103). As Azorín reported in "Cuestiones de actualidad," Fromentin thought Velázquez one of the few painters who could use the dullest of colors—black, gray, brown, white tinged with black—to create marvelous pictures (7:239).[31] Fromentin wrote that Veronese, Correggio, Titian, Giorgione, Rubens, Velázquez, Frans Hals, and Van Dyck, notwithstanding their disparate emphasis on and use of pigment, were all "colorists" because they depended more on color than on drawing to model form. The common denominator shared by all these masters, whether they used color exuberantly or with restraint, was their sensitivity to its nuances, an ability to choose a palette with great care, and to juxtapose color on their canvases with skill and accuracy (746–77). The opinion Fromentin expressed in *Les Maîtres d'autrefois* had already been voiced in the seventeenth century by Roger de Piles (1635–1709) who called both Rembrandt and Rubens great colorists because he considered the chromatic realism of the former and the saturated color of the latter as motivated by a shared concern for the potency of representation (Alpers 1976, 28). Azorín reached similar conclusions within the context of contemporary Spanish painting. Musing on how writers express color in modern prose, he points out that in painting the question of what color is and how we see it has never been resolved. "Is Zuloaga a colorist?," he asks; "Is there color in the work of Sorolla?" For Azorín the dichotomy between Zuloaga and Sorolla represented two sides of the same controversy: given that both painters used color to achieve great visual and symbolic effects, the real issue for Azorín was whether or not the palettes they used were consistent with the nature of the landscape or the people and objects they portrayed (6:240).

In Spain the question of Velázquez's use of color was addressed by Aureliano de Beruete who wrote that one of the very few instances where Velázquez appeared to be a "colorist, employing a violent opposition of brilliant tones instead of the dull tints rich in gray harmonies, which were usual to him" was in *The Coronation of the Virgin* (121). In his copy of Luis Pardo's *De arte contemporánea* (1900), Azorín annotated the landscape painter Casimiro Sainz's opinion that Velázquez had never been a great colorist, a fact Sainz claimed even the most reputable art historians in Spain could not deny (192). Ortega entered the fray on the side of the "non-colorists." Unlike Beruete, he thought Velázquez's *La rendición de Breda* represented the epitome of color in the master's work, but he went on to say that, despite the "Titianism" of this particular painting, Velázquez did not believe much in color, his favorite tones being limited to the cool scale of color values in which brown, black, olive, bluish-white, and ivory were dominant (8:643, 647–48).[32] Velázquez's preference for the infinite possibilities available within the gray-based color spectrum may offer yet another reason for the special place he occupied in Azorín's artistic pantheon. Azorín always described the landscape of his beloved Alicante in terms of its tenuous yet multi-hued and richly varied scale of gray tones, a "panorama of red grays, green grays, yellow grays" (9:87) that would be especially difficult to render in paint. While any artist could work with strong pigment, the intense Mediterranean sun challenged the painter with the ardous task of expressing himself by using only the infinite gray tonalities the landsape put at his disposal (8:601). A true native son whose taste apparently was determined by the coloration of the landscape into which he was born, Azorín considered Goya's best work to be his "portrait in gray" of Francisco Bayeu (8:437).

In his eagerness to resuscitate the classics of Spanish culture and to give them a new lease on life by showing their enduring relevance, Azorín wrote in the aptly titled "Cuestiones de actualidad" that there was no painter more modern or more universal than Velázquez (7:237). In *Lecturas españolas* he mentions that, although he could not play the piano, he owned a spinet and sheet music by Beethoven, Mozart, and Wagner; likewise, since he could not afford to buy original oil paintings, the walls of his home were hung with photographic reproductions of paintings by Titian, Goya, and Velázquez (2:640). Citations of Velázquez, his paintings, or visual art similes based on his style or specific works of art appear constantly in Azorín's writing. Toward the end of the first decade of the twentieth century, when both Azorín and Unamuno turned away from their initial eagerness to "Europeanize" Spain and, in Azorín's words, recommended a reaction against "these European tendencies," Velázquez began to represent for him the most profound, the most genuine, and therefore the least European, aspect of what was authentically Spanish.[33] Following the example of Giner and Cossío, who believed that literature and art could hypostatize the essential, unchanging characteristics of a race of people with greater efficacy than the official chronicles and archives of their national history, in Azorín's imagination Velázquez's *La fuente de los Tritones*, and *La rendición de Breda* represented the true meaning of *casticismo*. Referring to *La fuente de los Tritones* he observed in "La España de un pintor": "How many people see . . . all of seventeenth-century Spain, not in the kings and court fools painted by Velázquez, but in this small painting that represents a view of Aranjuez, and in which a gentleman bows every so slightly before a lady . . . in order to offer her a flower?" (7:247).[34] The diminutive figure of the *caballero* bowed before the lady emblematized the gallantry, gravity, and pride of the seventeenth century in Spain that was so different from the French way of life; this "supreme gesture, haughty and humble at the same time . . . without annoying effusiveness, without the least bit of French affectation, discrete, elegant, unlabored; this unique, marvelous gesture, is only to be had in Spain" (Fig. 3).[35]

In similar fashion, the embrace exchanged between the vanquished Nassau and the victorious Spínola in *La rendición de Breda* became a visual metaphor for the handshake Azorín witnessed in the halls of the Spanish Parliament between the political adversaries Lerroux and the conservative Maura (Fig. 4). He observed that "This . . . small gesture will pass into History; Richelieu, Tallyrand [sic], the great men of the world . . . would not have adopted this gesture of the most urbane, and at the same time

Fig. 3   Diego Rodríguez de Silva y Velázquez, *La fuente de los Tritones en el Jardín de la Isla, de Aranjuez*, 1657. Oil on canvas, 248 × 223 cm. Museo del Prado, Madrid.

Fig. 4 Diego Rodríguez de Silva y Velázquez, *La rendición de Breda*, c.1635. Oil on canvas, 307 × 367 cm. Museo del Prado, Madrid.

haughty cordiality, with their adversaries" (3:684). Azorín's visual contextualization of Spanish politics continues in another section of *Parlamentarismo español* where he refers to both *La fuente de los Tritones* and *La rendición de Breda* as two invaluable paintings that *document* the national tradition of Spanish urbane cordiality, expressed in Spínola's embrace of Nassau in *La rendición* and the gallant bow of the *caballero*, rose in hand, before the lady of *La fuente* (3:788). Once again comparing French customs to those of Spain, Azorín comments that "in these documents we are able to see that our tradition is one of sobriety that never approaches the surly . . . and a certain lilt of affability . . . that never descends into the overwhelming, sensational and, at times, inappropriate affability of our French neighbors" (3:788). *La rendición de Breda* is invoked for a

third time in *Parlamentarismo español* as a visual metaphor that condenses the magnanimity and nobility of spirit Azorín thought characterized the recently deceased politician Francisco Romero Robledo (1838–1906). Affiliated with the *Unión Liberal*, Romero Robledo—according to Azorín—was a "profoundly genuine Spaniard." If he had to summarize the nature of this *castizo español*, Azorín writes he could do so most eloquently by invoking a single gesture that expressed the political psychology of the illustrious parlamentarian: "the cordial, frank, effusive gesture with which Velázquez, in the *Surrender of Breda*, has General Spínola throw his arm around the shoulder of the vanquished Nassau" (3:801–2).

At times Azorín's references to Velázquez are purely decorative, used to establish atmosphere of place in the essays or the surroundings of a fictional character. In *La ruta de Don Quijote*, wishing to evoke the unchanged, seventeenth-century ambience of the Castilian towns, their inns and taverns which the self-styled knight-errant might have visited, Azorín describes an interior space as having generous balconies that allow the sun to stream into a room decorated with antique pottery and copies of Velázquez paintings (Ramsden 18). He dispatches the description of an aged vagabond with a simile based on a Velázquez painting, the old man, with "barbas intonsas y unos ojuelos malignos, perversos—como los del Menipo, de Velázquez—se ha dedicado a ir . . . corriendo a través de pueblos y aldeas" [4:97; shaggy beard and malicious, perverse, little eyes—like those of Velázquez's Mennipus—has devoted himself to wandering through towns and villages]. In "Génesis del *Quijote*," Azorín recreates the atmosphere of Cervantes's household in terms of a simile whose visual referent is also to a painting by Velázquez: "Y aquí, en la espaciosa estancia, quizá había un torno; en un rincón descansaría un huso; en el suelo se vería un tabaque lleno de gruesos ovillos de lana, y a par de él—como en *Las Hilanderas*, de Velázquez—reposaría . . . un gato ceniciento, a planchas blancas" [9:1168; And here, in the spacious room, there would perhaps be a spinning wheel; a spindle would rest in a corner; on the floor you'd see a wicker basket full of thick balls of wool, and next to it—like in Velázquez's *The Spinners*—would nap a gray cat with white patches].[36] In still other cases, Azorín used paintings by Velázquez to encode hermeneutic or ideological content. In *Antonio Azorín*, Velázquez's bust-length portrait of Felipe IV emblematizes the stupidity and impotence of his reign. The monarch, who was not of pure Spanish ancestry, is derisively referred to as an "Austrian King"; his waxed moustache and flabby cheeks emphasize a wide face and prominent jaw, while his "distracted, wandering eyes appear to look out stupidly at the irremediable decadence of a nation," an inertia and lack of direction Antonio Azorín compares to those still rampant in the Spain of his own day (48).

Of all Velázquez paintings, however, it is *Las Meninas* that seems to have had an ineffable magnetism for Azorín, enjoying a position of privilege in his intellectual and aesthetic views. The painting has many different functional values in his work, ranging from purely decorative intent, such as the carefully lit reproduction in Antonio Azorín's study (1:1009); a journalistic essay condemning a disfiguring coat of varnish applied to the painting in 1903 (*PCQ* 12); an essay-short story based on José Nieto, the small figure on the background steps of *Las Meninas*; an imaginary visit to Velázquez's studio in which a discussion of perspective in the painting takes place; and the photograph of a middle-aged Azorín standing in front of a reproduction of *Las Meninas* which appears on the back cover of Juan Manuel Rozas's edition of *Castilla*. When Azorín recalled Quechea, a village idiot in *Memorias Inmemoriales*, he compared the unfortunate to Mari Bárbola, the female dwarf in *Las Meninas* and to Zuloaga's *Gregorio, el Botero* (8:405–6). Azorín's imagination, ever susceptible to the suggestive potential of the seemingly trivial, was especially taken with the "puertecita de cuarterones" Velázquez painted at the deepest point of perspectival recession in his painting. The door is open, allowing the spectator to see a brightly lit, but indistinguishable space beyond. Azorín often speculated where that door might lead and why José Nieto was placed on the steps leading up to that door. In his "Recuadro a Velázquez" he observed that, just as the last rays of a setting sun glancing off a white wall in Rembrandt's *The Good Samaritan* become the focal point of that painting, in *Las Meninas* it is Don José Nieto, about to leave the room for some unknown reason, en route to some unspecified destination, who piques the imagination, allowing the observer to speculate on his plans and projects (*Recuadros* 81). The suggestive back door of *Las Meninas* proved to be a fruitful source of meditation for Azorín. In "Los místicos," he imagines the "puertecita de cuadernos" as opening onto a gallery surrounding an interior patio. The scene, in Azorín's imagination, would depict accurately the ambience of seventeenth-century Spain: "the gallery will surround a patio . . . and in the patio, at least—let us go on imagining—, there will be cypresses and rose bushes. And from the gallery . . . you will be able to hear the rustle of wide silk farthingales and the tric-trac of a sword."[37]

The same doorway, always expressed by some form of a diminutive, also functions as part of a visual arts simile Azorín used in "Las nubes," his rewriting of *La Celestina* (*Castilla*). Describing the upper floors of the house in which Calixto and Melibea live after their marriage, Azorín writes of "vast drawing rooms, removed studies, murky corridors with a little paneled door at the back, that—like the one in Velázquez's *Las Meninas*—allows the glimpse of a bright patio" (159). The evocation of Velázquez's masterpiece continues when Azorín includes in the same story a mirror that, much like the one in *Las Meninas*, reflects a painting not literally "in" the space described either by Azorín's prose or Velázquez's picture: ". . . in the center of the room, on a walnut table . . . with wrought iron studs, rests a pretty chess set with pieces made of ivory, mother-of-pearl and silver; the glass of a wide mirror reflects the aquiline figures against the gold background of a panel hanging on the opposite wall" (160).[38]

Velázquez was an intertextual painter. His canvases, including *Las Meninas*, often duplicate either his own work or that of other painters; in some cases, as Ortega pointed out, Velázquez recast ancient mythology, often in modern, irreverent terms within his own paintings. Perhaps Azorín's fondness for the *Meninas* can be accounted for by his own predilection for the self-reflexive: we have only to mention his 1925 novel *Doña Inés* and his fondness for Dutch and Flemish artists so proficient in the games of visual embedding. Considering Azorín's citation of such works by Memling, Van Eyck (*La Voluntad* 109), and Petrus Christus (*PCQ* 65), it is safe to assume that he knew Van Eyck's classic *Wedding Portrait of Giovanni Arnolfini* with its reflecting mirror strategically placed on the back wall, thus including in the painting the artist who presumably is standing in front of the couple, but not actually "in" the picture space.[39] Petrus Christus's *Saint Eligius* has a convex mirror in the foreground that reflects the street and two pedestrians before the shop window, all located outside the literal picture frame (Fig. 5). Like the mirror in Velázquez's *Las Meninas*, the mirror in the Saint Eligius painting functions as a "direct connection between pictorial space and the viewer's imagined location before the shop" (Upton 32). Azorín certainly knew *The Money Lender and His Wife* (also known as *The Money Changer and His Wife*) by Quentin Massys, the last pupil and artistic heir of Van Eyck. This canvas, housed in the Louvre, places the crucial mirror at an angle facing the spectator, reflecting not only the space represented, but also a street scene and figure painted in perspective within the mirror.[40]

Azorín's interest in the Flemish School may perhaps be attributed to what Giner de los Ríos noted was Van Eyck's, Memling's, and Massys's "conscious effort to study natural details" and their human subjects "who exude extraordinary veracity, lacking the mannered style and affectation that was then in vogue" (20:271–72). Well-known is Azorín's predilection for the mundane aspects of daily life—the "primores de lo vulgar" made famous by Ortega y Gasset—who likewise argued that Velázquez was the first modern painter to depict objects not in their idealistic, generic forms, but as displaying their quotidian, prosaic idiosyncrasies (8:523). Ortega dated the beginning of modern painting to the conscious attempt Velázquez made to introduce the element of time into the spatial medium of painting. Artists before Velázquez, in Ortega's view, avoided the temporal, while the great discovery of the Spanish master was that of "freezing the instant": "That is what he perpetuates, and that is, according to him, the mission of art: precisely to eternalize the moment" (8:487). Critics from Azorín to Foucault invariably have cited Velázquez as embodying the painter's intent to arrest an instant of action in space. Azorín wrote that traditional aesthetic rules did not apply to Velázquez since his painting was solely dependent on "la sensación y el momento." As he understood it, the master's work synthesized the two contrary sides of time: Jorge Manrique's sense of its fleeting nature and Berceo's sense of the eternal (*Recuadros* 81–82). Michel Foucault saw *Las Meninas* in terms of potentiality for movement that the painter suspended in his picture in an unrealized, immanent state: Velázquez portrays himself standing before a canvas, poised to begin work on his painting, "the arm holding the brush . . . is motionless, for an instant, between canvas and paints . . . the scene is about to yield up its volume" (3).[41] There is potential for movement as well in the figure of Don José Nieto whose raised leg indicates that he might step through the back door and out of the room, while the Infanta and her *meninas* appear to be surprised by the arrival of someone or something else located outside the frame of the painting. In his fictionalization of the life of José Nieto, Azorín also grasped the quality of immanent movement in the painting; his description of the scene emphasizes its unrealized potential through the use of verbs of motion as well as the subjunctive mood. He imagined that once arranged in the tableau we know as *Las*

Fig. 5   Petrus Christus, *Saint Eligius*, 1449. Oil on wood panel, 39 × 33½ in. The Metropolitan Museum of Art, New York. Robert Lehmann Collection, 1975. (1975.1.110)

Meninas, its human models "wait so that the painter might begin to work," but at the last moment Velázquez decides to step back from the canvas in order to have another look at the composition, and determines that José Nieto would be better placed "at the back of the corridor, ascending a few stone rungs" (2:463). Meanwhile, the rest of the group waits in their assigned positions for Don José to remove himself to the "little, panelled door" at the top of the steps.[42]

Velázquez's meditation on the nature of time and his desire to attenuate its chronological sequentiality were also of concern to Azorín who described his "dolorido sentir" (wistful melancholy) as an obsession with "that vague sensation . . . of time and things that go by in a vertiginous and formidable current" (2:90). In his desire to surprise and to suspend the present moment on its flight into history, Azorín engaged in the same kind of exercise as did Velázquez, albeit for different personal reasons. In separate essays on painter and writer this similarity of intent was noticed by the cultural historian José Antonio Maravall. In his monograph on the painter, Maravall notes that Velázquez tries to petrify instances of existence: "trapping the individual object at the moment that it passes through his consciousness . . . in a fully discrete instant" (1987, 80). By representing physical movement suspended in time, Velázquez introduced the issues of temporality and narrative sequence into painting, an inherently spatial form of art. Suggestive parallels can be drawn between Velázquez's freezing the instant on canvas and Azorín's continual subversion of linear time within the verbal medium in an attempt at what Ortega so perceptively called "an effort to salvage . . . the restless world that hurls onward toward its own destruction" (2:174). Azorín carried out his project by adopting the motto "vivir es ver volver" (to live is to see things repeat themselves), and by reconfiguring the linear time of narrative into the simultaneity of circular and self-replicating patterns. His revival and restoration of the Spanish literary classics to a kind of cultural eternal return is as much a part of his effort to efface distinctions between past, present, and future as is his preference for the present perfect or historical present tense in his writing. The present perfect enabled Azorín to freeze the subject in a state of immanence, or a perpetual present that Ortega dubbed "virtual stillness": a present that has not quite yet slipped into the irretrievable past (2:174).[43] In similar fashion, Velázquez also was able to capture both the eternal and the momentary in a single painting by depicting his subjects in "still movement," a painterly equivalent of the present perfect tense, something Ortega described as depicting "existence at the moment that it's condemned to stop existing" (8:847).

Azorín frequently attempted to suspend the inherent temporality of narrative through the spatializing poetics of ekphrasis, a topos that subverts the diachronicity of literature by re-creating within the parameter of language art forms the synchronic and spatio-visual qualities of the plastic arts. Ortega noted Azorín's ekphrastic imperative in his 1912 review of *Lecturas españolas*, which also happens to adumbrate similar observations Ortega would make in his future studies of Velázquez: "Azorín's craft consists in suspending the movement of things so that the attitude in which he surprises them is made eternal. . . . In this way the corrupting power of time is annulled. It's a question, then, of a sleight of hand similar to that used in painting" (1:239). Ortega's comment invokes the debate between the "sister arts" originated by the Greeks and taken up in neoclassical aesthetics by Lessing in the *Laocoön* (1766), a work in which the German philosopher distinguished painting from poetry by contrasting the successive, temporal nature of literature with the spatial and simultaneous characteristics of painting.

Azorín himself was aware of the time-space debate involving the sister arts. He considered Fromentin's theory of painting in "Ver y pintar," noting the French critic's distinction between Nature in which "everything is alive and consecutive. . . . Actions follow one after the other; continuity imprisons us. We co-exist with things as they evolve," whereas diachronicity was nonexistent in the visual arts that are changeless in the stillness of their tranquility (*PCQ* 237). Among the 100 books Azorín thought to place on an imaginary list of required reading he included, along with Cossío's *El Greco*, Lessing's *Laocoön* (9:1224–25), and he addressed the "discrepancies that had arisen regarding the limits of painting and poetry" in a chapter of *Capricho* titled "El crítico de arte." Refracting his voice in that of the art critic's, Azorín questions "Lessing's arguments in the *Laocoön*" as he considers whether painting can truly be said to represent a single, discrete episode apprehended synchronically by the human eye, and literature a series of moments meant to be perceived in diachronic progression. The art critic disagrees with Lessing's categorical separation of the genres by pointing out that Rembrandt's *The Good Samaritan* invokes an entire narrative of the protagonist's return home and his succoring of the battered traveler. The painting thus suggests a diachronic narration of all the successive moments pertinent to the telling of an adventure story. Although the art critic vacillates between his own intuitions and Lessing's dictates, in a later chapter he concludes that, contrary to Lessing's pronouncements, the plastic arts are nothing but a succession of diachronic moments (6:965).[44]

As James Heffernan, and other students of literary ekphrasis acknowledge, because the verbal and visual arts can never replace one another, they engage in a paragonal struggle of image against word, particularly the word of Lessing who deemed the visual arts had to remain silent, leaving verbal expression to literature (1993, 6–7). The verbally created plastic art object is, nevertheless, frequently interpolated into a literary work in an attempt to retard its linear movement. Because the plastic arts are essentially timeless and their "temporality" follows circular or repetitive patterns, superimposing the "frozen, stilled world of plastic relationships" upon literature has the effect, as Murray Krieger expressed it in his classic essay on the subject, of stilling "literature's turning world" (1992, 265–66).[45] The ekphrastic moment is therefore a conflictive one since it compels the work of verbal art to accommodate the inserted, generic "other" by temporarily suspending its internal laws of succession. The final aim of such literary mimesis is to coax the language art into imitating as closely as possible the style and technique of the visual arts. Literature is thereby empowered with the unique ability to reproduce the atemporal simultaneity of painting, sculpture, or even architectonic configurations within the confines of its own chronological irreversibility—although, as Krieger remarks, this type of literature will always be accompanied by an "archetypal principle of repetition, of eternal return" (1967, 125). Given Azorín's obsession with the notion of eternal return and his attempts to sabotage the forward march of time, it is not surprising that he would make exten-

sive use of the ekphrastic topos in his work. That he should also empathize with Velázquez, a painter intent on capturing the instantaneity of a scene or passing moment, is also understandable.[46]

Although a number of paintings by Velázquez engage in the exercise of freezing an instant of physical activity—Ortega mentions *Los borrachos* and *Las lanzas* as two examples (8:486)—it is *Las Meninas* that takes this theme to its limits as it portrays not one discrete action but, as we have seen, that of many. Foucault observed the circular pattern of movement to which *Las Meninas* impels a spectator's eye (13), and the figure of Velázquez himself "caught in a moment of stillness, at the neutral centre of this oscillation" (3). For these, and many other reasons that will become apparent, Azorín chose this painting as a structural fulcrum and visual emblem for his essay-short story "La casa cerrada" (*Castilla*, 1912).[47] Through his absorption of Velazquean techniques that we have come to identify as modern concepts of representation, Azorín, anticipating Ortega and Foucault, discerned in *Las Meninas* a contemporary phenomenology of vision. "La casa cerrada" thus becomes paradigmatic of the way in which Azorín engages a work of art in dialogue, utilizing Velázquez's painting as a visual referent for what, in reality, is an essay that interrogates the dialectical relations between word and image: a struggle in which painting—an art of natural signs—ultimately is displaced by literature, an art of arbitrary, linguistic signs. By allowing the word to usurp the image, Azorín asserts the priority and supremacy of language in the creation of visual reality and, in so doing, he endows the traditional ekphrastic topos with a decidedly modern flair.

"La casa cerrada"

On first consideration "La casa cerrada" appears to be a simple narrative about two men who return after a considerable absence to the home where one of them had lived as a child. Despite the passage of time and an important physiological change wrought in the protagonist, there have been no major transformations within or without the walls of the house: "todo está lo mismo que hace quince años." Neither the family portraits nor the photograph of *Las*

Meninas in the study has become discolored; the dining room, too, appears as if dinner had been served there just the evening before. While mention of *Las Meninas* seems rather casual and purely decorative, it is tempting to ask why Azorín chose to include this particular painting in his narrative, and why the protagonist would say that the figure of Don José Nieto has always had a profoundly suggestive effect upon him.[48] We note, first, that José Nieto is portrayed arrested in the motion of drawing back a curtain, "con un pie en un escalón y otro pie en otro," about to exit the room (202). Second, the protagonist speaks of Nieto as "ese hombre lejano— lejano en ese fondo del cuadro y en el tiempo" (203)—a figure remote both in time and the manner in which Velázquez has placed him within the painting (Fig. 6). Thus *Las Meninas* conflates the representation of time and space which so interested Azorín. In the same way that the painting preserves the "stilled movement" of a group of people as they were caught at a specific moment inside Velázquez's palace studio, Azorín's "La casa cerrada" is modeled along the lines of a "time capsule" that has just been reopened, disclosing its contents to the spectator-reader.[49]

Upon closer scrutiny, Azorín's verbal homage to the perspectival schematics that "frame" José Nieto in the doorway is not *sui generis*, but one among a congeries of frames, mirrors, windows, and paintings within *Las Meninas*, all bespeaking the structural organization of his vignette. From the outset "La casa cerrada" is situated within a visual arts paradigm through Azorín's constant use of frames and framing devices that tend to convert what is seen through them into a "picture." He begins the story with the protagonist's ascent to a mountain pass, from which the valley and town below can be seen in bird's eye perspective. The view described is seen through a window of the carriage in which the men travel, its borders marking off the interior of the vehicle from the scene beyond, effectively transforming the valley into a landscape framed by the carriage window.[50] Once Azorín's traveling companions enter the home, they repeat the ascensional movement that opened the essay, this time to a second-floor gallery from whose windows the protagonist remembers he liked to contemplate "el panorama de la vega" (201). The gallery windows, like the windows of the carriage, transform the view described into another framed

landscape. Proceeding to the library, the protagonist asks about the portraits that hang on its walls. Assured that neither moisture nor time has harmed them, the protagonist asks they be taken down so that he can run his hands over the paintings which he differentiates by their frames: "los distingo por sus marcos" (201). It is at this moment that Azorín makes two analeptic revelations: first, he confirms the reader's growing suspicion that the protagonist may be blind; therefore, the reader becomes aware that she experiences the narrative not through the protagonist's eyes, but through those of his companion who becomes metonymic not only for the protagonist's vision, but also for the eyes of the reader. What is "seen" is thereby doubly framed by the companion's eyes which themselves must peer through many different types of "frames" as they apprehend the narrated scene.[51]

The framed family portraits of "La casa cerrada" appropriate even greater significance when the reader is able to recognize them as belonging to a larger suite of verbally framed pictures and landscapes. As a structural device, the narrative frame possesses greatest importance when it juxtaposes a narrating present with a narrated past, leading a reader or fictional character to a "retrospective vision as an occasion for assessing the past and measuring one's present against it" (Dittmar 192). In the case of "La casa cerrada," the analeptic revelation of the protagonist's blindness, emphasized when he must feel the portraits of his ancestors with his hands, confronts not only the man's past with his present, but also functions as a narrative frame that establishes a considerably altered manner and scale of values by which to engage the essay in a second reading. Additionally, the two family portraits of "La casa," visual representations embedded within the already representational medium of literature, mimic the two pictures Velázquez painted on the rear wall of *Las Meninas*, itself a painting encompassing myriad portraits. These background pictures have been identified as paintings by Juan Bautista del Mazo after sketches made by Rubens, an artist twenty-two years older than Velázquez whom the Spanish painter came to know well during Rubens's eight month stay in Madrid in 1628. The inclusion of copies del Mazo made after Rubens allows Velázquez a paratactic evaluation of his own work against the legacy of both a precursor art-

Fig. 6   Diego Rodríguez de Silva y Velázquez, *Las Meninas*, 1656. Oil on canvas, 318 × 276 cm. Museo del Prado, Madrid.

ist and that of the younger, less talented pupil and "heir," del Mazo.[52] Just as Azorín invokes the illusion of depth and perspective through the use of both figurative (narrative) frames and literal (picture) frames, conflating time and space into one discrete sensory experience, he also introduces spatial qualities into the story by inserting three paintings—one historical, two fictional—within the text. On the other hand, Velázquez, as he responds to the work of Rubens and del Mazo in *Las Meninas*, also permits the entry of narrative time into the spatial medium of art.

From the portraits in the library the nameless protagonist of "La casa cerrada" and his equally nameless companion ascend to the highest level of the home where the blind man's study is located. The protagonist immediately proceeds to a window from which he says he liked to observe "los huertos de la vega" (202), often drawing the landscape closer to his eyes by using a pair of binoculars, creating another of the many "dual frame" structures that pervade the essay. It is in this room, above the desk, that the protagonist hung a framed reproduction of Velázquez's *Las Meninas*, its status as a photographic duplicate an adroit restatement of the self-reflexive nature of the original with its infinite regress of frames: Don José Nieto is framed by the doorway in which he stands; there are framed pictures hanging on the back wall of Velázquez's painting; these are reiterated by the heavy, protruding window frame on the right-hand side of the painting, revealed only by the light that streams from it into the studio. On the left-hand side of the painting is the framed canvas on which Velázquez is about to begin working, and finally, also on the back wall, hangs the framed mirror that reflects the visages of Felipe IV and Queen Mariana who are located outside the literal picture frame of *Las Meninas*. Ironically, it is this seemingly insignificant mirror that becomes a major player in the picture.

José Antonio Maravall suggests that a mirror, a window, or an open door such as those that appear in *Las Meninas* frequently are placed in a painting to make visible and to accommodate within the picture, spaces or vistas that otherwise would remain outside the purview of the work of art (1987, 110). As in some, but not all paintings by the Flemish masters who first explored self-reflexive art and whose work is the intertext for both Velázquez and Azorín, the

mirror in *Las Meninas* makes visible a scene located outside the frame of the canvas. As the spectator's eye attempts to decide whether the subject of the picture is the Infanta and her entourage located within the painting, or Felipe IV and Queen Mariana located outside the picture frame but made visible by the mirror, the eye is lured into an oscillatory dialogue between the interior and exterior contents of the picture.[53] A similar kind of dialogic exchange between the inner and the outer, the visible and the invisible, occurs in "La casa cerrada" as the reader's eye moves continuously between the inner spaces of vehicle and home to the exterior views of plain and town, doubly framed by the eyes of the protagonist's companion and the carriage, gallery, attic windows, and picture frames through which he sees.

The illusion of an eye(I)witness account given by the story's protagonist is induced by his constant use of verbs of perception: *divisar, contemplar, ver, mirar,* and *leer* (to discern, to contemplate, to see, to look, to read) occur several times on each page of this short narrative. The paradox, of course, is that the eye(I)witness is blind and sees nothing at all. The physiological act of vision is reconstructed through language; more specifically, through a rhetorical pattern of questions posed by the protagonist based on his surroundings as he remembers them in his "mind's eye," and the detailed, descriptive responses offered by his companion who confirms or completes the blind man's recollections:

—Tell me, can you see to the right . . . a white house that is barely visible through the trees?
—Yes, now it seems that the glass of a small window up high, glitters in the sun. (199)

—Are we passing by the plaza now? What I'd give to see that spacious plaza . . .!
—It's still there, they've opened up some new stores. In the center of the plaza they've made a small garden. (200)

—Can this be a small packet of letters? Among them there should be a photograph of me at eight years old.
—Yes, this is it, it's almost faded. (202)[54]

The entire visually perceptible reality of "La casa cerrada"—the town, its landscape, the interior of the house and the works of art it contains—is re-created through language in a series of speech acts emanating from the protagonist and his friend who verbally conjure the visual reality of the story.

The issue of focalization is as germane to *Las Meninas* as it is to "La casa cerrada." Blindness, as Mieke Bal has observed, is a crucial and self-reflexive theme in the visual arts as well as in literature, equally problematic in both because it presents the reader-observer with two focalizers: a blind protagonist who focalizes only verbally and a represented beholder who both speaks and focalizes visually for protagonist and viewer-reader.[55] Because the protagonist of "La casa cerrada" is blind, he must cede visual focalization to an "other" who functions as a point of exchange between the visible world of Azorín's story as apprehended by the reader, and the scene as the companion describes or helps to reconstruct it for the blind protagonist. Velázquez achieves reciprocity of contemplation in much the same way by entering his own canvas as subject, positioning himself at an interstitial location between the inner and outer realms of his painting. The process, however, substantially reduces Velázquez's ability to perceive his tableau as a composite whole since, by assuming the role of an intradiegetic narrator, he also becomes a character who sees and is himself part of the pictorial scene, thereby surrendering exclusivity of narrative voice and focalization to whomever occupies the position normally reserved for the artist's point of view located outside the canvas. Vision and narration in *Las Meninas* are thus mediated by two simultaneous points of view: Velázquez's partial vision from within the painting, and the mirror on the back wall whose function it is to restore visibility to the focalizer(s) who occupy the overdetermined point of view outside the picture frame and who otherwise would remain invisible: perhaps the King and Queen who observe Velázquez observing and painting them, while they observe their daughter and her ladies-in-waiting who, in turn, observe the royal couple. In similar fashion, the privilege of sight in "La casa cerrada" does not reside with the blind man but with an "other" whose controlling eyes, like the mirror in Velázquez's painting, restore absolute vision in Azorín's story as they focalize for the protagonist.

In *Las Meninas* the images of visibility and nonvisibility are so imbricate that they displace the intended subject of the painting. The royal couple, because of their location outside the picture frame, is seen only as an indistinct image reflected in the mirror on the back wall of Velázquez's studio. As Foucault points out, the paradox of *Las Meninas* is that the King and Queen are neither "in" the picture, nor are they depicted clearly, and no one "in" the picture is looking at the framed mirror which attests to their presence (7). In this way the ostensible subject of the painting is relegated to the status of object and the abstract notion of point of view replaces Felipe IV and Queen Mariana as the intended protagonists of the painting (Searle 257).[56] As the subject of both essay and painting slip out of focus, Azorín and Velázquez are able to create for themselves greater latitude in which to study the epistemology of vision.

Foucault proposes that the mirror in *Las Meninas*—and, I would add, the entire painting—"provides a metathesis of visibility" (8). Ortega, in a rewording of Kant's *Critique of Pure Reason*, concluded that Velázquez's masterpiece reached the pinnacle of what the visual arts could achieve: "the reduction of painting to pure visuality. *Las Meninas* becomes something like a critique of the pure retina" (8:477). Indeed, another Spaniard, Antonio Buero Vallejo, a painter before winning international recognition as a playwright, made similar determinations in his play *Las Meninas*, as well as in two critical essays on Velázquez. In his dramatic work, Buero portrays the painter's chief intellectual and technical pursuits as those of representing sight and the dynamics of vision. Responding to jealous accusations leveled at him by inferior palace artists, the character Diego Velázquez retorts, "All of you think that it's necessary to paint things. I paint vision" (1973, 275). Azorín's familiarity with critical literature on Velázquez, his special love for *Las Meninas*, and his invocation of the painting by a blind man in "La casa cerrada" are by no means without ulterior motive. Rather, the painting serves a hermeneutic purpose, conveying semiotic information the reader must have in order to grasp the deep structure of the text. As Velázquez's painting assumes dimensions other than those of a royal portrait, so "La casa cerrada" becomes Azorín's "metathesis of visibility." The images of sight, its lack, who sees, how they see, and what they see are the true subjects of both essay and painting.

A visual emblem instigates philosophical reflection "whenever the nature of images becomes linked with an account of the nature of man" (Mitchell 1986, 158). W. J. T. Mitchell designates a visual image that provokes speculation of this kind a "hypericon," and adduces Foucault's *Las Meninas* as precisely the kind of visual emblem that possesses an ontology beyond its status as a museum piece. For Michel Foucault, perhaps even for Velázquez himself, *Las Meninas* was not a royal portrait at all, but a (re)presentation of representation, a painting whose subject is vision itself. For Azorín, too, *Las Meninas* became a "hypericon" that he used to challenge Velázquez on his own ground, questioning the efficacy of the natural sign as the sole determinant of what the "mind's eye" could recognize and accept as visibly "real."

Throughout his long career as a writer, Azorín seems to have considered *Las Meninas* a painting that engaged him in dialogue not only on the nature of representation, but also on the nature of humankind. The protagonist of "La casa cerrada" is especially interested in whether or not the figure of José Nieto is still visible in his photographic reproduction of the painting. Nieto has always seemed extraordinarily real to him, simultaneously alive and eternal as are "heroes or geniuses," and he recalls whiling away many an hour of conversation with Nieto in the solitude of his study (203). Thirty years after publishing the essays of *Castilla*, Azorín invoked an imaginary visit to Velázquez's studio in "El tiempo pasado" (*Pensando en España*). In this short story Velázquez confides that the greatest issue to confront painters is that of perspective, of which there are two kinds: physical and metaphysical. Velázquez then inquires of his visitor whether he has not been successful in achieving both types of perspective in the small figure of José Nieto portrayed at nearly the innermost point of the deeply receding perspective in *Las Meninas*. For the fictional Velázquez, the figure of Nieto positioned on the rear steps leading to the *puertecita de cuarterones* and the blaze of light in the corridor beyond, speaks of hopes and joys we do not know, pain which we have yet to experience, of destiny itself (5:977–78). In short, he is a personage who engages "Velázquez-Azorín" in the same kind of meditation as he did the protagonist of "La casa cerrada."

Because of its status as a canonical work the "hypericon" may, with time, shift from an image that stimulates discussion to that of a reified sign, and as Mitchell observes, one of the aims of literary iconology is to breathe new life into visual emblems reified by time and commercial or intellectual exploitation (1996, 158–59). In his use of the *Meninas* as an iconographic metaphor and visual referent designed to unveil beneath the exquisite narrative "miniature" of "La casa cerrada," a debate on natural and arbitrary signs, Azorín reveals himself to be a true literary modern, taking up the enterprise of pouring new wine into old wineskins recommended by Mitchell.[57] In a penetrating essay on modern and post-modern aesthetics, Charles Newman referred to Ortega's metaphor of the window and the garden (*The Dehumanization of Art*) to illustrate the difference between nineteenth- and twentieth-century approaches to the perception of reality. While naturalism and realism assumed that the window glass was perfectly transparent, offering unobstructed views of the world, in the twentieth century the window of perception becomes "fogged with authorial breath as much as nature's mist." For Newman the twentieth-century metaphor for language is a cognitive process in which both observer and observed are dependent upon each other. "The window of language is no longer in a fact a window, but its own autotelic agency: Opacity as Reality" (66–67). This divorce of the arbitrary sign from the natural sign Newman sees at the core of modern aesthetics is also the keystone of Azorín's "La casa cerrada." The windows, literal and figurative, through which Azorín's reader "sees" are made possible by the protagonist's opacity; that is, his inability to see. If the reader perceives anything at all of the blind man's surroundings, it is due to the capacity language has of reproducing a visibly lived reality. And so well does the linguistic sign re-create the perceptibly real, that the protagonist's blindness never impedes understanding; in fact, it is not even confirmed until the essay's close.

Most likely Azorín chose *Las Meninas* to contextualize a reading of "La casa cerrada" because he clearly understood Velázquez's masterpiece to be a painting about the dynamics of vision. In Azorín's view, then, apprehension of the visibly real, generally associated with the natural signs of the plastic arts, could be crafted with equal validity through purely linguistic means. Language, because of its autotelic nature, could displace, perhaps even supersede, vision. For Azorín writing had—as Françoise Meltzer put it—finally "replaced the portrait" (137).

4

Lessons in Landscape: Essays on Art History

Of all the visual art genres, Azorín preferred landscape painting. He knew its history rather well and contributed essays, often accompanied by photographic illustrations, to the periodical press on his favorite landscape painters and paintings.[1] This enthusiasm for the genre derives not only from Azorín's personal aesthetic preferences, but was conditioned by his, and the preceding generation's, acceptance of the positivist credo that the environment—and landscape fell into this rubric—predisposed the character of peoples and nations. In 1904 Azorín wrote of the innate connection between the Castilian landscape and the character, gestures, art, literature, and even manner of dress of the Castilian people who, he thought, were epitomized by the "secret harmony" he inferred between the landscape of the *meseta* and Quevedo's prose which he characterized as "concise, austere, severe, rigid, lofty, untamable, inflexible" (4:121–22). As for Azorín's Spanish contemporaries, in *La obra de un ministro* (1910), he observed that to understand completely the character of Juan de la Cierva, one could not ignore the landscape into which the man was born and within which he spent his formative years: "si no se le relaciona estrechamente con el medio en que ha nacido y se ha formado en su educación primaria, con la *tierra* y con el *paisaje*" (3:33; emphasis Azorín).

The evolution of verbal description in the plastic arts—from mere objective summation to presenting the work of art filtered through a critic's subjective reactions and opinions—was perhaps initiated by Denis Diderot whose ekphrastic style of Salon reportage encouraged readers to participate in an alternative manner of reading about art. In a letter to Friedrich Melchior Grimm, reporting on paintings at the Salon of 1765, Diderot tells his friend, "I will describe the paintings to you, and my description will be such that with a bit of imagination and taste you'll be able to recreate them in space and situate the objects pretty much as I saw them on the canvas . . ." (14:26). As Norman Bryson points out, Diderot intended his verbal descriptions to evoke a mental image of the work on his reader's "eidetic screen" (1981, 183). The paintings Diderot praised most, especially in the early Salons of 1759, 1761, and 1763, appear to be either those that could be narrativized into "core texts," or descriptions of ideal paintings Diderot saw only in his own imagination; in his opinion, the more a work of art behaved like a discursive text demanding interpretation, the better it was (Bryson 1981, 183, 185, 188). As we shall see, Azorín was a great admirer of Diderot. He quoted the *Essais sur la peinture* with some frequency, and in *Me-*

95

morias Inmemoriales he observed that "X" judges works of art more or less as did Diderot: from a strictly emotional, subjective point of view (8:430). On one occasion Azorín wrote that a friend's father let his imagination fly when he commented on paintings, explaining them "in the manner of Diderot," seeing in the work of art not only the moment depicted by the artist, but everything that might have transpired before as well as everything that could have occurred afterward (7:779). Azorín defended his verbal exegesis of paintings by Zuloaga, saying that if Diderot had not been thought to talk nonsense when he wrote about his favorite painters, the "desbarros de un espíritu fino," although not necessarily always on the mark, certainly had their merit. Following Diderot's example, Azorín wrote, "by this I don't mean to say that I'm always right when I interpret Zuloaga; I give my explanation without much ado, and with that I've fulfilled my obligation" (8:433). It is through Diderot that Azorín's attraction to paintings overdetermined by narrative, his belief in the superiority of language to the natural signs of painting, his penchant for the ekphrastic topos, and, Cézanne excepted, his near silence on post-Impressionist art (e.g., painting that is not immediately legible), might be explained.[2]

Azorín himself was, and still continues to be, acknowledged as one of the greatest verbal landscapists in Spanish literary history. Although not a professional or even amateur painter, as were many of his generational writer-colleagues, Azorín's landscapes are as much the product of his own eidetic memory as they are of his sensitivity to perspective, color, light, and composition. His ekphrasis of the one painting by Aureliano de Beruete in his small personal collection (Pl. 18) is a fine example of the way in which Azorín utilized the verbal medium to re-create the style and specific color palette preferred by one of his favorite artists:

El mío (maravilloso paisaje de una suavidad y de una limpidez extraordinarias) representa una ladera verde en los aledaños de Madrid; más lejos aparecen unas casas rojizas; entre ellas un enhiesto chopo. Al fondo la centelleadura zarca del Guadarrama. Y por encima de todo . . . un cielo de un azul pálido, tenue. . . . Y de tal modo vive este pedazo de lienzo que a cada hora del día va cambiando la luz del paisaje con la luz real que entra por las ventanas; en poco más de medio metro de

tela amanece y anochece como en el mundo real. (7:244)

[My painting (a marvelous landscape of extraordinary softness and clarity) represents a green slope on the outskirts of Madrid; some reddish houses appear in the distance; among them an erect poplar. In the background, the light blue sparkle of the Guadarrama. And above it all . . . a sky of tenuous, pale blue. . . . And this bit of canvas is so alive that at each hour of the day the light of the landscape changes with the real light that enters through the windows; in little more than half a meter of canvas the sun rises and sets as it does in the real world.]

Azorín's landscape "originals" frequently are predicated on terminology and techniques borrowed from the art world; quite often they make overt allusion to the fact that the author intentionally creates a "painted" landscape, as in the following description of the Parque del Retiro in Madrid which verbally imitates the impressionistic painterly effect created by broken patches of dappled sunlight filtered through overhead foliage:

La alameda está desierta; el sol que se cuela por los resquicios de la fronda pone en el suelo fulgentes notas blancas . . . todo luz y sombra . . . todo verde en las hojas y negrura en los troncos, el vial de viejos olmos se pierde a lo lejos en una lontananza que nos recuerda el cuadro de un pintor. (3:1291)

[The promenade is deserted; the sunlight that filters through the chinks in the foliage deposits brilliant white notes on the ground . . . all light and shadow . . . all green in the leaves and blackness on the tree trunks, the path lined with old elms loses itself in a far distance that reminds us of an artist's painting].

The Castilian landscape that Azorín habitually describes as austere, noble, grand, and severe, "painting" it with the same color tones used by artists such as Beruete—"ocre, rojizo, negruzco, añil profundo, verde intenso" [ochre, red, black, deep indigo, intense green]—contrasts sharply with the other landscape in his repertoire: that of the Levantine provinces whose coloration the intense Mediterranean sun dilutes into a symphony of multi-hued gray tones. To describe the effect Azorín borrowed terminology from the art world: "I use the expression 'to tone down' (*aballar*), a technical term in painting, because nothing can express better the act of softening a spiritual landscape (just as you soften a painted landscape by toning down its colors)" (6:125). For Azorín the visual drama of Alicante was the drama of its "plethora of grays . . . in full daylight the color—due to the strong sun—absolutely disappears; everything is of an ashy vagueness" (9:1411). Unlike the Castilian landscape, admired by international tourists, the "invisible" landscape of Alicante is virtually unknown, even though its rich scale of gray tonalities, writes Azorín, was mastered neither by Goya nor by Titian (AE 74). At sundown, however, these same grays are coaxed from their hiding places by a "delicate and silent pastel artist who makes them emerge from his little box of colors," into a joyous concert of "red grays, green grays, blue grays, purple grays, violet grays. The scenery is splendid" (9:1411). The delicate colors of Alicante are further attenuated by the ethereal quality characteristic of its atmosphere, imparting to the landscape the washed-out properties of an old pastel drawing, an effect for which Azorín found concrete expression in a visual art simile: ". . . light that imparts a tone so delicate, so ethereal to colors that they resemble those of old pastel drawings that are in danger of rubbing off and that have been preserved—like the pastels of La Tour—behind a clear glass plate" (3:1244).[3]

Although Azorín obviously took great care and pleasure in creating his verbal landscapes, he wrote in 1931 that while landscape could be evoked either by words or in paint, the "personaje" who protagonizes his essay "La soledad de un pintor," prefers the painted variety.[4] Two years later, and this time without the circumlocutions of fictitious "personajes," Azorín reiterated that "es que he observado, a lo largo de la vida . . . que me impresiona más el paisaje pintado que el natural" [it's that I've observed throughout my life . . . that I'm more impressed by painted rather than by natural landscape]. In the same article Azorín mentions as his favorite painters "the beloved Turner," Corot and Théodore Rousseau.[5] Given his "bookish imagination," it is not at all surprising that Azorín would supplement firsthand observation of nature not only with actual paintings, but also with information he gathered from the many annotated books on art history, museum and exhibition catalogues, treatises on color, artist biographies, and gardening manuals in his personal library. As both his published writing and library holdings attest, Azorín had a respectable

knowledge of the history of landscape painting in Europe. While his commentary on the genre ranges from the work of Joachim Patinir (active 1480–d.1524) to Cézanne (1839–1906), and includes the Spanish landscapists who were his contemporaries, it is the French Impressionist painters whom Azorín addresses with greatest consistency in his essays and whose style he most often re-creates in his own landscape descriptions. Even more suggestive, it appears that the painters he most admired were those concerned with giving time plastic expression, and those whom art historians consider as the forerunners of the Impressionist movement. Azorín himself identified, within the course of landscape art history, evidence of his own notion of continuity and coherence. On a visit to the Louvre, as he proceeded from the landscapes of Poussin to Claude Lorrain, then from Lorrain to Corot and on to Renoir, Azorín noted that for him "the continuity of aesthetic creation affirmed itself from painting to painting" (PQ 135). Of greatest interest, however, was the evolution of Impressionism, and its parallel movement in literature, from the Barbizon School which Azorín described as "a group of painters—Corat [sic], Millet, Teodoro Rousseau, etc.,—who live and paint in the heart of Fontainebleau Forest. From this school, in turn, impressionism will evolve, the painting of Renoir, Pissarro, Monet, Degas, etc.; a school that develops alongside the realism and naturalism of the Goncourt brothers, Flaubert, Zola, etc."[6]

Within landscape history, the Dutch and Flemish painters are generally recognized as being the first to protagonize landscape in art. In his copy of Émile Michel's Nouvelles études sur l'histoire de l'art (1908), Azorín noted the author's assertion that prior to the Dutch, landscape production had been limited to playing decorative or subordinate roles to the sacred and mythological themes considered appropriate within traditional landscape decorum. "In Holland, on the other hand," Michel noted, "picturesque nature would be studied for itself alone" (187). Since the Low Countries had once formed part of the Spanish empire, Dutch and Flemish artists were well represented at the Prado Museum. For obvious reasons Azorín was quite taken with the "íntimo vulgar de los holandeses," as he wrote in an essay on Zuloaga (8:445). The painter most remote in time he studied was Patinir whose fantastic, eerie landscapes overwhelm the tiny human figures included in them. There are several important canvases by Patinir at the Prado. In one of his more obscure visual art similes, Azorín drew a literature-art parallel between the "boat that was crossing silently, hugging the coast" in Enrique Gil's novel *El señor de Bembibre* and Patinir's canvas *El paso de la Laguna Estigia* (Fig. 7). Both works of art emblematized something beyond the visible realities they represented: "Although the poet did not intend it, in that scene—resembling the paintings of Patinir— that slow ferryboat carries your soul . . . a song . . . speaks to you of life, of hope, of struggle; but another, more distinct and clear, speaks to you of the fugacity of time and things . . ." (3:1159). In "Ver y pintar," Azorín again mentions a painting by Patinir, very likely also *El paso de la Laguna Estigia*, which depicts "a ferryboat carrying a soul to Hades," and he proceeds to explain that Patinir "is one of the painters discussed by a group of writers that had always been attracted to art" (*PCQ* 238). Patinir may have appealed to the Generation of 1898 because, as recent critical studies have shown, he inaugurated a "modern" concept of landscape by diminishing the importance of the human

figure, thus freeing landscape from the shackles of medieval world views (Falkenberg 2). Although he did not have any formal training in art history, Azorín's acute sensitivity to, and profound understanding of the visual arts, led him to some surprisingly prescient conclusions. He wrote, for example, that as a genre landscape was not a modern concept. The "modern," in his view, could be identified as interpreting landscape through an artist's personality, a method of painting that he dated back to "Paul Bril, Hobbema, Ruisdael and the Spaniard Francisco Collantes, born in 1599" (7:1224).[7]

Paul Bril (1554–1626), a Flemish landscape painter who spent most of his career in Italy, was another favorite of Azorín's for whom the painter, together with Hobbema and Ruisdael, illustrates "the history of landscape genre."[8] In "El paisaje," Azorín states that in the days when he studied the history of landscape painting, "I used to know who was the first, among the primitives, to distance the horizon line; I don't recall it now" (*PQ* 214). The artist who so revolutionized the composition of painted landscape was none other than Paul Bril whom

Fig. 7   Joachim Patinir, *El Paso de la Laguna Estigia*, c. 1515–1524. Oil on wood panel, 64 × 103 cm. Museo del Prado, Madrid.

Azorín recalls by name in a passage of *El enfermo* in which the protagonist, Víctor Albert, engages in interior monologue: "Pablo Bril was the first landscapist who dared distance the horizon line. True landscape dates from Pablo Bril. Before his time landscape had been confined by a horizon line that we could touch with our hands" (6:829). Bril's contribution to the evolution of modern landscape seems to have appealed to Azorín: he returned to the subject again in the title essay of *Pintar como querer*, where he observed that in lowering and distancing the horizon line, Bril had come upon something obvious and simple, yet it was a vision no painter before had discovered: "he drops the line of the horizon. With that he creates landscape, he creates modern painting" (7). Yet Azorín was not, at least in this passage, as original as he might seem. A great deal of his writing on Bril, especially concerning the horizon line, was lifted from André Beaunier's *L'Art de regarder les tableaux* (1906). The French critic observes that until Paul Bril, landscape had been considered accessory to a painting's principal subject matter, whereas Bril aspired to carve out a niche for the genre by subordinating, or even eliminating, the human figure entirely from his canvases (179). Of equal significance, according to Beaunier, is the fact that "Paul Bril dropped the horizon line. That innovation had more consequences than one could ever imagine." According to Beaunier, this reform revolutionized composition and made possible the great landscape paintings of the seventeenth century (180).

By the mid-seventeenth century, Dutch landscape painting had turned its attention to capturing atmospheric effects in paint (Bachrach 26). The work of the Dutch painters, especially that of Jacob van Ruisdael (1628/29–1682) and his pupil, Meindert Hobbema (1638–1709), was to have significant impact on the British landscape pioneers John Constable and J. M. W. Turner who, in turn, would influence the Barbizon School and the Impressionists.[9] Ruisdael, dubbed by his modern biographer, Seymour Slive, as "Holland's greatest landscape painter" (13), was the first to express a sense of movement and impermanence on canvas, qualities that would be of obvious interest to the Impressionists. The techniques he used to depict atmospheric volatility in paint caught the imagination of the English landscapist John Constable (1776–1837), who observed the intrusion of narrative temporality into Ruisdael's portrayal of what he called "stories of the weather," something Constable thought was an attempt "to tell that which is out of the reach of art" (Paulson 1982, 110). The British painter himself would become famous for the narrative nature of his own "stories" of the sky, clouds, and weather-related atmospheric conditions. It is only natural that Constable would have been a favorite painter of Azorín's, who considered depiction of the sky essential to landscape painting, and clouds essential to any depiction of the sky (6:294). While in Azorín's pantheon of landscape painters, Paul Bril was significant for having distanced the horizon line, and Ruisdael and Hobbema for their accuracy of representation, Constable was valued for his skies and clouds which, in Azorín's opinion, many painters attempted to portray but only Constable succeeded in expressing well: "Constable distinguished himself for his skies. He has marvelous, fleecy skies. Many artists paint clouds, but few get them right" (6:294). When Azorín lived in Paris during the Spanish Civil War, he had the good fortune to see several important art exhibitions at the Louvre, among them a 1937 retrospective of English portraiture and landscape painting. Of the British painters, Azorín came away "bewitched" by the portraitist Thomas Lawrence; "full of passion" for his colleagues Romney, Reynolds, and Raeburn, and he wrote that he immediately purchased two or three books on English portrait painters. In "Iconografía" (*Memorias Inmemoriales*), he wrote that good portraiture, whether in literature or the visual arts, is an extremely difficult enterprise (8:404), and that the English painters, especially Lawrence who was once accused of not being able to draw, were masters of the genre (8:413).[10]

Portrait painting aside, referring to the Louvre exhibition, Azorín stated that he would not want to "fail to mention the skies of the landscapist Constable" (5:856). Recognized by art historians and the Impressionists themselves as a direct precursor, Constable—an avid student of landscape tradition—derived his interest in the portrayal of movement, the transient play of light, and the effect atmospheric changes had on material surfaces, from Ruisdael and Hobbema.[11] Constable was particularly impressed by Ruisdael's painting of the weather, sharing with his Dutch predecessor (as well as with Velázquez), a desire to freeze Nature and objects in motion, thereby not only transcending "change and motion in the very act of representing them" but, as Ruisdael had done before him, Constable allowed the temporal nature of narrative to intrude on his spatial medium (Heffernan 1987, 105). While the Impressionists used separate canvases to study the same landscape at different times of day or seasons of the year, Ronald Paulson points out that Constable, intent on capturing the moment of change from sun to rain or calm to storm, frequently portrayed the "before and after" effects of the weather in a single picture (1982, 111).

When Constable exhibited several paintings at the Paris Salon of 1824, his technique of using dabs of pure color, his unblended brushstroke, and his juxtaposition of tonal gradations to create depth and luminosity caused an immediate sensation (Simpson 17). One of the results was to encourage the French painters who would later constitute the Barbizon School to embark on revolutionizing landscape painting in France and to incite Delacroix to pursue his experimental use of pigment, openly challenging Ingres in his preference for color over line to model form. In Spain Aureliano de Beruete, in a necrological essay on his painter-friend Martín Rico, noted the hostility Constable met with in his own country, as well as the British landscapist's proto-impressionist techniques of depicting the play of light on objects, and his tendency to portray "the same subjects several times, according to the difference in illumination or movement of the skies" (534).[12] Ramiro de Maeztu, whose considerable and well-informed art criticism has yet to be collected and studied, established a line of continuity between the technique first used by Tintoretto and El Greco of juxtaposing tonal gradations of the same pigment to heighten color, and Constable's "re-discovery" of the same technique in his plein air painting "that so captivated Delacroix, and that Delacroix first impressed on the Barbizon painters, and then on the Impressionists" (1921, 55).

Constable abandoned history and religious painting for the exclusive study of landscape. Within that "inferior" genre, he preferred to concentrate on the depiction of transitory weather patterns that told temporal stories, as is evident in the titles he gave his paintings: *Noon Clouds Breaking Away after Rain* or *Dewentwater: Stormy Evening* (Heffernan 1987, 66–67). Constable's focus on the atmosphere

was concomitant with the development of scientific meteorology, coinciding with a rising interest in clouds in art and literature (Thornes 1979a, 499). In Spain, scientific studies of the atmosphere and its description in literature and painting began with realist writers like Pereda who incorporated observations on the mutability of clouds and atmosphere into his descriptions of nature (Litvak 1991, 44).[13] As was to be expected, the *Institución Libre de Enseñanza* was at the forefront of advances made in meteorological studies in Spain. The geologist José Macpherson, an excellent amateur photographer, invented an apparatus that recorded images more rapidly than a normal camera in order to photograph the ephemeral nature of cloud formations (Hernández Pacheco 282). The *Boletín de la Institución Libre de Enseñanza* was also active in keeping abreast of advances in the atmospheric sciences made abroad, and in 1891 closely followed the international debate on systems of cloud classification between Howard of Great Britain and the Swedish-British team of Hildebrandson and Abercromby who proposed a new, more refined version of cloud classification. In his chronicles of the debate for the *BILE*, Augusto Arcimis condemned Howard's system (which had been adopted in Spain) as "deficient," advocating instead the more specific categories proposed by Hildebrandson and Abercromby (348). Given Aureliano de Beruete's association with the *ILE*, the meteorological dispute undoubtedly was known to Spain's most prominent landscapist whose accurate portrayal of clouds and the sky in the area of Madrid was especially celebrated and often compared to those of Azorín and Baroja (Pena 1983, 20). In his 1912 review of *Castilla*, Ramón María Tenreiro observed that it was not surprising Azorín should dedicate his new book to the memory of Aureliano de Beruete since, in the work of both these "matchless landscapists," there was more than enough common ground—particularly in their ability to depict the mutable aspects of the Castilian landscape—to establish "delicate, fraternal bonds" between writer and painter (1912b, 425).

For Azorín, especially in stories such as "Las nubes" (*Castilla*) or the prologue to *Blanco en azul* (1929), the continuous weaving and unraveling of clouds in the sky become objective correlatives for his favorite thematic hobby-horses: eternity and inaccessibility; of diversity and sameness within the simultaneously mutable and changeless nature of time. In adapting Campoamor's dictum "vivir es ver pasar" (to live is to see life go by), to read "vivir es ver volver" (to live is to see things repeat themselves), Azorín chose clouds to give visual expression to the "invisible threads of human lives that cross and intersect in infinite space. The rule of chance. Chance in the clouds that go by, taking on different shapes, and chance in human lives. The sense of time disappears . . . and the clouds remain. White on blue. . . . The weaving and unraveling of human lives to a rhythm we don't recognize" (5:227).[14] From a very young age, Azorín expressed an interest in clouds. In *Memorias Inmemoriales* he wrote that while studying in Yecla, he attended classes in studio art and was especially moved by the skies of a much more talented student. From then on, "X" could never contemplate the sky without recalling those painted by his classmate: "without fail, on contemplating the sky, X would not see authentic reality, but the skies, sometimes clear with white cumulus clouds; at others, gray, painted by his classmate" (8:440). In another chapter of the memoirs, "X" recalls a favorite professor who happened to share with him an interest in clouds, and who believed that in landscape painting depicting the sky was of primary importance. In the professor's opinion, the clouds and skies of Velázquez and Constable were especially noteworthy (8:509).

In his annotated copy of Parada y Santín's *Las ciencias y la pintura* (1875), Azorín marked passages on the cloud formations that Velázquez painted in the backgrounds of his portraits: "With the exception of some Flemish backgrounds, Velázquez . . . gives us skies that are the best in the genre. The blue sky, stocked with white cirrus clouds, is the most common in the skyline of Madrid, and the one that characterizes it best . . ." (46).[15] It seems Azorín made it a point to master cloud nomenclature, for specialized terminology appears in most of his writing on the subject. Víctor Albert (*El enfermo*), spends a great deal of his time observing the sky: "he contemplates the blue vault where the snowy cumulus usually stroll. Víctor can't decide between the round cumulus clouds and the tattered cirrus. He's delighted by them all. And he winds up admiring the stratus and the nimbus clouds as well" (6:824). A pastime Azorín shared with the writer and fellow *alicantino* Gabriel Miró, was the contemplation of clouds in the sky, spending entire afternoons engaged in this diversion. Miró, wrote Azorín, seemed to prefer "cirrus clouds . . . above all when they resembled the spikes of an immense feather" (6:1020). More often than not, Azorín invoked clouds and Constable in the same breath. The British painter's skies were without equal in the history of art, and Azorín once observed that Constable, "painter of the firmament," would have found a variety of cloud-types in Spain to be able to paint to his heart's content: in the indigo-blue sky of Castile, the British landscapist would have found magnificent, burgeoning cumulus clouds, while in the diaphanous sky of Alicante, tenuous cirrus clouds predominate (9:1235). Like Constable, who embarked upon a project of "collecting" and classifying clouds, Azorín would write, "what I do is collect clouds. . . . I have a magnificent collection of cumulus, cirrus, stratus, and nimbus. . . . The clouds I am alluding to are depicted in the canvases of famous painters." He added that one of his personal favorites was Monet's *Remanso en Argenteuil* with its "marvel of clouds" that he had seen in the Louvre.[16] Having absorbed the lessons of art history, Azorín's description of clouds in "Las nubes" is a delightful skyscape, as accurate in its meteorological observations as it is aware of impressionistic color and light effects:

Hay nubes redondas, henchidas, de un blanco brillante. . . . Las hay como cendales tenues. . . . Las hay grises sobre una lejanía gris. Las hay de carmín y de oro en los ocasos. . . . Las hay como velloncitos iguales e innumerables. . . . Algunas, de color ceniza . . . dejan caer sobre la tierra una luz opaca, tamizada, gris, que presta su encanto a los paisajes otoñoles. (Fox 1991, 162)

[There are rounded, swollen clouds of a brilliant white. . . . There are thin, veiled ones. . . . There are gray ones against a gray background. Some are crimson and gold at sunset. . . . There are some that resemble countless little tufts of wool, all alike. . . . Some ash-colored ones . . . allow an opaque, filtered, gray light to fall upon the earth, lending enchantment to autumn landscapes.]

Constable's impact on the future painters of Barbizon indirectly affected the direction landscape painting would take in Spain. In 1850, on his way to study in Belgium, Carlos de Haes traveled through France where, according to Aureliano de Beruete, he undoubtedly encountered the painters who, under Constable's influence, set out to reinvent French landscape painting (1898, 379). Jaime Morera, a colleague of Beruete's who also studied with Haes, remarked that once Haes returned to Spain, the new vision and techniques he introduced caused as much furor in Madrid as Constable had when he exhibited at the French Salon of 1824 (271). Indeed, the catalogue introduction to a posthumous retrospective of Haes's work held in May 1899, supports Morera's argument, indicating that Haes was for Spanish painters what Constable had been to the English: "inspirer, not only of the modern British school of landscape painting, but also of that prodigious group of French painters named Rousseau, Troyon, Daubigny . . .".[17] Twentieth-century art historians in Spain go as far as to suggest that because he intended to record momentary landscape impressions, Haes's sketches are "instamatic snapshots" that anticipate techniques used by Impressionist painters. Joaquín de la Puente maintains that if Haes had introduced a little more light and brighter color into his oil paintings, while simultaneously reducing the breadth of his brushstroke, he would have become a true Impressionist (1898, 10). Enrique Lafuente Ferrari points out that Aureliano de Beruete inherited from Haes not only the influence of Barbizon, but that of Constable as well, although Beruete reformulated these influences into a vision that was "more spare and sober; in a word, more Spanish" (1941, 26).

While staying in London during the Franco-Prussian War, Monet and Pissarro were first able to see appreciable numbers of paintings by both Constable and Turner. The French painters were struck by the novel use of color in the canvases of both English painters, as well as by their ability to portray the transient qualities of atmosphere and light in paint, and the effects of time's passage on the perception of landscape. Like Velázquez, also acknowledged by the Impressionists as an important precursor, Constable became consumed with a "spots of time" theory, the intent of which was to "give 'to one brief moment caught from fleeting time,' a lasting and sober existence, and to render permanent many of those splendid but evanescent Exhibitions, which are ever occurring in the changes of external Nature" (Bermingham 151).[18] While Constable's preferred subject matter was the transformation of objects by the atmosphere surrounding them, his contemporary Joseph Mallord William Turner (1775–1851),

like the Dutch painters whose work served as a stylistic model for some of his own, painted the atmosphere itself.[19] Turner struck a responsive chord in Azorín. In the essay "Nada de particular" (1943), the protagonist, a painter as are so many of Azorín's fictive alter egos, observes that Turner's work, especially *The Evening Star* (1830–40), was marked by the artist's struggle to "define the undefinable: . . . to pin down a moment, a single moment" (*PCQ* 173).[20] In a series of interviews with Jorge Campos, Azorín revealed that he first saw a considerable number of paintings by Turner at the 1937 Louvre exhibition of British art which, he says, he visited several times and where he says he admired "the skies of Constable and Turner's *The Evening Star*" (162–63). The protagonist of "Nada de particular," however, writes that he had seen his first Turner some forty years before (i.e., at the turn of the century). Nevertheless, it was not until the Louvre exhibition that the narrator of "Nada de particular" mentions that he saw the (misidentified) *Evening Star* for the first time, and, he said, "ever since then Turner has invaded . . . my soul and I have not been able—nor have I wanted—to shake myself, release myself, free myself, of his influence" (*PCQ* 172).[21] So consuming does the protagonist's passion for *The Evening Star* become that he reduces his activity either to countless hours of contemplation before the painting, or to spoiling canvas after canvas in attempts to re-create in his own work a sense of the inaccessible and the ineffable that Turner conveyed so successfully in his (Pl. 19). The impossibility of doing so leads to fatigue and depression, causing the protagonist's family to urge consultation with a physician. It is to his doctor that the frustrated painter confides the true etiology of his enervated state, a condition Azorín would certainly have understood: "Doctor, I have spent hours and hours in front of that painting. And my mind has been taken over by the obsession of making concrete, like Turner, that which cannot be defined" (*PCQ* 173).

The Evening Star was an especially significant painting in Azorín's personal canon where it symbolized something akin to the indescribable, inconcrete, and unreachable. In the 1940 "Poeta sin nombre (Autobiografía)," an "anonymous" poet writes that throughout his life he had always hung an artistic masterwork above his desk: first it was Mategna's *Parnassus*, then a Santa María Egipciaca by Ribera; later Rembrandt's philosopher engrossed in thought before an open book; currently the place of honor was occupied by Turner's *The Evening Star* before which the poet reveals he spent long hours in meditation at a recent Louvre exhibition. Azorín more or less correctly describes the painting as portraying a "spacious beach with a lone human figure, and the sky which melds into the sea in the shadows of a nascent twilight. . . . And that figure, lost in the solitary vastness . . . what was it doing there? Was it waiting for something, or afraid of something? The evening star, a tiny star, was a little, scarcely discernable, white dot."[22] *The Evening Star* conjures in the "anonymous" poet visions of what twilight must be like in Spain, a reverie that leads him to consider the possibility that at the twilight of his career, spent far away from home, he may be entirely forgotten by a once-admiring public. In his view, only art that successfully evades time is immortal, and to achieve immortality the artist must discover a language that will remain valid for centuries to come: the verses of Jorge Manrique on the death of his father, being a good example.

Written during the melancholy isolation and insecurity of Azorín's Paris exile, this fictive autobiography evidently identifies *The Evening Star* as a pictorial equivalent of timelessness, as well as portraying the "poet" as lost and alone, in a state of suspended animation, on the vast beach of exile in a foreign land. This reading is confirmed in the novel *Capricho*, one of whose protagonists is an art critic who also recalls having contemplated *The Evening Star* on numerous occasions and who imagines that Turner might have included an isolated human figure in the painting "in order to make loneliness more striking and human" (6:916).[23] The consideration of time's inexorable progress, its inaccessibility and transitoriness made in passing in *Capricho*, come to the fore the following year in *La isla sin aurora*, a novel in which Azorín unexpectedly revises his notion of "vivir es ver volver" and in which Turner's *The Evening Star* is used once again as a visual image to instantiate the indefinable and the intangible. One of the protagonists is a novelist who was especially moved by one of Turner's paintings which he saw in Paris during "a show, at the Louvre, of British art" (7:75). Since that time the novelist dedicated himself to finding an identical confluence of images in nature: the same "yellowish, ineffable" light; the same

beach and vague horizon line in the distance; the same mysterious twinkle of the evening star (7:76). The novelist is rewarded for his perseverance but, rather than feeling gratified, he is disillusioned and disappointed. Although the scene he comes upon in nature is the same as the one in Turner's painting, the novelist realizes it is not identical: "The aura of art is missing. Turner, with his genius, knew how to rise above Nature." Life does, indeed, imitate art, but the truth of the matter is that the painted landscape is more beautiful and perfect than the natural one (7:76). As another protagonist in the novel concludes, "What is left unspecified (e.g., an imaginary, painted scene) is more beautiful" (7:128). The novelist realizes that although the evening star, painted by Turner in the nineteenth century, is the same one he now contemplates in the night sky, he and Turner are not the same person: unlike the star which remains impervious to the passage of time, the human being perishes, swept up in the rapidly moving currents of the universe (7:76).

The protagonists of *La isla sin aurora*—a poet, playwright, and novelist, all of them artists of the word as is their creator Azorín—conclude that the boat on which they are sailing, the "Sin Retorno," is a symbol of the world. The last words of the novel are spoken by the playwright who finally understands that one cannot recapture youth; illusion cannot be reclaimed; past enthusiasms cannot be relived. In a departure from his cherished adaptation of Nietzsche's eternal recurrence, in 1944 Azorín writes, "try as we might, those moments have already gone and cannot return . . . that boat we see, the 'Sin Retorno,' has provided us with the desired finale to the drama" (7:128). Azorín's abandoning the axiom "vivir es ver volver" is not as unexpected as it may seem. As early as the 1915 *Tomás Rueda* (*El licenciado vidriera*), the Heraclitean notion that one cannot bathe twice in the same river, begins to insinuate itself into Azorín's writing. When considering the resumption of his interrupted studies at Salamanca, Azorín's *licenciado* concedes that things do not repeat themselves exactly: Salamanca may be the same, but the house in which he lived, if it still stands, will certainly be different, as will the people of the city, not to mention the changes produced in the protagonist's own personality after having lived the bizarre experiences of the intervening years (3:312–13). By the time he wrote the essays of

Contingencia en América, most of which were composed in Paris between 1937 and 1938, Azorín, then 64 years old, postulated the relation of life to memory and reformulated his definition of what it meant to live: "Y si no cultivamos el recuerdo, ¿para qué queremos la vida? Y si no tenemos el culto de los seres queridos que nos precedieran en el viaje eterno, ¿para qué queremos vivir? Vivir es recordar" [7:1230; And if we don't cultivate remembrance, what do we want life for? And if we don't hold on to the memory of loved ones who preceded us on the eternal journey, what do we want to live for? To live is to remember]. As Inman Fox indicates, Azorín came to the conclusion that the concept of Time was a product of human consciousness and thereby ineluctably dependent on the individual will. Nothing truly remains in the past if we evoke it in memory: once remembered, the past is made present (1988, 154). But in *París* (1945), a collection of essays and remembrances of his years in the French capital, Azorín observed that in writing of the time he spent in exile, he attempted to relive past experience from the vantage point of the present, although he also admitted that should he return to the Parisian sites where some of the narrated events occurred, they could never be reproduced exactly (7:835). The solution is to bridge the gap through writing: art, therefore, is not a "game, but an evasion of reality," an exercise that actualizes the past as it enables the writer to escape the present (7:926). The *escritor* who authors *París* concludes that he prefers the past to life in a metamorphosed, alienated, post-exilic present: "Time passes, and it is not that time long-ago, but this one in the present. The writer has taken the road and would not wish to return to the reality that surrounds him" (7:928).[24]

Making our way back to J. M. W. Turner, however, in 1959 Azorín told Jorge Campos that Turner had always intrigued him as a personality (162–63). The one major piece on Turner that Azorín wrote before the Spanish Civil War—"La soledad de un pintor" (1931)—was undeniably the fruit of his having read Marcel Brion's 1929 anecdotal biography of the British landscapist.[25] Azorín was apparently quite moved, perhaps because it struck close to home, by the tale of Turner's constant artistic self-invention. He repeats the story of how, after years of struggle, Turner succeeded in winning a following and patrons, actually earning considerable sums of money, only to lose both accolades and patronage when his style evolved into something neither the public nor the critics cared to accept as "Turneresque." Turner symbolized the true artist who refused to be saddled with a style determined for him by his public, but rather renewed and transformed himself continuously, often running the risk of critical and public rejection. In Turner's case, the result was self-imposed isolation: the painter took refuge in drink and retreated to a lower middle-class suburb of London where he assumed the last name of a widow Booth with whom he had found lodging, successfully passing himself off in the neighborhood as Mr. Booth. The information Azorín includes in his review regarding the technical aspects of Turner's oeuvre is largely borrowed from the heavily annotated Brion. He bracketed discussion of the importance Turner accorded the sky and to atmospheric effects; also underlined is commentary on the sense of moving air and transparent atmospheric qualities no painter other than Turner could impart in so delicate a fashion (49–50). Accordingly, Azorín tells his Spanish readers, "No one has painted rocks like Turner; no one has painted the sky like Turner; no one has painted the sea like Turner. The sky, with its diverse tonalities, with its variety of clouds, is the great painter's speciality." He emphasized Brion's view that although Turner had no formal disciples, he was the ancestor and precursor of Impressionism (58). Azorín annotated a lengthy section of text pertinent to the painting *Rain, Steam, Speed—The Great Western Railway* (before 1844), which Brion considered anticipatory of impressionist technique. According to the French critic, at the end of his life Turner no longer painted landscape, the human figure, or architectural forms, but rather the "imponderable aspects" of the elements, of fog and water, projecting these into a fourth dimension to which he added the notion of speed, creating one of the "strangest paintings" ever realized in the history of art (45).

Azorín's review of Brion's biography actually begins as a meditation on how an unnamed artist might have come upon the extraordinary idea of painting a picture that depicts a train speeding through a typical English deluge (Pl. 20). Azorín's narrative teases the reader along with increasingly specific ekphrases until, faithful to his usual practice, both painting and painter are positively identified in the last paragraph of the review. Azorín imagines that one day a painter happened to observe the rapid passage of a train convoy scarcely discernible through a curtain of rain and the steam emanating from its locomotive. At this juncture he coyly drops the first clues to the painting's identity; clues intelligible only to readers familiar with nineteenth-century English painting: "Tres palabras se imponen al artista en este instante, condensadoras de las diversas sensaciones que está experimentando: lluvia, vapor, velocidad. En esas palabras va a encerrar todo el futuro cuadro el artista" [Three words take hold of the artist at this moment: rain, steam, speed. In those words the artist encapsulates the entire future painting]. As in the case of *The Evening Star*, this painting also becomes a metaphoric prompt leading to a meditation on life's uncertainties. The ashy gray of the picture's ambience appeals to Azorín because he intuits that from the "harmonious concert of these grays a supreme emotion will emerge." While the painting represents the mundane reality of a train enveloped by steam and speeding through a downpour, beyond its surface Azorín "sees" many other things: "Our own life, for example; our uncertain and vague destiny. . . . We see all that, and much more, whereas with the eyes, which see nothing, we go on contemplating the advancing locomotive enveloped in gray steam, beneath a gray sky from which falls a torrential rain."

By the early nineteenth century many English artists had embarked on painting campaigns to the north coast of France (Clarke 21). Eugène Delacroix (1798–1863) visited with Constable and Bonington in 1825, learning firsthand from the British painters a preference for intense color (Weil 1979). Already considered something of a maverick before Constable rocked the French art establishment in 1824, Delacroix would have a profound influence on the landscapists who later made Fontainebleau Forest their base of operations. In his exclusive use of color to model form, Delacroix challenged the academic, neoclassical style and technique of his contemporary Jean A. D. Ingres (1780–1867). Azorín made a note of this in his copy of Beadeker's *Paris et ses environs*: "Delacroix est le chef des coloristes et Ingres un fanatique de la forme, du dessin. Nôtre époque a généralement pris parti pour Delacroix" (14th ed., 1900). As is usually the case, much of what Azorín wrote about Delacroix was culled from

various books on art. Citing Benezit's *Diccionario de pintores* (Paris, 1925), he quotes the critic's opinion that while Delacroix's *Naufragio de la Medusa*, submitted to the 1819 Salon, and *Dante y Virgilio*, painted in 1822, both precipitated vociferous negative reaction, the movement to reinvigorate French art can be traced precisely to these two paintings (9:128). Azorín likewise cited an observation made by Fromentin in his travel diary, *Une année dans le Sahel*, that a black servant whom he interviewed and subsequently described in the diary, "makes a gesture to draw aside a curtain that is identical to another made by an African woman in Delacroix's *Women of Algiers*." Wanting to confirm Fromentin's homology, Azorín went to the Louvre to collate text with painting, and wrote that the experience was "unforgettable" (*PCQ* 237).[26] In the retrospective musings of *Ante Baroja*, he recalled that when he first came to Paris, by sheer accident yet quite appropriately, the Balzacian Baroja found himself renting what used to be Delacroix's studio (8:309). It was also in a former studio of Delacroix's, located near Saint Germain des Prés, one of Azorín's favorite churches, that Azorín himself was able to see the lithograph series Delacroix had made on themes from *Hamlet* (8:389).

While the Barbizon painters took courage from Delacroix's challenge to the French Academy, it was from Turner and Constable, both of whom were indebted to Ruisdael and other Dutch painters, that the young French landscapists inherited the example of the Dutch masters (Walford 189). The early work of Jean-Baptiste Camille Corot (1796–1875), father of the Barbizon School and the first painter to break with French academic tradition, owes much to both Ruisdael and Hobbema.[27] The landscapists of the Generation of 1830, as the Barbizon School is often called, were all inspired by artists from the Low Countries, frequently made copies of Dutch pictures in the Louvre, and collected Dutch painting. By the 1830s comparison between Barbizon painters and the Dutch landscapists was common currency in critical reviews.[28] The terminology "Generation of 1830" also entered the vernacular of Spanish art criticism. In *Recuerdos de mi vida*, Martín Rico, whose own work was significantly influenced by the Barbizon School, observed that the French "escuela de 1830—Decamps, Troyon, Corot, Daubigny, etc."—was indebted to Constable in particular because he was the first painter to put landscape on a modern footing (109). In his biography of Corot, Gustave Geoffroy made analogies between Corot and Constable whom he dubbed "the most determined of innovators as regards truth" because the British painter dared break with the conventions of historical and heroic painting, thus setting an example for the French landscapists to find "their way beyond roads bordered with temples, ruins, and tombs" (55).[29] Corot and those who followed in his footsteps were the first painters in France to turn their attention to the rural landscape of their nation, to sketch their motif from nature, and to render plein air effects in their oils and sketches, earning for themselves the sobriquet "precursors" of the Impressionists.[30] Corot's work has an "instantaneous quality" often compared to contemporary photography, an art form, like painting from nature, just beginning its process of evolution (Clarke 112). And like photography, the aim of painting out of doors, as Théodore Rousseau expressed it, was to capture "the virgin impression" of the subject (Rewald 95). As is evident from Rousseau's axiom, the word "impression" was bandied about by the Barbizon painters, as well as by their critics, years before Louis Leroy ostensibly coined the term in his biting *Charivari* review of the first Impressionist exhibition in 1874. Both Corot and Daubigny, who would exercise most influence on the Impressionists, were criticized for the lack of traditional finish in their work and a broader than usual color palette; Corot was singled out for the sketchiness of his technique, while Daubigny was called to task for giving only the "impression" of nature in his paintings.[31]

Corot was one of Azorín's favorite artists. He never tired of repeating the anecdote about a painting excursion made by Corot and Gustave Courbet. Legend had it that while Corot spent considerable time looking for an appropriate motif, Courbet randomly set down his equipment and began to paint, telling Corot that as long as he had Nature before him, one motif was as good as any other. The art critic of Azorín's novel *Capricho*, however, misattributes the quotation to Corot: "He had read . . . he did not know whether in reference to Corot . . . a maxim that made him doubt his memory. 'Wherever a painter might put his easel, there he will find his painting.'" (6:915). Shortly thereafter, the art critic corrects himself: "The

phrase in this chapter attributed to Corot is not Corot's, nor is it exactly as cited." After relating the care with which Corot identified an appropriate spot to paint, it was Courbet who observed, "For me, one place is the same as any other; they're all good as long as I have Nature in front of me." (6:917).[32] Most of Azorín's information about Corot appears to derive from Geffroy's 1924 biography of the French painter. He seems to have been intrigued by the story that Corot, together with the painters Boilly, Graindrant, and three architect friends, were portrayed in a humorous mural representing the six artists costumed as academicians crossing the Bridge of Arts to pay homage to the *Institut de France* that Boilly and Graindrant painted on the wall of an inn where the group liked to gather (45).[33] Anything having to do with the countryside interested Azorín, who wrote "campo" in the margin of the page where Geffroy related the story of the painted mural. He also underlined the titles of paintings Corot sent to Salon exhibitions between 1831 and 1834, all of which refer to the countryside: *Fôret de Fontainebleau*, *Vue d'Italie*, *Vue de la Fôret de Fontainebleau*, *Couvent sur les bords de l'Adriatique* (49–50). Despite painting numerous Italian scenes—no doubt motivated by visits made to that country in 1825, 1834, and 1843—Corot found his true calling in painting the French landscape. Azorín set off in brackets Geffroy's observation that Corot specialized in scenes from the outskirts of Paris, its forests, rivers, and the plains of Artois; in the same passage he also underlined commentary on Corot's "soft and gray sky of northern France" (54).[34] Azorín often compared the tenuous gray skies of Paris to those painted by Corot: "This morning's delicate, gray light—a light that makes us understand Corot—is made even softer when filtered through some thin curtains" (3:1038).

Azorín's most serious writing on Corot, however, took place in Paris during his self-imposed exile. As was true in the case of Turner, Corot's paintings became visual, tangible equivalents of Azorín's emotional state at the time. In "La aventura de Corot" (*Españoles en Paris*, 1939), Azorín wrote that whenever he fantasized about decorating the walls of an elegant Castilian mansion with paintings, he always included a landscape by Corot, although he admitted that he knew the painter's work only from books on art. Now that he was in Paris and had the Louvre at his disposal, Azorín looked forward to seeing Corot in the original. He was, however, in for a disappointment: "The impression I received—on my first visit to the Louvre—did not correspond to the inchoate one, crafted by desire. Corot was colorless. A painter without color is a false painter" (5:845–46). The deception led Azorín to remove the imaginary Corot landscape from the imaginary wall of his imaginary mansion because he did not find "the greens, the blues, the purples, the golds—the golds of dawn and the golds of evening sunsets—that I was hoping for." He simply could not understand how a painter of Nature could do without color to animate his work, and he considered replacing "his" Corot with a landscape by Haes, Beruete, Espina or, perhaps, Ruisdael (5:846–47).[35]

Although Corot won a second-class medal at the 1833 Salon for his *Forest of Fontainebleau*, a complaint was voiced by the critics that his tones were too gray and opaque: the criticism would haunt Corot for the rest of his life (Clarke 58).[36] Considering Azorín's preference for gray—the infinite gray tones of the Alicantine landscape; the grays of his favorite portrait by Vázquez Díaz—his initial rejection of Corot as "gray and colorless" merits investigation. An explanation can perhaps be found in his reading of Diderot: Azorín owned a copy of the *Essais sur la peinture* (Paris, 1795), and quoted from Diderot whenever the question of color arose in his own writing on art. In "El color" he cited the French encyclopaedist's view that color and line (i.e., draftsmanship) are one and the same. Paradoxically, this observation prompted Azorín to observe that each "color has its own scale; perhaps the most beautiful—and the most exacting—is the gray one. In sum, I believe that to paint is to draw" [pintar es dibujar] (*PCQ* 252). In the 1943 essay "Vázquez Díaz," Azorín again referred to Diderot's argument that color and line are inseparable: "el dibujo—lo dice Diderot—es el color mismo. Con el color lo ha de hacer un pintor todo" (*PCQ* 182).[37] In "Mes idées sur la couleur," it is evident that Diderot saw color as an artist's principal means of expression when he stated outright that while draftsmanship bestows form on objects, it is color that gives them life. In Diderot's view—and this was an opinion Azorín would have shared—the art world had many excellent draftsmen but very few great colorists, and he concluded that "it is the same in literature" (14:350). On reconsidering,

Azorín did not remove his imaginary Corot landscape because he decided it conveyed a sense of peace, the effect being that "any canvas by Corot calms our overwrought nerves" (5:848). Written during the early part of Azorín's exile, his essay on Corot's landscapes clearly turns to the work of art as a way of placating the confusion and sense of uprootedness of those tragic moments. As with Turner's *The Evening Star*, Azorín saw in Corot's pictures "beyond the tangible horizon . . . a suggestion of the eternal and the ineffable. And once more—a bit shamed by my imprudent decision—I rehang Corot's landscape on the bright, white wall" (5:849).

Corot was a close friend of Charles Daubigny (1817–1878), a leading member of the Barbizon group. A major influence on the Impressionist painters (as well as the Spaniards Rico and Beruete), Daubigny ruffled critical feathers with his almost exclusive dedication to plein air painting, the sense of improvisation his paintings conveyed, and his preference for an abbreviated, choppy brushstroke (Herbert 1962, 48, 56). Daubigny's work appealed to Azorín because of the painter's sensitivity to light, a concern which the Spanish author clearly shared. Azorín factored light into the "enigmas" of art, supporting his view with Daubigny's axiom that artists never employed enough of it in their work, and he cited Daubigny's opinion that light had its own language, that the duty of the painter was to make it speak, always taking care its voice never rose to the level of a shout (*PCQ* 169). Azorín's observation that Martín Rico and Beruete were influenced by Daubigny and the Barbizon School (6:294), was borne out by Aureliano de Beruete for whom the death knell of traditional landscape painting in France was rung by Constable in 1824 (Marín Valdés 94). By the time Rico traveled to Paris in hope of studying with Daubigny, the Barbizon painters had overcome long years of public resistence to their work, which at the time was selling respectably well due, in part, to the tireless efforts of their dealer Jean-Marie-Fortuné Durand-Ruel.[38]

Rural France, especially the life of her peasants, was the favorite motif of the Barbizon painter Jean-François Millet (1814–1875), whose "shaggy" finish incurred the displeasure of critics but was considered appropriate to his indecorous subject matter (Herbert 1988, 176). Millet's politically radical and populist tendencies appealed to the young Martínez Ruiz who noted in *Anarquistas literarios* that the great French painter thought art should not be considered the exclusive domain of a select few, but rather must nourish all humankind, "consecrating itself to the people, to uplifting the masses." When someone voiced the objection that the essence of art was inaccessible to those unequipped to appreciate it, Azorín reports that Millet simply shrugged his shoulders. One of Millet's favorite paintings, according to Azorín, was a canvas in which he portrayed the entry of Ruth and Boaz into a farmhouse during the farmhands' midday meal (1:183–84). Another Millet painting came to Azorín's attention when he commented on González Blanco's introduction to an anthology of Spanish poetry in which Blanco referred to his "honrosa misión de espigar en las trojes opimas de la lírica castellana" [honorable mission of gleaning in the fruitful granary of Castilian poetry]. As he took issue with Blanco's incorrect metaphor of gleaning "in" a granary, Azorín recalled "the famous painting—one of the famous paintings (e.g., *The Gleaners*)—by Juan Francisco Millet" (7:768). More than thirty years later, in a retrospective criticism he leveled at J.-K. Huysmans's acerbic condemnation of the Eiffel Tower and his censure of "Francisco Millet, painter of the gleaners," Azorín used both painting and Tower to give the abstract notions of human physical labor in time and space a visual analogy: "The Eiffel Tower is effort in space, and Millet . . . condenses in a few laborers, the idea of effort in time, everyday effort, at all hours, at all moments" (7:859–60). That Azorín was aware his frequent references to paintings and painters, particularly in the construction of visual art similes, might be interpreted as pretentious, is evident in an observation he made in *Memorias Inmemoriales*, the core of which, paradoxically, is a visual art simile whose relatum refers to the Barbizon painter Constant Troyon (1810–1865): "The Retiro is a beautiful park; in it there are ancient trees, like those in landscapes by Troyon. I haven't cited Troyon, a distinguished French landscapist in vain as they say; you'll see why later" (8:502–6).

Although not formally considered a member of the Barbizon School, because of proximity in age and genre preferences, Gustave Courbet has always been associated with the artists of Barbizon (Herbert 1962, 41). His objective realism contrasted sharply with the more subjective vi-

sion of the others, and his socialist political convictions went far beyond those Millet expressed on canvas. Courbet, a disciple of Proudhon, was active in the Paris Commune. Accused of playing a part in the destruction of the Vendôme Column, when the Commune capitulated to government forces Courbet was jailed and died in exile in Switzerland. Although Azorín recognized Delacroix as a great painter who infused his canvases with beautiful color, he wrote that Courbet had eclipsed Delacroix. He perceptively called attention to the fact that, while Courbet was considered a subversive revolutionary, there was nothing at all revolutionary in his purely classical technique. Referring to Courbet's *Enterrement à Ornans*, Azorín observed that while his "working methods did not differ from those of the great masters we see in the museums," it was the painter's choice of subject matter that the public found scandalous (8:302). Building on this brief excursion through nineteenth-century art history, Azorín remarked that people no longer remembered either Delacroix's "phantasmagorias" or Courbet's realism, and, in an unmistakable allusion to his favorite period in art history, he quoted Cézanne, fictionalized by Zola as Claude Lantier in the novel *L'Oeuvre*: what we need now, Lantier insists, is something that is neither Delacroix nor Courbet, but a completely new approach to painting, "and that painting is bright painting, in the open air, in full sun, without the vestiges of any school or traces of clouds" (*PCQ* 201; cf. *PQ* 119–20).

By 1859 the work of the Barbizon painters had begun to circulate on the European art market (Bouret 209), and their vision, once considered unacceptable, became "naturalized" by tradition. Public approval of the Barbizon artists was quickened by the emergence of Impressionism in the early 1870s which suddenly made the Barbizon landscape appear conventionally tame (Tucker 1995, 207). In the question of color versus line spawned by Delacroix's rebellion against classical tradition, the Impressionists fell into line behind the Romantic painter whose work confirmed their incipient theories on the juxtaposition of complementary color. Like their Barbizon forefathers, they were influenced by Turner and Constable, who were poorly represented in the Louvre, but whose work Monet and Pissarro had discovered while living in London during the Franco-Prussian War and the Commune.[39] They were particularly struck by the whiteness of Turner's snow and ice which they discovered was obtained not by a uniform application of white pigment, but by a "mass of different colours placed side by side and giving the desired effect when viewed from a distance" (Lindsay 160–61). In a letter Pissarro wrote in 1902 to Wynford Dewhurst, an English art critic who had studied painting in Paris in the 1890s and developed a friendship with both Monet and Pissarro, the French painter reminisced that "the watercolors and paintings of Turner and of Constable . . . have certainly had influence upon us. We admired Gainsborough, Lawrence, Reynolds, etc., but we were struck chiefly by the landscape painters, who shared more our aim with regard to plein air, light, and fugitive effects" (Rewald 258). In Turner's work especially the Impressionists found validation of their own concerns with depicting in paint the transient effects light had upon objects and the landscape.

Of all the Impressionists, Monet demonstrated the greatest interest in finding painterly solutions to the question of temporality. He attempted to resolve the problem in his series paintings where he presented the transformative effect light exercised on everything from wheatstacks to the Rouen Cathedral at different times of the day and different seasons of the year. It was during his work on the wheatstack group (1890), that Monet realized light and atmosphere changed with such rapidity that he required not two canvases (one for morning; the other for afternoon), but an entire series in order to capture what he called the "instantaneity" of nature's continuous metamorphoses. He moved from one canvas to the next as the visual effect changed "so as to get a true impression of a certain aspect . . . and not a composite picture" (Rewald 561–62). In their goal of capturing momentary effects, the Impressionists were also influenced by the nascent art of photography (Meyers 114); Impressionist painting is often described as a kind of "snapshot," an attempt to freeze the fleeting impression by isolating it from the temporal continuum. William Berg points out that the Impressionist "instant" embodies temporality in two different ways: at the same time that it emblematizes temporal sequentiality, the impressionist painting eternalizes the moment by immobilizing its dynamic and contingent qualities (193 n. 64).[40]

It is not surprising that Impressionism would have appealed to the sensibilites of the Genera-

tion of 1898. The openly heterodox nature of this peculiar manner of seeing the world, the personal Bohemianism of the painters, and their intent, at least in the early years, to portray modern life in art, was addressed in the Spanish periodical press during the Generation's formative years.[41] Taking Impressionism's aesthetic revolution as a model for their own, the Generation of 1898 set out to reform nineteenth-century Spanish literary style by transforming the abbreviated impressionist brushstroke into brief rhetorical periods; employing a succint literary syntax characterized by short clauses punctuated by commas; emphasizing the landscape in their written work; utilizing words loaded with color values; and adapting artistic techniques borrowed from the Impressionist painters to create vivid visual effects. They likewise abandoned realistic character development for "impressionistic" glimpses into personality traits and, like the French painters, in the first years of their activity as authors of fiction, the writers of '98 often portrayed scenes of modern life. In old age Pío Baroja reminisced that of all the Generation's writers, Azorín was the principal stylist who invented for himself and for Spanish literature— much like the Impressionists had in painting—a new literary tradition, "bringing clarity and concision to the language."[42] Aside from Azorín's adaptation of Impressionism's formal procedures to literary stylistics, Impressionism's concern with time appealed to him on thematic, aesthetic, and personal grounds. He found the popular debate regarding the relative merits of photography versus the visual arts addressed in a statement made by Auguste Rodin in *L'Art; entretiens, réunis par Paul Gsell*. In his copy of the interviews (2d ed., 1919), Azorín underscored passages in which Rodin stated that photography is a mendacious art because time could never really be stopped cold. Perhaps referring to the early Cubism of Braque and Picasso, Rodin observed that because the painter is capable of reproducing "l'impression d'un geste qui s'exécute en plusieurs instants," his work is much less conventional than a scientifically produced visual image in which time is abruptly suspended (92).

For Azorín, in much the same way that Castile was emblematized by the Burgos landscapes of Marceliano Santa María, Paris was emblematized by the sculpture of Auguste Rodin (1840–1917). Writing that he visited the

Rodin museum on many occasions, he noted that his favorite piece of sculpture was "la cabeza del hombre desnarigado" (i.e., *The Man with a Broken Nose*). In that sculpture Rodin distilled the spirit of both ancient and modern France which Azorín thought was characterized by deeply intense thought. It is not for nothing, he remarks, that Rodin is remembered as the creator of *The Thinker* (8:449–50). In addition to the collection of Rodin interviews, Azorín also read and annotated Rainer Maria Rilke's biography of the sculptor, *Auguste Rodin* (1st ed., 1903). He seems to have been especially taken by Rilke's observation of the open-ended, "unfinished" style characteristic of Rodin's work—statues with only parts of arms or noses—comparable to Impressionist paintings which often showed trees, clothing, or other objects brought to the very edge of a canvas that, when framed, gave the appearance of being arbitrarily truncated (53–54). Of greatest interest to Azorín, however, was Rilke's opinion that in the faces of Rodin's human subjects, the sculptor attempted to freeze a moment of eternity: "For him, to execute a portrait was to seek in a given face that bit of eternity through which he could partake of the great course of things eternal" (89). It is not surprising that Azorín would have identified with an artist who, like himself, attempted to experience a moment of eternity vicariously through his work.

The ineluctable, irreversible nature of time fascinated and horrified Azorín from a very young age. He remembers the "incessant hammering" of the grandfather clock in his boyhood home, especially unnerving as it ticked away the hours until he was packed off to the hated *colegio* at Yecla, or as the inevitable departure for the equally tiresome university drew near (8:427). Azorín could not have expressed his personal obsession more cogently than he did in the *Memorias* where he wrote that "it is the idea of time that enslaves me and forms the core of my spiritual personality" (8:543).[43] In rather deterministic fashion, Azorín attributed this preoccupation with time and fatality to his Alicantine ancestry, traceable to the Phoenicians who colonized the region and who shared "a sense of time with the Hellenes. The sense of time in Heraclitus," that he described as a "sharp, painful sensation of time" (5:369). Impressionist art and its attempts to paint the fugacity of time were defined in Heraclitean terms by André Beaunier in *L'Art de regarder*

les tableaux, a copy of which Azorín owned and annotated: "the Impressionists belong to the school of venerable Heraclitus who invented the philosophy of becoming and who summarized his views of reality with these melancholy words: 'everything slips away.' And he used to say that you cannot bathe twice in the same river because the river flows on, and even its banks are transformed . . ." (217). According to Beaunier, the painters Jongkind, Renoir, Monet, Pissarro, and Cézanne were the most eminent masters who subscribed to this philosophy and manner of artistic praxis.[44]

Azorín thought the French Impressionists to be "truly marvelous." Being the good art historian that he was, he always took care to point out that the term "impressionism" was merely one of convenience: "I say Impressionists for the sake of convenience, in order to embrace with an identical name, painters as inherently different as a Renoir and a Degas" (7:243). During his exile in Paris, a landscape by Sisley led Azorín to recall the landscapists of Spain and then to contrast the fine light of Paris with the intensity of Spanish light, and to compare the poplars along the Seine to those of the Castilian *meseta* (6:685). Azorín, however, was to suffer the same kind of deception vis-à-vis some of the Impressionists as he did with Corot. He observed that Manet's *Olympia*, "so controversial in its day," left him completely cold: on leaving the Louvre that day, he writes that he bought a colored postcard of Mategna's *Parnaso* with which to console himself (5:857). That Azorín kept up with the fortunes of the Barbizon and Impressionist painters is evident in his 1914 essay "Las sorpresas de la pintura" where he noted that during Corot's lifetime his paintings often sold for no more than 200–300 francs, and that in 1877 Degas was forced to trade paintings for oil paints. But he also observed that by 1912 a Degas painting had sold for 435,000 francs, and at recent sales landscapes by Corot had been going for 26,000 to 162,000 francs (*PCQ* 120).[45] Azorín was quite fond of Degas and in "El cuarto de costura" (*Valencia*) he used an unspecified Degas painting of laundresses not only to circumscribe his own, literary scene of women ironing, but to build a self-reflexive construct in which the verbal art (his story) duplicates a work of visual art (Degas's painting), that itself duplicates the feminine activity of washing and ironing clothes portrayed in the fictional room where the historically real, but verbally evoked, Degas painting is displayed: "Finally, the ironing and sewing room that has drawn the novelist like a magnet. Dresses on hangers and dresses on the chairs and a sofa. On the wall some marvelous women ironing by Edgar Degas. The painting is indicative of the discriminating spirit and sensibility of Elena Víu" (6:134). Writing about Degas in 1913 (*Clásicos y modernos*), Azorín called the painter "marvelous, incomparable," and related the unfortunate incident in which Pierre [sic] Wolff, art critic of *Le Figaro* and vitriolic opponent of the Impressionists, reviewed Degas's one-man show in 1876: "Le Pelletier [sic] street has suffered a misfortune. After the Opera burned down, a new calamity has befallen the neighborhood. Durand-Ruel has just mounted a show of so-called paintings" (2:792).[46]

In the art world, the name Durand-Ruel was synonymous with avant-garde painting. While the gallery founder, Jean-Marie-Fortuné championed the Barbizon painters and was largely responsible for the high value their work brought especially on the American market, his son Paul (1831–1922) was to play a similar role of agent, maecenas, and confidante to the Impressionists (Rewald 254, 271–72). His gallery became the principal archival repository of documents, letters, contracts, and photographs relating to the Impressionist movement. During the late 1930s when Azorín lived in Paris and frequented the gallery, it was still considered the foremost establishment dealing in Impressionist art. In an article published shortly after his return to Spain, Azorín stated that he returned with his eyes "full" of Monet, Sisley, Pissarro, and Renoir because he spent three years living near the Durand-Ruel gallery, "and whenever I went by—and I did so daily—I always stopped at the display window." In the last few months of his stay, Azorín was particularly taken by a Renoir landscape that depicted a "a lonely village street with a background of green fields" displayed in the gallery window.[47] In his eponymous memoir of life in Paris, Azorín not only commented on the historical significance of the Durand-Ruel gallery, but he also provided a more detailed description of the Renoir painting that made such an indelible impression upon him:

A poco trecho de la plaza de la Estrella . . . se encuentra la tienda de un mercader de cuadros, que en su tiempo valorizó el impresionismo: Durand-Ruel. En el escaparate hay siempre tres cuadros . . . de algún pintor impresionista. Durante dos meses he estado viendo una vista de los bulevares pintado por Sisley; y la entrada a una aldea por Renoir. En este último cuadro gustaba yo del verde de la pradería que se ve a lo lejos, entre las dos filas de casas, y de lo blanco de las viviendas. Y sugería la pintura, sin figuras, según costumbre de los impresionistas, un profundo silencio . . ." (7:980).[48]

[Not far from the Place d'Étoile . . . is the gallery of a dealer who in his day, held the Impressionists in high regard: Durand-Ruel. In the display window there are always three pictures . . . by some Impressionist painter. For two months I have been looking at a view of the boulevards painted by Sisley and the entrance to a village by Renoir. In this latter painting I found the green of the meadow seen in the background, between two rows of houses, and the whiteness of these dwellings, very pleasing. The painting, without human figures as is the Impressionists' custom, insinuated a profound silence].

The short fiction Azorín produced during and after his stay in Paris often includes protagonists involved with the gallerist Durand-Ruel. Like Azorín, the painter Gaspar Salgado (*Sintiendo a España*), lives near the gallery and makes a weekly pilgrimage there, his new work neatly rolled, hoping to make a sale at Durand-Ruel's (6:703). Lorenzo Lodares (*PQ*) divides his time between visits to the Louvre and Number 37, Avenue Friedland, address of the Durand-Ruel gallery. He frequently stands before the display window, mesmerized by the paintings of Renoir, Pissarro, Monet, and Sisley, "the Impressionist masters. And Impressionism, the painting of light, is what inspires Lorenzo Lodares": of all the paintings displayed, Sisley's view of the Place de la Madeleine on a foggy day is the one Lodares prefers (204–5).

Among the Impressionists, it was Monet who best expressed the passage of time in paint, devoting the second half of his career (beginning with the 1890 wheatstacks) to working in series. This new method of representing the landscape does not study motif as much as it constitutes experiments with the apprehension of time in paint. Late in life, Monet recalled that the idea for series paintings occurred to him nearly fifteen years before he began the views of Rouen Cathedral in 1892. He remembered that as he was painting a church at Vernon it occurred to him that it might be interesting "to study a single motif at different hours of the day and to note the effects of light that from one hour to the next modified so noticeably the appearance and the color of the building" (Tucker 1990, 84).[49] Azorín was familiar with some of the series paintings, having referred to them in his 1913 defense of El Greco against charges of "extravagant" vision, contending that El Greco's paintings were no more anomalous than Monet's latest production of waterlilies from the garden at his Giverny estate, or his earlier preference for cathedrals (PCQ 74). Azorín also frequently adapted the techniques of his beloved Impressionists to the verbal medium, a recourse, as we shall see in the following chapter, that entered his stylistic repertoire before the turn of the century, and remained a favorite technique that he used throughout his career to create vivid painterly images of changing light and color in the landscape.

5

Landscape into Prose: Essays on Impressionism; *La Voluntad, María Fontán*

In Chapter XIV of *La Voluntad* (1902), Yuste, mentor to the fictional Azorín and spokesman for many ideas held dear by José Martínez Ruiz, states emphatically that what proves an artist's true mettle is his ability to interpret the landscape. "In my opinion," he concludes, "landscape is the highest degree of literary art" (Fox 1968, 130).[1] Although Martínez Ruiz, of all the '98 writers, was the only one able to appreciate post-Impressionist landscape to a limited degree (e.g., Van Gogh, Gauguin, Cézanne), when he transposed landscape into prose, it is, without fail, mediated by an Impressionist vision.[2] Impressionism in the visual arts came late to Spain, and when it did, it was rejected by the art establishment as vituperatively as it had been in France some twenty-five years earlier. Given the reform-minded, antibourgeois attitude adopted by the '98 writers in their youth, it is not surprising they would be eager to incorporate impressionist stylistics learned from the French painters, as well as from the brothers Goncourt and Flaubert, to their own writing against the grain. In his memoir of Bohemian life and the literary *tertulia* in turn-of-the-century Madrid, Martínez Ruiz recalled this period of time as one in which feeling for the sake of feeling in literature was rampant, and color for the sake of color considered the ultimate accomplishment (6:287–88).

The present chapter considers Azorín's use of impressionist subjects, themes, and techniques in both fiction and the essay, and ranges in time from *Bohemia*, a collection of short stories published in 1897 to *María Fontán*, one of two novels Azorín published in 1944. With the exception of *La Voluntad*, I will study this body of work chronologically, postponing the 1902 novel for last, principally because Azorín included in its pages commentary on works of art and aesthetic theories in addition to those he drew from Impressionism, thereby establishing a paradigm for analyzing the role of visual art in works of fiction to be discussed in subsequent chapters.

In *El impresionismo en el lenguaje*, Charles Bally and Elise Richter observe that if anything can be defined as specifically "impressionist," it is the conscious representation of the emotions that things stir in the individual temperament and not the things themselves (1956, 108). More recently William Berg pointed out that painterly Impressionism is equivalent to metonymical structures in literature whereby much greater importance is attributed to an effect rather than to its cause.[3] Nature and objects thus become sources of pure sensation, "reproduced by the technique of small dots and strokes which instead of insisting on details—retained the general impression in all its richness of color and life" (Rewald 284). Insofar as an effect became more important than its cause, the subjective impression given more weight than material objectivity, and color rather than line preferable for the modeling of form, objects began to lose their well-delineated contours to assume more fluid properties expressed by juxtaposed spots and dabs of surface color. Color attributes of objects were themselves destabilized as they were now dependent on changes in the intensity and inclination of the sun's rays, the composition of the surrounding atmosphere, and reflections from the color spectrum or shadows thrown by adjacent bodies (Bally 111, 114 n. 1).

The short story "Paisajes" (Bohemia) initiates an impressionist vision of the landscape, and the adaptation of impressionist techniques to formal literary stylistics, that would continue to manifest themselves in Azorín's work for approximately the next forty years. The title of the story immediately connotes a visual art genre. Its protagonist is a writer who intends to produce a book of pure landscape scenes, and he intersperses the planned outline of his work with terms that carry inherent associations with the visual arts in general, and Impressionism in particular. The book, confesses its author, will be a subjective summa of his love affair with Nature. It, like Azorín's story, also will be titled Paisajes and, similar to the Impressionist modus operandi, it is projected as a "series of vignettes without human figures, of spots of color, of impressions . . . before a snippet of Nature, sensations of mother earth" (1:313). All the key formulas are present: dabs of color; impressions of emotional sensations induced by the spectacle of nature; absence of the human figure; a series of paintings. Furthermore, the author, like a good Impressionist painter, intends his landscape visions to be resplendent with vibrant light effects resembling "an album of watercolors." The projected chapter titles also recall those given by Impressionist painters to memorialize the effects the time of day or seasons of the year had upon landscape at the moment any given painting was executed: "Horas de siesta"; "Amanecer de estío"; "Tarde de invierno"; "Vendaval de otoño" (1:314).

In "Una visita," published in ABC, 1 July 1906, Azorín includes a description of the effects color and light reflections have upon childrens' clothing that demonstrates his awareness of the Impressionists' radical view that individual colors affect the tone of their neighbors: ". . . from the leaves of the acacias and plane trees fell a soft glow that bathed the white clothes of the children in a green halo" (EL 247–51).[4] Three years later, in the essay "Las montañas" (ABC, 7 September 1909), Azorín showed that he was also aware of the Impressionist discovery that light reflections existed everywhere in nature, even in supposedly colorless shadow. Having thoroughly assimilated the lessons of Impressionism, Azorín begins his étude of mountains by observing that changes in the angle of light alter the "physiognomy" of the ravines, peaks, rises, hillocks, and slopes which assume a completely different configuration as the play of light evolves from the first rays of dawn to midday sun, and then moves on toward afternoon. Similarly, "the shadows, in the mountains, have their special coloration; there are, as the Impressionist painters have seen, blue shadows, yellow shadows, violet shadows."

In a review of Lecturas españolas, published in the same year as Castilla, Ramón María Tenreiro lays out his essay in terms of an evocative visual art metaphor. Azorín's style, he writes, in no way resembles Dutch and Flemish masters in whose paintings every object is clearly outlined, "Cada [cosa] en su individualidad inquebrantable"; rather, Azorín presents objects enveloped by their own atmosphere as do Impressionist painters (1912a, 371). Although most critics, including Azorín's contemporaries, judge "La catedral" (Castilla) to be the most outstanding example of his literary impressionism, there are more beautiful and extended examples of impressionist technique in other essays, notably those of the Peñón de Ifach at Calpe in El paisaje de España, visto por los españoles (1917). As if to put his reader in the proper frame of mind, before he begins his splendid evocation of the atmospheric conditions that generate the shifting color harmonies surrounding the Peñón at sunset, Azorín first mentions Henri Fantin-Latour (1836–1904), a sometime impressionist-symbolist painter known for his portrayal of flowers and still life, before embarking on his description of the Peñón:

Desde lejos, al ir camino de Calpe, vemos erguirse el extraño y bello peñón de Ifach. Avanza en el mar una lengua de tierra; al final se levanta una especie de torre cuadrada o pilastra gigantesca. Tarea ardua el describir la coloración suave, en estas horas de la tarde declinante, del peñón de Ifach. Está teñido de un rosa tenue, que a la vez es violeta desleído; acaso en el violeta y el rosa se mezcla un poco de oro. Y . . . a estos tres colores se añade un tantico de morado. La coloración, sobre el azul del mar, va cambiando imperceptiblemente de minuto en minuto. La enorme masa cuadrada, en que antes predominaba el rosa . . . ahora parece teñida de violeta; minutos después, el violeta habrá desaparecido para dar predominio al oro . . . que enciende todo el horizonte y refulge sobre el azul del mar, que ahora es de añil intenso, oscuro. (3:1244)[5]

[From far away, on the road to Calpe, we can see the strange and beautiful peñón de Ifach rising in the distance. A tongue of land extends out into the sea; at its tip rises a kind of square tower or gigantic pilaster. It's an arduous task to describe the soft coloration of the *peñón* during the last hours of the afternoon. It's tinted with a tenuous rose color that at the same time appears to be a diluted violet; perhaps in that violet and rose a bit of gold is mixed in. And . . . to these three colors is added a little purple. The color, against the blue of the sea, keeps changing imperceptibly minute by minute. The enormous, square mass, in which rose predominated . . . now appears tinted with violet; minutes later, the violet gives way to a gold . . . that sets the horizon on fire and shimmers against the blue of the sea, now an intense, dark blue indigo].

Azorín's impressionist vision continues in the supposedly surrealist *Libro de Levante (Superrealismo*, 1929). Two evocations, one of the Levantine landscape, the other of the Castillo de Sax, are remarkably similar to Camille Mauclair's account of the Rouen Cathedral as interpreted by Monet on an overcast day, "scarcely discernible in the fog" (78). Aware of the degree to which atmospheric effects change human perception of color, Azorín "paints" the castle changing tonality as the day progresses: "The castle—four smooth walls—that are yellow, ochre, violet, purple, grey, according to variations in the color of the sky and the transparency of the air. And the castle that, with the slightest bit of moisture in the air, vanishes against the gray of the distant hills" (5:403).[6] As did the Impressionist painters, Azorín re-creates here the blurred qualities in which con-

tours and lines are imprecise and vague, and the atmosphere enveloping material objects contributes to the illusion of their melting into surrounding light and air.

Azorín's *Memorias Inmemoriales* includes a chapter titled "La Toledana" (8:552–55). The epigraph reveals that this was his "primera idea de mi novela *María Fontán*" (8:552). Like the novel's protagonist, Edit Maqueda—the heroine of Azorín's short story—disappears from Spain for an unspecified period of time. When she resurfaces in Madrid, like María Fontán, Edit returns enamored of the Impressionist painters and she decorates her new home on the calle Velázquez with paintings by Renoir, Sisley, Pissarro, and Monet (8:555). The novel Azorín would eventually publish in 1944 as *María Fontán (Novela Rosa)* is replete with artist characters, paintings, conversations about museums, color, lost paintings by Manet, and the collection of art work.

The orphaned daughter of Sephardic parents from Toledo, Edit Maqueda is sent abroad by her wealthy uncle-guardian to London and Paris where she is to acquire polish and, as her uncle specifies, to reinvent a new identity for herself as "María Fontán," a cultured woman of the world. After an unspecified period of time abroad, Edit-María acquires not only a new name and image identity, but also her uncle's estate, as well as the attentions of the elderly and very wealthy French duke, Lucien de Launoy. The two meet quite by accident in the Luxembourg Gardens where, in a few days, the Duke extends a curious invitation to María. Lonely and tired, he feels that having a lively, beautiful young woman living under the roof of his empty palace would be of great comfort to him. With no strings attached other than dining together twice a week, Lucien de Launoy suggests María come live in his mansion on the aristocratic rue de Monçeau.[7] María accepts the offer, and although she and the Duke see each other only at Sunday and Thursday dinner, the arrangement satisfies the aesthete in Lucien who finds personal fulfillment in sharing these short periods of time with an "obra de arte viviente" as he calls María, the most recent addition to his collection of precious *objets d'art* (7:531). Lucien de Launoy's fetishization of María as a work of art corresponds to the masculine voyeurism which typically sustains a patriarchal symbolic order. The artificial, objectified existence María willingly allows to be superimposed upon her earthy Toledan roots, undoubtedly decontextualizes her from the everyday world of contingency and causality with which ordinary human beings have to cope on a daily basis.[8] María, nevertheless, also displays another, more individual side of her personality that is difficult to reconcile with the young woman who accedes to the controlling fiats of the Duke's companionship. Even before she met Lucien de Launoy, in provocative departures from traditional Spanish gender norms, María would occasionally disguise herself as a naive shop girl from the provinces and in the company of her friends Denis Pravier and his fiancée Odette—authentic provincials whom she "adopts" precisely because they serve as her links to the real world—she engages in masquerades designed to test simultaneously the character of society jewelers, maîtres d'hôtel, and couturiers while undermining the myth of the proletarian as ignorant of exchange value and exploitation, by pretending to sell a spectacular diamond she'd "found in the street" to high-society dealers in luxury goods.

From time to time Denis and Odette join María and Lucien for dinner where the conversation usually revolves around art and artists. On one such occasion the four discuss the merits of the Parc Monçeau versus the Luxembourg Gardens. According to María, the Parc Monçeau, so near to the home she shares with Lucien, is a more aristocratic park: at the crossroads of four streets named after four great painters, the park has a certain "ambience of cultural gentility" that María feels is punctuated by its great masses of forested area; thicker and more solid than those of the Luxembourg Gardens, they remind her of the "masas de Corot o de Claudio Lorena" (7:532). Near the rue de Marcadet María also recently discovered a lovely square in which she found a bust of the Second Empire sculptor Jean-Baptiste Carpeaux; Denis observes that there is a street in the vicinity named after the sculptor (7:533). The passage stands out for two reasons: mention of Corot and Claude allows Azorín not only an allusion to two of his favorite landscape painters, but in assuming reader familiarity with the styles, whether Barbizon or Neoclassical, in which Corot and Claude painted their woodlands, Azorín is able to short-circuit unnecessarily lengthy verbal description by permitting the painters to make a visual evocation in his stead. Carpeaux (1827–1875), a fashion-

able sculptor famous for the scandalous dancing nymphs he executed for the new Paris Opera in 1869, was another favorite of Azorín's. In his essay "Los 'squares' de París," he again mentions the small plaza to which María had referred, and writes that Carpeaux was "one of my favorite sculptors; before or after, I really can't say, Auguste Rodin" (8:476).

Shortly after this dinner conversation takes place, Lucien appoints Denis Pravier his personal librarian. As Denis takes up his post in the ducal palace, María is nowhere to be found. Upon her return she appears tanned, as if she had been at a seaside resort. She confesses that she traveled to Brittany to persuade Odette's mother to come live in Paris, and reports that she was almost successful until something unexpected altered the mother's decision. Asked to explain, María produces a landscape in the Impressionist manner:

¡Qué bonito es lo blanco en lo verde, bajo un gris celeste! Pues esas manchas blancas que yo contemplaba entre los brezos de Bretaña, sobre el césped, entre el herbazal, era lo que impedía la venida de la buena anciana a París. Lo hubiera abandonado todo: su pradito, sus vacas, sus viejos muebles con los que ha convivido cincuenta años. No podía, sin embargo, abandonar sus ocas. (7:534)

[How pretty the white is against the green, beneath a gray sky! Well, those white daubs that I contemplated among the heather in Brittany, on the loam, in the pasture, was what kept the venerable old lady from coming to Paris. She would have given it all up: her meadow, her cows, the old furniture with which she had shared her life for fifty years. She could not, however, abandon her geese].

As the Impressionist painters had intended, the scattering of white daubs (*manchas blancas*) among the grass and heather María observes at a distance in the landscape, are reconstituted by her eyes into the geese that Odette's mother pastures on the green meadow of her farm.

María also has a sensitive eye for color. On a shopping expedition to a Paris fabric emporium, she remarks that her favorite colors are the faded pigments a painter from her native Toledo had told her were masterfully employed by "otro pintor toledano o de adoptiva tierra toledana" (7:528). Examining bolts of silk, María comes upon a dusty yellow that reminds her of a very special hue with which she has been obsessed ever since coming across the color in a *Manual del colorista* that Denis had given her. The yellow she looks for is called *jaune de Naples*: "it's barely yellow; it's a yellow that seems to be a vague memory of yellowness. What a pretty suit it would make! Other yellows are not as delicate as this one: mineral yellow, gold, saffron" (7:529). The color manual to which María refers exists in its original French edition in Azorín's personal library (A. M. Perrot, *Manuel de coloriste*; Paris, 1834). In the book there is, indeed, a yellow Perrot calls *jaune de Naples*, described as "a lovely straw yellow," the preparation of which the author explains in great detail since it is extremely difficult to produce commercially (xij–xiij). It is not at all surprising, then, that of all the colors in the spectrum, María Fontán would prefer an exquisite yellow hue quite difficult to mass-produce.[9]

Azorín substantially annotated the *Manuel de coloriste*, focussing specifically on the preparation of colors Perrot called *jasmine* (136) and *grenade* (140); on the back book flap, as was his custom, he made a personal index of colors he referred to as "claveles" (133); "azul cobalto" (39–40); "vermellón" (35) and "blanco" (27). He may have used the same color manual as a reference source for some detailed and technical passages on color composition in *La isla sin aurora* where Azorín's fictive novelist engages in a review of the myriad green tones he finds in an old book of color samples: "he had at his disposal the following greens: cobalt green, Prussian green, ash green, bile green. Because he'd seen the names of all these greens in an old book of color samples, he was not sure if the names would still be the same. . . . It was all a question of coming to an agreement with some painter" (7:37).

María's life as the Duc de Launoy's live-in work of art does not last long: the aged Duke falls gravely ill, and after a hastily arranged bedside marriage designed to facilitate inheritance legalities, María acquires yet another identity as the "duquesa viuda de Launoy." Because there is an ellipsis between the death of Lucien and the first dinner party María gives as a widowed duchess, we do not know how much time transpired between the two events. What we do know is that in a complete reversal of the role she had accepted and played for the benefit of her husband, now free of sublimated psychological trammels, upon inheriting his estate María

steps into the Duke's empty shoes, as it were, and herself becomes an important collector of art. In the process she also acquires what Carole-Anne Tyler calls "the phallus" that, unlike the penis, is not gender specific, but does have a frequent metaphoric or metonymic association with all the signs of power and privilege recognized by Western culture (207). María chooses the occasion of her dinner party to unveil her recent purchase of an unknown painting by Édouard Manet. Her instructions to the butler and maître d'hôtel are that the meal be exquisite, the palace be filled with yellow roses, and the Manet canvas be mounted in a new frame. One of her dinner guests is the painter Anastasio Arlegui, a great connoisseur of Manet, whom María plans to surprise with her recent acquisition. At the dinner itself, she leads the conversation around to Impressionist painting and to Arlegui's portrait of Verlaine which, she believes, captures the French poet very much in an impressionistic manner, "con toda su época en un instante de su vida" (7:543). Intending to corner Arlegui, María finally asks whether he is familiar with the entire Manet oeuvre. Arlegui responds positively, adding that the paintings he has not seen firsthand, he knows from photographs. María then reveals that after dinner she will show Arlegui a Manet he surely has never seen before, a "Manet with a Spanish subject, worthy of hanging beside the *Dead Toreador*" (7:544).

This is not the first time Azorín cited Manet's *Le Torero mort* (Fig. 8). In his prologue to Pedro Rocamora's *España*, he pointed out that the greatest influences upon an author are sometimes exercised by foreign writers with whom there exists an instinctive rapprochement despite the foreigner's stereotypical vision of Spain. To illustrate his argument, Azorín refers to Manet's *Torero Muerto* and Alfred de Musset's "escaleras azules" which the French poet situated in Madrid, a city he had never visited (9:1316–17). Evidently Azorín knew Manet's *Le Torero mort*, since María tells Arlegui her acquisition is worthy of being hung beside it. The painting, now at the National Gallery of Art in Washington, D.C., once formed part of a much larger canvas titled *Episode d'un combat de taureaux* that Manet exhibited in 1864. Because the painting was negatively received, Manet decided to cut the picture into pieces, retaining only the sections he found most satisfactory: the canvas in the

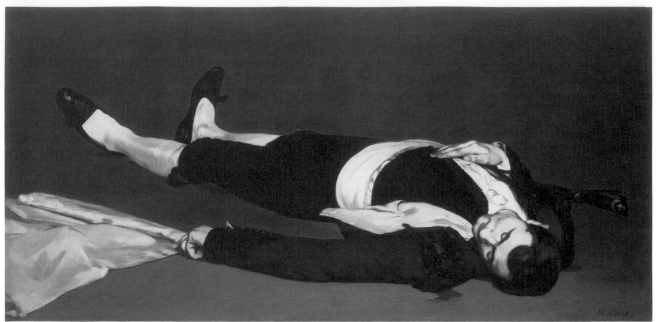

Fig. 8   Édouard Manet, *The Dead Toreador*, c. 1864. Oil on canvas, .759 × 1.533 m. The National Gallery of Art, Washington, D.C. The Widener Collection. By permission of the Board of Trustees, National Gallery of Art, Washington, D.C.

National Gallery and another titled *Episode in a Bullfight*, now at the Frick Collection in New York City. Undoubtedly Azorín was aware of the original painting's vicissitudes since, in his copy of Louis Hourticq's *Manet*, there is a piece of paper marking the page where Hourticq observes that the painting known as *Le Torero mort* had at one time been part of a larger canvas depicting a bull and the entourage of assistants which traditionally accompanies a bullfighter. Hourticq, however, states incorrectly that of the original picture the only known piece to have survived is the fragment titled *Le Torero mort*. Evidently basing himself on Hourticq's conclusions, Azorín seems to insinuate that María Fontán's unknown Manet is one of the missing pieces from the dismembered *Episode d'un combat de taureaux*.[10]

In a footnote, Angel Cruz Rueda, editor of Azorín's *Obras Completas*, reveals that Azorín modeled Arlegui on the painter Ignacio Zuloaga whom he came to know rather well during his exile in Paris where the Spanish artist made his home (7:542 n. 1). We also know that before the war Azorín did not care much for Zuloaga's work. In the lively debate the painter's realist style and Spanish themes generated among Spaniards, Azorín often sided with Zuloaga's critics who believed that he portrayed an excessively stereotypical *España negra*. During the

three years he spent in Paris, however, Azorín developed a close friendship with the painter, and he later wrote that he was able to appreciate the authenticity of Zuloaga's vision only after spending time away from his beloved country:

> Zuloaga ha creado un mundo poético. Ese mundo está formado con materiales de España. No se puede ver lo que es la España de Zuloaga . . . sino cuando se ha vivido algunos años fuera de España. No la he visto yo, que he pintado pueblos españoles . . . hasta después de haber vivido tres años en París. Tres años sin visión material, sin imaginativa, de la realidad española. Al volver a España, me dio en rostro, de pronto, la verdad de la pintura de Zuloaga. (8:433)

> [Zuloaga has created a poetic world. That world is made up of Spanish themes. You cannot see what Zuloaga's Spain is . . . until you've lived some years outside of Spain. I, who have painted Spanish villages, did not see it . . . until after I spent three years living in Paris. Three years without a material, imaginative vision of Spanish reality. On returning to Spain, the truth of Zuloaga's painting suddenly hit me in the face].

The evolution of Azorín's personal response to Zuloaga is, perhaps, encoded in the somewhat cryptic remark María directs to Arlegui, observing that while she has been able to unravel the secrets of other painters, she cannot decipher the enigma of her guest's manner because the key to appreciating his work "is the secret of Spain, of our Spain. And nobody knows that secret. Spain is multiple and profound" (7:544).

Zuloaga did not care for Velázquez, one of Manet's favorite sources, but he did admire Manet whose "Spanish" paintings were inspired by those of the great master.[11] Like Zuloaga and Azorín himself, Manet created a "poetic" vision of Spain and things Spanish; both painters' flat execution, smooth surfaces, somber palettes, and sense of enervation flickering in the faces of their human subjects, are rather comparable. In an article he wrote shortly after Zuloaga died in late 1945, Azorín observed that his thoughts invariably turned to the Spanish artist whenever he saw Manet's painting of the Spanish dancer *Lola de Valence* (1862) in the Louvre, and he attributed the association to the fact that Zuloaga's realism was undoubtedly derived from the same formula as Manet's.[12]

Possibly because the subject matter of her newly acquired painting stirs childhood memories, María Fontán decides to reacquaint herself with her Spanish roots. Returning to Madrid, she lodges at the Hotel Ritz just a short walk from the Prado Museum where she spends a great deal of time. At the museum she makes the acquaintance of Roberto Cisneros, a talented but impoverished *copista*, who specializes in the still lifes of a certain Menéndez.[13] Shortly thereafter, in yet another reversal of the traditionally prescribed gender role she had allowed a patriarchal culture to impose upon her, María becomes the benefactress of Roberto and his family. Her metamorphosis from a commodity "purchased" by the Duc de Launoy to a full-fledged commodities dealer in her own right, is completely realized in the novel's penultimate chapter, titled "Tenía que ser así," which recounts her inevitable marriage to Roberto. The wedding festivities include a tour of the Prado Museum arranged by Arlegui who shows off the Spanish masters to Guillermo Fabre, María's Parisian maître d'hôtel (7:563). In the meantime, María and Roberto board ship in Barcelona and sail for the Bosphorus, where they set up house in an old mansion with an abandoned garden whose stairway of worn stone leads down to the sea. María—a living work of art formerly belonging to the personal art collection of Lucien de Launoy; of late, friend to artists and herself a collector of art;

more recently benefactress and wife of an *artiste manqué*—brings her life to a closed, perfect circle as she exchanges her status of acquiescent object whose destiny was determined first by her uncle, and then by her husband, for that of a self-determining subject in full control of her own life. For Roberto, however, marriage does not signify any change at all in ontological status; rather, he exchanges one form of financial dependence for another, thereby prolonging *his* objectification, represented first by the role he was obliged to play as a copyist rather than a creator of original paintings, and second by the contract of marriage he incurs with María Fontán.

In appropriating Roberto, María not only duplicates Lucien de Launoy's proprietary role, but also adds a penis to "the phallus" she already possesses. And, again like the Duke, in ostensibly "freeing" her new husband's family from penury and Roberto from the drudgery of duplicating an "other's" pictures in the Prado, María ironically perpetuates the fetishism of which she herself had been a victim; a fetishism that characterizes the imaginary relations between different races, social classes, or genders "in which the signs of difference also signify phallic lack or wholeness" (Tyler 207). Furthermore, in returning to Constantinople, María repossesses her Sephardic origins by settling in what had been one of the most important centers of the Jewish exodus from Spain in 1492, a part of the world that also belonged to the same Byzantine milieu into which El Greco—the Toledan, or adopted Toledan painter who utilized María's favorite, muddy color palette—was born, and where he lived before leaving his native Crete to study art in Italy, and finally settling permanently in the Semitic and Arabic climate characteristic of late sixteenth-century Toledo.

As Inman Fox points out, one of the techniques Azorín used most frequently to throw his characters into relief, or to provide them with concrete frames of reference, was to describe their tastes in literature and the visual arts (1968, 41–42). Because the visual art paradigm in *La Voluntad* is expressed in such a variety of ways, it may be helpful to discuss this novel in terms of parameters established by Marianna Torgovnick for the study of visual arts and pictorialism in fiction. Torgovnick suggests a "continuum," or scale of values, along which she arranges categories assigned to an author's usage of visual art forms. She allots least importance to *decorative* uses of the arts where descriptive passages are recognizably influenced by an art-historical movement, a specific work of art, or the mention of an artist's name (14). Decorative usage includes the circumscription of allusion or metaphor by a visual art form, or instances in which characters happen to be artists whose vocation is only incidental to the novel as a whole. The same holds true when the art object is used as a mere prop in the overall scheme of a novel, having no significant impact, other than a purely decorative one, on its form and content (17, 72, 84). The next segment on Torgovnick's continuum is the *biographically* motivated usage of visual art which directs attention to the author's personal taste in, and experience of the arts, often placing him or her within a specific art-historical tradition (18). As the use of art work extends beyond an author's life and personal tastes into sociohistorical theory and artistic methodology, the continuum advances to *ideological* uses of the visual arts. This segment incorporates into artistic description, artist figures, pictorial metaphor or art objects, references to the author's political, historical or social views, the aims of which frequently are didactic or may lead to a "derivation of a theory of fiction from theories in the visual arts" (19). Frequently isolatable units within a novel, which may at first seem decorative, acquire ideological connotations they did not have in their original, visual art sources (20). Ideological usage of the visual arts may also direct a reader's attention to the central metaphors and thematic concerns of a novel (156). The last portion of Torgovnick's continuum focuses on *interpretive* usage which she subdivides into a *perceptual* or *psychological* sector, and a *hermeneutic* sector. The former refers to the manner in which characters experience art objects or pictorial scenes in ways that stimulate their minds in conscious or unconscious ways (22). Perceptual use of visual arts involves a character's "piecing together" of data that have the visual arts as a point of reference, or when characters register key novelistic moments as "pictures" in the visual imagination that subsequently yield vital knowledge or insight, leading to a verbal articulation of visual memory or a previously unconscious meditation on an art object (184, 191, 199). *Hermeneutic* use of the visual arts refers to the ways in which the arts or pictorial scenes motivate interpretive processes in readers' minds (23). Pictorialism and perceptual uses of the arts in the case of fictional characters, and hermeneutic ones in the case of readers, provide crucial interpretive clues to a novel's methods and meanings (213).

As Antonio Risco (1908, 34) and Inman Fox (1968, 46) have both observed, *La Voluntad* is one of the first examples of literary Impressionism in Spain and in Azorín's own writing. As long as Azorín limits his use of impressionistic technique to an evocation of the purely sensual effects of light and color in the landscape, such descriptions straddle the decorative-biographical segment of Torgovnick's continuum. As Azorín himself wrote in "Sobre pintura," a work of art is not merely a copy of nature; rather, it must be a harmonious ensemble based upon *a priori* observation of one's subject, the study of color nuances, and an awareness of the play of light and shadow (*PCQ* 26). He noted in *Memorias Inmemoriales* that atmospheric effects in painting and literature were always of special importance to him: "air has occupied, and continues to occupy, my interest; the air of life, and the air in painting and literature" (8:373). The opening paragraphs of *La Voluntad* suggest the visual arts through key words like *pintoresco, pincelada, tintas,* and by evoking a specifically Impressionist style through the use of color adjectives that are constantly modified due to changes in the atmosphere that surrounds them. The description, like an Impressionist painting, is infused with light that dissolves pigment into patches and dabs of color:

> El cielo comienza a clarear indeciso. La niebla se extiende en larga pincelada blanca sobre el campo. . . . En lo hondo, el poblado se esfuma al pie del cerro en mancha incierta. Dos, cuatro, seis blancos vellones que brotan de la negrura, crecen, se ensanchan, se desparraman en cendales tenues. . . .
>
> Poco a poco la lechosa claror del horizonte se tiñe en verde pálido. El abigarrado montón de casas va de la oscuridad saliendo lentamente. . . .
>
> La ciudad despierta. Las desiguales líneas de las fachadas fronterizas a Oriente, resaltan al sol en vívida blancura. . . . El cielo se extiende en tersa bóveda de joyante seda azul. Radiante, limpio, preciso aparece el pueblo en la falda del monte. Aquí y allá, en el mar gris de los tejados uniformes, emergen las notas rojas, amarillas, azules,

de pintorescas fachadas. En primer término destacan los dorados muros de la iglesia vieja. . . .
(61–62)

[The sky begins to brighten timidly. The mist extends in a long, white brushstroke over the fields.
. . . In the distance, the town dissolves in an indistinct blotch at the foot of the hill. Two, four, six
white tufts emerge from the darkness, grow, get
wider, and scatter in tenuous veils. . . .

Little by little the milky brightness of the horizon is tinted a pale green. The odd assortment of
houses emerges slowly from the darkness. . . .

The city awakens. The uneven lines of the facades facing East stand out in vivid whiteness
against the sun. . . . The sky stretches out in a
smooth vault of glossy blue silk. The town appears radiant and clear against the foothill of the
mountain. Here and there, in the gray sea of uniform rooftops, emerge the red, yellow, blue notes
of picturesque facades. The golden walls of the old
church stand out in the foreground . . .]

William Berg argues that metonomy, which
transposes meaning from literal to figurative
expression on the basis of causal relationships,
is the master trope of Impressionism. He further suggests that the principal motivators of
metonymical structure in Impressionist painting and literature are effects of light, color, and
movement which receive almost sui generis
treatment from Impressionist novelists and
painters for whom effect supersedes cause in
importance.[14] This is patently clear in Martínez
Ruiz's description of a sunrise over Yecla where
temporal effects appear to be much more significant than the increasing intensity of the sun
without which these effects would hardly exist.
Martínez Ruiz also takes great care in his verbal paintings to emphasize perspectival relationships. He achieves this effect not only by
using sharply contrasting colors placed in close
proximity to one another, but his choice of
verbs often demands ocular adjustments on a
reader's eidetic screen. The following landscape
is replete with verbs that connote the effect
light may have on the human eye; the contrast
of pale color against dark; of foreground against
background; and a line of trees that cuts
through the picture to create dimensional relationships among objects. I would also call attention to the way Martínez Ruiz incorporates
into this landscape a staccato-like arrangement
of adverbs and adjectives that appears to imitate
an Impressionist painter's application of pigment to canvas in broken spots of color:

En frente, sobre una colina verde, destacan edifi-
cios rojizos que marcan su silueta en el azul blan-
quecino del horizonte, y un enrejado de claros
árboles raya el cielo con su ramaje seco. A la de-
recha, aparecen los grandes cortados y socaves
amarillentos de los tejares, y acá y allá, los man-
chones rojos de las pilas de ladrillos; más lejos,
cerrando el panorama, la inmensa mole del Guadarrama, con las cúspides blancas de nieve, con
aristas y resaltos de azul negruzco. . . . Dos, tres
blancas humaredas se disuelven en la lejanía
suavemente (199).

[In front, against a green hill, reddish buildings
stand out, silhouetted against the blue-white horizon, and a latticework of thin trees crosses the sky
with their dry mass of branches. To the right appear the large, yellowish cuts and hollows of tiled
roofs, and here and there, the red stains of brick
buttresses; further away, enclosing the view, the
immense bulk of the Guadarrama, its peaks white
with snow, its angles and ridges of blackish-blue.
. . . Two, three white puffs of smoke dissolve
softly in the distance].

That verbs denoting optical reaction are just
as vital to color adjectives in the re-creation of
impressionist technique in literature is evident
in the following sunset. The adjectives of this
passage are especially notable since their evolving color intensity, generated by temporal
changes, compels them to assume the grammatical function of verbs: as they change in hue
these adjectives appear to evoke the psychody-
namics of vision inherent in shifts of ocular perception. The effect created with words is
comparable to sensations an observer might experience when viewing color metamorphoses
produced by changes in the atmosphere and
angle of light studied by Monet in his series
paintings. Equally suggestive are the dual adjective structures, composed of a color adjective
paired with a verbal-ocular adjective, that complement each other's function in the same way
an Impressionist painter might juxtapose complementary colors:

En la lejanía del horizonte el cielo *se enciende*
gradualmente en *imperceptible* púrpura, en *inten-
sos* carmines, en *deslumbradora* escarlata, que *inflama* la llanura en vivo *incendio* y *sonrosa* en lo
hondo, por encima de las espaciadas pinceladas
negras de una alameda joven, la silueta de la cor-
dillera de Salinas. . . . (121, emphasis added)

[In the distance, at the horizon line, the sky gradually *ignites* in *imperceptible* purple, *intense* car-
mine, *blinding* scarlet that *inflames* the plain in

vivid *conflagration*, and in the background, above the staggered, black brushstrokes of a line of young poplars, it *warms* the Salinas mountains into a rosy pink].

Although Impressionism in painting was not easily assimilated either by Spanish artists or the public, the '98 authors eagerly incorporated impressionist stylistics to their own writing. Martínez Ruiz was an avid reader of both the Goncourt brothers and Flaubert, and through his mouthpiece Yuste in *La Voluntad*, he proclaimed not only his admiration for the impressionist novel, but also used the opportunity to expound on what he considered to be a long overdue reform of Spanish literary tradition. On the occasions where Azorín links impressionist technique to textual production in the form of grammatical and syntactic structures, or to a derivation of a theory of literary stylistics, such as Yuste's musings in chapter 14 on the theory of the novel and his articulation of related socio-historical views, we move toward the ideological segment of Torgovnick's continuum. The first salvo Yuste fires in his "lesson on literary technique" (130) is aimed at the realist novel of Blasco Ibáñez whose landscapes, universally admired by others, he criticizes for being overly dependent on simile which, he says, is a fraudulent trope because it evades the challenge of direct, verbal evocation of nature. This is a rather odd opprobrium since Martínez Ruiz himself adopted the simile as his favorite trope, although he used it on a much more sophisticated level of comparison since his similes nearly always derive from the plastic arts, and thus involve reader visualization in the comparative process. Furthermore, as a sample of exemplary style, Yuste proceeds to cite a passage from Pío Baroja's *La casa de Aizgorri* that includes three uses of nonvisual simile (132). In chapter 15 of *La Voluntad* (137), Martínez Ruiz himself commits a similar transgression, utilizing four nonvisual examples of the very trope he condemns.

Reading a page from Blasco's *Entre naranjos*, Yuste notes the absence of plasticity, sound, movement, and color in the passage. He tells Azorín that an author must learn to handle these elements well in order to convey with maximum economy "small, suggestive details" to produce a total sensation of the scene described (131). Azorín chimes in with the observation that even more artificial than landscape description, the contemporary Spanish novel offends in the way it manages dialogue. As did Unamuno, "Yuste" prefers authors who duplicate uncensored human speech, "con incoherencias, con pausas, con párrafos breves, incorrectos . . . naturales" in their novels.[15] Anticipating twentieth-century narratological theory, Yuste blasts the realist novel of the nineteenth for attempting to make *fabula* and *sujet* coincide chronologically. As he remarks, real life does not unfold in logical, coherent fashion: "Esta misma coherencia y corrección anti-artísticas . . . se encuentran en la fábula toda. . . . Ante todo, no debe haber fábula . . . la vida no tiene fábula: es diversa, multiforme, ondulante, contradictoria" [133; This same anti-artistic coherence and correctness . . . are found in the entire plot. . . . Above all, there must not be a plot . . . life doesn't have a plot: it's diverse, has many forms; it is undulating and contradictory]. By privileging *sujet* (discours) over *fabula* (histoire), Yuste theorizes the Modern novel in which "synchronic relations *within* the text [take] precedence over diachronic referentiality" (Frank 1945, 207), thereby putting the responsibility of reconstructing *sujet* across the gaps in diachrony squarely upon a reader's shoulders as in a modern, "readerly" text. In Yuste's view, the Goncourt brothers came closest to the *desideratum*: rather than spelling out a character's comings and goings from morning to night, as was customary in the "novela del antiguo régimen," the brothers Goncourt suggested character via "fragmentos, sensaciones separadas" (134) in the same way that Impressionist painters, rather than rely on draftsmanship to achieve mimetic effect, depended upon a spectator's eye to recompose their juxtaposed dabs of complementary color into coherent pictures.

Pío Baroja wrote that Martínez Ruiz was a master stylist who created, almost ex nihilo, a new literary tradition for Spain. That Martínez Ruiz practiced what he preached, and that Baroja was not exaggerating, is apparent in a passage from *Memorias Inmemoriales*. Azorín recalls that his alter ego "Spoke just as he wrote: in short clauses. A dear friend, Melchor Fernández Almagro, said, in this regard, that I 'buried the *clausulón*'; that is, the long rhetorical period" (8:393). In "Estilo modernista," Baroja noted that because '98 writers rejected enervated, nineteenth-century literary rhetoric, they were generally censured for their use of neologisms, Gallicized syntax, and preference for "párrafos cortos, más que cortos, cortados" (8:846–47). The fragmented style Yuste praises in the impressionist novels of the Goncourt brothers is evident throughout *La Voluntad* in the form of narrative ellipses, uncomplicated syntax, sketchy character development, the introduction of protagonists in medias res, as well as the neologisms and short rhetorical periods to which Baroja had referred.[16] Martínez Ruiz himself recognized that when he first came to Madrid to seek his fortune as a journalist, his unusual style clashed with the bombast and flourish to which the public had been accustomed: "La entonación altisonante contrasta infelizmente con mi prosa menuda, detallista, hecha con pinceladas breves" [6:194; The high-flown arrogance of expression contrasts unhappily with my unremarkable, detailed prose rendered in abbreviated brushstrokes]. The comma became Martínez Ruiz's "pincelada breve," utilized not only to create a sense of movement in his writing, but also to deconstruct the flow and smooth facture of sentences rather similar to the comma-like brushstroke the Impressionists adopted not only to record visual impressions and the glimmer of light on objects with maximum speed, but also to defamiliarize the manner in which the human eye had traditionally apprehended reality.

The short, asyndetic clause so emblematic of Martínez Ruiz's literary style, created a rapid, jabbing rhythm that impressed itself on the senses rather than the intellect, recalling yet again the broken brushstroke characteristic of Impressionist painting technique.[17] A description of the Rastro in *La Voluntad* is a fine example of the manner in which Martínez Ruiz was able to create a frenetic dance of color, sound, light, and movement to produce the literary "sensación total" called for by Yuste; paratactic adjectival or noun combinations arranged in tripartite groupings reinforce the scene's lively visual nature, creating a rhythmically charged syntax which ineluctably sweeps the sentences onward in rapid flow:

> Resaltan las telas, rojas, azules, verdes, amarillas, de los tenderetes; brillan los vasos, tazas, jarrones, copas, floreros; llena la calle rumor de gritos, toses, rastreo de pies. Y los pregones saltan repentinos, largos, plañideros . . . revoltijo multiforme de caras barbadas y caras femininas, de capas negras, toquillas rojas, pañuelos verdes; flujo y reflujo de gentes que tropiezan, de vendedores que gritan, de carros que pasan. . . . Y un mozo cruza entre la multitud con un enorme espejo que lanza vivísimos destellos (231).[18]

[The fabric of red, blue, green, yellow awnings stands out; the glasses, cups, jugs, goblets, vases glimmer; the noise of shouts, coughs, shuffling of feet fills the street. And the vendors' cries suddenly leap out, long, plaintive . . . the many-formed jumble of bearded faces and womens' faces, black cloaks, red shawls, green kerchiefs, the ebb and flow of people stumbling into each other, vendors who shout, carts that pass by. . . . And a young man, with an enormous mirror that throws off vivid flashes, crosses through the midst of the crowd].

When inherited aesthetics and the techniques used to articulate them no longer express adequately a changed vision of the world, new techniques and aesthetics must be created. The Impressionists' novel manner of seeing the world was very much informed by the post-Kantian doctrine of *phénomenisme*, topical during the second half of the nineteenth century. Not to be confused with Husserlian phenomenology, *phénomenisme* maintained that only phenomena—the objects of actual sense experience—exist, and not the noumena behind them as postulated by Kant. This doctrine proposed that properly refined sensibilities could experience reality through appearances because nothing but appearances genuinely existed. The Impressionist painters never expressed their aims in precisely these terms, yet their goal of painting only what they saw amounted to a similar claim.[19] Although Martínez Ruiz himself contextualized the parable Yuste tells of two men who debate the question of noumena and phenomena within the parameters of Kantian philosophy, given that he was such an avid student of Impressionist painting, the parable assumes much richer dimensions when Impressionist aesthetic theories are also taken into account. The discussion between the two men centers on the proposal that reality is unknowable (101). One of them pushes the discussion further, arguing that "nadie conoce el noumenos." Indeed, agrees his companion, "yo no conozco el noumenos." Only phenomena are real, suggests the other. Again, the second man concurs, and both conclude that "Sólo vivimos por los fenómenos." As they go their separate ways, "convinced that they did not know the noumenos and that only phenomena were real," the reader discovers that one of them is a Kantian philosopher; the other a dealer in carnival booths (102). Since reality is determined by outward appearances only, evidently Martínez Ruiz put the ability of all human beings to apprehend it on an equal footing.

Contemporary art historians (e.g., Tucker and T. J. Clark) have shown that, contrary to the objectivity claimed by Impressionist painters, their vision was as selective as it was subjective, and rather than painting only what they saw, the Impressionists frequently adjusted or "corrected" reality to suit the aesthetic contingencies of any given painting, or series of paintings, on which they were working. Thus, while they pretended to record sensorial effects generated by external surroundings, working "impressionistically" from the outside in, the procedure was often reversed since it involved the projection of subjective intuition onto the outside world, a process we recognize immediately as tinged with expressionistic overtones.[20] Martínez Ruiz's emphasis on the subjective aspects of human experience inevitably raises the issue of Schopenhauer's world as a representation of individually willed images. As did the Impressionist painters whose images of reality were, in many cases, filtered through subjective, interior screens, Yuste convinces Azorín that "La sensación crea la conciencia; la conciencia crea el mundo. No hay más realidad que la imagen, ni más vida que la conciencia. No importa—con tal de que sea intensa—que la realidad interna no acople con la externa. El error y la verdad son indiferentes. La imagen lo es todo" [74; Sensation creates consciousness; consciousness creates the world. There is no reality other than the image, nor life other than consciousness. It does not matter—as long as it's intense—that internal reality does not jibe with the external. Right and wrong are immaterial. The image is everything]. Whether Kantian philosopher, American industrialist, empresario of carnival stalls, or a simple nun (137–38), all people are capable of constructing valid external realities through the projection of personal images drawn from the realm of the individual will or imagination. Thus Schopenhauerian reality as a product of willed images (representations), as were certain aspects of Impressionist paintings, can be said to skirt the borders of expressionism.

In the last chapter of the first section of *La Voluntad*, Martínez Ruiz presents an interesting conflation of Schopenhauerian philosophy with impressionist theory and technique that demonstrates my point. The same paragraph likewise illustrates what Torgovnick would call the hermeneutic sector of her continuum in which visual art forms stimulate interpretive processes in readers' minds. Alone in his room at night, accompanied by the flickering light of a sputtering candle that produces optical effects of motile color and shadow in the impressionist manner, Azorín broods on the Schopenhauerian intimations made earlier in the day by Yuste:

> Y piensa en las palabras del maestro: "¿Qué importa que la realidad interna no ensamble con la externa?" . . . La luz titila en ondulosos tembloteos. . . . Los amarillentos resplandores fluyen, refluyen en las blancas paredes. La roja mancha del fondo desaparece, aparece, desaparece. . . . "La imagen lo es todo," medita. "La realidad es mi conciencia". . . . La llama de la lamparilla se encoge formando en torno del encendido pábilo un diminuto nimbo de violeta. . . . La luz chisporrotea: una chispa . . . salta y se divide crujiendo en diminutas chispas de oro. . . . La luz se apaga: en la obscuridad los purpúreos grumos de la pavesa reflejan sobre la dorada lamparilla. . . . (194)

> [And he ponders the master's words: "What does it matter if internal reality doesn't mesh with the external?" . . . The light twinkles in undulating shivers. . . . The yellowish glare ebbs and flows on the white walls. The red stain in the depths disappears, appears, disappears. . . . "The image is everything," he meditates. "Reality is my consciousness". . . . The flame of the lamp shrinks forming a small, violet halo around the burning wick. The light sputters: a spark leaps out and splits, crackling in small, gold sparkles. . . . The light goes out: in the darkness, purplish lumps of burnt candlewick reflect against the gilt lamp. . .]

Given the influence of Schopenhauer on the Generation of 1898, the philosopher's voice refracted in that of Yuste–Azorín is undeniable. Yet I would suggest that beneath every articulation of the adage "la imagen lo es todo. . . . La realidad no importa; lo que importa es nuestro ensueño" [209; the image is everything. . . . Reality is unimportant; what matters is our fantasy], the word *imagen* can certainly be read as "appearance" or "impression-sensation," the only reality of any consequence that also mattered to the Impressionist painter.[21]

In addition to its association with *phénoménisme*, Impressionism was likewise the child of scientific theories advanced during the last third of the nineteenth century, proving yet again that this art movement was the expression of a novel consciousness. As we know, Modernism—of which Impressionist art is an early example—was obsessed with Time.[22] César Graña argued that impressionist technique was clearly influenced by quantum theory that postulated a "world in which *moments* can exist as total units of experience" (83). Wylie Sypher maintained that Impressionism was the artistic expression of the "science that was atomizing the world into an imponderable substance, pulverizing things into molecules that resemble the vibrant *foule des touches* in Seurat" (171). By the time Martínez Ruiz composed *La Voluntad*, scientific theory had generated a physical universe that was terrifyingly unstable and in a constant state of decomposition and recombination. Azorín's meditation on Nietzsche's eternal return in *La Voluntad* might be considered another example of the manner in which Martínez Ruiz conflates aesthetic, scientific, and philosophical notions common in the European Zeitgeist. The theories advanced by nineteenth-century physics, which postulated the fleeting, unstable nature of matter and informed the Impressionists' interest in freezing an instant of time in paint, perhaps also contextualize Azorín's subjective interpretation of the eternal recurrence. Early in the novel, Yuste reminds Azorín that nothing in the universe is permanent; that eternity itself, always a virtual present, should not be thought of as diachronic in nature (72). Against the backdrop of a ticking clock, Yuste expounds on the instability of matter: "La sucesión vertiginosa de los fenómenos no acaba. Los átomos en eterno movimiento crean y destruyen formas nuevas. A través del tiempo infinito, en las infinitas combinaciones del átomo incansable, acaso hayamos estado otra vez frente a frente en esta estancia . . . conversando, como ahora conversamos, en una tarde de invierno. . ." [73; The dizzying succession of phenomena never ends. The atoms in eternal movement create and destroy new forms. Through infinite time, in the infinite combinations of the untiring atom, perhaps we have been face to face in this room before, chatting as we are chatting now, on some winter afternoon . . .]. By his own admission, Azorín became as obsessed as Yuste with the concept of the infinite possibility of atomic recombination (221), and he

manages to link this idea overtly to Nietzsche later in the novel. Musing on the eternal dance of death reminds him that Nietzsche's eternal recurrence is nothing more than infinite human repetition based on the uniformly consistent recombination of atoms, implying that at some point in time, the combinations might well repeat themselves: "Entonces se dará el caso—como ya el maestro Yuste sospechaba—de que este mismo mundo en que vivimos ahora . . . vuelva a surgir de nuevo, y con él todos los seres, idénticos, que al presente lo habitan" [220; Then it will come to pass—just as Yuste already suspected—that this same universe in which we now live . . . might repeat itself all over again, and with it, all the identical beings that inhabit it now].

Beyond the impact Impressionist art and artistic theory had on aesthetics and literary stylistics in *La Voluntad*, Martínez Ruiz employed an impressively wide range of secular and religious works of art in his novel. While secular art forms span all the sectors of Torgovnick's continuum, religious art, for obvious reasons, is limited to its ideological and hermeneutic portions. In the second part of the novel Azorín declares, "yo soy un determinista convencido" (218).[23] As we have seen, Martínez Ruiz's determinism, to which he clung well into the 1940s, usually expressed itself as the belief that human beings are shaped by the environment into which they are born and, for him, environment meant nothing other than geography and landscape. While the Spanish are represented stereotypically as a happy, sunny people, the truth of the matter, states the fictional character Azorín, is that the desolate, parched landscape of Castile, violent in its contrasts of color and light, produces a rigidly unidimensional, gloomy national character responsible for the equally harsh and austere qualities that inform its literature and art. The inhospitable, asperous geography of Toledo, for example, is reflected in El Greco's "distorted and anguished characters." The works of art and literature Azorín adduces to illustrate his argument locate these passages somewhere between the ideological and hermeneutic sectors of Torgovnick's continuum since they are exponential of both the author's historical and social views, at the same time that they provide the reader with interpretive clues to decode the novel's form and content. Visual artist that he was, Martínez Ruiz even expressed his determinist views in terms of visual art analogies: because Castilian art was not animated by a broad and gentle humanism, in the hands of the sculptor Alonso Cano (1601–1667), the affable, ingenuous Saint Francis of Assisi is transformed into a "squalid, horrible" ascetic (211). The violently exaggerated and distorted characters of Quevedo's *Buscón* also are a clear revelation of the Castilian racial temperament, "hipertrofiado por la decadencia." For Azorín there is an undeniable bond between the literature of Quevedo, the painting of Zurbarán, and the sculpture of Alonso Cano: "between those pages, those canvases, those statues, and the rough terrain and endless, barren plains of the Castilian landscape, the affinity is logical and perfect" (213).

In his disquisition on the ephemeral nature of an artist's success or failure with contemporary critics, Yuste points out that the primitive Flemish painters—van Eyck, Memling, van der Weyden—did not bother to sign their work, a clear indication they had no worry concerning reception or critical acclaim (109).[24] Yuste is mistaken: the painters he mentions did sign at least some of their canvases which, ironically, makes his (and posterity's) attributions possible. Yuste's mention of the Flemish artists is purely decorative since neither they, nor their work, nor their style has any direct bearing on the themes or form of *La Voluntad*. Equally decorative in purpose is Yuste's observation that Jovellanos judged Mengs, rather than Goya, to be the better painter (106). Both passages, however, might approach the ideological sector of the arts continuum if they are read as visual art analogies to Martínez Ruiz's consoling himself for the indifferent and sometimes negative reception his own work suffered in Madrid during the early years of his career.

An author frequently uses decorative visual art allusions to avoid "explicit verbalizing that might flatten the novel," allowing the picture to make a vivid and succinct presentation for him (Torgovnick 212). Such is the case with the two visual art similes Martínez Ruiz constructs around the painting *El cambista y su mujer* by Marinus van Reymerswaele (1493?–after 1567). Walking along the streets of Toledo at nightfall, Azorín describes blotches of light thrown onto the pavement from shop windows: "Los escaparates pintan sobre el suelo vivos cuadros de luz; en el fondo de las tiendas, los viejos mercaderes—como en los cuadros de Marinus—cuentan sus monedas, repasan sus libros" (208;

The display windows paint vivid squares of light on the pavement; at the back of the shops, old merchants—like those in paintings by Marinus—count their money, review their accounts]. That Martínez Ruiz would contextualize Marinus's painting of a moneylender within the traditionally Sephardic milieu of Toledo is particularly a propos since, in the painter's native country, this occupation was common in the Jewish community. The association is made even more explicit in the second reference to Marinus where the physical appearance of Enrique Olaiz (aka Pío Baroja) is likened to that of a Jewish merchant or alchemist:

> Olaiz es calvo . . . su barba es rubia y puntiaguda. Y como su mirada es inteligente, escrutadora . . . esta calva y esta barba le dan cierto aspecto inquietante . . . algo así como uno de esos mercaderes que se ven en los cuadros de Marinus, o como un orfebre de la Edad Media, o como un judío que practica el cerrado arte de la crisopeya, metido allá en el fondo de una casucha toledada. (234)

> [Olaiz is bald . . . his beard is blond and pointed. And because his gaze is intelligent, scrutinizing this bald spot and this beard give him a certain disturbing appearance . . . something like one of those merchants you see in the paintings of Marinus, or like a goldsmith from the Middle Ages, or like a Jew who practices the occult art of alchemy down in the back room of some Toledan hovel].

Fictional characters often reveal vital aspects of their personalities through the art work they prefer. The artistic reproductions hanging on the walls of both Azorín's and Olaiz's studies encode a number of auto / biographical allusions, and because they extend beyond the realm of personal taste into sociohistorical commentary, they also straddle the ideological use of pictorial images on Torgovnick's continuum. In his study Antonio Azorín displays photographs of canonical works from the museum repertoire: Van Dyck's portrait of the Marquesa de Leganés, reproductions of paintings by Goya and Velázquez, and a drawing of an itinerant theatre troupe by Adolphe Willette.[25] There are also works of ecumenical art: two eighteenth-century German engravings depicting saints in ecstasy and a seventeenth-century Spanish print titled *Tabula regnum celorum* portraying worldly vices and sins, the Holy Trinity, the hierarchy of angels, etc. (93–94). The dual nature of this art collection is a visual analogy to Azorín's psyche, divided between the active, worldly life of an aspiring radical intellectual and another personality given to passive resignation. As we know, it is the latter persona that eventually dominates as Azorín accepts the life of provincial mediocrity, anonymity, and hollow religion practiced by rote. His final capitulation to the meaningless trivialities that define his marriage to Iluminada are similarly given visual-ideological expression through the vulgar religious art that a horrified J. Martínez Ruiz observes during a visit to the couple's home: "lithographs of the Sacred Heart of Jesus, the Heart of Virgin Mary, of Saint Michael the Archangel, the *Virgen del Carmen* . . . all done in loud reds, explosive greens, aggressive blues" (289).

Although I do not include a separate chapter here on Martínez Ruiz's 1903 novel *Antonio Azorín*, a cursory discussion of the protagonist's rooms is worthwhile because, although the works of art in them are sometimes identical to those of *La Voluntad*, they are more numerous and compress into one set of rooms, art work that is dispersed throughout the earlier novel. Rather than simply naming the titles of visual art reproductions, as he does in *La Voluntad*, here Martínez Ruiz engages in animated verbal ekphrases of the visual images he enumerates. Because this novel is dedicated to the painter, lithographer, and engraver Ricardo Baroja, an artist whose work Lafuente Ferrari termed of singular historic value due to its pictorial correspondence to what the literary Generation of 1898 stood for, Martínez Ruiz immediately situates *Antonio Azorín* within a visual arts context (1954, 38). The protagonist's study is crammed with books of drawings by Gavarni, a dictionary of art terminology, boxes of photographs of Spanish landscapes and important architectural monuments, reproductions of paintings in the Prado Museum, collections of Laurent's photographs of public figures from the 1860s, and daguerrotypes of "interesting women from the 1850s" (1:1008). On either side of the door hang reproductions of Van Dyck's "divina marquesa de Leganés" and Velázquez's *Las Meninas* (1:1009). Also by Velázquez is a bust-length portrait of Felipe IV, the ekphrasis of which is infused with ideological content emphasizing the King's "Austrian" physical deformities and his distracted, empty gaze looking out stupidly from the frame upon the irremediable decadence of his kingdom (1:1009). The ekphrasis of Velázquez's portrait

of Queen Mariana also bears ideological connotations as it comments on the Queen's "enormous farthingale and cambric handkerchief"; above the reproduction Azorín stuck a peacock feather, symbolic of the deadly sin of pride, and he describes Mariana as "haughty, scornful, with her eternal gesture of indifference perpetuated by Velázquez. . ." (1:1009).[26]

Antonio Azorín's study also includes landscapes. There is an original oil painting by Adelardo Parrilla, as well as vividly described photographs that bear titles reminiscent of those given by J. Laurent to his views of the principle cities and monuments in Spain: "Guadalajara. Vista de la carretera por las entrepeñas del Tajo" and "Salamanca. Vista del Seminario desde los Irlandeses" (1:1009–10). On the wall above the desk is a series of French lithographs representing female figures with the symbolic attributes of sculpture, poetry, painting, and music. These lithographs actually belonged to Martínez Ruiz and are still on view at the Casa-Museo in Monóvar. On another wall of the studio there is a drawing by Ramón Casas (a member of the Catalonian group of Moderns) portraying a femme fatale whose perverse beauty, the narrator remarks, Casas has been able to infuse with the essence of contemporary womanhood (1:1011). Above Azorín's desk hangs the ubiquitous self-portrait by El Greco. In the bedroom are reproductions of Goya tapestry cartoons depicting eighteenth-century, upper-class leisure activities, with the proverbial Guadarrama mountains in the background (1:1012).

In *La Voluntad*, Antonio Azorín shares visual art preferences with his friend Enrique Olaiz. The art work in Olaiz's study also points to Martínez Ruiz's ideological views. Because Olaiz was instrumental in bringing El Greco to the attention of young Castilian intellectuals, it is only natural that his work space contain reproductions of paintings by El Greco (234–35), including the *Entierro del Conde de Orgaz*, whose "hidalgos escúalidos, espiritualizados" were hewn by the harsh geographical environment of Toledo (244). There are etchings by Goya, engravings by Daumier and Gavarni, and a descent from the Cross by Metsys, or Massys (235).[27] This is not the first time Daumier and Gavarni, known for their social and political cartoons, are mentioned in *La Voluntad*. Earlier in the novel, the ideological orientation of both artists is worked into the relatum of a visual art simile through which Martínez Ruiz describes the world as a grotesque operatic carnival:

> Hay una famosa litografía de Daumier que representa el galop final de un baile en la Opera de París; es un caos pintoresco . . . de máscaras . . . que se atropellan, saltan, gesticulan . . . en un espasmo postrero de la orgía. . . . Pues bien, el mundo es como este dibujo de Daumier, en que el artista—como Gavarni en los suyos y como más tarde Forain . . . —ha sabido hacer revivir el austero y a la vez cómico espíritu de las antiguas Danzas de la Muerte. . . . ¡El mundo es una inmensa litografía de Daumier! (219)

> There is a famous lithograph by Daumier that represents the final gallop of a dance at the Paris Opera; it's a picturesque chaos . . . of masked figures . . . that run into each other, leap, gesticulate . . . in a last, orgiastic spasm. . . . Well, the world is like this Daumier vignette, in which the artist—like Gavarni and later Forain—knew how to bring to life the austere and, at the same time, comic spirit of ancient Dances of Death. . . . The world is an immense lithograph by Daumier!

The lithograph to which Martínez Ruiz alludes is Daumier's *Volià le grrrand galop charivarique*, and it has much more to do with Martínez Ruiz's publications prior to *La Voluntad* than meets the eye.

Honoré Daumier (1808–1879), whom Baudelaire called the Molière of caricature (1890, 378–79), made a name for himself as the creator of the modern political cartoon on the satirical magazine *Charivari*, founded in 1832 by Charles Philipon. The title for the magazine was particularly apt as its original meaning referred to a French custom in which young people assembled outside the home of social or moral offenders for the purpose of raising a tumultuous racket there by clanging pots and pans. During the period of the Restoration and Second Empire, the custom evolved from an expression of moral or social displeasure to the political arena, and the *charivari* became a popular form of political action (Tilly 78–79, 89). When Philipon and his team of draftsmen and writers set out to make "warfare every day upon the absurdities of the every day," aiming to keep Republican ideals alive by attacking the July Monarchy, they frequently suffered fines, persecution, intermittent closure, and even imprisonment (Larkin 14, 18). Because of onomastic coincidence, and similarity of ideological intent, it is highly probable that Martínez Ruiz

had Daumier in mind when he published his 1897 pamphlet "Charivari," a fierce criticism of literary, journalistic, and political circles in Madrid, naming names and, like the French magazine, often hitting below the belt. Martínez Ruiz's "Charivari" did, indeed, create such "racket" in the Spanish capital that the aspiring writer had to leave Madrid temporarily for fear of possible consequences.[28] Daumier's contemporary, Guillaume-Sulpice Chevalier (1804–1866) who adopted the *nom de plume* "Gavarni," frequently worked on the same magazines as Daumier, although he enjoyed greater popularity, perhaps because he specialized in the subtle, hence more palatable, lampooning of elegant Parisian society (Vincent 244 n. 2). Nevertheless, in the days that followed the July revolution, Gavarni turned to the political cartoon for the first time and began to contribute to various Philipon publications (Goncourt 70). In contrast to the humble, unpolished Daumier, Gavarni's caricatures of modern Parisian morals and mores were admired by Manet, Degas, Baudelaire, and the Goncourt brothers who wrote a biography of the artist. Aside from the obvious ideological connection, the interest Martínez Ruiz expressed in the work of Daumier and Gavarni may also have had stylistic reasons. The nature of caricature is very much like the simile, Martínez Ruiz's favorite rhetorical trope, in that caricature depends upon comparison and the recognition of sameness within a relatum that is so far-fetched or absurd, the likeness produced may be more true to life than at first imagined (Kris 190).

Martínez Ruiz engages in some social lampooning of his own in *La Voluntad* when he sends Azorín to the Biblioteca Nacional where he spends an afternoon leafing through a collection of photographs taken by Laurent in the 1860s and 1870s of notable personalities from Madrid's artistic, political, and financial worlds. While Azorín's ekphrases of these photographs are replete with irony, because his visual experience of them leads to a transformation of visual impression into verbal commentary on the lamentable state of the nation, which Azorín believes was brought on by the foibles of the generation represented in the photographs, the passage moves from the purely ideological to the interpretive-perceptual sector of Torgovnick's continuum. Although Azorín focuses especially on five photographs, the entire series becomes a grandiose representation of how quickly once-venerated public figures can seem absurdly gesticulating clowns whose "achievements" represent nothing but hollow mediocrity (248). The politically conservative journalist and poetaster Antonio María de Segovia (1808–1874) is a dandy "with gloves in his hand in the style of Velázquez," just as vacuous as the aristocrats in Velázquez's court portraits (251). The features of Archbishop Antonio Claret y Clará (1807–1870), who represents voluptuousness and was rumored to have had illicit relations with women, resemble those of the "perverse and decadent poet" Baudelaire. Cánovas del Castillo (1828–1897), who symbolizes brute strength, subdued the masses, and made and unmade governments through sheer force of will, is photographed with his left leg forward "in an attitude of invincible progress" (252). The impeccably coiffed and well-turned-out actor Julián Romea (1813–1868) represents elegance: a romantic tragedian, he "was adored by the public and by women especially." The financier and railroad magnate José de Salamanca (1806–1883), representing wealth, was in a position to disdain money because he was as equally adept at making it as he was of spending. Celebrated for his role in constructing the fashionable residential district in Madrid that bears his name, the Marqués de Salamanca reveals his character in "his mouth that folds scornfully and his supremely haughty gaze." The romantic poet Gustavo Adolfo Bécquer (1836–1870) symbolizes poetry. Standing against a backcloth representing "an exuberant, tropical, sensually mournful, romantic landscape" so popular with "our unforgettable grandmothers," Bécquer gazes wistfully into the distance, his eyes flickering with mysterious insinuations (253). Azorín mockingly assesses these photographs as depicting "the most intense of everything that mankind can achieve in life" (251).[29]

The last secular work of art in *La Voluntad* hangs in Yuste's study. Azorín describes it as a gloomy, old *vanitas* painting representing a woman holding a little girl by the hand; the child holds three carnations, two white and one red, in her free hand. To the right of the women is a table on top of which rests a skull; a legend on the back wall reads "nascendo morimur." The painting is a historically extant one titled *Dama y niña* by Adriaen Cronenburch (mid-sixteenth century), and forms part of the Flemish art collection at the Prado Museum (Fig. 9). Because as a pictorial image this painting provides the reader with interpretive clues necessary to understand a major thematic feature of the novel, its usage is hermeneutic and belongs to the last and most complex portion of Torgovnick's arts continuum. What is immediately remarkable about this painting is that both women are physiognomic mirror images of each other. Cronenburch further reinforces the notion of cyclic repetition through the background legend and by portraying the women holding hands as if to suggest a perpetual flow of vital forces between them. Why Martínez Ruiz hung this particular painting in Yuste's office becomes apparent since beneath its watchful presence Yuste's first peroration on the eternal return takes place:

la sucesión vertiginosa de los fenómenos, no acaba. . . . A través del tiempo infinito, en las infinitas combinaciones del átomo incansable, acaso las formas se repitan; acaso las formas presentes vuelvan a ser, o estas presentes sean reproducción de otras . . . como es la misma y distinta una idéntica imagen en dos espejos . . . (73)

[the dizzying succession of phenomena never ceases. . . . Through infinite time, in the infinite combinations of the untiring atom, perhaps forms repeat themselves; perhaps those in the present recur all over again, or these present ones might be a replication of others . . . just as the same image reflected in two mirrors is both identical and different].

Because a copy of Schopenhauer's *The World as Will and Representation* is prominently displayed on Yuste's worktable, and because Martínez Ruiz's ekphrasis of Cronenburch's painting, which he describes as "melancholy," follows in the next paragraph, the visual image, in addition to sustaining Nietzschean themes, also points the reader toward Schopenhauer.[30] The painting's legend functions as a visual correlative of the innate pessimism woven throughout the novel. The phlegmatic, wide-eyed gaze of both woman and child directly engages the viewer's eye, leading it ineluctably further into the picture to the "nascendo morimur" on the back wall to reinforce pronouncements such as Yuste's "observar es sentirse vivir . . . y sentirse vivir es sentir la muerte, es sentir la inexorable marcha . . . hacia el océano misterioso de la nada" [180; to observe is to feel oneself live . . . and to feel alive is to feel death,

Fig. 9   Adriaen Cronenburch, *Dama y niña*, 1537. Oil on wood panel, 105 × 78 cm. Museo del Prado, Madrid.

it's to feel the inexorable march . . . toward the mysterious ocean of the void].

In contrast to the secular art forms of *La Voluntad*, examples of ecclesiastical art occur only along the ideological and hermeneutic sectors of the visual arts continuum. The restriction is understandable given the anti-clerical posture adopted by most of the Generation of 1898 in its early years of anti-establishment militancy. The negative portrayal of priests and the monastic life in *La Voluntad* must be read in context of the scandalous premiere on 30 January 1901 of Pérez Galdos's *Electra*. Based on the notorious case of Adelaida de Ubao, who was persuaded by her confessor to enter a convent against the wishes of her family and her own misgivings, the play polarized Madrid and for a brief time made Galdós the darling of the younger writers. Although Martínez Ruiz's position in the *Electra* affair was equivocal, and provoked acrimonious public debate with Ramiro de Maeztu, the figure of Justina in *La Voluntad* was undeniably inspired by the unfortunate Adelaida de Ubao.[31] We first meet Puche, Justina's uncle and confessor, as his unctuous words "insinuate" to his young niece "the beatitude of the perfect life." Yet beneath Puche's apparent sweetness and resignation burns the apostolic fire of an "untamed beast . . . and the gentle cleric becomes ecstatic with the ardor of an ancient Hebrew prophet" (67). The walls of his sitting room are appropriately hung with crudely lit prints representing the Apostles John, Matthew, Peter, Paul, Bartholomew, and Simon. Above the sofa is a reproduction of a painting depicting the gentle submissiveness of Saint Francis de Paul that perhaps alludes to the way in which Justina abjures her inchoate personal wishes, placidly allowing Puche to lead her down the road toward professing as a novice. When she chooses to enter the Franciscan order of Saint Claire, pledged to accept poverty happily while depending only upon Divine Providence like the birds in the heavens, Martínez Ruiz observes that "one of those loveable, little birds will be Justina—a little bird locked up forever in her cage" (159). On taking her vows, Justina symbolically consents to the annihilation of personal volition ("su voluntad ha muerto"), while the earlier comparison to a caged bird is

substantiated visually by a painting on the wall of her cell which represents the "Notion of a mortified nun," showing her nailed to the Cross, lips chained shut, and feet treading the globe as if spurning worldly temptations (171). Justina herself perceives the similarity: "she looks at this nun nailed to the Cross and thinks of herself" (172).

The young cleric Ortuño also is personified by the works of art and books in his study. Too inexperienced and lightweight to have adopted a fixed ideological position, Ortuño has a library that covers a wide range of ecclesiastical literature, from the dangerously liberal to the intransigently Thomist (154). Two visual images in his study emblematize the unspecific nature of his personality: one depicts "a gaudy oleography of the Immaculate Conception"; the other a "flashy oleography of Velázquez's *Crucifixion*" (155). While the print of the Immaculate Conception denotes one of the most sublime articles of faith in Catholic dogma, Velázquez's *Crucifixion*, on the other hand, represents a highly unorthodox rendering of the Passion. The most sympathetic clerics in *La Voluntad* are Lasalde and Yuste whose religious vocations Martínez Ruiz undermines through their worldly intellectual pursuits and tastes in art. Father Lasalde is headmaster of a secondary school run by the Piarist fathers in Yecla, yet he spends most of his time pursuing archaeological interests by excavating the Cerro de los Santos where he finds the suggestive pagan statuettes that decorate his office and about whose lives he enjoys speculating with Azorín and Yuste (141–44). The walls of Yuste's residence, in addition to the Cronenburch *Dama y niña*, rather than being decorated with pictures of saints, are hung with large photographs of the principal cathedrals in Spain: Toledo, Santiago, Burgos, and León. The choice of pictorial images is meaningful because a cathedral is simultaneously a secular and a religious artifact whose construction is both a product of human religious fervor as well as that of human labor and aesthetic vision. The cathedral is thus a dual visual symbol emblematizing both Yuste's secular and spiritual nature, at the same time that it subtly alludes to the parochialism and questionable taste of Puche's preferences in art and to the unidimensional, tenacious brand of religion that he practices.

Part II
On Painters, Painting, and Writing:
Azorín's Language of the Eye

1

Azorín's Master Trope: The Visual Arts Simile

OF ALL THE FIGURES OF SPEECH, AZORÍN'S TROPE of choice was the simile. Given his stylistic preference for simplicity, condensation, and spareness, as well as his visual sensibility, the preference was a logical one. In his discussion of the metaphor of comparison in the *Rhetoric*, Aristotle connects *eikôn*, the Greek word for "image" or simile, to making the abstract concrete by "placing things before our eyes"; liveliness of style is to be got by compelling an audience to see things (Ricoeur 34). *Imago*, the Latin equivalent of *eikôn*, likewise connotes a visual sense of "image." In his handbook *On Tropes*, the first-century B.C. grammarian Trypho, defined *icon* as a comparison that attempts to liken visibly, but it is in post-Quintilianic treatises that *icon* and *imago* are used to signify pictorial description rather than straightforward comparison (McCall 243, 249, 253). Marcus Aurelius (Cornelius?) Fronto (b. A.D. 100) wrote that *icon* was particularly suitable for imagistic description because the figure derived from painting, and he advised the rhetor to proceed in the composition of *imago* in the manner of a painter who, above all, must depict clearly the characteristics of the object he paints (McCall 246, 248).

Modern theorists agree that, because the terms of comparison in simile are joined by some form of copulative "like" or "as if" structure, the simile exacts a much more visual relationship between its elements than does metaphor (Hawkes 3). Unlike metaphor, which presupposes substitution or replacement of identities, simile illustrates or illuminates rather than transforms, two unlike objects that, although drawn together by a copula of similitude, preserve their individual features because the same copula responsible for promoting their affiliation simultaneously disallows complete amalgamation of tenor and vehicle (Henry 59).[1] Terence Hawkes argues that simile often depends on sense impressions, especially the visual accuracy of reader imaging for its success (71–72). In comparison statements of the type "A is similar to B"—for example, the by now cliched "Achilles sprang up like a lion"—it is incumbent upon the reader to transfer the features of element B (the relatum "lion") to element A (the referent "Achilles"), and if, in the process, the reader imagines in the mind's eye Achilles' physical action in terms of the springing up of a lion, the simile will be that much more effective (Miller 217).[2] The relatum component of a simile—the lion in our case—is assumed to be part of a reader's general knowledge and its function is to indicate in what manner to qualify the referent: Achilles in the example we are using. The relatum is considered "old" information which the reader is assumed to have from previous life experience; the referent is the current topic, and the resulting comparison between old and current material, a construction of new information based on the statement of similarity between referent and relatum (Miller 217). Because the simile requires imaginative effort on a reader's part, it also fosters a pleasurable collaboration in the creation of the text itself.[3]

As I have shown in preceeding chapters, the similes Azorín uses with greatest frequency are doubly visual because their relata are drawn almost exclusively from the visual arts. When the painterly allusion that corresponds to the relatum component of a visual arts simile is well-known, such as "Don Antonio has taken out his fine cambric handkerchief and holds it in his hand—like Velázquez's little princesses—...", a reader will have no difficulty in disambiguating the metaphor (EL 64). However, Azorín frequently chose paintings for the associational value they had in his personal imaginative life rather than for their place in the art-historical canon. The inherent danger in cases where the work of art is either not specifically described, or well-known enough to form part of a reader's "old information," is that the simile fails as a sign system such as occurs in Azorín's description of Clodio from Cervantes's *Persiles*: "(Physically, did he also not resemble this bearded and corpulent man we see portrayed by Titian in the Pitti Gallery in Florence?)" (3:224). This simile, namely the comparison of Clodio to an unidentified portrait by Titian in the Pitti (Azorín probably was referring to a portrait of Pietro Aretino), raises more questions than it answers, and contributes neither to textual enrichment nor to evoking a specific image in a reader's imagination.

In general terms, authors rely on metaphor when they feel that the literal meaning of words does not express adequately what they want to say. Ortega y Gasset called metaphor a kind of "fishing rod" or "rifle" essential to the intellective process because it enables authors to grasp and to articulate elusive concepts beyond their immediate ideational capabilities in terms derived from more familiar realms of knowledge so that the remote idea becomes concrete, first to authors themselves, and subsequently to readers as well (2:390–91). Metaphor thus extends language by attributing a new sense to habitual signs and, in the process, expands reality by extracting new, figurative signifieds from old, literal signifiers. Once the basis of metaphoric comparison is understood, the path back to the author's literal meaning can be retraced.[4] In the case of Azorín's visual art similes, however, the verbally generated image frequently does not lead to a new, linguistic signifier, but to another image; namely, to a painting extant in the real, extratextual world. The visual arts simile thus fuses textuality and vision under the common aegis of the sign, a metalinguistic operation Norman Bryson calls "second-order semiological systems" (1981, 184), whereby the verbal allusion to a specific painting, which itself can be understood as a constellation of independent signifiers, plays two roles: as the relatum component of a simile, the painting—in its role as signifier—illustrates or qualifies the referent, and mediates meaning by enabling readers to decode the terms of comparison that leads to a new understanding of the verbal insinuation made first by the work of art as sign. The result is a "mixed metaphor" of sorts in which language is not a vehicle that conveys a new verbal signified; rather, its transforming function resides in compelling readers to produce referents from the realm of the visual rather than the language arts, although inevitably the paintings that constitute the relata of Azorín's visual art similes must first be engendered verbally. While in traditional forms of metaphor, passage from one level of reality to another is a gradual one, the visual arts metaphor entails a leap from verbal to visual means of expression. A metaphor of this type is a kind of "written visibility." Compare, for example, the two similes: "Her cheeks are red as roses" and "Her cheeks are as red as the roses in Monet's gardens." Because the visual arts metaphor provides instruction that encourages reader imaging, it is much richer and more performative than the exclusively language-based nature of traditional metaphor.

Azorín's partiality to the visual arts simile also explains his fondness for the ekphrastic topos, a verbally generated entity that must be *like* its pictorial object of reference in the real world. When we examine the underpinnings of Horace's proverbial "ut pictura poesis" (a poem is like a picture), rarely cited in its entirety: "*similisque* poesi / sit pictura" (and so a picture should try to be like a poem), we see that ekphrasis itself clearly is based on the principle of similitude.[5] Literary ekphrasis, like the visual arts simile, can exhibit both visually metonymic and visually synecdochic features in the sense that the verbally created art object must not only resemble its plastic art referent but is also drawn to it through contiguity. On the other hand, both ekphrasis and a simile whose relatum derives from a painting or an artist's general style, become synecdochic in cases where either one refers only to a salient detail or part of an art object or painting, and where the abbreviated description intends to represent the whole. For this kind of arrangement to function successfully, it is especially important that readers be familiar with the pictorial referent in order to reproduce it in the mind's eye and to be able to deduce from the verbal-visual fragment its larger, figurative meaning.[6] The synecdochic aspect of ekphrasis and the visual arts simile is constant in Azorín's literary portraits. When he describes a physically robust man playing with his infant daughter as a "coloso de bigotes a lo Velázquez" (mustachioed colossus in the style of Velázquez), Azorín short-circuits the need for a detailed description of the man's physiognomy by relying on a partial visual reference to Velázquez's unforgettable moustaches, which any reader who knows the painting *Las Meninas* will recall immediately.[7] A literary portrait like this one, which relies on the illustrative capabilities of a visual arts simile based on an actual painting, rather than purely linguistic forms of expression, is highly paradoxical because all three elements of the comparative structure prove to be "look-alike" clones, mirror images of each other, whereby the portrait-signifier (Velázquez's self-portrait in *Las Meninas*) stands in for both relatum-sign ("a lo Velázquez) and referent-signified ("los bigotes del coloso").

The visual arts metaphor is also metonymic in that the production of visual comparison between referent and a relatum drawn from the realm of painting, especially portraiture, is evoked through metonymy's customary contiguity. The result is what Albert Henry called an "evocative short-circuit between two metonymies" (40), convenient because it enables an author to have the image speak for him while circumventing the more traditional rhetorical strategies of quotation, allusion, or example, all more cumbersome forms of description. It is precisely the short-circuit effect of the visual arts simile, its ability to condense lengthy verbal description in more evocative fashion through the insinuation of visual characteristics, that appealed to Azorín's taste for concision and for making the intangible concrete and visible to his readers. "No hay en el arte plástico—y en literatura—" he observed in an article on the sculptor Sebastián Miranda, "cuestión tan magna como ésta de reducir a pocas especies, a pocos rasgos, un todo que se nos presenta inconcreto" [In the plastic arts—and in literature—there is no issue more important than this one of reducing to a few species, a few traits, a whole that presents itself inconcretely to us].[8]

Azorín maintained that portraiture, both literary and pictorial, posed the most difficult of challenges to the artist. He always cited the British portraitist Thomas Lawrence's adage that a successful portrait captured the sitter's essence by portraying no more than two or three representative features of the physiognomy while eliminating the rest (8:404). Traditional manuals of rhetoric and style recommended simile to writers of short narrative as a useful way to generate vivid yet brief descriptions of human beings, revealing hidden character traits through suggestion (Kleiser 12–13). Primarily a journalist and author of short fiction, Azorín frequently relied on the efficiency of visual art similes based on portraits to create both dramatic and lifelike visual contexts for his characters, and to evoke their physical appearance without having to describe them in detail himself. The formula is effective whether it entails the comparison of real people to historically extant portraits, such as a verbal sketch of Pío Baroja whose worn hat and roguish eyes are described as "debajo de estas alas cansadas [del sombrero]—como en algunos cuadros de Goya—fulgen, relumbran unos ojos vivos, perspicaces, siempre curiosos" [3:1143; beneath this brim of a tired hat—as in some of Goya's paintings—shine, sparkle, two lively, shrewd, always curious eyes], or the fictional portrait of a female character very much aware of the framing effect of the doorway within which she self-consciously poses for an imaginary portrait:

En la oscuridad . . . el amarillo joyante [del cobertor], entrevisto por la puerta, tiene un momento la atención de Virginia. Va Virginia vestida de negro; . . . lo negro de su traje, en la esbeltez de su persona, piensa Virginia que tendría en lo amarillo un fondo magnífico para un cuadro en que un pintor la retratase. Virginia Tous se levanta . . . abre del todo la puerta y se coloca en el umbral, de modo que su figura descuelle sobre lo amarillo brillante. (*PQ* 161–62)[9]

[In the darkness . . . the glossy yellow of the coverlet glimpsed through the door, catches Virginia's attention for a moment. Virginia is wearing black . . . she thinks that the black of her clothing, the slenderness of her figure, would look magnificent against the yellow background in a portrait an artist might paint of her. Virginia Tous gets up . . . opens the door wide and arranges herself on the threshold so that her figure is silhouetted against the brilliant yellow.]

The visual arts metaphor based on extant portraiture proved especially handy to Azorín, the aspiring dramatist, when he described the costumes he envisioned for the characters of his first play, *La fuerza del amor* (1901). Not yet the visual arts simile that would dominate his work in later years, the portraits to which Azorín alludes in the stage directions for *La fuerza* usually are announced by the referential command "véase" rather than a copula of similitude. Although less sophisticated than the visual arts simile, graphic stage directions such as these prove to be an unexpected windfall for any costumer who might design the show. Because the play is set in seventeenth-century Spain, Azorín draws his visual referents from the work of painters active during the period: the men's hats "are wide-brimmed, lined with black silk (see the portrait of infante Don Carlos by Velázquez" (1:742). In most cases, Azorín even reveals the location of the painting to which he refers: he describes the men's footwear as "shoes, without heels. See, in the Prado Museum, the painting by Eugenio Caxés *Don Fernando de Girón*, and better yet, an engraving after the portrait at the Calcografía Nacional" (1:742). The male protagonist, characterized as a "proper, sixteenth-century man of arms" [sic], wears a costume comparable to "engravings of the period; for example, a portrait of the handsome Captain Alonso de Céspedes, 'the Brave,' in the curious book . . . *Ensayos fotolitográficos, Madrid, 1873*" (1:742–43).

Use of the canonical portrait in the relatum component of a visual arts simile is already present in the previous year's *El alma castellana* (1900). As in the majority of portrait similes constructed by Azorín, these are often synecdochic in the sense that only a detail of the portrait is employed to evoke the entire image. Rather than offer his own, intricate description of women's hairstyles in Golden Age Spain, Azorín relies on portraits to do it for him: "There are hairdresses with charming buns that cover the ears, allowing only the heavy pearls of hanging earrings to show, like the divine Marquise of Leganés, by Van-Dyck [sic]; others are slick and flat, as in portraits by Sánchez Coello; still others have long plaits at both sides of the head, like the blond and melancholy Doña Mariana of Austria, painted by del Mazo" (1:604) (Fig. 10). Azorín frequently uses metaphors as visual codes to instantiate the purely conceptual, as in his comparison of a mature literary work to the "austere silver that we see in Titian's last paintings" (3:544). The portrait is also a favorite method Azorín employs to illustrate what he might subjectively envision in the "eye" of his own mind: he bestows corporeo-visual presence to Feliciana de la Voz in Cervantes's *Persiles* by comparing her to "a portrait by Palma, the Elder, or Titian: a handsome girl, blonde, with golden hair loose upon her bare shoulders and arms" (3:233). Criticizing the inappropriateness of prints by Isidro and Antonio Carnicero which illustrate a 1787 edition of *Don Quijote*, Azorín observes that the skirt Aldonza Lorenzo wears is not typically Spanish, but a "full skirt . . . by Fragonard, Boucher, Watteau. The whole engraving is taken over by that skirt" (*EdC* 198). The synecdochic evocation of an exquisitely billowing skirt emblematic of women's fashion as depicted in the rococo paintings of Fragonard or Boucher, establishes brilliantly the anachronism between Aldonza and her costume as interpreted by the Carnicero brothers.

The effervescent insouciance and sensuality of eighteenth-century French ladies are often represented with portrait similes drawn from the rivals and contemporaries of Boucher and Fragonard. The powdered, fabulously coiffed women of the aristocracy are as artificial as the manicured fantasy gardens in which they frolic: "the fine, slender ladies, with high, powdered coiffures, deep and luscious décolletage—like those we see in portraits by Van Loo, Larguillère, La Tour—; gardens like those of Chantilly . . ." (7:151). On the other hand, the grim, restricted lives Azorín imagined Spanish women to have led in the seventeenth century

Fig. 10   Anton Van Dyck, *Doña Policena Spínola, Marquesa de Leganés*, 1622. Oil on canvas, 204 × 130 cm. Museo del Prado, Madrid.

are suggested by the somber, confining dress depicted in court portraiture: "a short, black silk jacket, brocaded and decorated with embroidered flowers—one of those jackets with wide sleeves that you've seen in portraits by Sánchez Coello or Pantoja" (7:148).

Having reported for so many years on Spanish parliamentary affairs, Azorín inevitably found comparisons between members of Congress or ceremonial parliamentary occasions, and paintings from the classical Spanish repertoire. After an all-night session of Congress, Alonso Castrillo appears drawn, ghostly, "like a character out of El Greco, with a gray, dusty beard . . . and sunken eyes, encircled by deep shadows" (3:677); at the opening of Parliament in 1905, the royal crown and sceptre are displayed "on a small, covered table—like the ones we see in paintings by Pantoja and Velázquez" (3:724). Velázquez's contemporary, Antoon Van Dyck, gained international renown for the refined elegance, ease of manner, and aristocratic bearing with which he portrayed both his male and female subjects. It was the elegant quality of these models that Azorín wanted readers to recall when he authorized Van Dyck's portraits to represent his literary characters metonymically. He imagined Flaubert's Pecuchet as a tall, strong, dignified individual, perhaps somewhat arrogant, who, should he have dressed with greater care, "would resemble a wealthy magnate painted by Van Dyck" (1:391). The particularly refined manner in which the Flemish artist painted the human hand especially appealed to Azorín, and he often utilized the hands of Van Dyck's subjects as synecdochic visual instantiations of gentility and aristocratic breeding. Women's hands, wrote Azorín, can be extraordinarily beautiful, and those of a certain Conchita in *Veraneo sentimental* are "a little tapered—like those Van Dyck used to paint— white, delicate, soft, silky, light, ethereal" (7:289). Memorializing the hands of a Royal Academician, Azorín describes them as fine and elongated, slightly less pale than those of El Greco's "caballero de la espada," but rather more "masculine that Van Dyck's in his own self-portrait" (8:751).

On many occasions Azorín transforms a portrait into an icon that encodes abstract notions extending far beyond the frame of the painting. Two portraits of Erasmus by Holbein the Younger were a staple of his visual art simile repertoire. The German painter's reputation as

a portraitist rested on the accuracy, lifelike dimensionality, and seriousness of portrayal from which any insinuation of gratuitous flattery was wholly absent (Fromentin 1765). It was this simplicity and truthfulness of representation that Azorín read in Holbein's Louvre portrait of Erasmus (1523), a quality he felt elevated the painting beyond the sitter as an individual to that of a universal symbol designating "el hombre que escribe" (9:209).[10] In "Un Discurso de La Cierva," Azorín proposed Holbein's Erasmus to be emblematic of all men in public life: Erasmus represents not only a "man who writes," but also the intellectual who finds his way to understanding by seeking the path to truth and impartiality. He thus becomes "Our symbol: a man who, like the one in a painting by Holbein, would be attentively bent over a book in an attitude of comprehension . . . comprehension is the road to impartiality and truth" (3:148). In addition to Holbein's portrayal of Erasmus as an intellectual and writer (9:987), Azorín remarks that in the portraits of the Louvre and Parma [sic] Museums, Holbein portrayed the face of his model with such serenity that one could never suspect the drama of Erasmus's life flowing just beneath the sitter's unruffled exterior (9:1430).[11] Reviewing one of the five novels which comprise Georges Duhamel's *Vie et aventures de Salavin* (1920–1932), Azorín remarked that because there is nothing pretentious or pedantic about the work, its style resembles that of the great, sixteenth-century humanists, and he compared the clarity and simplicity of Duhamel's prose to that used by "a man Holbein painted in the act of writing, his hand extended on his desk and a large ring on his index finger" (*LM* 95–96).[12]

Azorín also frequently referred to Goya's portraits of representative figures from the Spanish Enlightenment as visual instantiations of abstract concepts. Whenever Jovellanos came to mind, Azorín invariably thought of the Spanish writer and social reformer as Goya had portrayed him: seated at a table, paper in hand, his face tinged with sadness, Jovellanos represents the "handsome man in his maturity, pensive, melancholy" (9:1430, 32). Azorín also maintained that the visual image most people would evoke in their imaginations of Moratín was the one immortalized by Goya: the playwright's delicate chin and perfectly arched eyebrows connoting his sharp intelligence (7:738). In reconstructing the youth of the politician the

Marqués de la Vega de Armijo (born in the 1820s), Azorín imagined the older women at court perhaps affixing artificial birthmarks to their temples in imitation of the natural one that so disfigured the visage of María Josefa, the King's sister, as she was portrayed by Goya in the famous group portrait *La familia de Carlos IV* (3:700).[13]

Although he compared the mischevous sauciness paired with demure gentility of a young Castilian woman in *Los pueblos* to a *maja* Goya depicted in *Capricho 16*, ("Perdone por Dios . . . , y era su madre"), in which an elderly female beggar is turned away disdainfully by a young woman, Azorín was careful to point out that his comparison was based on that of physical beauty alone rather than spiritual type. It is María's lithe, graceful figure and her elegant self-assurance that recall Goya's "manolas de la ermita de San Antonio" seductively balanced against a balcony railing (117), or the carefree *maja* of *Capricho 16* "with a smooth coiffure, a mantilla that reaches down to her eyes, and a fan resting against her mouth" (116).[14] Also from *Los pueblos* is the description of Aurelia whom Azorín "paints" leaning provocatively against a balustrade. The visual art metaphor he uses to evoke her pose and attitude, however, is more difficult to disambiguate because it refers to the relatively unknown French caricaturist Gavarni, famous for memorializing the foibles of elegant French women: "Aurelia leans on the parapet of the bridge, in one of those attitudes . . . of elegance and abandon in which Gavarni posed the refined and pale ladies of the 1850s on a garden terrace or on the arms of a divan" (111).

The two greatest painters in the world, in Azorín's opinion, were Peter Paul Rubens (1577–1640), "el más grande pintor de la materia," and Rembrandt (1606–1669), "el más grande pintor del espíritu," whose paintings of the story of Bathsheba offered two different interpretations of the same biblical episode: one carnal, the other intellectual (5:825–26). He wrote in *Memorias Inmemoriales* that, while living in Paris, "X" spent a great deal of time contemplating Rubens's lavish and exuberant paintings in the Médicis Gallery at the Louvre, and equally long periods of meditation before the Rembrandt canvases in adjacent rooms (8:585). Rembrandt, however, was by far Azorín's favorite of the two, and it is his paintings that figure most often as the relata of

Azorín's visual art similes and portrait metaphors. Pedro Laín Entralgo's scientific "dissection" of the Generation of 1898 conjured in Azorín's imagination an image of Rembrandt's *The Anatomy Lesson of Dr. Nicolaes Tulp* (9:1149). He admired this painting very much and referred to it often in his writing, remarking that *The Anatomy Lesson* embodied visually, if not the abstract notion we have of "surgery," then certainly that of "anatomical science" which supplies the knowledge that makes surgical intervention possible (*LM* 21). As is a great deal of art-historical writing and art criticism, Azorín's intricate commentary on various parts of *The Anatomy Lesson* coalesce into an ekphrastic re-creation of the painting, executed in 1632 when Rembrandt was only twenty-six and representative of the painter's early style (Fig. 11).[15] Azorín found it rather odd that Rembrandt would depict Professor Tulp wearing a wide-brimmed, misshapen hat while demonstrating techniques of practical anatomy. The "desmesurado chapeo," observes Azorín, looks as if Tulp had absentmindedly jammed it on his head on the way out for a brisk walk in the country, but passing by the medical school, decided to drop in to say a few words to his students. Citing Fromentin's opinion that, because this painting is a marvelous display of shimmering color, death seems to be entirely absent from the picture, Azorín observes that just as one does not perceive the presence of death in the painting, neither do the students seem to be paying any attention to what their professor is saying (21–22). He concludes that ultimately the internal dynamics among the picture's cast of characters is unimportant; what matters is that the painting is a great work of art because "anatomical science, the mother of surgery, is exalted there" (22).[16]

Of all Rembrandt's paintings in the Louvre, there were three that Azorín particularly admired: *Los peregrinos de Emaús*, *El buen samaritano*, and *La ascención del Arcángel Rafael*. It was the first painting, however, that he called the Dutch artist's masterpiece because its divine subject spoke more to his emotions than the other two (5:783). In fact, Azorín wrote that he would truly have been sorry should his life have ended before being able to see *Los peregrinos* (7:1220). In his memoir of exile in Paris, he recounted the anecdote of how, on one of his first visits to the Louvre, he set out to see Rembrandt's painting of Bath-

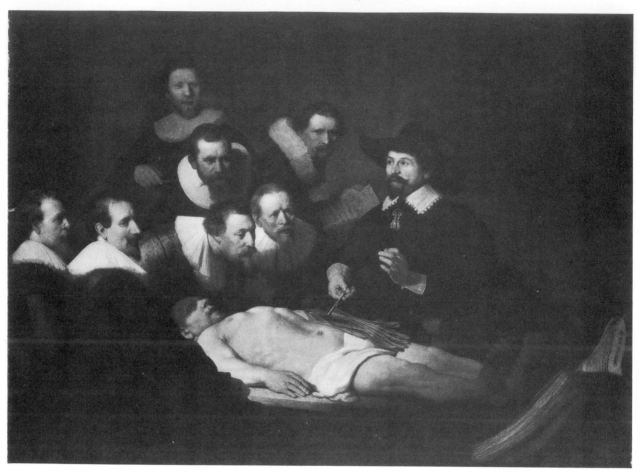

Fig. 11   Rembrandt Harmensz. van Rijn, *The Anatomy Lesson of Dr. Nicholas Tulp*, 1632. Oil on canvas, 1.69 × 2.16 m. Mauritshuis, The Hague, The Netherlands. Giraudon / Art Resource, New York.

sheba. Afterward he took a wrong turn into a corridor he had never explored before, only to find himself standing in front of the magnificent *Les Pélérins d'Emaüs*. Tongue planted firmly in his cheek, Azorín observed that without the intervention of Bathsheba "the *Peregrinos* would not exist. We could not begin to contemplate this painting had Bathsheba not existed" (5:831). It was the figure of Christ, whose face Rembrandt imbued with transcendent mysticism, that made the painting an emblem of the Divine for Azorín, and he was in complete agreement with a comment Fromentin made in *Les Maîtres d'autrefois* that no painter before or after Rembrandt made art "say" so many things beyond the surface of a canvas (*PCQ* 239–40). What Azorín found bewitching about Rembrandt was the painter's masterful use of light. One of the many fictional characters in *Sintiendo a España* who are either painters or art aficionados, Don Matías Peñalosa, like Azorín himself, is a Spanish exile

whose favorite form of recreation is visiting the great museums of Europe. It is not easy for Peñalosa to decide which painter he most admires, but after much rumination his choice falls upon Rembrandt whose incomparable manner of painting light mesmerizes him in much the same way that candlelight attracts moths (6:773). Vicente Llorer, a fictional painter and collector of work by Constable and Hogarth, is driven nearly insane in the short story "Su mejor obra" because in six years of work on a single canvas he cannot capture the light just so. "La luz me preocupa," he confesses to a friend. "No hay para el pintor nada como la luz." Llorer's favorite painter is Rembrandt precisely because he'd discovered the secret of painting light (*PCQ* 188–89). The art critic in the novel *Capricho*, who often voices Azorín's opinions on matters concerning the arts and aesthetics, reiterates that Rembrandt's most suggestive paintings are "the images of *The Good Samaritan* . . . ; *The Night Watch* and the *Disciples at Emmaus*" (6:914). Although he, too, concurs Rembrandt was a prodigious creator of painted light, that which he depicts in *Los peregrinos* is a light "not of this world." Equally unforgettable for the art critic is the last glimmer of late afternoon twilight reflecting off a small section of wall in *El buen samaritano* (6:914).[17]

Another painting Azorín thought superb was Rembrandt's *The Evangelist Matthew, inspired by an Angel*, also in the Louvre. The most suggestive feature of this Saint Matthew, shown seated with a pen in his raised hand as if awaiting inspiration, was his forehead which Azorín abstracted into the more emblematic notion of "poet-historian," "humanist," or "intellectual" whose profession is writing (6:56). In *Memorias Inmemoriales*, Azorín repeats his fondness for this painting, clearly seeing a resemblance between himself and the Evangelist as professionals of the pen: ". . . the similarity that "X" established between the sitter, in terms of writing, and "X" himself, always obsessed, pen raised in the air, by an enthusiasm for sheets of writing paper" (8:352). Contextualized by his own professional interests, portraits of the writer-thinker appealed to Azorín. Rembrandt's *Filósofo del libro abierto* led him to a detailed ekphrasis of the painting to which he appended his own interpretation of the mood it evoked. After describing the architectural details and furnishings of the room where Rembrandt posed his philosopher, Azorín sketched the man's apparel and observed that "The philosopher, seated a little away from the table . . . meditates, his hand on his cheek. The silence of this austere room must be profound; the imagination is not distracted by any piece of furniture since there is nothing more in the room than what we've just indicated" (8:697–98). Once again, a portrait by Rembrandt serves Azorín as a point of departure from which he distills the concrete representation of an intangible, abstract concept.

Azorín was aware that many seventeenth-century painters achieved the dramatic play of light and shadow in their canvases by working in darkened studios with only one, usually overhead, light source. When he noted the lack of windows in the Spanish Congressional building, he described the effect as "Everything is illuminated from above, as in a painter's studio" (3:823). Azorín also remembered coming across some notes he took in 1898 of a conversation he had with the Alicantine painter Lorenzo Casanova who told him of José de Ribera's technique of posing his models in a darkened room while "he positioned himself in a contiguous room, and painted looking through a peep-hole" (6:242). Years later, Azorín would have come across a discussion of Ribera's dramatic light effects in his copy of Georges Pillement's 1921 book on the Spanish painter. Referring to Pillement's study, Azorín noted that Ribera anticipated modern light effects in his work: "it is known that he painted in a dark room that had a little opening high up to one side of the ceiling through which the light entered. And in the master's canvases the contrasts of light and dense shadow are marvelous" (*PCQ* 153). Azorín writes that he always slowed his pace in the Louvre on reaching the Ribera gallery to savor the painter's incomparable mastery of light and shadow (6:219), which went beyond mere visual effect to something more tangible that could almost be felt with the hands (*PCQ* 58). One of Azorín's fictional painters duplicates Ribera's working methods: "In his studio he attempted to do what Ribera had done; heavy curtains covered the windows; in the darkened room a small window in the roof permitted a ray of bright light to fall on his model" (*PCQ* 169). Although Azorín said that control of light could be learned by studying the paintings of Rembrandt and Ribera, he wrote that Rembrandt was "the greatest luminist" of all.[18] On one occasion, he based not only the character description of a thinker-scientist on a portrait-simile whose relatum seems to point to Rembrandt's *Filósofo del libro abierto*, but he also attempted to reproduce verbally Rembrandt's chiaroscuro light effects: "Micael Salomón spent long hours seated in an armchair, submerged in the shadows, with a book in his hands. On seeing him, one recalled a certain venerable old man in a painting by Rembrandt. The white pages of the book Micael was reading picked up the soft light that fell from the skylight in the ceiling" (5:962).[19]

Although not a portrait, Rembrandt's *The Slaughtered Ox*, also known as *The Side of Beef*, had tremendous visual impact on Azorín (Pl. 21). Rembrandt painted several different versions of the butchered ox, but the canvas to which Azorín refers on many occasions is the magnificent painting executed in 1655 and acquired by the Louvre in 1857 (Vincent 92). The fictional novelist of *Capricho* reveals that he has always been obsessed by two masterworks, one literary; the other pictorial, that he considered models for his own writing: an unidentified exemplary novel by Cervantes and Rembrandt's "dressed carcass of an ox, and nothing more than that bloody carcass," a painting, the novelist argues, that is one of Rembrandt's most beautiful canvases (6:946). Always sensitive to color, Azorín thought *The Slaughtered Ox* a picture of "miraculous" chromaticity (9:355), and the work of one of his many fictional painter-protagonists is said to be adumbrated by "Rembrandt's painting—in the Louvre—that depicts the carcass of an ox" (*Posdata* 151). This painting seems to have acquired a hypostatic meaning for Azorín, akin to the notion of "aesthetic masterpiece," and he once wrote that of all Rembrandt's paintings the one he preferred was the "carcass of an ox at the Louvre" (*PCQ* 189).

The Portrait as Witness and Metaphor: *Don Juan* and *Comedia del Arte*

Two of Azorín's full-length literary works, the novel *Don Juan* (1922) and the play *Comedia del arte* (1927), are informed by portrait metaphors.[20] Don Gonzalo, father of the novel's ingenue, Jeannette, is a collector of art: his library walls display a portrait by Ingres, a landscape by Corot, as well as an unidentified portrait by Goya (4:254). In a sitting room of the bishop's palace hangs a portrait of the liberal Pope Leo XIII and a copy of Velázquez's highly unorthodox *Cristo*, both works of art likely visual references to the bishop's enlightened tendencies (4:70). The most suggestive works of art in the novel, however, are the colored lithographs that adorn the walls of the elderly Don Juan's bedroom. Although Azorín first mentions them early in the novel, he does not reveal what they represent until its conclusion. Throughout the story, the flirtatious Jeannette teases Don Juan mercilessly, even rather provocatively. Finally, during a soirée at the home of her parents just before the family's departure for an extended stay in Paris, Jeannette gives Don Juan a rose, "la rosa más roja, la rosa más lozana," loaded with all the clichéd symbolism evoked by the reddest of all roses (4:268). Several days later, Jeannette and her mother visit Don Juan's residence to say their good-byes. Don Juan is not at home, but his landlady allows the women into his rooms where for the

first time Azorín describes the content of the antique, French lithographs hanging on the wall: "they had wide frames of polished oak with gold roundels at the corners. They portrayed the story of Latude and Mme. de Pompadour" (4:269). The first lithograph represents the young and elegant Latude apparently declining a small bag of coins offered him by the beautiful Marquise de Pompadour, Louis XV's notorious and much-feared mistress. Another print depicts Latude, dressed in a lace nightshirt, dragged out of bed and apprehended by government agents. A third picture shows Latude in an apparent escape attempt from prison, lowering himself down a rope ladder from a tower under the cover of night. Jeannette reads aloud the epigraph of the first print: "Latude, born in 1725 . . . ambitious, but more foolish than culpable . . ." (4:269). She also comments on the charms of the fantastically coiffed and exquisitely dressed Mme. de Pompadour, noticing that Don Juan had anchored the rose she gave him several nights before between the glass and frame of the first lithograph. She coyly tranfers the rose to the second plate of the series which depicts Latude detained by the police.

Lithographs representing Latude and Mme. de Pompadour figure in other work by Azorín. In *El paisaje de España, visto por los españoles* he mentions having seen the series as a child while visiting a home in the mountainous region of Alicante, and recalls the epigraph of one print as reading, "He was arrested by order of the Marquise on the first of May, 1749." Azorín then observes, "During our life we've recalled Mme. de Pompadour offering a bag of coins to Latude so many times!" (3:1221–22). As described by Azorín in *Don Juan*, the lithograph series implies that some kind of illicit congress transpired between Latude and Mme. de Pompadour which Azorín obviously meant to emblematize the innuendoes beneath Jeannette's relationship to Don Juan, the difference being that Jeannette is much younger than the Marquise and Don Juan much older than Latude. This, at least, is the reading offered by Antonio Risco who writes that "the story of Latude and Mme. de Pompadour . . . resembles somewhat the action of the novel itself: Jeannette's temptation of don Juan with the simple rose she offers him" (1980, 240). The historial record, however, invalidates both Risco and Azorín, rather surprising in the case of the latter who knew the literature and history of the Spanish and French Enlightenments almost as well as any professional historian. The truth of the matter was that a certain Jean Danry who had served as assistant surgeon in the French army in Flanders found himself unemployed in Paris. Intelligent, attractive, but of somewhat dissolute character, Danry, who began calling himself "Henri Masers de la Tude," decided to turn a quick profit by exploiting national resentment against the King's favorite. In late April 1749, he and a friend manufactured a device from innocuous firecracker toys meant for children into a box that would pop loudly and spew forth powder upon opening. They mailed the box to the Marquise at Versailles hoping to gain handsome financial rewards for "denouncing" a plot against her life. Instead, Danry and his accomplice were arrested and hauled off to the Bastille from which Danry-Latude made several escape attempts, including one with the aid of a rope ladder constructed of shirts, stockings, and dinner napkins (Williams 116–32). He was finally released from prison in 1789 through the intervention of the grandson of Mme. de Pompadour's personal physician who had opened the fateful box of firecrackers forty years before. Clearly, the Latude-Pompadour story has nothing to do with sexual scandal but everything to do with a foolish young man's scheme to reap monetary rewards as quickly and effortlessly as possible. Why, then, would Azorín have chosen these lithographs as visual referents for the not-so-innocent dynamics between Jeannette and Don Juan? While it is unclear whether he was familiar with the true course of events in the Latude-Pompadour intrigue, it is obvious that the anonymous lithographer whose prints Azorín utilized as the visual background for his novel was either ignorant of the true facts, or purposefully chose to ignore them in order to add more spice to his art work. Whatever the case may be, Azorín elected to use the lithographer's version of events because it better served the hermeneutic significance he wanted his portrait-metaphors to convey.

In the "Autocrítica" that precedes the text of *Comedia del arte*, Azorín reveals that his play was inspired by a reproduction of an engraving by Watteau that he had picked up one day at the Rastro (4:980). While the "Autocrítica" situates the purchase somewhere between 1922 and 1927 (4:979), articles Azorín was publishing during the same period of time indicate that he was engaged in the reading of critical material on Watteau. In a 1920 essay on André Gide, published in *La Prensa* of Buenos Aires, Azorín mentions the Goncourt brothers' 1856 study of Watteau as the first in a series of critical appraisals of the artist; in "Un pintor a Buenos Aires," an article published in 1922, also in *La Prensa*, Azorín refers to the 1921 bicentennial commemorations of Watteau's death, mentioning a book he had read on the painter by Camille Mauclair.[21]

Not much is known about Antoine Watteau (1684–1721) other than the fact that when he first came to Paris he found employment with a painter of theatrical scenery, and that his first art teacher, Claude Gillot, specialized in paintings of scenes from the theater, a genre Watteau would transform and elevate to a refined and aristocratic, quality art form (Posner 12, 49). Watteau was born thirteen years after Louis XIV expelled the Italian commedia dell'arte players from Paris for insulting his mistress, Mme. de Maintenon, but he arrived in the French capital at a moment of growing public enthusiasm for the theater, and when the exodus of the Comédie Italienne had generated a demand for pictures of their characters or scenes from their plays (Posner 49). Although the Italian comedy did not return to Paris until 1716, five years before Watteau died, the artist's work in the genre is virtually synonymous with that of the Italian players (Goncourt 38). As is well-known, commedia dell'arte was improvised theater based on a loosely constructed plot outline performed by a company of actors each of whom specialized in a stock character role from which they rarely deviated. Allardyce Nicoll points out that Italian troupes began to visit France early in the seventeenth century; by 1661 there was a permanent company in Paris which had evolved such a uniquely French style of commedia that its center is often considered as being in Paris rather than Venice or Florence (160, 175–76). It was in the French theater that the oafish rogue Pedrolino was transformed into Pierrot, the melancholy and unlucky poet who often served as the unhappy middleman between his lady-love Colombine and her male admirers. One of Watteau's most beloved paintings is the slouched Pierrot dressed in his traditional white costume, wide, floppy hat and powdered face (Pl. 22).

Watteau's other generic specialty was the *fête galante* or the similar *fête champêtre* which portrayed authentic out-of-doors social activities pursued by the aristocracy at the center of which were musical or theatrical entertainments, coupled with amorous conversation and poetic innuendo of refined erotic behavior (Posner 151). Watteau seems to have recognized that the distinction between theater and reality was illusory, that dress was costume, and that human beings were actors on a social stage (Posner 58). His *fêtes galantes* or *champêtres* are peopled by real actors and actresses dressed in the costumes of their commedia roles, or conversely, ladies and gentlemen of the aristocracy wearing theatrical costume while they enjoy a pleasant outing to an elegant park. In both instances, the implication is that reality and fantasy are not only interchangeable but completely indistinguishable (Schneider 58). Whether the subject of Watteau's paintings was the Italian commedia, the *fête galante*, or a conflation of the two, his unifying theme was always the desire, pursuit, and attainment of love which he frequently emblematized with the Pierrot-Colombine duo.[22] Beneath the grace, wit, and poetic frivolity of these paintings there is always present, as Pierre Schneider observed, the silence that falls upon conversation when an angel passes, but the angel who brushes his wings "ever so lightly" over Watteau's actors and actresses, or the elegant participants of his outdoor parties, "causing them to hush, is the Angel of Death" (87). Watteau, who sought miracle cures for the tuberculosis that would kill him at age thirty-seven, was acutely conscious of the impermanent nature of love and pleasurable activity, as well as of the personal tragedy of time running out on his brilliant artistic career.

Rather than being inspired by a specific Watteau painting, I suggest that Azorín's *Comedia del arte* marries Watteau's interest in the theater, particularly the universal theme of illusion and reality as embodied by theatrical performance, to the ambience of a *fête galante* or *champêtre* which often situated the game of love in a bucolic setting. Azorín's play, much like a Watteau painting, is structured around the fulcrum of theatrical activity embedded within the parameters of the very text-performance we read or see, whereby the boundaries between reality and fantasy are purposefully blurred. The first act opens with a theater troupe relaxing in the country on one of its rare, free days. Despite admonitions from his colleagues, the lead actor

cannot help but escape into a secluded area of the park to rehearse his role for an upcoming production of Sophocles's *Oedipus at Colonos*. When Antonio Valdés is discovered studying his lines by José Vega, the troupe's dramaturge, the actor admits he is never off stage because fiction is everything to people of the theater. Vega adds that fiction is more attractive than reality and that ultimately actors are never able to distinguish whether reality resides in what they see or what they feign (4:982–83).[23] Unlike the commedia dell'arte where actors traditionally played one or two standard roles with which they were identified for life, the soubrette of Antonio Valdés's company, considered a lightweight by most of her colleagues, aspires to play Antigone in their production of *Oedipus*. In addition to advancing her career, Pacita Durán harbors a secret love for the middle-aged Valdés and sees the opportunity to play Antigone opposite his Oedipus as a way of bringing her closer to the actor whom she adores. Pacita confesses to José Vega, whose translation from the Greek the actors are using, that she has been learning the role of Antigone in secret and begs the poet to arrange an impromptu audition in the park. As the scene progresses, Vega realizes that the two actors have begun to stray from the text: Pacita, overwhelmed by the experience, uses the theater not only to disclose her potential as a tragic actress but also to facilitate a veiled declaration of love. The moment takes on the flavor of an Italian *commedia al improviso* which José Vega protests has nothing to do with his translation; Valdés, however, responds that such is the nature of commedia: "The author provides the plot, and the actor provides the dialogue" (4:995). Act 1 concludes with life imitating art when Valdés agrees to cast Pacita as Antigone and the young actress's fantasy at last becomes reality.

Act 2 takes place ten years later, and life once again imitates art, collapsing the boundaries between truth and fiction: we learn that two years after his triumph as Oedipus, Antonio Valdés lost his eyesight and had to retire from the stage. In the interim, Pacita Durán has become an internationally acclaimed tragedienne and is on her way back to Spain after a long tour of the Americas. The key to her success in the classical roles, according to Pacita's aged mentor, is that from the beginning she understood that theater is not so much about plot or the re-creation of period costume, as it is about revealing the archetypal nature of basic human affect. Pacita realizes that human beings experience hate, love, jealousy, and ambition in the same ways today as they did thousands of years ago; her "innovation" is merely to infuse these sentiments with a contemporary interpretation (4:1009). When she rejoins her former colleagues Pacita announces plans for a benefit performance of *Oedipus* for the impoverished poet José Vega. In a case of art now imitating life, she persuades Antonio Valdés to come out of retirement to re-create the role of Oedipus. Act 2 also reveals that in the intervening years, Antonio Valdés has been privately coaching Paco Méndez, the son of his company's former leading lady. Paco was only eight years old when Pacita triumphed as Antigone, but he was old enough to remember the electricity between Antonio and Pacita, and he now grills his mother as to whether Pacita Durán might have been in love with her leading man.

The third, and last, act takes place backstage during the benefit performance and afterward at the cast party. During the benefit itself, young Méndez approaches José Vega to confide his desire to debut opposite Pacita whom he also more than admires professionally. Recognizing that he will always be a groomsman and never a groom, Vega wistfully tells Paco that life is a theater in which only one play has been running since the birth of humanity. One of the acts in this long-playing drama, he says, is titled "Amor," and, because all the acts repeat themselves in perpetuity, Paco's confession reminds Vega of a day long ago when in a garden "a young woman approached me and anxiously requested . . . like you are doing now, to debut in a play that a great actor was going to stage" (4:1021–22). Always the facilitator of messages between couples, but never in love or able to declare himself openly (although he comes closest in a brief exchange with Pacita early in the play [4:991–92]), Vega points us in the direction of Watteau's many paintings of Gilles-Pierrot. This character, as he evolved in the French commedia, was typically associated with frustrated or hopeless love and, like José Vega, was a crucial go-between for lovers in commedia dell'arte scenarios. Watteau often depicted Pierrot as a tragic figure, usually placed at some distance from other company members, always costumed in white with a floppy baker's toque on his head, and posed in a slightly awkward physical posture (Pl. 22). Azorín captures the spirit of Watteau's Pierrot in an act 2 stage direction where he describes José Vega who has just returned from some financially disastrous and artistically unproductive years abroad: "José Vega appears in the door. He stops for a moment on the threshold, his head hanging, his arms limp, hands clasped together. He wears a wide hat. A long mane of hair shows from underneath" (4:1014).

In a reprise of his role as intermediary, Vega delicately communicates Paco Méndez's wish to debut opposite her to Pacita during the cast party. Pacita's reaction is the same as Don Antonio's had been years earlier: "Me . . . I control myself. He's a child." But Vega pursues the matter as he had also done with his friend Valdés: "You control yourself? Really? Your entire soul . . . all your enthusiasm only for art? And life that passes you by? And youth that slips away? Don't you feel love?" (4:1025).[24] The play concludes at daybreak as the group of old friends lifts their glasses in a toast to love, a toast during which Don Antonio passes away reciting lines from Calderón. An old flame has been extinguished, but a new day has dawned, and with it, a new debut and a new love: the play of life, as José Vega had predicted, repeats itself unchanged into eternity. In the same way that Watteau's highly theatrical paintings in which everyone plays a role and reality is inseparable from fantasy, Azorín, too, explores the indistinct boundaries between life and art. And like the Angel of Death who lurks beneath the superficial gaiety of Watteau's paintings, "comedia del arte," as the physician of Azorín's theatrical troupe observes, is really a "tragedia del arte": tragic because if art is truly a mirror held up to life, and if there is, indeed, no difference between illusion and reality, then art is forever doomed to mimic the tragedy of life's inexorable circularity (4:995).

2

Pictures on Exhibition

The Prado: A Garden of Fictional Delights

ONE OF AZORÍN'S FAVORITE PASTIMES WAS TO prowl museums both at home and abroad. A protagonist in the 1897 collection of short stories *Bohemia*, mentions that he goes to the Prado Museum every Sunday where he spends many hours contemplating the martyrs painted by José de Ribera (1:296). In the 1944 *Tiempos y cosas*, Azorín himself wrote that he regularly spent two or three hours in the Museum every morning (7:214). The Prado's labyrinthine exhibition halls provided Azorín an intimate refuge where he could pursue his cherished activities of visual contemplation, intellectual meditation, and the observation of fellow human beings completely unencumbered: "I walk through its exhibition halls with perfect ease; I sit on a divan and read the newspaper; I contemplate the paintings; I observe the pretty copyists who work in the Velázquez Gallery; I watch the incessant comings and goings of English tourists with their sturdy boots; the Germans with their frock coats . . . those pretty . . . Parisians who . . . appear with their high heels tapping ever so lightly" (7:214–15). Although Azorín loved the art treasures at the Prado, he was often appalled by the dilapidated condition of its physical plant, as well as by the irresponsi-

ble attitudes and lack of professional qualifications of some of the Museum's directors.

The projected sale of an unidentified painting by the Dutch artist Hugo van der Goes (1440?–1482) from the Prado collection stirred a protest of national dimensions in Spain that left Azorín rather nonplussed. Despite an outcry against the sale, in the essay "Lo del Van der Goes," he observed that when it came to raising money through public subscription designed to prevent the sale of the painting, only a few thousand *pesetas* had been collected (*PCQ* 63). He was truly perplexed as to the etiology of the national protest since the painting was not by a Spanish artist and represented nothing of "our spirit or our national aesthetics." The protest would be understandable, he observed, if the Prado were a museum within which the history of art was displayed in a chronological fashion that the projected sale would disrupt, but the Prado's holdings consisted of isolated groups of pictures between which there were tremendous chronological lacunae. Furthermore, Azorín pointed out that Germanic primitives were far better represented at the Museum by Patinir and Petrus Christus than by the single van der Goes canvas that had caused so much national consternation (*PCQ* 64–65). Even had the subscription been successful in raising the requisite one and one half million francs to pay for the painting, Azorín queried whether it might not be absurd to spend that kind of money in order to retain a non-Spanish work of art when, at the same time, the government was happily selling off abroad national art treasures in which breathed the authentic spirit of "our people and our race." The few *pesetas* that were gathered, he argued, would be better spent remedying the lamentable state of the Museum itself: for more than a month the damask upholstery on a sofa in the Murillo gallery remained torn, shamelessly displaying its tattered viscera for all to see, and perhaps leading foreign visitors to conclude that the Spanish people cared nothing for the upkeep of one of the world's greatest museums (*PCQ* 68–69).

Several months later (27 July 1913), Azorín was again outraged by events at the Prado: while the torn sofa still remained an eyesore in the Murillo gallery, the Museum had purchased a very expensive turnstile to be able to count automatically the number of daily visitors to the Prado. Since the apparatus was so costly, only one turnstile was installed and, in order to gather accurate statistics, all entrances to the Prado, save the principal one, had been closed, a decision that inconvenienced visitors to the Museum (*PCQ* 103). Because the space had originally been planned as a museum of natural history, light conditions at the Prado were not especially propitious to the exhibition and viewing of paintings (8:504). When he became aware of talk about constructing new space to accommodate a national theater company, Azorín protested vociferously, arguing that because the Prado was the only tourist attraction in Madrid, rather than build a home for a national theater, the government would do better to construct a building for the express purpose of displaying the nation's glorious art treasures that, more than anything else, sheltered the "soul of Spain" (7:1144–45).[1]

Occasioning most protest from Azorín, however, was what he called the annual autumnal "quadrille of paintings at the Museum" (7:482–83). Every year upon his return from the summer holiday, Azorín would immediately head to the Prado to witness with horror the incumbent director's gratuitous rearrangement of the collection: "Goya now hangs in the spot that El Greco used to occupy. . . . Rubens is dislodged by Titian . . . Raphael or Giorgione now replace Titian; how, in sum, large and small canvases are moved, replaced, and moved again in that chaotic and deafening sarabande . . ." (7:483). He observed that the constant rehanging of paintings that had been going on over a number of decades had begun to affect the works of art, invariably chipping the pigment and, in some cases, leaving significant bare patches in the Museum's "marvelous canvases" (7:484). Among the most heavily damaged were paintings by Goya (*PCQ* 11), especially a picture titled *La feria en el Rastro* (7:251). According to Azorín, this kind of collection "management" was the sport of choice among all the Museum's directors, and it provoked his rhadamanthine condemnation. As early as the 1903 article "En el Museo," published under the pseudonym "Pecuchet" in *El Globo*, Azorín called the Prado's newly appointed director "a man who has painted twelve or fourteen mediocre pictures," and he leveled harsh words at a system that entrusted art treasures symbolic of the country's history and past greatness to an unknown lightweight who engaged in further damaging the paintings by indulging in the game of musical art works (*PCQ* 11). The director, whom Azorín never identifies by name, had also undertaken inept restorations, leaving some of the Museum's paintings almost unrecognizable; the most notable and criminal being the "thick and ridiculous coat of automobile varnish" applied to Velázquez's *Las Meninas*, completely destroying the painting's ethereal light and diaphanous ambience. To add insult to injury, the painting had barely escaped even more serious damage when a window in the room where it was exhibited had fallen in. One could not help but feel sad when visiting the Prado, wrote Azorín, who witnessed the slow destruction of some of the greatest works of Spanish art (*PCQ* 12).[2] The greatest enthusiast of collection rearrangement at the Prado was a Mr. Villegas, an amateur painter whose thoughts Azorín said, randomly fluttered from one gallery of the Museum to the next. Villegas was an affable, correct individual, but whenever Azorín observed him in the Museum, spyglass in hand, about to rehang another picture, he wished Villegas would return to painting more "important" works on the order of his *La muerte del torero* (7:251).

When he finally had the opportunity to visit the Louvre during his Civil War exile in Paris, Azorín could not help but compare the arrangement of paintings in the French museum, which he termed a "museo hembra" (feminine museum) to that of the Prado, which he called a "museo macho" (masculine museum) (6:219). At the Louvre contemporary paintings were displayed in the very heart of the museum from which the visitor could radiate out into adjacent galleries that led to masterpieces from the past. This core of contemporary art functioned as a safe harbor, anchoring viewers in the present of their own familiar world from which they could then depart on a journey into the "preterit tense" of art history. At the Prado, on the other hand, a visitor was obliged to lose contact with the present immediately upon stepping over the threshold because he was plunged without transition into the "past tense" of the art-historical canon (6:707). For Azorín, museums were, indeed, places where the past and present assumed rather fluid properties, and perhaps this explains why he spent so much time in them in a kind of "suspended animation."

In the early decades of the twentieth century, museums in Spain, more often than not, displayed works of art in a jumbled, visual cacophony of arbitrarily arranged canvases. Contemporary photographs show exhibition galleries in which different genres, styles, and sizes of paintings are thrown together, all of them competing for space; many rooms were hung to the ceiling with art work, making for very difficult viewing indeed (Bernal 1990, 89). In his review of Rafael Laínez Alcalá's book on the painter Pedro Berruguete, Azorín meditated on the proper way to view paintings. He observed that each work of art in a museum required its own space, and that when hung too closely together, paintings begin to vie with one another for a visitor's attention, thus detracting from their own impact. Aware that the museum demands a time-bound, diachronic viewing of its collection, each picture urging the viewer to move forward in time, Azorín preferred a setting more conducive to an atemporal, synchronic apprehension of individual works that allowed each painting to reveal its mysteries on its own terms. Paradoxically, the best fate true lovers of art might wish for their favorite painters, he wrote, is that their work not be consigned to the walls of a museum, but to a special place where visitors could proceed at their own pace in a gentle stillness favorable to losing all sensation of time (*AE* 290–95).[3]

Works of art frequently served Azorín as sources of inspiration for his essays and short fiction. He visited museums assiduously, purchasing picture postcards of paintings he liked, as well as exhibition catalogues and books on art and artists (7:1015). While his penchant for "re-creating" works of classical Spanish literature in his own fiction is widely acclaimed, the role Azorín played in bringing important paintings from the Prado collection to general public attention in the essays and stories he published in popular magazines is not as well-known. In his biography of Azorín, Ramón Gómez de la Serna recalled the writer's inconclusive courtship of a young *copista* at the Prado early in the twentieth century. After describing the pair's timid encounters and brief verbal exchanges, Gómez de la Serna suggested that perhaps what really drew Azorín to the young lady, and held him in thrall for hours at a time on the "gran *puf* redondo" of the gallery where she worked, was the copyist's exercise of transferring onto a fresh canvas the reality of an old masterpiece, a process remarkably similar to Azorín's own technique of recasting the work of great painters or writers in his essays and fiction (1957, 240). One of Azorín's most remarkable achievements in this regard was a series of six vignettes he wrote in 1905–6 for the illustrated review *Blanco y Negro*. Each piece was based on a painting by a major artist from the Prado Museum and was accompanied by a photographic reproduction of the picture in question. Gómez de la Serna remembered that he always saw Azorín at the Prado alone, scrutinizing the paintings, his lips pursed in concentration, surveying the art-historical past as would a detective searching for mysteries as yet unrevealed to the public (1957, 55). He remarked that Azorín's fictive reconstructions in *Blanco y Negro* on what might be transpiring among a painting's cast of characters, and his analyses of what the painting might really be about, breathed new life into works of art and imbued them with a dramatic flair most visitors to the Prado had never before imagined. With Azorín's encouragement these pictures came magically alive, his essays providing a living catalogue of the Museum in lieu of the official guide "in which the dusty canvases came across as dry and rigid." At the time that Azorín's Prado series was published, Gómez de la Serna recalled that he awaited each piece with great anticipation, then headed directly to the Museum, Azorín's essay in hand, in order to (re)view the painting under discussion, allowing the written word to reveal to him "what there was in each picture of the homey, familiar, and secret" (1957, 154).

Azorín was not the first to engage in this kind of activity. In the "Pensées Detachées," Diderot comments that looking at paintings by great masters is as useful to writers as the reading of great literature is to painters (749). Azorín himself clearly appreciated the work of authors who were inspired by great works of art, as is evident in his commentary on José María Salaverría's *Los fantasmas del Prado* (1921), a collection of pieces that he described as a "series of refined 'sensations' before the pictures of the Prado Museum, stimulated by what those great paintings represent in history and in art" (*VH* 239). In his project of re-creating and narrating paintings with words, Azorín lent credence to Horace's adage that poetry gives voice to painting; he would have agreed with the argument Merleau-Ponty advanced in a polemical response to André Malraux's *Les voix du silence* in which the French philosopher posited that the arbitrary signs of written documents were superior to the natural signs of art because a painting is unable to resist time in the same way as could a manuscript. He argued that even in a torn or incomplete state, the signification of the word was embraced by the written text differently than works of art which do not possess the ductility of speech. Thus, in Merleau-Ponty's view, literature truly speaks, while the "voices" of painting are nothing but silence (G. Johnson 17).

The first essay in Azorín's *Blanco y Negro* series was "Don José Nieto," published on 11 November 1905. The piece is an imaginary biography of the male figure Velázquez painted at the top of a small staircase in the background of *Las Meninas*. Rather than accompany his article with a reproduction of the entire painting, Azorín chose only the portion of Velázquez's masterpiece that portrayed José Nieto, opting—as was frequently his custom—for a synecdochic fragment to represent the whole. After a brief description of *Las Meninas*, in which he referred to each character in the painting by his or her historically verifiable name, Azorín begins to weave his fictional tale. He suggests that José Nieto was depicted on the staircase because Velázquez modified his plans for the original composition of the picture during the last moments before actually beginning to paint.

Although it was known that José Nieto was a distant relative of Velázquez's, and that at the time *Las Meninas* was painted Don José was the director of the royal tapestry works, Azorín queried rhetorically, "Who is José Nieto?", and proceeded to invent possible responses. He may have been a soldier in Flanders or Italy, now retired to Madrid; perhaps he owns a collection of Petrarch's sonnets or a copy of the *Consolación filosófica* by the Roman philosopher Boethius. Perhaps Don José suffers from an irascible temper, threatening to defenestrate his servants as does a character in *La sirena de Tanacria* by Córdoba Figueroa. But when his temper is under control, José Nieto is most likely a good man who repents having wronged a fellow human being. Perhaps he calms himself by reading a little Petrarch and later finds his way to Velázquez's palace studio where Don Diego portrays him as the "very peaceable, very calm, very sweet man" whom we see in the painting today. Like most of the vignettes in the series, this picture "speaks" because Azorín animates it with a cautionary tone that produces a discretely modern, exemplary tale on the benefits of controlling one's temper.

The second installment of the series, "Un elegante" (25 November 1905), is based on a fragment Azorín writes he extracted from "a painting by Goya." The picture, titled *La vendimia* (Pl. 23), depicts a grape harvest scene in which a female peasant offers the bounty of the harvest to a well-dressed, upper-class couple and their child; farmhands and mountain peaks appear in the background. What interests Azorín most is the elegant husband who instantiates the typical eighteenth-century *petimetre*, or dandy. He uses this portion of Goya's picture as a point of departure for a meditation on the indignation eighteenth-century Spanish moralists expressed regarding the decadent frivolity of contemporary society as exemplified by the *petimetre*. Once we begin to read the essay, however, we realize that it is not so much a study of the dandy himself, as it is an examination of eighteenth-century diatribe against the loose morals of society women whom one Joaquín de Paz y Monroy condemns for allowing themselves to be coiffed by male hairdressers; Francisco López Salcedo berates them for putting rather bizarre ornaments into their elaborate coiffures; Alvarez de Toledo chastises women for speaking too loudly during social calls and for walking in too provocative a manner. Nevertheless, in Azorín's eyes, it is the *petimetre* of the painting, with his stylish frock coat, fine silk stockings, and "admirably simple" life of social entertainments and lapdogs, who epitomizes the "depraved" society of the eighteenth century. Once again Azorín depends upon a fragment of canvas to inform a painting in its entirety; in this case, the social mores of the Spanish Enlightenment, and he again couches his exegesis of visual text within the generic boundaries of an exemplary tale.[4]

Azorín based his third cautionary story, which he ironically titled "Un buen señor" (2 December 1905), on a fragment of Pedro Berruguete's painting *Auto de Fe* (Pl. 24). The picture depicts a detailed scene of victims condemned by the Inquisition to burn at the stake, jailers mounted on horseback, executioners, and a sizable group of church and civil functionaries who observe the proceedings from a raised platform above the scene. One of the officials witnessing the *auto* is a seated man who appears to have dozed off despite the goings-on all around him (Fig. 12). As in the case of his fictional biography of Don José Nieto, Azorín offers a meditation on who this personage might be, and why he seems so unconcerned by the horrifying events taking place before his eyes. Although our "buen señor" had been notified a few days previously that his presence would be required at today's solemn festivities, he had forgotten and overslept. Although the authorities send a page to fetch their absent colleague, by the time he arrives the executions have already begun and he is so exhausted that even while some victims are burned and others plead for their lives, all that concerns this good man is finding a comfortable position in which to snooze. When the quota of executions is fulfilled, he will calmly return to his palace, consume a midday repast, and retire to his garden for a siesta where, completely unaffected by the *auto de fe*, he will again drift off, perhaps recalling verses by the worldly medieval monk Berceo, "Ca estos son los arbores do debemos folgar . . . en cuya sombra suelen las aves organar" [For these are the trees under which we should rest . . . in whose shade the birds customarily trill]. Azorín uses a seemingly insignificant portion of Berruguete's canvas as a springboard to comment on the disparity between what might be of grave consequence for one individual, for another will have no moral or social importance whatsoever.

Miser Marsilio y su esposa, a painting by Lorenzo Lotto (1480–1556), leads Azorín to a meditation on hedonism that is the basis of the fourth essay in the series, titled "Un sensual" (9 December 1905). The painting depicts a young couple from the monied strata of Italian Renaissance society; the man is placing a ring on the woman's finger; above them hovers a maliciously smiling *putto*, his chubby arms embracing and drawing the couple closer together (Fig. 13). Azorín imagines the scene as taking place in the Milanese area of Bérgamo, perhaps during the autumn festival of Saint Alexander. The young man might be the son or grandson of merchants whose success has allowed him to move beyond his roots to a comfortable life of aristocratic leisure and an auspicious marriage to the Lauretta or Fiametta whom we see in the painting. Azorín observes that a passage in *La Celestina* cautions that one's inner virtues are revealed by the physiognomy. What he notices about the young man's face is his nose, "one of those noses—like Baudelaire's—of sensual, voluptuous men." But this young man, writes Azorín, although he sets a magnificent table, wears exquisite clothes, reads Boccaccio, and appreciates the undulating stride of beautiful women, also knows how to control his passions as counseled by his contemporary, Michel de Montaigne. And, because he exercises self-control, the young man of Lotto's picture will be able to enjoy the spectacle of life in Renaissance Italy with utmost intensity. The implied moral of the story that Azorín coaxes from the painting is that the tragedy of passions run amok, as occurs in *La Celestina*, will never devastate the lives of this Italian couple. "Our young friend" will make Lauretta or Fiametta happy because, at the same time that he is a consummate master of his emotions, he also is capable of living life to the fullest.

In keeping with the Christmas season, Azorín's fifth story, "Unos espectadores" (23 December 1905), is both an ekphrasis and a fictionalization of Hieronymus Bosch's triptych *La adoración de los Magos* (Fig. 14). His commentary, however, is restricted to the central panel that depicts a ramshackle hut in front of which three kings are grouped around the Madonna and Child. All around the hut—on its roof, climbing up its walls, and peeking through its broken windows—are what appear to be mercenary soldiers who have wandered off from the warring armies Bosch depicts in the distant

Blanco y Negro
Revista ilustrada

AÑO XV
MADRID
2 DICIEMBRE
DE 1905
NUM. 761

LOS AMIGOS DEL MUSEO. UN BUEN SEÑOR. Pedro Berruguete, en su tabla del Museo del Prado, nos ha conservado su figura inmortal. Es un hombre sencillo, discreto, apacible. No le sucede nada; le notificaron hace unos días que tenía que venir á presenciar este espectáculo, y después lo olvidó; esta mañana, cuando ya estaba todo preparado, cuando ya iban á subir los primeros reos al tablado, viendo que no venía, le han enviado un paje para llamarlo. El paje le ha encontrado todavía en la cama. D. Rodrigo, que es el mayordomo de su casa, se ha opuesto á que se le despertara; doña Giomar, la vieja dueña, que sabe las indignaciones terribles que el señor coge cuando se le despierta, levantaba ante el paje las manos al cielo é invocaba á la Virgen del Carmen y á la de las Angustias...

Sin embargo, había que proporcionarle este disgusto al señor; un segundo paje ha llegado, y ya entonces, D. Rodrigo ha entrado en la cámara del ilustre personaje y ha abierto las ventanas. Cuando el señor se ha enterado de por qué se le despertaba, ha dicho sencillamente: «¡Ah, sí, es verdad!», se ha vestido, ha tomado sosegadamente un refrigerio y se ha encaminado á la plaza de la ciudad. Al verle llegar, el auto ha comenzado: sólo faltaba él. Dos reos han sido aupados al cadalso, y allí se les ha hecho pagar con sus vidas sus delitos; después han de ser quemados sobre una hoguera. En tanto, nuestro amigo, acomodado en su sitio, se revolvía á una parte y á otra buscando una postura cómoda; acaso este asiento en que él está sentado se le antoja un tanto duro; tal vez piensa que él no hacía falta en esta función, y que mejor estaría á estas horas durmiendo. Bajo del estrado, á pocos pasos de él, otros dos reos son llevados al cadalso; á su izquierda, en el cadalso, los anteriores heresiarcas, muertos ya, muestran sus cuerpos rígidos, yertos. Y el excelente señor, á quien no interesa nada de esto, ha acabado—como nos lo muestra Berruguete en su tabla,—ha acabado por echar hacia atrás el busto, por entornar los ojos y por sumirse en un plácido y agradable estupor. Quizás los reos suplican, gimen, lanzan plañidos angustiosos; es posible que una multitud, que no vemos en la pintura, grite á lo lejos. Nuestro buen amigo dormita sosegado...

Y cuando acabe el auto volverá tranquilamente á su palacio. En él habrá anchas y confortables estancias: un huerto con frondosas avenidas de olmos se extenderá detrás del caserón. Y entre estos frescos olmos, después de un buen yantar, nuestro épico amigo dará unos paseítos antes de tomar su siesta inevitable. «Ca estos son los arbores do debemos folgar—pensará el buen señor con Gonzalo de Berceo;—en cuya sombra suelen las aves organar».

AZORIN

Fig. 12   Blanco y Negro, *Reproduction of 2 December 1905 issue.*

Fig. 13   Lorenzo Lotto, *Miser Marsilio y su esposa*, 1523. Oil on canvas, 71 × 84 cm. Museo del Prado, Madrid.

background of his painting. As Miguel Angel Lozano pointed out, it is in this essay that Azorín is most conscious that the impact of his piece is largely dependent upon whether or not his readers are able to see clearly details of the painting in the black and white reproduction provided by *Blanco y Negro* (37). He therefore describes the picture with painstaking care because he is unsure that "you will make all of this out in the photograph." As in the indifferent "buen señor" of Berruguete's canvas, Azorín contrasts Bosch's two armies about to clash in the background of the picture with the strolling lovers, thoroughly oblivious to the momentous event that has occurred on the outskirts of town, portrayed in the painting's middle ground. What intrigues Azorín most is the question "¿quiénes son estos espectadores de que vamos a hablar y que figuran en la tabla que tenemos ante la vista?" Who are these specta-

tors and what are they looking at? Azorín imagines them to be renegade soldiers who have momentarily wandered off from their squadrons to get a better look at the curious proceedings taking place in and around the shack. He imagines their stupefied reaction to the nativity scene they witness: three kings paying homage to the newborn son of a simple peasant woman. Paradoxically, these accidental tourists, men of war and representatives of armed force, happen to be present at the birth of the Prince of Peace. Bosch's triptych yields not only a timely meditation on the meaning of Christ's birth, but in his exegesis of who the secondary characters in Bosch's visual text might be, Azorín finds a logical way to connect the foreground portion of the painting to the presence of otherwise inexplicable armies, dogs, soldiers, and strolling lovers who people the middle and backgrounds of the picture and, once again, he relies on a synec-

Fig. 14   Hieronymus Bosch, *Tríptico de la Adoración de los Magos*, c. 1495. Oil on wood panel, 138 × 138 cm. Museo del Prado, Madrid.

dochic fragment from a larger painting to elucidate the sum of its parts.[5]

The last essay of the Prado series, and the most atypical, is titled "Un magistrado" (13 January 1906). It is based on Velázquez's portrait of the *licenciado* Don Diego del Corral, a relatively undistinguished subject compared to the popes, generals, kings, and queens normally associated with the Velázquez repertoire (Fig. 15). We might ask why Azorín would have chosen a portrait whose model did not enjoy immediate name recognition, either with readers or with visitors to the Prado Museum, but he cleverly contextualizes the subject not by weaving a semifictional tale around his life, but rather by considering the consequences a death war-

rant signed by Diego del Corral had not only for the condemned man, Don Rodrigo Calderón—court favorite and prime minister to Felipe IV—but perhaps also on the course of events in Spanish political and art history. Azorín thereby demonstrates in the subtle, indirect manner characteristic of his style, how an otherwise insignificant human being could overcome the limitations of an unremarkable existence, surpassing certain oblivion not by what he did with his own life, but by the effect his life had on that of greater men. There is, again, an exemplary tale to be culled from Azorín's commentary on the impermanent nature of power: Don Rodrigo Calderón, "one day so great, so powerful," now languishes in a mis-

Fig. 15 Diego Rodríguez de Silva y Velázquez, *Don Diego del Corral y Arellano*, 1631. Oil on canvas, 215 × 110 cm. Museo del Prado, Madrid.

erable jail cell, destroyed by gout and utterly abandoned. In building a meaningful scaffolding to support the historically unimportant Don Diego del Corral, Azorín provides Velázquez's painting with a context and meaning it would not otherwise have in the mind's eye of readers or museum visitors. At the same time he reinserts this seemingly inconsequential portrait, emblematic of a minuscule fraction of the Byzantine politics at the seventeenth-century Spanish court, into a much larger historical picture, made comprehensible through his brief foray into and through art history.

Strolling Through the Louvre: The Art of Exile

Despite having been to Paris in 1905 as part of the press delegation that reported an official visit young King Alfonso XIII made to the French capital, and again in 1918 as a war correspondent, Azorín did not visit the Louvre until his self-imposed exile to Paris where he lived from October 1936 to August 1939. Nevertheless, Azorín noted in *Españoles en París* that even before actually setting foot in the Louvre, he was familiar with the museum's collection from books, photographs, picture postcards, and various catalogue reproductions (5:853). During his nearly three years of exile, Azorín divided his time between writing articles for the Buenos Aires newspaper *La Prensa*, his only source of dependable income, and visiting libraries, churches, museums, public gardens, and the used-book stalls that lined the left bank of the Seine (3:21–22). However, as he observed in his memoirs, it was the museums of Paris that became his refuge from the pain, sadness, and disorientation of life in exile. Although Azorín frequented the Musée Grevin as well as the Carnavalet, the Louvre was clearly his favorite: he wrote that he visited the museum nearly three hundred times during his stay in Paris (8:413, 352).[6] Indeed, it appears that one of the very first things Azorín did on his arrival in Paris was to pay a visit to the Louvre, the excursion documented by an entry ticket to the museum dated 30 October 1936 tucked into his copy of Louis Hourticq's *Le Musée du Louvre . . . Guide de l'Art* (166–67).

Azorín wrote that while the experience of seeing his favorite paintings in the original confirmed his fondness for some, he found others thoroughly disappointing. He thought Rembrandt's *Bathsheba* superb and Giorgione's *Concert champêtre* without equal, but the absence of color in the work of Corot was not at all what he had imagined, and Manet's *Olympia*, "so controversial in its day," left him completely unmoved; on the other hand, Azorín was so impressed by Mantegna's *Parnassus* that on leaving the museum after his second visit there, he bought a colored postcard of the painting (5:856–57). The most splendid collection of paintings at the Louvre—perhaps even in the world, according to Azorín—belonged to the Italian Renaissance that represented "the pinnacle of color and line in art" (5:849–50). Leonardo da Vinci's *Saint John the Baptist* elicited a meditation on the artist's aphorism "Natura non rompa sua legge," which led Azorín to remark that the law of great art was similarly infrangible because the painter creates beautiful pictures just as naturally and spontaneously as an apple tree produces fruit (5:855). Azorín also liked the work of the nineteenth-century animal sculptor Antoine-Louis Barye, but he spent by far the greatest amount of time in the "small, deserted room . . . in which the woman found at Milo shows herself off."[7] In "Homero en el Louvre," Azorín first described the Venus de Milo as just another piece of sculpture and then, as he was often inclined to do, he added layer upon layer of increasingly specific detail so that when the statue is finally identified, a reader feels that she has known its name all along:

Pero al presente me hallo en presencia de otra mujer. No sé dónde la he conocido. No sé tampoco donde naciera. Tal vez, no en Atenas. . . . Sana y fuerte . . . ha ido avanzando en la vida. No podemos saber qué edad podrá tener ahora. Acaso veinte o veintidós años. . . . Sus labios, carnositos, se entreabren. Nos va a decir algo tal vez. . . . De un ángulo . . . nos trasladamos a otro. Y así la vamos contemplando en todos sus aspectos. . . . Preciso es que dejemos a la Venus de Milo. (5:850)[8]

[But at the moment I find myself in the presence of another woman. I don't know where I've met her. Neither do I know where she might have been born. Perhaps not in Athens. . . . She's gone through life healthy and strong. We cannot know how old she is now. Perhaps twenty or twenty-two. . . . Her full lips are half-open. Perhaps she's going to say something to us. . . . From one corner of the room we move to another. And thus we proceed to contemplate all of her features. It's necessary to take our leave now of the Venus de Milo].

There were also the magnificent Rembrandts. In "Atropos en el Louvre," Azorín reviewed some of his personal favorites: *The Good Samaritan*; *Saint Matthew*, deep in thought, pen in hand, the other softly caressing his beard; and one of several paintings representing Bathsheba. Adjacent to the Van Dyck gallery, Azorín found the exuberant paintings of Rubens, but it was Rubens's portrayal of the three Fates that caught his fancy, especially the figure of Atropos with the tiny scissors she uses to sever the thread of life woven by her two sisters. He found it ironic that Rubens, the painter of life's sensual pleasures, would have been equally adept at representing death. Azorín's attraction to questions concerning time, eternity, and the perishable nature of matter prevented him from seeing anything else in the same gallery: "With her tiny scissors, prepared to sever the thread of life, the young goddess is there, in my thoughts, and no longer in the painting. The obsession becomes so overwhelming that my eyes see nothing else of their surroundings . . ." (*PCQ* 221). When he returned from his reverie, Azorín was shaken anew because he saw the features of Atropos duplicated in the face of a female visitor to the gallery who had been contemplating the same painting: a friend tells him the woman is a famous actress. Thus Azorín had the rare experience of beholding a painted, mythological deity alongside a flesh and blood theater diva. But seeing the actress in performance later that evening dissipates the hallucination of the previous hours, and Azorín's obsession with Atropos recedes. It is the image of Rembrandt's *The Evangelist Matthew, inspired by an Angel* that remains in his mind's eye. He concludes that his experience was an excellent example of a case study in how fantasy is able to play tricks on the human mind, and how any aesthetic representation that is truly sublime can exercise a hypnotic effect on a viewer's imagination (*PCQ* 223–24).[9]

The Louvre became a conduit that enabled Azorín to forget temporarily the stresses of exile in a country whose language he did not speak very well, and the concomitant insecurity raised by lack of steady employment and a substantial loss of income: "Days have gone by. Visits to the Louvre have been more frequent. For someone who is distressed and finds himself far from his native land, the Louvre is a momentary Lethe" (5:846).[10] The Museum provided Azorín a source of spiritual consolation; its works of art inspired numerous essays and short stories, often serving as analogues of the author's distressed emotional state. Azorín had used works of art to instantiate personal emotions as early as the 1928 proto-surrealist novel *El caballero inactual* in which he commented briefly on the efficacy of creating visual images to emblematize inner sensation, or to express "an essential reality" (5:31). The process became much more constant in *Españoles en París* (1939) and *Sintiendo a España* (1942) which collect short fiction Azorín wrote during his Parisian exile.[11] The majority of the "fictional" characters in these stories are painters, art connoisseurs, collectors of art, or knowledgeable visitors to the Louvre. Whenever she visits Paris, the eponymous heroine of "Rebeca en París," never fails to pay an obligatory visit to the Louvre. One of her favorite paintings is Poussin's *Rebeca y Eliezer*; the modern-day Rebecca has a nearly symbiotic relationship with her painted counterpart, similar to that between Doña Inés and her medieval ancestor, Doña Beatriz, in Azorín's 1925 novel *Doña Inés (Historia de amor)*: "The two Rebeccas were symbiotic. For a moment, Rebecca was not herself, but the other one" (5:801). Now, during the Spanish Civil War, Azorín's Rebecca finds herself in the same emotional and moral quandary as her biblical namesake: she is the mother of twin boys and her husband Dámaso, like the biblical Issac, is also blind. Dámaso's favorite son, Enrique, has just been killed in the war and the Spanish Rebecca faces the same dilemma as did the mother of Jacob and Esau: "The biblical Rebecca declared to blind Issac . . . that the son he had in front of him was his first born. . . . But it was not Esau who stood before Issac. Rebecca was not telling the truth." In Paris, Rebecca stands in meditation before Poussin's canvas, hoping to find a solution to her predicament: whether or not to follow biblical example, and with the telling of a compassionate lie, spare her husband needless emotional heartache (5:801).

Azorín's writing on art during exile revolves around paintings into which he reads stories of loss, death, and ruin. The painter-protagonist of "La continuidad histórica" finds himself "withdrawn due to the heartache of absence" during which he is able to think of nothing but Spain

(6:679). The sixty-five year old landscape painter, Gaspar Salgado, who protagonizes many stories of *Sintiendo a España*, on one occasion has a quasi out-of-body experience in which, unsure of who or where he is, Salgado concludes he must be in Paris because he feels out of his element. The elderly painter, nearly the same age as Azorín, is so steeped in his "Spanishness," he confesses that of the "infinite number of canvases I have stained with paint," not a single one portrays a foreign landscape (6:702). Finding himself exiled in Paris, however, Salgado is so overwhelmed by nostalgia for his country that he decides to abandon landscape for history painting in the line of the great nineteenth-century Spanish artists Rosales, Gisbert, Casado del Alisal, and Pradilla (6:751).[12] While Salgado earns a living painting one canvas per week that he delivers on Saturdays to the Durand-Ruel gallery (6:703), Antonio Lara of "Edipo en París" spends his mornings at the Louvre where he observes that the canvases of the Italian Renaissance painters. provide a smooth transition to classical sculpture because the Italians learned to imitate classical beauty from the Greeks: "From a painting by Corregio [sic] or Titian, Antonio's eyes move on to the Venus de Milo or the commanding bust of Homer" (5:749). While meditating on the same bust of Homer, Azorín himself concludes, in another essay from the collection, that Greek literature—which on first consideration gives the appearance of clarity, simplicity, peace, and equanimity—has at its most recondite core an "irreducible surplus of infinite sadness." And, Azorín affirms dispiritedly, life in general is like that (5:853).

Gustave Courbet's *Burial at Ornans* was another painting Azorín personalized in terms of his own grief. After describing the scene of mourners gathered before an open grave, he writes that when he first saw Courbet's painting he understood immediately the deep emotion the artist obviously experienced in creating his picture. The weeping women on the right side of the composition become objective correlatives for Azorín's own pain: "Coming from Spain, feeling myself grief-stricken, these women were, indeed, the grieving women that I had left behind in my native land. In their faces was concentrated my own pain, and that of my entire country" (5:854–55). Azorín also was taken by three different interpretations of the martyrdom of Saint Sebastian that he dis-

covered at the Louvre. Writing as a poet exiled to Paris during the Spanish Civil War, the anonymous narrator of "San Sebastián en París" confesses to his personal physician that he suffers from three personalities: the one he had before the Spanish national catastrophe; the one he developed during the conflagration; and the personality of exile. To explain his case better, the poet illustrates his problem with a visual arts analogy focusing on the Saint Sebastian canvases painted by Pietro Perugino (c.1448–1523), Andrea Mantegna (1431–1506), and Guido Reni (1575–1642). Although Perugino depicts Saint Sebastian with several arrows piercing his side, the martyr's face appears serenely elegant and calm; Mantegna's Sebastian is also wounded by arrows, but his face reflects terrible pain and anguish; Reni portrays Sebastian with only one, barely distinguishable arrow that is half-submerged in shadow, although the Saint's face also reflects unmistakable physical pain (5:756–57). The poet observes that before the war he led a life of serenity comparable to that reflected in the visage of Perugino's Saint Sebastian; once civil war broke out, the poet felt himself accosted by the multiple arrows Mantegna depicts in his painting; and now, in exile, the poet feels he carries within himself the hidden, single arrow of Guido Reni's *Saint Sebastian in a Landscape*. He explains that, however the civil conflict in Spain might finally be resolved, nothing and no one will ever be able to tear Reni's hidden arrow from his breast because, for the first time, the poet has learned the meaning of hate: "That eternal and painful arrow piercing my breast, that they've stuck into my breast, is . . . the arrow of hate" (5:759).

In an essay from *En torno a José Hernández* (1939), also written during the exilic period, another of Azorín's poet-protagonists chooses a visual arts analogy to express his state of suspended animation between life and the abyss. The poet has only two works of art in his study: Guido Reni's *Aurora* and a bronze cast of Rodin's *Man with a Broken Nose*. Reni's painting proclaims life, while Rodin's bust emblematizes its destruction. The two works are metaphors for the state of the poet's own soul: at the same time that he yearns for the dawning of a new day, he must endure the wrenching pain of exile and is thus a living example of the strange harmony between life and the void (5:872–73).[13] Perhaps the most effective visual analogy Azorín made between a work of art and his devasted emotional state was to Hogarth's April 1764 print *Tailpiece, or the Bathos* (Fig. 16). As the painter-protagonist deliberates the question of which paintings might best express visually the complete demise of material existence, he considers whether Van Gogh's worn peasant boots would suffice, or perhaps Hogarth's mordant portrayal of the world's end which he describes in a rather detailed ekphrasis: ". . . en su cuadro [sic], puso todas estas zarandajas: una botella hecha vidrios, una escoba usada, una culata inservible de fusil, una campanilla rota, la muestra caída de un mesón titulado 'World's End,' la luna en menguante, un reloj de arena maltrecho, un drama en la última página con la acotación 'exunt [sic] omnes' . . ." [5:1040; . . . in his picture, he includes all these trivialities: a bottle broken into smithereens, a tired broom, a useless rifle butt, a cracked bell, the fallen signboard of an inn called 'World's End,' a waning moon, a damaged sand clock, the last page of a play with the stage direction 'exunt [sic] omnes']. Hogarth's agglomeration of material detritus, failure, and death finds resonance in the grief and despair of Azorín's poet for whom "Todo en España había acabado. . . . Todo lo

Fig. 16   William Hogarth, *Tailpiece, or The Bathos*, 1764. 10¼ × 12¹³⁄₁₆ in. (12⁹⁄₁₆ × 13¼ in., pl.). Print Collection, The Lewis Walpole Library, Yale University.

había visto derrumbarse" [5:758; Everything in Spain had come to an end. . . . He had seen everything demolished].

The Art of *Integrismo:* Inner Exile

When Azorín returned to Spain on 23 August 1939 he found himself, as did many intellectuals who did not overtly support the Franco regime during the Civil War—whether they had remained in Spain during the hostilities or left the country to seek refuge elsewhere—having to negotiate marginalization within the borders of their own country, an existential circumstance Paul Ilie aptly termed "inner exile."[14] One of the most difficult problems the inner exiles faced was that of resuming their professional careers: writers were refused publication, university professors access to the classroom, painters opportunities to exhibit, and journalists, like Azorín, were denied the government press identification cards without which no periodical or newspaper could employ them. Azorín obtained his *tarjeta de periodista* in early 1941 through the intervention of Ramón Serrano Suñer, Franco's Minister of the Interior as well as President of the "Junta Política de la Falange."[15]

On 1 June 1941, in the right-wing journal *Vértice,* Azorín published an essay titled "Ignacio Zuloaga," one of the most dexterous and, some would say, deplorable essays he wrote during the postwar period. He began the piece with an innocuous description of Zuloaga'a studio at number 7 on the Plaza de Gabriel Miró. Like the eye of a camera, Azorín sweeps over the studio furnishings, describes the views from a wall of windows, the artist's supplies littering the studio, the reproduction of Velázquez's *Las Meninas,* and the photographs of paintings by El Greco that hang on the studio walls. He then moves in for a close-up shot of the model whose portrait Zuloaga is painting. Relying on the same technique he used to describe the Venus de Milo, Azorín particularizes the portrait with increasing detail until the reader is able to identify the sitter for herself:

En una de las sillas está sentado el modelo, con el brazo derecho apoyado en la mesa, y la mano izguierda pendiente, por un dedo, del bolsillo del chaleco . . . (19)

[In one of the chairs sits the model, his right arm resting on the table, and the left hand hanging loose, hooked by one finger through the vest pocket.]

. . . Zuloaga le pregunta si se cansa; el modelo contesta que él, en París, en las estaciones del "Metro," solía estar . . . dos y tres horas viendo pasar los trenes, sumido en sus ensoñaciones . . . (20)

[Zuloaga asks him if he's tired; the model answers that in Paris he would often spend two or three hours in the subway stations watching the trains go by, immersed in his daydreams . . .]

. . . Zuloaga dice que la cabeza del modelo es muy difícil . . . el modelo replica que todos los pintores que le han retratado—Ramón Casas, José Villegas, Juan Echevarría, Sorolla, etc.—le han hecho observar lo arduo de pintar su cabeza . . . (20)

[Zuloaga says that the sitter's head is very difficult . . . the model replies that every painter who's done his portrait—Ramón Casas, José Villegas, Juan Echevarría, Sorolla, etc.—has commented on the difficulty of painting his head . . .]

El tiempo pasa; la figura va resaltando; al fondo hay un paisaje castellano, cerrado por un castillo roquero; el modelo está ante una mesa cargada de libros . . . (21)

[Time passes; the figure begins to emerge; there is a Castilian landscape in the background, closed off with a castle sitting on a rocky outcrop; the model is posed in front of a table loaded with books . . .]

Inevitably, the reader recognizes the painting as Zuloaga's portrait of Azorín in which the "model" is posed in the same manner described in the essay: his right arm resting on a table piled with books; the thumb of his left hand hooked into the watch pocket of his vest; a ruined castle on the bare Castilian plain in the background (Pl. 25). In a possible allusion to Edgar Allan Poe's "The Oval Portrait," Azorín indicates that Zuloaga "executed the portrait so faithfully that he transferred the poet's entire spirit to the canvas. The poet was left without a soul. And he could not write anymore" (21). The portrait itself is reproduced as the sixth and last photograph on the article's third page. What Azorín does not mention is that Zuloaga also portrayed him holding a copy of *Pensando en España,* a book of short stories written in exile (published in 1940) that carries a dedication to the artist. The book's inclusion in the portrait has the same effect as the mirror in Velázquez's *Las Meninas*, occasioning a self-referential dialogue between exterior and interior spaces; the painter and the writer; the natural signs of the visual arts and the arbitrary signs of writing.

All of this, however, tells only half the story. Anyone reading the essay would surely question the inclusion of two other photographs of portraits by Zuloaga reproduced on the preceding pages. The essay concludes in the same way as it began: with a description of an unnamed portrait Zuloaga plans to exhibit in a retrospective of his work. Of the myriad canvases waiting to be hung, Azorín's eye is drawn immediately to the picture of a man wrapped in the Spanish flag and wearing a Carlist red beret. He comments that the man in the portrait is an exceptional figure in Spanish history; his is a unique accomplishment (*gesta*), an epic tour de force. Azorín speculates that this portrait must have presented Zuloaga with the nearly insurmountable challenge of representing, in the same figure, a man who had been able to overcome and correct the errors of his nation's past, must now cope with the hard work and concerns of the present, but faces the promise of a splendid future. As in the case of the Venus de Milo, and his own portrait by Zuloaga, the model's identity is fully disclosed only at the last possible moment: it is the "Caudillo de España, iniciador del sacudimiento que ha de salvar a Europa . . . [y que] acaba de cumplir la empresa más heróica de nuestra historia" [22; Leader of Spain, initiator of the jolt that will save Europe . . . and who has just carried out the most heroic undertaking of our History]. Generalísimo Francisco Franco, dressed in the symbolic attri-

butes that brought victory to the Spanish people, is immediately recognizable from the very large reproduction of Zuloaga's portrait on the second page of the article where Franco is shown sporting the red beret of the *requetés*, a Falangist blue shirt, and the boots and jodphurs of a nationalist army officer. In another exhibition room, a second portrait catches Azorín's attention. The standing figure is clothed in Falangist accoutrements: white safari jacket and black trousers; gilded medals and military decorations adorn his chest; the model nonchalantly catches one of his hands on the belt around his waist. His casual pose connotes both subtlety and open sincerity, qualities Azorín compares to San Felipe Neri crossed with Machiavelli. The subject is none other than Ramón Serrano Suñer as depicted by Zuloaga and reproduced on the third page of the *Vértice* article, just above Azorín's own.

As appalling and distasteful as this obsequious essay might be, its visual text is extremely suggestive. While Azorín verbally describes his own portrait by Zuloaga as first in the series of three, physically it is placed last, in a subordinate position to those of Franco and Serrano Suñer. By grouping himself, at least in painted effigy courtesy of Zuloaga, alongside the new regime's two most powerful individuals, Azorín is able to align himself with the "right" political party, thereby allowing its representatives to see that he was prepared to be a team player. Zuloaga's portrait of Azorín thus proves to be an expedient means by which to negotiate extremely delicate political ends: the work of art mediates Azorín's desire for acceptance and integration, at the same time that it metaphorizes his much anticipated release from the sequestration of inner exile.

3
Affinities of Pen and Brush

Reader Reception as Visual Perception

AZORÍN'S 1952 COLLECTION OF ESSAYS, *El oasis de los clásicos*, includes one that he wrote in 1912, anticipating what we know today as reader reception theory. Azorín contends that analyzing opinions expressed about a work of literature by its contemporaries is invaluable to the study of aesthetic evolution. Taking the *Quijote* as his model, he points out that comparison between "how contemporaries of the masterwork have looked at it . . . and how, after years or centuries, it is seen and judged by posterity," often yields a tremendous disparity of judgment (9:1079). Always sensitive to the implications reader reception might have on literary criticism, in a 1944 essay on Espronceda, Azorín suggested that the most efficacious way to write a good literary history of the Romantic period was to peruse articles in the periodic press, a resource Spanish literary historians had yet to exploit properly, since there was not much interest in literature in Spain, and the study of aesthetics occupied only a secondary place in national life. Nevertheless, he continued, examining the transformations that occurred between 1840 and the present in the appreciation of Espronceda, or the Duque de Rivas, might produce extremely suggestive re-sults should the literary critic be willing to plumb the magazines, newspapers, and journals at his disposal (7:751).

As he did so often, Azorín found a way to contextualize his thoughts on reader reception within a visual arts paradigm. He observed that to Flaubert's contemporaries, the apothecary Homais (*Madame Bovary*) brims with irony and absurdity, his perorations designed to produce an "ostensible impression of the grotesque." Flaubert may have achieved the desired effect when his novel first appeared, but today Homais's disquisitions resemble nothing less than the speeches of some radical politician and do not at all seem ridiculous. The irony and humor have disappeared over time "as, with time, the brilliance of color fades in paintings" (9:962). Azorín's most seminal work as a response theorist, however, is to be found in the articles of *Rivas y Larra* (1916). He considered his essays on the two giants of Spanish Romanticism as models of a new critical methodology: "It's about time that literary history is written in a new way; the pages we've dedicated to Larra and Rivas are no more than an attempt, an experiment; other talents will come along to complete the task" (3:394–95).

Azorín began his new approach to Rivas by posing the questions, "What plays were staged immediately before *Don Alvaro*; which plays ran concurrently in the repertoire; which were put on following the play's close?" Equally significant, in Azorín's view, were attendance figures for the play and contemporary critical reviews (3:376–77). Since true literary history consisted of "a series of testimonials regarding the work or the author" (3:389), Azorín consulted the Madrid dailies for March 1835 in order to answer the questions he had posed (3:379). What results is a compendium, spread across several chapters, of theater statistics and contemporary critical reception of the revolutionary drama *Don Alvaro* that premiered on 22 March 1835 at the Teatro del Príncipe, although, according to Azorín's research, it did not cause nearly as much scandal as did the premiere of Victor Hugo's *Hernani* in Paris on 25 February 1830. What matters is that literary criticism, as Azorín restated in *Con bandera de Francia* (1950), not be limited to "a study of lexicon and grammar," but take into account the historical moment in which a work was written: possible antecedent influences upon the author, the relationship of the literary work to those produced by the author's contemporaries, coincidences between the work of literature studied and other cultural expressions (such as painting), correspondences between the author's aesthetic ideal and the sociopolitical milieu within which the work was conceived and written, innovative or traditional elements utilized by the author that might be in harmony or conflict with those of his time, as well as those which immediately followed. In Azorín's view, all these myriad elements had an impact on a work of literature, and it was the duty of the literary critic or historian to incorporate them to any stylistic analysis he might make (9:631).

As a critic of literature, Azorín always appreciated authors who, like himself, made use of visual and spatial effects in the verbal arts and were able to paint with the pen. It is not at all surprising, then, that he felt an affinity with the Duque de Rivas, who was also an accomplished painter. Azorín opened the third essay of *Castilla*, "Ventas, posadas y fondas," with a reference to Angel Saavedra's "El ventero" from the 1851 collection *Los españoles pintados por sí mismos*, a series of vignettes in which Spanish people from various geographical regions of the country describe themselves and their typical occupations in word and daguerrotype. As Inman Fox points out in his edition of *Castilla*

(1991, 199n. 1), Azorín cited this book with some frequency in his numerous publications on the Duque de Rivas. Azorín's own essay begins, "El Duque de Rivas ha descrito en su cuadro 'El ventero,' una de las clásicas ventas españolas" [The Duque de Rivas has described in his vignette 'El ventero,' a classic, Spanish inn] (Fox 1991, 119). Here, Azorín plays conceptually with the word *cuadro* which can mean both "scene" and "painting" in Spanish, but clearly it is the visual art connotation that he is after, implying that the painter in Angel Saavedra has described (*ha descrito*) the inns of his essay through verbal painting so as to bring them to life by encouraging readerly imaging. That Azorín was intrigued by the relationship between Angel Saavedra, the painter, and Angel Saavedra, the poet, is confirmed by the annotations he made in Pastor Díaz's 1842 biography of the Duke, all of which pertain to the importance painting had in his life. Underlined is information relative to the art lessons Saavedra received in his childhood from the French sculptor Verdiguier (7), to the school of painting the Duke established in Orleans while a political exile in France, the fact that he participated in an art exhibition held at the Louvre in 1831, and that his name figured in a list of painters active during that time in Paris (48–49).[1]

In the essay he included on the Duque de Rivas in *Clásicos y modernos* (1913), Azorín writes that in 1834 [sic] Angel Saavedra participated in an art exhibition in Paris and that while a diplomat posted to Naples in 1845, he continued to paint and show his work (2:775).[2] What matters most to Azorín, however, is that while the Duke's biographers frequently mention his artistic activities, they give insufficient weight to the relationship between Angel Saavedra's painting and his writing. He concludes that a study of the Duke's art could lead to a better understanding of his literature: "It would be interesting to look at paintings by the Duque de Rivas. From his canvases one could begin to derive some guidance to explain—or at least to understand—his literary manner and tendencies" (2:775). What follows is an inchoate attempt at an ekphrastic analysis of the Duke's literary corpus. As in the work of other painter-writers such as Gautier or the brothers Goncourt, Azorín notes that color, light, and shadow attract the Duque de Rivas, and that his literature is controlled by the visual, plastic, and painterly rather than by abstract concepts

(2:779). The pronounced contrast of light and shadow effects in some of the *Romances* remind Azorín of the chiaroscuro technique used by Rembrandt, while the riotous color and rapid annotation characteristic of the Duke's literary style recalls that of the Impressionists. Thus, the Duque de Rivas becomes "an artist who, using modern, impressionistic methods, executes paintings with romantic subjects. . . . We've recalled here the rapid technique of Impressionism because, at heart, Angel Saavedra is nothing less than a literary impressionist" (2:775–76). Saavedra was an Impressionist before the fact not only because his literature recorded momentary, visual sense impressions, but also because his impressionable temperament allowed the unchecked assimilation of other authors and literary currents within his own work. A contemporary of the Duke's, cited by Azorín, remarked that Angel Saavedra was far from politically astute, and that because his personality was as pliant as soft wax, it was marked by "every sensation due to the sole influence of enthusiasm, similar to how the modern daguerrotype transfers an image to a photographic plate due to the action of light" (9:1076–77, 1078).

Azorín noted favorably the Duke's unrestrained use of color: Saavedra's literature is the work of a painter and his painter's eye is evident in the "full-blown color" of *El moro expósito* (3:416), as well as the picturesque qualities, color contrasts, and elaborate descriptions of clothing, furniture, and landscape so conducive to stimulating readerly visualization in the *Romances históricos* (3:342).[3] According to Azorín, *El moro expósito*, an otherwise mediocre novel in verse, is salvaged by the author's use of color and detail. A kitchen scene in the home of the Arcipreste de Salas de los Infantes on a great feast day reminds Azorín of Dutch and Flemish genre painting. What is striking about his critical commentary here is that Azorín indulges in an ekphrasis of the Duque de Rivas's own ekphrastic moment, recognizing it as being inspired by the paintings of David Teniers or perhaps Adriaen Brouwer:

Se ha citado muchas veces la descripción de la cocina del cura de Salas de los Infantes en día grande de comilona . . . : el cacareo de los gallos en el corral, solivantados con la proximidad del degüello; las ollas, las sartenes y peroles; el espeso humo que llena la casa . . . una vieja, que apro-

vechándose del barullo, mete en el delantal una morcilla; una sirvienta que saca la mantelería de un armario; un chico que unta el dedo en miel y lo chupa. . . . Saavedra, pintor, tuvo presente aquí los cuadros de Teniers, Brower [sic] y otros maestros flamencos y holandeses. (3:416)[4]

[The description on a great feast day of the kitchen belonging to the priest of Salas de los Infantes has been cited many times . . . : the crowing of roosters in the yard, stirred up by the proximity of decapitation; the pots, pans, and kettles; the thick smoke that fills the house; an old woman, taking advantage of the commotion, slips a blood sausage into her apron; a servant fetches table linens from a great cupboard; a boy dips his finger into the honey pot, then sucks it . . . here Saavedra, the painter, had in mind pictures by Teniers, Brower [sic] and other Flemish and Dutch masters.]

In Azorín's opinion, however, Angel Saavedra was never able to supersede color and foreground in his writing, and when he was forced to get to the heart of literary matters, "our poet disappears" (3:419). Thus the Duque de Rivas wrote very much as would a painter; that is, he saw life "only as a flat surface; not as evolving, dynamic, but static. All his literary work is a vision of one moment. . . . There is no room for movement in Saavedra's aesthetic ideas . . ." (3:342). In other words, the Duke prefers to portray only one, synchronic moment in time, or what Lessing deemed in the *Laocoön* to be the exclusive domain of the painter.[5] Azorín's appraisal of the Duque de Rivas indicates that he intuited a conflictive opposition between the static, spatial nature of the visual arts and the temporal, diachronic characteristics of literature that have been examined in more recent studies of interarts relations. It is precisely when a verbally generated work of art is interpolated within a literary text that its temporality and diachronicity are temporarily interrupted by what Murray Krieger calls the "still movement" of the ekphrastic moment. In Azorín's opinion, the painter Angel Saavedra hampered the writer so that when he attempted to endow a literary scene with movement and temporality, the Duque de Rivas resorted to stringing together loosely a series of visual moments for as brief a time as possible in order to convey the illusion of cohesion. *Don Alvaro*, for instance, does not demonstrate coherently developed plot, character, or action; rather, it is a collection of colorful vignettes that Azorín calls "a collection of picturesque scenes" (3:343).[6]

Comparing the Duque de Rivas and Victor Hugo, the two representative figures of Spanish and French Romanticism, both of whom were talented artists, Azorín remarked that the Spanish poet-painter produced colorful miniatures in his art and literature, while the French poet-draftsman left fine sketches, notable for their contrasts of light and shadow, in the same way that his literature was characterized by "an energetic contrast between shadow and light; a continuous and formidable antinomy between good and evil, progress and regression" (9:203). In his preface to *Cromwell* (1827), Hugo defended his aesthetics of pairing the sublime with the grotesque as a way of creating artistic depth and richness. He cited Rubens, who used the same procedure of incorporating deformed and ugly court dwarfs into the otherwise sybaritic richness of his canvases. In his analysis of Hugo's aesthetics, Azorín remarked that this commingling of the ideal and the prosaic so prevalent in Spanish Golden Age literature had been abandoned until the Duque de Rivas, encouraged by the example of Hugo, brought it to the Spanish stage once again. He also noted in passing that Rubens's amalgamation of the beautiful and the grotesque had been taken up more recently in modern Spanish painting by Ignacio Zuloaga (3:395–96).

Azorín's interest in painters who were talented writers, or in writers who could also paint, and the derivation of parallels between writing and painting, did not stop with his essays on Angel Saavedra. In a 1933 article on the French caricaturist Jean Louis Forain (1852–1931), Azorín observed that, since so few visual artists had literary talent, famous painters and sculptors should make it a habit to be in the company of people who could record their experiences and thoughts on aesthetics. Exceptions to this general rule were, in Azorín's opinion, Leonardo da Vinci, Eugène Fromentin, and Eugène Delacroix, all three being equally talented writer-painters.[7] In the article "La pintura," Azorín remarked that writers had always been generous with painters and were often instrumental in disseminating information about visual artists, praising their work, and appreciating their struggles. He cited the rehabilitation of El Greco as the work of writers, and Delacroix's initial success as largely the achievement of Baudelaire (*PCQ* 234). In *El oasis de los clásicos* he observed that painters also had paid homage to contemporary authors, and referred to Fantin-Latour's 1864 group portrait evocatively titled *Hommage à Delacroix*, a painting that included Baudelaire among its sitters, and Vicente Carducho's 1632 portrait of Lope de Vega. He noted that coincidentally both Lope and Baudelaire loved cats, that both portraits were painted three years before their respective subjects' deaths, and that both men reveal "at this moment of their lives, a spiritualized physiognomy" (9:1004).

The literature-art parallels that seemed to intrigue Azorín most were drawn largely from the Spanish Golden Age. In the essay "La pintura" cited above, commenting on the parity of subject matter between Lope's sonnet on Judith's beheading of Holofernes, and Tintoretto's painting of the same theme, Azorín noted that Lope's *Rimas* could almost serve as a guide to the Prado. He made similar comparisons between Velázquez and Calderón, the ludic Quevedo and Bosch, and he compared the serious Quevedo to José de Ribera. Azorín also noted perspicaciously that, while the superficial comparison of subject matter shared by writers and painters was effortless, establishing an intimate equivalence of sensibility was quite another matter (*PCQ* 233). To illustrate his point, he contrasted Calderón's volatile personality with the phlegmatic aristocracy of Velázquez, capable of painting court dwarfs and the royal family with the same unruffled equanimity, whereas Calderón could not possibly have remained impassive before some Velázquez canvases (*PCQ* 234). As a matter of general principle, Azorín thought the greatest difference between painters and writers was that of "distance"; that is to say, while the painter must constantly be aware of placement, perspective, and composition, the novelist "doesn't even suspect the importance of such a requirement" (8:829). But even the cases of painter-poets could be equivocal. While the Duque de Rivas utilized color in both his painting and poetry, and Victor Hugo's talent as a draftsman is as evident in his writing as it is in his sketches, the poet-artist Juan de Jáuregui (1583–1614)—the painter of Cervantes's alleged portrait—is a colorless poet (9:203). On the other hand, Azorín also observed that extremely austere writers, such as Quevedo often was, might see brilliant color in paintings where, in fact, there was none. In a sonnet describing Guido Reni's portrait of the Duque de Osuna, Quevedo wrote that "the canvas is a riot of color." Although, in comparison to Quevedo, Guido Reni's canvas gives the impression of being colorful, Azorín observed that Reni could in no way be judged a true colorist among painters (*PCQ* 234).[8]

Azorín frequently saw parallel sensibilities between Quevedo and modern art and sculpture. In *Al margen de los clásicos* (1914), he compared the poet who "lived by the intellect and for the intellect" to Rodin's sculptures of Balzac and *The Thinker*, the work of both artists emblematic of their "constant and obstinate preoccupation with ideas" (3:239). Musing retrospectively on the author-painter José Gutiérrez Solana's two-volume *Madrid* (1913, 1918), Azorín observed that Solana's books, "strong, rough, harsh in color . . . have all the force, all the energy of the master's painting." Although he often disagreed with the harsh realism of Solana's literary descriptions, rejecting his aggressive pessimism, Azorín wrote that he found the electricity crackling throughout Solana's work, the violence of his line and the somber color palette he favored in both painting and writing, altogether captivating. Solana's *Madrid*, concluded Azorín, certainly would have been appreciated by the painter-writer's spiritual brothers, the poet Francisco de Quevedo and the painter José de Ribera (*AE* 205).[9]

In Lope de Vega, Azorín saw a master of the still life. Although a secondary genre, still life was appealing and had been practiced in both art and literature from the most remote of times. Himself a master still life "painter," Azorín remarked that the flavor and wit of act 2, scene 1 of Lope's *La francesilla*, set in a country inn, was a "model, albeit a little ridiculous, of what have been called still lifes in painting" (7:725). He also saw a similarity between El Greco's depiction of a menacing storm breaking over Toledo and a similar scene in Lope's *Rimas sacras*.[10] There was also a "profound, intimate" relationship of sensibility between Garcilaso's verse landscape descriptions of Toledo and landscapes painted by the foreigner Theotocópuli who managed to assimilate the spirit of Toledo in so marvelous a fashion that there was total spiritual harmony between the poet's "elegant, refined spirituality" and the painter's equally "subtle, ethereal, and tormented" vision (2:565). The literature-art parallels Azorín made between El Greco and various Spanish lit-

erary figures were rather numerous. He saw irrefutable proof of shared spiritual community between *El entierro del Conde de Orgaz*, whose upper half, depicting the heavenly host described as "celestial and delicate," contrasted with the earthbound mortals of the painting's "coarse and asperous" lower half, and a similar division of planes described with great color, relief and plasticity by the seventeenth-century nun, Sor María de Ágreda, in her verbal "painting" of Christ's burial in *La mística ciudad de Dios* (8:1110).[11] In appraising the cadre of Spanish Baroque painters whom he considered good candidates to paint a portrait of Don Quijote, Azorín toyed with, and rejected, Pantoja, Sánchez Coello, Ribera, Murillo, and even Velázquez, who surely would have produced a severe, dignified portrait of the Don; his choice, however, fell on El Greco whose classic portraits of Spanish noblemen Azorín had contemplated so often, and in whose faces he saw "a thirst for the ideal that is the same as Don Quijote's" (9:318–19).[12]

In his essay "Cejador y el Arcipreste" (*VL*, 1914), Azorín disagreed vehemently with Cejador's choice of El Greco as the ideal visual arts parallel to the *Libro de Bueno Amor*, protesting that no painter was less suitable for the comparison. Using his criterion of spiritual synchronism to establish true interarts parallels, Azorín pointed to the "profound difference of spiritual orientation, tendency, and manner" between the Archpriest of Hita and El Greco. In his view, the ideal painter to interpret Juan Ruiz's witty ribaldry would have been the sensualists Rubens, Jordaens, or Titian, "all painters of color, exuberance, gaiety, full of the joy of life" (2:980). Cejador's unfortunate choice of El Greco suggested that the Archpriest's editor had completely misread the *Libro de Buen Amor*, and Azorín cast his criticism of Cejador's argument that the *Libro* was meant for the "spiritual edification of readers," in terms of a visual arts analogy: if we are to believe Cejador, he wrote, we might as well concede that Rubens painted his lush nudes so that the public would abjure the pleasures of the flesh (Fig. 17). It is much more logical and rational, argued Azorín, to believe that Juan Ruiz wrote spontaneously, "without ethical or ascetic intent, in the same way that neither Jordaens, nor Rubens, nor Titian had such objectives in mind when they painted their nudes" (2:981).[13]

Azorín found a pictorial equivalent to Cer-

Fig. 17   Peter Paul Rubens, *The Hermit and Sleeping Anjelica*, c.1626–28. Oil on wood, 43 × 66 cm. Kunsthistorisches Museum, Vienna.

vantes's typical miscellany of realism and idealism in Murillo's painting *La cocina de los ángeles* that substitutes angels for a "cook and his scullions." As we have seen him do on occasion, Azorín's literary description of the painting becomes ekphrastic as it describes angels engaged in the mundane tasks of stirring large stew pots, setting tables, drawing water, and mashing something in a mortar; the kitchen itself is strewn with "red peppers, purple eggplants, tomatoes, a large squash, heads of garlic, meat" (Fig. 18). For Azorín the painting, with its angels placed in a worldly context and engaged in prosaic activities, communicates visually the commingling of literary realism and spiritual idealism with the same plenitude as does Cervantes in his novels (9:280). Cervantes's *La señora Cornelia* elicited from Azorín both an interarts analogy as well as an imaginary ekphrasis. The novel reminded him of Italian Renaissance paintings, and in his verbal recreation of the period style, Azorín employs color adjectives, perspective placement, and verbs that suggest ocular dynamics which might encourage readers to visualize along with the narrator: "veo una airosa columnata de mármol y una galería allá arriba. En el fondo se yerguen unos cipreses. Resalta un fragmento de rojo cortinón recogido . . . resplandece en lo alto un cielo limpio de azul intenso. Y en la galería se vuelve hacia nosotros . . . un varón envuelto en amplios verdes andularios" [I see a graceful marble colonnade with a gallery above it. Some cypresses rise up at the back. A drawn-back fragment of large, red curtain stands out . . . a clear sky of intense blue sparkles above. And in the gallery a man wrapped in a floor-length, green cloak turns toward us]. The scene has its pictorial equivalent, writes Azorín, as much in the austere Spain of Zurbarán as it does in the Renaissance Italy of Titian, Giorgione, Correggio, and Tintoretto.[14]

Góngora's sonnet on roses evoked a meditation on the autumnal roses in abandoned Spanish gardens, their delicate petals withering along with the yellowed leaves falling from the

Fig. 18 Bartolomé Esteban Murillo, *La cocina de los ángeles*, 1646. Oil on canvas, 1.80 × 4.50 m. Musée du Louvre, Paris. Giraudon / Art Resource, New York.

trees above, reminding Azorín of the roses painted by Zurbarán or those Velázquez placed in the delicate hands of his *infantas* (3:199). A nocturnal landscape by the same poet recalls an unspecified noctural landscape by Velázquez's son-in-law, Juan Bautista del Mazo, both literary and visual works sharing the same "broken crag," a "ray of moonlight," and a tree against whose trunk a lover sighs and laments his sorrows (3:215). The most suggestive comparison Azorín made between Spanish Golden Age literature and the visual arts, however, was between Calderón's *La vida es sueño* and Albrecht Dürer (1471–1528). In drawing an analogy between the play's opening scene to landscape engravings by Dürer, Azorín created a theatrically visual stage setting that metamorphosed both literary and pictorial intertexts into a highly original vignette of his own creation. He compared the anxiety, sense of melancholy, and mystery that undergird the typical medieval and early Renaissance Germanic landscape which frequently includes fantastic, menacing geography, and equally imaginary architectonic configurations in the distant background, to the sense of unease and the inhospitable milieu Calderón created in the first scene of *La vida es sueño* (Fig. 19). It is at this point that Azorín begins to embellish upon both Calderón and Dürer:

Una dama—disfrazada de varón—anda descarrilada por un monte; la acompaña un fiel escudero. Al dar vuelta a un recodo del vericueto, descubren una salida torre; son los últimos momentos del crepúsculo vespertino; se inflama el cielo con los resplandores de un ocaso sangriento; una nube de nácar acaso camina hacia Oriente. Desde lo alto de un lomazo . . . se divisa allá en la remota lontananza, por un gollizo abierto entre las montañas, la confusa masa de una gran ciudad. (3:247)

[A lady—disguised as a man—wanders lost in the mountains; a loyal page accompanies her. On turning a bend in the path, they come upon a prominent tower; dusk is falling; the sky is on fire with the blaze of a bloody sunset; perhaps a mother-of-pearl cloud drifts toward the east. From the top of a hill . . . over there, in the far distance, the confused mass of a city can be made out through an open cleft in the mountains.]

The blazing sunset, the distant city, and the sense of dramatic anticipation described here are original neither to Calderón nor to Dürer, but to Azorín's verbally generated "canvas."

There is a gap in Azorín's interartistic commentary between the Spanish Baroque and the late nineteenth and early twentieth centuries. He draws a brief parallel between Pedro Ruiz de Alarcón (1833–1891), whose surface joviality contrasts with Goya's profound lugubriousness (5:212); the fragile, delicate poetry of Gustavo Adolfo Bécquer is inseparable from the photographs J. Laurent took in 1868 of a certain type of woman: pale, blonde, with silken curls falling on her forehead (3:271). Azorín likewise perceived similarities between a scene in Enrique Gil's *El señor de Bembibre* (1844), in which a shepherdess sings a "moving, harmonious melody," while from a boat hugging the coastline,

Fig. 19   Albrecht Duerer, *View of Val d'Arco*, **1495. Water color on paper with body color and pen and ink, .223 ×
.223 m. Musée du Louvre, Paris. Giraudon / Art Resource, New York.**

her song is answered by a "war chant sung by the robust voice of a man," and a canvas by Joachim Patinir titled *El paso de la laguna Estigia* (which Azorín incorrectly titled *Barca del río Estigio*; see Fig. 7). Both novel and painting evoked in his imagination songs that speak of life, hope, and struggle on the one hand, while, on the other, they also imply "the fugaciousness of time and things" (3:1131). Gil's novel also demonstrates unmistakable "similarity and parallelism" to landscapes by Carlos de Haes, the two artists sharing a "technique of their time (a certain affectation, a certain coy, soft manner, a certain taste for rather theatrical composition)"; by the same token, there exists a felicitous rapport in the somewhat artificial and ingenuous way both painter and novelist reproduce the tonality and ambience of the landscape they portray (3:1128). Azorín argued that the Guadarrama mountains Velázquez included so often in his paintings, are the same today as they had appeared in the seventeenth century, proving that when artists of the pen or brush portray landscape faithfully, they leave documents that will remain valid for centuries to come (3:1117). Thus, although Enrique Gil set his novel in the Middle Ages, the landscape of the Bierzo region where the action takes place has not changed; it is as accurate in Gil's description as it would have been several hundred years earlier.[15]

Among his contemporaries, Azorín could not help but draw similarities between the Valencians Vicente Blasco Ibáñez and Joaquín Sorolla. Like the parallel between Enrique Gil and Carlos de Haes with the Bierzo, Azorín identified Blasco and Sorolla with the Mediterranean Sea and the Valencian coast, epitomized in the work of both writer and painter by the spiritual sensuality and grace of the women they portrayed (3:1233). In a visual arts simile that presupposes reader familiarity with the work of Sorolla, Azorín wrote that he always imagined Valencia in terms of a woman clothed in diaphanous white garments strolling through orange groves: "on a path through the orange groves, a figure dressed in sheer white—like in a painting by Sorolla—walks delicately toward us, from time to time she leans forward to clear away the branches . . . in everything about her person, her gestures, her manner, there is a supreme dignity fashioned of elegance, indolence, and spiritual sensuality," quite like the atmosphere Blasco Ibáñez evoked in his novel *Entre naranjos*

(3:1203–04). The coincidence of style Azorín perceived in Blasco and Sorolla was confirmed by the two parties concerned, as well as by more recent art criticism: while Blasco Ibáñez insisted that no one expressed the invisible color of the Valencian atmosphere, or the shimmering blue of the Mediterranean as well as Sorolla, Javier Tusell points out that Blasco might as well have been talking about the "carácter valencianista" of his own luminous and plastic verbal landscapes (361) (Pl. 26).[16]

Azorín's third prominent pairing of painter with writer in *El paisaje de España, visto por los españoles* (1917) was between the Basque novelist Pío Baroja, whose description of a small town led Azorín to recall "some paintings by Darío de Regoyos, pictures full of light, color, reverberations" (3:1147). Baroja and Regoyos often traveled together: their 1904 excursion to Córdoba was the basis of Baroja's novel *La feria de los discretos* (Barrio-Garay 50 n. 74); the same excursion led Regoyos to attempt to paint in the south of Spain, something both he and Baroja agreed was impossible to do because the sun tended to obliterate all color and sense of depth. Azorín, likewise, compared what he called Baroja's inattention to formal novelistic composition to a similar looseness of style in the work of Ignacio Zuloaga whose paintings "represented the totality of Spain" (*VH* 254).[17] With the healthy appetite of a Basque, Zuloaga found painterly inspiration throughout the country, visually devouring its cities, landscapes, and inhabitants (9:845). On the other hand, if he wanted to partake of the flavor and rhythms of Old Castile, Azorín invariably turned to a painter from Burgos, Marceliano Santa María (1866–1952). One of his personal favorites, Santa María painted landscapes that invoked the rhythms of medieval Castilian epic poetry. A relatively unknown painter, Santa María seems to have engaged Azorín on ideological as well as aesthetic levels. As a young man, the artist was commissioned to paint a scene from the history of Burgos that included the archetypal Castilian warrior-hero (Pl. 27). It is not by chance, then, writes Azorín, that a painter so steeped in the "entrails of the race" from the beginning of his career, would later wish to express the soul of the Burgos landscape in paint (9:846). Yet while Santa María maintained steadfast loyalty to his native province and to traditional Spain, in Azorín's view he also remained open to modern currents. And, because Santa María's character was forged in the quintessentially Castilian milieu of Burgos, the painter was able to renew, in the twentieth century, "with his brushes, that modality of spirit which Rodrigo Díaz de Vivar bequeathed to us so very long ago" (9:845–46).[18] Marceliano Santa María emerged as a paradigm for Azorín's beloved theory of coherence and continuity, whereby the permanent, unchangeable nature of Spanish tradition became the foundation upon which to build modern constructs germane to a socially, politically, and aesthetically regenerated nation in the twentieth century. The contemplation of a landscape by Santa María leads Azorín to an integrated "picture" of Spain: "Y ahora, ante un paisaje de Marceliano, hago la síntesis de toda España, varia en sus elementos, paisajes clásicos y paisajes románticos, y una en su espíritu" [9:847; And now, in front of a landscape by Marceliano, I reach a synthesis of Spain in her entirety, diverse in her elements, classic and romantic landscapes, but one in spirit].[19]

Spanish Contemporaries

As did his generational colleagues, Miguel de Unamuno and Pío Baroja, Azorín either knew or corresponded with Spanish painters who were his contemporaries. He often referred to the several modest oil paintings that hung in his study: a landscape with poplars along a river by fellow *alicantino* Adelardo Parrilla; a painting by Aureliano de Beruete of the Guadarrama mountains featuring the blue and ochre tones typical of that artist's palette; an etching by Ricardo Baroja.[20] Azorín's fictionalized selves, often refracted in protagonists who are either poets or painters, frequently work in studies or studios decorated with paintings by his favorite artists. The country home of an anonymous painter in "Mayo" displays photographic reproductions of paintings by Velázquez, Goya, Veronese, Sorolla, Zuloaga, and Beruete (*EL* 161); the newspaper editor of *Capricho* hangs pictures by Velázquez, Hobbema, Renoir, Sisley, and Pissarro in his office (6:932); in the same novel, a hotel owned by the father of one of the protagonists, features Danish porcelains and "four or six paintings" by Regoyos (6:938). A newspaperman in the novel *El enfermo* loves the visual arts and confesses his spiritual development was influenced by his favorite painters

and paintings: Velázquez, an unnamed landscape by Hobbema, and two or three paintings, also not named, by the "modern impressionists" (6:894). The physician's office in "Nada de particular" is decorated with a landscape by Juan de Espina that the narrator takes care to emphasize does *not* portray a humble cemetery in the Guadarrama; two paintings by Agustín Lhardy, one by Beruete, and another by Renoir. In a comparison of the Spanish Impressionist painters to Renoir, the narrator pointedly observes, "they do not compare unfavorably to the French" (*PCQ* 171). Elsewhere Azorín stresses the delicate quality of Beruete's canvases, the subdued nature of landscapes by Lhardy, and returns again to the "unaffected and modest" artist, Juan Espina (1848–1933), to whose painting of a small cemetery he now refers by name and describes in some detail. He reports that after seeing *Cementerio en el Guadarrama* at an art exhibition, the image has remained with him as a personal symbol of peace and solitude (6:705).[21] The ample study of the fictional poet Pablo Mansilla has only one work of art on its luminous white walls: a landscape by Corot (5:325); the sitting room of Salvadora de Olbena's paternal home contains a reproduction of Rodin's *Desnarigado*, some landscapes by Beruete, and a sketch by the nineteenth-century history painter Eduardo Rosales (7:646). Azorín commented again on Rosales (1836–1873) in *Pensando en España*, including the painter in a list of favorite artists. In his opinion, Rosales was one of Spain's greatest painters; an artist who withstood the test of time because he never capitulated to short-lived artistic trends. There was nothing more elegant than Rosales's *Presentación de don Juan de Austria a Carlos I* [sic], wrote Azorín, who then compiled a list of Spanish artists he most admired: "Después de Velázquez, Goya. Después de Goya, Rosales. Después de Rosales, Zuloaga" (5:981). The inclusion of Rosales is odd, given Azorín's vehement denunciation of nineteenth-century Spanish history painters whose academic inanities he routinely debunked at the turn of the century, calling the work of Pradilla, Plasencia, Domingo, Casado del Alisal, Carbonero, and Sala "anodyne," and the painters themselves a group of artists who were thought to be "awesome geniuses in their own day, and inconsequential daubers now" (*PCQ* 10–11).

Azorín was especially fond of contemporary Spanish landscape painters, most of whom spent varying lengths of time in the studios of Carlos dc Haes and formed a bridge between Beruete and the post-Impressionist landscapes of Marceliano Santa María, Daniel Vázquez Díaz, and Ignacio Zuloaga. Gaspar Salgado, the fictional painter of *Sintiendo a España*, voices his admiration for these artists from whom "he" learned so much, and to whose work Azorín himself often refers in his essays (6:704–05). The first artist Salgado recalls is Casimiro Sainz (1853–1898) who wandered the mountainous regions of Santander, painting its trees and rocks in the manner of his teacher Carlos de Haes (exhib. cat. *Centro y periferia* 391). Sainz left a legacy of beautiful, light-filled landscapes painted in and around Madrid, the towns of Old Castile, and at the source of the Ebro Rivcr. His lack of success with the art establishment, however, drove the sensitive painter to madness, and he died, institutionalized, at age forty-five.[22] The second painter to whom Salgado feels indebted is Joaquim Mir (1873–1940), who taught him the skill of controlling paint. A native of Catalonia, Mir is remembered for the riotous color and abstraction of his Mallorcan landscapes, similar in style to that of early Matisse, the French Fauves, or Gauguin's South Pacific canvases (Pl. 28). Josep Plá, Mir's biographer, left a marvelous description of the painter's extremely subjective vision of his beloved Mallorca:

A la dreta, la Cala Sant Vicenç, a posta de sol, vermella, de color de foc. El mar blau cobalt reflecteix aquelles roques encenses; queda vermell com sang. . . . L'aigua agafa, en aquest cantó, tons de plata. Afegeix'hi els morats de les algues de baix i de les figures salvatges que pengen fins a tocar l'aigua. . . . Quina bogeria de colors! (660)

[To the right, the cove of Saint Vincent, a vermilion sunset, the color of fire. The cobalt blue sea reflects the glowing rocks, drenched in a bloody red. . . . In this area the water acquires silvery tones. Add to that the various purples of the seaweed at the bottom and the overhanging, wild shapes of the vegetation that graze the water. . . . What a madness of colors!]

The description Azorín makes of a Mallorcan landscape in *El paisaje de España, visto por los españoles* (1917), a collection of essays in which he often compares literary with painterly visions of the same geographical regions in Spain, seems to approximate the Mallorcan canvases painted by Mir:

Y luego, desde un antepecho de piedra, ¿no se descubrc allá abajo un surgidero o cala en que las aguas se mueven y remueven suavemente? En el crepúsculo vespertino estas aguas son grana, morado, azul y oro. La visión es maravillosa. Contemplando ahora este mar, de tan espléndidas irisaciones, desde esta eminencia, tenemos la sensación de ir . . . en la proa de un barco. De ir, entre resplandores de oro, en busca de regiones desconocidas. (3:1234)[23]

[And then, from a stone parapet, can't you see there, down below, a cove or little bay in which the waters move and stir softly? At dusk the water is red, purple, blue, and gold. It's a marvelous sight. From this height, contemplating the sea now, with its splendid iridescence, we have the sensation of being . . . in the prow of a boat. Of going off, amidst a golden blaze, in search of unknown lands.]

Of course Salgado could not forget "don Aureliano de Beruete," nor the marvelous simplicity of Darío de Regoyos. Last on Salgado's list is the "elegant restauranteur of San Jerónimo Street, Agustín Lhardy" (1848–1918). Scion of the family that, in 1839, founded the chic café-restaurant Lhardy's still operating today at its original Madrid location, Agustín chose to become a painter: unfortunately, most of his small, delicate landscapes executed in the Impressionist manner, are in private collections and not available for public viewing.[24]

While Beruete was clearly Azorín's personal favorite among painters, he conceded that, in the same way the Generation's composer was Amadeu Vives, "their" painter was the Asturian, Darío de Regoyos (6:295–96). After spending an insignificant period of time at the Royal Academy of Fine Arts in Madrid in 1878, Regoyos (1857–1913) decided that not even Carlos de Haes had anything to teach him, and he left for Belgium where, with the exception of occasional visits to Spain made in the company of Belgian painters and writers, he lived until 1895 when he married and settled in the Spanish Basque country.[25] It was Regoyos's intimate contact with Belgian and French vanguard painting; his active involvement with important groups such as L'Essor and Les XX in Belgium; his friendships with Seurat, Signac, Pissarro, and Toulouse-Lautrec; his participation in the Salon des Indépendants beginning in 1890 and the Salon d'Automne beginning in 1905; and his acceptance by prestigious art dealers and gallerists in Paris (Durand-Ruel in 1897 and Druet in 1906), that made Regoyos the first Spanish landscape painter to achieve prominence on the international art scene. In his own country, however, the bourgeoisie and official art establishment continually censured the painter for his efforts to introduce to Spain the "modernismo de extranjis," as the new art movements in Europe were derisively termed (Pantorba 53).

Regoyos forged a highly personal style by combining a primitive naïveté of approach to the human figure with a pointillist execution, but his most characteristic paintings explore the effects that natural light, as well as artificial, nocturnal illumination, had on landscape. He wrote that since the Barbizon painters had studied afternoon light effects; Corot those of the morning; and the Impressionists the midday sun, it was left to him to paint "la noche y su luz obscura o mejor su obscuridad luminosa." He believed that moonlight changed the laws of color perception and was fascinated by the challenge of honoring "our lady the moon" in paint, a feat he thought few artists had ever attempted (exhib. cat. *D. de Regoyos* 85).[26] In a survey of the latest tendencies in the visual arts conducted by the *Mercure de France*, Regoyos responded on 15 August 1905 that if he were to begin his career over again, he would immediately adopt a lighter, brighter palette and paint nothing but landscape, delivering himself up entirely to recording the impressions he received from Nature's ever-changing physiognomy. Regarding the question of favorite painters, he remarked that among Spanish artists he most admired Sánchez Coello, Goya, Velázquez, and El Greco, but because he belonged to a different age, and because he was a man of his time, he also "adored" Corot, Manet, Monet, Whistler, Gauguin, and Cézanne (552–53).

Baroja recalled meeting Regoyos in San Sebastián in 1901 or 1902, and remembered the painter as being deeply interested in the work of Van Gogh, Pissarro, Gauguin, and Cézanne; he characterized Regoyos's personality as an intriguing mix of someone who was simultaneously judicious and sensible about his art, but had a streak of feckless ingenuousness that made him seem almost foolish or preposterous (7:888). Regoyos's guileless innocence, very much in evidence in his paintings, was noticed by his contemporaries who began calling him the "Saint Francis Assisi" of painting (Pl. 29).[27]

Unamuno referred to Regoyos as a "gran paisajista franciscano" because the gentle Bohemian painted landscape with a Christian, fraternal love for Nature (7:733); in "Las pinturas de Regoyos," Azorín noted that the artist was not only a painter of color and light whose work could not be further removed from academic tradition, but that the canvases themselves communicated a "profunda, dulce y graciosa ingenuidad," imparting to the viewer's eyes and spirit a soft contrast between light, color, sky and landscape, and the attitude suggested by Regoyos's rendition of the human figure (*PCQ* 32). Vázquez Díaz called Regoyos the "great painter of the Generation of 98," observing that he depicted the Spanish landscape as Fra Angelico might have painted his saints: kneeling, in humble submission (100). While Azorín will be remembered as the writer who immortalized the simple, everyday life and objects of the archetypal Spanish rustic town and peasant, it is Regoyos who recorded with his brushes and paints the "tranquil humanity" of the Spanish landscape, expressing loving empathy for its "menudas gentes" and the "minúsculos quehaceres y placeres" of their uneventful, humble lives (Rodríguez Alcalde 176, 190).[28]

As was the case with many radical artists and writers, during most of his life Regoyos's landscapes were judged peculiar and infantile, either because of the pointillist technique he preferred, or due to the arbitrarily explosive vibrancy of their color. The painter's work began to be appreciated only a few years before his death in 1913. This unfortunate situation elicited some interesting remarks from Azorín on canon formation, in "Las pinturas de Regoyos" written for *ABC* in 1908, on the occasion of Regoyos's one-man show at the Salón Vilches in Madrid. Azorín indicated that Regoyos was a classic example of how the passage of time "transforms heterodoxy into orthodoxy." Since Regoyos first appeared on the art scene, so many heresiarchs and such mind-boggling aesthetics had emerged, that perplexed critics "had to relent with Regoyos, given their hatred of the newest fanatics," having no choice but to dedicate a few lines in their articles to a painter whom they would otherwise have preferred to ignore (*PCQ* 51).[29]

Like Darío de Regoyos, the Catalonian painter and writer Santiago Rusiñol (1861–1931), spent a great deal of his early career in Paris where, together with Miquel Utrillo and

Ramón Casas, later joined by Ignacio Zuloaga, he formed an important part of the increasingly visible contingent of Spanish painters based in the French capital. A key figure in Catalonian modernism, Rusiñol played a significant role as importer and propagator of new European aesthetics in his native Barcelona. Azorín recognized the artist's importance in showing "us Castilians" the "abandon that breaks the rigidity of the solemn." It is through Catalonia, noted Azorín, that European innovation in philosophy and literature burst into Spain: first Romanticism, then Scottish philosophy, Naturalism, Ibsen and Nietzsche, followed by Impressionism in painting (9:1300). Rusiñol began his artistic career influenced by the gray palettes of Velázquez, Whistler, and the symbolist murals of the neoclassical revivalist, Pierre Puvis de Chavannes. Josep Plá writes that Rusiñol's connection to Puvis was more than superficial: when the art community held a banquet to honor the French muralist upon his completion of the huge wall frescos at the Sorbonne, all of Paris was in attendance, including Rusiñol who met Zola on the same occasion (371). In *Desde el molino*, his memoir of the Bohemian artist's life in Paris, Rusiñol recalled the extraordinary effect the restrained, dispassionate style of Puvis's large compositions had on the art world (148), observing that the muralist streamlined his art so much that it became the final word on spareness and simplicity, able to "say in a few words" what the elegant periphrases of Spanish orators could never hope to achieve (58). The influence of Puvis's decorative, Italianate medievalism can also be seen in the gothic-style tympana at Rusiñol's Cau Ferrat in Sitges (Plá 384). Vázquez Díaz explained the flat, mural-like effect of Rusiñol's painted gardens as the result of having studied Puvis's work (334), while Pantorba attributed Rusiñol's "calm, softly articulated and gray-toned figure paintings" to the influence of Puvis's melancholy, meditative serenity (124). Alfredo Opisso, reviewing Rusiñol's paintings *La Poesía* and *La Pintura* exhibited in 1896 at Barcelona's "Exposición de Bellas Artes e Industrias," wrote that Rusiñol's symbolism and Gothic pastiche could be compared only to Puvis de Chavannes whose work produced a similar, trance-like sensation of the intangible (175–76).

Rusiñol found his true calling and critical recognition only when he began to paint the classical gardens and parks of Spanish palaces and seigncurial homes (Plá 10, 395–96). Eduardo Marquina observed that the painter's overgrown, abandoned manor gardens were emblematic of the "vejez de España," visual instantiations that linked Rusiñol to the spirit of '98 (Plá 494) (Pl. 30). The painter's biographer, Josep Plá, noted that, similar to the activities of his generational contemporaries, Rusiñol's painting, writing, and collecting of classical Spanish art and artifacts all centered on his passionate need to "discover the nation" (496). Indeed, the opinions expressed by members of the Generation of 1898 regarding the thoughtless sqaundering of Spanish human and material resources in the seventeenth century, while the nation was ostensibly at the peak of imperial greatness, are analogous to Rusiñol's view that Spain was in irreversible decline, evident in statements he made repeatedly that his deserted gardens symbolized oases sown during the illusory splendor of an inert greatness; the lifeless issue of a dead past (1914, 1). But what beautiful death throes, he continued, what splendid defoliation, what fallen grandeur these neglected gardens represent. He described the *caserones* that his gardens surround as tombs "with weeping willows reclining on the balconies, life ebbing out of statues, the trees losing their leaves, and only the cypresses . . . shot their velvety crowns out above the garden's dead branches" (1914, 3). Similar to Azorín's melancholy predilection for "lo vetusto," Rusiñol set out to preserve not only the disintegrating parks of the past in paint, but also what Pantorba called the "musty nooks and crannies of dilapidated Spanish villages" (123). The painter urged the few poetic souls left in Spain to have one last glimpse of the gardens that remained intact because these, too, would soon vanish, some completely withered from neglect, others disguised by modern trappings, still others would be uprooted, and most would revert to "prosaic wastelands just like the wasteland that surrounds them" (1914, 4).

Critics often noted that Rusiñol, a successful author of bilingual Spanish-Catalonian poetry and drama, "fa literatura pintant i pinta fent literatura" (Plá 394), and they frequently compared his painted gardens to the decaying, modernist verbal landscapes of Rubén Darío, the early Antonio Machado, Juan Ramón Jiménez, and Valle-Inclán. Rusiñol's "poetry in a minor key . . . but frequently tremulous and effective" (Rodríguez Alcalde 232), shares, as well, noticeable features with Azorín's stylistic and aesthetic idiosyncracies.[30] Pompeyo Gener, a contemporary of the Generation of 1898, noted that Rusiñol's melancholy, pessimistic sadness tinted all his work with somber hues: if he had to identify the painter's favorite color, it would have to be violet; Gener also observed that Rusiñol was drawn to "calm, to a tranquility near death, to solitude" (Martínez Sierra 21), tendencies prevalent in Azorín's personal ontology, as well as in his own preference for the color gray. More recently Heidi Roch noted that the typical Rusiñol painting detains time, "comparable to . . . a still life, the antinomy, therefore, of the restless and agitated life of modern men." This contemplative turning inward and search for tranquility imparts a static quality to Rusiñol's most characteristic paintings which Roch called a kind of "pan-psychism" (13), qualities that approximate Azorín's preference for inclusive, first-person plural verb forms and possessive adjectives, and the diminutives that characterize his style, all of which create the intimacy we have come to associate with the minutiae of his literary descriptions.[31] Azorín defended Rusiñol in a retrospective essay where he recalled that an 1892 review of the Spanish National Art Exhibition written by Federico Balart lambasted a certain painter for banishing color, line, and drawing from his work, and critized "Señor X" for belonging to the contemporary contingent of "infantile nullities" in painting. Tongue planted firmly in his cheek, Azorín queries: "Who was the artist that among us, in 1892, represented a new aesthetic modality which so displeased the most eminent of our critics? It was Santiago Rusiñol," a painter who by 1913, the date of Azorín's essay, enjoyed recognition from all quarters (*PCQ* 117).

Because Ignacio Zuloaga (1870–1945) is so inextricably linked to the painting of Castilian landscape, and because he approached his theme from similar aesthetic and historical premises, Enrique Lafuente Ferrari, the most authoritative voice on matters concerning the Basque painter, associates Zuloaga's search for national authenticity with the spirit of '98. Reflecting the racially oriented anthropological theories of the moment, in his 1926 history of nineteenth-century Spanish painting, Aureliano de Beruete y Moret observed that Zuloaga portrayed the Hispanic "racial type" in his can-

vases (145–46).[32] Zuloaga's association with the Generation of 1898 appears to derive from the crucial year of the colonial disaster that coincided with his establishing a studio in Segovia where, until 1913, he spent each autumn on extensive painting campaigns. Like Regoyos and Rusiñol, Zuloaga went to Paris early in his career to seek his fortune, but unlike his predecessors, his success in the French capital won him almost immediate notoriety in Spain. To celebrate his accomplishments, the artists and writers of '98 held a banquet at Lhardy's restaurant on 13 December 1904. Attended by Azorín, the Baroja brothers, Eduardo Marquina, Rusiñol, Maeztu, Joaquín Dicenta, Eliseo Meifrén, Francisco Maura, and Marceliano Santa María, among others, Marquina took the opportunity to read an article Santiago Rusiñol published in Barcelona's *La Vanguardia*, recounting the anecdote of Zuloaga's "discovery" of El Greco and his donation of two El Greco paintings to Rusiñol's museum at Cau Ferrat. José María Salaverría noted that the piece was applauded so enthusiastically by the banquent participants the moment almost became an apotheosis of Santiago Rusiñol rather than Ignacio Zuloaga (Lafuente Ferrari 1950, 55).[33] Azorín recalled that, although he dedicated "Los toros" (*Los pueblos*, 1905) to Zuloaga, the *gente nueva* espoused Darío Regoyos as their painter for the simple reason that Zuloaga spent most of his time in Paris (6:295–96). That Azorín should have dedicated a story about bullfighting to Zuloaga is a reference to the painter's lifelong fondness for the sport which Lafuente Ferrari called his "tema eterno y apasionante." As a young man, Zuloaga practiced bullfighting semi-professionally in Andalusia, adopting the *nom de combat* "El Pintor" (Lafuente Ferrari 1950, 11, 42). After deciding to dedicate his talents to painting alone, his first successes abroad were with paintings whose subject matter was drawn from the *españolada*: scenes of bullfighters, flamenco dancers, and *majas* with their colorful shawls, fans, and spangles or, alternately, the beggars, procuresses, gypsies, witches, flagellants in religious processions, impoverished rural nobility and rogues associated with the *España negra* theme, all painted against theatrical backdrops of "threatening skies where blacks, browns, and leaden blues constituted a . . . lugubrious accompaniment meant to evoke, in the desolate landscape, a telluric fatality" (Jiménez Placer 493, see Pl. 5). Because these images seemed to correspond to a romanticized vision of Spain extant in the fantasies of the monied Parisian bourgeoisie, Zuloaga became enormously popular, and when the paintings began to sell extremely well, the artist, with his eye on the market, was only too happy to supply the demands of an expanding clientele.

The direction Zuloaga chose to follow professionally did not always sit well with his contemporaries. Many writers, artists, and intellectuals believed that he rendered a false, distorted, negative view of their country, "full of concessions to foreigners' ideas" about Spain.[34] The dispute between Zuloaga's detractors and supporters came to a head in 1910–12, in a notorious polemic between Ramiro de Maeztu and Azorín who debated the "cuestión Zuloaga" in the periodic press. At the beginning of his career Azorín was among the most vocal of the painter's critics, although, in retrospect, he confessed that it was not until he saw a Castilian landscape by Zuloaga in the offices of his physician in Paris that he realized, while Zuloaga might at first repel the viewer, it was precisely this negative reaction that gave birth to the most austere and severely dignified exponent of modern Spanish art (8:445).[35] The debate between Maeztu and Azorín began on 9 March 1910, prompted by a series of articles on Zuloaga that Maeztu had published in the *Heraldo de Madrid* and *Nuevo Mundo*, with responses from Azorín in *ABC*. The polemic continued through April 1912, although, as late as 1917, Unamuno would defend Zuloaga in an article titled "La labor patriótica de Zuloaga"; Luis Bonafoux weighed in on the side of Zuloaga, often in the pages of the *Heraldo*; Ortega y Gasset also entered the fray, summing up the issue in an essay composed between May and August 1910 (now collected in "Adán en el paraíso"), where he writes, "It is a characteristic of Zuloaga's paintings that, no sooner do we begin to speak about them, than we find ourselves embroiled in the question: 'Is Spain like this or not?'" (1:474). Writing in *Nuevo Mundo*, 28 April 1910, Ramiro de Maeztu chided Azorín for denying the existence of a "cuestión Zuloaga," and scolded him for being the spokesperson for those who believed erroneously that Zuloaga could not "see" properly when, in fact, at the moment "Ignacio Zuloaga represents Spanish painting abroad."[36] If Zuloaga's painting did not rouse public opinion, or if these opinions were all of a piece, Maeztu observed caustically, then there would be no "cuestión Zuloaga," but such was not the case. The issue was this: is Zuloaga visually "impaired," or are his critics? Maeztu argued that, whereas Azorín maintained Zuloaga's concept of Spain did not correspond to contemporary Spaniards' vision of their country, "I maintain that not only is it ours, but it's also expressed brilliantly in various canvases."

Azorín responded with the article "La España de un pintor," published in *ABC*, 7 April 1910. Zuloaga, he wrote, is a painter of literary character, but his vision corresponds to the fantastic view foreigners have always had of Spain, and "that is not the view we ourselves have of our affairs" (7:246). Zuloaga defended himself in a letter, excerpts of which Azorín included in "La pintura de Zuloaga" published in *ABC*, 27 March 1912, where the painter is quoted as saying that he seeks out "the daring, the openness of ideas, the strong, deep shout, the synthesis of the Castilian soul, the sacrifice of many details in order to emphasize the rudimentary." With the passage of time, and the calming of waters that ensued, perhaps Max Nordau provided the best assessment of both sides of the controversy when he wrote, in *Los grandes del arte español* (1921), that while all of Zuloaga's characters are real and their manifest verisimilitude arouses interest in his painting abroad, foreigners fall into the comic error of taking these paintings for a literal representation of Spanish reality. Although Zuloaga undeniably based his types on Spanish models, these did not represent the middle ground since the painter extrapolated them from bullfighting rings, popular festivals, and religious processions that did not constitute the daily fare of Spanish life. The difference was that Spanish people appreciated these characters for what they were: exceptional and colorful aspects of national life, whereas foreigners imagined all of Spain to be represented in a Zuloaga painting, leading them to draw completely false conclusions (422). Nordau's interpretation was borne out by Zuloaga himself in an interview with René Maizeroy in which the painter stated quite openly that what he detested most in the world was realism, "the grotesque art . . . of those who are content to copy . . . people and things, because I believe that a painter has the right to compose, transform, deform, and stylize nature in accordance with the character of his subjects."[37]

On the occasion of the painter Anselmo Miguel Nieto's departure for Argentina, Azorín published an essay on 6 August 1922, "Un pintor a Buenos Aires," in which he considered the issue of visual art reception, and compared the process to the reception of literature. In theory, he wrote, there exists an intimate relationship between the life of a nation and its art, but how is this correspondence expressed in practice, and how have a great artist's contemporaries responded to reality as interpreted by that artist? Referring to the French series "L'Art de nôtre temps," Azorín noted that it is both instructive, as well as amusing, to collate critical reception over the years, especially when it came to public opinion of innovative artists such as Courbet or Manet. After considering the reversal of critical fortune enjoyed by El Greco and Velázquez early in the twentieth century, Azorín finally gets to Zuloaga: like it or not, he writes, Zuloaga, in the same way as Pérez Galdós or Goya, created a highly subjective vision of Spain. The question of whether or not Spain, as interpreted by Zuloaga, had any parity with reality, he observed, is one that had been broached years ago and still continues to this day.[38] Azorín came to know Zuloaga, who made his home in Paris, on intimate terms during his Civil War exile in the French capital, and their friendship led him to rethink his opinions on the painter's work. In an article he published on Marceliano Santa María in *ABC*, 27 May 1943, Azorín stated that Zuloaga represented the totality of Spain: "his star extends throughout the whole area of Spain. With the enthusiasm of a Basque, Zuloaga launches himself upon cities, on character types, landscapes, and Spanish scenes" (*PCQ* 178). In his 1945 memoir of life in Paris, Azorín dedicated a chapter to Zuloaga where he reviewed the evolution of his relationship to the painter and his art (7:957–60). He admitted that at the beginning of Zuloaga's career he was engaged in an authentic struggle with the painter's vision, asking himself whether there could ever be any empathy or point of contact between them, remarking that he always tried very hard to find some way to reconcile their opposing views. It was during his sojourn in Paris that Azorín recalled buying some photographic reproductions of houses and streets painted by Zuloaga that made him realize all of Spain's immutable nature was caught in the facades of the artist's dilapidated "caserones vetustos" (7:960). He dedicated *Pensando en España* (1940), a nostalgic exile's tribute to

his sorely missed native land, to "Ignacio Zuloaga, pintor de España. Con la admiración y el cariño de un español" (5:913). In "El pintor de España," the final essay of the collection, Azorín reproduced a conversation that he had had with Zuloaga, in which he confessed that he learned to "see" Spain only during a three-year daily diet of Paris, observing that he learned to "feel" Spain intensely only after a prolonged absence from his country. Zuloaga agreed that the Spain that had emerged from his Paris studio could never have been painted within Spain itself. He reminisced that when he first came to Paris he noticed that the French ambience, coupled with the stimulus of homesickness, caused the mental images of his native land to acquire an emotional and lyrical intensity that even he found surprising (5:1080). In another essay on Zuloaga, from *Memorias Inmemoriales*, Azorín indicated that when he returned to Spain the full truth of Zuloaga's painting finally hit him in the face, and that, for the first time, his private image of Spain was in perfect accord with that of Zuloaga: "Indeed, those character types were those of authentic Spain. Those scenes were, indeed, clearly Spanish. The interior vision that I had of Spain finally connected with Zuloaga's." In the long run, Azorín concludes, what is important to keep in mind is not the extent to which Zuloaga achieves verisimilitude in his work, but that as an artist he "creates truth; that surrounding reality is an artistic creation" (8:443). The eulogistic article he published in *La Prensa* shortly after Zuloaga died is perhaps Azorín's greatest tribute to the artist. He recalled, yet again, the still extant debate between those who passionately insisted on denying veracity to Zuloaga's painting, and others who, scarcely avoiding hyperbole, staunchly defended him. As for himself, Azorín declared in no uncertain terms that "Zuloaga's Spain is the real one. . . . And I confess this after having held, regarding the painting of Zuloaga, disparate opinions: one critical; others supportive. When I look at Zuloaga's paintings, it is as if I were standing before Spain herself."[39]

Spanish art historians disagree as to whether the painter of '98 was Zuloaga or Daniel Vázquez Díaz (1882–1969). Angel Benito, Vázquez's biographer and compiler of the *catalogue raisonné*, agreed with Eugenio D'Ors who cast his vote in favor of the more "Spanish" painter Zuloaga, whose precepts and beliefs were more in keeping with those of the Generation of 1898.

Vázquez Díaz, a painter who lived the Cubist moment in Paris, and introduced his own version of the new, European art movements to Spain, better corresponds to what Benito calls "la generación de Alfonso XIII" (413). When Vázquez Díaz arrived in Paris in 1905–06 (he stayed until 1918), Cézanne had just died, the Fauves were at the zenith of their short-lived movement, and Picasso and Braque were just beginning to develop an artistic vision that would later be called Cubism. In the same way that Sorolla adapted impressionistic luminism to his fundamentally academic training, Vázquez Díaz assimilated Cubism's cerebral approach to painting and Cézanne's method of constructing architectural masses through volume, line, and plane without giving himself over entirely to a Cubist technique. In a 1921 article published in *Ultra*, Guillermo de Torre argued that Vázquez Díaz belonged to the school of painters who set out to look for a balance between "los medios expresivos y elementos plásticos," exemplified in the work of Vlaminck, Matisse, Lothe, and Luc-Albert Moreau (1). More than any other painter, it is the influence of Cézanne that art historians see in Vázquez Díaz, an assertion corroborated by the painter himself in an essay written for *ABC* in 1960 where he stated that, "Cézanne was a revelation for me from the time I was very young; I owe to him the direction of my training." Vázquez added that he also learned valuable lessons from Cézanne's fondness for El Greco (168–69).[40]

Despite his Cubist tendencies and the difference in age, Vázquez Díaz is often associated with the Generation of 1898 whose "official" portraitist he became; he also painted landscapes, usually executed during annual pilgrimages made to Spain in order to, as he said, "paint the intimate, personal *oeuvre* that I feel and to exhibit it in Paris." Sounding very much like Antonio Machado and Ortega, Vázquez Díaz added, "It is essential to build a nation" (Benito 105).[41] It was Vázquez Díaz's literary portraits that led critics to compare him to a number of his friends who belonged to the Generation of 1898, persuading some of them to name Vázquez the "pintor base de la generación del 98" (Benito 408). Lafuente Ferrari observed that it was logical for this painter to become the portraitist of '98 for the simple reason that the sensibilities of his generation had been awakened to landscape and the lyricism of color by the poets and writers of 1898 (1953, 36). Inevitably, Vázquez Díaz's close association with the cul-

tural giants of his day situated him within the ranks of artists, writers, and intellectuals who represent the best of Spanish Modernism (Fig. 20).

Vázquez Díaz embarked on his celebrated portraits due to the intervention of Azorín, who showed a sketch the artist had done of Ramón y Cajal to Luca de Tena, then editor of *ABC*, who immediately contracted Vázquez for a series of "cabezas de celebridades" (Benito 154). Because these portraits covered a wide range of celebrities—from Pérez Galdós and Menéndez Pidal to Rubén Darío, Adriano del Valle, Juan Ramón Jiménez; the seminal '98 group and their progeny, including Azorín, the Baroja brothers, Machado, Benavente, Salvador de Madariaga, Ortega y Gasset, Grandmontagne, Pérez de Ayala, Eugenio D'Ors, as well as the painters Sorolla and Zuloaga—critics have drawn parallels between Vázquez's work and that of his literary contemporaries. The writer and socialist politician Julián Zugazagoitia referred to Vázquez Díaz as the "Antonio Machado of painting," perceiving in his canvases the same Andalusian charm modulated by elegant sobriety that Machado had brought to poetry.[42] Lafuente Ferrari pointed to analogies between Juan Ramón Jiménez and Vázquez Díaz both of whom, without impressionistic emphasis on the Heraclitean nature of fluid and vibrating light, also set out to suspend and eternalize the fugitive moment through the "miracle" of their art. According to Lafuente, Vázquez's best work exudes, like the verses of Juan Ramón or Azorín's exquisite prose, a feeling of calm, stillness, and silence, all three artists sharing an instinct for composition and a talent for filtering the external, visual impression through their private, interior worlds, a process that spiritualized the sensory and, in Lafuente's opinion, was common to all "classical" works of art and literature (1953, 42). Angel Benito saw a relationship between the artist and both Juan Ramón Jiménez and Pío Baroja, while Moya Huertas, reviewing the *Exposición Nacional* for 1945, suggested that perhaps Vázquez Díaz was best compared to Azorín since the work of both masters integrated in different media an elegance of facture, purity, and synthesis, as well as "that flavor and effusion of distance that makes everything tremble with sadness . . . each object immersed in a melancholy and essential remoteness."[43]

Azorín, a great fan of Vázquez Díaz, considered him a "marvelous juggler of volume and

Fig. 20   Daniel Vázquez Díaz, *Los hermanos Baroja*, 1925. Oil on canvas, 187 × 147 cm. Courtesy Museo de la Real Academia de San Fernando, Madrid.

color" (8:446). In an article published in *ABC* in 1943, he wrote that when a painter like Vázquez Díaz leads his viewer from "one volume to another, from one color to another toward the unknown, toward the exquisite sensation of something unknown, that painter is a great painter" (*PCQ* 183). Vázquez Díaz shared Azorín's passion for gray, and in the same essay written for *ABC*, Azorín remarked that for painters and poets gray was the supreme color, observing that while Vázquez Díaz had all the colors of the spectrum at his disposal, he found only gray could express the high notes of his personality. Grey, wrote Azorín, "the color of ash, of the sky overcast with clouds that presage stormy weather, of the bare mountains [of the Mediterranean]," is the most difficult and delicate of colors to pin down (*PCQ* 183). In his opinion, Vázquez was at his best when he painted portraits in gray, in the same way that Goya was at his best in the predominantly gray portrait of his teacher and brother-in-law, Francisco Bayeu (*PCQ* 183, 8:437). Azorín himself sat for most of Spain's important post-Impressionists: the first, and perhaps oldest extant portrait, is a pastel by Ricardo Baroja of a youthful Azorín "en [sus] tiempos de incertidumbre" (8:412); Francisco Sancha painted the portrait of Azorín that appears on the cover of the first edition of *Los pueblos*; another early likeness was done by Ramón Casas; Joaquín Sorolla posed Azorín seated in a white wicker chair and dressed in a black suit (this portrait now hangs at the Hispanic Society in New York). The Basque painter Juan Echevarría needed eighty sittings to complete Azorín's portrait; Jenaro Lahuerta's portrait was awarded a prize at the 1948 *Exposición Nacional*. Sebastián Miranda made a small statue of Azorín in Paris, and the Valencian sculptor J. Alfonso executed a bronze bust of the writer, now in the vestibule of the Casa-Museo at Monóvar (1:cxiii–cxv). However, the two most famous portraits of Azorín, and the ones that he liked best, were those done by Ignacio Zuloaga and Daniel Vázquez Díaz. Azorín noted in *Memorias Inmemoriales* that "X" professed a sincere admiration for both artists and that there was a time when he had been "obsessed" with their painting (8:442–43). He called Zuloaga's portrait "superb," and he especially liked the allusive, ruined castle in its background (8:412). Although he thought both painters caught the "spiritual atmosphere" all good portraits should convey, of the two, Azorín's favorite, by far, was the portrait by Váz-quez Díaz (8:413) (Fig. 21). He observed that when painting, Vázquez, without a moment's hesitation, as if by instinct, went directly for the range of soft gray tones; the result, he wrote, "is a marvel of grays. The entire, nearly imperceptible scale of grays is in that canvas." Azorín found Vázquez Díaz's color preference seductive: "Gray dominates my whole portrait. And gray, that which is uttered in a low voice, is my element" (8:403). In a rare personal confession, Azorín admitted that it was through those grays that the painter had been able to externalize the sitter's innermost personality (8:447).[44]

French Contemporaries

The French Impressionists admired Pierre Puvis de Chavannes (1824–1898), an artist who specialized in large, decorative landscape murals with classical themes, and they acknowledged him as a "precursor" (Mauclair 198). Puvis's paintings, especially his rendition of the human figure, appear as if shrouded in palpable stillness, somehow existing outside of time and space—a characteristic that imparts an ethereal quality to his work, through which the artist intended to elicit mood more than subject, leading the viewer to private reverie (Wattenmaker 2, 13). Despite the traditional, academic foundation of his technique, Puvis was considered a vanguard artist and was frequently invited to exhibit with such groups as "La Libre Esthétique," successor to "Les XX" in Belgium where, in 1894, he showed three paintings alongside Pissarro, Sisley, Gauguin, Lautrec, and James Ensor (Wattenmaker 15). The artist developed a distinctive style that diverged from the illusory imitation of volume, depth, modeling, and natural color associated with nineteenth-century realistic practice; instead, he used the mural's extended, flat surface as an opportunity to create panoramic effects, harmonizing his pale, almost neutral palette with the stone on which he painted. Ironically, Puvis was as popular with artistic and literary moderns as he was with academic traditionalists. Literary symbolists, especially, saw in his work a reflection of their own striving for timeless, universal themes, while those with more conservative tastes found Puvis to be a follower of pre-Renaissance, Italian fresco painters or, alternately, the modern heir to Poussin (Kearns 241). Azorín defended Puvis in the face of the uncomprehending Spanish critic Rafael Balsa de la Vega

Fig. 21   Daniel Vázquez Díaz, *Retrato de José Martínez Ruiz*, 1942. Oil on canvas, 1.30 × 1.00 m. Courtesy Padres Escolapios, Madrid.

who, in an 1892 book on landscape painting, *Los bucólicos*, wrote that Puvis's work made him laugh. Although Azorín's rebuttal was written in 1914, by that time he was clearly familiar enough with Puvis to surmise that, while Balsa de la Vega referred to the painter's *Santa Genoveva* without specifying which of several paintings on the subject he had in mind, the critic must have been thinking of Puvis's *Encuentro de Santa Genoveva y San Germán*, since that particular canvas had a "most beautiful landscape in the background" (*PCQ* 118). Azorín probably saw Puvis's work for the first time during his 1905 trip to Paris when he reported the visit of Alfonso XIII to the French capital. In one of the "Crónicas del viaje regio" he describes the Paris City Hall, including a comment on the murals Puvis had made for its interior walls: "Up above, in one of the ample stair landings, materializes Puvis de Chavannes's *Invierno* with its delicate, milky colors" (3:853). It is understandable how Puvis's "tenuous color," his gray-based palette, and the static nature of his most characteristic work might have appealed to Azorín.[45]

Of the French post-Impressionist painters, although Azorín was interested in Van Gogh and Gauguin, it was to Cézanne that he responded most deeply. He wrote that he admired Gauguin and Van Gogh as two painters in whose lives misfortune played as important a role as inspiration. Noting that he saw a wonderful exhibition of paintings by Gauguin in Paris, Azorín also remarked that he envied Gauguin's retreat from modern civilization to the Pacific Islands, finding the lifestyle he chose, "like a compendium of solitude and withdrawal," extremely attractive (*PQ* 30, 9:1389). In his copy of Jean de Rotonchamp's *Gauguin: 1848–1903*, Azorín marked a passage in which Gauguin was quoted naming Cézanne, Van Gogh, and Émile Bernard as the masters from whom he learned all his "recipes" for painting and whose artistic issue he admitted to being, allegedly confessing, "Quel adroit pasticheur je fais!" (179). Despite the heartbreak of exile, life in Paris compensated Azorín by extending to him an almost unlimited bonanza of art exhibitions. In the retrospective *Valencia* (1941), he recalled life in the French capital as a continuous celebration of art shows subsidized either by the State or by individual gallerists and art dealers (6:32). The intense activity of the arts community in Paris allowed Azorín to see Gauguin "almost in his entirety," and he wrote that the

Edgar Degas retrospective held at the Orangerie in the spring of 1939 was so overwhelming that it "made him dizzy." It was at the Degas exhibition that Azorín accidentally stumbled upon a doorway above which a poster "makes our mouth water with anticipation." The doorway led to an "Exposition de Paul Cézanne": inside Azorín discovered a select group of well-chosen paintings by an artist whom he called "our painter" (6:32–33). There at last was this artist who, like his counterpart in Balzac's admirable novel, struggled so passionately with line and color, "that is, if line is something other than color" (6:33).[46] What Azorín found most suggestive about the exhibition was two rows of photographs: those in the top row displayed landscapes and villages in which Cézanne had actually worked; those in the bottom row reproduced paintings Cézanne executed at the sites portrayed in the top row of photographs. What struck Azorín about the juxtaposition was what he termed the "poder eliminatorio del pintor." His visual experience confirmed the full force and genius of Cézanne's intuitions, as well as the total lack of empathy for the painter on the part of his contemporaries. There is nothing more irritating to the masses, observed Azorín, than unembellished fundamentals, because "the essential in art" is always considered elite and somehow superior (6:33). Azorín's positive response to Cézanne—and for that matter, to Puvis de Chavannes—is explained by his belief that in the labyrinthine question of aesthetics, "elimination" in the sense of spareness and simplicity, rose above all other considerations "because the particular rhythm of prose is contingent upon economy" (6:32).

Azorín fictionalized his Orangerie experience in a story from *Sintiendo a España* whose protagonist, Gaspar Salgado, reveals that in Paris he had learned an unforgettable lesson from a modern French painter: the ability to see Spain better through contrast. In a transparent reference to Azorín's experience of the Cézanne exhibition, Salgado states that he saw something quite remarkable at a show of the painter's work: above reproductions of paintings by Cézanne, hung photographs of the sites represented.[47] What amazed Salgado was Cézanne's ability to expunge the inessential: "Of the landscape, Cézanne conserved only the indispensable. And that's what art is all about: elimination and simplification." Salgado confesses that he had already begun to move in a similar direction on his own, but that Cézanne

Fig. 22   Francisco Pradilla, *Dona Juana La Loca*, 1877. Oil on canvas, 340 × 500 cm. Casón del Buen Retiro, Museo del Prado, Madrid.

had put him on the right track. A landscape painter about to embark on his first attempt at history painting, Salgado questions whether he will be able to achieve the same kind of "essential simplicity" in his projected work: a scene from the regency of María de Molina, an early fourteenth-century queen who staved off numerous internecine conflicts in order to save the throne for her son, the future Fernando IV (6:751–52). As he ponders examples of history paintings by his nineteenth-century predecessors, Salgado juxtaposes Francisco Pradilla's *Doña Juana la Loca* (1877) with another, more restrained version of the unfortunate queen's life, *Demencia de Doña Juana de Castilla*, painted by Lorenzo Vallés in 1866. While the painting by Pradilla (Fig. 22) shows a crowd scene filled with the royal entourage and picturesque "period archaeology," the painting by Vallés is a model of simplicity (Fig. 23). The lessons Salgado has gleaned from Cézanne and Vallés serve him well in resolving the problem of "suppressing archaeology. Costumes and knick-knacks from other epochs" which he

feels only distract the viewer from concentrating on a work of art.[48]

As a writer Azorín had, for many years, subscribed to much the same approach to literature as Gaspar Salgado did to painting. In *El artista y el estilo* (1946), he affirmed that "style consists of elimination; it demands the exclusion of ornament and the conservation of the fundamental," and he wondered who it was that taught this secret to painters able to realize it in their work (8:654). The painter-protagonist of "La leticia en la egestad" confesses that lately he has been painting better than ever before because he achieved the pinnacle of tenuousness by eliminating useless detail from his work: "essence, divine essence, is what I put into my paintings" (5:1041). There is a clear affinity between the qualities Azorín admired in the visual arts and the stylistic features he valued most in literature: the artist's ability to single out the significant, evocative detail while suppressing all that proved inessential—"El secreto del arte de escribir," he declared, "consiste en eliminar" (5:987). He considered Cervantes a

Fig. 23 Lorenzo Vallés, *La Demencia de Doña Juana de Castilla*, 1866. Oil on canvas, 238 × 313 cm. Casón del Buen Retiro, Museo del Prado, Madrid.

master stylist whose ability to condense and eliminate the superficial was a feature common to the work of any mature artist (9:277). Among painters, Azorín singled out Rembrandt not only as a superb "painter of light," but also as one whose magical powers consisted in the ability to eliminate the extraneous. He used two different versions of Rembrandt's *Los peregrinos de Emaús* to illustrate his point. In one picture, Rembrandt depicted some figures by a window through which natural light streamed into the room; however, another, divine light also emanated from Jesus, creating a conflict between two light sources in the painting. In the definitive version of the *Peregrinos*, Rembrandt eliminated the window, an artistic decision Azorín correctly interprets as simplifying the painting by allowing only the light that streamed from Christ to dominate the canvas (5:784).

In Azorín's opinion, the modern painter who best exemplified the technique of elimination was Cézanne, and in a 1943 article on Zola's novel *L'Oeuvre*, he wrote that from Cézanne "originate . . . the innovations in art that were to come later" (*PCQ* 202).[49] Indeed, Mark Roskill argues that the pre-Cubist or early Cubist phase of art (1907–9) was a period of time in which Cézanne's star was in the ascendent among young painters who appreciated the "geometrizing and simplifying tendencies" in the older painter's work (1985, 32). Of all his generational contemporaries, it seems only Azorín was able to transcend Impressionism to appreciate painters like Van Gogh, Cézanne, and Gauguin. Writing in 1913, well into the Cubist revolution, Unamuno, for example, protested that Darío de Regoyos had been able to express "the soul of things" much better than those "insufferable cubists and futurists who claim to represent it" (7:745). The first phase of Cubism owed much to Cézanne's recuperation of volume, plane, and mass in art—the innately geometric forms of the natural world which he thought the Impressionists had ignored in their exclusive preoccupation with light (Habasque 28). The problem was duly noted in Spain by Vázquez Díaz who remarked that "Cézanne wanted to return to painting its corporeal dimension that had been lost . . . in the Impressionist carnival" (167). The Cézanne exhibit Azorín saw in Paris had a tremendous impact upon him: the experience seemed to coalesce much of his thought on literary and painterly style, evident in the articles he began to publish at this time on the "elimination effect," as he called it, and which he almost always associated with Cézanne. He continued to write on the "father" of Cubism after his return to Madrid, well into the 1950s. In "La cuestión Cé-

zanne" (1944), in much the same way that he had earlier debated the "cuestión Zuloaga," Azorín considered whether Claude Lantier, the protagonist of *L'Oeuvre*, was a true portrait of Cézanne, an issue that has been argued both ways by literary critics since the novel's publication (*PCQ* 207) (Fig. 24).[50] Most evocative, in the context of Cubism, is Azorín's 1944 novel *Salvadora de Olbena* where he experiments with multiple points of view, perspectivism, and the notion of simultaneity in time and space. Why Azorín would produce a novel in 1944 whose aesthetic foundations appear to be based on theories that informed intellectual and artistic life during the first two decades of the twentieth century (chiefly the return to form in art and the rejection of reality as static and unchanging in the sciences), is the subject of the last chapter in this book.

Fig. 24   Paul Cézanne, *La Maison du pendu à Auvers-sur-Oise*, c.1874. Oil on canvas, .55 × .66 m. Musée d'Orsay, Paris. Giraudon / Art Resource, New York.

4

The Cyclical Art of History:
Subversion of Time and Space in *Doña Inés*

AZORÍN'S PENCHANT FOR LITERARY ICONOLOGY is perhaps at its best in the 1925 novel *Doña Inés (Historia de amor)*, which incorporates most fully into a single work of fiction references to both historical and fictional painters, paintings, sculpture, architecture, and artistic movements as principal players. Although Elena Catena, editor of the most readily available text of *Doña Inés*, observes that painting inspires quite a bit of the novel (57), and she documents authorial references to extant paintings and painters, it was never Catena's aim to offer a taxonomy by which to study and categorize Azorín's use of the visual arts in the novel, nor does she establish a structural and thematic relationship between the visual art forms integral to the text and its stylistic composition.[1] In focussing on the many different interpretive values accorded to the plastic arts by Azorín in *Doña Inés*, the categories established by Marianna Torgovnick for the study of the visual arts and pictorialism in prose fiction are again extremely useful.

One of Azorín's favorite painterly genres was the still life which he re-created verbally in not a few of his essays and novels, frequently with a decorative purpose in mind. In "Los primitivos" (*Madrid*), for example, he includes a *bo-degón* inspired by those of Lucas Menéndez. In addition to revealing his source in the visual arts, Azorín discloses his literary source as Berceo's dictum "Non lo preciaba todo cuanto tres chirivías," and he uses the essay as a point of departure for commentary on the medieval Spanish poet:

> En un tablero de nogal . . . un vaso de buen vino— que será vino doncel—, una nuez . . . y tres chirivías. La luz entra por la ventana . . . y hace que se forme sobre la mesa una leve sombra. Delante están el vaso, la nuez y las chirivías. Detrás, el suave adumbramiento. El bodegón es bonito. No lo ha pintado mejor Lucas Menéndez. (6:289) (Pl. 31)[2]

> [On a walnut tabletop . . . a glass of good wine— most likely a young wine—, a walnut . . . and three parsnips. Light enters through the window . . . and throws a slight shadow onto the table. In the foreground are the glass, the nut, and the parsnips. In the background, the soft shade. The still life is pretty. Lucas Menéndez could not have painted it better.]

The decorative still life Azorín includes in chapter 40 of *Doña Inés* is a kitchen scene reminiscent of the Flemish style. Set in the boarding-house of Doña Eufemia where Diego Lodares resides, the verbal still life, as its visual arts counterpart, pays special attention to the effect light produces on various elements of the painting. Azorín provides the reader unequivocal instruction that what he has created is a *bodegón* and that his verbal "painting" should be interpreted as such: "Por la ventana entra el sol matinal. Brillantes y vivos van a dar los rayos en la panzuda limeta que, llena de vino claro, reposa sobre la mesa; a su lado se ven una dorada hogaza y cuatro o seis cuartales; manzanas, peras; rojos albérchigos forman un montón pintoresco" [184; The morning sun enters through the window. The sparkling and bright rays glance off a pot-bellied flask that, full of clear wine, sits on the table; beside it is a golden loaf of coarse bread and four or six smaller loaves; apples, pears; red peaches form a picturesque heap].

Equally decorative is the preceding chapter, "Aquelarre en Segovia," which establishes analogies between the conspiratory old "witches" from the four corners of Segovia—one of whom whispers "¡El jueves, trisagio en San Millán!"—and Ignacio Zuloaga's painting *Las brujas de San Millán* (Pl. 32). While Catena speculates that Azorín might have known the painting since he was a casual acquaintance of Zuloaga's (180, 56), in point of fact, both painter and writer were on friendly terms, and there is a great deal of intertextuality between Zuloaga's art and Azorín's prose. As we know, Azorín was not always approving of the painter's stereotypical vision of Spain, but he wrote a number of perceptive essays on Zuloaga's work and, on occasion, evoked the painter's general style as a visual referent for his own verbal-pictorial metaphor.[3] *Las brujas de San Millán* (1907), a relatively early piece in the Zuloaga corpus, was executed at the height of the painter's association with the Generation of 1898 writers. At the time of his closest association with '98, Zuloaga maintained a studio in Segovia, a city in Old Castile which the Generation's authors also frequented for its historic and symbolic significance to them. It is highly probable that, by the time Azorín wrote *Doña Inés*, he would certainly have known Zuloaga's painting of the Segovian "witches" modeled on actual women and servants from the town (Barrio-Garay 54). According to Lafuente Ferrari, *Segovia de noche*, another painting by Zuloaga that Catena reproduces in her edition of *Doña Inés*, also represents a "visión que llamaríamos azoriniana." Lafuente attributes the homology between

writer and painter to a shared need to depict in their respective media, human emotions confronted with time's passing, and both artists' effort to suspend time in order to portray "the eternal essence of things" (464).[4]

One of Zuloaga's strengths as a painter was his reputation as a master landscapist whose canvases of the Castilian countryside, together with its towns and villages, recall the prose landscapes of the Generation of 1898. Barrio-Garay writes that it was actually in 1898 that Zuloaga "discovered" Old Castile, especially Segovia, and that he executed a number of important paintings with a Segovian motif (53-54). Azorín, too, is known for his superb literary landscapes which, especially in his early work, are charged with ideological content. The landscapes of *Doña Inés*, however, are decorative rather than ideological, serving as lovely evocations of Segovia and its environs. Chapter 8, "Viaje a Segovia," is reminiscent of the Castilian landscapes painted by Aureliano de Beruete. On her way to Segovia from Madrid, Doña Inés draws back the curtain of her carriage to observe the panoramic vista stretched out before her:

> Las nubes dejan caer sus sombras densas entre la luminosidad viva en laderas y llanuras. Quedan entre las sombras . . . anchos fragmentos de paisaje en que resaltan peñas y árboles. Los colores del paisaje . . . son vivos y limpios. El azul oscuro bordea con el ocre. Un albero de tierra clara aparece entre un alijar sombrío con sus chaparros negros y redondos. (88)

> [The clouds allow their dense shadows to fall on the bright glow of the slopes and plains. Large chunks of landscape, in which boulders and trees are conspicuous, stand out in between the shadows. The colors of the landscape . . . are bright and clear. Dark blue borders on ochre. A mound of white-colored earth appears in a dark wasteland with its black and rounded thicket of small, evergreen oaks.]

What follows is an extended verbal landscape in which Azorín employs color words and color values to evoke concrete visual referents through language: the yellow and violet flowers of the wild broom and lavender contrast with the deep blue sky and ochre color of the soil against which Azorín places the various green hues of vegetation, the whole quite similar to the color palette used by Aureliano de Beruete. A second landscape in *Doña Inés* emphasizes the painterly qualities of Azorín's eye when he adds visual depth to the verbal landscape through a conscious use of perspective: "Las ventanas dan al campo y a la ciudad. La sierra se columbra en la lejanía. Cuatro o seis álamos, cerca de la casa, ponen sus cimas agudas—a causa de la perspectiva—junto a las últimas pinceladas blancas de la nieve de la montaña" [128; The windows open on to the countryside and the city. In the distance you have a glimpse of the mountains. Near the house, four or six poplars place their pointed crests—due to the laws of perspective—next to the last, white brushstrokes of snow on the mountain.]

A discussion of the Barbizon painters and its senior member, Jean-Baptiste Camille Corot in chapter 36, moves us toward the biographical sector of Torgovnick's continuum. It is through Tío Pablo, Azorín's alter ego in the novel who relates an 1836 visit to Paris, his meeting and spending some time in Fontainebleau Forest with the Barbizon painters, and his special fondness for Corot, that Azorín documents his own artistic preferences and inscribes his personal aesthetic values within a specific painterly tradition. As we have seen, Azorín knew the anecdotal history of Barbizon very well, and he wrote numerous essays on the individual painters of the group. He even included a reference in Doña Inés to the posada in which the Barbizon painters congregated: Tío Pablo remembers that the artists had decorated the doors, walls, and tables of the inn where they lodged and took their meals with curious sketches and rustic murals (172).[5] This mingling of documentable art history and identifiable painters with the purely fictional artist Taroncher, and his equally fictional portrait of Doña Inés—that receives its final touches while the discussion of Pablo's visit to Fontainebleau takes place—serves Azorín's thematic and artistic purpose of erasing boundaries between reality and fiction, while simultaneously providing the novel its overall thematic unity.

For Azorín, the crown jewel of landscape painting was the Impressionist school whose aesthetic and technical innovations were prepared for by the painters of Barbizon. Although impressionist technique was adopted by Spain's gente nueva at the turn of the century, because it was considered avant-garde, modern, and therefore highly charged ideologically due to its conscious intent to rattle the literary establishment, Azorín cultivated an impressionist style

throughout the better part of his very long literary career. Particularly evocative in context of Doña Inés is the technique Azorín used to describe the cathedral of Segovia that immediately recalls an earlier cathedral description from the essay "La catedral" (Castilla):

La luz de Segovia es más reverberante y fina que la luz de las otras ciudades españolas. . . . La hora del día, el tiempo, el sol, las nubes, hacen cambiar a la torre de color y aun de forma. Los resaltes de los ángulos son más salientes o desaparecen, y el matiz llega a rojizo, pasa por amarillo, se desvanece en un pajizo suave, según la luminosidad del momento. (92)

[The light in Segovia is more shimmering and fine than that of other Spanish cities. . . . The time of day, the weather, the sun, the clouds, make the cathedral's tower change color and even its shape. The ledges of its corners are more pronounced or disappear, and its hue becomes red, passes through yellow, dissolves into a soft straw color, according to the luminosity of the moment.]

In her notes to this passage, Catena speculates whether it would not be exceedingly risky to state that Azorín might have known Monet's 1894 Rouen Cathedral series (93 n. 14). As discussed earlier, Azorín was, indeed, familiar with the Rouen series paintings, most versions of which include, as do his verbal descriptions of the cathedrals at León and Segovia, visual commentary on the towers of the celebrated French cathedral.[6]

Well-read in the history and aesthetics of Impressionism, Azorín found his own ideas on color, light, and temporality reaffirmed in the work of Impressionist painters. In an essay on Spanish artists, he empathized with the exasperating instability and short duration of natural light when working out of doors, the ability of light to transform the appearance of objects in a matter of seconds, and the plein air painter's need to cope with these challenges:

Y todo lo transforma la luz; un árbol, un arroyo, unas rocas, una pared, no son lo mismo en todos los momentos de la mañana y de la tarde. No basta una hora para transformarlos; basta un brevísimo instante. . . . El ojo escrutador del pintor, la sensibilidad toda del pintor, que perciben este reflejo sutilísimo y fugaz, ¿cómo se compondrán para poder aprehenderlo en la tela? (PCQ 148–49)

[And light transforms everything; a tree, a rivulet, some rocks, a wall are not the same at all moments of the morning and the afternoon. An hour doesn't even suffice for them to be transformed; a brief instant is enough. . . . The painter's scrutinizing eye, his entire sensibility which can perceive the extremely subtle, fleeting reflection, how do they organize themselves in order to capture it all on canvas?].

Azorín surely recognized his own sensibilities in the Impressionists' keen awareness of temporality both as a technical challenge and also as the exclusive subject of a canvas as occurred in the mature work of Claude Monet (Sypher 178). Marianna Torgovnick observes that the depiction of light on canvas is the painterly equivalent of time in the verbal arts (131), and time, recorded as gradually changing color values, in Wylie Sypher's opinion, may become a formula for space (178). As the painter he always wanted to be, and often imagined that he was, in his cathedral descriptions Azorín intuitively made use of temporality in the form of changing color values to simulate the visually apprehended sensations of light and space within the verbal medium, coaxing the written page into yielding a sense of dimensionality in much the same way a painter would employ perspective in order to impart a sense of space and depth to a canvas.

While Azorín's preference for literary and plastic Impressionism spanned, at different moments of his career, the decorative, biographical, and ideological segments of Torgovnick's visual arts continuum, his use of a portrait of the Queen Regent, María Cristina, as a visual referent for the events of chapter 45, "Diego ante el jefe político," is purely ideological. Don Santiago Benaya, the civil authority in Segovia, summons Diego Lodares to an audience, ostensibly to berate him for the public scandal generated by Diego's amorous encounter with Doña Inés in the cathedral. While Diego waits for the discussion of his indiscretion to begin, the omniscient narrator observes, not without some irony, that from her perch on the wall, María Cristina, widow of Fernando VII, known for her sexual proclivities, looks upon the scene with the hint of a knowing smile playing upon her lips (198–99). María Cristina scandalized the Spanish court during her regency by marrying a much younger bodyguard; her portrait in Don Benaya's office thus becomes a visual image that Azorín uses to encode the parallel situation of Inés and Diego whose relationship,

made public, scandalizes Segovian society and, as in the case of the Queen Regent, symbolizes the beginning of Doña Inés's fall from grace.[7] Azorín, however, expresses utter contempt for Segovian prudery by suddenly deviating from Don Benaya's expected course of action, and has the governor merely scold Diego for publishing an article in the Romantic journal *Semanario Pintoresco* in which the young poet dared make a scathing attack on the intransigence of literary classicism.

On the interpretive portion of Torgovnick's continuum, perceptual or psychological usage of the visual arts refers to the ways in which characters experience art, or pictorial objects and scenes, in ways that stimulate their minds either on conscious or unconscious levels (22). "Daguerrotipo," the second chapter of *Doña Inés*, literally "frames" two portraits of the eponymous heroine: Azorín begins with a detailed verbal description not only of the costume Doña Inés is wearing, but also of her physical beauty which, he notes, is beginning to show "un imperceptible principio de flaccidez" (73). Within its borders this verbal portrait contains the description of a daguerrotype taken of Inés, dressed in the same clothing just described by the narrator, but the effects of sun and time have already caused the image to fade. In her study of portraits in literature, Françoise Meltzer argues that contemplation of a photograph or portrait indicates the desire to enter a distant or by-gone world (136). Azorín not only situates his novel from the very first sentence within a specific frame of time past—"En 1840 y en Madrid"—but the fading daguerrotype he emphasizes was also taken in 1840 by the historically identifiable Marqués de la Remisa, serves first, as an additional topical reference to contextualize the novel's ambience, and second, as a visual memento of the protagonist as she appeared before time had begun to ravage her beauty. In his description of the fading daguerrotype ("time and the sun have nearly erased the image"), Azorín once again utilizes time and color to mimic space and light in such a painterly fashion as to lend dimensionality to the form, as well as to the symbolic content, of his verbal portrait.[8]

The knowledge characters receive through visual impressions, or contact with art objects, may cause them pain or discomfort (Torgovnick 191). When she receives a letter from Don Juan, severing their relationship, Inés contemplates her own "portrait" in the mirror of her dressing table, smoothing her fingertips over her skin "softly, in order to test its firmness" (85). As she reflects on her break with Don Juan, the gold coins Doña Inés caresses while contemplating her reflection in the mirror bring a melancholy acknowledgment that no amount of money can stem the passage of time, an especially disconcerting realization for an unmarried woman on the verge of middle age.[9] The room where Doña Inés reads Don Juan's letter is dominated by a lithograph of Buenos Aires, hung in a wide mahogany frame. The lithograph, we are told, is "inseparable from the time she whiles away in this room" (76), and it seems to have acquired an unspecified importance in her life. Azorín himself intuits the "fatality that unites us, without our wanting it, to some piece of furniture or knick-knack" (76), the same psychological meaning Torgovnick argued an *objet d'art* could acquire in a fictional character's life. The lithograph, of course, is proleptic to the voyage Doña Inés will make to Buenos Aires as the final episode and containing "frame" of her biography placed at the novel's conclusion.[10]

The invocation of framing, whether by reference to literal pictures in frames, or metaphoric to the viewing or placement of scenes and characters in the frames of windows, doors, and balconies, places the text in "perspective," creating an illusion of pictorial space within the normally temporal and linear flow of narrative (Kestner 1981, 110–11). Azorín's tale of Doña Inés, her broken affair with one lover and the beginning of a new liaison in Segovia with Diego ("el de Garcillán") Lodares, is a "frame" story within which a parallel novel unfolds, titled *Doña Beatriz (Historia de amor)*, written by Tío Pablo. The medieval legend of Doña Beatriz de Silva and her tragic love for the adolescent troubadour Guillén, although not an exact duplication of the primary discourse, demonstrates enough significant coincidence with the frame story to move it into the realm of self-reflexive fiction.[11] Not only do the names of both sets of protagonists bear similar oxytonic inflection—Inés / Beatriz; Guillén / Garcillán—but Inés also happens to be the last descendant of the Silva bloodline and, like Beatriz, "she was in the autumn of her life . . . and had never savored love" (157). Like their lovers, both of them blue-eyed and blond young men, the two women bear a striking physical resemblance to one another. The two tales finally intrude upon

each other's diegetic spaces when the fictional painter Taroncher, commissioned by Tío Pablo to paint a portrait of Doña Beatriz, simultaneously produces a portrait of Doña Inés in which she appears as a mirror image of Beatriz. A portrait is by definition a copy, a metaphor of what it represents; the relation between representation and represented is therefore also necessarily metaphorical (Weinsheimer 79). But, as Weinsheimer suggests, while a copy indicates a referent that is not itself, the mirror image has no existence outside of itself: it is effaced since as a "virtual" duplication of its referent, the mirror image "has no image, for the image is of the thing itself that it reflects" (Weinsheimer 108). Seeing her own portrait as a mirror image of Doña Beatriz, Inés recognizes that a line of demarcation between herself and her medieval ancestor has been erased: "Doña Inés, pensativa, absorta, volvía a experimentar . . . la sensación extraña, indefinible, que experimentara al poner la mano días antes sobre la estatua de Doña Beatriz. ¿Existe el tiempo? ¿Quién era ella: Inés o Beatriz?" [174–75; Doña Inés, pensive, absorbed, experienced once again . . . the strange, indefinable sensation that she had felt, days before, when she put her hand on the statue of Doña Beatriz. Does time exist? Who was she: Inés or Beatriz?]. In this instance the two portraits, like the two narratives created by Azorín and Tío Pablo, evolve synchronically in time as a "double-text-in-progress" (Caws 10), in which the framing narrative is circumscribed by the embedded story, the double texts held together by the painter Taroncher who moves in and out of Azorín's novel *Doña Inés*, as well as Tío Pablo's "historical" reconstruction based on the life of Doña Beatriz.

The two pairs of self-reflexive visual and verbal texts produce a complex hierarchy of novelistic frame structures. The literary portrait by nature is a verbal (re)presentation of a character created through language within the already representational medium of literature. It likewise adumbrates the superiority writers strive to impart to the verbal medium as it competes with plastic art forms (Meltzer 215). Azorín engages in this type of hierarchization by situating writing on a higher scale of values than the graphic image as he translates the visual impact of the two portraits to the verbal medium. Art objects often intend to record history by preserving it as "visual text" (Dubois 12). Azorín, however, attempts to reverse this process when he indicates that Taroncher's portrait of Beatriz is actually an imaginary reconstruction based on her sarcophagus sculpture. The painter reduces and textualizes the original, three-dimensional statue to a graphic image which he represents on the two-dimensional plane of canvas or sketch pad. This image is, in turn, transformed into the verbal discourse of Tío Pablo's history and, finally, the past is retextualized and retransmitted to a depersonalized reading public in the novel that Azorín titles *Doña Inés (Historia de amor)*.

Although Inés had all along perceived analogies between her own life and that of Doña Beatriz, it is the uncanny resemblance between Taroncher's portraits that serves as the catalyst for a strong reaction on her part, leading to a second visit to the cathedral chapel where Beatriz is interred. While prior to this moment, Inés had an exclusively perceptual interaction with the art objects that filled her life—the daguerrotype, lithograph of Buenos Aires, and Taroncher's two portraits—her visit to the funerary statue moves us from the perceptual sector of Torgovnick's continuum (of value to the character only), toward the hermeneutic sector, indispensable to a reader's interpretive competence. It is also a moment when Azorín's poetics of framing moves away from the realm of aesthetics to assume more semiotic functions. As Doña Inés wanders about the cathedral, she ponders the fluid nature of time and space, the possibility that a past life might flicker within a present one, the spark of a remote consciousness live within her own, or that perhaps she had already experienced the present moment in some prior life. Inevitably she finds herself in the Silva chapel, standing before the funerary statue of Doña Beatriz. The relationship between sculpture and characterization is extensive in the tradition of literary ekphrasis. Classical rhetoricians used ekphrasis to give voice to the mute work of art, especially to the funerary statue, and through the trope of *enargeia*, to re-create the work of art with such verbal vividness as to give it the illusion of life (Kestner 1978, 68). Azorín's description of Doña Beatriz's sarcophagus sculpture takes care to endow the statue with precisely the kind of energy ancient rhetors strove to produce: "La escuela de escultura funeraria que se placía en marcar las huellas de la muerte en los personajes representados, no es la que ha esculpido estas estatuas. . . . La faz de la dama es serena y

sus ojos van a pestañear" [169; The school of funerary sculpture that took pleasure in showing the traces of death in the personages represented, is not the one that produced these statues. . . . The lady's face is serene and her eyes are about to blink]. Shortly thereafter, Tío Pablo observes that the statues of Beatriz and her husband seem to be in a deep sleep from which they will awaken shortly and return to their palace, Don Enrique bearing with him the marble laurel wreath that crowns the head of his sarcophagus sculpture.

Although there is no sepulchral statue of any woman in the cathedral at Segovia (Catena 58), Azorín's "notional ekphrasis," the representation of an imaginary work of art, may have been inspired by Ricardo de Orueta's *Escultura funeraria en España* (1919), a copy of which exists in the library at Monóvar. Commenting on the sepulchre of Gómez Carrillo de Albornoz (d. 1441) in the cathedral at Sigüenza, Orueta remarks that the anonymous sculptor who executed the statues of Gómez Carrillo and his wife appears to belong to a school of artisans that intended to disguise any direct evocation of death: "The sepulchre here is merely a monument to the glory and honor of the deceased . . . with something, not much, of religious thought, and certainly nothing, or the least possible amount, of funereal suggestion: sleeping statues abound . . ." (57). Orueta describes the head of Gómez Carrillo's statue as resting on an alabaster laurel wreath, a portion of text Azorín bracketed, writing the word "laureles" in the margin (60). A description of the sepulchral niches of Don Juan Fernández Pacheco and his wife Doña Inés Téllez de Meneses in the church at San Bartolomé (Cuenca) is even more suggestive. Observing that there are indications the original statues may have been recumbent rather than kneeling as they are today (307), Orueta remarks in passing that Doña Inés Téllez was first cousin to Doña Beatriz, wife of Don Juan I of Castile, and that the lordship of Belmonte was awarded to Doña Inés's husband, Juan Fernández Pacheco, by King Enrique III on 16 May 1398 (310). The coincidence of names—Inés, Beatriz, Enrique—surely caught Azorín's attention since, on the back jacket of the book, he wrote the words "matrimonio 305," noting the initial page number of Orueta's description of the church at San Bartolomé where Doña Inés Téllez and her husband are interred.[12] The illusion that the funerary statues of Beatriz and

Pl. 17 Dominico Theotocopuli (El Greco), *Cardinal Juan de Tavera*, c.1608. Oil on canvas, 1.03 × .82 m. Hospital de San Juan Bautista de Afuera, Toledo, Spain. Giraudon / Art Resource, New York.

Pl. 18 Aureliano de Beruete, *Paisaje con el Guadarrama al fondo*, c.1903. Oil on canvas, 44 × 57 cm. Courtesy Casa-Museo Azorín, Monóvar (Alicante), Spain / Obras Sociales de la Caja de Ahorros del Mediterráneo.

Pl. 19 Joseph Mallord William Turner, *The Evening Star*, c.1830–40. Oil on canvas, 91.1 × 122.6 cm. The National Gallery of Art, London. Turner Bequest, 1856.

Pl. 20 Joseph Mallord William Turner, *Rain, Steam, Speed—The Great Western Railway,* before 1844. Oil on canvas, 90.8 × 121.9 cm. The National Gallery of Art, London. Turner Bequest, 1856.

Pl. 22 Jean Antoine Watteau, *Gilles*, c.1717–19. Oil on canvas, 184.5 × 149.5 cm. Musée du Louvre, Paris. Scala / Art Resource, New York.

Pl. 21 Rembrandt Harmensz. van Rijn, *The Slaughtered Ox*, 1655. Oil on wood panel, 94 × 69 cm. Musée du Louvre, Paris. Giraudon / Art Resource, New York.

Pl. 23 Francisco de Goya y Lucientes, *La Vendimia*, c.1786. Oil on canvas, 275 × 190 cm. Museo del Prado, Madrid.

Pl. 24 Pedro Berruguete, *Auto de fe presidido por Santo Domingo de Guzmán*, c.1495. Tempera and oil on wood panel, 154 × 92 cm. Museo del Prado, Madrid.

Pl. 25   Ignacio Zuloago, *Portrait of José Martínez Ruiz, "Azorín"*, 1941. Oil on canvas, 145 × 173 cm. Private Collection, Madrid.

Pl. 26   Joaquín Sorolla, *Entre naranjos*, 1903. Oil on canvas, 100 × 150 cm. Museo Nacional de Cuba, Havana. Photograph courtesy Fundación Cultural MAPFRE Vida, Madrid.

Pl. 27   Marceliano Santa María, *El triunfo de la Santa Cruz en la Batalla de las Navas de Tolosa*, 1891–92. Oil on canvas, 450 × 600 cm. Courtesy Museo Marceliano Santa María, Burgos, Spain.

Pl. 28   Joaquim Mir i Trinxet, *La cala encantada*, c.1901. Oil on canvas, 86 × 120.5 cm. Museu Nacional d'Art de Catalunya, Barcelona. © MNAC (Calaveras/Mérida/Sagristà).

Pl. 30 Santiago Rusiñol, *Jardí del Palau Víznar*, 1898. Oil on canvas, 125 × 121 cm. Museo de Cau Ferrat, Sitges, Spain. © 1998 Artists Rights Society (ARS), New York / VEGAP, Madrid.

Pl. 29 Darío de Regoyos, *El gallinero*, c.1912. Oil on canvas, 65 × 55 cm. Casón del Buen Retiro, Museo del Prado, Madrid.

Pl. 31   Luis Egidio Meléndez, *Bodegón: membrillos, melocotones, uvas y calabaza*, 1771. Oil on canvas, 42 × 62 cm. Museo del Prado, Madrid.

Pl. 32   Ignacio Zuloaga, *Las Brujas de San Millán*, 1907. Oil on canvas, 190 × 204 cm. Courtesy Colección del Museo Nacional de Bellas Artes, Buenos Aires, Argentina.

Enrique are alive is the very quality that subsequently permits Doña Inés to experience the hallucinatory (con)fusion of her own identity with that of Doña Beatriz in the following chapter: "¿Es ella Doña Beatriz? ¿Doña Beatriz es Doña Inés? Las manos de la dama se extienden hacia el rostro mamóreo. La alucinación llena el cerebro de Doña Inés. La cabeza de la señora se inclina; sus labios húmedos, rojos, ponen en el blancor del mármol un beso largo, implorador" [177; Is she Doña Beatriz? Is Doña Beatriz, Doña Inés? The lady's hands reach out toward the marble face. A hallucination fills her brain. She inclines her head; her moist, red lips place a long, imploring kiss on the whiteness of the marble]. In this climactic, almost cinematic scene, Inés and Beatriz finally meld into one persona, and Azorín finally arrives at the thematic core of his novel: the conflation of time and space into one, atemporal present within which humankind from across all the ages, and from the most heterogenous of circumstances, recognize affinities and resonances amongst themselves, a notion Ortega dubbed *sinfronismo* in his seminal essay "Azorín: Primores de lo vulgar" (2:163, 167–68).[13]

For Azorín, who consciously sought to introduce the spatiality and inherent simultaneity of plastic art forms within the linear and temporally irreversible arts of the word, sculpture proved to be an especially useful way to incorporate the property of volume into literature. As sensitive as he was to the issue of temporality and the notion of the eternal return, it is not surprising that Azorín would find literary ekphrasis attractive not only for aesthetic reasons, but for ontological ones as well. As it is forced to make way for the inserted verbal description of an art object, a literay work "frames" the ekphrastic moment, setting it apart from the containing narrative. While the frame accommodates the intruding generic "other," literature's diachronic movement is temporarily subverted by the synchronic and self-reflective ekphrasis that "spatializes" text by arresting its linear progression. Thus the ekphrasis is self-contained and spatial rather than temporal and sequential. Originally intended as rhetorical embellishment, ekphrasis, as it is understood by modern critics, has the potential to "still" literature's turning world as well as to aspire to metaesthetic commentary.[14]

Chapters 35 and 37 of *Doña Inés* create a hiatus in the text's linear sequence to make room for the rather elaborate descriptions of the funerary statues of Doña Beatriz and her husband, appropriating in the process language evocative of the plasticity and geometrical shape of sculpture.[15] The special capacity literary ekphrasis has to still the temporality of narrative by subverting its diachronicity into a self-contained, circular movement is in specular relation to Azorín's novel which also follows a circular pattern. The structure of *Doña Inés* resembles that of two concentric circles, one revolving within the other; a tale of two parallel novels that tell the story of two parallel lives. Located at the nucleus of these circles lies the self-replicating, stilled and "rounded" movement of the ekphrasis, restating once again Azorín's thematic intentions, as well as his personal concern to stem the flow of time in order to convert its linear nature, if not into the perfect circularity of Nietzsche's eternal recurrence, then certainly into a self-begetting spiral that allows for variation of character and situation while retaining the same thematic content and human emotion.

Unlike Doña Beatriz, who lost her mind after the murder of her young troubadour, Doña Inés, as presaged by the lithograph of Buenos Aires hanging in the vestibule of her Madrid home, departs for Argentina. In escaping to the New World, she follows in reverse order the trajectory of Diego Lodares who abandoned Argentina to return to Spain. Our last glimpse of Doña Inés is framed by a window from which she observes children at play in the garden of her school, one of whom, perhaps as Diego had done years before, might be seen musing over a book of poems in the shade of a "venerable y amado ombú" (220). In this light the refrain from Bellini's opera sung earlier in the novel by Tía Pompilia, a refrain that causes Inés to ponder the repeatable nature of the past (108), assumes its full significance: because it is circular, time, indeed, repeats itself, often in tragic or ironic ways. Murray Krieger's observation that the ekphrastic moment "through all sorts of repetitions, echoes, complexes of internal relations converts linearity into circularity" can be equally valid when said of self-reflexive literature (1992, 263). It accounts for the reasons why Azorín may have favored involute works of art such as *Las Meninas* and why, within his own writing, he might have chosen the ekphrastic topos to contextualize the hermeneutic processes of reading, writing, seeing, painting, and framing. Students of twentieth-century aesthetics agree that Modernism considers history as self-reflexive, cyclical, and atemporal.[16] Krieger holds that the art form, be it visual or literary, that finds its end in its beginning, exemplifies the Modernist implosion of time and space, and leads to a circularity of form characteristic of Modern formalism and thematics: the self-begetting circle becomes a Modernist emblem thematizing form as well as content (1992, 227–28). Azorín explores the circularity of time and space not only in the conflationary moment when Doña Inés kisses the marble statue of Doña Beatriz, but also in the symbolic bouquet of roses, beautiful but short-lived, and the sand clock prominently displayed on Tío Pablo's worktable as he recounts the final years of Doña Beatriz. The uroboric nature of time as marked by the sand clock is especially conspicuous for its self-contained and circular method of telling time: one has only to turn this type of clock over to renew its capacity of repeating the process into infinity. Azorín also juxtaposes the disjunction between narrative time and story time by noting that, while it took Tío Pablo only one hour to relate the last installment of the Doña Beatriz story, the events themselves occurred over a much longer period: "Ha pasado una hora, una hora como otra hora en la sucesión de los siglos. Las rosas dan su fragancia; rojas como la sangre del trovador. Y en los espacios inmensos los astros trazan sus órbitas" [162; An hour has passed, an hour like any other in the succession of centuries. The roses, red like the blood of the troubadour, perfume the air. And in the vastness of space, the stars sketch out their orbits].[17]

Although many topical references situate *Doña Inés* in mid-nineteenth-century Spain (the novel ends with Tío Pablo's death in 1849), Azorín writes as an unmistakable literary Modern affected by the social and aesthetic upheavals of his own day. In old age "Tío Pablo" takes stock of a Europe shaken by the revolutions of 1848 and moving inexorably toward something unknown and disturbing: a vulgar and materialistic bourgeoisie dying a slow death; an exhausted and meaningless system of Roman law that had left Humanity without direction, plunged into a dark, barbaric chaos; in short, civilization as Tío Pablo has known it, "was moving toward a profound and frightening social transformation" from which it might never recover or, alternately, emerge metamorphosed

beyond recognition.[18] Ricardo Quinones pointed out that because of its self-reflexive nature, Modernism was concerned with the simultaneously perennial and dynamic, producing an aesthetics of circularity whereby conclusive endings give way to "resolutions that re-start, endings that re-commence" (118). More than any other member of the Generation of 1898, it was Azorín who responded to the modern view of time as circular and human existence as tragically and ineluctably repeatable. In the epilogue to *Las confesiones de un pequeño filósofo* (1904), he announced that, " 'todo es uno y lo mismo,' como decía otro filósofo no tan pequeño; es decir, de que era yo en persona que tornaba a vivir en estos claustros; de que eran mis afanes, mis inquietudes y mis anhelos que volvían a comenzar en un ritornello doloroso y perdurable" [2:91–92; 'everything is one and the same,' as one not so inconsiderable philosopher used to say; that is, it was I, in person, who came back to live in those cloisters; it was my cares, my worries, and my longings that began all over again in a melancholy and eternal ritornello]. As valid in 1904 as it was in 1934 when Azorín wrote that the eternal circle was the greatest tragedy of humankind, trapped "per secula seculorum" within the concepts of time and space; of material existence and the void; of being and not being, the notion that life was an unbreachable circle governed not only Azorín's personal philosophy from the early twentieth century onward, but it also adumbrated philosophical points of view that would dominate European thought in the century's middle decades.[19]

The transubstantiation of linear time into the circular pattern of eternal return contributed to the Modernist transformation of history into myth (Krieger 1992, 222). Azorín addressed this issue in chapter 41 of *Doña Inés*, "La historia y la leyenda." In the guise of a humorous, even rather crude mishearing of Don Larrea's public defense of Doña Inés's sullied reputation, Larrea's challenge is metamorphosed by two old women into a "pregón de pescado" [fishwife's cry]. Attributed either to the women or, perhaps more accurately, to a satirical journalist who made some pointed remarks regarding the scandalous kiss exchanged in the cathedral by Inés and Diego, and whom Larrea meant to neutralize with his challenge, the phrase "pregón de pescado" enters the Segovian vernacular as meaning "una conferencia chirle . . . vana . . .

una noticia falsa, de palabras . . . que merecen desdén" [188; an insipid exchange . . . hollow . . . false information . . . words deserving of contempt]. As he juxtaposes story and discourse, Azorín entertains the process by which objective factual content can be altered by the subjective nature of the discursive form chosen to relate that content, thereby transmuting fact into legend. He concludes, as did Unamuno, that "el hecho . . . auténtico, se ha desvanecido en la noche de los tiempos. Y en cambio subsiste . . . la frase ideada con posterioridad al hecho, por un escritor chocarrero. La leyenda ha vencido la historia. La leyenda es más verdad que la historia" [188–89; the authentic fact has dissolved into the mists of time. And, on the other hand, the phrase conceived after the fact by a crude writer persists. Legend has overcome history. Legend is more authentic than history]. The concept of history as an aesthetic narrative construct had always fascinated Azorín. Like Cervantes, one of his favorite authors, he was aware that in Renaissance Spain the word *historia* could refer to both fiction and history. And while history is ostensibly based on empirical fact, in *Doña Inés* Azorín flirts, much like Cervantes had in the *Quijote*, with the illusion of historical verisimilitude. The embedded story of Tío Pablo's archival reconstruction of the historically "real" Doña Beatriz de Silva promotes the reality of the frame story within which it is contained. But, as occurs in *Don Quijote*, the conflict in Azorín's novel is not between a fictional, idealized reality and an extra-textual, empirical one; rather, it is between textualized versions of the real and the ideal. The clues to Azorín's views on the narrative nature of historiography, and his opinion that historical narration was determined by the subjectivity of the historian, are traceable to rather unexpected sources which belie contemporary argument that the conception of history and fiction as human aesthetic constructs is a post-Modern phenomenon (Smith 200 n. 5).[20] In "Elena Víu" (*Valencia*), Azorín comments that the novel is a graft form of history; that, in fact, a novel *is* History and it is impossible to know "which are the characters who have lived an authentic and real life: whether they are the personages of History, or the characters of a novel" (6:131). Without much explanation, he traces this notion to Menéndez y Pelayo (1856–1912), and to the French poet and novelist, Alfred de Vigny (1797–1863).

Azorín develops this allusion further in "África en el arte" (*Con bandera de Francia*). Insisting that the creation of Africa as an empirical entity in nineteenth-century French art and literature was just as valid as the one elaborated and memorialized in contemporary historical annals, he observes that in the prologue to his novel *Cinq-Mars*, Alfred de Vigny proposed a unique theory of History according to which the "hecho *estético* es tan verdad como el hecho *histórico*: o sea que la belleza—en la creación histórica— es tan cierta, o más cierta, que la verdad auténtica y positiva" [9:758; the *aesthetic* fact is as verisimilar as the *historical* fact: in other words, beauty—in historical creation—is as accurate, or more so, as authentic and positive truth]. More interesting for our purposes, however, Azorín remarks that in his "Discurso de ingreso en la Real Academia de la Historia" (1883), Menéndez y Pelayo subscribes to de Vigny's view of History as an aesthetic discursive event (9:758).[21] The approach to historiography suggested by Menéndez y Pelayo is surprisingly *unlike* that of the typical, nineteenth-century historian who, according to Hayden White, did not realize that "facts do not speak for themselves, but that the historian speaks for them . . . and fashions the fragments of the past into a whole whose integrity is—in its *representation*—a purely discursive one" (1978, 125).

Menéndez y Pelayo began "De la historia considerada como obra artística," his investiture speech at the Royal Academy of History, by warning his new colleagues that he did not intend to address the issue of the philosophy of history properly speaking; rather, he preferred to explore "the aesthetic notion of history," considering it a fine art, and readmitting to the realm of legitimate historians, writers such as Thucydides, Tacitus, and Machiavelli whom modern historians tended to exclude from their ranks (178).[22] Menéndez y Pelayo argued further that the concept of history as art was as old as Aristotle's suggestion that both history and poetry utilized artistic discursive forms. "If we moderns are guilty of anything," the new Academician observed, "it's that we've been overly forgetful of this fact" (180). In similar fashion, Hayden White maintains that it is only the prejudice of modern historical theorists which holds that truth must be represented in statements of fact, and explanation must conform to scientific, noetic models which exclude the interpretative or speculative element from historiography, thereby also evading the intrusion of literary, poetic aspects into historical narrative (1987, 48). White argues that the process by which historians choose to order fragments extracted from the historical record into coherent narrative is a verbal performance substantially the same as the "ways that novelists use to put together figments of their imaginations to display an ordered world" (1978, 125). Historical account, in White's opinion, is as much an artistic *inventio* as is the writing of fiction with which historiography shares the same discursive strategies and techniques (1978, 54, 121). What differentiates historical from fictional writing is not the discursive form used to encode content but the content itself; namely, the real events that comprise the plot (*histoire*) of historical narrative or the imaginary events of fiction (1987, 27).

Citing the British historian Thomas Macaulay's (1800–1859) position that poetry is as necessary as philosophy to historiography, Menéndez y Pelayo, like Hayden White, deploys the argument that historians depend on art to give coherent narrative form to the factual content they extract from the historical record: "And who was ever an excellent historian without a good dose of fantasy and feeling? The facts are nothing more than bricks for the edifice that art will raise" (177). As does Hayden White, who maintains that the historian, as literary artist, interprets rather than objectively explains facts because he fashions them into a "story" by suppressing or subordinating some while emphasizing others, thereby redescribing the historical event "in such a way as to justify a recoding of it in another mode" (1978, 84, 98), Menéndez y Pelayo states that even though interpretation is a genuine aesthetic faculty, "the masters of poetry and history partake of it to an almost equal degree" (179). While both historian and poet engage in giving form to and interpreting scattered fragments of reality, according to Menéndez y Pelayo it is the explanation of the content of the form and not the form itself that distinguishes poet from historian (179). He explains that while the poet is master of his content in the sense that he can manipulate the lives and psyches of his characters at will, the historian, although engaged in similar activity, can proceed only by conjecture, probability, and speculation because he lacks any certitude or authority over his content (179). In the same

way that Cervantes explored textualized versions of the real and the ideal in *Don Quijote*, Menéndez y Pelayo indicated that although both poet and historian feed on reality, they also conspire to transmit, under the guise of the verisimilar, truths that are ideal and textual. To illustrate his argument, he pointed to the difficulty of determining primogeniture with respect to the twin sisters history and poetry, observing that while in some cases poetry, in the form of the *cantar de gesta*, often predated historical narration of the same event in prose, in others the unembellished listing of fact in annal or chronicle was given literary form after the fact by poets such as Lope de Vega or Shakespeare, so that history then found its way back to the "hands of the people transformed into poetic material and the only history that many of them knew." In his opinion Tacitus was one of the greatest "artistic creators of men," possibly excepting Shakespeare, and the archival research involved in the composition of Schiller's historical dramas or the historical novels of Sir Walter Scott, must surely have renewed and influenced advances made by historiogaphy as an art form (180–81).

This, then, is the frame of reference for Azorín's allusions to Alfred de Vigny and Menéndez y Pelayo, and the context for his own belief that the real and the ideal are often impossible to distinguish; that even the most rigorous of historical accounts cannot avoid the insidious creep of the imaginary. Most likely Azorín had in mind historians such as Tacitus, Thucydides, or even Carlyle when he concluded that "Los antiguos historiadores gustan de poner en boca de personajes notorios largos parlamentos. ¿Se definen esos personajes, o se define el propio historiador? Aun en los análisis más sutiles, la discriminación entre la realidad y la fantasía es imposible" [6:324; Ancient historians like to put notoriously long speeches in the mouths of characters. Do those personages define themselves, or is it the historian who defines himself? Even in the most subtle of analyses, the difference between reality and fantasy is unobtainable].[23] Azorín found "interpretation" of historical data—what Hayden White called a historian's "excluding certain facts from his account" or "filling in the gaps in his information on influential or speculative grounds" (1978, 51)—repugnant, commenting that "lo que evito (evito y me repugna) [es] la interpretación de cualquier realidad histórica. Con los hechos escuetos me basta" [8:364; what I avoid (it revolts me and I avoid it), is the interpretation of any historical reality. The bare facts are all I need]. Azorín's meditations on historiography were not entirely the fruit of his mature years. As early as *El alma castellana* (1900), he already considered historiography a form of necromancy conjured by the discursive form a historian chose to impose upon content, which could just as easily prove that the Inquisition was responsible for the decline of Golden Age literature in Spain; that the same literature flourished thanks to the Inquisition; or alternately, that the Inquisition had no effect on literature at all. The facts of the historical record are meaningless in themselves; the sorcery "está en escogerlos, agruparlos, generalizarlos, agrandarlos, hacerlos decir lo que el historiador quiere que digan. He aquí la nigromancia" [1:680; is in choosing them, assembling them, generalizing them, expanding them, making them express what the historian wants them to say. There's the magic].[24]

The innate divergence that might arise between *histoire* and *discours* in the field of historiography, and thus the notion that historical narrative is an interpretative art form circumscribed by the historian's subjective arrangement of the facts, is also the basis of a 1904 essay Azorín wrote on Francisco Silvela one year before the statesman's death. Any period of a nation's history, he notes, can be represented in a variety of ways, determined by the nature of the "pequeños hechos" from which the historian derives his conclusions and the manner in which he chooses to arrange them in narrative form (4:78). The eternal problem of history, observed Azorín, in "Al pie del acueducto," is that the introduction of an apparently insignificant variant into historical discourse can supplant truth with fiction (*PQ* 169). Following a lengthy discussion of the fictional aspects of historiography, Luis García Robledo, the narrator of Azorín's story, acquiesces to the publication of a second party's history of Segovia's aqueduct provided that this "apocryphal" version be accompanied by Robledo's own, "authentic" account (171). In rather Borgesian or Cervantine fashion, Azorín proceeds to undermine the veracity of Robledo's supposedly "genuine" history by attributing different baptismal and surnames to his narrator(s): when he's asleep, his name is Daniel Sojo; when awake, it's José Fernández; al-

legedly either Sojo or Fernández has gone to Segovia to count the number of stones used to build the aqueduct; García Robledo claims he's been sent to Segovia to study the stones' chemical composition in order to determine the correct date of the aqueduct's construction.[25] Azorín experienced firsthand the effect discrepancies in the historical record could produce in his own writing. Having meticulously researched the ambience of 1840s Madrid so that he could create an authentic context for *Doña Inés*, a contemporary review of the novel chided Azorín for erroneously introducing gas lighting to the Spanish capital in 1840. The reviewer, Roberto Castrovido, based his criticism on the 1854 edition of Mesonero Romanos's *Manual de Madrid* which states that, although by 1832 gas lights were installed in the "plaza de palacio," by 1847 gas lighting extended only to a few streets around the Prado, and it was not until 1849 that gas lighting became general throughout Madrid. Therefore Doña Inés could not possibly have seen gas lights in the neighborhood where she lived. Azorín responded to the criticism with a 1925 essay, "El problema de la historia." He began by arguing that history only approximates reality because reality is fluid, subject to modifications imposed by the passage of time and the changeable nature of human sensibilities (9:1122). On examining Castrovido's historical sources, he discovered that in the second edition of the *Manual de Madrid* (1833), Mesonero Romanos stated there were 201 streetlights in Madrid fueled by "el gas hidrógeno carbonado extraído del aceite." A gasometer and condensors were installed in the garden of the Café de la Victoria. In the 1845 appendix to the *Manual*, Mesonero wrote that gas lighting was definitively established in the plazas around the Palace (9:1124). In the 1844 edition of the *Manual*, however, Mesonero laments that extended use of gas lighting in Madrid had to be abandoned because of the high cost and dangers of extracting gas from olive oil. By the final, 1854 edition of the *Manual*—the one utilized by Castrovido in his review—Azorín discovered that Mesonero himself introduced a variant into his previous accounts. Inexplicably he now stated that in 1845 "the new lighting was permanently installed only at the plaza in front of the Palace—"now," writes Azorín, "it is singular *plaza* and not plural *plazas* . . ." (9:1125).

Since Mesonero Romanos introduced variants into the historical record he himself had generated, he proved to be an unreliable narrator, and Azorín had to look to other sources if he was to acquit himself of Castrovido's accusations. He found exactly what he needed in Fermín Caballero's *Noticias topográficas*, conveniently published in 1840, and unarguably the source for the ambiental gas lighting Azorín incorporated to his novel since there is copy of Caballero's book in the Casa-Museo library at Monóvar. In his article Azorín refers to page fourteen of Caballero's book which describes the "barrio de las Afueras de Segovia," the geographical territory where the opening scene of *Doña Inés* is situated, as beginning "en la Fábrica de Gas" (9:1125).[26] Azorín finds additional support in Caballero's 1844 *Manual geográfico-administrativo de la Monarquía española* which definitively establishes gas lighting in the "cercanías de Palacio" and, therefore, the verity of gas light in 1840 around the Palace, not far, observes Azorín, from the "barrio de Segovia" where the first scene of his novel takes place. Thus it was entirely plausible for Don Juan to have a "mechero de gas" in the corridor of his home situated in the neighborhood of the Palace. Although Azorín admitted that in *Doña Inés* he described multiple streets and squares as being illuminated by gas, he promised to rectify the error in future editions of his novel (9:1126). The dispute over whether the streets of Madrid were illuminated by gas in 1840 was not important in and of itself, remarked Azorín, but it did illustrate the larger issue of accuracy and certitude in historical narrative. If we cannot agree on something as recent and uncomplicated such as the names of the streets in Madrid that may have been lit by gas in 1840, how can historians establish with any degree of authority what actually transpired between Felipe II and his son Carlos in the depths of the Royal Palace in 1568; or, even more recently, in the Queen's apartments between Isabel II and her prime minister Salustiano Olózaga in 1843? (9:1123)

While in *Doña Inés* Azorín broaches the question of legend and history, and what it means to construct written as well as oral records within the ideal, textualized world of fictional discourse, the novel itself generated a debate on the very same issues in the extratextual milieu of the real world, thereby singularly reinforcing Azorín's position—and it is one many writers have shared throughout the ages—that History straddles an indeterminate no-man's-land somewhere between fiction and reality. There are no absolutes, whether ideal or empirical, concludes Azorín, because "Everything is unstable, variable, and contradictory in the reality of History" (9:1126).

5

A Simultaneity of Vision: *Salvadora de Olbena*, Cubism, Relativity, and the Cinema

THE WORK OF PAUL CÉZANNE (1839–1906) WAS not well-known to the younger generation of painters working in Paris until a year after Cézanne's death when an extensive memorial exhibition was mounted at the Salon d'Automne of October 1907 (Habasque 21). Cézanne's vision was truly a revolutionary one in that he was the first modern artist for whom the unifying factor in painting was not single-point perspective, but the innate geometric shape of all objects, each of whose sides or planes was oriented toward a central point unique unto itself (Laporte 1949, 245). Unlike his contemporaries, the Impressionist painters who were engaged by the phenomenological and transitory nature of their surroundings, Cézanne adopted a more cerebral approach to painting as he investigated the permanent, absolute foundations of the natural world (Gray 50). Contrary to the Impressionists' method of registering the instantaneous present, Cézanne's manner of depicting the successive, diachronic visual experience of his motif within the synchronic space of a canvas has often been compared to the continuous evolution of a remembered past that Henri Bergson postulated in his concept of *durée* (McClain 47).

In his evocative study of high Modernism (1880–1918), Stephen Kern argues that this was a culture obsessed with the quantifying, relativizing, standardizing, measuring, and even painting of time. As early as Jean Guyau's *La Genèse de l'idée de temps* (1890), the French philosopher reversed Kant's notion that "our sense of time is an a priori form of perception," and suggested that the idea of time derived from a future orientation of experience, together with an individual's psychological development. Constructing what Kern termed "a philosophy of the future in the active mode," Guyau, in some ways anticipating the suggestion of process in Bergsonian thought, maintained that the sense of time originates in desire and the idea of a future toward which the human being evolves (102). Influenced by the ideas of Nietzsche, Bergson, and pragmatic philosophy, the painters who would eventually be grouped together as "Cubists" rejected the idea of the artist as a passive contemplator, choosing instead a more active role in creating new realities more pertinent to the rapidly changing world in which they lived (Gray 160).

The dynamism implied in Bergson's notion of psychological time, whereby our sense of the present is augmented by a cumulative memory of the past, contributed to liberating modern painters from the limiting factor of a single point of view, stimulating artistic interest in the representation of objects as remembered from successive and subjective experiences of them in time and space.[1] While, in *An Introduction to Metaphysics*, Bergson proposed that in its desire to embrace the object, "analysis multiplies . . . the number of points of view in order to complete its always imperfect translation," analytical Cubism attempted, and ultimately failed, to portray the artist's perception of objects through the integration of multiple views, or concepts of them, in order to re-create an object's totality in time *and* space (Gray 87–88). Although, for reasons that are obvious, a painting cannot convey the idea of a ceaseless elaboration of new forms inherent in Bergsonian *durée* on the single, unitary surface of a canvas, Cubist painters found common ground with Bergson in the notion of simultaneity, and it has been argued that the philosopher's insistence that the concept of the world as static and unchanging was utterly false "explains more satisfactorily than any reference to Einstein or Minkowski the repeated discussions of time in Cubist writings" (T. Mitchell 177). The connection between Cubist art and Bergson seems to have been made first by Léon Werth in a review of work Picasso completed between 1908 and 1909, but did not exhibit until May 1910. Referring to the dynamism of form and the opposition of planes in these pictures, Werth made a comment on the "thought" to which Picasso's work may be equivalent; that is, the painter's expression on canvas of "the sensations and reflections which we experience over time" (Roskill 1985, 31). By 1910 Bergson was widely read and his thinking on the interaction of time and space well-known in the French intellectual community. As early as the 1889 *Essai sur les donées immédiates de la conscience*, the philosopher included advice to artists on how to portray reality by freeing themselves from the spatiality of external objects, using the expression "interpenetration" to refer to the concept of duration and space (Roskill 1985, 35).[2]

The breakdown of superannuated, nineteenth-century epistemologies that occurred in the European Zeitgeist at this time is particularly evocative. As Ricardo Quinones pointed out, one of the first effects Modernism had on the intellectual milieu was that of disassembling temporal linearity, looking "to leaps of experience, to juxtapositions that could be startling and unexpected" (58). In physics Bertrand Russell, influenced by A. N. Whitehead, conceived of the world as a construction rather than an inference, and suggested that the appearance of things changes with the point of view of the observer, arguing as well the possible existence of unperceived perspectives (Gauss 76). Max Planck's publications on quantum theory (1900) and Ernest Rutherford's work on radioactivity (1902), moved science away from Euclidean geometry and Newtonian physics: Albert Gleizes and Jean Metzinger, Cubist painters who would become the movement's most important theoreticians, wrote in *Du Cubisme* (1912), that if the Cubist depiction of space were to be related "to a particular geometry," it would have to be that developed by "non-Euclidean scientists" (Roskill 1985, 30). In 1905 Einstein published his work on the special theory of relativity which recognized that space and time could no longer be thought as absolute, but rather existed in a functional relationship to each other; the Cézanne retrospective which so influenced Picasso and Braque's initial elaboration of Cubist art (1908–1912) was mounted in 1907; Minkowski had formulated the space-time continuum by 1908; Bergson's *Évolution créatrice*, which had an immediate and significant impact on French thought, was likewise published in 1907. While Bergson conceived of "duration" as a dynamic force that effected change by elaborating new forms of life and experience, Cubist simultaneity dismantled the uniform pictorial perspective and temporal limitations that had governed painting since the Renaissance.[3]

In 1916 Einstein developed his work on relativity further, publishing his research as the General Theory of Relativity, perhaps the most significant revision of the modern view of time in which temporality is no longer presented as constant, but as a function of relative motion; the phenomenological subject, like time and space, became inseparable from, and bound by, the limitations of specific events (Ermarth 8). On the other hand, Niels Bohr eliminated the notion of continuity from classical physics, explaining the successive nature of phenomena with the notion of "quantum leaps" which he postulated drive the world while emitting energy in blocks of discontinuous, radiative emissions. The Cubists' intent to present several angles of vision simultaneously, and their suggestion that a new aggregate be assembled from the discontinuous planes comparable to quanta implied by the physics of discontinuity, has been argued both ways. Alex Keller maintains that to see in the Cubist "mosaic of fragments" a correspondence to quanta "is not a suggestion that can be demonstrated" (105), while the Spanish art historian José Camón Aznar argues that Cubist idiom coincided both chronologically and theoretically with the development of quantum theory. Aznar holds that the Cubist concept of time is similarly discontinuous due to the superposition of disassembled planes not linked by the flow of uninterrupted surface transitions, gradations of light, or the illusion of depth considered the norm in traditional art (1958, 360). Picasso, however, observed that the series of "independent snatches" Cézanne depicted in his canvases was not sequential but simultaneous (Marling 95). Perhaps Martin Pollock assessed the issue best in his observation that "it is the relativity of space, not the Theory of Relativity" that allowed the Cubist painter to represent at least some of the meaning implied in the concept of four-dimensional space (132), by fusing several different perspectives of an object into a single image, thereby reconstituting it in time and suggesting to the viewer a sense of movement in space (Marling 95).

Cubist theory implied a relativity of knowledge at the same time that it subscribed to the epistemological notion that the intellect is superior to the senses as a tool with which to comprehend the world. In its first stages of development Cubism still relied to some extent on visual models, but the paintings produced were not so much a record of the artist's sensory reaction to the motif as they were a pictorial expression of the painter's knowledge or idea of the subject: Ramón Gómez de la Serna reported Picasso as having said, "Yo hago los objetos tal como los pienso, no tal como los veo" [1929, 100; I make objects as I think them, not as I see them]. The story of Cubism begins in 1907 with the meeting of Braque and Picasso who together developed the movement's initial phase between 1908–12, a phase abruptly ended by the outbreak of war and Braque's mobilization in 1914.[4] Like Cézanne, who threw over Impressionist concerns with the instant in favor of a multiplicity of perspectives to achieve a more composite view of reality, Cubist painters believed that all points in space had equal status relative to each other, and they incorporated into their paintings multiple

views of their motifs, combining abstract as well as representational elements within the same canvas (Golding 10) (Fig. 25). In Spain, Cubist paintings by Gleizes, Gris, Léger, Le Fauconnier, Duchamp, and Metzinger were first shown at Barcelona's Dalmau Gallery in April and May of 1912 (Cooper 101–2). In 1915 Ramón Gómez de la Serna organized the first exhibition of Cubist art in Madrid at the Galería Arte Moderno (Barrio-Garay 85). Writing in 1922, in the *Archivos de Neurobiología*, Gonzalo Lafora remembered that he and fellow medical students thronged to the Madrid gallery, "full of curiosity, to see that much-talked-about artistic phenomenon." To Lafora and his companions, students of psychiatry, Cubist paintings appeared to resemble the drawings of their patients, and he remarked that when shown these drawings "some of the exhibitors . . . agreed with us on their frequent similarities" (119). Among the members of the Generation of 1898, the reaction to Cubism, when there was any, proved uniformly negative. In a 1912 article, "De arte pictórica," Unamuno wrote that what could not and must not happen in art was to paint simply for the pleasure of shocking the public as occurred in the case of that "aberración del llamado cubismo," which he predicted would be no more than a passing fashion among "blasé snobs." To buttress his argument Unamuno quoted from a letter sent him by Darío de Regoyos who, while an artistic innovator himself, found Cubism "detestable." Unamuno quoted Regoyos as writing that he preferred the excesses of Romantics like Martínez de la Rosa to the calamity wreaked upon the art world by a "Catalonian named Picasso who's done orientalism, pointillism, cézannism, van goghism, gauguinism, etc., . . . and I won't go on because I'd need a lot more paper to relate his infinite transformations" (7:739). Baroja thought that "those Cubist hustlers" (7:885) had invented a short-lived art form which evidently "has collapsed and doesn't count anymore. I doubt that that style of painting will endure; neither do I believe that painters like Matisse will last. . ." (7:899). He took particular umbrage at the notion that a "stupidity like Cubism" received more public attention than scientific developments relative to the disintegration of the atom (7:823), writing that at one time intellectual "snobs" even said that Picasso's style evolved from a blue period to absolutism: "What nonsense! What can

Fig. 25   Pablo Picasso, *Les Demoiselles d'Avignon*, June–July 1907. Oil on canvas, 243.9 × 233.7 cm. The Museum of Modern Art, New York. Acquired through the Lillie P. Bliss Bequest. Photograph © 1998 The Museum of Modern Art, New York. © 1998 Estate of Pablo Picasso / Artists Rights Society (ARS), New York.

'absolute' painting mean? Nothing, I think. That you can see the nape of a man's neck and his forehead at the same time; his chest and his back; his belly and his rear end? That's sheer eccentricity'' (7:898). Baroja, for whom psychoanalysis was "something like the Cubism of the medical profession," thought the former a terrific way to fleece a gullible public and the latter an insignificant postwar "swindle," concluding that its only conquests as an art form "have been posters for movie and fashion houses. It has not gone beyond that modification of window displays" (7:435).

Surprisingly, Azorín seems not to have had a public reaction to Cubism when the movement was at its zenith but, of all his contemporaries, he was the only one to develop a retrospective appreciation for Cézanne. As discussed earlier, an exhibition of Cézanne's work at the Orangerie had significant impact on Azorín, both as a visual experience as well as a catalyst which stimulated a flurry of articles on "cézannisms" and literary style in 1944. It also may have prompted Azorín to reread and write about Zola's novel *L'Oeuvre*, whose protagonist was said to have been modeled on Cézanne. He again commented on Cézanne in "La pintura" which appeared in *ABC*, 8 December 1951. Here Azorín observed that, while Velázquez equals nature in his painting, modern art set out to surmount nature, reducing itself to lines and planes. But nature cannot be outdone, he observed, and no matter what "los pintores de la línea" attempt, their work—Cézanne's geometry, for example—is prefigured in natural crystallography. And, despite striking similarities between Ortega's philosophy of perspectivism, developed precisely during the heyday of Cubist art, and his ongoing dialogue with Einstein, in a 1946 lecture, "Idea del teatro," Ortega observed that "Painting lies in ruins—its rubble is Cubism—; that's why Picasso's paintings resemble a demolished house or a corner in the Rastro flea market" (7:450).

Ortega developed his theory of *perspectivismo*—the relativity of reality—in the 1916 "Verdad y perspectiva." He intentionally linked his theory to Einstein's General Theory of Relativity, published in the same year, by arguing that the coincidence between his and Einstein's positions was a sign of the times since both repudiated the notion that a single, absolute reality exists in a single, absolute space (Quinones 115). In words resonant with Cubist idiom, Ortega described his view of the "truth, the real,

the universe, life" as being broken into "innumerable facets, countless directions, every one of which opens out onto an individual" (2:19). Like Cubist painting, which intends to present the viewer a picture of reality from an individual painter's perspective, Ortega wrote that when the individual remains faithful to his point of view what he sees will be a real aspect of the world (2:19). Similar to the Cubists who recognized the significance to their aesthetics of the new physical theories of relativity, Ortega rejected what he called the erroneous belief in one absolute vision, acknowledging that diversity in no way diminished the validity of individual perspective; rather, "it seems to me that the individual point of view is the only one from which you can genuinely see the universe" (2:18).

Ortega elaborated his theory in the 1923 "La doctrina del punto de vista," collected in *El tema de nuestro tiempo*. Developing an analogy he first introduced in "Verdad y perspectiva," he illustrated the notion of *perspectivismo* by proposing that two individuals could view the same landscape, yet neither would perceive the same thing. What for one constitutes important foreground material, for the other might appear indistinctly in the background, and each individual will apprehend an aspect of the landscape that the other will never see (3:199). In the same essay Ortega carefully documented the evolution of his theory in an apparent attempt to establish priority of publication vis-à-vis Einstein: "From 1913," he insisted, "I have set out in my university courses this doctrine of perspectivism which appears formulated unambiguously in *El Espectador, I*" (e.g., the 1916 "Verdad y perspectiva"). Ortega refers his readers to an appendix he added to *El tema de nuestro tiempo*, titled "El sentido histórico de la teoría de Einstein" (3:231–42), where he further discusses the ways in which Einstein's work on general relativity is a "magnificent confirmation" of his own thoughts on perspectivism (3:200 n. 1). He emphasized yet again that "Verdad y perspectiva" was in print "when nothing had yet been published on the general theory of relativity," and that while space and time are the objective ingredients of perspectivism in physics, his own "doctrine of perspectivism," went beyond physics to embrace all reality (3:235).[5] Ortega again called Einstein's theory a "marvelous justification of the harmonious multiplicity of all points of view," and suggested that because both theories allowed individual truths to exist within a plurality of perspectives, when extended to morals and aesthetics, it would produce a new understanding of life and history, leading to tolerance and the admissibility of alternative life experiences. Rather than viewing non-European cultures as barbaric, for instance, the Westerner could now begin to respect them as equally valid as his; the Chinese perspective of the universe thus became as reasonable as the Occidental (3:237).

When, in "La doctrina del punto de vista," Ortega writes that knowledge (e.g., perception) is relative to the individual perceiver, and that "by juxtaposing everybody's partial vision one can produce the fabric of an absolute and all-embracing truth" to yield a more complete picture of reality akin to the absolute omniscience we attribute to God (3:202), philosophically he draws near Einstein's reinvention of the universe as contingent upon individual perceptual capabilities (Smith 14), and he comes interestingly close to the Cubist manner of composition via multiple points of view.[6] In *Du Cubisme*, Gleizes and Metzinger write that "If so many eyes contemplate an object, there are so many images of that object; if so many minds comprehend it, there are so many essential images." And like Ortega and Einstein, for the Cubist painter "an object has not one absolute form: it has as many as there are planes in the region of perception" (Gray 76). Ortega would have been in complete agreement with the Cubist theoreticians for whom "true reality" was a highly subjective notion, dependent, as Christopher Gray observed, "on the ideas and attitudes of the observer, as . . . on the sense stimuli from the external world . . . true reality . . . can no longer remain fixed and permanent, but must be dynamic" (76). In "Reflexiones sobre la nueva pintura," published in Ortega's own *Revista de Occidente* in 1925, Marjan Paskiewicz wrote that the most important feature of Cubist painting was its simultaneity of form. Since it was impossible to represent a succession of forms over time in painting due to the two-dimensional nature of the medium, Cubism discovered a way to create the effect of total reality by tabulating partial visual images to produce a sensation of simultaneity on the plane surface of a canvas, substituting illusion of visual plenitude for the sense of touch and three-dimensionality that only space made possible (305). Ricardo Quinones observed that perspectivism was central to the Modern consciousness,

intent as it was on presenting a multiplicity of views on the world, all of which were "true," thereby eliminating any need to append disclaimers of subjectivity (117). Because the Cubist painter relied on a "mobile perspective" by moving around the motif to depict simultaneously its successive aspects as perceived in space, when brought together on canvas and reassembled in time, these works of art presented images ordinarily disallowed by normal retinal vision (Habasque 125; Roskill 1985, 31). Modern literature, like science, philosophy, and the visual arts, was also affected by the spirit of the times, and writers, particularly novelists and playwrights, began to explore ways of including all the component parts of reality within textual discourse. Sartre wrote in 1947 that the theory of relativity applied to the novel as well as it did to the world of physics, and that "in a true novel, there is no more place than in the world of Einstein for the privileged observer."[7] As they acknowledged the insufficiency of a single perspective, writers surrendered their omniscience, disrupted linear time, and, like Bergson and Whitehead who suggested the spatialization of time, began to experiment with simultaneity, leading to what Joseph Frank, in 1945, called a "spatialization" of the novel. More recently Wendy Steiner proposed that Modern literary experimentation with point of view grew out of both the relativism of modern philosophy as well as the Cubist explosion of the notion that the work of art must limit itself to presenting one, atemporal moment of vision portrayed by a perceptor standing in a single, fixed position (1982, 180). In the same way that Cubist art is self-reflexive, especially in its synthetic phase that focused attention on its own creative processes, Modern literature turned inward to examine the ways in which the literary artifact was conceived and produced.[8] Perhaps stimulated by Bergson's *durée*, because the Cubist painter, as Steiner observed, interacts with the past and "makes a simultaneity of it," Cubist art encouraged viewers to perceive history not as linear, but as a spatial construct of interrelations between the anachronous and the contemporary (1982, 191).

Among the novelists responding to the new ways of thinking about reality being proposed by scientists, philosophers, and painters, Wylie Sypher suggested Aldous Huxley and Philip Toynbee as two writers who employed the simultaneous perspectives of Cubism in their work (296). Jennifer Stone drew analogies between Cubist simultaneity and Luigi Pirandello's break with narrative linearity in *Six Characters in Search of an Author* (1921), a work that accommodates multiple and contradictory views of the same event without ever moving toward a resolution of absolute truth as to their interpretation (56–57). Mark Roskill compared Pirandello's shifts between dramatic fiction and dramatic production in the same play to the self-conscious aspects of synthetic Cubism (1985, 163), while Sharon Spencer likened the development of Cubist painting to what she called the "open-structured" novel evolved during the same period of time. As an example of one of the first novels to explore deliberately the relationship between an author and his fictional characters, Spencer's choice falls, rather curiously, on Miguel de Unamuno's 1902 *Amor y pedagogía*. While in the appendix Unamuno introduces a conflictive interpretation of events (e.g., the effect Apolodoro Carrascal's suicide has on his father's subsequent behavior), I do not believe this novel can in any way be called a "Cubist" work of literature. Spencer further argues that Unamuno was writing *Niebla* (1914), "which contains an even more elaborate and astute analysis of the motives and processes of novel creation than *Amor y pedagogía*," during the same years that Braque and Picasso experimented with mixed media, and the notion of Cubist art as a self-conscious artifact (55). Although *Niebla* is undeniably a modern, self-reflexive novel insofar as its unresolved internal contradictions, the extradiegetic narrator's unexpected metamorphosis into an intradiegetic-homodiegetic protagonist, and the novel's awareness of its own process of production qua literature is concerned, self-reflexivity is not necessarily a feature exclusive to Cubist painting and literature; rather, it is a theoretically buttressed and conceptually accepted aesthetic code concomitant with the notion that experience is multi-leveled, time no longer sequential, and the human being or fictional character free to transit between different strata of experience and existence (Quinones 91).

Like Einstein who revolutionized classical physics; Picasso and Braque who dismantled traditional perspective and rethought pictorial form and space; Ortega who reappraised philosophical relativism; and Unamuno who pioneered both theological and literary Modernism

in Spain, Azorín, too, was a man of his time, a modern writer who dismissed traditional forms of narrative linearity from his work and began to experiment with self-reflexivity, simultaneity, and spatialization in his 1925 novel *Doña Inés*, the "super-realist" novels and short stories of the 1920s and 1930s, and finally, the 1944 *Salvadora de Olbena (Novela romántica)*, a text, I will argue, inspired by the Cézanne retrospective Azorín had seen in Paris. Robert E. Lott was the first to notice the perspectivism of *Doña Inés*, pointing out that the novel's plurality of viewpoints resulted in protagonists "who are seen in multiple and partial perspectives" (1968, 88). In 1927 Azorín commented on what he called the "polyvalency of images" in an essay titled "El cine y el teatro," published in *ABC* on May 26. Using terminology similar to that developed by Ortega, he observed that an image produced different effects in different people. While reality itself is immutable, not only do the eyes that look at it perceive different things, but reality can even produce a "polyvalency of representations" in the same individual. Azorín illustrated his point by suggesting that seeing one's childhood home after an absence of twenty years will produce a succession of images drawn from past memories as well as current perceptions on the eidetic screen of the mind's eye (9:107).[9]

Talk of scientific and philosophical relativity did not peak in pre–World War I European culture. Ortega published his definitive "La doctrina del punto de vista" in 1923 and the decade 1925–35 witnessed the work of the physicists Heisenberg and Schrödinger that even Einstein himself had difficulty accepting. Heisenberg's uncertainty principle posited that the human being cannot be dismissed from physics because observations cannot be made independently of an observer, while Bohr declared that humankind must "become conscious of the fact that we are not merely observers but also actors on the stage of life" (Bazarov 95). When Azorín wrote *Salvadora de Olbena* in 1944, he no more set out consciously to write a Cubist novel than did Unamuno when he wrote *Niebla*, but the wartime climate of the 1940s undoubtedly witnessed a revival of talk about atomic theory, energy, and relativity that, when linked to the impact the Cézanne exhibition in Paris had upon Azorín in the late 1930s, the series of essays he wrote on Cézanne's influence on "pure" literary style, as well as the articles he published on Zola's *L'Oeuvre* in the 1940s, suggest that Azorín was at least reassessing the incipient phase of Cubist art at the time that he wrote *Salvadora de Olbena*. It would follow that his intellectual ruminations would inevitably make themselves felt in his creative work.

While the Impressionists had already come upon the idea of presenting a series of views on the same landscape painted at different times of the day and/or seasons of the year, it was Cézanne who first explored the different geometric planes of a single object or landscape in the same canvas. Although Zola was ultimately disappointed by the "failure" of Impressionist painting, and by the "failed genius" of his boyhood comrade Paul Cézanne, in his early *Salons* he was among the first to support the Impressionists at the beginning of their careers, and in his own novels he often employed multiple points of view on the same scene, whether emanating from the same character or from different characters at the same time (Berg 1992, 116). Although he died in 1902, Zola's recognition of the relativity of human perception moves some of his novels "toward a cubist-like multiplicity" (Berg 1992, 147).[10] Among other features of *Salvadora de Olbena* is a cubist-like fragmentation of the novel's time-space continuum. In the first four chapters Azorín stops time dead in its tracks by freezing the action of all four within the same fifteen minutes of time, between 1:45 and 2:00 A.M. as he travels through the space of Olbena describing the many different kinds of clocks there are in the town, and presenting partial views of the activities in which certain of the town's residents are simultaneously engaged at two o'clock in the morning on 15 December of an unspecified year (7:758).[11] He begins by insinuating that time itself is a relative concept, for not all clocks in Olbena strike two synchronously and therefore not all residents pass from one hour to the next at the same moment in time; the farmers of Olbena do not own mechanical clocks at all, preferring to consult the stars because they consider them more reliable (7:569–70). He further explores the notion that time yields different meanings for different people by describing the contexts in which Olbena's residents experience the moment marked as "two o'clock in the morning," a notion to which he returns later in the novel when Paco Ardales insists on taking a photograph of Salvadora posed against

a laurel bush whose perennial nature he contrasts with the more beautiful, but fugitive qualities of the rose (7:610). The conversation then turns briefly to individual perspectives on objects as Paco observes that the mountain they all see in the distance "is not the same when I've said that it's beautiful and when you look at it in order to see whether it is really beautiful or not" (7:611). The ensuing conversation reverts to the eternal symbolism of the laurel and closes with the omniscient narrator's musing on the relative and elastic nature of the time-space continuum: "Time passes . . . but it is not the same everywhere; it is not the same in Olbena as it is in Madrid or London. It is not the same for some people as it is for others; it is not identical, at these moments, for Salvadora as it is for Ardales, for Ardales as it is for Valdecebro" (7:612).

Within the synchronic novelistic space of Olbena, comparable to cinematic montage or a Cubist painter's canvas with its superposition of planes melting into and rising out of each other, Azorín constantly shifts back and forth in space and time, annihilating sequential chronology and thereby spatializing his narrative. Chapter 4 moves backward in time from two o'clock in the morning, where it began, to the 1:45 A.M. arrival of the express train from Madrid which not only delivers the mail, but also Ricardo Valdecebro whom the reader had previously encountered already comfortably ensconced in the "Hotel del Comercio" (7:571, 573). At the chapter's conclusion we see Valdecebro engaged in the writing of a letter, yet the narration of the count's arrival at the hotel lobby does not occur until chapter 7 (7:583), and the letter he is seen writing is not composed until Valdecebro finds writing paper in his room (7:584): it is at this point that the scene comes full circle to the count's frustrated crumpling of the letter that closes chapter 4 (7:586). The letter is thrown out the window onto the street where Paco Ardales retrieves it the following morning, but the incident is not related textually until chapter 12 (7:596). Equally suggestive is Azorín's conscious manipulation of story time and discourse time. Although he takes four chapters to narrate the course of events in Olbena from 1:45 to 2:00 A.M., he proceeds to jump, as José Antonio Maravall suggested, in a discrete "quantum leap," from two to three o'clock in one sentence at the conclusion of chapter 4: "And at dawn, at two, deep silence returns to Olbena. In a room at the 'Hotel del Comercio' where the traveller has just arrived, you can hear the scratching of pen on paper: then, after a brief pause, the noise of paper being crumpled fills the air. The bells at the Church of the Assumption have struck 2:30; they've struck 2:45; they've struck 3" (7:577–78).[12]

Faithful to his usual practice, in a chapter evocatively titled "El pasado," Azorín explores, perhaps with some Bergsonian connotations, the possibility of experiencing past time and events from a vantage point in the present. Wandering about her house in the predawn hours, Salvadora finds herself at the door of what used to be her father's study. As she crosses the threshold, Azorín writes that without being aware of it, Salvadora "penetrated into a space where the past had taken refuge"; sitting down in her father's worn armchair, Salvadora has a strange, out-of-body experience, as if it were her own father who sat in the chair: "she entered the past completely; the present was abolished; the future did not exist" (7:581). In a technique Azorín had used previously in "La fragancia del vaso" (Castilla), an old flask of perfume whose contents evaporated long ago that Salvadora finds in her father's desk, along with some yellowed letters and dried roses, like the Proustian madeleine, are crystallizations of the past that momentarily transport her backward in time.[13] The implosion of time and space, as well as the relativity of perception, receive more elaborate treatment in chapter 18, "La mano." Doctor Casal owns some statuettes and pottery recently excavated at an archaeological site near Olbena. One of the items is a beautiful marble hand, fashioned with such vitality and skill, that it appears about to grasp something; yet as Casal indicates, the hand must have been sculpted some three or four thousand years before.[14] When Paco Ardales suggests that Salvadora place her hand next to the marble artifact, the juxtaposition transfigures the moment in time and space in which the group finds itself, transporting them backward three thousand years. Similar to Salvadora's reaction when she sat in her father's armchair, she now comments that "a small piece of marble has the power to make citizens of the twentieth century live a moment in the remote past." Paco observes that each time he looks at the hand, he sees it "in a different way"; Valdecebro thinks of the hand as reaching out toward an abstract, indefinite ideal,

whereas Dr. Casal interprets it as about to grasp something tangible and concrete (7:614–15).[15]

Like a Cubist painter, who presents a multitude of changes in focalization accumulated over time within the spatial limitations of a single canvas, Azorín devotes the greater part of his novel to assembling a multiplicity of perspectives on Salvadora as a personality, and then on the possible explanations for her alleged contretemps with don Juan Pimentel.[16] Similar to Cubist painters who assumed the role of principal focalizers, moving freely about their motif, studying it from various points of view before reassembling the fragments into a composite whole, in chapter 21 Azorín introduces an intradiegetic-homodiegetic narrator who speaks in the first person and whose role it is to collate and reconstitute snippets of information he gathers about Salvadora into a composite picture of her character (7:623). In the process, mirroring the spatiotemporal discontinuity of his narrative, Azorín, like a Cubist painter, rejects the sequentiality of single-point perspective to create what Eric Rabkin termed a dialectic between the spatiality of story and the temporality of plot that forces readers to suspend the construction of logically coherent discourse until supplied with as complete information as possible (267–68). Although Rabkin argues that throughout the history of literature all narrative has, to some extent, played with the diachronic and synchronic modes of reading, deliberate attenuation of the linear aspects of story and the defamiliarization of plot become important features of the Modern idiolect which places a greater burden on readers' active participation in textual (re)construction than does traditional narrative (253–54). Azorín clearly set out to engage the readers of Salvadora de Olbena in the perceptual-intellective activity of reading diachronically in time, while simultaneously attempting to apprehend and reassemble the story's plot in synchronic fashion.[17]

Chapters 23 through 27 present five different exchanges the narrator has with five different people who supply five distinct, but not contradictory, opinions of Salvadora's personal and unaffected generosity. Luis Magraner, the bodegonero of Olbena, relates Salvadora's visit to his establishment and the long tour she made with his wife of its pantries and kitchen (7:630–33). Anselmo Gutiérrez, owner of the "Hotel del Comercio," insists on his reliability as a source by stating that he never tells a lie; he then re-counts how Salvadora came to the aid of a client who unexpectedly took ill at the Hotel by housing the young lady in her own home and providing her with expert medical care (7:635–36). Arturo Astudillo, director of the Academia Astudillo, also insists that he will tell "the truth and nothing but the truth" regarding Salvadora (7:636). He narrates how she discretely came to his rescue when the Academia was in dire financial straits (7:639); Paulino Gras, administrator of the local post office, illustrates Salvadora's appreciation of the small favors he does for her by sending his children toys and candy (7:641). María Rodríguez, although she claims reliability because she and Salvadora are "childhood friends," also states that recently her memory has begun to fail her (7:642), and although she intends to demonstrate Salvadora's mischievous nature by relating what she calls "the episode in the attic" (7:644), her mind wanders so much that despite several attempts to recoup the point of her story, which she says "certainly illustrates Salvadora's character from the first moment of her life," María never reveals anything at all about the episode, leaving the narrator with only a partial perspective, an incomplete vision (7:645).

It is through María Rodríguez that Azorín begins to undermine the seeming unity of perspective and the reliability of his narrator's sources. While at the beginning of the novel he leads the reader to believe that Salvadora is thirty-two years old (7:594) to Valdecebro's forty-something (7:584), in her rambling conversation with the narrator María states that she is only twelve years older than Salvadora, making her forty-four years old and much too young for the onset of the senility from which she claims to suffer (7:642). On the other hand, earlier in the novel, Paco Ardales engages in interior monologue consisting of an imaginary conversation with María Rodríguez where she says that she is seventy-eight years old, an entirely plausible age at which to begin to lose one's mental acuity (7:602). This scenario, however, would make Salvadora sixty-six years old, certainly not the beautiful, young widow Azorín would like us to believe that she is. Solidity and stability of unified perspective are thoroughly shattered in the chapters that follow the narrator's interview with María Rodríguez. All titled "De la historia," chapters 30 through 34 present five different perspec-tives on the supposed rift between Salvadora and don Juan Pimentel. Pimentel is the first to speak, telling the narrator that rumor of discord between the two originated when Salvadora did not acknowledge his formal bow to her at a social gathering by rising from the sofa where she was seated (7:655). Although social protocol would have required Salvadora to rise for a number of reasons, Pimentel himself never reveals his true feelings about the matter, commenting only that town gossips "deduce from all this that I had a falling out with Salvadora. There's nothing more: this is the story that, like the justice meted out in days gone by, the people *demand*; the masses demand it" (7:656). The notary, Claudio Minguella, who "knows everything," provides a completely different view of the affair. The falling out, he says, occurred because Salvadora once owned a house contiguous to Pimentel's, and refused him permission to incorporate part of an unused alley-way separating the two homes into his own property when don Juan wished to reconstruct his residence (7:657). But, according to Minguella, it is important to add that at the time this happened, Salvadora was in the process of selling her property and it has never been ascertained whether it was she or the new owner who refused Pimentel permission to make use of the alleyway (7:658). We are left, as before, with an inconclusive, partial view of the incident.

A third interpretation is supplied by Amparo Testor, wife of the local exporter of olive oil, who precedes her version of events with the disclaimer, "don't you believe me, eh!" (7:659). According to Amparo, don Juan unsuccessfully courted Salvadora, accounting for the tension between the two. She states outrightly that the episode of Salvadora's so-called *descortesía* is thoroughly false, as is also the "legend" regarding the alleyway: Amparo knows who bought Salvadora's house and she knows that it was the new owner who tangled with Pimentel. Amparo, however, takes leave of the narrator once more appending her disclaimer, "no me crea usted a mí," to which she adds that further investigation of the case might even prove her version of the story to be false, and that "neither was the old rebuff a motive for any bad feelings between Juan and Salvadora" (7:661). The fourth take on the episode, told by Leandro Castaño, concierge of the old Casino, does, indeed, contradict Amparo Testor's. Leandro, like

Claudio Minguella, "knows everything"; he claims that Amparo Testor carried on a flirtation with Pimentel in Valencia where she lived and don Juan was a law student at the university. According to Castaño, after leading Amparo on for a number of years, Pimentel left her for Salvadora. "Then," the narrator asks, "everything that Amparo says about Salvadora and Pimentel is a lie?" "She's full of resentment," is Leandro's final reply (7:663). The fifth, and most suggestive, account is given by Doctor Bretaño who begins his story by saying that Leandro Castaño is a teller of tall tales (7:665). Bretaño claims reliability because he knew Pimentel when they were both students in Valencia. It is true, he says, that Amparo Testor and don Juan carried on a flirtation, but it sputtered out of its own accord without acrimony from either party. It is also true, however, that Salvadora and don Juan carried on a correspondence but it was initiated quite some time after Amparo and don Juan had broken off. The truth of the matter is that don Juan and Salvadora still continue to see each other, but their meetings take place at Salvadora's property in Gamonel, about eight kilometers from Olbena (7:667). The real issue, according to Doctor Bretaño, is why Salvadora and don Juan do not wish anyone to know that they call on each other, only perpetuating gossip about the alleged misunderstanding between them. Bretaño can only speculate as to the reasons. The lesson to be learned from this, he says, is that "how from the most crass material, from what people accumulate, we've arrived at the most unsubstantial" (7:667). In any case, as the good doctor observed before beginning his version of the story, "Life is multiple and changeable; history cannot capture life. Historical matter is in a perpetual state of evolution." There is always something that upsets our plans and preconceptions, and our judgment of the past is modified continually by the upheavals and reactions we experience in the present (7:666). The chapter concludes with a surprise appearance by the author who supports Doctor Bretaño's point with a parable drawn from a historically verifiable incident involving the distortion of literary text, some verses by Camprodón, the zarzuela *María* adapted by Emilio Arrieta, and the actor Enrique Chicote's 1944 recollection of the lines he spoke in that zarzuela that he uses as an example of how difficult it is to establish textual accuracy: in the case of literature the issue can be settled by consulting manuscripts and first editions, whereas establishing the true nature of human relationships is quite another matter.

This conclusion restates ideas to which Azorín had merely alluded in chapter 3 when he wrote that the first two chapters of *Salvadora de Olbena* are meant as historical exposé and that in the chapters that followed he planned to write a novel, giving free rein to all possible flights of fancy. As he takes leave of history to enter novelistic territory, Azorín steps onto the terrain of what he calls the "truer truth" of fiction (7:574). But throughout the course of the novel he consistently deconstructs his claim by questioning the reliability of his characters whose multiple, often contradictory perspectivism, reiterates his point that no decisive conclusions can be made about anything at all since absolute truth does not exist either in the fictional or the empirical universes.[18] Azorín reinforces his thematic nucleus stylistically by shattering linear sequentiality and disrupting the reader's temporary suspension of disbelief when he introduces metafictional commentary on the novel's process of production into the narrative. In a burst of self-referential parabasis reminiscent of Unamuno or Pirandello, a narratorial "yo" erupts on to the novelistic scene in chapter 21, identifying itself shortly thereafter as a writer (7:625), and subsequently revealing that he had known Salvadora's father in Madrid (7:646). Unlike Unamuno's "yo" which eventually identifies itself as the author of *Niebla* and then enters the narrative as a fictionalized character, Azorín keeps the narratorial "yo" of *Salvadora de Olbena* separate from the brief authorial intervention he interpolated into chapter 34 when commenting on textual distortions (7:668–69).

Like Unamuno, Azorín also experiments with author-character conflict when he declares that he created Ricardo Valdecebro in spite of himself, and that once created, the character issued forth different from his authorial intentions, forcing him to take Valdecebro by the hand in order to walk him through his paces (7:605). Valdecebro's aimless existence, his thoughts on the misty, illusory nature of life, and his revelations to Filomena, Salvadora's lady's maid, that she too, may be a fictional creation, all evoke shades of Unamuno's Augusto Pérez:

Tú también debes formar parte integrante de la
concepción del autor . . . de la idea primordial que
el autor formó de su libro. No creas que desvarío
. . . aunque voy por la vida como al descuido,
pongo atención en todo. ¿Y sabes tú lo que es la
vida? La vida es una ilusión, vivimos y no sabe-
mos que vivimos. Somos como fantasmas que
cruzan un momento por el inmenso espacio de las
constelaciones. (7:606)

[You too must form an integral part of the author's
concept . . . of the primordial idea that the author
formed about his book. Don't think that I'm delir-
ious . . . although I appear to go through life absentmindedly, I pay attention to everything. And
you know what life is? Life is an illusion; we live
and we don't know that we're alive. We're like ap-
paritions that momentarily pass through the immense space of the constellations.]

Internal contradictions and multiple perspectives designed to reveal the subject from as
many different, but simultaneous exposures as
possible, are characteristic of the "open-structured" novel that shares with Cubist art an
awareness of the fluid, constantly evolving nature of reality whose multiple facets, as Wylie
Sypher once said, are both fact and fiction.[19] A
response to the fragmented, unstable universe
formulated by science and philosophy in the
first three decades of the twentieth century, the
use of multiple perspective in the visual and
verbal arts was both an attempt to provide a coherent view of reality as well as to depict its
newly postulated mutability. Perhaps a somewhat belated reaction on Azorín's part, *Salvadora de Olbena* is informed by ideas he culled
from related sources, among them Bergson,
Proust, and the relativity of perspective filtered
through Ortega on the one hand, and modern
art on the other. Azorín's refusal to establish a
hierarchy of opinion among his fictional characters, his juxtaposition of fragmented and contradictory, yet equally valid perspectives on
Salvadora, are all symptomatic of new directions being followed in Modern literature as
well as Cubist art which resorted to similar
paratactical arrangements of synchronic and
diachronic aspects of visual apprehension. As
Herbert Read imaginatively described the effect, a Cubist object "emerges from the canvas
like the image of a lantern-slide in the process
of focussing, but the result is never a familiar,
mimetic image, rather it establishes a new
order of reality by suggestion or association"
(Roskill 1985, 157).[20]

As it set out to challenge the aesthetics of
representation, the disintegration of the sign, as
Roland Barthes put it, became "modernity's
grand affair" (148). Azorín concluded, as did the
scientific relativists, modern painters, filmmakers, and also Ortega, that reality is polyva-
lent and fractured, that all truths are valid, and
that the only false perspective is the one that
claims to be absolute. In Ortega's view, this was
a radical revision of philosophy and the human
concept of the universe because, rather than
being exclusionary, it accepted divergence and
contradiction as complementary views of the
world (3:200). As did many creative minds that
responded to the crisis in mimetic realism engendered in twentieth-century culture, Azorín
merged the conflicting claims to verisimilitude
made by idealistic fiction and empirical history
when he admitted the validity of all points of
view by working on the premise that to apprehend reality an observer must see it from as
many angles as possible. It seems that for
Azorín, vision rather than the intellect or intuition, was the supreme judge of the empirically
verifiable. The last words of his novel are uttered by the old orchard-garden that insists on
the accuracy of its opinions because it has visually witnessed events in Salvadora's life: "Decía
que yo he visto muchas veces a Salvadora; la he
visto risueña y la he visto encapotada; la he
visto barzoneadora cuando niña . . ." [7:675; I
was saying that I've seen Salvadora many times;
I have seen her cheerful and I have seen her
down; I have seen her wander about here as a
child. . .]. The garden takes care not to attribute
to Salvadora thoughts and feelings she may not
have had, nor does it want to offer interpretations of reality that could be misleading: "no
quiero urdir . . . unos pensamientos que verosí-
milmente ella no tenía. Ni quiero tampoco
forjar una historia romántica, basada en lo que
ahora voy a contar" [7:676; I don't want to spin
. . . ideas she never really had. Neither do I wish
to fabricate a romantic story based on what I am
going to relate]. The garden knows only what it
saw with its own eyes: after a long absence from
Olbena,

vi con placer que una tarde aparecía Salvadora. . . .
Trascendía su persona a tristeza, que no vi en ella
nunca. . . . Se sentó, al cabo, al pie del laurel y sacó
un libro. . . . Puedo asegurar que era un libro de
versos. Leyó largo rato; al levantarse, estuvo
mirando atenta al laurel; arrancó una hoja y la in-
tercaló en el libro. Ya sonaba el Angelus; se encen-

dían en puntitos brillantes las luces de la ciudad. (7:677)

I was pleased to see Salvadora appear one afternoon. . . . Her person exuded a sadness I had never seen . . . finally she sat down at the foot of the laurel and took out a book. . . . I can confirm that it was a book of verses. She read for a long while; when she got up, she spent a long time contemplating the laurel; she tore off a leaf and put it into the book. The church bells were already announcing evening prayer; the lights of the city glowed in brilliant little dots].

As far as the garden is concerned, there is no more and no less to Salvadora's story—all else is mere conjecture, incomplete fragments, and partial truths.

Salvadora de Olbena and the Cinema

Cinema was introduced to Spain in 1896, some ten years before Picasso began to elaborate Cubist art forms.[21] In many ways the cinema anticipated the Cubist manner of looking at the world due to its ability to spatialize time through montage, a technique that juxtaposed a plurality of actions occurring simultaneously in different locations. Blaise Cendrars, active in Cubist circles from 1912 to 1924, saw montage techniques borrowed from the cinema as a means by which to combine image and rhythm in poetry and painting (Butler 161). For writers and painters, cinematic montage provided an example of structure and organization as well as the effects that could be obtained by combining multiple perspectives without the need for transitions or explanatory passages (Spencer 113). Filmmakers likewise discovered that space could be temporalized by expanding, compressing, and even reversing the sequentiality of temporal order through the use of flashback or creative editing. As Stephen Kern has documented, some early twentieth-century novelists (and I would add, painters), found solutions to the problem of representing the passage of time in the innovative spatiotemporal manipulations suggested by the cinema (30). The freedom to move around a motif in order to observe it from many different points of view implied by the roving eye of a moving camera also may have suggested to writers and painters that the disruption of sequentiality in prose narrative, or linear perspective in the visual arts, and the reconstruction of objects or events in time, could be attained most easily through

juxtaposition, a technique—in the words of Arnold Hauser—"corresponding exactly to that mixture of space and time in which the film moves" (Spencer 156).

Allusions to the cinema begin to appear in Azorín's work in the 1920s. His passing reference in *Félix Vargas* (1928), later retitled *El caballero inactual*, to the fact that "The spectacle of things will unfold in front of Félix like a cinematographic film ribbon in which there were no images" (5:47), shows his awareness that a stream of visual images might create the effect of a continual present, so dear to his personal ontology. In his review of *Félix Vargas*, Antonio Espina wrote that through the use of ellipsis in time, Azorín's novel exhibited the effects of cinematic simultaneity, demonstrating rather effectively the protagonist's dual psyche (116).[22] I would have to agree, nonetheless, with Montes Huidobro's assertion that the unsophisticated character of the cinema as it was practiced in Spain in the 1920s would have had little impact on the complex, refined narrative techniques Azorín had developed by that time. I would again agree with Montes Huidobro that, more than any other art form, it was painting that exerted the greatest influence on Azorín when he created his major narrative work (29–30).

In an interview published in *Primer Plano* in 1940, one year after his return from exile, Azorín told Fernando Castan Palomar that he had not been to the movies in perhaps as many as fifteen years (i.e., since 1925), "because my eyesight is not good." But he also told Palomar that he was aware "great things" were being achieved in the medium, and that there was much room for development. Without elaborating, Azorín also stated that he had a generally negative opinion of the cinema: "I believe that it has been harmful because of the immorality. I am not referring to sexuality alone." Ever sensitive to the plasticity of art forms, he concluded the interview by declaring that the most important element in the cinema was the play of light and shadow.[23] Substantiating the confession he had made to Castan Palomar on the "immorality" of the cinema, in his personal copy of Marcel Lapierre's 1946 *Anthologie du Cinéma*, Azorín annotated entire paragraphs in an essay by Cecil B. DeMille in which the great filmmaker addressed the question of how to convey female "sex appeal" and the "problèmes d'ordre sexuel" to the screen with taste and decorum (118–21).[24] Failing eyesight or not, during the mid- to late 1940s Azorín attended the movies with such regularity that the theatre consortium of Madrid honored him with a permanent free pass to its establishments. The fruits of these "labors" are the articles collected in *El cine y el momento* (1953) and *El efímero cine* (1955).[25]

In the first of the two books, Azorín declares himself to be "a movie fanatic" (87), stating that in the past three years he had seen some six hundred films (107); in the second book he notes that in one five-month period, he went to as many as two films per day (144), sometimes seeing the same picture, such as Henry James's *The Heiress*, five or six times (156). Perhaps the explanation for his passionate interest in the cinema can be found in Montero Padilla's suggestion that "it is through the notion of time that we can explain Azorín's rapprochement with the cinema" (360). The observation is confirmed by Azorín himself in the titles he chose for his two books, both pregnant with temporal allusion. The prologue of *El cine y el momento* begins with the observation that "I find two things in the cinema: the explanation of time and a legitimate communication with the rest of the world." He proceeds to observe that everything in the film medium is momentary and perishable, from the fragile and flammable nature of the film ribbon, to the actors, aesthetics, and fashions that come and go with such rapidity one is simply overwhelmed by the sensation of life's evanescence and instability. Modern life, he remarks, is epitomized by the instantaneous in which the technology of the radio, the airplane, and the moving picture all converge (5). An identical set of ideas appears two years later in *El efímero cine*, a title also laden with temporal reference and whose epigraph reads: "Temática del tiempo, ¿cómo no me había de atraer el cine, que es el tiempo en concreto?" [The theme of time. How could the cinema, which is time itself, not have attracted me?"]. In the introduction Azorín again addresses the ephemeral nature of the film medium, and remarks that the cinema, the radio, and the airplane made their appearance roughly at the same time, all three emblematic of the rapidity of modern life. The movies, he observes, try to "freeze the moment; the moment becomes visible through the image" (12–13).[26] In articles Azorín wrote on the cinema subsequent to his two books, the concept of temporality reap-

pears with overwhelming insistence. In "Clave del Cine. II," published in *ABC*, 7 June 1957, Azorín writes that when he goes to the movies and is confronted with the spectacle of vertiginously moving images, he's seized by an awareness of "Eternity."[27] He appears to have become captivated by the movies for the same reasons that he appreciated Velázquez's attempts to freeze the instant as it evolved in time and the temporal nature of Impressionist painting; ironically, although cinema was the first art form in which temporality became malleable and fluid, it is precisely for the same reasons that the time-bound nature of film became one of its most prominent characteristics.[28]

Musing on what meaning the idea of time had for him, Azorín remarked that he always associated time with melancholy; that it was only through melancholy that he could become aware of the depth and breadth of time. His thoughts jumped immediately to the novels *Doña Inés* and *Salvadora de Olbena*, both of whose protagonists are intelligent, single women approaching middle age. According to Azorín, a woman who is acutely sensitive to the passage of time is extremely difficult to portray because there are so many different facets to her psyche and personality (*EdC* 94–95). *Salvadora de Olbena* is, indeed, a study in time. If the cinema, in addition to modern art, philosophical perspectivism, and scientific relativism influenced this novel, it would be manifest in, among other aspects, the cinema's Bergsonian recognition of the fluid nature of time and its acknowledgment of "the extent to which the past exists in our conscious experience as a function of present awareness" (Ermarth 74). During the night in which she roams about her house in Olbena, Salvadora stops to sort out her visiting cards: one set, that she eventually throws into the fire, reads "Salvadora López de Ledona, viuda de Argüelles"; the other bears a new identity she has chosen for herself, the unadorned "Salvadora de Olbena." As flames consume the first set of cards, Salvadora removes her gold wedding band, but as she does so, she realizes that she can never break with the past completely because, despite all her efforts, the past forms an ineradicable part of her present: "No se puede romper con el pasado: imposible abolir el tiempo. . . . Como pasa ahora el tiempo, en este ámbito compreso por la noche y la lluvia, así ha pasado también en la vida de Salvadora hasta llegar a este trance decisivo"

[7:594–95; You cannot break with the past: it is impossible to abolish time. . . . Just as time passes now, in this ambience circumscribed by night and rain, time has also passed in Salvadora's life until coming to this decisive juncture]. That Salvadora finds herself at the same crossroad of time and space that constitutes Bergsonian *durée*, was confirmed retrospectively by Azorín in "Actitudes de Artista," published in *La Prensa* of Buenos Aires, 18 April 1948. He sets the scene of his essay by describing the city clocks of Olbena as they mark the passage of time, a backdrop against which Salvadora burns her first set of visiting cards, emphasizing that this particular moment marks the division of time in her life into the past and future; the life that she has already lived and the life that she is going to live. There is nothing more to the novel, insists Azorín, than "two, three, four hours in the deepest night, in solitude, in time, in history, in legend."

One of the things that most intrigued Azorín about the movies was the medium's ability to fracture time: in his copy of André Berthomieu's *Essai de Grammaire cinématographique*, he annotated a statement that "the unity of time does not exist in the cinema," and proceeded to bracket a paragraph describing the American invention of "flash-back" technique that displaces linear chronology by allowing one to go back and forth in time. In the same paragraph Berthomieu points out that quite a number of films use this technique to intensify dramatic interest, commenting that the maneuver is as common in the novel as it is in the cinema (26). The dialogical relationship between sequentiality and simultaneity was an issue explored in all aspects of modern culture. Thus, the juxtaposed multiple perspectives Azorín offers in *Salvadora de Olbena* can be attributed just as easily to the influence of Cubist art or the philosophy of Henri Bergson, as they can to the influence of the cinema that disrupted homogeneous visual space in order to consider new spatiotemporal relations (Kern 142). In "El cine" (*ABC*, 11 February 1950), Azorín notes the unlimited spatiality the film medium has at its disposal, allowing the spectator to transcend both time and space, an idea he developed further in "El nuevo mundo" (*ABC*, 24 May 1950). In the same spirit that Stephen Kern observed that cinema ended time's tyranny over space by compressing, expanding, and reversing it through editing techniques (30),

Azorín wrote that film creates a new sense of time through "retrospection, simultaneity, and anticipation," and that for the first time in the history of art, the spectator, rather than being stifled by time, is finally able to transcend its limitations.

Similar to William Carlos Williams who related multiple points of view in art to the quick cutting of cinema (Marling 128), it is entirely possible that Azorín borrowed the technique either from the film or from modern art. Although Berthomieu's study on the "grammar" of cinema appeared two years after *Salvadora de Olbena*, Azorín surely found his intuitions on novelistic "editing and cutting" endorsed in passages which he annotated that described similar procedures in movie making: "It is a question of writing the script on separate sheets of unnumbered paper and numbering only the scenes or sequences in such a way that their continuity can be rearranged and recomposed at any time simply by changing or inverting the scenes or sequences already set" (30). Equally suggestive is an article by Marcel Carné in which Azorín annotated how the traveling camera (similar to the narrator in *Salvadora de Olbena*, or a Cubist painter who collates and orders multiple views of a motif), can become a character in a movie plot: "Placed on a moving carriage, the camera glided, rose, panned or flew to wherever the plot needed it. It was no longer conventionally fixed on a tripod, but participated in the action, itself becoming a *character in the drama.*"[29] Sharon Spencer's argument that the highly visual nature of cinematic juxtaposition of perspective, often on the same person, event or object, tends to produce in the *nouveau roman* a spatial rather than a temporal orientation to reality (112), is equally true in the case of *Salvadora de Olbena*.[30] In the same way that Cubist painters arranged spatially organized views of objects accumulated over time through juxtaposition, the filmmaker employed montage to rearrange the ostensibly irreversible sequentiality of time, and philosophers as well as scientists postulated the nonexistence of absolute perspective, modern novelists, including Azorín, employed the same, or similar, techniques in narrative to explore the issue of space and time, often reducing time to isolated moments of perception without any obligation to maintain sequential development, provide connective transitions, or to contextualize their material within existing frames of reference.[31]

Notes

Introduction

1. Since the Academy's founding in 1713, by the Marqués de Villena, only two Spanish-American writers—one Colombian, the other Mexican—have preceded Vargas Llosa at the Real Academia: both were elected to membership in the nineteenth century. Although Vargas Llosa became a Spanish citizen in 1993, he is the first non-Spanish national to be elected to the Royal Academy in the twentieth century. I quote from Vargas Llosa's address as it was reproduced in *ABC* (Madrid) for 16 January 1996.

2. Fox's seminal essay, first published in *Cuadernos Hispanoamericanos* (January 1967), has been reprinted numerous times. He argues that books were invariably the point of departure for Azorín's "artistic inspiration and we can even say that books supplied him with almost the entirety of his literary idiom" (Fox 1988, 121).

3. The citations are from *Obras Completas* (1963, 8:440–41). Cf. Campos (162). All further references to the *Obras Completas* are cited in the text by volume and page number. References to Azorín's work collected apart from the *Obras Completas* will be cited parenthetically in the text by an abbreviated title (see List of Abbreviations), with the appropriate page number.

4. Azorín's diagnosis of his memory as visual apparently was based on classifications proposed by the French neurophysiologist Jean Martin Charcot (1825–1893) whom Azorín quoted on several occasions. In "La memoria," for example, he states that because his memory is eidetic, a visual image facilitates his total recall of "what I experienced on such and such an occasion, with all its circumstances of place, people, time, light, etc." (*Agenda* 150). See also "El damasco rojo" (*París*), that Azorín calls a homage to "Juan Martín Charcot," and in which he observes that, with the passage of time, his visual memory most easily retained the colors of former surroundings: in this case, the intense red damask wall coverings in the home of Victor Hugo that he had visited in Paris many years before (7:956).

5. The essay appeared in *La Prensa* (Buenos Aires) on 18 February 1940. All further references to *La Prensa* are to the Buenos Aires periodical. In a piece on Maurice Vlaminck, Azorín again noted that he felt great empathy with painters and that "we learn to persevere from painters more than from any other artists" (*La Prensa*, 20 December 1931).

6. An observation Bram Dijkstra made regarding Wallace Stevens's inability to write "without having the stimulus of a new painting to kindle his imagination" as being symptomatic of people who are either unable or unwilling to scrutinize concrete reality, but who *are* capable of imitating the simulacra produced by others, might also be said of Azorín (165).

7. Today ekphrasis has been extended by some to mean any kind of reference to the visual or graphic arts: Mack Smith writes of the ekphrastic use of film (34), while James Heffernan proposes that ekphrastic theory also include any form of writing *about* the visual arts, such as art criticism (1991, 304).

8. Heffernan (1993, 93, 118); Foucault (9). The distinction between natural and artificial signs was made by Plato, in the *Cratylus*, where he postulated the visual image to be a natural sign because it resembles what it represents whereas, with the exception of onomatopoeia, words expressed meaning only through arbitrary convention (Burwick 123).

9. The quotation is from Ortega's *Obras Completas* (2:174). Subsequent references are made parenthetically in the text by volume and page number. Elise Richter noted that the use of the historical present relocates narration of a past event to the present "in order to give a listener the illusion of participating in the event described" (Bally et al. 1956, 101–2)

10. I borrow the term "forever now" from Krieger (1992, 287). Vargas Llosa remarked that all aspects of

214

Azorín's writing are directed toward suspending time in order to avoid death: "This is the profound meaning of the present or present perfect of the indicative in which he customarily wrote his texts . . . a way of immobilizing the world, of freezing life" (51). For additional discussion of the present perfect in Azorín's work, see Ramsden's edition of *La ruta de Don Quijote* (203).

11. Azorín's copy of *A Rebours* was published in Paris by Charpentier (1903); the annotations are on page 71. Cf. Meltzer's comments on the same passage by Huysmans in her *Salomé and the Dance of Writing* (41).

Part I, Chapter 1

1. Cf. "A contemporary writer on aesthetics has argued that landscape does not exist until the artist expresses it in painting or literature. Only then—when it is created in art—do we really begin to see the landscape" (3:1171). For similar thoughts see 3:1143, 3:1186, and 9:758. Azorín was exactly on target with his intuition: the idea of the French Near East as a literary and painterly construct still obtains today, as was evident in the 1982 art exhibition "Orientalism: The Near East in French Painting, 1800–1880," held at the Memorial Art Gallery of the University of Rochester and the Neuberger Museum of the State University of New York at Purchase. See especially, Linda Nochlin's contribution to the exhibition catalogue: "The Imaginary Orient," repr. in her *The Politics of Vision* (1989, 33–59).

2. Allowing for some degree of variation, the following painters are usually associated with the Generation of 1898: Aureliano de Beruete, Darío de Regoyos, Ignacio Zuloaga, Joaquín Sorolla, José Gutiérrez Solana, Agustín Lhardy, Agustín Riancho, Casimiro Sainz, Juan Espina, Santiago Rusiñol, Gustavo de Maeztu, and Ricardo Baroja (see Azorín, *PCQ* 248, 6:264; Fernández Almagro 1948, 189; Lafuente Ferrari 1948b, 453, 458; Laín Entralgo 385; Rozas 79). Azorín went as far as to include in the Generation's ranks the young Pablo Picasso "who has published handsome, traditional ink portraits in the group's magazine: *Arte Joven*" (6:239). Baroja indicated that Picasso contributed two or three illustrations for his novel *Inventos y mistificaciones de Silvestre Paradox* when it was serialized in *Arte Joven*, as well as the charcoal portrait of the author featured on the magazine's cover (*Obras Completas* 7:897). Subsequent references to Baroja's *Obras Completas* will be cited parenthetically in the text by volume and page number.

3. Azorín (6:218), Baroja (7:718), and Unamuno (7:731) all comment on their museum attendance. Both Azorín and Unamuno took art lessons as youngsters, and Azorín often mused on his desire to have been a painter, but of all the Generation's writers, it is Azorín who pursued with greatest consistency a painterly sensibility in his creative work. Baroja wrote that he was sorry he never seriously followed his inclination toward art; had he done so, he indicated he might have become a landscape Impressionist (7:431–32, 7:437–38).

4. For the political situation leading to the founding of the Institución Libre de Enseñanza, I am indebted to the work of Dolores Gómez Molleda (1966), and Juan López Morrillas, especially the latter's *The Krausist Movement in Spain* (1981). Giner maintained that, "Of all the great

problems pertinent to the regeneration of our people, I am aware of none so underestimated as national education" (7:87). Cf. his *Ensayos y cartas* (1965, 152).

5. Giner, influenced by German Volksgeist theorists, took great care to differentiate the expression "pueblo" from the more prevalent, somewhat derogatory connotation it carried in the nineteenth century as meaning "common, vulgar humanity," and the more general meaning he and the '98 writers preferred as "the entire nation . . . as a State" (Giner 1969, 28). Speaking of the Spanish *pueblo*, Unamuno wrote that the majority "do not love it, they do not study it, and they do not know it well enough to love it" (1:868). The idea that geography was the basis of national pride was not a new one. In his copy of Antonio Ramírez Arcas's *Manual descriptivo y estadístico de las Españas . . .* (1859), Azorín annotated passages in the prologue dedicated to "studious youth" in which the author exhorts his young readers: "As much as you hear it said . . . that we're seized by social dissolution, don't pay any heed to that kind of slander . . . pay attention to the general study of the nation if you want to become familiar with what defines our authentic condition . . ."(6).

6. To meet those needs, Giner attracted to the *ILE* a distinguished faculty of natural scientists, including the celebrated geologist José Macpherson, responsible for preparing, along with Antonio Machado Núñez, the first geological studies of the province of Seville. Macpherson (1839–1902), born in Cadiz to a wealthy Scotsman and a Spanish mother, received his geological training in Paris. Settling in Madrid in 1874, he pioneered orogenic study in Spain and was an internationally recognized authority on the subject (see Lapworth 1903). While teaching at the *ILE*, Macpherson offered post-graduate instruction in geography and geology to the Institute's own faculty. Antonio Machado Núñez (1812–1895), paternal grandfather of the poet Antonio Machado, was professor of natural sciences at the University of Seville; in 1883 he was appointed to Madrid's Universidad Central. A free-thinking liberal and champion of Darwinism, Machado Núñez belonged to Giner's intellectual circle and to the *ILE* where he founded the first Gabinete de Historia Natural (Giner 1965, 174–75). Antonio and Manuel Machado were students at the *ILE* from 1883 to 1889 where the future poet of the Generation of 1898 undoubtedly was exposed to the Institute's excursionist pedagogy and respect for the Spanish landscape. When Machado's *Campos de Castilla* appeared in 1912, Azorín wrote that "Machado's recent poems are a collection of Castilian landscapes," noting in the poetry the unmistakable presence of a landscape artist (2:805).

7. For the formation and by-laws of the "Sociedad para el Estudio del Guadarrama," see *BILE* (vol. 10, no. 236; 15 December 1886). Also Pena López (1982, 86), and Calvo Serraller's contribution to the exhib. cat. *Aureliano de Beruete* (1983, 35). For the growth of geology and geography in Spain and its influence on literature and art, see Pena (1982).

8. In this respect Spain was no exception to the European order: the Barbizon painters of France, who became active in the late 1820s, were the first to protagonize landscape in their country, but until the innovations of the Impressionists made their work pale by comparison, the French Academy ostracized the painters of Fontainebleau

Forest for rebelling against academically sanctioned land-scape decorum (Rewald 21).

9. In one of his several editions of Richard Ford's *A Handbook for Travellers in Spain* (3d ed., 1855), Azorín annotated a passage where Ford appears to repeat Bowles's observation verbatim: "The Castilians have a classical non-perception of landscape . . . while the farmers imagine that the branches [of trees] harbour birds which eat up corn" (2:653).

10. For example, Unamuno wrote in *Por tierras de Portugal y de España*, "It has been said . . . that the aesthetic feeling for Nature is a modern sentiment, that with the ancients it was merely sketched in, that it's of romantic origin, and not a few add that its high priest was Rousseau" (quoted in Orozco 17–18). Cf. Azorín's statement that "The taste for nature, in literature, is completely modern; in France, Rousseau . . . inaugurates literary landscape . . ." (3:1147; also "Paisajes" in *Correo Español*, 27 December 1930). In *Lecturas españolas* (1912), Azorín observed that a truly modern feeling for landscape entered Castilian literature for the first time with José Mor de Fuentes's 1786 novel *La Serafina* (2:625; cf. 7:392). Elsewhere, however, he wrote that it was in Enrique Gil's 1844 novel *El señor de Bembibre* that "for the first time in Spain landscape in the literary arts was born" (3:1126). Cf. Baroja, "Estilo modernista" (8:847).

11. At the time of the posthumous exhibition Beruete's son, the art historian Aureliano de Beruete y Moret, noted that the 666 paintings displayed represented only one-third of his father's oeuvre (exhib. cat. *Aureliano de Beruete, 1845–1912* 10). Isabel Cajide calculated the number of Beruete's extant paintings at near 2,000 (5–6). Beruete enjoyed greater recognition abroad than he did at home: in 1893 he won the only medal awarded at the Chicago International (Pantorba 50); he was inducted into the Hispanic Society of New York in 1908 and donated several paintings as a gift to commemorate the occasion; in 1887, and again in 1910, he was on the panel of judges for the Paris International (exhib. cat. *Aureliano de Beruete* 114 and Domenech 1912, 422).

12. The liberal politician Segismundo Moret, a relative of Beruete's and an avid collector of art, was intermittently on the faculty of the *ILE* and became its president in 1879 (Giner 1965, 178–80).

13. Ford, *A Handbook for Travellers in Spain* (1855, 2:653). For an in-depth study of the invention of a Castilianophile nationalism in turn-of-the-century Spain, see Fox (1997).

14. From "Tópicos del momento" (1909), reproduced in Fox (1991, 289–90). In the seminal essays of *En torno al casticismo*, Unamuno, too, identified *castizo* (i.e., pure) Spanishness with Castile; the metaphors he preferred throughout the five essays allude to external referents in the Castilian landscape.

15. At the beginning of his career Beruete, like his teacher Haes, preferred northern landscapes executed in a style similar to that of the Barbizon painters whose technique he learned firsthand on a trip to Paris, and from Martín Rico, a Spanish painter living in France at the time of Beruete's visit. Rico also admired the Barbizon School and studied the work of its painters assiduously; he and Beruete developed a lifelong friendship, and Rico's influence is patent in Beruete's early work (exhib. cat. *A. de Beruete* 18, 94; Pena 1982, 49). As Beruete became more deeply involved with the ideological orientation of the *ILE*, he changed not only his palette and subject matter, but also his technique which evolved from a Barbizon-type landscape to an impressionist manner. Beruete knew the Impressionist movement rather well due to his frequent travel to Paris, and he used impressionist technique in his own painting almost exclusively from approximately 1903 until his death in 1912. Many '98 writers, especially Azorín (perhaps under Beruete's influence), also expressed a decided preference for Barbizon and Impressionist painters (cf. Azorín 1:183; 5:325; 845–46; 6:915; Baroja 7:718; 7:884).

16. Denis Cosgrove, *Social Formation and Symbolic Landscape* (15) quoted by A. Jensen Adams in W. J. T. Mitchell (1994b, 66). Murray Krieger recently observed that artistic praxis might reflect not only the sociopolitical orientation of a specific group, but that art itself may be a product of rhetoric generated by that group (1992, 256). In this sense Spain was not an exception to developments in the rest of Europe: Mark Roskill recently pointed out that landscape, as a nineteenth-century phenomenon, went hand-in-hand with "a movement . . . to rediscover those rustic and primitive patterns of existence in nature that have a seemingly timeless strain to them . . . to find roots in the countryside, in the shape of an inheritance of customs and practices binding the generations together" (1997, 121).

17. Reprinted in *La Lectura* (1915, 1:361–70). Calvo Serraller noticed that since its inception in Spain, landscape painting invoked "une conception morale" (1985, 76). Azorín pointed out the "moral attitude" toward landscape held by Nietzsche, Giner, and Fray Luis de Granada (4:151–52).

18. Giner's excursions to the "monumental cities" of Spain as he called them had unmistakable ideological connotations: in her article "Nation, Narration, Naturalization," Jo Labayni notes that archaeological sites and ruins play an important role in the formation of national mythologies because they present a synthesis of cultural relic embedded in nature (135).

19. In his study of Ortega's writing on landscape, Thomas Mermall showed that it provided the philosopher with a constant source of meditation in the early stages of his career (1983, 110–11). As it did for Giner, landscape for Ortega had pedagogical, moral, aesthetic, patriotic, and hermeneutic functions.

20. Subsequent references to Cossío's *El Greco* will be cited parenthetically in the text by volume and page number. It is an error to attribute to the Generation of 1898 sole responsibility for rehabilitating El Greco and Velázquez. Manuel B. Cossío and Aureliano de Beruete produced the first modern scholarship and cataloguing of work by the two artists before the turn of the century. Although Cossío's two-volume study of El Greco appeared in 1908 (the book carries a 1908 imprint but was actually released in November of the previous year), he began to publish his research in the *BILE* during the last years of the nineteenth century. Beruete's monograph on Velázquez was published in France in 1898.

21. Cf. ". . . better than any Castilian writer from Castile, isn't Zuloaga bringing to light in his painting the eternal entrails of Castile?" (Unamuno 7:743). In his seminal study of Zuloaga, Lafuente Ferrari included a revelatory footnote in which he cited a German critic, Moeller van

der Bruck, who made an observation in an article published in *Die Wage* for October 1903, that Zuloaga "possesses the highest quality according to Nietzsche: that of race" (1950, 200 n. 1). The German critic's point was to demonstrate that the "decadence" of Zuloaga's Spanish peasants and villages proved the general decline of Latin nations while affirming the corresponding rise of Germanic peoples. In 1909, Christian Brinton, editor of *Art in America* and the first American critic to write seriously on Zuloaga and Sorolla, observed that although both artists were diametrical opposites, their art "is equally typical and equally racial" (26). Although Sorolla is not usually associated with the nationalistic landscape ideology spawned by the *ILE*, it is important to keep in mind that he met and became fast friends with Aureliano de Beruete in 1889, and through him entered the intellectual circle of the *Institución Libre* (Jiménez Burillo 27).

22. From "Una visita a Zuloaga" published in *La Prensa*, 2 December 1917.

23. In the ten years that elapsed between the initial composition of *La España negra* and its publication in Spain, Regoyos had moved away from his work as a graphic artist, abandoning what Maeztu called his Goyesque, "sinister fantasies," for oils and a lighter palette, concentrating almost exclusively on landscape. His aesthetics had so evolved that Regoyos felt obliged to append a disclaimer to the Spanish edition regarding the book's paternity (San Nicolás 124–25, 136).

24. Salaverría's article appeared in *Hermes* (Bilbao) for April 1917; the issue carries no volume or page numbers. On Regoyos as precursor of the expressionism of Zuloaga and Solana, and his affinities with '98 ideology, see Carmen Pena (1993, 97).

25. Baroja's reference to the artist's "faulty technique" is a swipe at the criticism directed at Regoyos's naive and primitive manner of rendering the human figure. The simple Spanish peasant of his canvases recalls the same archetypal figure that peoples the work of Machado, Azorín, and Baroja, and the artist's preference for what Rodríguez Alcalde (176) called "las menudas gentes y los menudos gestos" [ordinary people and ordinary gestures], is reminiscent of Azorín's "menudos hechos" [ordinary events]. For additional '98 commentary on Regoyos, see Baroja (7:880, 891), Unamuno (7:733, 745–50), and Azorín (*PCQ* 32).

26. Beruete, as did many painters of his day, also tried his hand at writing: his play, *Entre rocas*, which premiered in 1900 to unfavorable reviews, discouraged the artist from further attempts at creative writing (exhib. cat. *A. de Beruete* 17).

27. Two years prior to this 1914 contribution to *Jardines de España*, Azorín's sense of plasticity led him to assume the role of an "artista ante el paisaje," and to paint with words the emotions that "this brown and solitary Castilian plain" produced in him. The result was a Rusiñol-like gardenscape:

. . . esta callejuela con sus tiendecillas de abaceros . . . este viejo palacio con los cristales rotos y polvorientos, cerradas las ventanas, con su jardín de adelfas, rosales y cipreses, obstruídos los viales por los hierbajos, saturado el ambiente por denso olor de humedad, llenas de hojas, las aguas inmóviles, negras, de una fuente" [2:604–605]

. . . this back street with its grocers' shops . . . this old mansion with its closed windows, the glass broken and dusty; with its garden of oleanders, roses, and cypresses; the paths overgrown by weeds; the atmosphere saturated with a dense odor of dampness; the still, black waters of a fountain full of leaves].

28. In *El caballero inactual* (*Félix Vargas* 1928), one of Azorín's experimental, "surrealist" novels, he writes that the locomotive represents for him "time, anxieties, hopes, happiness, sadness, personal tragedies of people who haul them around from one end of the earth to the other" (106). On another occasion Azorín juxtaposed the historically symbolic and, in his day, abandoned gardens of the palace at Aranjuez—emblematic of the eternal aspects of both Spain and time—with the whistle of a passing locomotive: ". . . Aranjuez, Aranjuez: in the gray, overcast autumn days, when we wander along the deserted promenades, a vague sadness invades our soul . . . the leaves fall; in the distance, blows the high-pitched whistle of a train" (2:1144). Rusiñol painted the palace gardens at Aranjuez with such frequency that Alfonso XIII granted him the title of "honorary gates keeper."

29. See Azorín's "Antonio y Manuel Machado" first published in *ABC*, 13 April 1947, now collected in *Varios hombres y alguna mujer* (259); also *Ante Baroja* (8:266). Cf. Baroja's own 1903 "Estilo modernista" (8:845).

30. See the exhib. cat. *Darío de Regoyos* (33, 309, 311, and the appendix).

31. The editorial was printed in the 30 November 1901 issue. In the annotated copy available at the Casa-Museo Azorín in Monóvar, Azorín underscored passages that prove to be significant, especially in regard to the verbal landscapes of his 1902 novel *La Voluntad*:

Seducidos por los infinitos cambios de la naturaleza, consiguen [los impresionistas], mediante *una ejecución rápida*, fijar sobre el lienzo las movilidades de la atmósfera; en una palabra, *son los pintores de los efectos fugaces*, de las impresiones pasajeras, quizás las más sublimes, *sobre todo en el arte del paisaje* y de la marina, pero también las más difíciles de interpretar [emphasis Martínez Ruiz].

[Seduced by the infinite changes of nature, the Impressionists, through *rapid execution*, succeed in fixing the mobility of atmosphere on canvas; in a word, *they are the painters of transitory effects*, of passing impressions, perhaps the most sublime, *above all the art of landscape* and marines, but also the most difficult to interpret].

Among the signatories of the protest were Ignacio Zuloaga, Darío de Regoyos, Santiago Rusiñol, Pablo de Uranga, Adolfo Guiard, Miquel Utrillo, and Daniel Zuloaga; conspicuously absent is the name of Joaquín Sorolla. The new Academician against whom the protest was directed was Mariano Benlliure (1862–1956), who titled his investiture speech "Arte y anarquía."

32. Regoyos's claim is qualified by Giner de los Ríos who published an extremely informed, and informative, 1895 article on Impressionism in the *BILE*. Aside from correctly telling his readers that the Impressionist landscape, especially in the cases of Monet and Pissarro, originated with the British painter Joseph Mallord William Turner, Giner mentions that in the next to last Exposición de Bellas Artes held in Madrid (no date), the public had the opportunity to see two canvases by Whistler: the portraits of his mother and that of Sarasate "which have gone almost unnoticed here by the great majority of our artists and critics, but were acquired shortly thereafter by the French government for the Luxembourg, its museum of contemporary art" (87). In the same article Giner names, as exponents of new tendencies in Spanish art, the painters Santiago Rusiñol and Ramón Casas (83).

33. "Joaquín Sorolla y Bastida" was published in *La*

Lectura 1 (1901); it is reproduced in *Eight Essays on Joaquín Sorolla* (77).

34. Rico left Madrid hoping to study with the Barbizon painter Charles Daubigny, but the French artist refused him lessons. In his memoirs Rico recalled that he learned subsequently Daubigny probably felt no empathy for him since another Spanish painter had once copied his work without permission (41). Azorín owned a copy of Rico's memoirs in which he made interesting annotations.

35. The article was published in *Revista Nueva* 1 (1899):615–20.

36. For what follows on postwar French art and politics, I am indebted to Richard Brettell's marvelous essay "The Impressionist Landscape and the Image of France" (1984).

37. T. J. Clark, one of the most prominent historians of Impressionist art writing today, noted its "moral aspect" (3), as did Robert Herbert who observed that for the Barbizon painters "moral and social truth [in art] gradually became synonymous with contemporary life" (1988, 38), echoing the moral subtext Giner, the Generation of 1898, and Ortega saw in the canvases of the modern Spanish landscapists.

38. Lemonnier quoted in Clark (259); Brandes in Rewald (496).

39. The reconstruction of Paris was begun in 1853 when Haussmann was appointed Prefect of the Seine, and lasted fifteen years, until 1868, taking place during the formative years of the Impressionists: the revolutionary Salon des Refusés took place in 1863; the term "impressionism" was coined by Louis Leroy, a *Charivari* critic reviewing a painting Monet showed at the first Impressionist exhibition in 1874. The "Haussmannization" of Paris has a singular analogy to a similar reconfiguration of Madrid when inner-city congestion was alleviated by the, then, fashionable Gran Vía. Although the project was first conceived in 1862, plans were not authorized until 1898. A public auction of bonds to float the Gran Vía was not held until February and again in April 1905, but there were no investors. Money was not raised successfully until 1909; the project commenced in April 1910; an initial phase was completed and opened by 1915; and the project was declared complete in 1917 (Corral 371–74). Gómez de la Serna remembered that the artists and writers of his generation—Gutiérrez Solana among them—grew up in a city "full of rubble caused by the eagerness to repair and enlarge it" (1944, 64).

40. "Las sorpresas de la pintura" was first published on 30 March 1914 in *ABC*. Amid consistently mounting criticism of his theorizing a "Generation of 1898," Azorín argued that a "generation" is an aesthetic construct which, in turn, is governed by a commonality of ethics, politics, and history. Within that aesthetic entity, however, it was entirely possible for members to be as diverse and contradictory as all the citizens comprising the Spanish nation (9:1151).

41. Rather than call the new painters "impressionists," Zola at first employed the term "les naturalistes" who, he said, were increasing in numbers and represented the modern movement in art that would soon have to be reckoned with. When Monet first arrived on the Paris art scene, Castagnary welcomed him as a new member of the "naturalist" group of painters (Rewald 189, 148). Spanish art critics also equated French naturalism with Impressionism. Beruete y Moret wrote that as "naturalist" paint-

ers became progressively more interested in atmosphere and light, they became more "impressionistic," establishing, with time, an independent art movement (137).

42. Azorín addressed the cultural interdependence of Nietzsche, Wagner, and landscape painting in his essay "Martín Rico." It is also useful to recall here the triad Azorín said circumscribed Spanish aesthetics at the turn of the century: "la escuela del 98, el wagnerismo y los paisajistas" (6:292–93).

43. Given Azorín's personality, it is understandable that he would admire restraint in all forms of artistic expression. He returns again and again to Lessing's contention that the Laocoön statue is a superb example of controlling expression of emotion so as to leave something to the imagination of the viewer. In his own writing Azorín often referred to the statue itself, or to Lessing's interpretation of its significance, as an instantiation of "the moderation that we admire in the famous sculpture . . . put forth as a model of restraint by Lessing; restraint in the expression of pain" (*CM* 46; cf. *EC* 49, 134).

44. I quote from the 1924 edition of *La españa negra* (46).

45. See Pena (1982, 56, 117). Lily Litvak (1991) suggests that Wagner's influence (e.g., giving voice to Nature) can be seen in the animism of the vegetal motifs Antonio Gaudí incorporated into the capitals and pedestals of the columns in the Sagrada Familia Cathedral of Barcelona.

46. Vayreda spent two months in Paris in 1871. See Opisso (195), Pantorba (129), Jiménez-Placer (15:218), and the exhib. cat. *L'Escola d'Olot* (27, 106).

47. I follow here the thought of T. J. Clark on the socio-economic underpinnings of the Impressionist art movement, although I disagree with his argument that its "painters discovered the limits and insufficiency of their own ideology" (258), since a false class consciousness must always be subliminal for it to be false. Its "discovery" necessarily entails a conscious confrontation with, and reaction to, its casuistry.

48. Carlos Blanco Aguinaga's *Juventud del 98* (Madrid: Siglo XXI, 1970) is fundamental to understanding the equivocal ideology and class alienation of the Generation of 1898. Thomas Mermall presents an excellent summary of Blanco's position, as well as those of his detractors and supporters, in "La ideología del 98 bajo el franquismo" in *Divergencias y unidad: Perspectivas sobre la Generación del '98*, edited by John P. Gabriele (Madrid: Orígenes, 1990), 49–60.

49. On pictorial minimization of industry in the impressionist landscape, see Herbert (1988, 202), Clark (161), and Buchloh et al. (125–26). Tucker writes that by the 1870s, 450,000 kilograms of sewage were flowing into the Seine daily, creating a terrible stench as well as environmental problems. At Argenteuil the water in the boat basin foamed due to the sludge collected at its bottom (1995, 100).

50. The quotation is from Lafuente Ferrari's essay in the exhib. cat. *Aureliano de Beruete* (9); cf. Pantorba (50), Faraldo (31), Jove (39), and Jiménez-Placer (923).

51. Bazille quoted in Sypher (172). In "La destruction du sujet," Georges Bataille wrote that emotional disengagement in French painting began with Manet: because he was more interested in *how* he painted his subjects than in attaching any meaning to them, paintings such as *L'Execution de Maximilien* or the famous *Olympia*, focus

on painting for its own sake and anticipate the Impressionists' "destruction" of subject matter (56).

52. The quotation is from Beruete y Moret's 1926 history of nineteenth-century Spanish painting (131–32). See Marín Valdés (exhib. cat. *Aureliano de Beruete* 100) for an excellent comparison of Azorín's prose to Beruete's art. For, in my opinion, misguided comparisons of Beruete to Baroja, see Calvo Serraller (1985, 36, 38), Faraldo (30–31), and Rodríguez Alcalde (107). At the beginning of his career (1883–1890), Santiago Rusiñol, who lived and painted in Paris for many years, showed canvases that protagonized factories, workshops, and the *banlieue* on the outskirts of Barcelona before finding his metier in the painting of gardenscapes. Rusiñol's "vulgar thematics" offended the refined sensibilities of some art critics who dubbed him a "champion of realism" (Trenc Ballester 305).

53. In his history of railroads in France, Pierre Dauzet confirms Herbert's argument. According to Dauzet, because France's defeat was so sudden and unexpected, young people who were students at the Collège Impérial during the "Disaster of 1870" did not have enough time to lose their image of France as a great nation. These were the same young engineers, writes Dauzet, whose confidence and courage helped rebuild the damaged railway system within ten years after the war's end (140).

54. Coincidental with nascent scientific experiments in locomotion as a means of mass transport in the 1830s and 40s, it is worth mentioning that the first experiments in photography occurred during the same period of time. Modernity's speeding up of time, as it were, accounts for a reciprocal desire to arrest the fleeting moment of which both Impressionism and photography, its contemporary sister art, are emblematic.

55. The Gare Saint-Lazare, redesigned by Eugène Flachat in the 1860s, was considered a marvel of engineering and architectural style. Monet's paintings of the depot are as much a tribute to Flachat as they are to the train as an emblem of modern life (Herbert 1988, 28).

56. From surviving correspondence with his brother Amancio, it is clear that Azorín had been accumulating publications relative to trains and locomotion for quite some time. Cf. a letter in the Monóvar archive, dated 18 June 1912, where he asks his brother to forward some of this material to Madrid. Although I have verified the date of the letter, Fox reproduces the same with slight textual variants and a different date (1991, 101 n. 1). "Los ferrocarriles," the essay that opens *Castilla*, includes a description of steam enveloping a train engine and the glass dome of the station that are remarkably similar to Monet's views of trains in the Gare Saint-Lazare.

57. In *El Enfermo* (1943), the sudden appearance of a train in a landscape once again prompts an association with modern life: "And suddenly, at a bend in the road, we saw the glimmer of railroad tracks. The feeling of solitude had disappeared and was replaced, to our satisfaction, by the sensation of modern life" (6:810).

58. Also dating from 1944 is *Veraneo sentimental* where much of the landscape Azorín describes on his way to a summer resort is seen from the windows of a train hurtling through eight tunnels. The blurred countryside is juxtaposed against a trackside rivulet, its water slipping calmly and silently alongside the railroad tracks (7:270). Schivelbusch indicates that not only the speed of trains, but railroad tunnels in particular, contribute to a passenger's sense of loss of contact with the landscape (25).

59. Cf. "Un viaje a Francia," first published in *ABC* on 4 July 1925, now collected in *EL* (226).

Part I, Chapter 2

1. Although Cossío is customarily recognized as the moving force behind awakening interest in El Greco, he himself gave credit to Théophile Gautier and the French Romantics for disseminating information about the painter outside Spain (1907, 337). As an indication of how important a scholarly contribution Cossío's work on El Greco really was, Bermúdez-Cañete writes that Rainer Maria Rilke expressed a desire to learn Spanish so that he could read the book in the original (1:163).

2. It is easy to see from the example of Cossío's Tainean view of El Greco how the *institucionistas* and, subsequently, the *gente nueva* made the leap from a revalorization of classical literature and art to thematizing the Castilian landscape as a vital ingredient in their interpretation and explanation of Spanish cultural heritage, and their inherent "Spanishness" first to themselves, and then to the public at large.

3. For example: "Catalonia has always been distinguished by its lively intellectual curiosity; she revealed to us the forgotten El Greco . . . it was there, before anywhere else in Spain, that great authors like Ibsen became known . . ." (9:956; cf. 2:913–14).

4. Azorín observed that meditation on a painting by El Greco could lead, through a quasi-mystical experience, directly to the very marrow of "Spanish History" (6:306). For other commentary by Azorín on El Greco, the Castilian landscape, and the role the Generation of 1898 played in popularizing the painter's work, see "El color" (6:239) and "Generaciones de escritores" (9:1142).

5. As I have shown (note 1, above), Cossío always credited the Romantics with bringing El Greco to the attention of Europeans on the vanguard cultural fringe. Elsewhere in his book, he writes that the Romantic restitution of El Greco was carried to its conclusion by the "contemporary neo-romanticism that we call modernism" (1:535). Cf. Cossío (December 1907, 379).

6. Baroja also wrote that El Greco's neurasthenic imagination was the same ember that smoldered in the canvases of Santiago Rusiñol (8:883).

7. It is worth noting that the revalorization of Góngora clearly began at a much earlier date than the famous homage to commemorate the tercentenary of his death (23 May 1627) organized by the Generation of 1927 which adopted the poet as an emblem of the new direction they hoped to give Spanish poetry.

8. Given Azorín's personal interest in the fleeting nature of time and an entire career devoted to literary experiments in its apprehension, it is not surprising that he would find in Góngora and El Greco spirits kindred to his own. In the first pages of his essay "*Diario de un enfermo*, de Azorín: El momento y la sensación," Laureano Bonet also discusses parallels between El Greco and Góngora (1990, 81–84).

9. Góngora was very much aware of the relationship between the sister arts of painting and poetry. Emilie Bergmann studied his literary ekphrases in "Painting in

Poetry: Góngora's Ekphrasis" where she writes that, "Through language Góngora is able to elaborate upon the possible ambiguities of the visual image as a symbol," always choosing to bifurcate the relationship between visual and literary symbols and their meaning(s) (1976, 248).

10. Cf. Cossío's "El arte en Toledo" where he notes El Greco's "clear understanding of the effect of complementary colors and of the oozing of some into others" (1925, 282). Without expressly saying so, in the same essay, Cossío even has El Greco anticipating the "divisionist" (pointillist) technique of Seurat and Signac.

11. First published in the May 1921 issue of *Hermes*; reproduced in the exhib. cat. *Darío de Regoyos* (55).

12. See Lafuente Ferrari (1950, 55) and Joaquín de la Puente (1976, 74 and 233 n. 16).

13. Muther quoted in Cossío (1907, 377). The original is from *Geschichte der Malerei im Neunzehnten Jahrundert* (1893, 2:508). A similar notion was taken up by José Ortega y Gasset who maintained that, while his official duties as court painter to Felipe IV obliged Velázquez to paint nobility, popes, military heroes and the like, what really interested him was the seemingly inconsequential business of painting light and atmosphere (1:200).

14. The book subsequently was translated into English (London: Methuen) and German (Berlin: Photographische Gesellschaft) in 1906. Ironically, a Spanish edition never appeared. Art historians continue to recognize the importance of Beruete's study: Lafuente Ferrari calls the book "un libro magistral" (exhib. cat. *A. de Beruete* 9), while Calvo Serraller writes that Beruete's most important contribution was to show Spaniards how to "see" Velázquez, a skill fundamental to appreciating the modernity of his painting (exhib. cat. *A. de Beruete* 34).

15. There is something to be said in support of Ritter's argument. Cossío wrote that El Greco's color palette of silver-violet tones was the result of his having settled in Castile, and that one of El Greco's most patent influences on Velázquez was his distinctive, gray-based palette (1:512). In descriptions of his native Alicante, Azorín used the same gray color scheme that Ritter described as endemic to the work of Velázquez and Beruete, to which Azorín would often add the refrain "el gris es mi elemento."

16. See Pena (1982, 66) and her essay in the exhib. cat. *Aureliano de Beruete* (18). She supports her views by pointing out that although Beruete's interest in luminous atmospheric effects stemmed from his study of Velázquez, impressionist technique did not surface in his own painting until 1905–6. On the following page, however, Pena appears to reverse herself when she observes that Velázquez is "of essential importance to understanding French pre-Impressionism" (1982, 93, 94).

17. Lafuente Ferrari maintains that, rather than Sorolla, it was the mature landscapes of Beruete—marked by a warmer, more colorful palette, an abbreviated, unblended brushstroke, and vibrating atmospheric effects—that demonstrate an ideal synthesis of Velazquean technique and the intoxication with light characteristic of Impressionist painting (1957, 278).

18. For a complete chronology of Ortega's writing, lecturing, and publication on Velázquez, see Lafuente Ferrari (1970, 154 n. 2).

19. Ortega frequently associated the fortunes of Velázquez with those of the Impressionist painters. Cf. his 1954 "Introducción a Velázquez": "In 1870 the French Impressionists, the 'plein air' painters, in turn influenced by the English, elevated the fame of our painter to its zenith. But the inverse also occured: about 1920 Impressionism waned, and with it, the triumph of Velázquez" (8:619).

20. Cf. Cossío who wrote that the contemporaneity of El Greco and Velázquez was embodied in their "transposing [to canvas] the purely individual, the contemporary . . ." (1907, 377).

21. Given his personal preferences for the trivial and the everyday, rather than the heroic or historically significant, it is not surprising that Azorín would have a deep appreciation for Velázquez. Ortega's interpretation of Velázquez coincides with his appraisal of Azorín's style which he thought was determined by a taste for "los primores de lo vulgar" [exquisite vulgarity of the commonplace].

22. In *Meditaciones del Quijote*, Ortega observed that "Velázquez seeks out the impression of things. The impression is formless and accentuates the material substance—satin, velvet, canvas, wood, organic protoplasm—from which things are made" (1:387).

23. César Graña noted the pleasure Impressionists took in the suspenseful and intriguing possibilities latent in the "indirection" of vision, as well as the apprehension of a subject in a moment of "candid camera" surprise (92). Unlike the objective eye of a camera which encompasses all that it "sees," Velázquez was the first to understand that a painter's eye could be selective, even indifferent, to what it perceived: therein his "asombrosa anticipación a su tiempo" (Lafuente 1970, 214).

24. Nina Mallory dates the inception of "impressionist" technique in Velázquez's painting to after the first trip he made to Italy (1629–30). On his return to Spain, Velázquez began to portray "what he saw in terms of the impression it made in the viewer's eye, and not its tactile substance" (144). According to Mallory, Velázquez's experiments with impressionist technique culminate in his portraits of palace fools, dwarfs, and idiots because it was with this "base" subject matter that he felt most unencumbered by self-censorship and other deterrents imposed by the restraints of convention (153).

25. As an indication of how preferences change within the art-historical canon, it is worth noting that, although he mentions *Las Meninas* and *Las Hilanderas* as masterpieces of the highest order, in an 1885 article titled "Los cuadros más importantes del Museo del Prado," Cossío maintained that should the museum visitor have no time to see anything else, she should make it a point to view *La rendición de Breda*, Velázquez's most famous painting (in *BILE*, 15 October 1885:301–3).

26. Gaya Nuño (1974, 2); S. Brown (1958, 204). On the Impressionism of the Villa Medici landscapes, also see Ortega (8:645) and Rodríguez Alcalde (21); Pantorba observed that both paintings suggest "a marvelous anticipation of 'Impressionism' " (19).

27. In the opinion of Spanish art critics, Velázquez and either Goya or El Greco, depending on the personal views of the individual, were "Impressionist" painters because they considered visuality of foremost importance and continually explored solutions to the "problem of vision in their painting" (Sánchez Marín 1968a, 326). Elizabeth Tufts goes so far as to suggest that Manet's still-life paint-

ings were influenced by Luis Meléndez, the foremost still-life painter in eighteenth-century Spain (51).

28. The citation is from de la Encina's article "El arte de Ignacio Zuloaga" published in an unpaginated issue of *Hermes* for August 1917. Cf. Christian Brinton: "He [Zuloaga] continues unbroken the aristocratic dignity of Velázquez, the picaresque note which few Peninsular painters have been without, and the restless diabolism of Goya" (1909, 32).

Part I, Chapter 3

1. See Weinsheimer (1990, 149, 142, 147, 138). As did T. S. Eliot in the twentieth century, Giner de los Ríos observed that as a generation reaches maturity it establishes a style consonant with its own historical moment, supplanting the "classics" of the immediate past with its own. With time, these, too, will become "classics" in the eyes of future generations (3:236).

2. See especially Fox's "Azorín y la coherencia (Ideología, política y crítica literaria)" (1988, 65–93). In his copy of the Catalonian art critic Torres-García's *Notes*, Azorín bracketed a passage that corroborated his own ideas on national continuity and coherence: "And it's not everyone who can be a genius, creator, inventor of new forms and manners of working. In the end, according to what Xenius said, the genius is the one who perpetuates tradition" (86–87).

3. Juan de la Cierva (1864–1938), mayor of Madrid, also held ministerial posts in various governments, notably as Ministro de Gobernación (Interior) under Maura (1907–9). Azorín was most adulatory of de la Cierva in *La obra de un ministro* (1910) and *Un discurso de La Cierva* (1914), both collected in vol. 3 of the *Obras Completas*.

4. Azorín's position comes close to that of Unamuno who, in 1906, abandoned his notion of "Europeanizing" Spain and proposed, instead, that Spaniards "Hispanize" Europe. Cf. Unamuno's "Sobre la europeización" in vol. 4 of the *Obras Completas*.

5. Azorín continued to subscribe to this notion throughout his life. In *Sintiendo a España*, a collection of stories written during the Civil War and published in 1942, the painter-protagonist Gaspar Salgado pays a visit to his physician asking that his "gland" regulating patriotism and historical consciousness be removed. The doctor reminds him that should he fulfill his wishes, Salgado would no longer feel the need to relate the present to the past, and would remain indifferent to improving the Spanish circumstance because, as the doctor puts it, "there is no real moral progress which matters without that close link to tradition" (6:680).

6. As early as 1907 Azorín remarked that concomitant with the Generation's project of reacquainting itself with authentic Spanish life and landscape, was an "eagerness to renew, to expand the language" by unearthing and returning to circulation a *castizo* lexicon that had lain dormant far too long (*PCQ* 24).

7. Azorín's literary salvage operation was most active after 1910: *Lecturas españolas* (1912); *Clásicos y modernos* (1913); *Los valores literarios* (1914); *Al margen de los clásicos* (1915). As Inman Fox reminds us, Azorín was also instrumental, through his popular and widely read book reviews and literary essays, in bringing to public at-tention the "Clásicos Castellanos" series which began to issue the first popular and reasonably priced editions of classical Spanish literature in 1910 (1988, 141).

8. That Azorín was familiar with Cossío's publications on El Greco is evident in his references to the fundamental essay from 1897, cited in "La cuestión *Greco*" (*PCQ* 80) and "El tricentenario del Greco" (2:842).

9. Elsewhere in the *Memorias*, Azorín again remarks that, "In addition to a preference for the unadorned in literature, we have to mention X's inclinations in the visual arts. He began, many years ago, by admiring certain painters: El Greco, for example, was one of his favorites. I don't believe that's true now" (8:585).

10. The review of *Contemporary Review* was published in *La Lectura*, 1914.2 (103–4). More recently, Laureano Bonet has suggested that "El Greco" and "Toledo" were magic words that appealed to Azorín, Baroja, and Valle-Inclán because they identified in the painter's alleged "neurosis," his tortured representation of the human figure, and his violent, eye-catching use of color, "spiritual and ideological states of the Generation of '98: melancholy and pessimism; meditation on the decadence of Spain . . ." (1987, 149–50).

11. Also from *Castilla* is the pensive gentleman of "Una ciudad y un balcón" whose pale, extenuated visage, finished off by a small, pointed, gray beard, and eyes veiled with profound sadness, Fox again suggests Azorín lifted from El Greco's *Caballero de la mano al pecho* (1991, 139 n. 10).

12. Although in the Campos interviews, Azorín states that the trip occurred in 1901, Fox dates it to December 1900 (1968, 205 n. 91). In "Luna en Toledo" (chap. 24 of *Madrid*), Azorín also dates the trip to December 1900, and describes not only the episode of the child's coffin, but also his finding in the street-level window grating of a "decrepit manor house . . . a very old, small book among the potsherds and rags . . . the text began thus: 'It's better to avoid sinning than to flee death' . . ." (6:244). Baroja probably referred to the same incident in *Camino de perfección* when Fernando Ossorio comes upon some pages of Ignacio Loyola among the trash caught in the window grates of an old mansion in Toledo. Baroja recounts his version of the same trip to Toledo in *Desde la última vuelta del camino* (543–44).

13. As Lafuente Ferrari points out, the designation "modernista" and "impresionista" was applied indiscriminately in the late nineteenth and early twentieth centuries to anything or anyone that could be associated with innovation and the modern (1950, 117). Baroja's labeling Zuloaga a "pintor impresionista" is understandable given the period of time in which it was made, and Zuloaga's friendship with the Barcelona *modernistas* Utrillo, Rusiñol, and Casas. Cf. Ortega's 1911 meditation on Zuloaga's painting *Gregorio, el botero*: ". . . Zuloaga is a realist, a colorist, an impressionist. Besides, he assimilates the tradition of our classics: Greco, Velázquez, Goya. And as for classical tradition, he is somewhat romantic" (1:537).

14. Baroja's visit to Toledo, including the viewing of *El entierro* at night in the company of Burell, is recounted in *Exposición-Homenaje a Ricardo Baroja* (29). In addition to Lafuente Ferrari's version of Rusiñol's account, Zuloaga's whimsical excursion to Toledo was also told by Ramiro de Maeztu in "Nueva pintura," where Rusiñol's torchlight and Baroja's candles are replaced by matches

(1903, 17). Cf. Valdivieso (exhib. cat. *Centro y periferia* 92).

15. Laureano Bonet sees Valle-Inclán's *esperpento* as originating within the "modernist entrails" of El Greco's expressionistic style, broken lines, and arbitrary but symbolic use of color. Similarly, he considers the topic of El Greco and Toledo in *La lámpara maravillosa* as emblematic of Spanish Modernism, pointing out that Santiago Rusiñol considered El Greco the "home modernista de son temps" (1987, 141, 148, 140).

16. The trick of creating a substitute to refract the voice of the real author is an old one and often serves as a point of departure for constructing a narration *en abyme* (Dällenbach 76); the structure of *Diario*, however, is not so much catoptric as it is, perhaps, of Martínez Ruiz attempting to show versatility as a writer in response to early criticism of his narrative style.

17. In "La creación de Toledo," published in *La Prensa* of Buenos Aires on 16 January 1927, Azorín returns to his oft-repeated theory that landscape is created by artists of the pen and brush, attributing the notion to Balzac and to an anonymous "English writer." He noted that "Zorrilla, Bécquer, Galdós, Baroja, and among the foreigners, Gautier, Barrès and others, contributed to the creation of Toledo." As a point of curiosity, Azorín is often credited with coining the adage, "Africa begins at the Pyrenees." Yet Barrès made the following remark about Spain in *Du sang*: "It's Africa: Spain instills in the soul a sudden burning like a red pepper in your mouth" (209). Azorín owned and annotated a 1909 edition of this monograph, as well as Rafaëlli's *Mes promenades* in which Barrès's observation is also quoted (115). In "La pintura española juzgada en el extranjero," Angel Ganivet attributes the quip "El Africa empieza en los Pirineos" to Dumas (1:997–98).

18. Cf. Marguerite Rand, who noted that "one should not look for a relationship between Azorín and El Greco in their use of color, but in the interpretation of a spiritual essence" (394).

19. As early as his 1885 essay "La pintura española," Cossío argued that to qualify as a "Spanish painter," one did not necessarily have to be born in Spain. Rather, the criterion was to demonstrate a "national character" in the finished product: "Origins are influential and, above all, the ambience and environment in which the artist is formed . . ." (375). The determinist Barrès speculated that El Greco's childhood, spent in the Eastern, Byzantine milieu of his native Crete, accounted for his empathy with the Catholic and Moorish population of Toledo. He suggested that perhaps because El Greco carried within his psyche a spiritual familiarity with Islam, he was drawn to Toledo in the first place, "predestined" by circumstance to become the interpreter par excellence of its semitic atmosphere (102).

20. In his article "Impresionismo español," Camón Aznar speculates whether it might have been El Greco's "spirited treatment of the brushstroke, this tenuousness of pictorial material" that determined his "synthetic and tremulous" brushstrokes, leading Pacheco to observe, "Who would believe that Domenico Greco brought the paints back and retouched the pigment time and again in order to leave the colors separate and unblended and to produce those striking blotches in order to affect boldness?" Aznar goes on to trace Velázquez's "diaphanous

manner and unblended brushstroke" to the precedent set by El Greco (1955, 37–38).

21. Antonio Risco points out that in his desire to convey visual impressions with greatest fidelity, Azorín often began by eliminating, like an Impressionist painter, "all definite modeling or substantive weight." He preferred, instead, to indicate objects through the use of "daubs, sketches, brushstrokes, like those in a painting by Aureliano de Beruete or Darío de Regoyos" (1980, 114). I would also add the name of the "proto-Impressionist" El Greco to this roster of painters emulated by Azorín.

22. James Abbott writes that Azorín maintained a "determinist vision" until at least 1946 (1963, 48). Cf. the following passage from *El caballero inactual* (1928): "Not to exaggerate the dependence of men upon the environment; but to seek in the land, the habitat, the air, the landscape, the soul of the person studied" (5:79); also "De Unamuno a Ruskin" of 1926: "As negligibly determinist as we might be, we must always recognize that to understand a personality, familiarity with the environment around it is indispensable" (24).

23. The tendency of the Castilian to general apathy and inertia, which could only be roused momentarily into violent enthusiasm or reaction before subsiding just as quickly into torpid somnolescence, was also noted by Unamuno in *En torno al casticismo* (1:859–60). In *Idearium español* Angel Ganivet criticized the same irrational aspect of the Castilian personality: "Nothing interests it, ordinarily nothing moves it; but suddenly, an *idée fixe*, not being able to reconcile itself with others, produces an uncontrollable drive" (1:289).

24. It would not be out of place to recall here Unamuno's "El Cristo de Velázquez" and Manuel Machado's ekphrastic poems on paintings by Velázquez in *Apolo. Teatro pictórico* and the "Museo" section of *Alma*.

25. The essays, written in 1913, are reproduced in *Pintar como querer*. "Cuestiones de actualidad" also devotes some commentary to Jean-François Rafaëlli's *Mes promenades au Musée du Louvre* (Paris, 1913), which includes discussion of paintings by Velázquez housed in the Paris museum.

26. In his review Azorín renders quotations from the French into Spanish. Aman-Jean's original reads as follows: "L'Espagne plus encore que tout autre pays méditerranéen est sans couleur" (122). "Au demeurant, on ne saurait soutenir que Velázquez soit parmi les grands coloristes: Rembrandt, Delacroix, Watteau. Il n'est pas de cette famille" (123). While traveling in French North Africa, Eugène Fromentin made a similar observation that "the color of this semitropical region was essentially gray" (quoted in Schapiro 129).

27. In "El Museo y Velázquez" Azorín questioned Aman-Jean's implication that Spanish painters were conditioned by environmental factors to eschew color by pointing out that "our marvelous landscapist Beruete," a Spaniard no different from Velázquez, was, indeed, a great colorist (*PCQ* 105). Azorín was clearly thinking of the artist's last phase, distinguished by a markedly impressionistic color palette and technique.

28. The quotation is from "La poesía de Castilla" (2:481–83). Cf. "Un pequeño homenaje: los jardines" where Azorín nearly duplicates Aman-Jean's description of the Infanta Margarita. Referring to women at the seventeenth-century Spanish court, Azorín evokes "ladies with

blue, somewhat distracted and melancholy eyes, these women who carry a rose or a fine linen handkerchief in their hand" (7:152). Aman-Jean also relates the anecdote, repeated by Azorín, although I cannot recall where, of the cash-strapped household of Felipe IV: the pastry chef refused to supply the Queen with sweetmeats, obliging her to borrow money for her indulgences from court buffoons; the Infanta was once served rotten capon; and Velázquez, who had been appointed chief of staff to the royal household, was driven to distraction by constant struggles to procure funds with which to pay the palace staff (139).

29. The commentary on deterioration of pigment and the greater freshness of painting on wood panels, rather than on canvas, is from "Montañas de Carigó" (*PQ* 47); the extended metaphor on navigating the oceans of color, in "Vázquez Díaz" (*Memorias Inmemoriales* 8:447).

30. As is the case with Aman-Jean's book, Azorín translates Rafaëlli's French into Spanish. The original is as follows: "Je ne peux definir son dessein. Il ne se formule jamais, ni sa manière de composer; mais il est le coloriste plus fameux que je connaisse . . ." (116).

31. The original French that Azorín paraphrases in Spanish is as follows: "Il faut dire aussi qu'il n'est pas nécessaire de *colorier* beaucoup pour faire oeuvre de grand coloriste. Il y a des hommes, témoin Velásquez [sic], qui colorent à merveille avec les couleurs plus tristes. Du noir, du gris, du brun, du blanc teinté de bitume, que de chefs-d'oeuvre n'a-t-on pas exécutés avec ses quelques notes un peu sourdes!" (647)

32. The question whether Spanish painters were colorists or not also involved Goya. Azorín was familiar with Paul Valéry's *Pièces sur l'art* since he defended Goya against Valéry's assertion that the Spanish painter was among the "pintores decolorados." Following arguments made by Fromentin, Rafaëlli, and Aman-Jean, Azorín contended that Goya attained the pinnacle of chromaticity precisely at the moment when experience counseled him to use pigment with greatest restraint (5:847).

33. Cf. "La invasión extranjera" published in *ABC* on 23 May 1910; I quote from *Pintar como querer* (47).

34. Since Azorín knew Aureliano de Beruete's book on Velázquez, he must have been aware that Beruete reattributed *La fuente de los Tritones* to Velázquez's son-in-law, Juan Bautista del Mazo (1906, 33 n. 1). The attribution was accepted immediately by art historians; Azorín, however, in whose writing *La fuente* played such a vital role precisely as a painting by Velázquez, apparently found it convenient to ignore the reassignment of authorship to del Mazo. Today the painting is again attributed to Velázquez.

35. Azorín's reference to *La fuente de los Tritones* also appears in "Un hidalgo," a chapter from *Los pueblos* (Valverde 1982, 203–4). Elsewhere Azorín writes that the Spanish *caballero*, often impoverished but always maintaining his stiff upper lip in the face of adversity, is the best literary synthesis of the "essence of Castile" ("Lazarillo de Tormes" in Fox 1991, 294).

36. "Las sombrereras," from *España* (1909), although re-creating the workshop of milliners rather than spinners, compares the scattering about of silk and linen cloth, and other tools of the trade, to the scene depicted by Velázquez in *Las Hilanderas* (2:446). Azorín evokes *The Spinners* again in "Un hidalgo" where weavers of cotton cloth have a workshop near the *hidalgo's* home: "You can hear the rhythmic sound . . . the weavers make with their spin-

ning wheels . . . you've seen these wheels in Velázquez's painting" (Fox 1991, 249–50).

37. The essay was first published on 10 November 1917. It was subsequently included in the *Obras completas* (*La cabeza de Castilla* 9:934) and reprinted in *Ni sí, ni no* (204–7). In *Sintiendo a España*, written in Paris during the Spanish Civil War, Azorín imagined how it might feel to be able to meditate once again "in front of that small, panelled door that you see in the background of Velázquez's *Las Meninas*" (6:708).

38. In similar fashion, Azorín's story "El espejo del fondo" transposes the huge, ornate mirror that still hangs today on the back wall of Lhardy's confectionary to the seventeenth century, imagining Quevedo, his friend Adán de la Parra, don Ferrand, the brother of Carlos I, the poet Cristóbal de Castillejo, Don Juan de Austria, and Cervantes, all gathered in the main dining room of Lhardy's for afternoon pastry while "the mirror at the back reflects their images" (6:265).

39. Without including dates, Svetlana Alpers mentions that Van Eyck's portrait of Arnolfini had, at one time, hung at the Spanish court (1983, 31). I assume the painting left Spain centuries before Azorín was born.

40. Azorín owned a copy of Hourticq's *Le Musée du Louvre* (Hachette, 1921) in which Massys's *Le Banquier et sa femme* is described (83). J. Laurent also photographed a painting in the Prado Museum by Marinus de Reymerswale titled *El cambista y su mujer* (177). Either of the two paintings may have been the source for Azorín's vivid description in *La isla sin aurora* of an old man and his wife lovingly engaged in the most "delicate operation" of weighing gold coins (7:80–81). Although Azorín visited Paris in 1905, and again in 1918, he never set foot in the Louvre until his exile to Paris during the Spanish Civil War. In his memoirs, however, he does say that before actually visiting the museum, he knew its contents quite well: "por libros, fotografías, por postales, por reproducciones varias, conocía yo estas obras" (5:853). For discussion of Memling and Van Eyck, see Dällenbach (10–11); for Petrus Christus, see Risco (1980, 69 n. 26), Maravall (1987, 109), and Upton (32–34).

41. Cf. Maravall (1987, 80–82), Ortega (8:486–87) and Searle (248).

42. The inclusion of a staircase in any work of art suggested to Azorín the implied portrayal of diachronicity (successive movement) frozen within the synchronicity (spatiality) of a painting. Cf. "Lo inexpresable" where he describes just such an instant with a visual art simile: "Todo ha durado un instante como un instante dura la subida de los dos o tres escalones en el cuadro de Rembrandt *El buen samaritano*" [6:820; It all lasted but an instant, just like climbing the two or three steps in Rembrandt's *The Good Samaritan* lasts only an instant].

43. Elizabeth Ermarth observes that the postmodern subversion of chronology began with the Moderns' "refusal to slip into the past tense, the tense of history and of traditional narrative" (72). Azorín's preference for the present perfect not only served his personal psychological needs, but underscores his use of decidedly modern stylistic techniques.

44. Azorín occasionally returned to the sister arts debate. In *Ante las candilejas* he pointed out that generic boundaries could only be sustained while a kind of superstition had it that painting could not breach the frontiers

of literature, or sculpture those of painting. Only with the Romantic reaction to Neo-classical literary theory were these limitations thoroughly disregarded, enabling literary production to reach the level of complexity and intensity it achieved in modern times (9:29). On the other hand, in *Con permiso de los Cervantistas,* Azorín exclaims: "What can we do but resign ourselves to the teachings of the *Laocoön*?" (9:344). Cf. "Dos peligros" (*EC* 134).

45. Joseph Frank was the first to study the subversion of narrative linearity via spatializing effects in his groundbreaking essay "Spatial Form in Modern Literature" (1945). Although unrelated to the intrusion of verbally generated works of art into literature, similar displacements of narrative linearity were explored by Gérard Genette who classified the techniques that might induce conflict between story (*histoire*) and the manner in which that story is told (*discours*) in *Narrative Discourse: An Essay in Method* (French edition, 1972).

46. Enrique Lafuente Ferrari noted that one of Velázquez's greatest achievements was to "realize in painting, a spatial art, the capturing of time" (1970, 131). Particularly suggestive in terms of the aesthetic inclinations and artistic techniques preferred by Velázquez and Azorín, see Wendy Steiner who describes literary ekphrasis as a topos "in which poetry is to imitate the visual arts by stopping time, or more precisely, by referring to an action through a still moment that implies it" (1982, 41).

47. Another favorite painting of Azorín's was Rembrandt's *The Evangelist Matthew,* most likely because he saw in the picture another instance in which an artist arrested his subject in motion: "he saw the subject with pen raised . . . abstracted, thinking about what he was going to write" (8:352).

48. The citation is from Fox (1991, 203). All further references to "La casa cerrada" are from Fox's 1991 edition of *Castilla* and will be included parenthetically in the text.

49. The return to a closed or abandoned home is a symbol Azorín habitually used to represent "time capsule" effects. "La lucecita roja" (*Castilla*), "La casa vieja," and "La casa abandonada" (*Leyendo a los clásicos*) recapitulate similar themes. Murray Krieger has remarked that circular structure narratives which find their ends in their beginnings are "spots of time" demonstrating a conflation of time and space (quoted in Kestner 1978, 77). Inman Fox proposes that in his battle against the clock, Azorín conflates time and space purposefully in order to nullify the destructive power of time and to create a new reality in which past and present coexist (1988, 154).

50. Mary Ann Caws mentions that placing a protagonist or an action at an unusual height, or "enclosed in a noticeable set of limits and openings," contributes to the creation of a framing effect (22). In his "Meditación del Marco," Ortega argues that the window frame as a compositional structure is similar to a picture frame since both isolate their contents from the reality that surrounds them, moving what is seen through either picture or window frame closer toward the aesthetic-ideal (2:311).

51. Cf. Caws (262, 28–29) on the metonymic function of an included observer and the framing technique of "seeing an observer see." Viola Hopkins suggests that it is at moments where sight (in Azorín's case, the lack thereof) merges with insight (the reader's awareness of Azorín's visual games as fundamental elements of plot, theme, and structure) that the framing device is used to

greatest effect (563). Azorín used a similar device in "El hijo y la madre" where the child's blindness is revealed only through insinuation, allowing the reader to draw her own conclusions at any given moment of the text (*PQ* 109–12).

52. Nina Ayala Mallory identifies the two paintings as copies of Rubens's *Minerva y Aracne* and Jordaens's *Apolo y Marsias* (162). Eric Rabkin notes the modernist use of parataxis to promote a "dialectic between the synchronic and the diachronic aspects of reading to retrieve a coherent value system . . ." (270). Although *Las Meninas* represents three generations of painters diachronically, the spectator apprehends the painting synchronically as she looks at the picture. Velázquez's inclusion of works by contemporary artists in *Las Meninas* leads the intertextuality and perspective embedding in the painting to even greater depths, taking the number of framed pictures in the masterwork to an unprecedented level of complication.

53. In fact the mirror may not be reflecting the King and Queen in the flesh at all, but their portraits Velázquez is painting on the angled canvas within *Las Meninas.* Cf. Buero Vallejo (1992, 3).

54. The technique of evoking visual reality through a pattern of questions and answers was also used by Antonio Machado in "A José María Palacio" (*Campos de Castilla*). The poet, like Azorín, employs the future of probability to confirm visual memory of place: "Do the old elm trees have any new leaves? / Even the acacias must still be bare. . . . / Are the brambles flowering / among the grey rocks? . . . . / The storks will have already been arriving on the belfries" (187).

Quintilian and later rhetoricians advised the use of verbs of perception as a means to achieve *enargeia;* that is, to describe something so vividly that the image is recreated in all its volume and solidity before the eyes of a reader or listener to produce the illusion of an eyewitness account (Bergmann 1976, 248). *Enargeia* is also an important feature of the ekphrastic topos (Krieger 1992, 68, 126). Elizabeth Esrock argues that the engagement of fictional characters in visual perception encourages visualization on the part of readers (183).

55. For Bal on blindness and dual focalization, see 1991, 290, 408 n. 49, 425–26 n. 30.

56. Foucault attributes this dynamics to the impossibility of portraying both artist and King as having equal importance in the same painting. As the intended subject of *Las Meninas* is elided, "representation freed finally from the relation that was impeding it, can offer itself as representation in its pure form" (16). Svetlana Alpers proposes an ideological interpretation, suggesting that "Velázquez sees himself as part of the very court he sees through" (1983, 40).

57. In his study of Ortega's identifying Velázquez as exemplary of the "modern," Thomas Mermall argues that what concerned Ortega most were the "historical variations of the subject as creator of meaning" (240). In "La casa cerrada" Azorín appears to suggest a comparable idea: he who controls the verbal sign has the capacity not only to create meaning, but to create meaningful visual reality through language alone. Eric Rabkin adds that the tendency to spatialize narrative—as does literary ekphrasis—is characteristic of the modern imperative to revitalize literary forms (270). In the paragonal struggle be-

tween the verbal and the visual arts, ultimately it is the verbal art that implodes the still, circular movement of literary ekphrases, framing them within the boundaries of the narrative's dominant, linear progression.

Part I, Chapter 4

1. These photographs, unfortunately, did not accompany the essays when they were reprinted in the *Obras Completas*. To appreciate the full impact of Azorín's illustrated writing on the visual arts, one must go to the original newspaper sources.

2. Rémy Saisselin noted that Diderot's *Salons* were not art criticism at all, "but literature inspired by paintings" (152). This often proves to be true in Azorín's writing on art, artists, and museums in which the ostensible subject often serves as a point of departure for literary meditations. Bryson, however, points out that after 1769, Diderot began to express increasing interest in paintings that resisted "translation into discourse" (1981, 200).

3. Azorín refers here to the eighteenth-century French pastel artist Maurice Quentin de Latour (1704–1788), and alludes to the delicate, impermanent nature of the medium.

4. Published in *La Prensa*, 20 September 1931.

5. "Dos escenas del tiempo," published in *La Prensa*, 22 October 1933.

6. From "La pintura de Zuloaga" published in *ABC*, 27 March 1912. Azorín was also one of the first to recognize—as did art historians decades later—that the painters comprising the so-called Impressionist movement were much too diverse to form a unified "school." Writing on nineteenth-century art, Azorín commented that after the Barbizon and Courbet "appears Eduardo Manet and the coterie of 'impressionists,' grouping in this way, as a whole, painters of different nuances. Here we have Claude Monet, the marvelous Degas, Pissarro, Sisley, Cézanne. Can we [i.e., Spaniards] count on a falange of artists like this one?" (7:243). Azorín may have borrowed the expression "falange" from Zola who referred to the young landscape Impressionists that he supported as a "nouvelle phalange" of painters (Adams 186).

7. In an essay on Martín Rico in *Madrid*, Azorín contradicted himself on this issue. Although he continued to write that landscape painting was a modern phenomenon, in the sense that it should be filtered through the subjective vision of the artist's personality, he concluded in this article that, "Neither Hobbema, nor Paul Bril, for example, have painted landscapes like a Claude Monet or a Daubigny" (6:293).

8. The quotation is from "Los pintores" published in *La Prensa*, 12 December 1940. Azorín's intuition regarding the importance of Paul, and his brother Matthew, Bril proved correct. Cf. Manuela Mena who recently studied the significance of the Bril brothers to the development of landscape painting in early sixteenth-century Europe (exhib. cat. *Paisajes del Prado* 151). In the same essay Azorín writes that "modern landscape in Spain began with Haes," and he refers to Haes's inaugural address at the Academy of Fine Arts which he says he'd read several times. In the address Haes himself referred to Paul Bril as important precursor (287–88).

9. Sir Kenneth Clark wrote that Ruisdael was "the greatest master of the natural vision before Constable" and that the East Anglian landscapists would take Ruisdael as their model (64). Camille Mauclair also indicated that the Impressionists considered Ruisdael an important precursor, and were especially interested in the blues of his horizons as well as the blue notes in his landscapes (16). For the influence of Ruisdael and Hobbema on the British landscapists, see Bazarov (63), Slive (13), and Walford (229 n. 63).

10. Elsewhere Azorín called Lawrence "one of the greatest English portraitists," and recounted an anecdote that Lawrence always told his students: the secret to good portraiture consisted of isolating the sitter's most essential feature; once this was accomplished, the rest would take care of itself (*LM* 158).

11. On Constable and Impressionism, see Bazarov (98); on the influence of Ruisdael and Hobbema on Constable, see Clark (147) and Paulson (1976, 253 and 1982, 126).

12. This notion was fully realized by the Impressionists in their mature work which, by repeating the same subject under a diversity of atmospheric conditions, intended to capture the concept of difference within sameness (Bermingham 148). In his history of nineteenth-century art, Aureliano de Beruete y Moret noted that Constable particularly influenced the Barbizon painters Rousseau, Troyon, Corot, Millet, and Daubigny (135–36).

13. Azorín noted that Pereda's landscapes were somewhat old-fashioned because they were reminiscent of the style, admirable though it was, of Hobbema and Ruysdael [sic] (6:301).

14. As late as *Sintiendo a España* (1941), Azorín observed the mutable yet permanent nature of clouds that "pass through the limpid sky of Castile, eternal in their fugacity" (6:756).

15. To underscore the significance of his annotations, on the back flap of the book, Azorín penciled in "nubes-Velázquez-46." One of the "fictional" characters in a short story from *Sintinedo a España*, happens to own "a little treatise in which blue pencil marks are seen on the pages that deal with clouds" (6:770–71).

16. When he needed to describe an overcast sky, Azorín did so with a visual art simile whose relatum he based on a Constable sky: "un cielo plomizo o un cielo aborregado. Como algunos del gran pintor de cielos: John Constable" [9:1299; a leaden or fleecy sky, like those done by the great painter of the atmosphere: John Constable]. On both Constable and Monet, see "Cervantes exagera" in *La Prensa*, 8 June 1941. In this essay Azorín, while praising Monet, insists that "Constable's clouds are without equal. Nobody has painted the sky like Constable."

17. Reprinted in *Los estudios de paisaje de Carlos de Haes, (1826–1889)*. Madrid: Dirección General de Bellas Artes, 1971. The catalogue is unpaginated.

18. Cf. Paulson (1982, 143) and Bazarov (100). Given Constable's near-obsession with giving time painterly expression, it is not surprising that his work so appealed to Azorín.

19. Of the Dutch masters, Jacob van Ruisdael especially influenced Turner's work (Bachrach 9). On Turner and the atmosphere, see Paulson (1982, 112) and Heffernan (1984, 147).

20. In this essay Azorín mistakenly describes *The Evening Star* as depicting a violent snowstorm at sea. It is a curious error since the painting was one of his favorite

landscapes and he describes it accurately on many occasions, most notably in the novels *Capricho* and *La isla sin aurora*, where the painting protagonizes several chapters. Turner did, however, paint several pictures of violent snowstorms on land and at sea. Perhaps Azorín was referring in this case to a canvas titled *Snowstorm—Steamboat off a Harbour's Mouth* (1842).

21. With the exception of "La soledad de un pintor" (1931), Azorín's writing on Turner was produced after the Louvre exhibition: "El poeta sin nombre" (1940); "Nada de particular" (1943); *Capricho* (1943); *La isla sin aurora* (1944). Cf. mention of *The Evening Star* in "La rara apuesta" (*Cada cosa en su sitio*).

22. Published in *La Prensa*, 18 February 1940. Here Azorín dates the exhibition to 1939 and incorrectly identifies the human figure in Turner's painting as female. He also neglects to mention the presence of what appears to be a frolicking dog which accompanies its master on the deserted beach at twilight.

23. Another of the protagonists in *Capricho* is a stage director who is especially fond of the visual arts. He surrounds himself with paintings by artists that exercise particular influence on his soul: Velázquez, Hobbema, the Impressionists (6:894). Azorín "identifies" these paintings as "a character who resembles a beggar or a philosopher, by Velázquez; a meadow and rivulet by Hobbema; the entrance to a village by Renoir; a street in Paris by Sisley; a rustic town by Pissarro" (6:934).

24. In his interviews with Jorge Campos (1958–59), Azorín commented on the futility of Proust's attempts to recover the past, observing that "it is always another past that is recuperated" (238). It is a past with a different twist, a different flavor, a different hue, and one that we view with changed sensibilities (125).

25. "La soledad de un pintor" appeared in *La Prensa*, 20 September 1931.

26. Azorín reported that he found nothing more pleasurable than reading books on art and artists written by painters. Among his favorites were Delacroix's *Journal* and Rafaëlli's *Les promenades d'un artiste au Musée du Louvre* (*PCQ* 122).

27. See Clarke (49) and Herbert, who also writes that the Dutch and British painters (e.g., Turner and Constable), influenced Delacroix and Courbert (1988, 282).

28. See Clarke (139), Walford (191), Herbert (1962, 19), and Rosenfeld (12). Avid students of artistic tradition, the Impressionists learned the Dutch manner from the Barbizon painters, as well as from the collection of Dutch Baroque painting at the Louvre (T. J. Clark 183).

29. A radical journalist and novelist of the realist school, Gustave Geffroy (1855–1926) became an intimate friend of the Impressionist painters and wrote some of the most significant and perceptive criticism on the history of Impressionism and the life and work of its painters. Azorín owned and annotated Geffroy's biography of Corot.

30. Corot first exhibited an outdoor study in 1849 and his first plein air oil in 1852 (Herbert 1962, 84). It is important to recall that, while Geffroy refers to Corot's rehabilitation of the French landscape (54), the truth of the matter is that the French countryside, including Fontainebleau Forest, was beginning to suffer the ravages of industrial and urban encroachment. The situation is not without parallels to that of the Impressionist landscape which, although it began as a chronicle of modern life, ended as an evasion of the contemporary despoliation of Nature.

31. On Corot, see Clarke (7); for Daubigny (Herbert 1962, 63, 106). Criticism of Daubigny's "impressionism" began in 1861 with Théophile Gautier who argued that while objects should be delineated by contour, the "landscapes of M. Daubigny offer little more than a juxtaposition of spots of color" (Herbert 1962, 48).

32. In his 1962 essay "Ante unas esculturas de Sebastián Miranda" (*ABC*, 13 February 1962), Azorín again misattributed the quip to Corot. Most likely he culled the anecdote from his copy of Henri Guerlin's *Le Paysage*: ". . . Corot eut du mal a trouver sa place; il cherchait son motif, elignait les yeux, penchait la tête. . . . Quant a Courbet, il s'était installé, n'importe où: 'Ou que je me mette, déclare-t-il, ça m'est égal; c'est toujours bon pourvu qu'on ait la nature sous les yeux' " [94–95; Corot had a hard time finding the right place . . . he looked for a motif, he shaded his eyes, hung his head. . . . As for Courbet, he would settle down anywhere: 'Wherever I am,' he said, 'makes no difference to me; it's all good as long as I have nature before my eyes.' "]

33. The Academie des Beaux-Arts was a branch of the state-sponsored Institut de France. It was abolished during the French Revolution but reinstated in 1816. The legends of who painted whose walls and where, have many avatars in Barbizon-Impressionist lore, and many are probably based on fact. Michael Clarke recounts that Corot and others decorated the walls of Souvent's Inn at Bougival with views of riverbanks and hills (117). Bouret tells the story of Corot and Daumier decorating the walls of Daubigny's home in Auvers in 1868 (169). Cf. Charles Yriarte for variations of the Daubigny story (402–3).

34. In Guerlin's *Le Paysage*, Azorín made the following annotations on the back jacket relative to Barbizon: "aire, luz (Daubigny)"; "cielo (Constable)"; "Millet (la mar)," with additional notes on Théodore Rousseau.

35. In "La experiencia del Louvre," another essay from *Españoles en París*, Azorín stated that he found Courbet, though not a great painter, enchanting, and repeated that Corot "no corresponde del todo—por su ausencia de color—a lo que de él esperaba" (5:856–57).

36. Martín Rico found that Corot's and Daubigny's slate gray tones reminded him of those used by Velázquez; Beruete agreed with critics who observed similarities between the "general tone" of landscapes painted by Velázquez and a certain poetical simplicity in those executed by Corot (1906, 34).

37. The chapter on Vázquez Díaz in *Memorias Inmemoriales* (1946), contains a variation on the same theme: "Our painter is bewitched by color; color and drawing are the same thing; I think that Diderot already made that observation" (8:436). In the 1940 "Los pintores" (*La Prensa*, 15 December 1940), Azorín speculates that color is what constitutes landscape painting and again refers to Diderot's *Essais sur la peinture* to support his position. In his personal copy of the *Essais* there are significant annotations in the chapter on color.

38. For Beruete's comments on Constable, Barbizon, and Rico, see "Martín Rico" (1908, 533–34). Rico commented in his memoirs that he had met Manet at the beginning of the French painter's career, and wrote that at the time Manet "was very keen on Spain and extraordinarily taken by our customs and physical types." Rico also

spent a summer painting with Pissarro at Varenne Saint Mar (112). On the importance of the senior Durand-Ruel to the success of the Barbizon painters, see Rewald (94). This man's son, Paul Durand-Ruel, took over the family business in 1865 and played a significant role in the success of the Impressionist painters (Denvir 77).

39. Paul H. Tucker notes that there were no paintings by Constable or Turner in the Louvre until 1873 and 1967, respectively (1995, 48). According to Tucker, Monet admired seventeenth-century Dutch painters as well as Watteau (1995, 37). T. J. Clark notes that many of Turner's paintings that are highly valued today (such as *The Evening Star*), were not brought up from London's National Gallery storage until 1906 (173).

40. Capturing the transient impression in paint has also been called the visual equivalent of Bergson's *instantané* (Berg 1992, 192).

41. See, for example, Giner de los Ríos "La pintura impresionista francesa" in *BILE* (31 March 1895) and Fernando Araujo's article "El impresionismo" (1909).

42. Baroja quoted in Azorín's *Obras Completas* (3:1320). In the same observation, Baroja made the questionable statement that Azorín had a much harder time of it than did the Impressionist painters because, while everyone presumes to voice an opinion on literature, art tends to be judged only by a "público culto."

43. Azorín found his nightmarish idea of time shared by Baudelaire, bracketing in his copy of the poet's *Journaux intimes*, the following passage: "We're always overwhelmed by the idea and the sensation of time. And there are only two ways to escape this nightmare, to forget it: pleasure and work. Pleasure wears us down. Work strengthens us. We must choose" (103). To lose himself in hedonistic pleasures was not an option for the ascetic Azorín who chose instead to submerge himself in his creative work, utilizing the literary medium to exorcise his personal demons.

44. So visual was Azorín's imagination that he even couched the passage of historical time within an aesthetic paradigm: "This moment in which a rose sparkles and perfumes, what is it in the eternity of time? A moment from 1600, or 1800, or 1900; a moment in which . . . a painting by Velázquez, or a scene by Goya, or a landscape by Beruete has just been hung . . . a moment in which human emotion is at its most delicate and intense, what do you represent between the two eternities that circumscribe and imprison us between the past and the future, the two eternities of past and present?" (3:200).

45. Evidently Azorín was engaged in reading about Degas at the time he wrote "Las sorpresas" since, in his copy of P. A. Lemoisne's *Degas*, he stuck a newspaper clipping from *Le Matin* which carried an item on the painter, "Chez le peintre Degas," dated 12 December 1922 (61). Azorín is somewhat incorrect regarding the miseries of the Barbizon painters. According to Steven Adams, the Barbizon painters began to receive official and critical recognition in the mid-1860s, and with it, a measure of financial success (183–84).

46. The art critic of *Le Figaro* was not Pierre, as Azorín wrote, but Albert Wolff (1835–1891), and the correct street on which the Paris Opera stood was rue Le Peletier.

47. From "Los pintores" published in *La Prensa*, 15 December 1940. This Renoir landscape is the same one Azorín mentions three years later in *Capricho* (6:934).

That Renoir was one of Azorín's favorite Impressionists is attested to by the newspaper clipping of an article by Georges Lecomte, "Beaux jours avec Auguste Renoir" (*Candide*, 12 February 1941), which Azorín stuck into his copy of Beaunier's *L'Art de regarder les tableaux*.

48. For many years it was commonplace to believe that the Impressionists excluded the human figure from their work. Azorín repeats this widely held notion again in "Los pintores" ("Sabida es la repugnancia de los impresionistas a pintar figuras en sus paisajes"), and again in the essay "El paisaje": "Sabido es también que los impresionistas franceses se impusieron la exclusión en el paisaje de toda figura humana" (6:216). This was certainly not the case while the Impressionists dedicated themselves to the painting of "modern life"; nor is it entirely true of their "pure" landscapes. The adage can be associated most accurately with Monet's series paintings in which the subject is not the ostensible wheatstack, poplar, or cathedral, but painting itself.

49. Paul H. Tucker points out that it was the church at Vetheuil that Monet was painting; because the gestation period seems excessively long, he suspects that Monet's statement is largely apocryphal (1995, 153).

Part I, Chapter 5

1. All further references to *La Voluntad* are to Fox's 1968 Castalia edition, and will be cited parenthetically in the text.

2. Martínez Ruiz's Impressionism, though much talked about, has been studied only superficially. See Pena (1982, 91), Risco (1980, 214–15), Sabater (50). Granell (191) and Abbott (1973, 143–45) both argue incorrectly that impressionist technique is limited to Martínez Ruiz's early work.

3. See Berg (1992, 228–29 and 1985, 43–44).

4. The terms "sensation" and "impression" were used interchangeably by contemporary critics in talking about Impressionist paintings. It is likely that Azorín would have known that Jules Castagnary (1830–1888), one of the few art critics who reacted positively to the first Impressionist exhibition in 1874, observed in his review that the painters "are Impressionists in the sense that they render not a landscape but the sensation produced by a landscape" (quoted in Vitz 75). Cf., more recently, Richard Shiff: "The impression, then, can be both a phenomenon of nature and of the artist's own being. Albert Boime notes . . . the importance of the parallel concept of the effect (*effet*). He states that the term *impression* was nearly interchangeable with *effect*" (1986, 70). Azorín's verbal recreation of the effect adjacent colors have upon each other is explained technically by Camille Mauclair: ". . . depending on the time of day; that is to say, the greater or less inclination of the sun's rays . . . the green of the leaves and the brown of tree trunks modify each other. It is necessary to study . . . the composition of the atmosphere that comes between the painter and his gaze" (30).

5. When he first embarked on his series paintings, Monet complained that the landscape changed so rapidly he needed many more canvases than the two he first envisioned would be adequate for morning and afternoon effects. In "Mayo," Azorín demonstrates similar awareness of the volatility of landscape perception: "Landscapes are

not the same during all four seasons. They're not the same in the morning as they are during the afternoon. During the morning they also change from hour to hour, from minute to minute" (*EL* 162–63).

6. Cf. also, *Libro de Levante*: ". . . changes in the delicate landscape dictated by the light of the moment; changes each minute; each minute, a new landscape; the shades of gray, different from what they were a moment before. Change according to the degree of dryness or moisture in the atmosphere . . ." (5:427).

7. It is curious that Azorín would have María and Lucien meet in the Luxembourg Gardens where traditionally Parisian *filles* would come to seek male admirers (see Corbin 209). The rue de Monçeau where the Duke lives is close to the Parc Monçeau, painted on several occasions by Monet in 1876 and again in 1878.

8. For my reading of María Fontán's "ekphrastic power" as an isolated visual art object, I am indebted to ideas Wendy Steiner elaborates in "The Causes of Effect: Edith Wharton and the Economics of Ekphrasis" (1989, 290). It is important to note that during the Impressionist era one way that women could pursue a profession was through painting, as the examples of Rosa Bonheur, Berthe Morisot, Mary Cassatt, Eva Gonzalès, and Suzanne Valadon prove so eloquently.

9. Yellow was also Azorín's favorite color. In an essay on the painter Daniel Vázquez Díaz (*ABC*, 6 June 1943), he wrote that of all the colors used by El Greco, "diluted yellow" was the one that took root in his own sensibility (*PCQ* 182). Yellow is likewise the favorite color of Víctor Albert, protagonist of the novel *El enfermo*, who is partial to yellow roses and on excursions to the countryside gathers yellow wildflowers (8:881–82). The eponymous heroine of *Salvadora de Olbena* prefers yellow roses, a preference the novel's omniscient narrator reveals he shares: "Among all [the roses] (that is our preference also), her favorites were the yellow ones" (7:618).

10. On Manet's mutilated painting, see Joel Issacson's essay "Manet and Spain" in the 1969 exhib. cat. *Manet and Spain. Prints and Drawings* (9–16); also Fried (91, 308).

11. On Zuloaga, Manet, and Velázquez, see Azorín's "Recuadro a Velázquez" (*ABC*, 10 December 1960). Georges Bataille observed that Manet copied the placement of his dead matador from a Velázquez canvas (50). The reference is to a painting known as *Orlando Muerto*, thought to have been painted by Velázquez, but since then attributed to an anonymous, seventeenth-century Italian painter. Manet probably saw this painting at the sale of the Pourtalès collection in early 1865, and it may have given him the idea to isolate and partially repaint the dead matador of his *Episode in a Bullfight* (Fried 11, 97; Wilson-Bareau 21).

12. The article "Ignacio Zuloaga" is marred by an unfortunate misprint that robs it of the analogy Azorín intended to make between Zuloaga and Manet: "El realismo de Zuloaga tiene, sin duda, la misma fórmula de Zuloaga [sic]" (read Manet). Published in *La Prensa* on 13 January 1946, the piece was accompanied by five reproductions of paintings by Zuloaga. Michael Fried's argument that the "notorious flatness" of Manet's pictures derives from his attempt to break the conventional "fourth wall" observed by previous generations of French painters in an effort to "make painting . . . *face* the beholder as never before"

(266), may account for the same flatness in Zuloaga's work for similar reasons.

13. Azorín was probably referring to Luis Egidio Meléndez (1716–1780), a leading still-life painter at the eighteenth-century Spanish court. For more on Azorín's literary references to Luis Meléndez, see Part II, chapter 4, below.

14. See Berg (1992, 228–29 and 1985, 43–44).

15. For Unamuno on natural dialogue, see Jurkevich (1992a, 571–73).

16. Cf. Abbott (1973, 136), Fox (1968, 30), and Risco (1980, 32) for remarks made in passing on Martínez Ruiz's fragmentary structures and literary impressionism.

17. On the Impressionist brushstroke, see Reutersvärd, Bally (113–14 n. 1), and Torgovnick (40). On the adaptation of Impressionism to literary stylistics, see Bally (120–22). For specifically Azorinian variations, Risco (1980, 133) and Ramsden (1966, 211).

18. The section in *La Voluntad* (Part II, Chapter 2) that describes the passing of black and white hearses is another example of the manner in which Martínez Ruiz assembles a visual tableau using color, light, sound, and movement to produce the "blurred" effect of teeming city life reminiscent of boulevard scenes crowded with pedestrians, coaches, and shops painted by Monet (*Boulevard des Capucines*, 1873) or Pissarro (*The Boulevard Montmartre on a Winter Morning*, 1897 and *Boulevard des Italiens; Morning, Sunlight*, 1897).

19. For my discussion of *phénoménisme* I am indebted to Roger Shattuck's stimulating essay, "Claude Monet: Approaching the Abyss" (1984).

20. Kearns observes that in perfecting the means by which to suggest the luminous atmosphere surrounding all objects, Monet created "decorative designs which represented the point of balance between visual truth and subjective interpretation . . ." (244–45). Antonio Fuster argues that from the moment Impressionism "does not propose to embellish nature, but simply to capture its essence and presence" at any given instant, it comes into close contact with expressionism (49). If we consider Impressionism as that which refers to how the individual eye perceives appearances here and now, and expressionism as that which is speculative and intuitive (Bally 52, 90), we would have to conclude that the painting of Monet and his colleagues was informed by both tendencies. This is also true of the impressionist novel which, because it tended to represent external reality in terms of "sensory and psychic experiences of an exceptional, exquisite, exotic, pathological, and unhealthy kind," also manifested expressionistic tendencies (Bally 134–35). Cf. Peter Selz who writes, "Impressionism itself was, of course, much more than mere rendition of optical appearances: it was a very subjective way of seeing and painting" (18). On Impressionism's shift from objective observation to subjective expression, see also Richard Shiff (1986, 87 n. 1).

21. Ernest Mach (1838–1916)—Austrian philosopher, scientist, and one of the leaders of modern positivism—felt that science should confine itself to the description of phenomena that could be perceived by the senses, a position Paul Vitz and Arnold Glimcher argue is "worthy of Monet" (86).

22. See especially Kern (passim) and Enguídanos (25) both of whom see, respectively, in Proust's and Martínez Ruiz's "angustia del tiempo" a telltale sign of Modernism.

23. It is interesting to note that, while Azorín consistently advocates the notion that modifying the mediocre, unhealthy environment in which the Spanish people, from the most "grosero, inintelectual" (80–81) to government representatives (113) live, in the end, he too, is reduced to passive mediocrity by the very environment he so criticized in the first two parts of the novel.

24. "El divino Van der Weyden," as Yuste calls him, surfaces again in a 1903 short story by Martínez Ruiz where the painter's style functions as the relatum of a visual arts simile: "A lo lejos viene lentamente un anciano de larga y vellida barba, con un pequeño gorro morado en la cabeza—como un cuadro de Wan der Weyden [sic]—vestido de rojo, abrigado con un corto gabán guarnecido de suaves pieles" (Valverde 1972, 211–12) [From far away an old man with a long, fleecy beard approaches, there's a purple cap on his head—as in a painting by Wan der Weyden [sic]—he's dressed in red and wears a short overcoat adorned with soft fur]. The painter in question is Rogier van der Weyden (1399/1400–1464).

25. As Inman Fox points out, the Marquesa de Leganés was the daughter of Ambrosio de Spínola, victor at the battle of Breda. Velázquez immortalized the general in the painting *The Surrender of Breda*. Van Dyck's portrait of Doña Policena Spínola is in the Prado Museum and in *El alma castellana*, Martínez Ruiz incorporated the portrait to the relatum of a visual art simile he used to describe the hairdresses of elegant, seventeenth-century court ladies: "Los hay [peinados] en graciosas bandas que cubren las orejas y sólo dejan ver las gruesas perlas de las arracadas, como en la divina marquesa de Leganés, de Van Dyck . . ." [1:603; There are hair styles in charming buns that cover the ears and only allow the heavy pearls of earrings to show, as in Van Dyck's portrait of the divine Marquesa de Leganés].

26. On the peacock as emblem of vanity and pride, see Schwartz (106). The library at the Casa-Museo Azorín in Monóvar has what appears to be a guide to the Prado Museum from which the first 114 pages are missing. In the margin of that guide, next to a reproduction of Velázquez's full-length portrait of a young Felipe IV, Azorín wrote "este" in blue pencil. There are also blue pencil markings beside Velázquez's portrait of Mariana of Austria, described in the guide as having "in her left hand a very large cambric handkerchief." In the same guide, Van Dyck's portrait of the Marquesa de Leganés is marked in red pencil and Marinus de Reymerswaele's painting of Saint Jerome is set off in blue.

27. Inman Fox points out that it is possible Martínez Ruiz meant to refer to the celebrated *Descendimiento* in the Prado by Rogier van der Weyden, rather than one by Metsys (1968, 235 n. 117).

28. Azorín continued to refer to Daumier throughout his writing. In *Los valores literarios* (1914), he not only mentions Daumier as a "satírico violento y elocuente," but also praises his oil paintings based on scenes from the *Quijote* (2:957). In "La íntima filosofía de un escultor," he compares the ability of Sebastián Miranda and the "great caricaturist Daumier" to zero in on the one physical feature that most dominates and defines the faces of their subjects (*PCQ* 145–46). Azorín's assessment regarding Daumier is supported by Focillon's observation that Daumier "draws . . . the little fact which means nothing . . . and projects it into absolute space where it acquires the

enormousness of a symbolic representation" (Vincent 212). Azorín also made a passing reference to Daumier's series of lithographs pillorying lawyers and judges in *París* (7:949). For Gavarni lithographs portraying "bailes locos, ruidosos," see Azorín's 1906 "Las mujeres" (*PCQ* 19).

29. Azorín toned down the vitriol in three of these ekphrastic portraits, republishing them with accompanying photographs in a "Retratos históricos" series on 16 June, 23 June, and 8 September 1906 in the illustrated magazine *Blanco y Negro* (cf. Lozano Marco 27, 42).

30. Regardless of the Schopenhauerian connotations evoked by Cronenburch's painting, its self-referential qualities most successfully restate in visual form the notion of perpetual replication that is constant throughout *La Voluntad*. Cf. "Todo . . . cambia en la apariencia y se repite a través de las edades . . . la humanidad es un círculo" (168; Everything . . . changes in appearance and repeats itself through the ages . . . humanity is a circle]. In the guide to the Prado Museum referred to in note 26 above, Martínez Ruiz placed four heavy blue hieroglyphs beside a description of Cronenburch's *Dama y niña*.

31. Inman Fox provides an excellent analysis of the historical and literary circumstances surrounding the *Electra* affair in "*Electra*, de Pérez Galdós (Historia, Literatura y la Polémica entre Martínez Ruiz y Maeztu)" (1988, 75–77).

Part II, Chapter 1

1. It is generally agreed that simile is either a developed metaphor, and therefore all metaphor an implicit comparison or simile (Ricoeur 25), or that metaphor is an abbreviated form of comparison (Henry 53).

2. In my study of simile in the work of Azorín, I prefer to employ terminology for the elements of comparison currently used by students of metaphor such as George A. Miller—A (the referent) is like B (the relatum)—rather than those coined by I. A. Richards, for whom Achilles would be the tenor and the lion a vehicle.

3. For the role of imagination and visualization in structures of similitude, see Black (225), Brogan (177), Colley (157 n. 3), and Kleiser (17).

4. On the extension of language and the expansion of literal reality through metaphor, see Black (224–26), Hawkes (63, 71), Ortega y Gasset (2:394; 6:259), and Ricoeur (150).

5. I reproduce the quotation from Horace and its translation as it appears in Paulson (1971, 1:262–63). Traditionally, the relation between poetry and painting is attributed to the Greek poet Simonides of Ceos, who is reported to have said that "painting is mute poetry and poetry a speaking picture."

6. On the synecdochic and metonymic aspects of ekphrasis, see Heffernan (1993, 82) and Dubois (18). Mack Smith holds that there is also a synecdochical relation between literary ekphrasis and the frame narrative within which it occurs (19).

7. William Berg, drawing on Roman Jackobson's argument that synecdoche was the central trope of late nineteenth-century literary imagery, studies the importance of synecdoche in Émile Zola's creation of impressionistic visual images (1992, 217–18). Linda Nochlin suggests that synecdoche constituted a modern pictorial element in the Impressionist idiom, especially in the work of Manet and

Degas whose paintings often feature truncated human figures as a way of avoiding the sense of closure upon which traditional artistic (and, I would add, narrative) composition had been predicated (78–79). The Impressionists' visual substitution of part for whole elicited accusations of inept composition or of not properly finishing a canvas from their critics. Rodin, too, was chastised for "mutilating" his sculptures by "hacking off arms, decapitating torsos, etc." (Berger 1969, 133).

8. "Sebastián Miranda" was published on 30 January 1960 in *ABC*. In "La plástica de un siglo," a summary of early twentieth-century aesthetics, Azorín noted that a symbol (he probably meant to say "metaphor") condenses reality and makes visible in one instant what otherwise would take "hours" to describe (*ABC*, 17 April 1950). In his study of the visual in Zola, William Berg argues that while metonymy was the favorite trope of the realists, metaphor was the figure that literary Moderns preferred (1992, 217–18).

9. Azorín again uses a portrait-simile, as well as a doorway, to create a "picture frame" effect for Sor Natividad in the novel *Don Juan*: "En el fondo luce el altar mayor de la iglesia. Multitud de luces, en límpidas arandelas de cristal, brillan, entre ramos, sobre los dorados esplendentes. Sor Natividad permanece un momento en la puerta, encuadrada en el marco como la figura de un retablo" (4:227).

10. In similar fashion, the intense spirituality of a painting by the artist Ary Scheffer (1759–1858) of Saint Augustine and his mother Saint Monica raised the painting, in Azorín's opinion, beyond its ostensible subjects to the more archetypal emblem of "a mother and son who are in ecstasy" (9:209–10).

11. The ekphrasis of Holbein's Louvre portrait appears to rely heavily on Jean-François Rafaëlli's description of the painting in *Mes promenades au Musée du Louvre*, a book Azorín knew and cited: "All of Erasmus is there, painted by his friend. . . . This portrait will always be for us an image of the philosopher, the writer, committing his thoughts to paper with care despite everything that threatens him from the outside . . ." (164).

12. The jeweled rings on Erasmus's fingers seemed to fascinate Azorín. He describes them in detail as, "On the left hand . . . you see: a ring on the index finger; on the middle finger, two rings, one of them with a green stone; on the little finger, a thin band of gold" (9:307). Elsewhere Azorín remembered the rings as being on Erasmus's right hand (9:987). A photograph of the Louvre portrait in Rafaëlli's *Mes promenades* shows two rings on Erasmus's left hand (167). The portrait *Erasmus of Rotterdam, writing* at Basel (1523) shows two rings on the left ring finger and one large ring on the left index finger. *Erasmus of Rotterdam, writing* at the Louvre (1523–24) shows one ring on the left little finger, two on the left ring finger, and one on the left index finger. Azorín returned to Holbein's portraits of Erasmus and the rings on his fingers in "La sortija de Claudette" (*CM* 98–99).

13. Of the Spanish Romantic painters only the society portraitist Antonio María Esquivel (1806–1857), figures prominently in Azorín's repertoire of portrait-metaphors. In *Rivas y Larra* he describes José Fluixá, a young man who participated in the 1901 pilgrimage to Larra's tomb, as wearing a hat "with a flat, straight, brim; a long mane of hair . . . a black cravat was wound three times around his neck. You could say he looked like a typical figure in a painting by Esquivel" (4:483–84).

14. In *Rivas y Larra* Azorín turned to a portrait-simile based on Goya's general manner of depicting the *maja* or *manola* to describe Tomasita, a character in Bretón de los Herreros's play *Me voy de Madrid*: ". . . menuda, vivaracha, con unos ojos negros, relampagueantes, con tu mantilla y tu peineta alta como en un cuadro de Goya" (3:495). In conjuring a panoramic vista of Madrid as seen from the outskirts of town, Azorín used a visual arts simile based on a well-known painting by Goya to do it for him: ". . . veríamos la ciudad a lo lejos (como en este lindo cuadrito de Goya titulado *La romería de San Isidro* . . ." (*EL* 209–10).

15. In his book on Velázquez, Aureliano de Beruete pointed out that Rembrandt's *Lesson in Anatomy* and Velázquez's *Los Borrachos* were the two most renowned pictures in Europe at the time they were painted, and that both exhibited similar tendencies because their creators aimed at depicting "the most absolute realism" in their canvases (1906, 30). In his copy of René Ménard's *Histoire des Beaux-Arts*, Azorín marked passages relevant to the author's analysis of Rembrandt's "two different styles: *The Anatomy Lesson of Dr. Tulp* belongs to the first . . . a clear day rules, the color of the flesh is light and the painter's touch, smooth." The *Ronde de nuit*, another Rembrandt painting Azorín admired, represented the artist's mature style, characterized by "the contrast of great masses of shadow with a vivid stream of light illuminating isolated objects" (211–12). On the back jacket of the book Azorín added a mnemonic "Dr. Tulp–211."

16. In another essay from *Los médicos* Azorín writes that whenever he thought of the life-death antinomy, he always visualized Rembrandt's *La lección de anatomía* (162). Reminiscing about his own brother Ramón, a medical doctor, Azorín observed that while the surgeon of Rembrandt's painting appears flabbergasted both by the presence of his students as well as by the cadaver in front of him, Ramón would never conduct himself in such a way at the sickbed of a patient (8:465).

17. In the essay "En Aranjuez," Azorín calls Rembrandt the "poet of light" and again uses the crepuscular light reflecting off a white wall in *El buen samaritano* as a point of reference (*ABC*, 20 March 1956). The portrait-simile that draws on relata from the Rembrandt oeuvre in which light is a major factor is not uncommon with Azorín, as in the following example: "But a young girl has come in carrying a candle in her hand. . . . I saw that the glow of light—as in a face painted by Rembrandt—sharply illuminated a little oval face" (Ramsden 1966, 48).

18. The observation was made in "Lo castizo" (*ABC*, 28 April 1954; cf. *PCQ* 169).

19. Rembrandt's striking use of light and shadow was so unusual that the highly regarded writer, art critic, and painter Eugène Fromentin, whose critical work Azorín knew well, utilized Rembrandt's *La Ronde de nuit* in a portrait-simile of his own. Recounting his presence among a group of Arabs dancing around a campfire in the French Sahara, Fromentin was surprised to discover that the Orient was not at all as Delacroix had depicted it; rather, the desert was a place in which all color is washed out, leaving only a "sketch somewhat blurred by confused shadows, scored by long shafts of light, creating . . . unusually in-

tense effects. It was something like Rembrandt's *Night Watch* . . ." (31).

20. Although the action of the play *Brandy, mucho brandy* (1927) is motivated entirely by nefarious effects the portrait of a deceased uncle has upon the protagonists, because the picture serves neither as a metaphor nor does it encode the action of the play, I do not include it in the discussion of portrait metaphors that follows.

21. "Andrés Gide" dates from 30 May 1920 and "Un pintor a Buenos Aires" from 6 August 1922. It is impossible to determine which of the several books Camille Mauclair published on Watteau Azorín may have read since none exists in his personal library.

22. For love as a structuring element in the painting of Watteau, see Robin Ironside's introduction to the Goncourt's *French Eighteenth-Century Painters* (4, 7) and Donald Posner (8, 176). Azorín may have culled similar information from his copy of Louis Hourticq's *Histoire generale de l'art*: "Watteau dressed his models in fantastic costumes . . . largely inspired by the theatre. . . . His universe is that of the stage. He was especially fond of actors from the Italian comedy, their picturesque costumes . . . that great character Gilles or Pierrot [whom Hourticq calls "a sad, dreamy personage"] belongs to this series" (142).

23. José Vega voices the fiction-reality dichotomy at other moments of act 1: "la ficción es la realidad" (4:980) and "La ficción es mejor [que la Naturaleza]" (4:993).

24. Cf. the exchange in act 1 between Valdés and Vega: "She's passionately in love with you."; "She's a girl; I've no right to sacrifice her."; "Can you restrain yourself?"; "I'll try." (4:996).

Part II, Chapter 2

1. Azorín had always been interested in the permutations of the national art collection. In one of several copies of Ford's guide to Spain, he annotated observations regarding the devastation of the national collection during the Napoleonic invasion as well as the periodic, inept restorations that had ruined some of the Museum's best pieces (1855, 2:682–83).

2. The situation at the Prado has not changed dramatically since 1903. In the early 1990s the Museum went through four directors in a little over three years: Calvo Serraller, for example, resigned on 14 May 1994, alleging government neglect and apathy (cf. "Prado Chief Quits over Photo Shoot" in the *Guardian*, 16 May 1994). In 1994 the ceiling over *Las Meninas* was still leaking (cf. "Trouble at the Prado: Even the Roof Leaks" in the *New York Times*, 18 July 1994). On 1 May 1995 the *New York Times* ran an article by Alan Riding ("The Prado Embarks on Plans to Expand into a Complex") which described the Museum's state of disrepair, the rats in its basement storage rooms, and celebrated the long overdue allocation of funds for repair, restoration, and updating. On 16 May 1995, however, William D. Montalbano, writing for the *Los Angeles Times* ("Artistic Heart of Spain Is Scheduled for Surgery"), wrote of the discord that ensued in the Ministry of Culture over just how much money to spend on repairs at the Prado.

3. The opinions Azorín expresses here anticipate Maurice Merleau-Ponty's view that "the museum gives us a . . . sense that these works were not . . . intended to end

up between these morose walls. . . ." For Merleau-Ponty the museum as "meditative necropolis" was not the ideal way to display works of art at all because it tended to convert "living historicity into official and pompous historicity" that was nothing more than the "historicity of death" (quoted in G. Johnson 99–100).

4. That Azorín thought of the eighteenth century primarily in visual terms is patent in an essay on Cadalso where he observes that "I think of the eighteenth century as symbolized by a frock coat—dark red-purple with little embroidered flowers—. . . , a miniature of a beautiful lady dancing a minuet, a large room with gilt mirrors and candelabra . . . , a garden with symmetrical walks, a poem by Meléndez or Cadalso" (7:721).

5. Azorín enjoyed recasting biblical stories in modern, fictional guise. "El primer milagro" is one of several variations on the Nativity theme (5:299–306).

6. In *Pasos quedos*, however, Azorín wrote that he visited the Louvre some two hundred times during his four-year [sic] stay in Paris (109). For Grevin, see *París* (7:907); on Carnavalet, *Españoles en París* (5:835). Another favorite haunt was the twelfth-century Greek Catholic church, Saint Julien le Pauvre (5:795).

7. From "Ante unas esculturas de Sebastián Miranda" (*ABC*, 13 February 1962).

8. Azorín's withholding the statue's identity until the last possible moment of his description may not be as original as it appears. Louis Viardot uses a similar sleight of hand in a passage of *Les merveilles de la sculpture*, which Azorín owned and annotated: ". . . alone on her pedestal like a god . . . a statue of a woman, large, severe, her thighs girded by a floating dress . . . rather unfinished, because she's missing both arms. . . . That mutilated statue is the most precious debris of ancient art that Paris can boast of: it's the Venus de Milo." (79). Azorín was fond of this sculpture: in his copy of Hourticq's guide to the Louvre he underlined a passage where the author refers to the Venus de Milo as the most beautiful woman in the world (151), and he left a newspaper clipping about the statue from *Le Figaro*, 10 November 1936, between the pages of Hourticq's commentary.

9. Azorín refers again to Rubens's painting of the three Fates in *Contingencia en América* (7:1219).

10. The allusion is to the River Lethe in Hades whose waters would cause anyone who drank from them to forget the past.

11. In general, any aesthetic product could, in Azorín's view, exteriorize feelings that would otherwise not be discerned easily: ". . . emotions . . . are exteriorized . . . through a painting by Velázquez, some pages from Cervantes, some verses by Lope de Vega, a scene from Calderón" (*VH* 181).

12. Azorín had a soft spot for these artists whose work is typical of the grand, academic manner associated with Western European history painting in the nineteenth century. He occasionally referred to Gisbert's *Los comuneros de Castilla*, Pradilla's *Doña Juana la Loca*, Rosales's *El testamento de Isabel la Católica*, and Emilio Sala's *La expulsión de los judíos* in his writing (cf. 9:1034; *Los pueblos* 100, and *VH* 254).

13. Ten years later, in the short story "Entre dos luces" (published in *La Prensa*, 30 January 1949), Azorín made a similar analogy. The two favorite moments of the day for the protagonist are sunrise and sunset: artistically speak-

ing, Joaquín Chies might be said to live between Guido Reni's *Aurora* and J. M. W. Turner's *The Evening Star*. Azorín repeated almost the same metaphor in "El último Don Juan," where he retained the "virginal" morning light of Reni's painting, but substituted Turner's picture with the "dying," crepuscular light Rembrandt portrayed in *The Good Samaritan* (*EC* 42).

14. See esp. Chapter 4 ("Two Exiles: A Comparative Morphology") and Chapter 5 ("Alienation and Exilic Homology") of Ilie's *Literature and Inner Exile* (1980).

15. The negotiations relative to Azorín's return to Spain and his subsequent ambiguous relations with the regime are amply discussed by Inman Fox (1993, 81–85).

Part II, Chapter 3

1. Although in his article "El Duque de Rivas, pintor," Antonio Rumeu strongly disagrees with most of what Azorín wrote on Angel Saavedra, he does concur that "Duque de Rivas, the painter, exercised a patent influence on Duque de Rivas, the poet" (345).

2. Much of the same essay is reproduced in "El Duque de Rivas" from *El oasis de los clásicos* (9:1075–79).

3. Elsewhere Azorín again commented on the "heightened sense of color" in the *Romances históricos*, observing that Angel Saavedra was a writer for whom the exterior world is much more important than the analysis of psychological passions (9:1076–77). Cf. essentially the same essay in *Clásicos y modernos* (2:775–76); there is additional commentary on the Duke's use of color in *Pasos quedos* (37).

4. These observations were most likely drawn from Pastor Díaz's comments on the same scene from *El moro expósito*, which Azorín underlined and annotated in his copy of the biography (47–48). He also annotated another episode of gluttonous feasting in his copy of Saavedra's *El parador de Bailén* (2:xii). Azorín mentions the painter David Teniers (1610–1690) again in *Con bandera de Francia*, also in context of exquisite and bountiful table settings (9:514). Known for his genre scenes representing the wealthy Dutch bourgeoisie, perhaps Tenier's *La Cuisine* (Prado Museum) is the intertext for Azorín's allusions. Adriaen Brouwer (1608–1640) was admired for his use of color and chiaroscuro; he specialized in scenes of village inns and country life, was collected by Rubens and Rembrandt, and his style imitated by Teniers, among others (see Fromentin 1754 and 1779).

5. Cf. Diderot: "The unity of time is even more rigorous for the painter than for the poet. The painter has at his disposal no more than an almost invisible instant, whereas the poet's description is made of successive instants that would fill up a long gallery with paintings" (1959, 774).

6. Azorín saw the lack of coherence in the work of the Duque de Rivas as symptomatic of Spanish life in general, and as another proof of his own theory of "coherencia y continuidad" in particular. He noted in an aside, "(Later we'll argue that this incoherence and superficiality [in Saavedra's work] are the capital defects of Spanish life)" (3:343).

7. The essay on Forain appeared in *La Prensa*, 19 March 1933; "La pintura," discussion of which follows, was published in *ABC*, 8 December 1951.

8. Since I have not been able to locate any portrait of the Duque de Osuna by Guido Reni, I suspect Azorín's attribution might be incorrect. Azorín also compared the writer Manuel José Quintana (1772–1857), whom he called a sensual poet "who trembles and is moved by exquisiteness of form," to certain Italian painters, among them Guido Reni, in whose work he found a similar alliance of splendorous display coupled with morbid refinement (7:762–63).

9. In "El Madrid de Solana" Azorín commented that, "The painting of José Gutiérrez Solana has its logical analogy in the literary art of the painter," and pointed again to the realistic aspects of Solana's painting and writing (9:1357).

10. From "Memoria de Barrès a la belleza de Toledo" (*La Prensa*, 6 July 1924). In the same article Azorín drew parallels between El Greco's imaginary storm over Toledo and a literary passage that described a real storm in the Imperial City as experienced and memorialized by Antonio Martín Gamero in *Los cigarrales de Toledo* (1835).

11. Sor María de Ágreda (1602–1665), a Franciscan abbess and mystic, was an epistolary spiritual adviser to Felipe IV. She authored a biography of the Virgin, *La mística ciudad de Dios*, of which there are numerous editions, some quite rare, in Azorín's personal library.

12. In *Con Cervantes*, Azorín chose the painters Federico de Madrazo, Casto Plasencia, Antonio Muñoz Degrain, and Emilio Sala for the task of painting a portrait of Cervantes that was to be based on literary descriptions other writers had made of Don Quijote's creator (8:1054). Azorín's choice of artists is curious, since they were all history or society portrait painters of the traditional, garden-variety. Azorín was also quite fond of the unassuming statue of Cervantes in a small park in Madrid's Plaza de las Cortes. Not the work of a famous sculptor, wrote Azorín, the statue had been censured many times, no one ever referred to it, and the park was never visited by the "friends of Cervantes." The unfortunate statue, he noted, was scorned and abandoned much as Cervantes had been in his own lifetime (8:1091–92).

13. What is interesting about Azorín's reading of the *Libro de Buen Amor* is his favorable interpretation of the book's ludic nature and salacious content.

14. From "Poeta sin nombre" (*La Prensa*, 18 February 1940). In *Con permiso de los cervantistas* Azorín makes a rather curious analogy between a Gauguin seascape painted in Brittany and a phrase culled from Cervantes that described the "waters of the sea as a shirred coverlet, and they made blue shimmers over the green plain" (9:277). Elsewhere, referring to the *Persiles*, Azorín remarked that Cervantes's last works might be compared only to the superb, last paintings of Velázquez (3:219).

15. Of the more contemporary nineteenth-century authors, Azorín commented only on Clarín's lack of visual sensitivity, observing that Leopoldo Alas was more interested in the portrayal of spiritual realities than in "the depiction of a realistic ambience" (7:1164). Among the Generation of 1927 writers, Azorín singled out Antonio Espina, whose satiric bent and strong visual sense would have delighted Goya, but he disapproved of Espina's penchant for using typographical settings to make visual statements with words: "Why, being a poet, does he engage in this typographical confusion? Today's typographical caprices are nothing new" (7:787).

16. Pérez Rojas also compared Blasco's *Entre naranjos* to paintings by Sorolla (exhib. cat. *Centro y periferia* 170). Sorolla, indeed, titled one of his canvases *Entre naranjos*, now at the Museo Nacional de Cuba in Havana. Nancy Norris has observed similarities between the quasi-impressionism of Sorolla's technique and the chromaticity of Blasco's *La barraca* (382). Pablo Jiménez Burillo and others argue that Sorolla's early painterly interest in social themes (i.e., to 1900), was nurtured by his involvement with the socialist and republican political climate of his native Valencia, and especially the socialist ideals of his lifelong friend Vicente Blasco Ibáñez (exhib. cat. *Joaquín Sorolla (1863–1923)* 27). When *Alma española*, a turn-of-century literary magazine associated with the *gente nueva*, ran a series on the "soul" of different geographical regions in Spain, Blasco was asked to contribute the piece on "el alma valenciana."

17. Baroja rejected comparison between himself and Zuloaga. Commenting on Sorolla and Zuloaga in *Galería de los tipos de la época*, he observed that "Sorolla was one of the best painters of the time; but that doesn't interest me very much. Sorolla and Zuloaga opted for style: they painted, for better or worse, by recipes, with technique, but without emotion" (7:902; cf. 7:900–901).

18. The literary nature of Santa María's work is confirmed by the art historian Jiménez Placer who identified in the decorative and stylized rhetoric of paintings such as *Figuras de romance* "the literary nature of this kind of painting" (988). Carmen Pena writes that Marceliano Santamaría [sic] was one of the artists most instrumental in disseminating a Castilian-centered ideology in Spain (1982, 120).

19. "Marceliano Santa María" was first published in *ABC*, 27 May 1943; it is reproduced in *Pintar como querer* (177–80).

20. For Adelardo Parilla, see (1:cxxv and 8:441); for Beruete and Baroja, see Campos (21–22).

21. Espina, as did many painters of his generation, preferred Castilian themes: the outskirts of Madrid, the Guadarrama mountains, the Escorial. Like Beruete's mature work, Espina also preferred color over line for modeling landscape, and he too, showed a Castile of subdued, graduated color rather than as a land of stereotyped, monotonous majesty (Rodríguez Alcalde 101; Pantorba 64–65).

22. See Pantorba (82–83) and Rodríguez Alcalde (130).

23. Azorín was intrigued by painters who succumbed to madness, perhaps, as he wrote, the result of their daily struggle with paint and canvas, carried out in silent loneliness and solitude. He specifically mentioned as victims Vincent Van Gooh [sic], Joaquim Mir, and Casimiro Sainz (*PCQ* 149–50), and discussed a book written by two French physicians who studied Van Gogh's descent into madness in "Pintores españoles: inquietud" (*PCQ* 147). Although not exactly mad in the sense of Van Gogh or Sainz, Mir experienced a period of time during which he feared other painters, notably his friend Rusiñol who was also on a Mallorcan campaign, and accused him of trying to steal his ideas. Mir's paranoia and need to distance himself physically from contact with other painters became so overwhelming that he began to seek out the most inaccessible of cliffs on which to paint, suffering serious injuries from a fall that ultimately caused his family to remove him to the Instituto Pedro Mata in Reus for an enforced period of treatment from January 1905 to October 1906 (Jardí 72).

24. I would like to express my gratitude to Antonio Tránchez, manager of Lhardy's, who in the summer of 1993 graciously allowed me to view the small collection of paintings by Agustín on display in the maze of private dining rooms on the upper floors of the restaurant.

25. Juan San Nicolás is the first art historian to contradict the popularly accepted notion that Regoyos studied with, or was a disciple of, Carlos de Haes. He presents supporting evidence in a recent biography, *Darío de Regoyos* (1990; 1:19), as well as in his contribution to the exhibition catalogue *Darío de Regoyos* (303–11).

26. Regoyos pursued his interest in nocturnal illumination throughout his career, as is evident in paintings such as *Efectos de luz* (1881), a trolley-car stop, perhaps at the Puerta del Sol, during evening hours; *La Plaza del Palacio, nevada* (1882), a study of gas-light reflections on snow; *Resplandor de velas* (1886), portraying the glow of lit tapers during an All-Soul's Eve pilgrimage to a rural cemetery; a sea and moonscape titled *Nocturno* (1902); several fireworks displays from 1904 and 1905; *La Concha. Nocturno* (1906), a painting of the famous beach at San Sebastián; a moonscape illuminating factory chimneys belching smoke titled *Humo de fábrica. Luna* (1908), and a late canvas depicting Barcelona's *El Paseo de Gracia de noche* (1912). These paintings are beautifully reproduced in color plates in the exhib. cat. *Darío de Regoyos, 1857–1913*.

27. Lily Litvak writes that interest in Saint Francis of Assisi was rekindled at the end of the nineteenth century, especially by movements such as Art Nouveau that discovered in the Saint "la arcáica estética de lo humilde" (1980, 198–99). Cf. Juan de la Encina, "Nuestro pintor franciscano" (exhib. cat. *D. de Regoyos* 48–50).

28. In "Primores de lo vulgar" Ortega drew analogies between the vision of primitive painters, who brought all sorts of minutiae to the foregrounds of their paintings, and similar techniques utilized not only by Azorín, but also by some contemporary painters (2:191), perhaps having the example of Regoyos before him as he wrote the essay: Ortega owned a painting by Regoyos that hung in his study (cf. "Meditación del marco" 2:307–13).

29. In "Las sorpresas de la pintura" (*ABC*, 30 March 1914), Azorín took up canon formation again, writing that "Today's heresy is tomorrow's othodoxy; history is able to cure us of many outrages. The vicissitudes and evolution of artistic works through the ages, can imbue our spirit with a little calm, equanimity, and caution when considering a painting by this innovative young man or a poem by that daring poet" (*PCQ* 115–16). The article concludes with a cautionary note to the "señores tradicionalistas" who typically become indignant when confronted with innovative works of art, not to rush so quickly to judgment for time, as in the case of Regoyos, might prove them wrong (*PCQ* 120).

30. For comparison of Rusiñol's painted gardens to turn-of-century literary landscapes, see Lafuente Ferrari (1948a, 447) and Litvak (1980, 163–64). Azorín discusses Rusiñol's play *El místico* in "La psicología del teatro" (7:1115–22).

31. Roch attributes the *fin de siècle*, neo-Romantic turning toward interior and fantastic spaces, the recuperation of landscape, and the "decadent" literature of then-marginalized authors such as D'Annunzio, Wilde, and

Baudelaire, to the crisis in faith in scientific and technical progress experienced by the industrialized West. In Spain these repercussions were especially acute in Catalonia (21). Unlike most Spanish landscapists of his generation, who preferred to paint natural scenes, Rusiñol was partial to the artificial, geometric layout of the formal garden or park setting (Plá 398). Perhaps as a way of retaining a sense of order in the modern, chaotic world in which he lived, Rusiñol told Vázquez Díaz that "my paintings explain my tendency to create architecture with trees and plants" (Roch 41).

32. Although Zuloaga was a much sought after portraitist by Spanish, French, and American cultural and political dignitaries, industrialists, and society ladies, he is best remembered for his Castilian landscapes. See Lafuente Ferrari (1948b, 455 and 1950, 440). Regarding nineteenth-century racial theories, José Francés expressed a similar opinion in his article "La peinture espagnole depuis le milieu du XIXè siècle," in which he referred to Zuloaga as a "chercheur des types de sa race" (323).

33. The only dissenting voice regarding Zuloaga's connection to '98 is that of Julio Caro Baroja, who believes that Zuloaga neither shared decisive moments of his life and career with the writers of his own time, nor that there are any meaningful similarities between his painting and the prose of Baroja and Azorín, or Machado's poetry (64–65).

34. In the following discussion regarding the verisimilitude of Zuloaga's vision, I draw on the chapter "Revisión y antología de la 'cuestión Zuloaga' " in the third edition of Lafuente Ferrari's La vida y el arte de Ignacio Zuloaga (Barcelona: Planeta, 1990). The textual citation is found on page 301. The one foreign critic who seems to have understood Zuloaga was the American, Christian Brinton, who observed in 1909 that "There is nothing salubrious in the work of Zuloaga; these faces are . . . scarred by sin or covered with a heavy coating of rice powder. . . . Like much of the Spanish art of his own or former days, that of Zuloaga is defiantly histrionic" (32).

35. In the same passage of Memorias Inmemoriales, in language reminiscent of opinions he expressed on El Greco at the beginning of the twentieth century, Azorín observed that while Zuloaga did not treat mystical subject matter, his work transformed failed sensuality into the asceticism of a Rembrandt, Ribera, or Zurbarán, the entire oeuvre exuding aspiration toward the Infinite (8:445). He subsequently revealed both the identity of the painting he had seen in Paris (Las tierras de la Bureba), and the name of his physician (Doctor Amuedo), in "El paisaje" (ABC, 22 March 1949). Cf. discussion of the same painting in "Cajal y el cine" (EC 120)

36. There is a complete bibliography on the "cuestión Zuloaga" in Lafuente Ferrari's La vida y el arte de Ignacio Zuloaga. Maeztu's claim that art critics from all over the world had begun to write about Zuloaga is corroborated by the bibliography and the list of exhibitions Zuloaga held abroad detailed in Lafuente Ferrari's appendices.

37. The interview is quoted by Juan de la Encina in "El arte de Zuloaga" published in Hermes, August 1917. In all fairness to Azorín, even Lafuente Ferrari conceded that as far as he could ascertain, Zuloaga took great liberties in his landscapes: "I have been able to corroborate . . . that Zuloaga modified topographical details as he pleased . . . to make them suit his composition" (1948a, 171).

38. "Un pintor a Buenos Aires" was published in La Prensa, 6 August 1922. This was not the first time Azorín addressed the public reception of visual art. In "Los pintores" he observed that on considering Courbet, Degas, and Puvis de Chavannes, "one experiences a strange feeling on seeing how contemporary criticism judged these paintings that we admire so earnestly today" (PCQ 60–61). In an essay on Zola's novel L'Oeuvre he noted that when in 1886 Pierre Sandoz (i.e., Zola) negatively appraised the work of Claude Lantier (i.e., Paul Cézanne), he had no way of knowing that by 1907 Rémy de Gourmont would write that all artistic innovations of the early twentieth century would evolve from Cézanne (PCQ 201).

39. "Ignacio Zuloaga" appeared on 13 January 1946 in La Prensa of Buenos Aires.

40. For Vázquez Díaz's early development in Paris, see Benito (106), Jiménez Placer (1027), and Guillermo de Torre (1921, 1). Sánchez Marín made the suggestive observation that had Vázquez Díaz participated more fully in the Cubist adventure, he would have joined Pablo Picasso and Juan Gris as the third painter of a powerful "Spanish Cubist trilogy" in Paris (1968b, 327).

41. Benito points out that from 1918, the date of the painter's return to Spain, until about 1936, Vázquez Díaz devoted himself almost exclusively to landscape painting (309). Like his older colleague Darío de Regoyos, Vázquez Díaz, although a native of Andalusia, was repelled by the strong light and coloration of the south. In an interview with Camilo José Cela, then a fledgling newspaper reporter, Vázquez confessed, "I don't respond to the sunny landscape; I paint the north, the Basque country, with greater pleasure" (Benito 332).

42. Many of Vázquez Díaz's portraits were exhibited in Spring 1968 in a show titled "Generación del 98" mounted at the Galería Theo in Madrid (Sánchez Marín 1968b, 327). Cf. Azorín, "Dos artistas," published in La Prensa for 26 November 1922. The Zugazagoitia quotation is from Benito (408; cf. 412). Vázquez Díaz published four sketches interpreting Machado's epic poem "La tierra de Alvargonzález" in the journal Mundial for January 1912 (Benito 11 n. 72). Cf. Lafuente Ferrari (1976, 103 n. 18).

43. Quoted in Benito (408), the article "La pintura en la Exposición Nacional" was published in La Estafeta Literaria (number 28, 1945).

44. Angel Benito writes that Vázquez Díaz dated his slow evolution toward the simplification of form and a return to his "beloved grays" to the period 1920–30 (440, 443). Of all the portraits he painted, Vázquez himself was most taken by the one he did of Miguel de Unamuno. At the first sitting Unamuno requested the picture include a blank sheet of writing paper on which he planned to write something in his own hand. Begun in early July 1936, the sessions were interrupted by the outbreak of civil war and Unamuno's death at the end of the same year. Although Vázquez completed the portrait from memory, he left the sheet of paper blank and, in his article "El retrato de la cuartilla blanca," he speculated on what don Miguel might have written there had he lived to see the portrait completed (254).

45. Azorín would have found his positive initial reaction to Puvis confirmed and reiterated by André Beaunier in L'Art de regarder les tableaux. Referring to Puvis's supposed archaism, Beaunier argues that it was more a matter of extreme purification, noting that among his contempo-

raries, Puvis "is one of those who reacted . . . against forms of beauty that had ceased to be beautiful but which continued to debase themselves" (252). He went on to comment on Puvis's idiosyncratic predilection for silvery gray color (252–53), and his manner of insinuating "notions of order and calm" even in his decorative murals (257).

46. Azorín added that the Orangerie exhibit led him to recall Cézanne's picture of two cardplayers and a superb landscape he had already seen in the Camondo collection at the Louvre. The same Cézanne exhibition is mentioned again in "La pintura" (*ABC*, 8 December 1951; now collected in *PCQ* 235). Although Azorín does not name the novel directly, his oblique reference is to Balzac's *Le Chef d'oeuvre inconnu*. The association is curious since Cézanne is most often linked to Claude Lantier from Zola's novel *L'Oeuvre*.

47. The contrast of paintings juxtaposed against photographs of the sites where Cézanne executed his canvases is as suggestive today as it was for Azorín in 1939. Pavel Machotka, a professor of psychology and art, repeats the exercise in his recent study of how Cézanne transformed nature into art: *Cézanne. Landscape into Art* (New Haven: Yale University Press, 1996).

48. Before it was collected in volume 4 of the *Obras Completas*, "Doña María de Molina" appeared on 14 April 1910 in *La Prensa* of Buenos Aires. Azorín may be attributing to Salgado a painting based on the life of María de Molina titled *Jura de Fernando IV en las Cortes de Valladolid* painted in 1863 by Antonio Gisbert (1834–1901). Lorenzo Vallés's *Demencia de Doña Juana de Castilla* won a second-class medal at the 1866 Exposición Nacional, where it attracted attention because the artist "eliminated all superficial details from his picture" (exhib. cat. *La Pintura de Historia del Siglo XIX en España* 252). Both Gisbert's painting, as well as the two interpretations of Doña Juana de Castilla by Vallés and Pradilla, are beautifully reproduced in color in this exhibition catalogue. Elimination of extraneous detail may also be the reason why Azorín responded well to Vázquez Díaz. Enrique Lafuente Ferrari observed that, paradoxically, Vázquez's elimination of detail transmitted to the viewer something more than would a mere documentary description of material objects (1953, 40).

49. Azorín included Cézanne among the stylistic moderns Góngora, Mallarmé, and Rimbaud, all dissidents who fought "to express the inexpressible" (6:152).

50. See Robert J. Niess (1968) for extensive discussion relevant to this question. Azorín discusses Lantier (repeatedly misspelled "Lautier") and *L'Oeuvre* in "La cuestión Cézanne" (*Destino*, 22 January 1944), and also in "En el estudio" (*Destino*, 16 October 1943). He returned to Zola's novel in "Cine realista" (*CM*). Cf. discussion of Cézanne's painting *La Maison du Pendu* in the introduction to *Pintar como querer* (1954).

Part II, Chapter 4

1. All further references to *Doña Inés* are to Catena's 1981 Castalia edition, and will be cited parenthetically in the text.

2. I have not been able to trace Lucas Menéndez to any historical painter. Most likely Azorín was referring to Luis Egidio Meléndez de Rivero Durazo y Santo Padre (1716–1780), a still-life painter at the eighteenth-century Spanish court. Meléndez's lush canvases are still housed today in their own gallery at the Prado Museum. Although he frequently spelled his name Menéndez, in petitions the artist sent to the king, and in the signature of his 1746 self-portrait, the painter referred to himself as Luis Meléndez (Tufts 6 n. 8). An essay Azorín actually titled "Bodegón," is a still life set in a rustic kitchen complete with frying pans, red peppers, a codfish, and flagons of oil and vinegar that recall an early *bodegón* by Velázquez of a woman frying eggs (6:106–7).

3. For example: "El caballero en negro era segoviano; no olvidaré nunca su señoril silueta, adecuada a Zuloaga" [7:1056; The gentleman in black was Segovian; I'll never forget his aristocratic figure, worthy of Zuloaga]. Unfortunately, this type of visually synecdochic allusion so common with Azorín, is robbed of its full impact unless a reader is familiar with the style of the painter or specific painting to which the author refers.

4. In the essay "Zuloaga" (*París*), Azorín observed that from painting the human figure Zuloaga moved on to depict the "immutable" essence of Spain as exemplified in the "portraiture" of archetypal houses and streets (7:960). In a 1961 article "Ignacio Zuloaga," published in *ABC*, another of Azorín's painter-friends, Daniel Vázquez Díaz, remembered the "somber, dramatic Spain" of Azorín and Baroja as having affinities with Zuloaga's artistic interpretation of Spain (185). Emilio Orozco made observations similar to those of Lafuente Ferrari's regarding Zuloaga's painting as being analogous in spirit to the Generation of 1898's concern with time: the human emotions stimulated by an awareness of time's passing and a desire to still its inexorable, forward progress (185–86).

5. Azorín could be conflating in this reference an 1868 episode in which Corot and Honoré Daumier decorated the interior of Charles Daubigny's home in Auvers with landscape murals (Yriarte 403), and the "Cabaret de la Mère Anthony," a café-inn located near Fontainebleau Forest, that was popular with the younger Impressionist painters who decorated its interior with murals and caricatures. Renoir memorialized the cabaret in his 1866 painting *Le Cabaret de la Mère Anthony, Marlotte* in which he used the painter Alfred Sisley as one of his models and included in the background one of his own caricatures (Denvir 37).

6. Cf. Camille Mauclair's observation that in the canvases Monet painted at Rouen, "the towers fill up the paintings: at the bottom of some canvases a bit of space scarcely shows, a corner of a plaza at the foot of some enormous shafts of stone that rise almost to the top of the picture frame" (77–78). For Azorín's comments on Monet's Rouen paintings, see *Pintar como querer* (74, 77).

7. In Azorín's personal library there is a book by Luis Pérez Bueno, *Retratos de mujeres españolas del siglo XIX* (1924), that includes a portrait of María Cristina de Borbón strikingly similar to the one he describes in *Doña Inés*.

8. Antonio Risco's observation that Azorín frequently associated photographs with the transitory nature of time (1980, 242), is borne out by a comment Azorín himself made in "Capilla desierta" to the effect that "Primitive, discolored photographs. . . . Give us the feeling of an instantaneous past that will never return. The photograph captures a fugacious instant. And this perpetuation of the

fleeting—in photographs that have faded with time—plunges us into sadness" (5:836).

9. In context of Azorín's interest in the ephemeral nature of feminine beauty, an item of bibliographic curiosity is commentary on the subject made by Auguste Rodin that Azorín annotated in his copy of interviews with the French sculptor: "Beauty changes quickly. I would not say that a woman is like a landscape that is constantly modified by the inclination of the sun's rays, but the comparison is almost exact. True youth, that of virginal puberty . . . that moment scarcely lasts a few months." (139). Azorín paraphrases the quip in Spanish in *El efímero cine* (50). Rodin was one of Azorín's favorite sculptors, along with Carpeaux and Houdon (cf. "Sebastián Miranda" in *ABC*, 30 January 1960) and *Pintar como querer* (162).

10. The poetics of frame structure in *Doña Inés* are reinforced by the balcony scenes at the novel's beginning and end: after she reads Don Juan's letter of farewell, Inés tears it to pieces and, framed by the windows of her balcony, "her hand extended, she flings out a hundred little pieces of white paper" (81). The novel concludes with a glimpse of a much aged "mamá Inés," again framed by a balcony, from which her hands throw kisses to her adoptive children playing in the garden below (220).

11. Joseph Kestner argues that use of the framing device to produce a *structure en abyme* also tends to spatialize textual discourse as the element of one narrative obviously recedes and becomes background to a larger narrative (1981, 73).

12. It is worth noting that significant portions of *Doña Inés* are informed by books Azorín had in his library. The only pages he cut in L. Roch's *Vistas de Segovia* (1921) are those pertaining to the city's cathedral and *alcázar*. His discussion in the first pages of the novel, regarding the introduction of gas lighting to limited sections of Madrid in 1840, derives from Fermín Caballero's *Noticias topográficas-estadísticas sobre la administración de Madrid* (1840). Equally topical is a description of the *juego de prendas* called "Vuelen, vuelen" that the young people play at Tía Pompilia's soirée: Azorín culled his information from page thirty-seven of Mariano de Rementería y Fica's *Manual completo de juegos de sociedad o tertulia, y de prendas* (2d ed., 1839), a translation, "with additions from the Spanish," of a text first published in French by a Mme. Celnart.

13. In "La luna y el ciprés," Azorín writes of the vertigo a fictional protagonist experiences when he mentally conflates "una alacena entreabierta" depicted by Delacroix in the painting *Les Femmes d'Algers* (1834), with "una alacena idéntica" described by Fromentin in his travel diary *Une anée dans le Sahel*. The exact resemblance across time, space, and different aesthetic media overwhelms the protagonist much as it does Doña Inés, and for the same reasons: ". . . I felt dizzy. The vertigo of time and space abolished. The vertigo of that which is identical yet different" (*PQ* 25–26). Cf. "La puerta cerrada" (also in *PQ*) for another reference to Delacroix's *Mujeres de Argel* (204).

14. See Krieger (1992, 256–66) and Mandelker (2). Because literary ekphrasis describes a generic "other," it is also unavoidably self-conscious and melds extremely well with the self-conscious nature of the *structure en abyme* in Azorín's novel. David Mickelsen notes that spatial form appears in textual discourse when chronology is eliminated or severely attenuated (69). Another technique

of spatializing text is through parataxis, an ingenious but impractical attempt to force a synchronic reading of events that occur simultaneously within a novel but which, because of the temporal nature of narrative, must inevitably be represented by the author, and apprehended by readers, in diachronic fashion. Azorín uses this technique to retard time, thereby spatializing discourse, in chapter 27, "Obsesión (Ella)" and chapter 28, "Obsesión (El)" that describe the simultaneous awakening of romantic feelings between Doña Inés and Diego.

15. Thomas Meehan also noted the importance of plastic art forms in *Doña Inés*, and observed Azorín's intent to transcend the temporal limitations of the verbal medium by lending it sculptural and spatial qualities through "juegos de perspectiva . . . y mundos dentro de mundos" that lend the novel a three-dimensional quality while forcing it to assume static or circular rhythmic properties (134–35, 147). As if to contrast the "stilled" movement of chapers 35 and 37, which contain the notional ekphrases of the funerary statues, Azorín increases the pace of chapter 38, "Tolvanera," to a feverish pitch of human physical activity, extreme weather conditions, and cinematic cuts in sharp contrast to the atemporal qualities of the preceding chapters.

16. See, for example, Davidson (71), Lodge (50), Quinones (118).

17. In the following chapter Azorín again considers the relativity of time and space when, in a dream, God asks Tío Pablo how long he thinks it might take to pour a handful of sand between His fingers. "Lord, I think two or three seconds," responds Pablo. God then observes that those two or three seconds would be measured in "thousands and thousands of centuries" by the ordinary mortals who inhabit the earth (165).

18. Tío Pablo's ruminations on societal and aesthetic upheavals, and the transformation of traditional values that he witnessed, were articulated in comparable fashion by Francisco Giner de los Ríos in 1865 (cf. his thoughts on the culture of crisis in "Del género de poesía más propio de nuestro siglo" in López Morillas 1969, 43). The lack of closure in *Doña Inés* is likewise symptomatic of modern aesthetics (e.g., chapter 49, "¿Epílogo? No; todavía no"; chapter 51, "Tampoco es esto epílogo"; chapter 52, "Epílogo.").

19. "El círculo eterno" was published in *La Prensa*, 11 February 1934.

20. Particularly evocative in this regard is a statement Azorín made in "El reinado de Alfonso XIII" (19 December 1935), to the effect that "History is . . . a subjectivism. History is the historian. As is the historian, so shall History be" (*Dicho y hecho* 176). For the preceding discussion of Cervantes, I am indebted to Mack Smith's chapter on *Don Quijote* in *Literary Realism and the Ekphrastic Tradition* (1995, 27, 55).

21. Cf. *Rivas y Larra* where Azorín writes that in the prologue to *Cinq-Mars* de Vigny develops "a profound doctrine regarding aesthetic truth and historical truth that, many years later, merited the support of Menéndez y Pelayo in his *Ideas estéticas*" (3:396).

22. All references to Menéndez y Pelayo's lecture to the Royal Academy of History are from Azorín's copy of volume 7 of *Estudios y discursos de crítica histórica y literaria*, edited by Sánchez Munian (1893).

23. Unamuno covered similar ground in his study of

imaginary dialogues penned by Carlyle, Cellini, and Thucydides. See his essay "Maese Pedro: Notas sobre Carlyle" (1:1025; 1029–30); for Cellini and Thucydides (7:834; 3:360, 367).

24. Cf. Hayden White: ". . . historians might choose on aesthetic grounds different plot structures by which to encode sequences of events with different meanings . . ."; "The events are *made* into a story by the suppression . . . of certain of them and the highlighting of others, by . . . all of the techniques that we would expect to find in the emplotment of a novel or play" (1978, 53, 84).

25. Azorín also explores the art of historical narration as a human, hence fallible, construct in "El arte de la historia" (1934), an allegory similar to "Al pie del acueducto," in which he proposes three stages for the construction of historical narrative. The first is an oral account told by an eyewitness participant in the historical event; the second, another oral account, is repeated to an historian by someone who was present at the eyewitness's narration. This second party, however, invariably distorts the record by suppressing some facts while emphasizing others, thus introducing variants that contribute to the production of legend and not history. The third, and last phase, is the historian's written record, based on the second account, that not only introduces additional variants into the narrative, but might also include a moral interpretation of the event and its perpetrator(s) (*Dicho y hecho* 66–70).

26. The first paragraph of the novel begins as follows: "En 1840 y en Madrid. . . . Por una callejuela avanza un transeunte. La callejuela pertenece al barrio de Segovia. Las afueras del barrio de Segovia son extensas. Están comprendidas en su área la Casa de Campo, el Campo del Moro, el Parque de Palacio. . . . En las afueras del barrio de Segovia está enclavada la Fábrica del Gas" [In 1840 and in Madrid. . . . A pedestrian moves forward along a narrow street. The street is in the Segovia neighborhood. The outskirts of this district are extensive. They include the Casa de Campo, the Campo del Moro, the Parque de Palacio. . . . The gasworks are situated on the outskirts of the community].

Part II, Chapter 5

1. Cf. McClain (51) and Butler (141–42). It is important to bear in mind that before Leon Battista Alberti's (1404–1472) theory of perspective shackled artists to painting only what they could see from one point of view at any given moment in time, painters often represented diachronic narrative in their pictures. Religious art that depicts the lives of saints is a good example of this technique (Heffernan 1993, 14).

2. For Bergson's centrality to cultural debate in France between 1900 and the beginning of World War I, see Antliff (3–10); also T. Mitchell (179). Roskill observed that on one occasion an interviewer showed Bergson some reproductions of Cubist art in which the philosopher expressed interest, "but was not inclined to go further" (1985, 35). Standish Lawder writes that Bergson found in the cinema a plastic expression of his theories on *durée* and the simultaneous perception of form, and that film, as well as Bergsonian thought, was integral to the intellectual milieu

within which European painting was developing on the eve of the first World War (20, 248 n. 31).

3. The moment the element of time is incorporated into painting, the object is "spread out" in space; Charles Gauss observed that if it is located anywhere at all, it would be at the intersection of time and space (76). In *Studies in Child Language and Aphasia*, Roman Jakobson made the interesting observation that Cubist perspectivism transformed the object "into a set of synecdoches," an effect that holds equally true in literature as it does in Cubist painting (Halter 117). The revisionism occurring in physics and philosophy in the early twentieth century was not the only factor ushering in cultural change: the new art of cinema also played a role in the multiplicity and mobility of perspective that began to surface in the visual arts and the novel. In Spain, Ortega y Gasset (more about whom shortly), began to develop his own theory of *perspectivismo* in the 1913 *Meditaciones del Quijote*, where he implied the existence of as many spaces as there were points of view (Kern 132).

4. Guy Habasque suggested that the twenty paintings by El Greco exhibited at the Salon d'Automne of 1908 also contributed to Picasso and Braque's new way of looking at reality (7). R. Gómez de la Serna recalls that in the early 1900s, Picasso's studio walls in Paris were hung with photographs of paintings by El Greco, and that Picasso was also tangentially influenced by Puvis de Chavannes (1929, 69).

5. Topical commentary in Spain on the link between Ortega and Einstein was also careful to point out that the theory of relativity did not uphold the general relativity of knowledge, but the relativity (i.e., *perspectivismo*) of the physical universe, nearly always ascribing to Ortega priority over Einstein in the formulation of this idea. See, for example, Manuel G. Morente's 1923 review "El tema de nuestro tiempo. Filosofía de la perspectiva" (211).

6. Ortega immediately pointed out that in the empirical universe omniscient vision of this kind did not exist (3:202), and he remarked that the absolute, *species aeternitatis* point of view Spinoza had postulated was a fiction (3:199). When he translated Charles Maurron's essay "On Reading Einstein" for a 1930 issue of the *Criterion*, T. S. Eliot coined an expression similar to Ortega's, writing that since no "observer-elect" existed, it would follow that there could be no single reality (Quinones 116).

7. From "M. François Mauriac et la literature," *Situations I* (quoted in Spencer 76). Sartre's "privileged observer" is similar to what Ortega and Eliot respectively called the omniscient point of view or the "observer-elect" (see note 6, above).

8. On the self-reflexive nature of Cubist art and literature of the 1920s and 30s, see Steiner (1982, 181), Spencer (56), and Roskill (1985, 163). Steiner adds that "the complication of space relations in Cubist painting could quite persuasively be approximated by a complication in temporal relations in Cubist writing" (182).

9. Mark Roskill observed that the "adjacency" of early film images may have contributed to the use of similar techniques in literature and art (1985, 35); it is suggestive that Azorín would comment on the simultaneity of visual images in an article on theatre and cinema. His implication that the past continues to flow into the present invokes Bergsonian connotations; conceptually Azorín also somewhat anticipates Wendy Steiner's argument that

"Cubist interaction with the past makes a simultaneity of it" whereby history is altered in context but not in substance (1982, 191). In Azorín's personal library there is an undated edition of Bergson's *Reflexions sur le temps, l'espace et la vie* as well as a 1923 edition of Guyau's *La Genèse de l'idée de temps*.

10. Joiner and Zdenek argue that the question of perspective was a lesson Azorín learned from the Impressionists (114). Given the period of time and the personal context in which he wrote *Salvadora de Olbena*, it is highly unlikely Azorín was inspired by Impressionist painting in this case, especially in view of the fact that in the same year he also published *María Fontán*, a novel undeniably inspired by Impressionist art, but one that has nothing in common with the stylistics, context, or thematics of *Salvadora de Olbena*.

11. Sharon Spencer writes that when an event in time is "halted for an exploration or exposure of its elements, it has been spatialized" (156). Jerome Klinkowitz points out that all Western literature needed to do to end "time's tyranny over space" was to replace the illusion of linear sequentiality in narrative with the self-conscious device of fiddling with compositional order (40). The tyranny of time also tyrannized Azorín and, as Gómez de la Serna shrewdly observed, Azorín's persistent attempts to commingle time and space are symptomatic of "la más develadora doctrina actual" (1957, 13). Cf. the prologue to *Angelita* where Azorín writes, "The sensation of time in the sensibility of a writer; the sensation of time and its double, space" (5:447).

12. In his important study "Azorín, idea y sentido de la microhistoria," Maravall not only discusses the effect quantum physics had on modern concepts of time, but he also makes an interesting case for Azorín being aware that time consisted of fundamentally discrete units. Similar to the postulates of quantum physics, Azorín's world view "is always discontinuous in its texture; the only thing that re-establishes continuity is repetition. Microhistory is a consciousness of discontinuities that repeat themselves. . . . Those 'moments'—we've called them quanta of meaning—that Azorín tries to capture through observation, do not play the role of facts . . ." (1968, 52–53; cf. 28–29).

13. Azorín was a great fan of Proust's, once commenting that he had read the entire oeuvre (5:179). What seems to have been of greatest interest to him was the manner in which Proust dealt with the concept of time that, for obvious reasons, Azorín felt resembled his own: "Three great facets or ideas prevail . . . in his work: first, the general detailing; second, the work of the subconscious; third, the sensation of time" (5:178). Azorín felt that it was Proust's detailed, rather than generic, descriptions which produced in the reader a tangible sensation of time's passing: "The idea of time is communicated through detail . . . to detail is to make things come alive. . . . And here's how Proust, thanks to meticulous and prolix detail, transmits to the reader the overwhelming sensation of time" ("Las dos ideas de Proust" in *La Prensa*, 22 October 1925; cf. 5:150). In his copy of Ortega's *El Espectador, VIII*, Azorín found the essay "Tiempo, distancia y forma en el arte de Proust" especially suggestive (it was first published in 1923, the same year as "La doctrina de perspectiva," and two years prior to Azorín's own essays on Proust in *La Prensa*, the second of which was published on 25 October 1925). Azorín annotated Ortega's passages on Proust's

"elasticizing" of time and space as well as his commentary on Proust's expansion of space through *detallismo* (99). Cf. Azorín's essay "La Mancha" (*EdC* 55); on the stylistic use of detail in the incipient stages of Azorín's own writing, see Alfaro López (225).

14. Dr. Casal, who studied medicine in England, also appreciates British art: "He was an enthusiastic admirer of . . . Turner, Hoggart [sic], Constable and the portraitists" (7:7587). Salvadora's father owned a reproduction of Rodin's *Desnarigado*, a landscape by Beruete, a sketch by Eduardo Rosales, and a portrait of Salvadora's mother painted in Paris by Francisco Domingo Marqués (7:646).

15. This thematic aspect of *Salvadora de Olbena* might also be considered an example of what Ortega called *sinfronismo*, the ability of human beings to establish currents of empathetic identification with civilizations remote in time from their own: "We surprise Azorín time and again in this maneuver of sampling the vital sentiment of the ages. His art consists of reviving that basic human affect across all time ("Azorín: Primores de lo vulgar," published in the same year as "Verdad y perspectiva." The quotation is from Ortega's *Obras completas* 2:163).

16. Cf. Camón Aznar: "Simultaneist paintings are composed of phenomena distant in time but concurrent in the space of the canvas itself" (1958, 355). In the same study Aznar quotes the Cubist painter Jacques Villon as saying that Cubism must present "in a mysterious but united whole, the different aspects of an object" (363).

17. Peter Halter observes that abandoning linear perspective in the visual arts coincided with the annihilation of narrative continuity in Modern literature (215).

18. Although I agree with Kathleen Glenn's assertion that for Azorín "ultimate reality is unknowable" (53), for the reasons just stated, I cannot concur that Azorín also considered fiction to be the "truest truth" (56).

19. Quoted in Spencer (52), the reference is to Sypher's *Rococo to Cubism in Art and Literature* (270). Cf. Berg on the parallels between simultaneous vision in literature and the efforts of Cézanne and the Cubists to remove objects from the "contingencies of relative perception" by depicting them from several angles at once (1992, 120). Without making any connection to Cubism, philosophical or scientific relativity, María Josefa Díez de Revenga comments in passing on Azorín's "práctica del simultaneísmo," observing that the thematic nucleus of *Salvadora de Olbena* consists in the presentation of diverse perspectives on the "impossibility of getting to the truth about human beings and their affects" (345–46). Cf. similar conclusions by Joiner and Zdenek (115).

20. Azorín's novel may not be as anachronistic as it first appears: it was only during the 1940s that the first serious scholarship on Cubism and the scientific-philosophical and literary ambience within which it evolved began to appear. Cf. Charles E. Gauss, *Aesthetic Theories of French Artists* (1949); Christopher Gray, *Cubist Aesthetic Theories* (1953); Joseph Frank, "Spatial Form in Modern Literature" (1945); Paul M. Laporte, "Cubism and Science" (1949) and "The Space-Time Concept in the Work of Picasso" (1948); Daniel-Henry Kahnweiler, *The Rise of Cubism* (English trans., 1949) and *Juan Gris, sa vie, son oeuvre, ses écrits* (1946); A. H. Barr, *Cubism and Abstract Art* (1936); the exhibition catalogue *Picasso, Fifty Years of his Art* (1946); Herbert Read, "The Situation

of Art in Europe at the End of the Second World War" (1948), repr. in *The Philosophy of Modern Art* (1955).

21. For cinema in Europe, see Kern (70); in Spain, Montes Huidobro (31). The influence of film on Cubism is borne out by the career of the Cubist painter Fernand Léger who was also an important avant-garde filmmaker.

22. Azorín wrote a handful of articles on the cinema in the 1920s, collected in Payá Bernabé and Rigual Bonastre (5–22). In "Lo azoriniano en *Doña Inés*," Elena Catena argues for the influence of the cinema as early as 1925 (*Cuadernos Hispanoamericanos*, no. 226–27, 1968). Also referring to *Doña Inés*, Thomas Meehan pointed to the "desdoblamiento temporal" (i.e., spatialization) that Azorín achieved in chapters 27 and 28 which relate the moment Diego and Inés realize, independently of each other, that they have fallen in love. Although this moment occurs simultaneously in time, it takes place in two different locations in space and must necessarily be narrated and apprehended diachroncially by author and reader. Cf. Eric Rabkin's observation that to speak of "spatializing" narrative is to speak metaphorically since readers can only actualize plot in the imagination *through* time (253).

23. The interview, "Los académicos y el cine," appeared in *Primer Plano* for 20 October 1940. A week later, Azorín published in the same periodical "El encanto de la luz," where he reiterated his statement on the importance of light and shadow in the cinema (Payá Bernabé and Rigual Bonastre 23).

24. Perhaps Azorín's preoccupation with the "temática amatoria" in the cinema would explain the appearance of related themes in his two 1944 novels, *María Fontán* and *Salvadora de Olbena* which he subtitled, respectively, "novela rosa" and "novela romántica." He actually quotes De Mille's commentary on feminine beauty in "La eterna cuestión" collected in *El cine y el momento* (45).

25. For a contemporary account of Azorín's cinematic activities, see José Montero Padilla, "'Azorín' y el cine" in *Revista de Literatura*, 4 (1953):359–65. Azorín's newly found interest in moving pictures is additionally documented by the respectable collection of books on the topic in his library.

26. Cf. the same observation Azorín made regarding J. M. W. Turner's intent to "freeze the moment" in paint (see part I, chapter 4). In the interview with Marino Gómez Santos appended to *El efímero cine*, Azorín says that the cinema is a product of the most salient features of modern life: multiplicity, speed, and fugacity (155). He confirms Stephen Kern's observation that modern artists, novelists, and poets responded to the notion of simultaneity made possible by new technologies such as the wireless, high-speed rotary presses, the cinema, and the telephone (68).

27. In "El primer arte" (*EC*), Azorín remarks that in the movies time and space are limitless (23), and in "Don José Soriano" (*VH*), he indicates an awareness of the dialectic between synchrony and diachrony implied by the space-time continuum: ". . . time implies the chronology of things; eternity is not chronological" (40).

28. Cf. Arnold Hauser's observation that time is "the real medium of film and the basic category of its world-picture" (quoted in Spencer 155).

29. Reproduced in Lapierre (234). The italics are Carné's, but Azorín underscored them in his copy of the book. He quotes directly from Berthomieu's *Grammaire* in *El cine y el momento* (131).

30. In "El cine," Azorín observes that, while film can provide both partial and complete views of persons, objects, or events, in many instances it is the partial perspective that is more evocative (*EC* 17). Mario Vargas Llosa recently observed that Azorín's novelistic world is rather similar to the Cubist fragmentation of perception, and commented on his "prose submitted to such merciless purification that it seems only the visual element survives." Vargas Llosa argues that *Doña Inés*, *Don Juan*, and *Salvadora de Olbena* anticipate the formal features of the *nouveaux romans* by Robbe-Grillet, Claude Simon, and Nathalie Sarraute (53).

31. Cf. Azorín's comment that, "For me—and for many others—there is no present, nor future, or past: everything is present. And if everything is present, why should I maintain a chronological order that does not exist in reality?" (8:342). And, speaking of frames of reference, Azorín even contextualized the cinema within a visual arts paradigm, suggesting that film rehabilitated traditional history painting since both art forms depend on composition for their realization. He used Emilio Sala's painting *La expulsión de los judíos* (1889), as an example of the skill the history painter, qua film director, needed to have in order to arrange crowd scenes successfully ("El director" in *El efímero cine* 139). Azorín made a similar allusion to Rembrandt's *The Anatomy Lesson of Dr. Nicholas Tulp*, a painting reproduced as the frontispiece of *El cine y el momento* (cf. Fig. 11), which he considered an admirable example of painterly composition that also could be taken "as a model of cinematic composition" (*ABC*, 30 November 1960). Elsewhere Azorín argued that realism in film should not take the truculence of Zola's *L'Oeuvre* to be exemplary; rather, the norm should be modelled on Murillo's *La cocina de los ángeles* (cf. Fig. 18) whose angel-cooks are portrayed as realistically as the "two gentlemen and a monk—who contemplate the scene, and like the other monk who is depicted levitating in the air" in the same painting (*CM* 63).

Works Cited

Abbott, James H. 1963. "Azorín and Taine's Determinism." 46.3:476–79.

———. 1973. *Azorín y Francia*. Madrid: Seminarios y Ediciones.

Adams, Steven. 1994. *The Barbizon School and the Origins of Impressionism*. London: Phaidon.

A Day in the Country. Impressionism and the French Landscape, exhib. cat. 1984. Los Angeles: Los Angeles County Museum of Art, 28 June–16 September.

Aldritt, Keith. 1971. *The Visual Imagination of D. H. Lawrence*. London: Edward Arnold.

Alfaro López, José. 1979. *Madrid: Primera década del siglo XX (1901–1910)*. Madrid: Magisterio.

Almagro San Martín, Melchor de. 1944. "Zuloaga y su arte o vindicación de la 'españolada.' " *El Español* (22 January):16, 12.

Alpers, Svetlana. 1976. "Describe or Narrate? A Problem in Realistic Representation." *New Literary History* 8:15–41.

———. 1983. "Interpretation without Representation, or, the Viewing of *Las Meninas*." *Representations* 1:31–42.

———. 1988. *Rembrandt's Enterprise: The Studio and Market*. Chicago: University of Chicago Press.

Altamira, Rafael. 1898a. *De Historia y Arte (estudios críticos)*. Madrid: Victoriano Suárez.

———. 1898b. "El movimiento histórico en España." *BILE* (June 30): 178–87.

Álvarez Lopera, José. 1987. *De Cean a Cossío: La fortuna crítica del Greco en el siglo XIX. Textos, documentos y bibliografía*. Madrid: Fundación Universitaria Española.

Aman-Jean, Edmond. 1913. *Velázquez*. Paris: Alcan.

Antliff, Mark. 1993. *Inventing Bergson: Cultural Politics and the Parisian Avant Garde*. Princeton: Princeton University Press.

Araújo, Fernando. 1909. "El Impresionsimo." *La España Moderna* 21:174–77.

Arcimis, Augusto. 1891. "Clasificación de las nubes." *BILE* (November 30):348–52.

Arteaga, Cristina de. 1926. "Una tarde con Zuloaga." *Arte Español* 8, no. 4:144–48.

Ashton, Peter Shaw, Seymour Slive, and Alice Davies. 1982. "Jacob van Ruisdael's Trees." *Arnoldia* 42:2–31.

Aureliano de Beruete (1845–1912), exhib. cat. 1983. (Madrid: Caja de Pensiones, 22 March–14 May). Madrid: Caja de Pensiones.

Azcoaga, Enrique. 1972. "Azorín y la Pintura." *Homenaje Nacional al Maestro Azorín*. Alicante: Diputación Nacional.

Azorín: see entries for Martínez Ruiz, José.

Babelon, Jean. 1952. "La España de Manet y el Manet de España." *Clavileño* 14: 15–20.

Bachrach, A. G. H. 1980. "Turner, Ruisdael and the Dutch." *Turner Studies* 1: 19–30.

Bahamonde Magro, Angel y Julián Mérida. 1978. *Burguesía, especulación y cuestión social en el Madrid del siglo XX*. Madrid: Siglo XXI.

Bal, Mieke. 1991. *Reading Rembrandt: Beyond the Word-Image Opposition*. Cambridge: Cambridge University Press.

——— and Norman Bryson. 1991. "Semiotics and Art History." *Art Bulletin* 73, no. 2 (June): 174–208.

Balart, Federico. 1894. *Impresionismo. Literatura y Arte*. Madrid: Fernando Fe.

Bally, Charles, Elise Richter, Amado Alonso, and Raimundo Lida. 1956. *El impresionsimo en el lenguaje*. 3d ed. Trans. Amado Alonso and Raimundo Lida. Buenos Aires: University of Buenos Aires Press.

Balsa de la Vega, Rafael. 1891. *Artistas y críticos españoles*. Barcelona: Arte y Letras.

Barán, A. L. de. [Miquel Utrillo]. 1898. "Darío de Regoyos." *Luz* 8 (December):n.p.

Baroja, Pío. 1949. *Obras Completas*. Vol. 7. Madrid: Biblioteca Nueva.

———. 1951. *Obras Completas*. Vol. 8. Madrid: Biblioteca Nueva.

———. 1970. *Desde la última vuelta del camino*. Barcelona: Planeta.

———. n.d. *Camino de perfección. (Pasión mística)*. New York: Las Américas.

Baroja, Ricardo. 1952. *Gente del 98*. Barcelona: Editorial Juventud.

Barrès, Maurice. 1988. *Greco, ou le secret de Tolède*. Edited by Jean-Marie Domenach. Brussels: Editions Complexe.

Barrio-Garay, José Luis. 1978. *José Gutiérrez Solana: Paintings and Writings*. Lewisburg: Bucknell University Press.

Barrois, Charles. 1902. "Don José Macpherson. Notice nécrologique." *Société Géologique du Nord* 31:213–17.

Barth, John. 1980. "The Literature of Replenishment: Postmodernist Fiction." *Atlantic Monthly* 245, no. 1:65–71.

Barthes, Roland. 1986. "The Reality Effect." Trans. Richard Howard. *The Rustle of Language*. New York: Hill & Wang, 141–48.

Bataille, Georges. 1983. *Manet*. Geneva: Skira.

Baudelaire, Charles. 1890. *Curiosités esthétiques*. Paris: n.p.

———. 1919. *Journaux intimes*. Paris: G. Crès.

———. 1965. *The Painter of Modern Life and Other Essays*. Trans. and ed. Jonathan Mayne. London: Phaidon.

Bazarov, Konstantin. 1981. *Landscape Painting*. New York: Octopus Books.

Beaunier, André. 1906. *L'Art de regarder les tableaux*. Paris: Librairie Centrale des Beaux-Arts.

Becker, George J., and Edith Philips, eds. and trans. 1971. *Paris and the Arts, 1851–1896: From the Goncourt Journal*. Ithaca: Cornell University Press.

Benito, Angel. 1991. *Vázquez Díaz: Vida y Pintura*. Madrid: Dirección General de Bellas Artes.

Berg, William J. 1985. "*L'Oeuvre*: Naturalism and Impressionism." *L'Esprit Créateur* 25, no. 4:42–50.

———. 1992. *The Visual Novel. Émile Zola and the Art of His Times*. University Park: Penn State University Press.

Berger, John. 1969. *The Moment of Cubism and other Essays*. London: Weidenfeld and Nicolson.

Bergmann, Emilie. 1976. "Painting in Poetry: Góngora's Ekphrasis." In *The Analysis of Hispanic Texts: Current Trends in Metholodogy*, ed. by Mary Ann Beck, Lisa E. Davis, et al. New York: Bilingual Press. 242–55.

———. 1978. *Art Inscribed: Essays on Ekphrasis in Spanish Golden Age Poetry*. Cambridge, MA: Harvard University Press.

Bermingham, Ann. 1989. *Landscape and Ideology: The English Rustic Tradition, 1740–1860*. Berkeley: University of California Press.

Bermúdez Cañete, Federico. 1979. "Notas sobre el paisaje en Baroja." In *Estudios sobre literatura y arte dedicados al Profesor Orozco-Díaz*, ed. A. Andrés Soria Gallego Morrell. 3 vols. Granada: Granada University Press. 1:143–67.

Bernal Muñoz, José Luis. 1990. "Museos y exposiciones en el cambio del siglo, 1897–1903." *Cuadernos de arte e iconografía* 3, no. 6:77–89.

———. 1991. "Regoyos visto por Regoyos." *Goya*, no. 220:220–29.

———. 1992. "Las vanguardias artísticas vistas por Pío Baroja." *Cuadernos de arte e iconografía* 4, no. 9:205–16.

Bernaldo de Quirós y Pérez, Constancio, and J. M. Llanas Aguilaniedo. 1901. *La mala vida en Madrid*. Madrid: Rodríguez Serra.

Berthomieu, André. 1946. *Essai de Grammaire Cinématographique*. Paris: La Nouvelle Edition.

Beruete, Aureliano de. 1898. "Carlos de Haes." *La Ilustración Española y Americana* (June 30):379.

———. 1900. *Entre Rocas*. Madrid: Velasco-Sociedad de Autores Españoles.

———. 1906. *Velázquez*. Translated by Hugh E. Poynter. London: Methuen.

———. 1908. "Martín Rico." *Cultura Española*, no. 10:527–47.

Beruete y Moret, Aureliano de. 1926. *Historia de la pintura española en el siglo XIX: Elementos nacionales y extranjeros que han influído en ella*. Madrid: Ruiz Hermanos.

Black, Max. 1962. "Metaphor." In *Philosophy Looks at the Arts: Contemporary Readings in Aesthetics*, ed. Joseph Margolis. New York: Scribner's. 218–35.

Bly, Peter A. 1986. *Vision and the Visual Arts in Galdós: A Study of the Novels and Newspaper Articles*. Liverpool: Francis Cairns.

Bonet, Laureano. 1987. "El Greco como tópico literario en *La lámpara maravillosa*." In *Genio y virtuosismo de Valle-Inclán*, ed. John P. Gabriele. Madrid: Orígenes. 139–50.

———. 1990. "*Diario de un enfermo*, de Azorín: El momento y la sensación." In *Divergencias y Unidad: Perspectivas sobre la Generación del 98 y Antonio Machado*, ed. John P. Gabriele. Madrid: Orígenes. 81–97.

Borrell, Félix. 1912. *El wagnerismo en Madrid*. Madrid: Ducazcal.

Bouret, Jean. 1973. *The Barbizon School and 19th Century French Landscape Painting*. Greenwich, CT: New York Graphic Society.

Brettell, Richard. 1984. "The Impressionist Landscape and the Image of France." In exhib. cat. *A Day in the Country: Impressionism and the French Landscape*. Los Angeles: Los Angeles County Museum of Art. 27–49.

———. 1991. "French Painting and the European Vanguard." In *Impressionism and European Modernism*, ed. Norma Roberts. Seattle: University of Washington Press. 12–17.

Brinton, Christian. 1909. "Two Great Spanish Painters: Sorolla and Zuloaga." *Century Magazine* 78, no. 1 (May):26–36.

Brion, Marcel. 1929. *Turner*. Paris: Rieder.

Brogan, Jacqueline Vaught. 1986. *Stevens and Simile: A*

Theory of Language. Princeton: Princeton University Press.

Brown, David Blayney. 1990. *The Art of J. M. W. Turner.* London: Headline.

Brown, Sara. 1958. "Velázquez." *Cuadernos Americanos* 97, no. 1: 239–59; 98, no. 2:190–216.

Burnetière, Ferdinand. 1883. "L'Impressionnisme dans le roman." *Le Roman naturaliste.* Paris: Calman Levy. 75–104.

Bryson, Norman. 1981. "Diderot and the Image." *Word and Image: French Painting of the Ancien Régime.* Cambridge: Cambridge University Press. 179–203.

———. 1988. "Intertextuality and Visual Poetics." *Style* 22, no. 2:183–93.

———, Michael Ann Holly, and Keith Mosey, eds. 1991. *Visual Theory: Painting and Interpretation.* Cambridge: Polity.

Buchloh, Benjamin H. D., Serge Guilbaut, and David Solkin, eds. 1983. *Modernism and Modernity: The Vancouver Conference Papers.* Halifax, Nova Scotia: The Press of the Nova Scotia College of Art and Design.

Buero Vallejo, Antonio. 1973. "El espejo de *Las Meninas.*" *Tres maestros ante el público (Valle-Inclán, Velázquez, Lorca).* Madrid: Alianza. 55–93.

———. 1992. "Acerca de *Las Meninas.*" *Insula,* no. 541 (January):1–2, 27–28.

Burwick, Frederick. 1990. "The Grotesque: Illusion vs. Delusion." In *Aesthetic Illusion: Theoretical and Historial Approaches,* ed. Frederick Burwick and Walter Pape. Berlin and New York: Walter de Gruyter, 122–37.

Butler, Christopher. 1994. *Early Modernism: Literature, Music, and Painting in Europe, 1900–1916.* New York: Oxford University Press.

Caballero, Fermín. 1840. *Noticias topográficas-estadísticas sobre la administración de Madrid.* Madrid: Yenes.

Cajide, Isabel. 1969. "Aureliano de Beruete, renovador del paisaje." *Artes,* no. 100:3–6.

Calvo Serraller, Francisco. 1985. "Identification du XIXè siècle espagnol." *Revue de l'Art,* no. 70:75–82.

Camón Aznar, José. 1947. "El espacio en la estética de Azorín." *ABC,* 8 February.

———. 1955. "El impresionismo español." *Un siglo de arte español (1856–1956).* Madrid. 37–53.

———. 1957. "El arte de Azorín." *ABC,* 3 July.

———. 1958. *El tiempo en el arte.* Madrid: Sociedad de Estudios y Publicaciones.

———. 1968. "*Las Meninas* de Velázquez, según Picasso." *Goya,* no. 86 (September–October):88–93.

Campos, Jorge. 1964. *Conversaciones con Azorín.* Madrid: Taurus.

Cardenal de Iracheta, Manuel. 1954. "Don Ricardo Baroja, escritor." *Clavileño* 5:43–50.

Carlos de Haes. Un maestro del paisaje del siglo XIX, exhib. cat. 1996. (Zaragoza: Centro de Exposiciones y Congresos, May–June 1996). Zaragoza: Ibercaja.

Carné, Marcel. 1946. "La caméra, personnage du drame." In *Anthologie du cinéma,* ed. Marcel Lapierre. Paris: La Nouvelle Edition. 233–35.

Caro Baroja, Julio. 1957. "El paisaje en la obra de los hermanos Baroja." *Clavileño* 8:64–69.

Carrier, David. 1987. "Ekphrasis and Interpretation: Two Modes of Art History Writing." *British Journal of Aesthetics* 27, no. 1:20–31.

Carroll, David, ed. 1990. *The States of "Theory": History, Art, and Critical Discourse.* New York: Columbia University Press.

Castan Palomar, Fernando. 1940. "Los académicos españoles y el cine." *Primer Plano,* 20 October.

Catena, Elena, ed. 1981. *Doña Inés (Historia de amor),* by José Martínez Ruiz. 2d ed. Madrid: Castalia.

Caws, Mary Ann. 1985. *Reading Frames in Modern Fiction.* Princeton: Princeton University Press.

Centro y periferia en la modernización de la pintura española (1880–1918), exhib. cat. 1993. (Madrid: Palacio de Velázquez; Bilbao: Museo de Bellas Artes, 1993–94). Barcelona: Ambit.

Chaffee, Diane. 1984. "Visual Art in Literature: The Role of Time and Space in Ekphrastic Creation." *Revista Canadiense de Estudios Hispánicos* 8, no. 3:311–20.

Clark, Kenneth. 1976. *Landscape into Art.* New York: Harper & Row.

Clark, T. J. 1986. *The Painting of Modern Life: Paris in the Art of Manet and His Followers.* Princeton: Princeton University Press.

Clarke, Michael. 1991. *Corot and the Art of Landscape.* New York: Cross River.

Clavería, Carlos. 1953. "Azorín, intérprete de los clásicos." *Insula,* no. 94 (15 October):3, 11.

Cobb, Christopher H. 1977. "Barrès, Azorín y el ideal conservador." *Neophilologus* 61, no. 3:384–395.

Cohen, Ted. 1978. "Metaphor and the Cultivation of Intimacy." *Critical Inquiry* 5, no. 1:3–12.

Colley, Ann C. 1990. *The Search for Synthesis in Literature and Art: The Paradox of Space.* Athens: University of Georgia Press.

Collier, Peter, and Robert Lethbridge, eds. 1994. *Artistic Relations and the Visual Arts in Nineteenth-Century France.* New Haven: Yale University Press.

Cooper, Douglas. 1971. *The Cubist Epoch.* London: Phaidon.

Corbin, Alain. 1982. *Les filles de noce (misère sexuelle et prostitution au XIXème siècle).* Paris: Flammarion.

Corral José del. 1967. "La Gran Vía de José Antonio. Datos sobre su historia y construcciones." *Anales del Instituto de Estudios Madrileños* 2:369–89.

Cossío, Manuel B. 1897. "Preparación para el estudio del arte." *BILE,* no. 442 (January):4–9.

———. 1907. "El Greco, Velázquez y el arte moderno." *BILE* 31 (November):336- 46; 31 (December):373–81.

———. 1908. *El Greco.* 2 vols. Madrid: Victoriano Suárez.

———. 1925a. "Las 'Conferencias de Arte' de Aureliano Beruete y Moret." *BILE* 49:25–29.

———. 1925b. "El arte en Toledo." *BILE* 49:245–86.

———. 1931. "El Greco." *BILE* 55:273–78.

Costello, Bonnie. 1985. "Effects of an Analogy: Wallace Stevens and Painting." In *Wallace Stevens: The Poetics of Modernism,* ed. Albert Gelpi. New York: Cambridge University Press.

Dällenbach, Lucien. 1989. *The Mirror in the Text.* Trans.

Jeremy Whiteley with Emma Hughes. Chicago: University of Chicago Press.

Darío de Regoyos (1857–1913), exhib. cat. 1986. (Madrid: Sala de Exposiciones de la Fundación Caja de Pensiones, 21 November 1986–12 January 1987). Madrid: Caja de Pensiones.

Dauzet, Pierre. 1948. *Le Siècle des chemins de fer en France*. Paris: Bellenand.

Diderot, Denis. 1959. "Pensées détachées sur la peinture." In *Oeuvres esthétiques*, ed. Paul Vernière. Paris: Garnier. 741–840.

———. 1984. *Salon de 1765. Essais sur la peinture*. Ed. Else Marie Bukdahl, Annette Lorenceau, and Gita May. Paris: Hermann.

Díez de Revenga, Francisco Javier. 1976. "Cromatismo y sensibilidad de Azorín." *Homenaje a Azorín*. Alicante: Instituto de Estudios Alicantinos. 105–14.

Díez de Revenga, María Josefa. 1993. "Azorín novelista. De *Don Juan* a *Salvadora de Olbena*." *Anales Azorinianos* 4:335–48.

Dijkstra, Bram. 1971. "Wallace Stevens and William Carlos Williams: Poetry, Painting, and the Function of Reality." In *Encounters: Essays on Literature and the Visual Arts*, ed. John Dixon Hunt. New York: Norton.

Discursos leídos en las recepciones y actos públicos celebrados por la Academia de las Tres Nobles Artes de San Fernando desde 1859. 1872. Madrid: Manuel Tello.

Dittmar, Linda. 1983. "Fashioning and Re-Fashioning: Framing Narratives in the Novel and Film." *Mosaic* 16:189–203.

Domenech, Rafael. 1901. "Santiago Rusiñol." *La Lectura* 2:727–42; 850–67.

———. 1912. "Aureliano de Beruete." *Museum* 2:421–34.

Dubois, J., F. Edeline, J-M. Klinkenberg, et al. 1981. *A General Rhetoric*. Trans. Paul B. Burrell and Edgar M. Slotkin. Baltimore: Johns Hopkins University Press.

Dubois, Page. 1982. *History, Rhetorical Description and the Epic: From Homer to Spenser*. Totowa, NJ: D.S. Brewer.

Duncan, Philip. 1985. "The 'Art' of Landscape in Zola's *L'Oeuvre*." *Symposium* 39:167–76.

Eight Essays on Joaquín Sorolla y Batista. 1909. 2 vols. New York: The Hispanic Society of New York.

Eliot, T. S. 1945. *What Is a Classic?* London: Faber & Faber.

Embeita, María. 1973. "El impresionismo como visión filosófica de *La Voluntad* de Martínez Ruiz." *Boletín de la Asociación Europea de Profesores de Español* 5, no. 9:67–73.

Encina, Juan de la. [Ricardo Gutiérrez Abascal]. 1917. "El arte de Ignacio Zuloaga." *Hermes*, no. 8 (August): n.p.

Enguídanos, Miguel. 1959. "Azorín en busca del tiempo divinal." *Papeles de Son Armadans* 15:13–22.

Ermarth, Elizabeth. 1992. *Sequel to History: Postmodernism and the Crisis of Representational Time*. Princeton: Princeton University Press.

Espí Valdés, Adrián. 1976 "José Martínez Ruiz y los pintores de Alicante." In *Homenaje a Azorín. Ponencias y Comunicaciones, Monóvar, 1973*. Monóvar: Instituto de Estudios Alicantinos.

Esrock, Ellen. 1994. *The Reader's Eye: Visual Imaging as Reader Response*. Baltimore: Johns Hopkins University Press.

Exposición-Homenaje a Ricardo Baroja. 1957. Exhib. cat. with intro. by Enrique Lafuente Ferrari. Madrid: Museo Nacional de Arte Moderno.

Falkenburg, Reindert L. 1988. *Joachim Patinir: Landscape as an Image of the Pilgrimage of Life*. Trans. Michael Hoyle. Amsterdam & Philadelphia: John Benjamins.

Faraldo, Ramón D. n.d. *Aureliano de Beruete, pintor*. Barcelona: Omega.

Fernández Almagro, Melchor. 1948. *En torno al 98*. Madrid: Jordan.

———. 1962. "Vázquez Díaz y la literatura." *ABC*, 4 April.

Ferrand, Manuel. 1974. "Azorín y la pintura." *Azorín, Cien Años (1873–1973)*. Seville: University of Seville Press. 173–84.

Fiesta de Aranjuez en Honor de Azorín. 1915. Madrid: Publicaciones de la Residencia de Estudiantes.

Fontanella, Lee. 1981. *La historia de la fotografía en España desde sus orígenes hasta 1900*. Madrid: El Viso.

Foster, Hal, ed. 1988. *Vision and Visuality*. Seattle: Bay Press for Dia Art Foundation.

Foucault, Michel. 1973. "Las Meninas." *The Order of Things. An Archaeology of the Human Sciences*. New York: Vintage. 3–16.

Fox, E. Inman. 1988. *Ideología y política en las letras de fin de siglo*. Madrid: Espasa Calpe.

———. 1989. "Spanish Writers as Political Intellectuals." *Romance Quarterly* 36, no. 3:299–306.

———. 1990. "Hacia una nueva historia literaria para España." *Dai modernisimi alle Avanguardie*. Palermo: Flaccovio. 7–17.

———. 1993. "Azorín y el franquismo. Un escritor entre el silencio y la propaganda." *Anales Azorinianos* 4:81–117.

———. 1997. *La invención de Castilla. Nacionalismo liberal e identidad nacional*. Madrid: Cátedra.

———, ed. 1968. *La Voluntad*, by José Martínez Ruiz. Madrid: Castalia.

———, ed. 1970. *Antonio Azorín*, by José Martínez Ruiz. Barcelona: Labor.

———, ed. 1991. *Castilla*, by José Martínez Ruiz. Madrid: Espasa-Calpe.

Francés, José. 1924. "La peinture espagnole depuis le milieu du XIXè siècle." *La Revue de l'Art Ancien et Moderne* 45:25–34, 96–105, 165–74, 323–34; 46: 265–73.

Frank, Joseph. 1945. "Spatial Form in Modern Literature." *Sewanee Review* 53: 221–40, 433–56, 643–63.

Fried, Michael. 1996. *Manet's Modernism or, the Face of Painting in the 1860s*. Chicago: University of Chicago Press.

Fromentin, Eugène. 1984. *Oeuvres Complètes*. 2 vols. Ed. Guy Sagnes. Paris: Gallimard.

Fromrich, Yane, 1997. "Watteau et la gravure." *Pèlerinage à Watteau*. 4 vols. Paris: Hotel de la Monnaie. 1:149–66.

Fuster, Antonio F. 1970. *Impresionismo español*. Madrid: Valera.

Ganivet, Angel. 1961–62. *Obras Completas*. 3d ed. 2 vols. Madrid: Aguilar.

García Antón, Irene. 1990. "El mundo de Azorín visto por Ignacio Zuloaga." *Lecturas de Historia de Arte* 2:500–504.

Gauss, Charles E. 1949. *Aesthetic Theories of French Artists, 1885 to the Present.* Baltimore: Johns Hopkins University Press.

Gaya Nuño, Juan Antonio. 1974. *El Impresionismo en España.* Madrid: Comisaría General de Exposiciones.

Geffroy, Gustave. 1924. *Corot.* Paris: Nilsson.

Geikie, Archibald. [1898] 1970. *Types of Scenery and Their Influence on Literature.* Port Washington and London: Kennikat Press.

Giner de los Ríos, Francisco. 1895. "La pintura impresionista francesa." *BILE* 19 (March):83–88.

———. 1897. "Espíritu y naturaleza." *BILE* 21 (June): 165–69.

———. 1915. "Paisaje." *La Lectura* 1:361–70.

———. 1919. *Estudios de literatura y arte.* Vol. 3 of *Obras Completas.* Madrid: La Lectura.

———. 1924. *Pedagogía universitaria. Problemas y noticias.* Vol. 10 of *Obras Completas.* Madrid: La Lectura.

———. 1925. *Filosofía y sociología. Estudios de exposición y crítica.* Vol. 11 of *Obras Completas.* Madrid: Espasa-Calpe.

———. 1933a. *Estudios sobre educación.* 2d ed. Vol. 7 of *Obras Completas.* Madrid: Espasa-Calpe.

———. 1933b. *Educación y enseñanza.* 2d ed. Vol. 12 of *Obras Completas.* Madrid: Espasa-Calpe.

———. 1936. *Arqueología artística de la Península.* Vol. 20 of *Obras Completas.* Madrid: Espasa-Calpe.

———. 1965. *Ensayos y cartas.* Mexico: Fondo de Cultura Económica.

Giner Pantoja, José. 1977. "La educación estética en la Institución." *En el centenario de la Institución Libre de Enseñanza.* Madrid: Tecnos. 51–56.

Glenn, Kathleen M. 1976. "Azorín's *Salvadora de Olbena*: Reality and the Artist." *Hispanófila* 19:53–62.

Golding, John. 1988. *Cubism. A History and an Analysis, 1907–1914.* 3d ed. Cambridge, MA: Harvard University Press.

Gómez Carrillo, Enrique. 1920. "El cubismo y su estética." *El Liberal* 30 June: 1–2.

Gómez de la Serna, Gaspar. 1960. "Velázquez y el 98." *Villa de Madrid* 3, no. 14:40–44.

Gómez de la Serna, Ramón. 1929. "Completa y verídica historia de Picasso y el Cubismo." *Revista de Occidente* 73 (July):63–102; 73 (August):224–50.

———. 1943. *Don Diego Velázquez.* Buenos Aires: Poseidon.

———. 1944. *José Gutiérrez Solana.* Buenos Aires: Poseidon.

———. 1957. *Azorín.* 3d ed. Buenos Aires: Losada.

Gómez Martínez, José Luis. 1987. "Krausismo, modernismo y ensayo." In *Nuevos Asedios al Modernismo,* ed. Ivan A. Schulman. Madrid: Taurus. 210–26.

Gómez Molleda, Dolores. 1966. *Los reformadores de la España contemporánea.* Madrid: Consejo Superior de Investigaciones Científicas.

Goncourt, Edmond and Jules de. 1873. *Gavarni. L'homme et l'oeuvre.* Paris: Flammarion.

Gowing, Lawrence. 1966. *Turner: Imagination and Reality.* New York: Museum of Modern Art.

Graña, César. 1971. *Fact and Symbol: Essays in the Sociology of Art and Literature.* New York: Oxford University Press.

Granell, Manuel. 1949. *Estética de Azorín.* Madrid: Biblioteca Nueva.

Granjel, Luis. 1958. *Retrato de Azorín.* Madrid: Guadarrama.

Gray, Christopher. 1953. *Cubist Aesthetic Theories.* Baltimore: Johns Hopkins University Press.

Guerlin, Henri, ed. n.d. *Le Paysage.* Paris: Henri Laurens.

Gullón, Ricardo. 1952. "El impresionista Darío de Regoyos." *Clavileño* 3: 37–45.

Gysin, Fritz. 1989. "Paintings in the House of Fiction: The Example of Hawthorne." *Word and Image* 5:159–72.

Habasque, Guy. 1959. *Cubism: Biographical and Critical Study.* Trans. Stuart Gilbert. Lausanne: Skira.

Haes, Carlos. 1872. "De la pintura del paisaje antigua y moderna." *Discursos leídos en las recepciones de actos públicos, celebrados por la Academia de las Tres Nobles Artes de San Fernando desde el 19 de junio de 1859.* Madrid: 281–96.

Halter, Peter. 1994. *The Revolution in the Visual Arts and the Poetry of William Carlos Williams.* Cambridge: Cambridge University Press.

Hanson, Anne Coffin. 1972. "Popular Imagery and the Work of Édouard Manet." In *French Nineteenth-Century Painting and Literature,* ed. Ulrich Finke. Manchester: Manchester University Press. 133–63.

Hawkes, Terence. 1972. *Metaphor.* London: Methuen.

Heffernan, James A. W. 1984. *The Re-Creation of Landscape: A Study of Wordsworth, Coleridge, Constable, and Turner.* Hanover, NH: University Press of New England.

———. 1985. "Resemblance, Sign and Metaphor in the Visual Arts." *Journal of Aesthetics and Art Criticism* 44, no. 2:167–80.

———. 1987. "Space and Time in Literature and the Visual Arts." *Soundings* 70, nos. 1–2:95–119.

———. 1991. "Ekphrasis and Representation." *New Literary History* 22, no. 2: 297–316.

———. 1993. *Museum of Words. The Poetics of Ekphrasis from Homer to Ashbery.* Chicago: University of Chicago Press.

———, ed. 1987. *Space, Time, Image, Sign. Essays on Literature and the Visual Arts.* New York: Peter Lang.

Helsinger, Elizabeth. 1989. "Constable: The Making of a National Painter." *Critical Inquiry* 15:253–79.

Henderson, Linda D. 1971. "A New Facet of Cubism: 'The Fourth Dimension' and 'Non-Euclidean Geometry' Reinterpreted." *Art Quarterly* 34, no. 4:410–33.

Henry, Albert. 1971. *Métonymie et Métaphore.* Paris: Klincksieck.

Herbert, Robert L. 1962. *Barbizon Revisited.* Boston: Museum of Fine Arts.

———. 1981. "Industry and the Changing Landscape from Daubigny to Monet." In *French Cities in the Nineteenth Century,* ed. John Merriman. New York: Holmes & Meier. 139–64.

———. 1988. *Impressionism: Art, Leisure, and Parisian Society.* New Haven: Yale University Press.

Hermes. 1917. Número consagrado a Ignacio Zuloaga. August.

Hernández Pacheco, E. 1927. "El geólogo D. José de Macpherson y su influencia en la ciencia española." *BILE* 51 (31 August):252–56; 51 (30 September): 280–84.

Hinterhauser, Hans. 1980. *Fin de siglo. Figuras y mitos.* Trans. María Teresa Martínez. Madrid: Taurus.

Hollander, John. 1988. "The Poetics of Ekphrasis." *Word and Image* 4:209–19.

Hopkins, Viola. 1961. "Visual Art Devices and Parallels in the Fiction of Henry James." *PMLA* 76:561–74.

Hourticq, Louis. n.d. *Manet.* Paris: Librairie Centrale des Beaux-Arts.

Ilie, Paul. 1980. *Literature and Inner Exile. Authoritarian Spain, 1939–1975.* Baltimore: Johns Hopkins University Press.

Ironside, Robert, ed. and trans. 1948. *French XVIII Century Painters,* by Edmond and Jules de Goncourt. New York: Phaidon.

Isaccson, Joel. 1969. "Manet and Spain." *Manet and Spain: Prints and Drawings.* Ann Arbor: University of Michigan Press. 9–16.

Jardí, Enric. 1989. *Joaquim Mir.* Barcelona: Ediciones Polígrafa.

Jay, Martin. 1988. "Scopic Regimes of Modernity." In *Vision and Visuality,* ed. Hal Foster. Seattle: Bay Press. 3–23.

Jiménez Burillo, Pablo and Florencio de Santa-Ana Álvarez-Ossorio, eds. 1995. *Joaquín Sorolla (1863–1923).* Madrid: Fundación Cultural MAPFRE VIDA.

Jiménez-García, Antonio. 1986. *El Krausismo y la Institución Libre de Enseñanza.* Madrid: Cincel.

Jiménez Landi, J. 1977. "Científicos en la Institución Libre de Enseñanza." *En el Centenario de la Institución Libre de Enseñanza.* Madrid: Tecnos.

Jiménez Placer, Fernando. 1955. *Historia del Arte Español.* Barcelona: Labor.

J. Laurent, I. 1983. Exhib. cat. Madrid: Ministerio de Cultura-Museo Español de Arte Contemporáneo.

Johnson, Galen A., ed. 1993. *The Merleau-Ponty Aesthetics Reader: Philosophy and Painting.* Evanston: Northwestern University Press.

Johnson, Roberta L., ed. 1996. *Las bibliotecas de Azorín.* Alicante: Caja de Ahorros del Mediterráneo.

Joiner, L. D., and J. W. Zdeneck. 1976. "*Salvadora de Olbena*: A Summa of Azorín's Artistic Credo." *Research Studies* 44:111–19.

Jongh-Rossel, Elena de. 1985. *El Krausismo y La Generación de 1898.* Valencia and Chapel Hill: Albatrós-Hispanófila.

———. 1986. "El paisaje castellano y sus descubridores: anticipando el 98." *Hispanic Journal* 7:73–80.

———. 1991. "El Krausismo gineriano del joven Azorín." *Letras Peninsulares* 4, no.1:139–53.

Jove, José María. 1952. "El impresionismo y los impresionistas españoles." *Arbor* 22:24–45.

Jurkevich, Gayana. 1991. *The Elusive Self: Archetypal Approaches to the Novels of Miguel de Unamuno.* Columbia and London: University of Missouri Press.

———. 1992a. "Maese Pedro Unamuno: Carlyle and Narrative Experiment in *Niebla.*" *Canadian Review of Comparative Literature* 19, no. 4:569–83.

———. 1992b. "'Abulia', Nineteenth-Century Psychology and the Generation of 1898." *Hispanic Review* 60, no. 2:181–94.

Kearns, James. 1994. "The Writing on the Wall: Description of Painting in the Art Criticism of the French Symbolists." In *Artistic Relations in the Visual Arts in Nineteenth-Century France,* ed. Peter Collier and Robert Lethbridge. New Haven: Yale University Press. 239–52.

Keller, Alex. 1983. "Continuity and Discontinuity in Early Twentieth-Century Physics and Early Twentieth-Century Painting." In *Common Denominators in Art and Science,* ed. Martin Pollock. Aberdeen: Aberdeen University Press. 97–106.

Kern, Stephen. 1983. *The Culture of Time and Space, 1880–1918.* Cambridge: Harvard University Press.

Kestner, Joseph. 1978. *The Spatiality of the Novel.* Detroit: Wayne State University Press.

———. 1981. "Secondary Illusion: The Novel and the Spatial Arts." In *Spatial Form in Narrative,* ed. Jeffrey R. Smitten and Ann Daghistany. Ithaca: Cornell University Press. 100–28.

Kinmont, David. 1983. "Vitalism and Creativity: Bergson, Driesch, Maritain and the Visual Arts, 1900–1914." In *Common Denominators in Art and Science,* ed. Martin Pollock. Aberdeen: Aberdeen University Press. 69–77.

Kleiser, Grenville. 1925. *Similes and Their Use.* New York: Grosset & Dunlap.

Klinkowitz, Jerome. 1981. "The Novel as Artifact: Spatial Form in Contemporary Fiction." In *Spatial Form in Narrative,* ed. Jeffrey R. Smitten and Ann Daghistany. Ithaca: Cornell University Press. 37–47.

Krieger, Murray. 1967. "The Ekphrastic Principle and the Still Movement of Poetry; or Laokoön Revisited." In *The Play and the Place of Criticism.* Baltimore: Johns Hopkins University Press. 105–28.

———. 1992. *Ekphrasis. The Illusion of the Natural Sign.* Baltimore: Johns Hopkins University Press.

Labanyi, Jo. 1994. "Nation, Narration, Naturalization: A Barthesian Critique of the 1898 Generation." In *New Hispanisms: Literature, Culture, Theory.* ed. Mark I. Millington and Paul Julian Smith. Ottowa: Dovehouse. 127–49.

Lafond, Paul. 1912. "Darío de Regoyos." *Museum* 2:277–92.

Lafora, Gonzalo R. 1922. "Estudio psicológico del cubismo y expresionismo." *Archivos de Neurobiología* 3, no. 2:119–55.

Laforgue, Jules. 1919. *Mélanges posthumes. Pensées et paradoxes. Pierrot fumiste. Notes sur la femme. L'Art impressioniste.* 6th ed. Paris: Mercure de France.

Lafuente Ferrari, Enrique. 1941. "Aureliano de Beruete y Moret." *Arte Español* 13:25–27.

———. 1948a. "Los paisajes de Ignacio Zuloaga." *Príncipe de Viana* 9:433–66.

———. 1948b. "Pintura española y Generación del '98." *Arbor*, no. 36:449–58.

———. 1950. *La vida y el arte de Ignacio Zuloaga*. San Sebastián: Editora Internacional.

———. 1953. "Lirismo y color en Vázquez Díaz." *Clavileño* 4:34–43.

———. 1954. "Ricardo Baroja y su arte." *Clavileño* 5:33–42.

———. 1957. "Un siglo de paisaje en la pintura española." *Goya*, no. 17: 276–87.

———. 1970. *Ortega y las artes visuales*. Madrid: Revista de Occidente.

———. 1976. "Antonio Machado y su mundo visual." In *Antonio Machado y Soria*, ed. Heliodoro Carpintero. Madrid: CSIC. 71–112.

Laín Entralgo, Pedro. 1962. "La Generación del Noventa y Ocho." In *España como problema*. Madrid: Aguilar. 343–633.

Lapierre, Marcel. 1946. *Anthologie du cinéma*. Paris: La Nouvelle Edition.

Laporte, Paul M. 1949. "Cubism and Science." *Journal of Aesthetics and Art Criticism* 7, no. 3:243–56.

———. 1966. "Cubism and Relativity." *Art Journal* 25, no. 3:246–48.

Lapworth, Charles. 1903. "The Anniversary Address of the President." In *Quarterly Journal of the Geological Society of London* 59:lvii–lx.

Larkin, Oliver W. 1968. *Daumier: Man of His Time*. Boston: Beacon.

Laviña, Matías. 1876. *La catedral de León*. Ed. Manuel M. Fernández y González. Madrid: Eduardo de Medina.

Lawder, Standish D. 1975. *The Cubist Cinema*. New York: New York University Press.

Le Guern, Michel. 1973. *Sémantique de la métaphore et de la métonymie*. Paris: Larousse.

Leiris, Alain de. 1980. "Manet and El Greco: The 'Opera Ball'." *The Arts* 55: 95–99.

Lemoisne, P. A. n.d. *Degas*. Paris: Beaux-Arts.

L'Escola d'Olot. J. Berga, J. Vayreda, M. Vayreda, exhib. cat. 1993. (Olot: Museu Comarcal de la Garrotxa, 19 February–12 April; Barcelona: Fundació La Caixa, 22 April–30 May). Barcelona: Fundació La Caixa.

Levin, David Michael, ed. 1993. *Modernity and the Hegemony of Vision*. Berkeley and Los Angeles: University of California Press.

Levin, Harry. 1966. "What Was Modernism?" In *Refractions: Essays in Comparative Literature*. New York: Oxford University Press. 271–95.

Levine, Steven Z. 1978. "Monet, Lumière and Cinematic Time." *Journal of Aesthetics and Art Criticism* 36:441–47.

Lindsay, Jack. 1995. *Turner. The Man and His Art*. New York: Franklin Watts.

Litvak, Lily. 1980. *Transformación industrial y literatura en España (1895–1905)*. Madrid: Taurus.

———. 1991. *El tiempo de los trenes. El paisaje español en el arte y la literatura del realismo (1849–1918)*. Barcelona: Serbal.

Lodge, David. 1988. *The Modes of Modern Writing: Metaphor, Metonymy and the Typology of Modern Literature*. Chicago: University of Chicago Press.

López-Morillas, Juan. 1975. "La Institución, Cossío y el 'arte de ver.'" *Insula* 30 (July–August):1, 18.

———. 1981. *The Krausist Movement and Ideological Change in Spain, 1854–1874*. Trans. Frances López-Morillas. Cambridge: Cambridge University Press.

———, ed. 1969. *Francisco Giner de los Ríos: Ensayos*. Madrid: Alianza

———, ed. 1973. *Krausismo: Estética y literatura*. Barcelona: Labor.

López Rey, J. 1937. *Realismo e Impresionismo: El arte español en el siglo XIX*. Vol. 15 of *Historia del Arte Labor*. Barcelona: Labor.

Los paisajes del Prado, exhib. cat. 1993. Madrid: Nerea.

Lott, Robert E. 1968. "Sobre el método narrativo y el estilo en las novelas de Azorín." *Cuadernos Hispanoamericanos*, nos. 226–27:192–219.

———. 1971. "Considerations on Azorín's Literary Techniques and the Other Arts." *Kentucky Romance Quarterly* 18:423–34.

Loyarte, Adrián de. 1909. "El arte en el país basco: La pintura. Darío de Regoyos y Pablo Uranga." *La Lectura* 2:154–60.

Lozano Marco, Miguel Angel. 1990. "Las colaboraciones de Azorín en *Blanco y Negro*. El camino hacia *España. Hombres y Paisajes*." *España Contemporánea* 3, no. 1:25–46.

Lubar, Robert S. 1996. "Narrating the Nation: Picasso and the Myth of El Greco." In *Picasso and the Spanish Tradition*, ed. Jonathan Brown. New Haven: Yale University Press. 27–60.

Machado, Antonio. 1915. "D. Francisco Giner de los Ríos." *BILE*, no. 659–600: 220–21.

———. 1991. *Campos de Castilla*. 2d ed. Ed. Geoffrey Ribbans. Madrid: Cátedra.

MacLeod, Glen. 1993. *Wallace Stevens and Modern Art: From the Armory Show to Abstract Expressionism*. New Haven: Yale University Press.

Maeztu, Ramiro de. 1903. "La nueva pintura española en París y en Bilbao." *La Lectura* 2:14–34.

———. 1921. "Homenaje a Regoyos." In exhib. cat. *Darío de Regoyos*. 53–59.

Mallory, Nina Ayala. 1991. *Del Greco a Murillo. La pintura española del Siglo de Oro, 1556–1700*. Madrid: Alianza.

Mandelker, Amy. 1990. "A Painted Lady: Ekphrasis in *Anna Karenina*." *Comparative Literature* 43, no. 1: 1–19.

Maravall, José Antonio. 1968. "Azorín, idea y sentido de la microhistoria." *Cuadernos Hispanoamericanos* 76:28–77.

———. 1987. *Velázquez y el espíritu de la modernidad*. Madrid: Alianza.

Maravall Casesnoves, Darío. 1983–84. "Ortega y Gasset y la física de su tiempo." *Aporia* 6:9–22.

Marín Valdés, Fernando A. 1993. "Textos biográficos y críticos en torno a Aureliano de Beruete." *Aureliano de Beruete, 1845–1912*. Madrid: Caja de Pensiones. 85–101.

Markiewicz, Henryk. 1987. "Ut Pictura Poesis . . . A History of the Topos and the Problem." *New Literary History* 18:535–58.

Marling, William. 1982. *William Carlos Williams and the Painters, 1909–1923.* Athens: Ohio University Press.

Martínez Ruiz, José. 1959. *Obras Completas.* 2d ed. Vols. 1–2. Ed. Angel Cruz Rueda. Madrid: Aguilar.

———. 1947. *Obras Completas.* Vol. 3. Ed. Angel Cruz Rueda. Madrid: Aguilar.

———. 1948. *Obras Completas.* Vols. 4–7. Ed. Angel Cruz Rueda. Madrid: Aguilar.

———. 1963. *Obras Completas.* 2d ed. Vols. 8–9. Ed. Angel Cruz Rueda. Madrid: Aguilar.

———. 1953. *El cine y el momento.* Madrid: Biblioteca Nueva.

———. 1954. *Pintar Como Querer.* Madrid: Biblioteca Nueva.

———. 1955. *El efímero cine.* Madrid: Afrodisio Aguado.

———. 1957. *Dicho y hecho.* Barcelona: Destino.

———. 1959a. *Posdata.* Madrid: Biblioteca Nueva.

———. 1959b. *Agenda.* Madrid: Biblioteca Nueva.

———. 1959c. *Pasos Quedos.* Ed. José García Mercadal. Madrid: Escelicer.

———. 1960. *Ejercicios de castellano.* Madrid: Biblioteca Nueva.

———. 1962. *Varios hombres y alguna mujer.* Ed. José García Mercadal. Barcelona: Aedos.

———. 1963a. *En Lontananza.* Madrid: Bullón.

———. 1963b. *Los Recuadros.* Madrid: Biblioteca Nueva.

———. 1965. *Ni sí, ni no.* Barcelona: Destino.

———. 1966. *Los Médicos.* Valencia: Prometeo.

———. 1967. *La Amada España.* Barcelona: Destino.

———. 1973. *Cada cosa en su sitio.* Barcelona: Destino.

———. 1898. "Mis Montañas." *Madrid Cómico,* 9 April.

———. 1901. "El Museo. Una sala para El Greco." *La Correspondencia de España,* 17 December.

———. 1902. "El Museo Moderno." *La Correspondencia de España,* 6 April.

———. 1904. "Arte y Utilidad." *Alma Española* 2 (3 January): 4–5.

———. 1908a. "Los ferrocarriles." *ABC,* 26 September.

———. 1908b. "Las Pinturas de Regoyos." *ABC,* 4 April.

———. 1909a. "Las Montañas." *ABC,* 7 September.

———. 1909b. "Un Tren que Pasa." *Diario de Barcelona,* 28 December.

———. 1910a. "Geología y Política." *ABC,* 3 February.

———. 1910b. "Falso Casticismo." *ABC,* 26 April.

———. 1911. "Recuerdos de Mallorca." *La Vanguardia,* 12 September.

———. 1912. "La Pintura de Zuloaga." *ABC,* 27 March.

———. 1913. "Andanzas y Lecturas. El Espíritu de Barrès." *La Vanguardia,* 8 April.

———. 1916a. "Don Francisco Giner." *ABC,* 18 February.

———. 1916b. "Las Obras de Giner." *La Prensa,* 30 March.

———. 1917a. "Andanzas y Lecturas. Los ferrocarriles." *La Prensa,* 10 May.

———. 1917b. "Andanzas y Lecturas. Una visita a Zuloaga." *La Prensa,* 2 December.

———. 1920a. "Hugo. Su influencia en los impresionistas." *La Prensa,* 25 April.

———. 1920b. "Andanzas y Lecturas. El problema ferroviario." *La Prensa,* 4 May.

———. 1920c. "Andanzas y Lecturas. Andrés Gide." *La Prensa* 30 May.

———. 1921. "La Vida Española. Estudios de artistas." *La Prensa,* 7 August.

———. 1922a. "La Vida Española. Un Pintor a Buenos Aires." *La Prensa,* 6 August.

———. 1922b. "La Vida Española. Dos Artistas." *La Prensa,* 26 November.

———. 1924. "La Memoria de Barrès y la Belleza de Toledo." *La Prensa,* 6 July.

———. 1925a. "Marcel Proust." *La Prensa,* 18 October.

———. 1925b. "Las Dos Ideas de Proust." *La Prensa,* 22 October.

———. 1926. "De Unamuno a Ruskin." *Repertorio Americano* 12:24, 27.

———. 1927. "El Pasado y Nosotros." *La Prensa,* 4 August.

———. 1929. "Ferrocarriles. Guerra." *ABC,* 26 September.

———. 1930a. "Los ferrocarriles." *La Prensa,* 1 January.

———. 1930b. "España. Ferrocarriles. *ABC,* 22 July.

———. 1931a. "La soledad de un pintor." *La Prensa,* 20 September.

———. 1931b. "En el estudio de Vlaminck." *La Prensa,* 20 December.

———. 1939. "El pintor de España." *La Prensa,* 7 May.

———. 1940a. "En el Museo del Prado." *La Prensa,* 11 February.

———. 1940b. "Los Pintores." *La Prensa,* 15 December.

———. 1941. "Ignacio Zuloaga." *Vértice,* no. 45 (June): 19–22.

———. 1942. "El pintor y sus lienzos." *La Prensa,* 22 November.

———. 1943. "Las ideas estéticas en la España de Franco." *ABC,* 1 October.

———. 1944. "Museo Grevin." *ABC,* 3 September.

———. 1946a. "Ignacio Zuloaga." *La Prensa,* 13 January.

———. 1946b. "Con Goya un Momento." *ABC,* 29 March.

———. 1946c. "El arte y la actualidad." *Diario de Barcelona,* 4 May.

———. 1950a. "Salvador Dalí." *La Prensa,* 8 January.

———. 1950b. "La plástica de un siglo." *ABC,* 15 April.

———. 1951a. "André Gide." *ABC,* 31 March.

———. 1951b. "La Pintura." *ABC,* 8 December.

———. 1952. "Wagnerismo." *ABC,* 5 April.

———. 1959. "La Catedral de Gaudí." *Papeles de Son Armadans,* 1 December.

———. 1960a. "Sebastián Miranda." *ABC,* 30 January.

———. 1960b. "Recuadro a Velázquez." *ABC,* 10 December.

———. 1962. "Ante unas esculturas de Sebastián Miranda." *ABC,* 13 February.

Martínez Sierra, Gregorio, ed. n.d. *Santiago Rusiñol.* 2 vols. Madrid: Saturnino Calleja.

Martínez de Lahidalga, Rosa. 1975. *Gustavo de Maeztu.*

Madrid: Servicio de Publicaciones del Ministerio de Educación y Ciencia.

Mauclair, Camille. 1904. *L'Impressionisme. Son histoire, son esthétique, ses maîtres.* 2d ed. Paris: Librairie de l'Art Ancien et Moderne.

McCall, Marsh H. 1969. *Ancient Rhetorical Theories of Simile and Comparison.* Cambridge, MA: Harvard University Press.

McClain, Jeoraldean. 1985. "Time in the Visual Arts: Lessing and Modern Criticism." *Journal of Aesthetics and Art Criticism* 44:41–58.

Meehan, Thomas C. 1969. "El desdoblamiento interior en *Doña Inés.*" *Cuadernos Hispanoamericanos,* no. 237:644–68.

Meltzer, Françoise. 1987. *Salomé and the Dance of Writing. Portraits of Mimesis in Literature.* Chicago: University of Chicago Press.

Mermall, Thomas. 1983–84. "El paisaje pedagógico de Ortega y Gasset." *Aporia* 6:109–23.

———. 1989. "Ortega's Velázquez and the Topics of Modernity." In *Ortega y Gasset and the Question of Modernity,* ed. Patrick H. Dust. Hispanic Issues 5. Minneapolis: Prisma Institute. 223–42.

Meyers, Jeffrey. 1975. *Painting and the Novel.* Manchester: Manchester University Press and New York: Barnes and Noble.

Michel, Émile. 1908. *Nouvelles études sur l'histoire de l'art.* Paris: Hachette.

Mickel, Emanuel I., Jr. 1981. *Eugène Fromentin.* Boston: Twayne.

Miller, George A. 1979. "Images and Models, Similes and Metaphor." In *Metaphor and Thought,* ed. Andrew Ortony. London and New York: Cambridge University Press. 202–50.

Mitchell, Timothy. 1977. "Bergson, Le Bon, and Hermetic Cubism." *Journal of Aesthetics and Art Criticism* 36:175–83.

Mitchell, W. J. T. 1986. *Iconology. Image, Text, Ideology.* Chicago: University of Chicago Press.

———. 1989. "Space, Ideology, and Literary Representation." *Poetics Today* 10: 91–103.

———. 1992. "Ekphrasis and the Other." *South Atlantic Quarterly* 91:695–719.

———. 1994. *Picture Theory. Essays on Verbal and Visual Representation.* Chicago: University of Chicago Press.

———, ed. 1994. *Landscape and Power.* Chicago: University of Chicago Press.

Montero Padilla, José. 1953. "'Azorín' y el cine." *Revista de Literatura* 4: 359–65.

Montes Huidobro, Matías. 1994. "Azorín: Teoría y práctica del cine." *España Contemporánea* 7, no. 1:29–46.

Moral, Carmen del. 1974. *La sociedad madrileña fin de siglo y Baroja.* Madrid: Turner.

Morente, Manuel G. 1923. "El tema de nuestro tiempo. Filosofía de la perspectiva." *Revista de Occidente* 1, no. 5 (November): 201–17.

Morera, Jaime. 1899. "Don Carlos de Haes." *La Ilustración Española y Americana,* 8 May.

Mukarovsky, Jan. 1977. "Between Literature and the Visual Arts." In *The Word and Art,* trans. and ed. John Bur-

bank and Peter Steiner. New Haven: Yale University Press. 205–34.

Navarro Ledesma, F. 1903. "Del pobre don Luis de Góngora." *Helios* 7:477–80.

Newman, Charles. 1984. "The Post-Modern Aura. The Act of Fiction in an Age of Inflation." *Salmagundi,* nos. 63–64: 3–199.

Nicoll, Allardyce. 1976. *The World of Harlequin: A Critical Study of the Commedia dell'Arte.* Cambridge: Cambridge University Press.

Niess, Robert J. 1968. *Zola, Cézanne, and Manet: A Study of* L'Oeuvre. Ann Arbor: University of Michigan Press.

Nochlin, Linda. 1989. *The Politics of Vision: Essays on Nineteenth-Century Art and Society.* New York: Harper & Row.

Nordau, Max. 1921. *Los grandes del arte español.* Trans. Rafael Cansinos Assens. Barcelona: Artes y Letras.

Norris, Nancy Ann. 1983. "Visión azoriniana del paisaje español." *Cuadernos de Aldeeu* 1, nos. 2–3:373–83.

Opisso, Alfredo. 1900. *Arte y artistas catalanes.* Barcelona: La Vanguardia.

Orozco-Díaz, Emilio. 1974. *Paisaje y sentimiento de la naturaleza en la poesía española.* Madrid: Ediciones del Centro.

Ortega y Gasset, José. 1963–83. *Obras Completas.* 6th ed. 12 vols. Madrid: Revista de Occidente.

Orueta, Ricardo de. 1919. *Escultura funeraria en España.* Madrid: Centro de Estudios Históricos.

Paisaje y figura del 98, exhib. cat. 1997. Madrid: Fundación Central Hispano.

Panofsky, Doris. 1952. "Gilles or Pierrot? Iconographic Notes on Watteau." *Gazette des Beaux-Arts* 39:319–40.

Pantorba, Bernardino de. 1943. *El paisaje y los paisajistas españoles.* Madrid: A. Carmona.

Parada y Santín, José. 1875. *Las ciencias y la pintura. Estudios de crítica científica sobre los cuadros del Museo de Pinturas de Madrid.* Madrid: Minuesa.

Park, Roy. 1969. "Ut Pictura Poesis: The Nineteenth-Century Aftermath." *Journal of Aesthetics and Art Criticism* 28:155–64.

Paskiewickz, Marjan. 1925. "Reflexiones sobre la pintura nueva." *Revista de Occidente* 9:302–16.

Paulson, Ronald. 1971. *Hogarth: His Life, Art, and Times.* 2 vols. New Haven: Yale University Press.

———. 1976–77. "Toward the Constable Bicentenary: Thoughts on Landscape Theory." *Eighteenth Century Studies* 10, no. 2:245–61.

———. 1982. *Literary Landscape: Turner and Constable.* New Haven: Yale University Press.

Payá Bernabé, José and Magdalena Rigual Bonastre, eds. 1995. *El cinematógrafo. Artículos sobre cine y guiones de películas.* Valencia: Pre-Textos.

Pèl i Ploma. 1900. Número monográfico dedicado a Santiago Rusiñol, no. 13 (December).

Pena López, María del Carmen. 1973. "Aureliano de Beruete y la Generación del 98." *Revista de la Universidad Complutense de Madrid,* no. 86:143–47.

———. 1982. *Pintura de paisaje e ideología. La Generación del '98.* Madrid: Taurus.

———. 1983. "Aureliano de Buerete y Moret, personaje y

paisajista español de fin de siglo." In exhib. cat. *Aureliano de Beruete (1845–1912)* Madrid: Caja de Pensiones. 12–72.

———. 1993. "La modernización del paisaje realista. Castilla como centro de la imagen de España." In exhib. cat. *Centro y periferia en la modernización de la pintura española, (1880–1918).* Barcelona: Ambit. 42–48.

Perrot, A. M. 1834. *Manuel de coloriste.* Paris: Librairie Roret.

La Pintura de Historia del Siglo XIX en España, exhib. cat. 1992–93. (Madrid: Prado Museum, October 1992–January 1993). Ed. José Luis Díez. Madrid: Museo del Prado.

Plá, Josep. 1970. *Tres artistes.* Vol. 15 of *Obras Completas.* Barcelona: Destino.

Pollock, Martin, ed. 1983. *Common Denominators in Art and Science.* Aberdeen: Aberdeen University Press.

Posner, Donald. 1984. *Antoine Watteau.* Ithaca: Cornell University Press.

Puente, Joaquín de la, ed. 1971. *Los estudios de paisaje de Carlos de Haes, (1826–1889).* Madrid: Valera.

———. 1976. *Marceliano Santa María.* Burgos: Obra Cultural de la Caja de Ahorros del Círculo Católico de Obreros.

Quinones, Ricardo J. 1985. *Mapping Literary Modernism: Time and Development.* Princeton: Princeton University Press.

Rabkin, Eric S. 1981. "Spatial Form and Plot." In *Spatial Form in Narrative,* ed. Jeffrey R. Smitten and Ann Daghistany. Ithaca: Cornell University Press. 79–99. First pub. *Critical Inquiry* 4 (1977):253–70.

Raffaëlli, Jean-François. 1913. *Les promenades d'un artiste au Musée du Louvre.* Paris: n.p.

Ramsden, Herbert, ed. 1966. *La ruta de Don Quijote,* by José Martínez Ruiz. Manchester: Manchester University Press.

Rand, Marguerite C. 1956. *Castilla en Azorín.* Madrid: Revista de Occidente.

Regoyos, Darío de. 1901. "El Impresionismo en Francia. Protesta de los impresionistas españoles contra el discurso de Benlliure." *Juventud. Revista Popular Contemporánea* 1 (30 November): 8–10.

"Regeneración estética de España, la." 1898. *Luz,* no. 6:86–87.

Rementería y Fica, Mariano de. 1839. *Manual completo de juegos de sociedad o tertulia, y de prendas.* 2d ed. Madrid: Norberto Llorenci.

Reutersvärd, Oscar. 1952. "The Accentuated Brush Stroke of the Impressionists." *Journal of Aesthetics and Art Criticism* 10, no.3:273–78.

Rewald, John. 1973. *The History of Impressionism.* 4th ed. rev. New York: The Museum of Modern Art.

Richardson, John A. 1971. *Modern Art and Scientific Thought.* Urbana: University of Illinois Press.

Rico, Martín. n.d. *Recuerdos de mi vida.* Madrid: Ibérica.

Rico Verdú, José. 1973. *Un Azorín desconocido. Estudio psicológico de su obra.* Alicante: Instituto de Estudios Alicantinos.

Ricoeur, Paul. 1977. *The Rule of Metaphor.* Trans. Robert Czerny with Kathleen McLaughlin and John Costello, Jr. Toronto: University of Toronto Press.

Risco, Antonio. 1980. *Azorín y la ruptura con la novela tradicional.* Madrid: Alhambra.

———. 1985. "El paisaje en Azorín: Su elaboración y destrucción." *Actes du Premier Colloque International José Martínez Ruiz (Azorín).* Pau: Université de Pau. 331–38.

Ritter, William. 1907. "Beruete, paysagiste castillan." *L'Art et les Artistes* 5:197–99.

Robinson, Marian S. 1983. "Zola and Monet: The Poetry of the Railways." *Journal of Modern Literature* 10:55–70.

Roch, Heidi, ed. 1981. *Santiago Rusiñol.* Barcelona: Departament de Cultura i Mitjanes de Comunicació de la Generalitat de Catalunya.

Rodin, Auguste. 1919. *L'Art.* Paris: Grasset.

Rodríguez Alcalde, L. 1978. *Los maestros del impresionsimo español.* Madrid: Ibérico Europca de Ediciones.

Rosenfeld, Daniel. 1986. *The Spirit of Barbizon.* San Francisco: The Art Museum Association of America.

Roskill, Mark. 1985. *The Interpretation of Cubism.* Philadelphia: Art Alliance Press.

———. 1997. *The Languages of Landscape.* University Park: Penn State University Press.

Rowe, John Carlos. 1982. "James's Rhetoric of the Eye: Remarking the Impression." *Criticism* 24, no.3:233–60.

Rozas, Juan Manuel, ed. 1973. *Castilla,* by José Martínez Ruiz. Barcelona: Labor.

Rumeu, Antonio. 1935. "El Duque de Rivas, pintor." *Arte Español* 12:345–52.

Rusiñol, María. 1983. *Santiago Rusiñol, visto por su hija.* 2d ed. Barcelona: Juventud.

Rusiñol, Santiago. n.d. *Desde el Molino.* Barcelona-Madrid: Iberoamericana.

———. 1914. *Jardines de España.* Barcelona: Renacimiento.

Sabater, Gaspar. 1944. *Azorín, o la plasticidad.* Barcelona: Juventud.

Saisselin, Remy G. 1961. "Ut Pictura Poesis: Dubos to Diderot." *Journal of Aesthetics and Art Criticism* 20:145–56.

Salaverría, José María. 1917. "Darío de Regoyos." *Hermes* (April): n.p.

Sánchez-Camargo, Manuel. 1962. *Solana. Vida y pintura.* Madrid: Taurus.

Sánchez Marín, Venancio. 1961. "Tres maestros del paisaje español." *Goya,* no. 41 (March–April): 369–71.

———. 1968a. "Maestros del Impresionismo Español." *Goya,* no. 83 (March–April): 325–26.

———. 1968b. "Retratos de Vázquez Díaz." *Goya,* no. 83 (March–April): 326–27.

Sánchez Munian, José María. 1956. *Antología General de Menéndez Pelayo.* 2 vols. Madrid: Biblioteca de Autores Cristianos.

San Nicolás Santamaría, Juan. 1990. *Darío de Regoyos (1857–1913).* Barcelona: Edicions Catalanes.

Schapiro, Meyer. 1994. "Eugène Fromentin." *Theory and Philosophy of Art: Style, Artist, and Society.* New York: George Braziller. 103–34.

Schivelbusch, Wolfgang. 1979. *The Railway Journey: Trains and Travel in the Nineteenth Century*. Trans. Anselm Hollo. New York: Urizen Books.

Schneider, Pierre. 1967. *The World of Watteau, 1684–1721*. New York: Time-Life.

Schwarz, Heinrich. 1952. "The Mirror in Art." *Art Quarterly* 15:96–118.

Scott, Grant Fraser. 1991. "The Rhetoric of Dilation: Ekphrasis and Ideology." *Word and Image* 7, no. 4:301–10.

Scott, Nina M. 1975. "Unamuno and Painting." *Hispanófila* 19:57–66.

Searle, John R. 1980. "*Las Meninas* and the Paradoxes of Pictorial Representation." In *The Language of Images*, ed. W. J. T. Mitchell. Chicago: University of Chicago Press. 247–58.

Selz, Peter. 1991. "German Expressionism in the Context of the European Avant-Garde." In *Impressionism and European Modernism*, ed. Norma Roberts. Seattle: University of Washington Press. 18–21.

Sesé, Bernard. 1980. *Antonio Machado (1875–1939). El hombre. El poeta. El pensador.* Trans. Soledad García Mouton. 2 vols. Madrid: Gredos.

Shattuck, Roger. 1984. "Claude Monet: Approaching the Abyss." *The Innocent Eye: On Modern Literature and the Arts*. New York: Farrar, Straus & Giroux. 221–39.

Shiff, Richard. 1978. "Art and Life: A Metaphoric Relationship." *Critical Inquiry* 5, no. 1:107–22.

———. 1986. "The End of Impressionism." In exhib. cat. *The New Painting: Impressionism, 1874–1886*, ed. Charles S. Moffet. National Gallery of Art, Washington, D.C. (17 January–6 April 1986). 61–89.

Silver, Larry. 1983. "Step-Sister of the Muses: Painting as Liberal and Sister Art." In *Articulate Images: The Sister Arts from Hogarth to Tennyson*, ed. Richard Wendorf. Minneapolis: University of Minnesota Press. 36–69.

Simpson, Lisa A. 1987. *From Arcadia to Barbizon: A Journey in French Landscape Painting*. Memphis, Tenn: The Dixon Gallery and Gardens.

Slive, Seymour. 1991. *Jacob van Ruisdael*. New York: Abbeville.

Smith, Mack. 1995. *Literary Realism and the Ekphrastic Tradition*. University Park: Penn State University Press.

Snyder, Joel. 1980. "Picturing Vision." *Critical Inquiry* 6:499–526.

——— and Ted Cohen. 1980. "Reflexions on *Las Meninas*: Paradox Lost." *Critical Inquiry* 7:429–47.

Souriau, Etienne. 1949. "Time in the Plastic Arts." *Journal of Aesthetics and Art Criticism* 7:294–307.

Spencer, Sharon. 1971. *Space, Time and Structure in the Modern Novel*. New York: New York University Press.

Steinberg, Leo. 1981. "Velasquez's *Las Meninas*." *October* 19:45–54.

Steiner, Wendy. 1982. *The Colors of Rhetoric*. Chicago: University of Chicago Press.

———. 1989. "The Causes of Effect: Edith Wharton and the Economics of Ekphrasis." *Poetics Today* 10, no. 2:279–97.

Stone, Jennifer. 1989. *Pirandello's Naked Prompt. The Structure of Repetition in Modernism*. Ravenna: Longo.

Swart, Koenraad W. 1964. *The Sense of Decadence in Nineteenth-Century France*. The Hague: M. Nijhoff.

Sypher, Wylie. 1960. *Rococo to Cubism in Art and Literature*. New York: Random House.

Tenreiro, Ramón María. 1912a. "El nuevo libro de Azorín. *Lecturas españolas.*" *La Lectura* 1:366–76.

———. 1912b. "El nuevo libro de Azorín. *Castilla.*" *La Lectura* 3:424–28.

Thornes, John E. 1979a. "Landscape and Clouds. Artists as Meteorologists." *Geographical Magazine* 51, no. 7:492–99.

———. 1979b. "Constable's Clouds." *Burlington Magazine* 121:697–704.

Tilly, Charles. 1981. "Charivari, Repertoire and Urban Politics." In *French Cities in the Nineteenth Century*, ed. John Merriman. New York: Holmes & Meier. 72–91.

Torgovnick, Marianna. 1985. *The Visual Arts, Pictorialism, and the Novel. James, Lawrence, and Woolf*. Princeton: Princeton University Press.

Torre, Guillermo de. 1921. "La ascensión colorista de Vázquez Díaz." *Ultra*, no. 8 (20 April): 1.

———. 1963. "Ut pictura poesis." *Papeles de Son Armadans* 28 (January): 9–44.

Torrente Ballester, Gonzalo. 1965. *Panorama de la literatura española*. 3d ed. Madrid: Guadarrama.

Torres-García, J. 1913. *Notes sobre art*. Barcelona: Masó.

Toscano, Nicolás. 1991. "Unamuno, pintor." *Cuadernos Hispanoamericanos* (June): 89–96.

Tren Ballester, Eliseo. 1988. "Costumbrismo, realismo y naturalismo en la pintura catalana de la Restauración (1880–1893)." In *Realismo y naturalismo en España en la segunda mitad del siglo XIX*, ed. Yvan Lissorgues. Barcelona: Anthropos. 299–310.

Trimpi, Wesley. 1973. "The Meaning of Horace's *Ut Pictura Poesis*." *Journal of the Warburg and Courtauld Institutes* 36:1–34.

Tucker, Paul Hayes. 1990. *Monet in the '90s. The Series Paintings*. New Haven: Yale University Press.

———. 1995. *Claude Monet: Life and Art*. New Haven: Yale University Press.

Tufts, Eleanor. 1985. *Luis Meléndez: Eighteenth-Century Master of the Spanish Still-Life*. Columbia: University of Missouri Press.

Tuñón de Lara, Manuel. 1977. "Institución Libre de Enseñanza e 'Institucionismo' en el primer tercio del siglo XX." *Actas del Quinto Congreso Internacional de Hispanistas*. 2 vols. Burdeos: Instituto de Estudios Ibéricos e Iberoamericanos. 2:839–51.

Tusell, Javier. 1993. "El paisaje como símbolo de la identidad nacional en la España contemporánea." In exhib. cat. *Los Paisajes del Prado*. Madrid: Nerea. 351–35.

Tyler, Carole-Anne. 1990. "The Feminine Look." In *Theory Between the Disciplines. Authority / Vision / Politics*, ed. Martin Kreiswirth and Mark A. Cheetham. Ann Arbor: University of Michigan Press. 191–212.

Unamuno y Jugo, Miguel de. 1899. "Puesta del sol (recuerdo del 16 de diciembre de 1897)." *Revista Nueva* 1:615–20.

———. 1966–71. *Obras Completas*. 9 vols. Ed. Manuel García Blanco. Madrid: Escelicer.

Upton, Joel M. 1990. *Petrus Christus. His Place in Fifteenth-Century Painting*. University Park: Penn State University Press.

Utrillo, Miquel. 1900. "Los jardines de España de Santiago Rusiñol." *Pel & Ploma*, no. 13 (December): 11.

Valverde, José María, ed. 1972. *Artículos olvidados de José Martínez Ruiz*. Madrid: Narcea.

———, ed. 1982. *Los Pueblos. La Andalucía trágica y otros artículos*, by José Martínez Ruiz. Madrid: Castalia.

Vargas Llosa, Mario. 1996. "Las discretas ficciones de Azorín." *ABC*, 16 January: 50–54.

Vázquez Díaz, Daniel. 1974. *Mis artículos en ABC*. Madrid: Ibérico-Europea.

Vincent, Howard P. 1968. *Daumier and his World*. Evanston: Northwestern University Press.

Vitz, Paul C., and Arnold B. Glimcher. 1984. *Modern Art and Modern Science: The Parallel Analysis of Vision*. New York: Praeger.

Wagner, Anne M. 1986. *Jean-Baptiste Carpeaux: Sculptor of the Second Empire*. New Haven: Yale University Press.

Walford, E. John. 1991. *Jacob van Ruisdael and the Perception of Landscape*. New Haven: Yale University Press.

Wattenmaker, Richard J. 1975. *Puvis de Chavannes and the Modern Tradition*. Toronto: Art Gallery of Ontario.

Weil, Al. 1979. "Turner and Impressionism." *Turner Society News* 13:n.p.

Weinsheimer, Joel. 1991. *Philosophical Hermeneutics and Literary Theory*. New Haven: Yale University Press.

White, Hayden. 1978. *Tropics of Discourse*. Baltimore: Johns Hopkins University Press.

———. 1987. *The Content of the Form. Narrative Discourse and Historical Representation*. Baltimore: Johns Hopkins University Press.

Williams, H. Noel. 1925. *Madame de Pompadour*. London: Harper.

Wilson-Bareau, Juliet. 1988. *Édouard Manet: Voyage en Espagne*. Caen: Échoppe.

Wood, Christopher S. 1993. *Albrecht Altdorfer and the Origins of Landscape*. Chicago: University of Chicago Press.

Yriarte, Charles. 1868. "Courrier de Paris." *Le Monde Illustré*, 27 June:402–403.

Index